Survey
of
Science Fiction
Literature

**FIVE HUNDRED 2,000-WORD ESSAY REVIEWS OF
WORLD-FAMOUS SCIENCE FICTION NOVELS
WITH 2,500 BIBLIOGRAPHICAL REFERENCES**

Edited by
FRANK N. MAGILL

Volume Two
Dea - Imm
513 - 1018

SALEM PRESS

Englewood Cliffs

LIBRARY OF CONGRESS CATALOG CARD NUMBER: 79-64639

Complete Set: ISBN 0-89356-194-0
Volume II: ISBN 0-89356-196-7

PRINTED IN THE UNITED STATES OF AMERICA

LIST OF TITLES IN VOLUME TWO

THE DEATH OF THE EARTH
(LE MORT DE LA TERRE)

Author: J. H. Rosny (the Elder) (1856-1940)
First book publication: 1910
English translation: 1978
Type of work: Novella
Time: The end of organic life on Earth
Locale: A series of "oases" in the midst of endless desert: Big-Springs, Red-Lands, Dune Equator

An entropic vision of the death of mankind on an Earth, without water, animals, or plants, one last hero struggles in vain against evolution and the inevitable rise of metallic life forms called the ferromagnetics

> *Principal characters:*
> TARG, the Planetary Watcher of Big-Springs oasis
> ARVA, his sister
> MANO, a widower of Big-Springs, later Arva's husband
> ERE, a beautiful girl with blonde hair
> REM, head water-master
> OLD DANE, a centenarian and spokesman for the resigned majority
> of mankind

Though little-known in the English-speaking world, *The Death of the Earth* is an important early work of scientific fantasy, one whose treatment of the evolutionary theme rivals H. G. Wells in sophistication. "Rosny ainé" (Rosny the Elder) is the pen name (along with his brother Séraphin J. F. Boëx) of Joseph Henri Boëx, a Belgian who became a Parisian man of letters. Esteemed in his own time (he won a Prix Goncourt), he is virtually ignored by critics today. Highly prolific, he wrote in a variety of genres: fantastic tales, "lost race" novels, as well as a number of potboiling social novels in the naturalist mode of Zola and his followers. These latter may account for his critical eclipse — in fact, in his declining years he resorted to the purest sensationalism, as his *Vie amoureuse de Balzac* attests. His early fantasies, however — the first, *The Xipéhuz*, was published in 1887, and thus antedates Wells by eight years — are both original and imaginative. *The Death of the Earth* is a milestone in the history of what is today called science fiction.

In form, *The Death of the Earth* is closer to Wells than to the work of Rosny's illustrious countryman Jules Verne; it is a cautionary moral tale rather than a narrative of adventure. What is more, its basic premise — that evolution as an entropic process, with organic life "running down" — seems to echo *The Time Machine*. It looks, therefore, as if Wells may have inspired Rosny. On closer examination, however, we see that Rosny's story comes from a different source, and ultimately heads in a different direction from that of Wells's; from the beginning, all his work sinks roots in a native tradition. *The Xipéhuz* is a *conte philosophique*: if nascent mankind encounters alien mineral beings, it is only so that they might better understand their own limits. But if in this early evolutionary meeting of organic and mineral life the struggle is won by man, things are exactly reversed in *The Death of the Earth*: the time for the metal kingdom has come, and man must pass.

It would seem, then, that this tale is meant to humble us, to show us our limits and teach us broader respect for natural law. However, there is more here than a dutiful Enlightenment message. The garden the last men seek to cultivate is not Candide's narrow space, but a new Eden; and Rosny's figures are not treated satirically, but with almost elegaic tenderness. The thrust of the novella is therefore oddly ambiguous; it is simultaneously an implacable "scientific" account of evolution and a protracted lament for the death of a unique and irreplacable mankind. For if Rosny's intellect seems to accept natural selection, his heart blindly rejects it.

As befits a moral tale, the emphasis of this short narrative is neither on plot nor on character development. Action is minimal. Planetary Watcher Targ, standing by his Great Shell which links scattered and distant oases on a drying Earth, dreams of distant times when growing things flourished. All at once the message comes that earthquakes have destroyed the sister oasis of Red-Lands: mankind's ultimate agony has begun. Crowds gather — a few bewail man's fate, but most sink into apathy, awaiting the moment when they must slip out of life with painless euthanasia. Opposed to this defeated type of man is the hero Targ, a romantic individual whose dream of the green past enfolds a vision of rebirth. He is supported by his sister Arva and her lover-husband Mano. The former follows because of blood bonds: she shares the family capacity to dream. The latter is driven by more selfish reasons, such as loneliness and physical necessity. Mano is a widower who has recently been "reclassified," permitted within the tight demographic norms of these oasis worlds to remarry and found a new family. Now, in Arva's presence, he too dreams of a rebirth, but on a much lesser level. From this moment forward, *The Death of the Earth* is a protracted tale of dashed hopes, of the gradual but inevitable decline of man.

The basic form of Rosny's narrative is a curving fall. Along the way, however, numerous seismic tremors occur, brief flareups of heroism and love in the ancient manner. Targ undertakes a long and arduous journey underground, and ultimately discovers water; but ultimately his invasion of the mineral kingdom proves futile; this water too will dry up. He searches on and in the end makes another find, although it is too late to save himself or mankind. In the ruins of Red-Lands he unearths another treasure: a miraculously unharmed girl with golden hair. Like all other last men, Targ is dark and sunburnt, with a huge chest cage that comes from breathing dry, rarefied air. In his eyes this "atavistic" creature — her name is Ere — becomes more than a wife: she is the symbol of man's rebirth. Wrested from the mineral enemy, she is his new Eve. With her he actually seeks to create his own Eden at the end of human time.

As with the water, however, the Earth again takes back what it has given: Eden and Ere both perish in one final earthquake. After this long string of cruel deceptions the end comes as we knew it must. The protagonists yield to this fatality according to their different personalities. Where Mano once rebelled in the name of physical pleasure, now despair falls upon him in an equally physical fashion, "like a stone." Arva is leaving with Targ, Ere, and the children for the Equatorial Oasis and the hope of a new start. He refuses to go: a pleasant euthanasia is better than "a horrible death out there in the desert." Arva gives up when this new enclave collapses. With all the children gone, brother and sister can spawn no new race: faced with this biological end of the dream — a stone wall nonetheless, even if on a higher plane — she accepts the death drug. Targ as last man, however, refuses to take his life in this manner; his final protest takes the form of a vast recapitulatory hymn that sings the rise and fall of organic life on Earth, brought forward "in an unbroken line" until it ultimately comes to rest in him. Targ will not break it; he lays himself humbly yet consciously among the ferromagnetic beings to die: "In this way some small bit of the last human life entered freely into the New Order of Things."

The message seems simple and clear: only when man abandons the vain heroics of a vanished past can he attain new wisdom and a truly evolutionary consciousness. In reality, however, things are not so simple for Rosny, and his work is full of irreconcilable tensions. Set against evolutionary men — with their "petrified" faces, shrunken stomachs, and huge lungs, these oasis dwellers seem themselves to be changing from animal to mineral. There are special men, such as Targ with his ancient vision, Ere with her primeval vigor and blonde hair. It is not enough for Rosny to call these figures "atavisms," for they form a strange island in the stream of evolution, constants that defy the idea of physical change. Throughout the narrative, Targ's dream of a new beginning is set, mirror-fashion, against the fact of man's end. If Ere means "era" — man's has passed — it also suggests (if we wish to make it do so) Eve. This yearned-for Eden at the end of human time can only be postlapsarian: the most that can come of it is another cycle of organic life.

But there is more here than soulless counterdynamic. Opposing linear evolution is a circularity that, instead of merely conserving energy, preserves essences: at the center of this system of life is man himself. Nor is it any man: we have Adam and Eve, Targ and Ere — aristocratic progenitors. Rosny's title itself offers a further echo of the curiously irrational homocentricity of this novel. Man's death is not the death of the Earth. And yet it is, for with him dies human consciousness, leaving only senseless mineral forces.

In this way then, man's greatness is like that of Pascal's thinking reed: conscious of his cosmic frailty, he at least knows the mineral realm crushes him, while the mineral knows not. For Rosny, however, the thinking reed has become a lamenting one. For his man, it is no longer enough to know that he perishes. As Targ laments his own passing, he seems at the same time to be striving to preserve in a realm of poetic elegy what is lost in that of matter. And beyond this he seeks to do even more: through his lyrical power of imagination he actually strives to remake the "enemy" in his own image. In the great mineral cavern at the core of the Earth, it is Targ's light that sets off the kaleidoscopic magic of the crystals. This underground world has remained dark and dead until human daring penetrates it, and human imagination unlocks its beauty. Ultimately the gems' durability, as well as our own ephemerality, becomes no more than a function of the human consciousness of time. Rosny seeks everywhere through paradox to make his ferromagnetics seem genuinely alien — their molecular structure of "living iron" is fluid and yet contains no liquid, their magnetic fields are so erratic that man can reduce them to no law but randomness. And yet Targ, in his lyrical musings, fits them easily into the human paradigm. The evolutionary path he sees them following is ours: now concerned only to grow and multiply, perhaps later they will achieve "consciousness" of a human sort.

If mankind is dying in Rosny's tale, he is also evolving, but this time on a spiritual plane. Clearly the development of Targ is opposed to the sterile waning and waxing of material beings: last men and ferromagnetics. If humanity has value, it resides only in this lyrical consciousness that rises as the special man passes beyond heroic aggression to humility and resignation. The Christian overtones are obvious. The ferromagnetics destroy man so that he can be reborn, and in doing so circumscribe this new life form, visit upon them his new understanding as a spark of grace. The scenario is a strange one of fall and redemption. It was man (it turns out) who first gave the mineral being life: in classic manner the molecular structure of metals was altered by human technology in its race for progress — the sin of intellectual pride again creates its monster. And if Targ, in his elegaic meditations, comes to accept this responsibility, he simultaneously wipes away all guilt with his final sacrifice: as if to insure that these alien creatures will develop a human type of consciousness, he bestows the spark by consciously laying down his own last human life. The time traveler in John W. Campbell's later "Twilight" bestows a similar human gift on the machines that inhabit the humanless world he finds at the end of time: curiosity. In doing so he not only preserves what is most essential in man, but in a single stroke eradicates original sin: what once made man fall will now lift him to the state of superman. Rosny's tale, though perhaps more orthodox, remains the original model for this process of "Christianizing" evolution; merges with the alien only to be preserved in his most essential part, and in turn to lift it out of the grooves of natural selection to some new — yet thoroughly human — glory.

In his introduction to the novel, Rosny prides himself on its concision: "*The Death of the Earth* is a small novel which I could have easily expanded to three hundred pages. I didn't do so because in my opinion scientific fantasy (*le merveilleux scientifique*) is a genre that demands brevity." And yet, in spite of its taut, often crabbed style, the novel is still somehow too long. Whatever of man is preserved, Targ remains the last man, and with him the human form dies. Reluctance to let go of Targ may have caused the author to ignore his own dictum; for where Targ is doomed in his body — he too is dark and huge-chested — he grows in presence in his lyrical musings, and Rosny seems to multiply these at random. The author sets in motion an artificial rhythm of crises that provokes outbursts — cries of hope or agonizing laments — and allows evolution to run its necessary course. There is a certain verbal resistance to the stream of time, leading to repetitive soul-searching which rapidly degenerates into set pieces.

For instance, the epic at the center of the Earth, as Targ trudges on in search of water, is Interminable: we find ourselves seesawing up and down as the hero discovers and then loses the way. There are few if any dramatic encounters in the novella; the long gaps in this excruciatingly slow-moving tale are filled by Targ's outpourings. Oddly enough, man is present here only insofar as he bewails his future absence. There is something almost sado-masochistic about Rosny's forcing the reader to watch this prolonged and futile death struggle. The blatant emphasis on scientific method (Targ in his searchings for water is obviously the perfect empirical observer) obliges us on one hand to be "objective," to accept evolution and the inevitability of man's end.

On the other hand, however, we are shown (as with Pascal) that the human heart has reasons that reason does not know. Targ is doomed by other, more human laws — he who would rise by science must fall by it. Ironically we see him let his second Eden perish through an error in technical observation: he forgets to check the stress on its foundations, and it crumbles in an earthquake. We are then made to sit back and watch as Targ grasps futilely at straws in the wake of the doubly unavoidable. Our sorrow at his elegiac outcries — the human vision preserved — is mingled with an almost voyeuristic fascination with the spectacle of loss itself.

Such, apparently, was Rosny's attitude: here was a proponent of positivism with the deepest aversions to science, a man (to use Arnold's phrase) "wandering between two worlds, one dead, the other powerless to be born." In *Jean Barois*, Rosny's contemporary, Roger Martin du Gard, records a similar scientific agony: we watch the positivist and agnostic revert to faith in the face of pain and death. That faith, however, is no more viable than Targ's dream of a new Eden. It is the spectacle of death itself that has become fascinating and significant.

George Slusser

Sources for Further Study

Criticism:

The Encyclopedia of Science Fiction and Fantasy. Compiled by Donald H. Tuck. Chicago: Advent Publishers, Inc., 1978, pp. 371-372. Tuck notes Rosny's science fiction to be the best of French origin.

THE DEATHWORLD TRILOGY

Author: Harry Harrison (1925-   )
First book publications: Deathworld (1960); *Deathworld II* (1964); *Deathworld III*
  (1968)
Type of work: Novels
Time: An indefinite future
Locale: Three imaginary planets

Three works in which soldier-of-fortune Jason dinAlt contends with the lethal environments and dangerous politics of three bizarre planets

Principal characters:
  JASON DINALT, a gambler
  KERK, leader of the Pyrran
  META, a Pyrran woman
  MIKAH SAMON, a religious fanatic
  IJALE, a slave woman
  TEMUCHIN, warlord of the nomad tribes on Felicity

Pyrrus is a world so deadly that in order simply to survive, one must be trained from birth instinctively to recognize and kill anything hostile. Pyrrus is a heavy gravity planet, apparently at war with mankind, where native life forms evolve and mutate, becoming more deadly each day that one survives. In addition to unending war, the planet is plagued with volcanic activity and extremes of temperature. Harry Harrison presents three such "deathworld" planets, which test the ingenuity, strength, and intelligence of his main character, Jason dinAlt. The novels in the trilogy are about survival in the physical sense, as situations, environments, plants, animals, and people actively attempt to kill Jason. The three *Deathworld* novels are exciting adventures depicting the hero's ability to survive and to overcome immense odds.

Since science fiction heroes take many shapes and forms and enjoy diverse abilities and technological advances, it is surprising that Harrison chose to give his main character only sporadic telekinetic powers and limited native intelligence. Jason is cast initially in the role of a successful wandering gambler, a sophisticated type drifting from casino to casino in search of a challenge which will make his life meaningful. The deathworld planets provide a background against which he can pit all his talents and discover his worth. Each planet has its unique dangers and obstacles to overcome; each is the setting for a game whose stakes are Jason's life.

Deathworld, the first novel of the trilogy, begins when Jason dinAlt receives a message capsule in his suite on the casino planet Cassilia. He knows no one who could be aware of his identity, so he prepares to welcome his visitor by hiding his gun under a pillow on the couch. His visitor is Kerk from the planet Pyrrus, and he resembles a heavyweight wrestler. Thinking that Kerk must be sent by the police or by an old enemy, Jason insists that he remove his gun. When he attempts to enforce the request by drawing his own weapon, Kerk outdraws him with superhuman speed. With the barrel of his enormous gun pointed directly between Jason's eyes, Kerk impatiently explains his proposition. Kerk must raise three billion credits by morning; gambling is the only way to do it. Having looked into Jason's past exploits, he offers him a bankroll of twenty-seven million credits to play with. Anything over the three billion which Jason wins is his to keep. Should he lose, Kerk will kill him.

The theme of risking one's life is repeated throughout the trilogy. Life must be put on the line in order to live fully. Fascinated by the large sums of money, the urgency, and by the remarkable Pyrran man, Jason agrees to the gambling venture; he gambles and wins. The management is not exhilarated by his good luck and attempts to prevent his departure. Kerk intervenes to help Jason collect his winnings; the two shoot their way to freedom, stop later for a quiet meal, and then battle their way off the planet.

Over Kerk's strenuous objections, Jason then decides to go to the Pyrran planet to see what he has risked his life for and to see what kind of place breeds men like Kerk. On the journey he meets Meta, a Pyrran woman who moves and thinks with the same speed and precision as Kerk. She is the pilot of the sole Pyrran spaceship, which is transporting the cargo paid for by Jason's gambling venture. The cargo turns out to be guns, ammunition, and military supplies with which to fight the hostile planet Pyrrus. During the long trip, Jason and Meta gravitate towards each other and finally become lovers; but as soon as the journey ends, both Kerk and Meta become singleminded in pursuit of their objective. Meta no longer pays attention to Jason, leaving him perplexed and angry.

The reason for the Pyrrans' caution is that the planet Pyrrus is deadly. Even the crew of the spaceship, who are far superior physically to Jason, must be unloaded like cargo in armored cases; they have been away too long, and need to be brought up to date concerning the latest dangers facing man. Jason is injected and innoculated against all the microbiological dangers, and forced to go through classes with the Pyrran children. In a simulated environment, he is drilled to perfection to respond instinctually to danger. At the end of many months of training, however, he realizes he will never become proficient enough to survive unattended.

Meta's rejection, together with his dependent position, prompts Jason to investigate the history of the settlement. Just as he begins to understand the Pyrran character and to uncover taboos surrounding the mysterious war, the city suffers another attack and Jason inadvertently causes the death of a Pyrran. Imprisoned, he awaits the return of the spaceship to take him away from Pyrrus. During his confinement, he learns that there are settlers who live outside the armored city, and that only limited trade and communication between them and the city dwellers is allowed. Jason then bribes a guard and escapes into the wilderness, where he meets the settlers, who, he learns, are hated by the city dwellers because they have learned to live with the planet. A state of war exists between the two groups, and the outside settlers, who have been cut off from the benefits of technology, ask Jason for his help and return him to the city.

Realizing that the city dwellers' problem is their own hatred of their environment, amplified and turned back against them, Jason organizes the outsiders to capture the spaceship. The control of offworld access will force the city dwellers to listen. The raid is successful and Jason dramatically demonstrates the truth of his discovery. Reluctantly, the city Pyrrans accept Jason. Meta realizes Jason's true worth and they are reunited.

No sooner is Jason accepted into Pyrran society, however, than he is kidnaped and then shipwrecked on "Deathworld II." In the second novel of the trilogy he faces a planet cut off from civilization, a world whose culture has lost most of its technological heritage. *Deathworld II* takes Jason on an evolutionary journey, beginning with his capture and nomadic slavehood. He advances up the evolutionary ladder by being captured by a more "advanced" group. He gains privileges by demonstrating his knowledge of proprietary scientific secrets and makes his escape, only to be captured again by another group still higher on the ladder. In hopes of finding the means to contact his Pyrran friends, he begins seeking the highest level of technology on the planet. As time passes, Jason tires of being passed from one power group to another and decides to change the medieval social structure by consolidating all the scientific knowledge in the hands of one group and introducing advanced technology. In spite of his successful campaign he is seriously wounded and only at the last moment rescued from certain death by the arrival of his Pyrran companion Meta.

In *Deathworld III*, the Pyrrans battle the nomadic inhabitants of Felicity, a heavy gravity planet containing enormous mineral resources. Although the natives fiercely defend themselves from outside exploitation, Jason decides that the Pyrrans need a new challenge, and ought to invade the planet. It takes more than stamina and physical skill, however, to overcome the resistance of Felicity's inhabitants; the Pyrran strategy of overwhelming the barbarians by sheer strength fails. With the help of his shipboard computer library, Jason recalls the experience of the Mongolians in attacking the Chinese civilization, and tricks the barbarian warlord into conquering the more civilized lowlands. Jason's recognition of the historical precedent yields him the final victory, and the conquerors are assimilated.

In each of the three deathworlds, Jason appears to be the underdog, weak, slow, and ill-adapted to the environment. But he comes prepared with knowledge, experience, and the determination to overcome all obstacles. As a gambler, he has learned to stretch the odds; he risks his life and wins.

At times Harrison is a better, more subtle writer than appears on the surface of his action-packed stories. His subtlety is most evident in the character of his disparate heroes, and is particularly evidenced by the developing nature of Jason dinAlt himself. To understand this development, we must remember that these novels were written for John W. Campbell, Jr., when *Astounding-Analog* dominated the science fiction magazine field. Harrison worked very closely with Campbell and, in fact, edited a collection of the Campbell's provocative and sometimes controversial editorials for book publication. Campbell had a rather restricted notion of what constituted a hero, and authors often tailored their lead characters according to the editor's specifications. Usually two-dimensional men who have their greatness thrust upon them, Campbell's heroes often solve problems by studying them from a unique viewpoint.

Harrison began the *Deathworld* series by creating Jason in the image that Campbell desired. Thus, in *Deathworld I*, Jason is the apotheosis of the Campbellian hero: at odds with society, he is trapped in circumstances he can neither understand nor comprehend. If he accepts the situation as defined by the almost superhuman Pyrrans, he will very likely die. Only when Jason refuses to take at face value the continuing war being fought by his captors does he begin to see the possibilities for survival. Surely this situation was typical of many stories printed by Campbell, and Harrison's treatment differs little from the Campbellian prototype. However, even in the first book, Harrison violates one of Campbell's unspoken edicts: Do not give the hero a love interest. Jason falls deeply in love with Meta, a situation that rarely occurred in standard *Astounding-Analog* fiction. Yet Harrison makes this happening crucial to Jason's growth, and his consequent development as a person depends upon this circumstance as well as upon Jason's increasing ability to look "otherwise" at the situations he finds himself in.

Harrison once remarked that he got terribly tired of Jason in *Deathworld II* and *Deathworld III*. The more he considered the devious yet "heroic" person he had invented, the more he became aware of Jason's essentially paradoxical, exaggerated nature. At this point, Harrison's irrepressible sense of the ridiculous took over, and to rid himself of the last vestiges of Campbellian "jasonism," he created a new "hero" in his 1965 novel, *Bill, The Galactic Hero*. Bill is such a bumbling idiot and the book about him so hilariously funny that no reader would ever again be able to take Campbell or Jason seriously. Therefore, the *Deathworld* series can be viewed as the culmination of the development of the classic science fiction hero, leading directly into its opposite, the creation of the anti-hero.

However, Harrison is far too good a craftsman to let his notion of the ambiguous hero get in the way of telling a story. All three novels are filled with action and suspense guaranteed to hold the reader's interest, although they are not equally successful: Harrison's interest in *Deathworld III* seems to flag and the plot becomes somewhat laborious at the end. *Deathworld IV* turned into *Bill, The Galactic Hero*, and science fiction finally proved that it could laugh at itself after the penny-dreadful seriousness of the first three books, which, if they lack the brilliant comedic invention of Harrison's later work, are still well worth reading, if only as period pieces.

Peter Brajer

Sources for Further Study

Reviews:

Amazing Stories. XXXV, January, 1961, p. 134.

Analog. LXVII, June, 1961, p. 165, LXXV, March, 1965, p. 87 and LXXXII, April, 1969, p. 167.

Magazine of Fantasy and Science Fiction. XX, January, 1961, p. 96.

New Worlds. CI, December, 1960, p. 128.

Publisher's Weekly. CXCIII, April 29, 1968, p. 79.

Punch. CCLVI, April 2, 1969, p. 511.

Times Literary Supplement. March 20, 1969, p. 287.

Visions of Tomorrow. I, December, 1969, pp. 61-62.

DEEP WATERS

Author: William Hope Hodgson (1877-1918)
First book publication: 1967
Type of work: Short stories

A collection of fantastic sea stories peopled with fearsome monsters and bizarre creatures

Deep Waters is a collection of fantastic stories of the sea, some of which first appeared in the collections *Men of the Deep Waters* (1914) and *The Luck of the Strong* (1916). Of the remainder, some had not been reprinted since their magazine appearances before World War I, and three were found among Hodgson's papers after his death. Two of these three had first appeared in earlier Arkham House anthologies edited by August Derleth.

Hodgson ran away to sea during his teens, and had a thoroughly miserable time as a shipboard apprentice. When he later turned his hand to writing, he wrote numerous journalistic pieces about life at sea and campaigned for better conditions for seamen. His first short stories were not sea stories, but after the publication of "From the Tideless Sea" in 1906, he began to use sailing ships as a frequent setting for his fiction, and in particular for the special brand of fantasy which is featured in *Deep Waters*. Much of the fiction he produced during his brief career — including two of his novels, *The Boats of the Glen Carrig* (1907) and *The Ghost Pirates* (1909) — was devoted to the elaboration of the old adage that "stranger things happen at sea." He portrayed the sea as an alien wilderness, uncertain in her moods and sheltering countless foul monsters. He applied himself especially to the development of the mythology of the Sargasso Sea, a region of the North Atlantic infested with great expanses of floating weed which were superstitiously held responsible for the entrapment and disappearance of many ships. (These masses of weed no longer infest the region to any marked degree, and the mystique of the Sargasso has been partly transferred to the so-called Bermuda Triangle.)

The basic structure of Hodgson's characteristic fantasies of the sea is identical with that of classic horror stories: they are tales of superstitious dread, filled with fogs and strange noises, each climaxing in some kind of monstrous visitation. At their best they are marvelously eerie. What distinguishes them from the normal run of Victorian and Edwardian horror stories, however, is that they forsake entirely the vocabulary of symbols characteristically employed by tales of the supernatural. They are exercises in speculative biology and teratology, investing heavily in the affective qualities of natural grotesquerie and operating entirely within a naturalistic world view. (Even *The Ghost Pirates*, which is a brilliant account of the "haunting" of a ship, rationalizes its effects by means of the notion of a dimensional "slip" which becalms the vessel in a limbo between two parallel worlds.)

"From the Tideless Sea" is a standardized "manuscript found in a bottle" story, offering two messages released from a ship named the *Homebird*, lost in 1873 — twenty-nine years before the discovery of the first message. The missive tells how the *Homebird*, crippled by a cyclone, became entangled by the weeds of the Sargasso. Its author is Arthur Samuel Phillips, who, with his wife and baby daughter, is left alive when all the crew have perished in an attempt to rescue the ship from her predicament. It ends with an ironic note to the effect that the ship has sufficient provisions to last the survivors for seventeen years, and that they are hopeful that they may be found eventually. The story continues with a further message picked up by a different ship, which relates the story of the survivors' sixth year aboard the stranded *Homebird*, and in particular their encounter with a gigantic flesh-eating crab.

This popular story set the pattern for several other stories, including a direct sequel ("More News from the *Homebird*," 1907) not included in *Deep Waters*. The stories seem like different versions of a recurrent nightmare whose essential features are invariable: a ship, somehow lost at sea and alienated from the civilized world from which it set out, falls under the sway of the sea's monsters and mysteries, and is irrevocably claimed by that horrific "other world."

Apart from the sequel to "From the Tideless Sea," Hodgson published four other such stories in 1907. One was the novel *Boats of the Glen Carrig*, in which a ship is becalmed offshore from an island inhabited by all manner of bizarre and horrific creatures, ranging from predatory mollusks to maleficent fungi. The other three stories are all in *Deep Waters*. "The Mystery of the Derelict," the weakest of the three, is a straightforward account of the discovery of an abandoned ship which turns out to be infested by unnaturally large and fearsome rats.

Much more impressive is Hodgson's most famous and most frequently reprinted story, "The Voice in the Night," in which a ship becalmed in a misty haze is hailed by a small boat whose occupant begs for food but refuses to come aboard or even to approach closely enough to be seen. Eventually, those aboard the ship persuade him to tell his story, and he explains how he and his fiancée were shipwrecked on a small island where nothing grows except a strange gray fungus, which proved to be edible but addictive. When the dawn breaks, the small craft pulls away hastily, but the narrator gains a fleeting glimpse of what their visitor, as a result of eating the fungus, has become.

Also in 1907, Hodgson published an article on cyclones and the curious meteorological effects that can sometimes be seen in association with them. This material he subsequently wove into his fourth sea fantasy of the year, "The *Shamraken* Homeward-Bounder," in which an ancient sailing ship making her last voyage sails toward what appears to be a vast arch of red-lit cloud, which her crew believes to be the gate of Heaven. The conclusion is metaphorically justified when the cyclone responsible for the strange phenomenon tears the old ship apart.

The Ghost Pirates ended the first wave of Hodgson's fantasies of the sea, and for the next couple of years he devoted himself principally to the "occult detective" stories featuring Carnacki, and to his extravagant futuristic fantasy *The Night Land* (1912). In the same year that this last novel appeared, however, he began publishing more stories of monstrosities of the sea. "The Thing in the Weeds" features the most famous marine terror of them all, the giant squid, while "The Island of the Ud" features a savage tribe of islanders who worship a gargantuan crab. (This story and its sequel, "The Adventure of the Headland," are, however, primarily treasure-hunt stories rather than fantasies.) A much more adventurous story published later in the year was "The Derelict," in which a debate on the nature of life and the possible existence of some essential animating principle forms the prelude to an illustrative narrative about a derelict vessel completely covered by a strange "mould" which animates parts of its structure.

Hodgson's speculations grew even more daring in another particularly extravagant story, "The Stone Ship" (1914), in which a group of sailors in a longboat fight their way through a sea infested with giant eels to a ship thrown up from the seabed by a volcanic eruption. The wood of her hull has been petrified, and so have the bodies of the men aboard her, one of whom bears a writhing mass of "red hair" upon his head — a sea caterpillar of rather startling appearance.

The posthumous stories recovered by August Derleth from papers in the possession of Hodgson's sister extend the author's range of the bizarre still further. "The Habitants of Middle Islet" and "The Crew of the *Lancing*" appear to be different drafts developing the same notion. The former features a derelict ship haunted by beautiful sirens who appear as beguiling faces in the water but then reach out with claws like talons; the latter also has faces in the water belonging to seallike humanoids with curved tails and jaws like the beak of an octopus, and makes more explicit the implication that the monsters are the crew-members of the derelict ships, who have undergone a sea-change. An altogether more enigmatic story is "The Call in the Dawn," in which members of a ship's crew hear the frequently repeated cry "Son of Man!" drifting over the water, emanating from a vast mass of weed which might (or might not) have gathered about a derelict ship. Here the mystery is left deliberately unresolved, the cry remaining nothing but an imaginative challenge, essentially inexplicable.

Considered together, the stories in *Deep Waters* (with the single exception of an anomalous sentimental tragedy, "The Sea Horses," which actually takes place on shore) comprise a remarkably coherent and consistent mythology. There is nothing else quite like it in fantastic fiction, though it has obvious affinities with Thomas A. Janvier's *In the Sargasso Sea* (1898) and E. H. Visiak's classic *Medusa* (1929). One of the collection's most curious features is that it is so anachronistic, for by the time Hodgson was writing these stories, the conquest of the seas by steam was already well under way. It is essential to the mythology of the stories that the characters should be at the mercy of the ocean, entirely dependent upon the whims of the wind and the frequent malice of the storm. Hodgson's marine wilderness is an environment where man emphatically does not belong: it is alien, and therefore inimical.

There are, of course, many bodies of work within imaginative literature which express a consciousness of the universe as an essentially baleful and menacing place. It is a sensation which everyone experiences from time to time, and the function commonly served by horror stories (for both their writers and their readers) presumably has much to do with the prevalence of the sensation and the need for catharsis of its pressures. What makes Hodgson particularly interesting as a writer in this vein is not so much his choice of the sea as a *milieu*, but the manner in which he populates that *milieu* with figures of menace. He stands at the interface of the supernatural imagination and the scientific imagination, being one of the first writers to abandon the traditional apparatus of ghosts, demons, and supernatural forces in favor of a new set of images.

In the twentieth century we have seen the rapid growth and proliferation of new teratologies which provide the essential figures of menace to inhabit our nightmare scenarios. Some writers — notably Algernon Blackwood and H. P. Lovecraft, in their different ways — have achieved considerable success in remodeling the traditional vocabulary of symbols into a more naturalistic form, but the predominant trend has followed Hodgson in replacing the vocabulary. Science fiction has made prolific use of biological oddities made horrific by enlargement or by investment with horrific powers of personal encroachment.

One further comment which may be made regarding the psychological profile of the stories in *Deep Waters* is their persistent emphasis on pollution. In virtually every situation described, attention is called to noxious odors, and frequent reference is made to slime. This is particularly obvious in "The Derelict" and "The Stone Ship," although "The Voice in the Night" can be construed as the ultimate story of personal pollution. This emphasis is something which became very marked as the concept of the alien slowly invaded (and eventually took over) stories of menace; the alien invasion stories of the pulp magazines are almost obsessive in their recapitulation of the personal violation idea.

Although he dealt with a watery sea rather than the "sea of space," Hodgson was a pioneer in the characterization of alien environments (it is interesting that in the novel he considered to be his masterpiece, *The Night Land*, the entire world falls prey to eternal night and fog and becomes infested with the same kind of horrific creatures, enlarged by a further order of magnitude, that menaced the *Glen Carrig*). It is for this reason that Hodgson invites description as one of the forefathers of modern science fiction.

Brian Stableford

Sources for Further Study

Criticism:

The Encyclopedia of Science Fiction and Fantasy. Compiled by Donald H. Tuck. Chicago: Advent Publishers, Inc., 1978, pp. 224-225. This article gives a biographical and bibliographical review of Hodgson's career.

Reviews:

Startling Mystery Stories. I, Summer, 1967, p. 117.

THE DEMOLISHED MAN

Author: Alfred Bester (1913-   )
First book publication: 1953
Type of work: Novel
Time: The twenty-fourth century
Locale: New York City

A first degree murder is committed in a future society where telepathy makes premeditated crime almost impossible

Principal characters:
BEN REICH, a successful business mogul
CRAYE D'COURTNEY, a rival businessman
BARBARA D'COURTNEY, his daughter
LINCOLN POWELL, the telepathic ("Esper") prefect of police
MARY NOYES, a telepath who acts as Powell's hostess
GUS TATE, a telepath who assists in planning the murder

Alfred Bester's *The Demolished Man* was one of the first novels published in *Galaxy Science Fiction* in the early 1950's. It became an instant success, and it has rarely been out of print since, gaining fans with each successive generation of readers. Its appreciation is well-deserved, for science fiction writers and readers alike still admire its pace, its distinctive style, its depth of characterization, and its brilliant depiction of a future society where mind-readers, known as "espers" (derived from "extra sensory perception") and nonespers intermingle in a fast-paced, hectic futuristic society.

Two stories run parallel through *The Demolished Man*. First we see Ben Reich, business mogul and entrepreneur, whose Monarch Utilities and Resources, Incorporated, is a multinational conglomerate. Reich has been haunted by a recurring nightmare, the vision of The Man with No Face. He identifies this shadowy figure with Craye D'Courtney, whose D'Courtney Cartel, another conglomerate, has been slowly eroding Reich's profits. Reich resolves to kill D'Courtney, a near-impossible task in a society where crime is rendered almost impossible by the large number of espers who will "peep" the thought prior to the deed itself and treat the potential criminal before the crime is committed. Reich is a brilliant man and a bold executive. In planning the murder of D'Courtney he leaves a trail of false clues, suborns a Class I Esper, and acquires a mind-block to make his identification extremely difficult.

Parallel to Reich's story run the efforts of his counterport, or foil, Lincoln Powell, Esper I prefect of police. If Reich is the conventional "bad guy" in Bester's portrayal, Powell is certainly the traditional hero in almost every sense of the word, except for one thing; while he is certainly brilliant, attractive, witty, sensitive, humane, able, and caring, he nonetheless harbors a negative *persona* within him, the irrepressible liar and practical joker he calls "Dishonest Abe."

Reich and Powell first meet after Reich's murder plans are carried out almost to perfection. Only the sudden, unexpected appearance of Barbara D'Courtney, who witnesses her father's murder, has frustrated Reich's plans. When the two men meet, Powell carefully traps Reich into an admission of guilt — and the chase and hunt is underway. In this crucial scene of the book Bester very carefully indicates that the two men, quite different in many significant ways, are more alike than might actually appear. Both are ethical, although it is their own code of ethics. Both are unscrupulous but charming, both are supremely capable, and both are instantly attracted to each other in a brother-brother or love-hate relationship. They could become fast friends, even as esper and nonesper, but they vow to become enemies — and the chase to find Barbara, the attempt to ascertain a motive for the murder and to make it stand up to "Old Man Mose," the mosaic multiplex prosecution computer, comprise most of the remainder of the novel.

The Demolished Man is not only brilliant science fiction, it is also one of the rare examples of the detective story within the genre. While the reader knows the identity of the killer from the first page of the book, he is swept along by the story of crime and punishment, motive and opportunity, hunter and hunted, even justice and mercy. The fact that Reich is no conventional villain, that he is, indeed, a good but almost fatally flawed individual, holds the reader's attention throughout the book. We wonder if Reich will be able to get away with his crime against the almost impossible odds presented by the espers of the society. Indeed, at times Powell is so pompous, so impossibly "goody-goody" that we almost hope for Reich to escape justice, and for Powell to fall on his insufferably smug face.

Yet Powell is, in the conventional sense of the word, the hero, at least the protagonist. As readers, we may not appreciate Powell's heroic nature, but we do recognize, in justice, that Reich must not be permitted to go unpunished. It is only when we realize that Bester has very carefully drawn a double hero, or, for that matter, a double villain in the composite character of Powell-Reich or Reich-Powell, that we can understand Bester's purpose. All men are flawed, he seems to say; all men are potential devils, but they are potential angels as well.

Thus ambiguity permeates *The Demolished Man*, an ambiguity arising from depth of construction and characterization. Bester does not portray his twenty-fourth century society in terms of black and white, either-or, wrong or right. The "normals" of that society are not intrinsically less capable than the espers, just as supernormal peeping ability on the part of the espers does not mean that they are supermoral or superethical human beings. For example, Dr. Jeems, the psychiatric head of Kingston Hospital where Reich is demolished, is a "normal," and both Gus Tate and Jerry Church, supremely talented espers, are corrupted by Reich, or, more properly, by their own innate greed and lust for power. These ambiguities are welcome and lend a depth to the novel that other science fiction works of the early 1950's often lacked.

Philosophically and psychologically, also, *The Demolished Man* was far beyond most of what was being published at the time. Bester was, among other things, trained in psychology, and that training is evident almost everywhere in the novel. What is particularly interesting about this work is that, while Bester employs the jargon and method of Freudian analysis, an examination of the novel in terms of the Adlerian power-drive or Jungian archetypal analysis would be equally fruitful. Thus the identity of The Man with No Face can be, in Freudian terms, the overpowering demands of the Superego, or, in Jungian terms, the final meeting of the *persona* with the Shadow. Both explanations are equally satisfactory. However, other deeper, ancient themes permeate the novel: the search for a father by the son, or the search for the son by the father, for it should come as no surprise to the reader to discover that D'Courtney is Reich's natural father and that Barbara is his half-sister. D'Courtney had once denied his natural son and is now seeking atonement with him, while Reich's primitive unconsciousness has driven him in turn to seek revenge on the father who abandoned him. The motive for the killing is passion, not profit, but everyone, including Powell, is unaware of it, assuming, with Reich, the profit motive.

Philosophically, Bester resurrects the ancient notion of solipsism to indicate the power and singleness of Reich's vision. If he alone is real in his universe, he will become a galactic focal point, immune to the reality of either espers or normals. He will become the creator of his own universe and the deadly enemy of galactic reason and reality. "I'll own you," Reich shouts. "I'll own you all. Bodies, passions, and souls." In facing this challenge, Powell concentrates all of the latent psychic esper energy in the Mass Cathexis Measure to force Reich to face himself, and thus The Man with No Face. Reich must understand that he has lost the Cosmic Game, that it cannot be won by "theft, terror, hatred, lust, murder, rapine."

In the end, *The Demolished Man* is not simply a work of science fiction wedded to the detective story, but a novel of death, rebirth, and resurrection as well, a novel of mothering and fathering, a story of growth, development, and final maturity of both "heroes." Demolition, the reader is at first surprised to discover, is not capital punishment. Rather, it is a process of slow extinction of consciousness leading to the rebirth of the totally mature person. In this sense, then, Powell fathers Reich, just as he had previously "fathered" Barbara D'Courtney who had been rendered a helpless infant as a result of witnessing her father's murder. Powell, in fact, feels that he and esper society are nursemaids to the universe. He has nursed both Ben Reich and his half-sister Barbara from unconsciousness to awareness.

Powell, however, is not infallible. He has missed some rather obvious clues planted throughout the book, and even in his deep psychological penetration of Barbara's psyche, he does not discover at first that Barbara is a latent esper. Thus is should come as no surprise to the reader to discover on the very last page of the novel that Ben Reich is a latent esper as well, although Powell seems singularly unaware of what is now fairly obvious. Bester has given us enough clues to enable us to arrive at this discovery ourselves (although most readers miss them the first time around): the fact that Bester *never* uses italics for anything except peeper transmission; the knowledge that esper ability is genetic, that Ben's half-sister Barbara is a latent peeper, and so on.

Both Barbara and Ben, having died to "normal" society and to themselves, are reborn to esper society, having been fathered or brothered by Powell. For example, on the first page of the novel, Reich has been sleeping in a womblike hydropathic bed; on the last page, although still undergoing demolition, he has been reborn enough to think, *"Powell-peeper-Powell-friend,"* and eventually awaken into peeper society.

Bester's handling of his women characters in the novel also mark it as an achievement far ahead of its time. The panoply of women — Barbara D'Courtney, the daughter in search of a father; Duffy, the virgin seductress; Mary Noyes, the long-suffering mistress of Powell's house but not of his body; Maria Beaumont, the Gilded Corpse at whose decadent party Reich murders his father — all are well drawn, even though they sometimes have only minor roles. Bester has the ability to sketch his characters with only a few words, or an incisive bit of action. If not distinguished, they are at least memorable.

Nearly thirty years have elapsed since the first publication of *The Demolished Man*, but the brilliance of its stylistic development, the ingenuity of its plot construction, and the sheer vigor of its execution make it still a distinguished science fiction novel.

Willis E. McNelly

Sources for Further Study

Reviews:

Analog. LII, December, 1953, pp. 149-150.

Authentic Science Fiction. XLI, January, 1954, pp. 149-150.

Fantastic Universe Science Fiction. I, August–September, 1953, p. 191.

Galaxy. VI, September, 1953, pp. 121-122.

Imagination Science Fiction. IV, August, 1953, p. 144.

Magazine of Fantasy and Science Fiction. V, July, 1953, p. 84.

DHALGREN

Author: Samuel R. Delany (1942-   )
First book publication: 1975
Type of work: Novel
Time: Indeterminate, but most likely the late 1970's
Locale: The city of Bellona, somewhere in the United States

A lengthy, serious attempt to fuse science fiction and avant-garde literary modes of expression in a grim odyssey through a mysteriously shattered city

Principal characters:
THE KID, a nameless wanderer who becomes a poet and street gang leader
LANYA COLSON, an upper-class woman, also a wanderer; a musician and teacher, and the Kid's lover
DENNY, a teen-age boy, a street gang member and the Kid's lover
TAK LOUFER, an engineer who welcomes newcomers to Bellona
GEORGE HARRISON, a black rapist who assumes symbolic importance for the city's inhabitants
ROGER CALKINS, publisher of the Bellona *Times* and leader of the city's cultural elite
ERNEST NEWBOY, an established poet visiting Bellona
SCORPIONS, members of street gangs, interracial but largely black
PAUL FENSTER, a former civil rights activist
MICHAEL KAMP, a former astronaut who has landed on the Moon
THE RICHARDS FAMILY, the last middle-class family in Bellona

The science fiction novel shares with its so-called "mainstream" counterpart an evolution from the contradictory ancestry of satirical and melodramatic romance. Science fiction readers are usually well enough aware of the struggle for acceptance their genre has always faced in the American literary community, but focusing on the negative implications of segregation in the pulp ghetto, they generally forget that novelists of all varieties once had to fight the same battles. Writers such as Henry James, now thoroughly canonized by established critics, once felt pressed to defend their artistic aspirations against the simultaneous charges that their medium was disreputable and that their attempts at art were pretentious distractions for readers seeking a vaguely defined "entertainment." The issues seem to surface repeatedly in debates surrounding the development of any new art form, particularly those growing from a base in popular culture. While seeking communication with an audience, the artist is nonetheless concerned with perfecting both the tools and the modes of execution: meeting self-defined standards of merit. These standards may challenge, either explicitly or implicitly, the assumptions underlying previously existing tastes. On the other hand, an audience must be reached on its own terms if it is to respond voluntarily to a piece of work. Resolving these often contradictory demands becomes a necessary task for any artist seeking both quality and popular recognition.

Beginning his novelist's career at nineteen, Samuel R. Delany early established a reputation for fusing traditional science fiction themes and formats with his own artistic concerns for mythology and the use of language. But this reputation exists more among writers, who honored Delany with the Science Fiction Writers of America's Nebula Award four times between 1966 and 1969, than among fans, who have extended their Hugo Award only once. In all his early books, Delany was working in two new areas. He was adding depth to the genre's traditional adventure formats, consciously wedding his plots to the myth-building processes of folklore while simultaneously developing the ability to use small nuances of speech or behavior to define character or situation. Among the genre's few black writers (and the first of these to achieve prominence), he also has a vision — bred in Harlem and sharpened into poetry in Athens and Istanbul — of life on the streets of an urban underworld which gives his mythology enough social edge to be historical and political in the most complete sense. The culmination of this literary growth is *Dhalgren*, perhaps the most complex and intellectually demanding novel ever published by a writer within the science fiction community.

Dhalgren bears many signs of its pulp magazine ancestry, although its literary pretensions mask many of the similarities. A nameless wanderer has a fleeting confrontation with a dark woman on the outskirts of a city called Bellona. While the graphically described sexual encounter (the first of many, both heterosexual and homosexual, throughout the book) is something no pulp editor could have permitted, it is thoroughly traditional in its form and consequences — in everything, in fact except its explicitness. Following the coupling, the woman disappears. Searching for her, the wanderer enters the city, which has been cut off from the remainder of the United States as the result of some unexplained and undefined cataclysm. Remembering his biography but not his name, this wanderer, the Kid, soon embarks on a dual quest. He explores the city, seeking to understand how it can function shorn of established law and social relationships, in an environment shrouded in smoke, lacking clocks and calendars, in which even the separation of night and day and the order of days in the week are completely arbitrary. Equipped with a strange and terrifying weapon, a gauntlet of knives surrounding a chain mail glove, and a mysterious set of chains studded with glass prisms, the Kid seems embarked on exactly the sort of adventure which science fiction writers have always enjoyed. There is an environment to explore, and there is a mystery of social situation to understand, along with its possibly cosmic implications.

But there is a second mystery, which is much less a part of science fiction convention. As the Kid is told when he enters the city, Bellona is a place where people become exactly what they are and do exactly what they want to do. The Kid knows neither who he is nor what he wants to do, and the exploration of this alien environment becomes his quest for his true identity.

Hardly an actual veteran of science fiction's pulp magazines, Delany does, however, possess the strong sense for an interesting story of which critics from among the genre writers themselves are so proud. Bellona's smoke-shrouded streets, whose configuration changes from one moment to the next, lead from one bit of the puzzle to the next. What happened here? And what did it mean? Who has stayed in the city and why? Who has come here since the disaster and why? At first even the novel's pretentiousness contributes to the fun of the paired mysteries as literary devices become carefully concealed clues, evidence for exploration. But in the long run Delany never manages to resolve the conflicting demands his high ambitions place on his work.

Practicing the novelist's contradictory art, Delany revels in paradox. He is a fantasist in subject and a grim realist in language, style, manner, and even, to a large measure, in structure. At times this is a powerful combination, with individual scenes and bits of dialogue that have a great dramatic impact. To read *Dhalgren* and sense Delany's fascination for urban life existing outside the reach of a larger law while holding a mental image of America's festering ghettoes is a truly frightening experience. But if Bellona's fate is the subject of a social novel, the Kid's search for himself creates a psychological novel. Both sides of the book describe surrealistic situations in very realistic language, and rely on the confusion of the real and the surreal. Each requires a great deal of the reader. Delany the storyteller creates mysteries whose fascination encourages one to plunge ever faster and deeper into the book, but Delany the artist, like Henry James, writes for those upon whom nothing is lost. With his careful layers of meaning and almost microscopic attention to detail, he creates a rich and dense work which has its intellectual satisfactions, but which also slows down at precisely those points at which some forward motion might be required.

This is no accident, for it is rooted in the Kid's growing awareness of himself and in the way he is received in the city. He is rapidly introduced to most of the important people in what has become a very small city, and soon becomes a figure of note in his own right. His exploits, some legitimately heroic, others merely colorful, become part of the city's emerging folklore and his notes, observations, and poetry become the focus of its cultural life. But such success, even acceptance, only heightens the Kid's self-doubt. To a certain extent this deepens and rounds him as a character, and Delany uses the process as a tool to explore the very personal experience of writing and literary acceptance. But the Kid is the narrator as well as the principal character, and his growing introspection and self-involvement change the quality of his narration as well as of his life. He stops exploring the city and begins living in it, no longer questioning his environment and finding his most settled home as the leader of a street gang. Living his new *persona* as a celebrity, the Kid's thoughts and the book's pages focus on his efforts to separate the elements of myth and image accumulated in the city from his often equally frightening but "true" identity.

It is this introspection on Delany's part that overburdens *Dhalgren*. Distrusting his artist's *persona*, the Kid soon rejects the artist's implicit but necessary role as an interpreter of reality. At the start Delany deliberately creates the impression that the novel itself is drawn from the Kid's scribbled journal, but the narrative point of view switches from first to third person often enough to give an objective picture of the wanderer and his quests. By the novel's final chapters, this device has been abandoned and the adaptation of a journal is made explicit. Not only is the outside perspective on the Kid lost, but since the Kid has lost any confidence in his ability to interpret reality correctly, the novel itself explicitly abandons the attempt to understand what has happened in Bellona. The Kid's rejection of the attempt to interpret the structure of reality is even tied to the suggestion that paranoia, the insanity of which the Kid is terrified, is the perception of nonexistent patterns in the random relationship of events. All that is left is the telling of the story, with the inundation of microscopic detail at last complete, and sequence and structure obliterated.

Delany has always been fascinated with the mythmaking process — the creation of new patterns with which to interpret the world. Seen from the inside, with the Kid able to note the difference between his own experience and people's perceptions of him, mythmaking is destructive of the myth figure's "true" or human identity. By the time the Kid does remember part of his name, his past identity has become quite irrelevant. The knowledge thus symbolized is partial and completely useless in either understanding or controlling Bellona's destructive environment. With the sequence of days in the week arbitrarily altered by the town's only newspaper, with two moons passing through the night and the sun filling half the daytime sky, the concrete has become mysterious. At the same time, ubiquitous motorcyclists' chains studded with jeweled lights and projecting holographic images of mythological beasts (the only overt presence of advanced technology in the novel) are at first mysterious icons fraught with meaning for those initiated into the city's secrets, then traced to their banal source, a novelties warehouse. Even the patterns of myth are subject to the disorganization of entropy, and each new reference point or source of information dissolves under the Kid's very glance.

Yet for all its mythmaking overtones, *Dhalgren* is a social novel. Although many of the book's characters are black, the issue of race is both central to Bellona's history (the city's cataclysm, while mysterious, is always associated with a race riot) and largely submerged. As in American life at large, Bellona's black population is generally invisible. But race and racial politics retain their volatility. The assassination of a civil rights activist sets off a second racial upheaval in which the Kid is expelled from the city. Moreover, the cyclical theories of history with which science fiction is replete are brought to an extreme degree here: like *Finnegans Wake*, *Dhalgren* ends on the same sentence with which it opens. Thus, the closing events become the mysterious past which the Kid has been seeking, the only explanation Delany ever gives for what has happened to the city.

So Bellona's disaster is social, even political: through its shattered streets run all the archetypes that science fiction and the larger society from which it springs consider the movers and shakers, not of power necessarily, but of culture. During the 1960's in particular the civil rights martyrs, the homeless outlaws, the poets from the filthy streets, the artists, the hippies in the parks, the street gang leaders (black and white), and the space-exploring engineers and astronauts were all heroes. Some supported the social *status quo*, others sought its reformation or abolition. Yet all were accepted by one segment of society or another as the agents of American culture's future vitality. All are in Bellona or arrive there as part of the story, but none of them can discover the city's secret. Neither can they help the Kid. They have all lost their power to influence the environment in any direction other than increased entropy: the destruction of even *ad hoc* social institutions, disorder, personal disorientation, and a massive increase in violence. At every turn, people attempt the modes of expression and action which seemed reasonable in the 1960's, and at every turn their failures illuminate the failures of the American culture in which they were rooted and the lies and violence inherent in both the original situation and the inevitably failing efforts at retrieval. Crucial among these failures is the absence of even the traces of organized, cooperative activity above the volatile level of a street gang. If entropy is triumphant in Bellona, it is to a great extent by default. The Kid, and all the others, engage in their quests pursuing solely their individual goals at the inevitable cost of violent death. Sufficiently aware of the condition to make it an object of explicit satire, Delany is as much a victim of this decadence as any of his characters, for the failures and lies in the novel extend as far as the eye can see and there are no alternatives in sight.

Dhalgren marks the nadir of pessimism in science fiction's tradition of social criticism. An entire culture is caught in a trap, desperate for a way out but provided with only unreliable information on which to act and limited to choices of action which can only make the situation worse. In Delany's circular structure, one can venture forth on quests for knowledge, but Vasco da Gama, Columbus, even Neil Armstrong, now seem as mythical as Lancelot and Gawain. No learning is possible. All growth and movement merely bring one back to the starting point, the gates of the great city, preparing yet another doomed foray into a world at once fascinating but violent, familiar yet alien, never consumed but always burning.

Albert I. Berger

Sources for Further Study

Criticism:

Scholes, Robert and Eric S. Raskin. *Science Fiction*. New York: Oxford University Press, 1977, pp. 95-96. Delany's *Dhalgren* is described as being "richly characterized fiction" in this book.

Reviews:

Booklist. LXXI, June 1, 1975, p. 991.

Library Journal. C, March 15, 1975, p. 604.

Magazine of Fantasy and Science Fiction. XLIX, November, 1975, p. 50.

New York Times Book Review. February 16, 1975, p. 27.

DIMENSION OF MIRACLES

Author: Robert Sheckley (1928-   )
First book publication: 1968
Type of work: Novel
Time: The present
Locale: Earth and several alternate Earths

A satirical picaresque novel about a man who, having journeyed to the Galactic Center to collect his prize for winning an intergalactic sweepstakes, has no idea how to return to his own Earth amid a multitude of possible Earths

Principal characters:
> TOM CARMODY, Everyman in search of his home
> THE PRIZE, an object/animal/being capable of shapechanging
> MELICHRONE, a god
> MAUDSLEY, a contractor, builder of Earth
> CARMODY'S PREDATOR, a thing with the sole purpose of eating Carmody

Robert Sheckley's books refuse to be categorized. Are they fantasy, science fiction, Zen philosophy, or the work of a sane madman? There is no one answer. The only choice is to say that whatever they are, they are the best in that field. It is easy to make comparisons to other art forms to explain Sheckley: he is Magritte, he is Dali, he is surrealism in prose form. But his is a surrealism with rules. There is a beginning, a middle, and an end — a framework — but what happens within that framework is pure Sheckley. *Abandon preconceived notions of reality, all you who read here* is the watchword of any Sheckley novel. Sheckley's writing is not, however, experimentation for experimentation's sake; it also entertains, and allows the reader a glimpse into a very intriguing mind.

Dimension of Miracles is the "simple" story of a simple man in search of his homeland — a topic familiar since ancient times. In this case the hero is Tom Carmody, who is informed that he has won first prize in the Galactic Sweepstakes; caught up in the joy of winning, he fails to take into account what such a prize might entail. He is told that the prize has value, but nowhere is he told what sort of value that might be. The Prize is a *yenta*, a whiner, and a half-baked philosopher, but it must have some value — it is, after all, a prize. Sheckley makes the point that our civilization is too prone to consider prizes — be they material gain, fame, or being named best in class — as an end in themselves rather than as a possibly dubious honor that might prove to be more trouble than it is worth.

After being given his Prize, Carmody is told he must find his way home on his own — and not merely to a point in time and space, but to a point in several possible dimensions. There are many Earths. Which one is Carmody's Earth? And which Earth does he really want? Carmody seeks an answer from the autochthonous Melichrone, but finds that he too needs answers. A god who has tried all aspects of godliness, who has been worshiped by countless billions, and who has created both Heaven and Hell, he has grown bored with it all; Melichrone wonders what a god's ultimate purpose is in life.

Carmody comes up with an answer. Because Melichrone has been a god of one planet, in one section of space, he has internalized his godhood. Now, to have purpose, he must externalize his power — and the only way to do that, Carmody explains, is to aid others outside his own world, which is, in reality, himself. Carmody is external to Melichrone, needs help, and is, therefore, Melichrone's purpose in life. Unable to get around the skewed logic of all this, Melichrone agrees to help Carmody. Logic taken to its most absurd conclusions is the hallmark of a Sheckley book. So skilled is he at this art that after working his way through the dizzying prose, the reader finds himself convinced, for the length of the book, that the author's *reductio ad absurdum* is indeed the height of logical thought.

Melichrone's aid takes the form of sending Carmody on to Maudsley, the world contractor. But before he allows Carmody to leave, he warns him of impending doom: a Carmody predator is after him because he is the only Carmody. The theory is that all creatures fit into the chain of life as the eaters and the eaten. All things have their predators, but such predators are native to the habitat of the eaten. Carmody, by removing himself from his home, had also removed himself from the sphere of his natural predators — and so it was necessary for the Universe to create a predator especially for Carmody: a Carmody eater. The predator is very wily, knowing all the tricks a Carmody might use to avoid him; and, worst of all, the Carmody eater is hungry. There is but one Carmody, just as there is but one Carmody eater.

Duly warned about his predator, Carmody goes to Maudsley in hopes that the latter can remember the contracting job — Carmody's Earth — done for an elderly chap with a beard and long nightgown. Maudsley does remember the job, and with some shame. He cut several corners on the job and cheated his customer, the God of Earth. But God accepted Maudsley's flawed creation and even stated he would turn the flaws into something useful — his people would have something to wonder about, something to puzzle their minds with, and, not being gods, they would come up with many explanations of the inconsistency of the world, thus giving them something to do with their lives. God and Maudsley had between them invented science.

Maudsley agrees to construct a machine that will take Carmody back to the Earth (or one of them), but while waiting for the device to be completed Carmody has his first brush with his predator. Cleverly disguised as a girl in distress, a hero-scientist, and a rocket ship all at the same time, the predator almost succeeds in eating Carmody. The description of the incident is pure space opera. Sheckley masterfully dissects the genre and points out all of its absurdities, while Carmody falls for the predator's ploy. Only the quick action of the Prize and Maudsley saves Carmody from his fate. The Prize has some use, after all.

Maudsley explains further the laws of predators and warns Carmody that he must in the future be extremely cautious. The predator will strike again and again, and since it is Carmody's fate to be eaten, the predator will more than likely win in the end. Carmody's only hope is to find his own world — the only place that does not need a Carmody predator. Maudsley points out that Carmody has an additional problem: will he be able to tell if the Earth he is on is *his* Earth? Maudsley's machine can take him to Earth, but only to *Where* Earth. Where Earth is only the first of the three W's involved in finding Carmody's Earth; the second W is When and the third is Which. The Earth Carmody will find on the first try is bound to be the wrong one, but Maudsley will give him a letter of introduction to someone who can help him with the temporal problems. Carmody is not amused by the limitations of Maudsley's help, but anything is better than doing nothing at all to get home.

The first Earth is definitely the wrong one — or possibly the right one at the wrong time. It is the Cretaceous Period on a world with talking, intelligent dinosaurs, and is not Carmody's idea of his world at all. He meets a dinosaur named Borg and engages in a very carefully constructed discussion of the future without telling the creature that in his Earth dinosaurs have been extinct for some sixty million years. One wrong step in this conversation could go badly for Carmody. He doubts very much that Borg would enjoy hearing the truth and might get violent.

Carmody's predator next appears in the guise of an IRS representative, but this is too obvious — even Carmody knows that IRS agents are predators.

Carmody's next contact proves to be the head of the Galactic Placement Bureau, one Clyde Beedle Seethwright. Seethwright, after a Lewis Carroll-style discussion on the realness of reality, agrees to send Carmody on to a Where and a When Earth, but he is not able to solve the Which Earth problem; Carmody must do that himself. But with reality being what it is, any Which world might seem like the right world to Carmody, since he will fit into each and not realize that it is not his Which. The only clue will come from the Carmody eater. As long as the predator is still after him, Carmody will know he is on the wrong Which Earth. But the only way he may find out for sure that he is on the wrong Which Earth is if the predator eats him, in which case the knowledge is of little use. Carmody is faced with a problem of no small dimensions.

Seethwright sends Carmody next to an Earth with a City that is perfectly willing to look after him for the rest of his life, but with certain restrictions. Carmody must do what the City asks of him, because all the City's requests are for his own good. The City is Big Brother, or Big Momma, with a vengeance. This is not Carmody's idea of life, nor is it a suitable world for him, and he exits quickly.

The next Which Earth seems to be New York City, but the fact that Carmody's predator almost manages to eat him by disguising itself as an IRT subway is proof enough that this is not Carmody's Earth. The next Earth, where advertising is a way of life, almost convinces Carmody, until the appearance of a second Carmody, whose Earth it really is, sends our hero out again on his quest.

The next Earth was the Earth of Carmody's childhood — or rather, of the childhood he wished he had had — a world where Lana Turner was a school chum, and Burt Lancaster was the friendly village policeman. It was a world of dreams found only in the back row of a movie theater with a box of popcorn and some jujubes. Carmody leaves this world only when he realizes that it contains background music to each scene, and thus cannot be real. Reality does have the flaw of lacking dramatic music to set off its high points.

Finally, Carmody locates his real home, the Earth we know and live in, an Earth with soot-browned trees, carbon monoxide air, PCP, muggers, and more waste than we know what to do with. But Carmody, safely home at last, free of his predator, decides he does not wish to live here; he throws himself back onto the probability wheel and goes in search of other Earths. He may not find a Utopia, and his predator is now back on his trail, but at least he is alive in a Universe full of possibilities.

Carmody, like all of us on Spaceship Earth, may only have moments to live, or a lifetime, but he will make each minute count. That, perhaps, is Robert Sheckley's message: in a world of possible realities, we must make each minute count. We alone can make reality real.

Kathleen Sky

Sources for Further Study

Criticism:

The Encyclopedia of Science Fiction and Fantasy. Compiled by Donald H. Tuck. Chicago: Advent Publishers, Inc., 1978, p. 386. This article gives a brief summary of Sheckley's career.

Reviews:

Publisher's Weekly. CXCIII, May 20, 1968, p. 63.

Times Literary Supplement. October 16, 1969, p. 1215.

THE DISAPPEARANCE

Author: Philip Wylie (1902-1971)
First book publication: 1951
Type of work: Novel
Time: 1950-1954
Locale: The United States

The fictional account of a four-year period during which the women have disappeared from the men, and the men from the women, focusing on the worldwide ramifications to the instantaneous disappearance of one sex from the other

Principal characters:
> DR. WILLIAM PERCIVAL GAUNT, a well-respected "generalist" scholar, husband, and father
> PAULA GAUNT, a Ph.D. in foreign languages, wife, and mother
> EDWINNA GAUNT, their divorced daughter
> ALICIA GAUNT, her daughter

Philip Wylie's inventive book *The Disappearance* might cause even the most seasoned science fiction veteran to raise a skeptical eyebrow. The avid science fiction reader has been through invasions from unknown areas of the galaxy, cosmic catastrophes of monumental scale, and physical anomalies of the strangest kinds. This seasoned reader, while vigilant in spotting inconsistency, is reasonably openminded when confronted by the implausible. Whether Wylie's strangely disturbing tale is science fiction, fantasy, allegory, or a combination of all three, remains to be seen. What is certain is that it departs from precedent and stands alone in an often inbred world of science fiction and the literature of fantasy.

The sudden wresting away of one sex from the other provides the author with an excellent setting for his relentless tirade against all that he considers wrong with American attitudes. When, without reason or explanation, "the females of the species vanished on the afternoon of the second Tuesday in February at four minutes and fifty-two seconds past four o'clock, Eastern Standard Time," Dr. William Percival Gaunt, like the rest of the men in the world, is baffled by the curious event. Likewise, Paula Gaunt, while working in her garden, gazes up to smile at her husband, and right before her eyes he disappears. So begins Philip Wylie's poignant account of a world suddenly separated into two parallel worlds, existing simultaneously, each without the presence of the opposite sex.

In *The Disappearance*, originally written in 1951 and reprinted in 1978, the iconoclastic Wylie, noted most for his diatribe against American values in *Generation of Vipers* (1942) and his collaboration with Edwin Balmer in *When Worlds Collide* (1932) and *After Worlds Collide* (1933), once again takes on the gadfly role. The tale is actually a vehicle through which the author expresses his sometimes heavy-handed views on religion, war, science, morality, and specifically, the idiocies perpetuated by prescribed sexual roles.

The book is really two novels within one. It succeeds because of Wylie's ability to combine an inventive plot with dynamic action and characters who respond believably to four long years of chaos, disaster, and suffering. Dr. William Percival Gaunt, the foremost philosopher of his time, and Paula, a Ph.D. in foreign languages, his wife and a mother, are the leading characters in the story. In separate yet parallel roles, they each help organize and reconstruct their single-sexed worlds. Through their individual struggles and eventual reunion they illustrate Wylie's central themes. He views a "person" as being an androgynous construct, and that only through the symbiotic functioning of both male *and* female qualities can human potential be realized. The author's enchantment with Jungian concepts is apparent throughout the book, and whether the reader accepts the premise that instincts are the primary determinant of human behavior, he will find the story provocative and intellectually challenging.

After opening the story with the Disappearance itself, Wylie uses flashback techniques to introduce his characters. The Gaunts have had an ordinary life together. William is a well-respected "generalist," and although Paula is a capable linguist, she is trapped in the limited role of wife and mother. After conceiving and rearing two unimpressive children, they continue to endure the years together. Their daughter Edwinna, living with them, embodies the conflicting qualities of beauty, cruelty, and intelligence so often found in Wylie's characters.

The narration of *The Disappearance* is unique. Wylie, concerned with the criticism of his treatment of women in *Generation of Vipers*, takes on the formidable task of alternating chapters from male to female point of view. The technique is effective, allowing the author to fill out and explore the various ramifications of his fantastic situation. If at times he seems to be propagandizing his own ideas too strongly, he does so without losing his reader. With the exception of a twenty-four page didactic essay (which is an entire chapter in the text), Wylie is able to infuse the most static situations with movement or the potential for movement.

The plot development personifies the underlying premise of the story: creative wholeness is only possible in the person who is "a-man-plus-a-woman." With one or the other gender missing, there is likely to be hate and destruction, but no creativity and love. Throughout the book, as the author alternates between male and female worlds, it is destruction and hardship that is depicted. The sense of loss and emptiness in each world slowly grows into resentment and hate. Most of the story is the chronicle of mankind's physical and spiritual disintegration. On one level, it depicts two separate worlds disintegrating. On another level, it scolds society for forcing men and women into separate psychological and material domains. The war between the sexes is the result of an unenlightened attitude which overlooks a fundamental truth: man and woman are but halves of the one true sex.

Wylie begins his allegory in the male world. The men are taken by surprise when the women physically disappear, unaware that they are already spiritually separate from the women. The immediate aftermath of the Disappearance is bewilderment more than anything else. Although the male dominated government and business world function fairly well, the international reverberations are quite different. Wylie, unable to resist the opportunity to play on popular fears, has the Soviet Union blame the United States for the disappearance of their women, justifying an atomic attack on the United States. In typical Wylie fashion, the intensive three-day atomic war is gruesomely described. While the United States loses three cities, the Soviet Union loses seventeen and the war itself. The men revert to primitive savagery. Law and order breaks down and men begin to run in packs killing and looting. Men also turn to homosexuality and female impersonation. Throughout all of this, William Gaunt's committee of scientists, scholars, and philosophers cannot explain the rationale behind the Disappearance.

The women, in their separate world, are in worse shape than the men. Left to their own resources after the Disappearance, the women are woefully unprepared for even the simplest tasks confronting them. They are barely capable of survival, being wives of politicians rather than politicians themselves, and consumers of products rather than businessmen. Through the organizational skills of women like Paula and Edwinna Gaunt, a government comprised of congressmen's wives is set up. Having sidestepped the disaster of atomic war with the Russian women, the American women are plagued with various natural disasters and epidemics. Unable to run the equipment necessary for mining or operate complicated machinery, they suffer from inadequate food supplies, lack of medical treatment, and the general breakdown of morality. The women soon become resentful and hateful toward the men who had made them so dependent. Again, destructive forces are promulgated in the absence of the other sex.

The sexes are reunited on the four-year anniversary of the Disappearance, ironically Valentine's Day. Suddenly, the world is restored to the way it was four years earlier. Men and women once again walk the same streets. Loved ones who had died in the separation period are restored to life. Individuals who had spent four hellish years apart join together for celebrative orgies. Without ever understanding why the Disappearance occurred, people are back together, understanding now that men and women are one.

In Franz Kafka's *Metamorphosis*, the main character, Gregor, is so dehumanized in life that he actually wakes up one morning to find himself transformed into an enormous cockroach. In Wylie's *The Disappearance*, the men and women are so separated from their own vital male and female qualities that they actually disappear into separate worlds. Unlike Kafka, Wylie gives his characters a second chance. When the men and women are rejoined and given a moment to reflect, they realize that it is only through both male and female energies that the creative forces of the universe work. Men and women are equal parts of life's creative wholeness, separate and different only in their individual functions.

Wylie, in this allegorical fable, has moved away from his earlier evangelistic fervor. No longer is a personal God reaping havoc upon humanity. There are no images of the familiar old man sitting on his throne in judgment. There is rather, the allusion to a creative principle or force that is universally present in the collective unconscious. The author's continued use of archetypal concepts and symbolism indicates his discovery of another, more esoteric, explanation for the irrationalities of mankind. The closest explanation for the Disappearance itself is couched in these symbols. An obscure character in the story, cryptically at work building a mandala-shaped room in his house, suddenly begins to have vivid and accurate dreams of the women in their separate world. He does not know why he built the structure, only that he was compelled to build it. Nevertheless, the room brings him into contact with the instinctual make up of the species, the unified collective unconscious; and he is momentarily able to transcend the separateness. There is a fire; the room is destroyed; the dreams stop; the story continues.

The Disappearance will be stimulating to some and disquieting to others. There is, of course, the Wyliean sideshow of atomic warfare and its aftermath of rioting and rebellion in the male world. There is natural calamity and disease in the female world. These opportunities for projected horror had been present in Wylie's earliest work, and they continue up to his posthumously published *The End of the Dream*. They are his particular trademark. But *The Disappearance* represents a change in Wylie's writing. It is less vitriolic than his earlier work and more subdued than some of his later work. Its message, as evidenced by the book's reappearance in 1978, is timeless. Its literary merit speaks for itself.

Clifford P. Bendau

Sources for Further Study

Reviews:

Analog. XLVIII, December, 1951, pp. 160-161.

Catholic World. CLXXII, March, 1951, p. 472.

Chicago Sunday Tribune. January 14, 1951, p. 3.

Kirkus Reviews. November 1, 1950, p. 662.

Magazine of Fantasy and Science Fiction. II, June, 1951, pp. 84-85.

New York Herald Tribune Book Review. January 14, 1951, p. 4.

New York Times. January 14, 1951, p. 5.

San Francisco Chronicle. January 7, 1951, p. 17.

Saturday Review of Literature. XXXIV, January 20, 1951, p. 10.

Time. LVII, January 15, 1951, p. 82.

THE DISPOSSESSED

Author: Ursula K. Le Guin (1929-   )
First book publication: 1974
Type of work: Novel
Time: Several hundred years in the future
Locale: The twin planets of Urras and Anarres, orbiting the star Tau Ceti

One rebel's attempt to bridge the gap between an anarchist commune, once liber-tarian and now petrifying, and the lush but tyrannical parent culture from which it developed

> *Principal characters:*
> SHEVEK, an Anarresti physicist, author of the General Temporal theory
> TAKVER, a fish geneticist, his partner
> RULAG, an engineer, Shevek's mother
> BEDAP, a science teacher and Shevek's ally as a social reformer
> SABUL, a physicist, first Shevek's sponsor, then his rival
> ATRO, an aristocratic Urrasti physicist
> SAIO PAE, an Urrasti physicist and secret government agent
> DEMAERE OIIE, an Urrasti physicist, a product of upward mobility
> VEA DOEM OIIE, his flirtatious sister

The popular American science fiction of the twentieth century has always paid homage to the long tradition of speculative Utopian literature. However, homage quite often stops short of actual practice, and while thoughtful commentators from within the genre might pay tribute to the Utopian writings of Thomas More, William Morris, Samuel Butler, and Edward Bellamy, few have chosen to emulate their creative endeavors. Indeed, in the shadow of real developments giving flesh to the dystopian speculations of Aldous Huxley and George Orwell, science fiction writers and their readers often seem to have forgotten that genre tradition includes the literary construction of better worlds than their own. But literature cannot remain isolated from the time and place where it is created, and in troubled times writers and audiences alike search as much for visions of a new world coming as they do for those celebrating a rejection of the old. Far more difficult to find than its history of violence, America has a heritage of communitarian Utopia which was reawakened (if far from truly rejuvenated) parallel to the larger antiwar protests and political resistance of the 1960's. Committed to their vision of technology as civilization's prime mover, however, few science fiction writers were willing to examine the alternative views of human nature, creativity, and possibility underlying any Utopian speculation.

In fact, science fiction had seemingly rejected the Utopia. After Belsen and Hiroshima, no Utopia seemed adequately to reflect the human capacity for evil once people were armed with the most powerful of technologies. The very will to power needed to control the vast arsenals suggested that every attempt to control them would inevitably worsen the situation by extending the practical reach of the worst human impulses. Faced with the daily evidence buttressing such a grim view, few science fiction writers are willing to admit the creative, nonaggressive powers of the human intelligence, recognition of which lies at the root of any Utopian speculation. Even in an age of terrible environmental stress, faceless organizations, and the possibility of apocalypse, human beings are part of the environment in which they live, and they are capable (within limits) of shaping their own niche within it. The balance of such a niche in the literary ecology is as precarious as any in the biological realm, however. Aware of everything militating against a conception at once Utopian and realistic, Ursula K. Le Guin, in *The Dispossessed*, is artist enough to retain the qualifications and ambiguities, while simultaneously restoring a sense of possibility to science fiction's shattered landscape.

Le Guin makes good use of traditional science fiction elements: an unconventional scientist whose work is rejected by his elders, the search for a faster-than-light spaceship drive, even the American myth of the frontier. *The Dispossessed* has a circular structure in which all travel within the story, and the novel's narrative structure itself is a form of return to a starting point. But unlike most other science fiction writers, Le Guin has abandoned technological determinism, replacing it with a vision of science and technology as varieties of human creativity existing in an environment of other varieties: art, music, love, and politics. The journey to knowledge and the attempt to reform a petrifying community are simultaneous processes which change both the traveler and the environment through which he moves. As Shevek (Le Guin's unorthodox physicist) knows, one can go home again if one realizes that home is a place one has never been.

This understanding of growth processes, and the attendant faith in learning (however limited), rescues *The Dispossessed* from the twin traps of didactic sentimentality (so characteristic of Utopian literature) and murderous nihilism (equally characteristic of the popular culture of the 1970's). Le Guin translates her understanding into literature not only by making Shevek the principal character, but by partially recounting the story from his point of view. It is told in two narrative lines: scenes on Urras in the present, which dramatize the immediate conflicts, are juxtaposed against flashback scenes on Anarres, which chronicle Shevek's past from his birth to his departure for Urras. Thus, in the rather broad sense implied by a society without a formal government, Shevek is a political figure, a revolutionary. However, his growing understanding of physics, his appreciation of his society's organization, his awareness of his own life, and his deepening bonds with other people all develop in an intimate, mutually reinforcing relationship with one another.

A brilliant scientist, and a lonely incurable individualist, Shevek is nevertheless alienated from his society more by the way his friends are treated than by the equally shabby treatment accorded him. Educated to distrust his own individuality in a society interested only in collective experience, Shevek eventually sees, through his friends' experiences, that his recurring nightmare of an impenetrable wall which he must penetrate is not the symbol of his own inadequacies, but of the obstacles placed in his path by his society in violation of that society's own rules. His political alienation grows as he gradually becomes aware of the existence of kindred spirits and of the burdens placed upon them. In turn, this awareness of others makes him sufficiently self-aware to realize that to be a revolutionary in a society which erroneously considers itself revolutionary requires a commitment from the very center of one's soul.

Only after having reached that matched awareness of self and others, and of the political implications of such awareness, does Shevek find a partner with whom he can share the road he has chosen to take. Later, politically more aware and personally happy, Shevek is still unable to complete his work in physics until he satisfactorily answers the rude questions an egalitarian society puts to any outstanding or wrongheaded individual living outside the norms. Only after realizing that the relationship between individual creativity and social order is reciprocal, that society provides a security and stability which individual existence cannot, and that only the power of moral choice inherent in an individual creative mind can force change, can the physicist complete his most important work. And he must engage in a political act in order to save his life and return home with the lessons he has learned.

To accomplish all this, Shevek must leave his anarchist commune of Anarres to seek recognition for his physics among people whose entire ideology, modeled on contemporary capitalism, recognizes individual talent. Parallel circles of narrative juxtapose different stations of the journey in a fashion illuminating the virtues and limitations of both Anarres and Urras, its capitalistic parent culture. The Anarresti have made their harsh desert planet a reasonable, if occasionally difficult, place to live; but the society has been growing rigid. Bureaucracy has gained a great deal of control over daily life, and group solidarity has made it nearly impossible for talent such as Shevek's to find outlet. Social criticism is recognizable only as mental illness. At the same time, Urras, far more pleasant than its arid moon, is still the dictatorial home of warring nation-states from which the anarchists had escaped eight score and ten years earlier.

Such a double vision could easily lead to cynicism and despair, but Le Guin refuses to see either Anarres or Urras as static or closed systems. Shevek remains committed to the basic principle of Anarres's founding, that change is basic in both individual and social organisms. For him, physics is not the study of power, but of relationships. Shevek cannot complete his Temporal Theory until a deadly enemy presents him with a needed key, a copy of Einstein's Theory of Relativity from an alien Earth. Neither Urras nor Anarres can be fully understood without understanding the two together: neither's achievements appreciated, the horrors of neither's limitations accurately grasped. And of course neither can change without interaction between them, and Shevek's journey is the first real contact between the people of the twin planets in their mutual history.

The process Le Guin sketches is more complex than saying that neither society is correct and that given time and goodwill they will gradually come to resemble each other. Valuing freedom and initiative rather than property or power, Shevek repeatedly underestimates the real influence the latter two have. Overwhelmed by the lushness and complexity of life on Urras, Shevek almost fails to recognize that both his personal life and his professional creativity are becoming submerged in power plays. Here again, the personal and the political are intimately related. Rebuffed after misreading the seductive wiles of an Urrasti flirt as honest sexual invitation, he recognizes how far down the equally seductive path of political cooperation with Urras he has actually traveled — and by this time he is aware that from the Urrasti point of view his mission of communication is but a front for an intelligence operation placing control of his physics in military hands. Shevek flees Urras convinced that his trip to the home planet has been a failure and a mistake, the consequences of which he will bear for the rest of his life. The Urrasti (of all political persuasions) are interested only in converting his freely offered gift into exclusively controlled property. Everything that happens to him confirms his belief in his original rebellious intuitions that the existence of a revolutionary regime presupposes nothing more than the continuation of a revolutionary tradition, and that only continual and active commitment to that tradition can fulfill its original promise of a better life (explicitly defined in noneconomic terms).

Central to this system of belief is the concept that the organization of society is a human activity, not a predetermined structure. All Anarresti are, or should be, revolutionaries, constantly questioning the social organisms within which they live. Ideally, Anarres is never a finished creation, only a promise made and kept by the struggle and effort of people who believe in it. Secure behind the walls of their quarantine, most Anarresti have forgotten this perspective on their own culture. As Shevek's own experiences demonstrate, the promise is demanding and dangerous, but it is a promise of freedom, not of safety. These are crucial perceptions, because they bring creativity out of the past and into the present and future and direct human endeavor to the shaping of history rather than to the resisting of it.

Le Guin both admits politics to the realm of the reasonable in science fiction and raises the perception of political activity well above the mechanistic concept of electoral and legislative maneuvering so characteristic of American political debate (inside science fiction or out). As a human activity, politics requires a realistic but positive view of people if it is to be anything larger than cynical manipulation of the powerless. But a realistic view of people requires consideration of the cynical, the self-serving, and the stupid if a work of either fiction or political theory is to be more than sentimental. Here again the acceptance of even Utopia as ambiguous and continually an unfinished promise provides, not an answer, but a path for action.

This glimpse of possible action makes Le Guin a singular writer in the 1970's, and she illuminates with her singularity the apocalyptic dead end reached by so much of the popular culture. Le Guin's physicist hero, ostracized by his own society, his theoretical work towards a faster-than-light spaceship, even the *deus ex machina* of alien intervention saving him to return to Anarres are all typical science fiction devices. In other hands, Shevek might have been reduced to a galaxy-roving adventurer, or crushed between two rigid societies. But here he is both too strong to be crushed by society and too human to exist outside of it. The difference is the awareness of social relationships and historical context, as well as of great personal strength. It is this dynamic vision, rather than the genre conventions which Le Guin uses so freely, that is at odds with science fiction's traditional determinism. She has not changed the artifacts, only the context within which they are considered.

Le Guin is far from a sentimental writer, however, and her future is entirely open. The forces binding individual purpose and creativity into social action are shared pain and suffering, not benevolence and certainly not an indiscriminate love. As one component part of the environment, human activities are not exempt from the blind judgment of natural law. They can fail, often horribly. There are guarantees of nothing. But they may also succeed, although success may have to be defined carefully and the definitions may change from time to time. In light of the odds, hope must be qualified indeed. But hope is there. The tension between human and environment, and between the individual and society, makes creativity possible. Social context determines the uses to which the products of individual creativity are put. This recognition is at the root of hope, for so conceived, the present is not the end of history, but the beginning of tomorrow.

Albert I. Berger

Sources for Further Study

Criticism:

Bierman, Judah. "Ambiguity in Utopia: *The Dispossessed*," in *Science Fiction Studies*. II (1975), pp. 249-255. Bierman shows the theme of evil in Utopia.

Slusser, George E. *The Farthest Shores of Ursula K. Le Guin*. San Bernardino, Calif.: Borgo, 1976, pp. 46-56. Slusser calls this novel an almost puritanical probing of man's social conscience.

Reviews:

Booklist. LXX, June 15, 1974, p. 1132.

Christian Science Monitor. LXVI, June 26, 1974, p. F4.

Kirkus Reviews. XLII, March 1, 1974, p. 266.

Library Journal. XCIX, April 1, 1974, p. 1061.

New York Times Book Review. October 26, 1975, p. 48.

Observer. October 6, 1974, p. 30.

Publisher's Weekly. CCV, March 18, 1974, p. 48.

Time. CIV, August 5, 1974, p. 84.

Yale Review. LXV, December, 1975, p. 256.

DO ANDROIDS DREAM OF ELECTRIC SHEEP?

Author: Philip K. Dick (1928-1982)
First book publication: 1968
Type of work: Novel
Time: The late 1990's following World War Terminus
Locale: West coast of the United States, principally San Francisco

The attempt by a professional bounty hunter to track down a group of escaped androids becomes a provocative exploration of the question of what it is to be "truly human"

> *Principal characters:*
> RICK DECKARD, a bounty hunter of androids for the San Francisco police
> IRAN DECKARD, his moody housewife
> WILBUR MERCER, messianic hero of an electronic religious cult
> BUSTER FRIENDLY, a TV talk show host and popular idol
> JOHN R. ISADORE, a radiation brain-damaged clerk at a pet hospital for electric animals
> HANNIBAL SLOAT, the cynical owner of the pet hospital
> RACHEL ROSEN, android model of the Nexus-6 type of Rosen Associates
> PHIL RESCH, a veteran android bounty hunter
> INSPECTOR POLOKOV,
> LUBA LUFT,
> INSPECTOR GARLAND,
> PRIS STRATTON,
> ROY BATY, and
> IRMGARD BATY, escaped Nexus-6 type androids

In this novel of life in the future upon a nearly ruined earth, Philip K. Dick brings together humans and their manufactured android surrogates in a crisis of identity. Elements of the detective story, the western, and the psychological melodrama combine with a subtly developed science fiction post-catastrophe story to produce a work that aspires to be read as a philosophic novel. The claims implied in *Do Androids Dream of Electric Sheep?* are therefore large and challenging.

One of the achievements of this novel is the creation of the post-catastrophe world following World War Terminus. Earth is a dying planet, almost purged of animal life by clouds of radioactive dust which still move about upon the winds, threatening remaining life forms with sterility, degeneration, and finally death. Following the atomic war, there has been a great migration of Americans to Mars. Migration is encouraged for "normals," those not physically or mentally impaired by radiation poisoning. Commercials on the government-owned television channel warn of the longterm effects of fallout and promise to each qualified settler in the Martian New America a free android, made to order as slave or companion. The ownership of a private android servant is the reward for immigration of "normals," a reward which the government claims "duplicates the halcyon days of the pre-Civil War Southern States."

Androids are manufactured biological creatures first produced during the war as "Synthetic Freedom Fighters." Following the war, the state of the art advanced to the point that the most recent model, the Nexus-6 android, is superior to humans in many ways. However, increasing the intelligence and sophistication of the androids has produced problems. The most serious is the need to identify, apprehend, and retire (that is, destroy) renegade androids who have killed or abandoned their human owners and, passing as human, have escaped to earth. The parallels here to the social and moral evils of black slavery in America are obvious and effectively rendered. The ethical and cultural implications of android existence are central themes in this novel and the focus of many of the author's best effects.

The environmental, ecological, and cultural impact of radiation fallout is managed masterfully, especially as these matters intersect the novel's exploration of what being human means in terms of social values and behavior. The direct impact of the war on human civilization is no less severe than its effect on both the earth's biosystem and on human social ecology. The distortions and dysfunctions of human cultural experience may be blamed on the war, but they seem more fundamental still, lying perhaps at the root of humanity's abuse of technology and scientific knowledge. The compelling symbols of the dry rot at the core of modern civilization are the empty apartment buildings, the cities falling into neglected ruin, and the great radioactive dust heaps whose poison is blown everywhere as the wind shifts.

Dick's choice of dust symbolism recalls Vonnegut's *Mother Night* in tone and Walter Miller's similar treatment in *A Canticle for Leibowitz*. We may be reminded of F. Scott Fitzgerald's Long Island waste land in *The Great Gatsby*, and we may recall the more remote dust heaps of Dickens' *Our Mutual Friend,* which serve as symbols of a culture similarly choking on ruined lives, lost hopes, and a general decay produced as a by-product of a society concerned with getting along, patched together largely by its commercial interests. Perhaps Dick's postwar future has not lost its soul entirely, but the remedies in his novel seem less clear than they did a century ago to Dickens and also less efficacious for a society beginning to wonder if it can tell the difference any more between a human and an android.

The question of whether androids have souls does not receive any clear answer until the end of the novel, by which time the reader's sympathies have been pulled about for and against the renegade androids. The answer is no, androids have no souls. They do not represent a life form as Wilbur Mercer, the great lover and protector of life, recognizes it. Androids are merely intelligent computers, and the only reason they might elicit human sympathy is because humans cannot imagine having no souls, and might tend to view androids anthropomorphically. The question of the title is also answered implicitly in the action; androids would not dream unless programed to do so. If they did dream they would not distinguish between electric and real sheep, of if they did they would not value real sheep over electric ones. Despite living in a world of imitation life forms, humans prefer real animals and people to their mechanical surrogates.

Nevertheless, the survivors of World War Terminus live an almost vicarious daily life in a world of ersatz reality. The Penfield Mood Organ is waiting to control moods and consciousness: simply dial the appropriate code. Depressed? Dial 481: "Awareness of the manifold possibilities open to me in the future." An 888 gets you "the desire to watch TV, no matter what's on it," and so on. But even electronic mood control is a drug of uncertain remedy for loneliness, the depression that comes from being left behind by emigration because, perversely enough, humans will sometimes prefer genuine depression to artificially induced ecstasy. Such indeed is the case with Iran, Deckard's wife. Neither state applies to androids, however.

Electronic saturation of consciousness through television has become part of the lifestyle, and reinforces the theme of the perversion of life processes from organic and natural forms to artificial and electronic ones. Buster Friendly and his Friendly Friends dominate commercial television, filling the day with a nonstop series of interviews and not-too-goodnatured inanities. Buster's wit and frequent truculence seem to keep his devoted audience amused, but the audience's satisfaction is also a measure for the reader of the cultural bankruptcy of the people.

Buster Friendly's only effective rival for attention and influence is an electronically processed religion of the future known as Mercerism. In a way, Mercerism is the key to the problem of human identity in the novel. Union with Mercer is experienced electronically by means of the "empathy box." When engaged, the subject experiences a mental and spiritual identification with the consciousness of Wilbur Mercer, a sort of middle-class messiah, and through him with the collective mind of all those absorbed in Mercer's videotaped struggle upward from the tomb world of death consciousness to ecstatic triumph. En route, Wilbur Mercer must brave natural hazards and the stones cast at him by the enemies of natural life known as "the killers." This drama of ascending and descending fortunes offers a perpetual catharsis for Mercer's followers. The real benefit seems to come from making contact with an electronically projected collective consciousness, a temporary awareness that is the key to the psychic healing experienced by users. Indeed, it is finally the power of empathy that separates android from human consciousness.

As the novel opens, Rick Deckard begins his day arguing with Iran, his wife, about the ethics of retiring androids. He reminds her that they are either killers or potential killers. Before going off to his office, Deckard visits his electric sheep grazing on the apartment roof and daydreams about one day owning another real animal. The opportunity of earning enough bounty money for a real animal presents itself when Deckard is informed by Inspector Bryant that he will be taking the place of the chief bounty hunter who was wounded by an escaped android posing as Polokov, a Russian secret policeman. Deckard is sent to the android plant in Seattle to verify the accuracy of the only effective android detection test, the Voigt-Kampff Altered Scale test. Deckard proves the test's validity by discovering that the beautiful Rachel Rosen is in fact a Nexus-6 model android, legally living an apparently normal human existence because she is a production model. Armed with a valid test, Deckard begins the hunt for six androids at large in northern California.

One by one, Deckard locates, tracks down, and retires the androids, but each case is more difficult than the last and involves unexpected reversals of thinking for the reader. In the course of his android hunt, Deckard finds himself denounced as an android to police who turn out to be androids led by an android, Inspector Garland. Garland, in turn, denounces a human bounty hunter, Phil Resch, as an android whose memory had been so programed that he was not aware that he is an android. Deckard and Resch find it necessary to satisfy one another that each is indeed human. After retiring a beautiful opera singer android, Deckard finds that he reacts with revulsion at the destruction of a great talent, android or not, and worries that he is beginning to feel an empathetic identification with androids. Resch argues that such empathy would be suicidal, because bounty hunters are all that stand between the Nexus-6 and humans, the "barrier which keeps the two distinct."

Unsure of his ability to deal with the remaining Nexus androids, Deckard appeals for assistance to Rachel Rosen, who instead traps him into a liaison designed to paralyze his will to retire any more androids, especially since one of the target androids, Pris Stratton, is Rachel's duplicate. Nonetheless, Deckard resolves to finish the assignment he had begun the day before.

The escaped androids have taken refuge in a ruined apartment complex inhabited by one lone tenant, John R. Isadore, a chickenhead (an individual brain damaged by radiation) who works as a clerk in the Van Ness Animal Hospital for electric animals. Isadore is a goodnatured, insecure, and minimally competent "special" person who often sees things more clearly than normals. Isadore intuitively understands that Buster Friendly, who turns out to be an android, and Wilbur Mercer, who turns out to be a fiction, are fighting for control of the psychic selves of the population. Buster represents critical reason and Wilbur sympathetic intuition.

The final action of the novel brings together the various plotlines. Buster Friendly explodes Mercerism as a hoax, producing the aged actor who played Mercer for the filming of the saga. Friendly concludes triumphantly but erroneously that the idea of human empathy is a lie. As these revelations are shocking the world, the androids reveal, in their treatment of the solicitous Isadore and in Pris's experimental torture of a live spider, that they lack a crucial element in their composition. In the final analysis they are monstrous, and deserve their fate.

Deckard manages to destroy the androids, but not before he is nearly killed himself. The most difficult of the three proves to be Pris, the android *femme fatale*, who uses Deckard's empathetic feelings against him. Without the intervention of Wilbur Mercer, who warns Deckard in a vision of the coming attack, he could not have defended himself. At least we must presume that it is a vision, and one which at least symbolically validates the truth of Mercerism, if only as a source of psychic force. Mercer assures Deckard that disposing of the androids is disagreeable but necessary, and it will not make Deckard one of the killers of life. If we are to take Mercer's argument as an authorial view, we may conclude that the really distinctively human traits are not rational or intellectual but intuitive and sympathetic.

One characteristic of Phil Dick's work, and an important feature of *Do Androids Dream of Electric Sheep?*, is the logical discontinuity which disturbs the reader's equilibrium. A writer runs the risk of manipulating reader expectations in this way. Although the reader is not alienated in this novel, the calculated reversals blur the definition of the characters, particularly of the hero, Deckard. More seriously, they limit the full development of the plot and the successful resolution of its elements. Since these elements are carefully interrelated, the damage is greater than it would have been if the design had been less ambitious. The result is that *Do Androids Dream of Electric Sheep?* is more suggestive of meaning than expressive, and the reader is left wondering whether the novel's failure to fulfill its own potential is the result of too much or too little thought from the author. There is no doubt that the novel suffers the effects of hasty composition in the lost opportunities for fuller development of its themes, in the many loose ends left unresolved, and in embarrassing lapses of style.

Despite these shortcomings, *Do Androids Dream of Electric Sheep?* is a stimulating science fiction novel that compels the reader to face serious moral and existential issues growing out of humanity's interactions with its own science and technology. Dick's novel succeeds better than most science fiction works in stimulating the mind and imagination of the reader and in providing some unforgettable symbols of a world we already partly inhabit.

Donald L. Lawler

Sources for Further Study

Criticism:

Gillespie, Bruce. *Philip K. Dick: Electric Shepherd*. Melbourne, Australia: Nostrilla, 1975, Gillespie's main theme is based on this work.

Reviews:

Analog. LXXXII, September, 1968, p. 171.

Books and Bookmen. XIV, June, 1969, p. 57.

Kirkus Reviews. XXXVI, January 15, 1968, p. 76.

Library Journal. XCIII, March 1, 1968, p. 1018.

Magazine of Fantasy and Science Fiction. XXXV. August, 1968, pp. 19-23.

New Worlds. CXC, May 1969, p. 59.

Publisher's Weekly. CXCIII, January 29, 1968, p. 92.

SF Commentary. VII, November, 1969, p. 33 and IX, February, 1970, pp. 11-25.

Spectator. CCXXII, April 4, 1969, p. 446.

Times Literary Supplement. June 12, 1969, p. 643.

LE DOCTEUR LERNE
(Doctor Lerne)

Author: Maurice Renard (1875-1939)
First book publication: 1908
Type of work: Novel
Time: 1908
Locale: France

A scientist succeeds in transplanting brains and personalities between different living beings

Principal characters:
    DOCTOR LERNE, a famous surgeon
    NICOLAS VERMONT, the doctor's nephew
    EMMA BOURDICHET, Lerne's mistress
    OTTO KLOTZ, the doctor's German assistant

Maurice Renard was an early practitioner in science fiction both as a critic and a writer. Although his production was modest, he stands out as one of the most original authors to emerge at the beginning of the twentieth century. Because of its many screen adaptations, *Les mains d'orlac* (The Hands of Orlac) is undoubtedly his best-known work. However, the novel in which Maurice Renard displayed the most depth and creative power was his first, *Le Docteur Lerne*.

The novel chronicles the fate of Doctor Lerne, a world-renowned surgeon, who suddenly withdraws from the spotlight of public life in order to carry out unconventional transplant experiments in a secluded retreat. After successfully transplanting plants into animals and vice versa, he gains enough skill to switch brains between two organisms. But at that point he is murdered by his assistant, Otto Klotz, who, with his German helpers, transplants his own brain into Doctor Lerne's body. Under everybody's nose, he takes the famous surgeon's place and proceeds to perform all sorts of daring and unnatural operations.

This is how Nicolas Vermont, the doctor's nephew, finds the situation upon his arrival at the chateau. Puzzled by certain changes in his uncle's behavior, the nephew begins a risky investigation into what the scientist is involved in. It becomes even more dangerous when he falls in love with Lerne's protégée and mistress, the beautiful Emma Bourdichet. Meanwhile, Lerne-Klotz has embarked on a series of experiments in mind transfer without surgery. He is on the verge of a breakthrough when he dies, struck down by a heart attack. Nicolas then discovers Lerne's true identity. He thinks the nightmare is over until it appears that Klotz' mind has taken control of his car, "an organic body never having been alive" in which the invading mind has no need to struggle with the one already there. One last battle begins. Here we have a plot that has been laid out by a master who adroitly keeps everyone from knowing, until

Nicolas makes the discovery, that Klotz has killed Lerne. The inquiring nephew's deductions soon bring the opposite to light.

Presented in this way, the final unexpected turn of events can hardly be considered serious, so it is to Renard's credit that the suspense remains taut up to the very last line, however improbable the events may seem.

Three characters are met in the course of the action: a handsome young man who is a bit scatterbrained; a good-looking woman to rescue more or less in spite of herself; and the complex being created by joining Lerne's body to Klotz's mind.

To begin with, Lerne's nephew, Nicolas Vermont must be considered the character who is by far the easiest to place. If one compares Lerne's chateau and its distress-laden aura (even for those who seem to be in control of the situation) to a powder keg, Nicolas' sudden appearance provides the spark that ignites it. In order to create and maintain the necessary friction between the tense atmosphere of the chateau, while treating the newcomer as effectively as possible, Renard has developed his characters with great precision. Nicolas shows all the attributes expected of a middle-class young man in 1908. To these qualities he adds a doggedness typical of the newspaper man in an American crime novel of the 1920's and 1930's, a doggedness which has been caused for the most part by Emma, Lerne's well-endowed mistress, with whom he has fallen madly in love.

Like Klotz-Lerne, Emma is a double personality, except that she knows how to stay on the side of good. At first she appears simply to be a beautiful young woman kept by an unattractive old man. But Renard has no use for stereotypes, and little by little, while remaining quite physically attractive, Emma reveals what she really is, an uneducated and unmannered streetwalker. At the end of the novel she leaves Nicolas to return to her previous life, shedding once and for all the thin veneer of breeding which had deceived the hero as well as the reader. Pre-World War I stories in which the heroine is a "loose woman" are so rare that the fact is worthy of mention.

Klotz-Lerne presents quite another problem. In the first place Lerne's true personality must be taken into account since the signs Nicolas recognizes in the course of the novel emphasize the contrast between the surgeon's present behavior and what it was in the past. The real Doctor Lerne was the epitome of the enlightened scientist who worked to spread discoveries beneficial to humanity; his decision to withdraw to an isolated spot in order to devote himself to his last work reflects his dedication.

Otto Klotz represents the other side of the coin: the image people have of the scientist at a time when science frightens them. Moreover, the fact that Klotz is German further indicated villainy, given the nationalistic, anti-German mood that prevailed in prewar France. In defining his characters well (as he did with Nicolas) Renard is less exacting with the details regarding the "wicked" leading character's nationality. As for Germany's motives, they are personified in Klotz: fame, fortune, and women (Emma, in this instance).

The two personalities immediately clash within the body of Doctor Lerne, but the struggle between his body and the invading mind is an unequal one. The doctor's behavior changes very quickly in a thousand little ways, which is his downfall in the final analysis, while in the background the benefactor becomes a sorcerer's apprentice. Nicolas' arrival on the scene upsets the tense and oppressive chateau atmosphere that has weakened all the other characters.

In view of these details, one might question whether *Le Docteur Lerne* is really a science fiction novel, or whether it is fantasy. Certainly at the outset it is a typical science fiction story with some fantastic patterns woven into it; but this fantastic element becomes more and more dominant as the novel progresses. To begin with, if the basic assumption is made that it is possible, in the wake of biological research, to transplant living tissue and organs from one plant or animal phylum to another and then to transplant whole brains, it is obvious that *Le Docteur Lerne* is a work of science fiction. But the setting itself is pure fantasy. A chateau beyond the lines of communication, even entered *via* a secret passageway, gives the book a close resemblance to gothic and modern fantasy. Next, the atmosphere of Lerne's domain reinforces this feeling. Everything is in a state of neglect, fear lurks in every nook and cranny, periodically monsters escape from strange laboratories, a madman with brains oozing out (one of the doctor's assistants unwise enough to give in to Emma's advances) is locked up in a room, and a number of other things gradually nudge the reader away from science fiction and into horror fantasy. The point in *Le Docteur Lerne* where the shift into irrational fantasy takes place, comes in the second part when Klotz-Lerne begins to mastermind transference.

The reference is perfectly clear; it is demonic possession. Cloaked behind a thin scientific veil (a vague allusion to experiments connected with the metaphysics of the period), but possession nevertheless. Perhaps today the theme can be justified as science fiction on the grounds that a mutant might be endowed with extrasensory powers. When viewed from the state of science and mentality in 1908, however, such mind transference is pure fantasy. Even "possession" of Nicolas' car does no damage to this statement; for example, North American Indian legends ascribe a manitou to all beings on Earth whether living or not.

Thus, *Le Docteur Lerne* is probably one of those hybrid works located on the ill-defined (and ultimately very subjective) borderline that separates science fiction from fantasy. And Renard also adds a dash of thriller to his recipe, which brings us to the writing itself.

The novel is structured like a serial with a cliffhanger ending for each chapter. The overall narrative develops like a police story with a trail of clues leading everyone on a wild-goose chase followed by an unexpected turn of events which unmasks the true guilty party. It also resembles a mystery in the way reality progressively deteriorates before the reader's eyes. This is exactly what makes Renard's style impressive; he creates real and human characters that touch us, even while projecting against a background of extraordinary adventures. Although the fantastic elements crop up constantly, the characters and situations are so believable that the reader accepts the story as real. Renard has forced only a few details to make the plot flow smoothly, and they do not hinder us from accepting the characters as being totally human.

One last point to bring out regarding Renard's originality is the eroticism that emerges from certain passages in the novel. Considering the degree to which science fiction was sanitized from sex before the 1960's, *Le Docteur Lerne* stands as proof of a rarely encountered audacity. Some of the episodes in the novel are strikingly graphic and sensual, even by today's liberal standards. Beyond its purely literary qualities, *Le Docteur Lerne* impresses the reader with its up-to-date flavor and topicality. In his best pages, Maurice Renard comes across as someone far ahead of his time, someone who could be called a science fiction visionary.

Richard D. Nolane

DR. BLOODMONEY
or How We Got Along After the Bomb

Author: Philip K. Dick (1928-1982)
First book publication: 1965
Type of work: Novel
Time: 1981 and 1988
Locale: The San Francisco Bay Area and inland; also a manned satellite circling the Earth

A satirical and at times nightmarish evocation of America after a nuclear war, a world dominated by shortages of food and the loss of technological expertise

> *Principal characters:*
> BRUNO BLUTHGELD (ALIAS JACK TREE), a nuclear scientist-turned-shepherd
> BONNY KELLER, a wife and mother who engages in compulsive affairs
> EDIE KELLER, Bonny's seven-year-old daughter
> BILL KELLER, a homunculus, in Edie
> ANDREW GILL, a manufacturer of cigarettes and fine liquor
> HAL BARNES, a schoolteacher
> WALTER DANGERFIELD, a man trapped in a satellite orbiting the Earth
> DR. STOCKSTILL, a psychiatrist
> STUART MCCONCHIE, a young, ambitious black salesman
> HOPPY HARRIGAN, a mutant created by a nuclear "accident"

Philip K. Dick's *Dr. Bloodmoney* is primarily a postdisaster novel, and in its creation of a historical period that is essentially an "alternate reality," the work has merits comparable to those of Dick's famous *The Man in the High Castle* (1962). The latter novel credibly described an alternative history that most Americans would consider unimaginably horrifying (the victory of the Axis in World War II), and also a historical impossibility. By contrast, *Dr. Bloodmoney* (1965) depicts a world shattered and temporarily reduced to primitivism, starvation, and genetic chaos by nuclear war, a possibility that, however frightening, seemed all too likely in 1965, and also seems distinctly believable more than a decade later. Set in the 1970's and the 1980's, *Dr. Bloodmoney* extrapolates a postdisaster model of our industrial society with power and conviction.

Dr. Bloodmoney was written in one of Dick's most fertile periods, the years 1964-1966, which also produced, among other novels, *The Martian Time-Slip* and *The Three Stigmata of Palmer Eldritch*, which most perceptive readers of Dick would consider high on his list of achievements. The pulpy title of the novel probably owes as much to the film *Dr. Strangelove* (1964), a black comedy about the beginning of a nuclear holocaust, as to the inspiration of the author or publisher. The title character of Dick's novel is a nuclear scientist, Bruno Bluthgeld (the name means "bloodmoney" in German), whose genius had produced a nuclear malfunction in 1972, and who is later held responsible for the "hydrogen war" of 1981. Bluthgeld is characterized as a more human-ized version of the film's caricature of the demented nuclear scientist, Dr. Strangelove.

Unlike the film — and these parallels are meant to be only suggestive — Dick's novel does not depict the experience of nuclear disaster in a melodra-matic or sensationalized fashion. On the contrary, *Dr. Bloodmoney* portrays the effects of disaster on American society. The novel begins in 1981 in a society much like that of 1965. There has been a nuclear "accident" in 1972 which has produced some mutants; but society has gone on mechanically with its mindless commitment to nuclear weaponry. The major concerns in 1981, in Dick's 1965 view, are the liberalism of employer Jim Fergesson in hiring not only a black salesman, but a "phocemelus" or mutant without arms and legs created by the malfunction of 1972. Here Dick's extrapolation seems partially dated: the tensions over black equality in the 1960's seem already largely a thing of the past in the 1970's.

Instead of disaster itself, Dick is concerned with the effects of disaster, as he depicts it in the lives of several characters. After an initial period of chaos and terror, Dick shows his world slowly stabilizing at a level of communal primitivism. Food supplies are scarce, technology has largely been destroyed, and the belief in magic arises again. Paper money becomes worthless, while the value of silver coins increases enormously. People are reduced to eating rats in order to survive, and a boiled fish head becomes a delicacy. Transporta-tion reverts to the level of horse-drawn vehicles, although there are some wood-burning engines. Communal justice descends to a crude vigilante form.

For some, the postdisaster world turns out to be beneficial. Stuart McCon-chie, a black salesman who survives on a diet of rats, finds that his intelligence has greatly increased thanks to radiation effects. Likewise, many rats and other animals are transformed into more intelligent creatures. People with the knowledge of handicrafts, like Andrew Gill, the tobacco and liquor expert, become widely respected businessmen. Those with some technological train-ing, like Hal Barnes, are in demand as teachers.

Perhaps most interesting is the change in the status of mutants. Before the "emergency" (as it is called), the mutant phocemelus Hoppy Harrigan was a freak in the older sense of the word: a grotesque aberration barely tolerated by "normal" people. Afraid to show his developing talent for psychokinesis — the ability to control objects by the mind — before the disaster, Hoppy emerges after the chaos has settled as a "handy" or repairman of formidable skills and considerable importance to his community.

If these transformations in the wake of universal disaster are ironic, they help to establish the ironic tone of the novel. Dick's irony can frequently be Kafkaesque (as it often is in other novels), a fact illustrated in the scene where McConchie thinks about gathering up worthless paper money while eating a rat and playing a chess game with a dying man. This particular scene tends to crystallize the horror of nuclear devastation in a brief but impressive vignette.

One of the most imaginative ironies is the transformation of the status of Walter Dangerfield after the devastation. Dangerfield and his wife had volunteered to be the first colonists on Mars, but a failure in their rocket had occurred, and their ship had become a manned satellite endlessly circling the Earth. Before the "emergency," Dangerfield had been an object of pity: his wife had died, dooming him to a life of solitude while his ship continued its meaningless orbits. But after the disaster, Dangerfield finds a sense of purpose: his broadcasts to the Earth, including recordings of pop music and readings from novels, serve to encourage the survivors of the destruction below. In fact, Dangerfield becomes a unifying force for his listeners, as well as a reminder of the civilization they have lost and might, to some degree, be able to recover. Dangerfield's courageous acceptance of his predicament makes him the spiritual and moral center of the novel.

Dangerfield is in fact typical of many Dick heroes, and perhaps symbolic of Dick himself as an artist. Apparently doomed to a meaningless life of entrapment and absurd solipsism, Dangerfield accepts his condition courageously with a wry and self-deprecating irony, becoming an image of human gallantry and determination for others. Separated from his fellow humans in his satellite, Dangerfield establishes a friendly and meaningful communication — one might almost say "communion" — with them. (Similarly, Dick the writer attempts to bridge the gap between himself and his readers.) One of Dangerfield's most significant acts is his reading of W. Somerset Maugham's novel, *Of Human Bondage*. Dangerfield, making the best of his ironic predicament, reads the novel to encourage the survivors of the nuclear holocaust to make the best of *their* bondage to unpleasant and impoverished conditions.

Similar ironies in the novel occur in other characters' reactions to the post-disaster world. Bonny Keller, Dick's heroine, unlike most women retains her beauty despite the radiation; so she embarks on a series of compulsive affairs, though remaining married to her dull husband. Her infidelities are related to a curious father-fixation she feels for Bruno Bluthgeld, the nuclear scientist, and her concern over his increasing withdrawal into a world of private obsession with guilt. Her indiscretion on the day of the "emergency" produces a curious mutation: a daughter, Edie, who carries her twin in the form of a homunculus (whom she calls Bill) inside her.

Both Edie's homunculus and the "phocemelus" Hoppy are symbols of the grotesque world created by nuclear destruction; but the two creatures develop in opposite directions. Whereas Hoppy attains new importance as a "handy" and develops an inhuman arrogance that becomes destructive, the homunculus, though able to talk only to his sister Edie, becomes a sympathetic figure and a symbol of redemptive innocence.

Of all the characters affected by the disaster, perhaps the most disappointingly realized from an artistic standpoint is Dick's Bluthgeld, the "Dr. Blood-money" of the title. Dick's treatment of Bluthgeld is compassionate rather than satirical, but the characterization is neither convincing nor memorable. At the beginning of the novel, Bluthgeld is already guilt-ridden because of the first nuclear accident, for which he feels responsible. Yet he seems to be continuing with his nuclear work. After the disaster strikes, Bluthgeld is depicted as retreating to a life as a shepherd in a remote rural area in an attempt to atone for his sin of developing nuclear weapons. Moreover, he is portrayed as slowly lapsing into a kind of insanity because of his guilt. Yet toward the end of the novel, the sight of McConchie, who had seen Bluthgeld on the day of the disaster, triggers a reaction of hostility and fear from Bluthgeld: afraid that his alias of "Jack Tree" will be destroyed and his true identity revealed, Bluthgeld begins to set off a new series of explosions. The circumstances are shadowy and unconvincing: the reader is not told how Bluthgeld retains his scientific mastery when his mind is deteriorating, or where he gets the materials to create new bombs, or why he would have been constructing nuclear devices while suffering from guilt. In short, although Dick has attempted to characterize Bluthgeld as humanely as he can, and to break away from stereotyped conceptions of the mad nuclear scientist, he has failed to do so.

Bluthgeld's last attempt to re-create nuclear devastation precipitates the crisis of Dick's novel. From the disaster and the reactions of the characters to it, the story has proceeded rather quietly, without the usual melodrama found in a Dick novel. But Bluthgeld's action triggers a response: Harrigan the mutant demonstrates his psychokinetic abilities by lifting Bluthgeld in the air several hundred feet and then dropping him to his death. From this point, Harrigan becomes the major element of menace to Dick's characters. Separated from humanity by his lack of arms and legs, and possessing nearly superhuman powers from his "wild talents" or psychokinetic abilities, Harrigan is portrayed as contemptuous of his fellows and desirous of a bizarre kind of power. He is represented as gradually strangling Dangerfield, the voice of hope and human solidarity, by using his psychic talents whenever Dangerfield passes over Marin County in the satellite. Harrigan schemes to take over the satellite by remote control and thus dominate Dangerfield's listeners.

This grotesque effort to seize power poses a nightmarish threat to Dick's characters that is as surrealistic as anything Dick has imagined. But the menace to Dangerfield and the human community is defeated in an equally bizarre way. The homunculus mutant, Bill Keller, is endowed by Dick with the power to leave his sister's body and take residence in another body, forcing the mind in that body to take Keller's place. This nonmaterialist phenomenon is one of the "given" elements of the novel: it is never rationalized with a scientific or pseudoscientific explanation other than mutation. Bill also has the ability to hear the voices of the dead, a feat which defies rational explanation. After trying existence in the bodies of a worm and an owl, Bill manages to exchange places with Harrigan, who then dies in Bill's tiny stunted body.

On the symbolic level, Dick's plot suggests the defeat of egotism and pride by redemptive innocence, and after Hoppy Harrigan's death, the Marin County postdisaster is depicted as stabilizing and beginning an upward struggle toward the recovery of a more complex technology and civilization. Various new beginnings are announced: Dangerfield recovers; Bonny Keller decides to cease her affairs and settle down with Gill; Gill and McConchie plan to industrialize Gill's industry in tobacco and liquor; and so on. Thus Dick's novel ends on an affirmative note.

The chief problem with the novel, however, is that while the plot may function on a symbolic level, the incidents of Bluthgeld's death, Harrigan's threat, and Bill Keller's salvation of society are rather bizarre and lacking in credibility, even for science fiction. Aside from Dick's difficulty in characterizing Bluthgeld, the novel lacks an impressive concluding action once the world after the disaster is described. This must be taken into account in any final assessment of *Dr. Bloodmoney*.

But granted the novel's weaknesses, a moderately favorable judgment on it can still be made. As in many other Dick novels, most notably *The Man in the High Castle*, Dick portrays a nightmarish situation credibly in *Dr. Bloodmoney*: the novel's vision of the impact of nuclear disaster on its people seems credible. As in several Dick novels, an interesting assortment of unusual characters is presented believably, the main exception being Bluthgeld. Finally, in Bill Keller, the innocent homunculus, Dick has created a memorable figure who virtually steals the last third of the book. If *Dr. Bloodmoney* is below the level of Dick's best work, it is also well above the level of unsuccessful fiction.

Edgar L. Chapman

Sources for Further Study

Criticism:

Gillespie, Bruce. *Philip K. Dick: Electric Shepherd*. Melbourne, Australia: Nostrillia, 1975, Gillespie praises the theme of *Dr. Bloodmoney*.

Jameson, Frederic. "After Armageddon: Character Systems in *Dr. Bloodmoney*," in *Science-Fiction Studies*. II (1975), pp. 31-42. Jameson dissects the portrayal of the characters.

Reviews:

New Worlds. CL, March, 1966, p. 157.

SF Commentary. I, January, 1969, p. 48.

DOCTOR MIRABILIS

Author: James Blish (1921-1975)
First book publication: 1964
Type of work: Novel
Time: 1231-1294
Locale: England, France, and Italy

As Volume 1 of a trilogy with the theology overall title After Such Knowledge, *which includes studies of science and theology as uneasy bedfellows, and the thousand-year period of retreat from learning,* Doctor Mirabilis *offers a life of Roger Bacon, a scientist-theologian of sorts who believes he has a devine mission*

Principal characters:
> ROGER BACON, a scientist, lay Franciscan, and lecturer at Oxford
> ADAM MARSH, a scientist at Oxford and the confessor of Eleanor of Pembroke
> ROBERT GROSSETESTE, the Chancellor of the University, later the Bishop of Lincoln
> ELEANOR OF PEMBROKE, the sister of the King and wife of Simon de Montfort
> HENRY III OF WINCHESTER, the King of England
> PIERRE DE MARICOURT (PETER THE PEREGRINE), an alchemist and teacher
> THOMAS BUNGAY, an astronomer at Oxford, and a Franciscan provincial minister
> ALBERTUS MAGNUS, a Dominican and Regent Master at the University of Paris
> LORENZA PICCOLOMINI, the Marquis of Modena, a patron of the arts
> RICHARD RUFUS OF CORNWALL, a Regent Master at Paris and Oxford

In *Doctor Mirabilis*, James Blish blends three "languages": Middle English when the characters are *speaking* Middle English, modern English when they are speaking French or Latin, and medieval Latin for direct quotations from the writings of the person speaking. The combination gives the book an aura of magic appropriate to those dark ages of struggling science, abortive politics, and fragmented histories. As if to exorcise that aura, Blish adds an "Argument" (a chapter by chapter plot summary), a "Dramatis Personae," and Notes.

Roger Bacon never doubts that the secrets of the universe are God's secrets (early in the novel, at seventeen, he understands that knowledge is "theology's handmaiden"); and he sees the function of the scientist as that of probing those secrets and making the discoveries available for man's use. To the wealthy Marquis of Modena in Tivoli, with whom he spends two years of blissful research, Bacon explains his three "dignities," on which rest the scientific method and natural philosophy. *Faith* he finds necessary regarding previous scholars, for "perfect skepticism is paralyzing" when it demands unprofitable repetition of experiments. *Experience* enables the scientist to understand relationships among the several branches of service, and *reason* guides in the use of knowledge for the protection of Christianity, the greater glory of God, and the greater welfare of man. But ethics, he says, is the pinnacle of the schema. He has dreamed of a universal science.

Roger begins his career as a scientist at a time when Aristotle's works have been banned at Paris but encouraged by Grosseteste at Oxford, where Bacon hopes to become a teacher of Aristotle's science. His problem, then, is to interpret Aristotle in a manner least likely to cause offense. The main problem seems to be the plurality of forms — Aristotle's layering of the soul in vegetative, sensitive, and intellectual forms. So stated, the implication is that animals, which have vegetative and sensitive souls, must also have immortality, a faculty of the intellectual soul. Also, if matter is one in number and the same in all things, then it must be both God and Creator. But Bacon argues that matter is incomplete and imperfect and saves the day for Aristotle by his distinctions between potentiality and actuality. Scholars were then highly trained in disputation; and Blish dramatizes the Aristotelian problem in one magnificent confrontation between Roger Bacon and Albertus Magnus, his master and the chief theologian in Paris. Roger succeeds in confounding his superior and forever after condemns Albertus Magnus, whose reputation remained superior to his own, as an ignoramus.

Blish recounts Bacon's early experiments with magnifying lenses at Ilchester; later Bacon wrote on optics. Blish features a gunpowder demonstration in a lecture confuting Richard Cornwall, Bacon's rival at Oxford. An explosion dramatically ends the lecture and gives Bacon the title of magician; but in leading up to it, albeit amid catcalls and derisive laughter, Bacon makes — as extensions of his present knowledge — the predictions for which he is to become famous: the automobile, flying machines, underwater locomotion, suspension bridges, and circumnavigation of the globe. Although he repeats basic experiments endlessly, he investigates any phenomenon; he seeks "anything at all that an omnivorous soul could call knowledge." His chief fame today rests on his contribution to the scientific way of thought.

Bacon's reputation as a magician stems from his serious study of alchemy while at Oxford and his association in Paris with certain underground scholars, among whom Blish identifies Raimundo del Rey, who was a student of Peter the Peregrine, an alchemist who conducted a kind of unofficial university. In a dark basement laboratory, complete with athanor and alembic, students first experience the effects of del Rey's concoction that he calls "sweet vitriol" — actually ether. Del Rey tutors Bacon in Arabic so that Bacon may read Aristotle and other writers in authentic texts; and, always striving for authenticity, Bacon in old age would publish a Hebrew as well as a Greek grammar. Blish dismisses as unfounded the legend of Bacon's talking brass head, mentioning it only in connection with Albertus Magnus; actual experiments, however, occasionally seem equally strange. Blish dramatizes the possibility of the use of

goat's blood to cut a diamond, for example: Bacon keeps a goat with a ban-
daged leg in his room in Paris.

Whereas most students have no money with which to buy diamonds or other
equipment for experiments, Bacon has a bag of two thousand pounds in mixed
coinage salvaged from his father's ransacked estate in Ilchester. His apparent
poverty (his attending Oxford as a charity student supported by Grosseteste's
use of the Frideswyde Chest while working for a master's degree) contributes
to the mystery surrounding his name. Nor does Blish directly comment on the
alchemical possibility of an elixir of life to extend longevity, although Roger
Bacon later alters an early book he has begun writing on old age; when summoned to trial at sixty-three years of age he surprises even himself with his
powers of recollection. He thereafter survives thirteen years in prison in
hobblegyves, often without food for several days at a time, and lives to the age
of seventy-eight. According to other records, Albertus Magnus, also an alchemist, lived to be eighty-seven.

The ordinary unlikelihood of such longevity can be deduced from Blish's
dramatization of the perils of thirteenth century life. He graphically pictures
ecclesiastical power struggles and political intrigues; capricious and cruel im-
prisonments; uneducated, conniving serfs; grinding poverty that can make a
thief or cutthroat of nearly any citizen; and cells and streets in London and
Paris reeking with animal wastes. At Westminster, for example, Bacon nearly
faints in his room, upon which Adam Marsh shouts "*Stercor!*"; and on his
return to it, carrying a torch, Bacon unwittingly ignites its accumulated sewer
gas, causing a great explosion. Everywhere there are restrictions on individual
liberties, including the Church's burden of heavy guilt laid on such apparent
innocents as Eleanor of Pembroke and Adam Marsh.

For all his defense of the Church, however, Bacon seems blessed by the
absence of a nagging conscience; he has, instead, an inner voice that Blish
constructs for him, in place of the brazen head, and which he calls "the self";
at times, however, it speaks so plainly that it seems to be external rather than
internal. A mischievous familiar, at times it prompts him to incautious statements. But its higher function reveals to him in a dream a "cipher," a message
composed, he thinks, of several languages unknown to him. His weakened
physical condition, added to the effects of the vitriol taken during a week of
illness, produces a second stage, a shamanistic vision which he is appointed
The Man to "bring back into the world the *scientia universalis.*" The "self"
concludes with a warning that "Time is Past." From this, Bacon concludes
that God has revealed all knowledge to his patriarchs and prophets since the
beginning of the world, but that it has been largely lost by the accumulated
sins of men, even as their lives have been shortened. He understands the elixir
to be in the nature of "a medicine called the ineffable glory and the treasure of
philosophers, which completely rectifies the whole human body." Before his
collapse and vision, Bacon had been reading *The Secrets of Secrets*, which he

had taken to be an authentic letter to Alexander the Great from his teacher Aristotle and which he comes to regard as an important key to knowledge.

After this vision, Bacon determines to become a scientist, not a theologian; having received his doctorate at Paris, he becomes a lay Franciscan and goes to Rome. Searching there for more obscure books in order to interpret the cryptic message of his dream, he attracts the attention of the Marquis of Modena and enters a two-year idyllic period. Eventually he understands that the *U*'s of the vision's message are *V*'s, actually Roman numerals, and that the message gives the proportions of saltpeter, charcoal, and sulphur, the ingredients of gunpowder. Accepting that all knowledge had been once given by God to man, Bacon knows that subsequent knowledge can never be discovered, but only rediscovered. So he realizes that in his message he has found the *"ignis volans*, the flying fire of the Hellenes which had been lost for all these many centuries."

Recalled to Oxford, Bacon writes a "gloss," an introduction for *The Secret of Secrets*, begins his *Metaphysica*, and masters alchemy; but for his outspokenness he becomes known as a dangerous sciolist. His choice of the Franciscan Order becomes a problem in that, with their vows of poverty, the Franciscans threaten the ordinary clergy who enjoy secular comforts and powers. In addition, Joachim of Flora, a Cistercian, had proclaimed three ages in the history of man: the age of the Father, the age of the Son, and a new age of the Holy Spirit in which the Church would be freed from its worldliness. Bacon thinks that the Antichrist, now imminent at the dawn of the new age, will be a scientist; and he is suspected of being a Joachite. When his arch rival, Richard of Cornwall, succeeds to the post of regent master at Oxford, Cornwall has adequate reason to banish Bacon, in the year 1260, to a monastery in Paris. There, under corrective discipline, he performs menial chores; the new Constitutions of the Chapter, reacting to the threat to their very existence, prohibit all writing and publication.

Relief comes in the form of a mandate from Rome that Bacon's books be sent there, but it is so cautiously worded that the means of producing the books cannot be stipulated, nor the money given to hire the necessary copyists. Dated June, 1266, the mandate requests Bacon's remedies for evils, but urges secrecy. With the letter, however, Roger gains some freedom of movement and becomes a beggar (metaphorically taking up "the bowl of Belisarus," although he finds that his habitual neglect of his friends makes approaching them in time of need a near impossibility. Thomas of Bungay sacrifices his own safety to further Bacon's work; and Eleanor Pembroke, now reduced to poverty and guilt, surrenders a keepsake worth thirty-five pounds. Bacon succeeds in gathering together several of his earlier writings and sends to Rome the *Opus Majus* and some lesser works; but the Pope, Clement IV, dies. Bacon's denunciation of other scholars, even though he had been meticulously protective of official religion, causes him to be sent to prison as a writer of "schisms."

Blish gives considerable attention to political backgrounds, for in this down-phase of the cycle of history, political uncertainties and instabilities militate against the discoveries of scientists. Bacon has no recourse, either from Church or State, against his imprisonment; and his eventual release from prison has no explanation except a change of administration. Returned to England and tended by Thomas Bungay, he attempts to write his *Compendium of Theology*; but it shows the effects of a mind weakened by age. Thomas notes sorrowfully that of four announced causes of error, for example, Bacon deals with only three. He dies while still writing his great work.

Roger Bacon, firm in his belief in both revelation and science, and known to posterity as *doctor mirabilis*, exemplifies the type of theologian-scientist that Blish sees reborn in the succeeding ages of his trilogy — Father Domenico of the twentieth century in *Black Easter* and *The Day After Judgment*, and Father Ruiz-Sanchez of the twenty-first century in *A Case of Conscience*. As in the other works, the state remains helpless in the crises it faces; and the Church — both entrenched and protecting its flanks — seriously undermines the possibilities for either revealed or experimental knowledge.

Grace Eckley

Sources for Further Study

Reviews:

Amazing Stories. XXXIX, March, 1965, pp. 123-124.

America. CXXV, October 9, 1971, p. 269.

Booklist. LXVII, July 15, 1971, p. 929.

Kirkus Reviews. XXXIX, February 1, 1971, p. 128.

New York Times Book Reviews. September 6, 1971, p. 35.

Wall Street Journal. July 7, 1971, p. 16.

DOES ANYONE ELSE HAVE SOMETHING FURTHER TO ADD?
Stories About Secret Places and Mean Men

Author: R.A. Lafferty (1914-   )
First book publication: 1974
Type of work: Short stories

A collection of sixteen stories by a satirist whose fantasies are peopled with appealing grotesqueries

R.A. Lafferty's unique imaginative world, sardonic and strange, is shown to its best advantage in his short fiction. Given the continuing popularity of *Nine Hundred Grandmothers* (1970), perhaps the most widely known of the several anthologies of his collected works, it is surprising that Lafferty's work remains somewhat unfamiliar to general science fiction readers and fantasy fiction audiences alike. For behind Lafferty's lilting cadences and oddly tilted perspectives is the shrewd vision of a satirist who laughs all the while he draws blood.

And it is precisely the matter of Lafferty's peculiarly curved point of view that makes his work so engaging and so startling. Confronted with the unexpected, we find our discoveries unpleasant. It is as if we were invited into the fun house only to find the house of horrors occupying the same space. We're taken in by Lafferty's revels and frolics where the only negative command is to avoid seriousness. Though the key word in Lafferty's fictive vocabulary may be "humor," the laughter he elicits from us is soured by discomfort, and with good reason. We sense the laugh is on us.

Yet we learn to be lured into the "secret places" and encounters with "mean men" that the subtitle of the work promises. Like some Gaelic magician of a bygone era, Lafferty incants for us the strange names and stranger places of another reality, always fantastic, often allegorical and parabolic. His cast of characters includes the meanest man alive, who marries the most beautiful woman in the universe (producing rather bizarre results); a bogus interplanetary con man playing the first Adam; and three men called "Magi" in search of the missing link. Everywhere are victims and victimizers, always capable of transformation before our eyes, as Lafferty conjures up a bestiary of humans exhibiting themselves for our amazement or wonder or vilification against a background drawn by one who can comfortably manage the absurd.

In *Does Anyone Else Have Something Further To Add?* we are treated to a full complement of Lafferty's malicious virtuosity and sly tomfoolery. The style and tone of the stories are set for us by the title of the collection and by the opening story, entitled "About a Secret Crocodile," which has to do with the secret societies controlling the world. The most powerful of these societies, "Crocodile," directs "attitudes and dispositions," while its subsidiary, ABNC, also known as "Crocodile's Mouth," manufactures "all the catchwords and slogans of the world." Lafferty exploits the satiric possibilities in deliciously direct ways. ABNC chiefs John Candor and Jim Dandy admit to being in serious trouble because they've been "caught" in the network of their own catchwords and "slaughtered" by their own slogans. Hope is held out at the end by the promise of a new, but as yet nameless and powerless, society of "good guys and good gals" who may yet take on the challenge of the secret crocodile.

That rather wistful optimism is savagely undercut for us by Lafferty's parading sideshow of "mean men." After all, "good guys" smacks of the kind of catchword manipulation used by crocodile mouths, so perhaps we should not expect too much, especially from an author who seems such a "good guy," but is mean enough to hold the mirror up to a nature contrived for our delight and ridicule.

We should know by now that we are being amply forewarned. Lafferty's talent for naming the unnameable — Velik Vonk and Willy McGilly, Crayola Catfish and Guiseppe Juan Schlome O'Hanlon — surely reveals the whimsical side of his art. But scratch the surface of these stories and you find insight into what Lafferty himself has characterized as our "writhing underminds."

This darker side of Lafferty's fictions is adroitly managed in the story of "The Man Underneath." The tone is light. This story of a magician trickster undone by his own trickery is strewn with benign sarcasm and deft ironic touches. Charles Chartel, called the "Great Zambesi," winds up a victim of his own "deadly seriousness" (an echo, perhaps, of Matthew Arnold's "high seriousness") as a magic man. In the process, Lafferty creates some marvelously outrageous moments. For instance, Chartel's woman-in-the-box disappearing trick begins to yield up more than anyone bargains for — a clown dressed like the little tramp, who cavorts about the stage changing "his garb six times in a minute and a half" while he has his hands in his pockets. Chartel recognizes the intruder as someone faintly familiar, and by story's end so do we. He says he is "sub-c" or "just little c," and his master's greatest trick. He has joined the act because, he explains to Charles, "one of us became too serious" and to be serious "is the only capital crime." So the lid literally comes down on the serious Chartel, but success opens its door to the new Great Zambesi because there never was an act "with such variety and fun in it." The fluid and changeable "sub-c," like the man underneath, emerges to achieve new heights.

Like the irrepressible subconscious of "The Man Underneath," Lafferty's wit and ingenuity bob to the surface and mock our "deadly seriousness." If Lafferty's authorial shenanigans bear little resemblance to those of that rotter Charles Chartel, his kinship with the rejuvenated Great Zambesi, performing with variety and fun, is his little joke on us.

Lafferty's linguistically oriented playfulness and authorial self-consciousness, though, are not only devices for heightening our sense of the outrageous and the droll; they are also techniques for fostering and underlining the source of the magic of fiction's illusion. In Lafferty's case, the self-consciousness and self-reference caricatured in "The Man Underneath" point a mischievous finger at several things simultaneously: the relationship between "little c" and the Great CC, Charles Chartel; between the underplayed subconscious and the repressive and ponderous ego; between the creator and his creation. But that wily finger points us also the "capital crime" of which capital CC stands charged. Here is a delicious instance of Lafferty's gamesmanship, where the word "capital" signifies at one and the same time the first letters of Charles Chartel's name, the head or skull (as in "decapitate" or "caput"), and a kind of offense punishable by death (the consequence, we know, of "deadly seriousness"). Not only, then, do the little letters and lower case words hold out the prospect of a fun-filled variety act, one that we've really been witnessing all along courtesy of Lafferty the word magician himself, but they illuminate a whole realm of expectations about Lafferty's fictional world. Whatever else it may be, that world will not be "deadly" serious. Whatever else it may do, it will certainly capitalize with heady abandon on the possibilities of wordsmanship.

Whenever Lafferty exposes what he calls our "writhing undermind," he manages also to undermine the attitudes and dispositions controlled by those capital letters (one is tempted to say "capital criminals") ANBC, and the slaughter their slogans and catchwords inflict on the language. It is somehow reassuring to know that Lafferty makes capital of our folly only after he's burlesqued his own.

Because the impact of a Lafferty story comes from its ironic perspective, we are prepared to accept the weird logic by which phantasmagoric dreams become fitting subjects of comedy, and indirection is the shortest distance between two points. Lafferty's commitment to the idea that we see ourselves clearly only after we've seen ourselves distorted is cunningly dramatized in this collection's concluding "secret place" story, "The Weirdest World."

The story concerns itself with the fate of an inept alien commander who is marooned by his crew on the "planet" of Florida. In a rather hilarious parody of the theme of the noble savage, we watch the innocent extraterrestrial huckstered and exploited by the owner of a reptile ranch. Called the "blob" by his host-captors, he in turn calls them "grubs." Playing these bipeds at their own game, and winning because he can see *both* sides of the cards at the same time, the blob seems close to achieving his aspiration: he wishes to gain control over his environment. In the end he is outwitted and undone by the treachery and hypocrisy of his erstwhile friends. But before he dies, the outcast alien sends a communication abroad into the Galactic drift. It is a warning to those who would leave their worlds: avoid this one where "ingratitude is the rule and cruelty the main sport." It is a place where unfinished grubs, having crawled out from under the rocks, "walk this world upside down with their heads in the air."

Since "The Weirdest World" is the next to last story in the book, it is appropriate that it end with the blob's declaration: "I am near my end." Put nothing past Lafferty. "The Weirdest World" is not the last word — "The Ultimate Creature" is. And the last word in secret places may be our "writh-ing underminds," or Lafferty's own self-reflective *writing* undermind with which he is so often preoccupied. For the landscape of his stories is often a spiritually barren place, where beings seem endlessly to search for identity, for origins, for first causes, for Utopian ends. So in "Maybe Jones and the City," a parody of the utopian impulse, the protagonist has searched the universe for twenty years looking to recover the Perfect Place. He finally gets summoned to the Bureau of Wonderful Cities, set up to accommodate the good time crowd, folks with "the golden flaw" in their characters. Their plan is to construct Heaven *and* Hell "on the premise that one man's Heaven is another man's Hell." What Maybe Jones contributes is his modestly titled proposal "The Empyrean According to Maybe Jones." The narrator winds up soliciting sug-gestions for the Perfect Place from the "raffish elite" who want to get so high they never have to come down. As for the art and philosophy crowd, or the "peace and benevolence beat," they can go to hell, their "own appropriate bureau." In the end, of course, nothing is recoverable. Our only recourse is to start again in the company of the likes of High-Life Higgins, Good-Time Charley Wu, and Margaret the Houri.

In another story, "In the Garden," visitors to another world search for a source of superior thought. What they find is a man named Ha-Adamah and a woman the man says is named Hawwah. After an invitation to eat the apples, since they are "the finest fruit in the garden," the visitors conclude that they are in an unspoiled Paradise. The tycoon of the group plans to market the place to Earthlings as Eden Acres Unlimited because, we are told, folks have a "feverish passion to befoul and poison what is unspoiled." When the visitors find they've been the victims of a hoax, they're not too disappointed. They decide it was really paradise after all since the "Eve" there never spoke a word.

The magic of Lafferty's words is that they can damn and praise all at once. In the last story of his collection, "The Ultimate Creature" has the form of a woman and she represents "the ultimate treasure of the worlds." In a universe of Floating Justice, inequities are reconciled when the meanest and weakest man can possess that Ultimate Treasure. The ridiculous and the sublime are thus united and perfection is achieved by a reconciliation of opposites. Even Peter Feeney can woo and win the universal Ultimate. Still, we sense some-thing fishy about this union of outrageously incongruous superlatives. What of a Peter who, unlike his biblical namesake, prepares his "pretty fishy kids" not for salvation, but for the frying pan?

Clearly, the realm of Lafferty's satiric vision is one where extremes meet. And where extremes meet, the grotesque and the beautiful, the mean and the marvelous, the horrible and the comic, the appearance and the reality, the credible and the absurd, also are joined. The incongruity of Peter Feeney's salty tears spicing up a tasty dish of fish kids makes us laugh and wince at the same time. We're assured that Floating Justice grins in the face of ultimates, even perfection, since it seeks proportion in all things. Though we may shed a tear for Feeney's culinary fate, we chuckle to think he's getting his just dessert.

Is there anything further to add? From John Candor to Peter Feeney, Lafferty marks off the parameters of his fictive world. It is, strangely enough, a world promoting and endorsing the possibilities inherent in human nature. Because Lafferty can see around corners, we come to believe with him that the situation is hopeless, but not serious. For man is the creature that laughs. He laughs occasionally as a release from terror and pity, sometimes as an escape from pain, often as an expression of delight, always as a challenge to all the hostile universes, without and within, to which Lafferty makes us privy. Because man can laugh at himself — absurd and outrageous and ridiculous as that self may be — he may yet survive both the frying pan and the fire. In the end, we face up to the fact that crocodile tears don't necessarily inhibit our taste for self-mockery.

One of Lafferty's fictional characters once observed that there has been entirely too much solemnity in the universe. *Does Anyone Else Have Something Further To Add?*, like Floating Justice itself, helps to redress the balance.

Greta Eisner

DONOVAN'S BRAIN

Author: Curt Siodmak (1902-   )
First book publication: 1943
Type of work: Novel
Time: The 1940's
Locale: The United States; specifically, the cities of Phoenix and Los Angeles, and the small town of Washington Junction

The brain of a powerful millionaire, kept alive after he dies, develops the power to control living human beings for selfish and vengeful interests

Principal characters:
FRANKLIN SCHRATT, an immigrant physician from Europe
PATRICK CORY, a young research doctor
JANICE CORY, his wife
WARREN HORACE DONOVAN, a mailorder magnate
HOWARD DONOVAN, his son
CHLOE BARTON, his daughter
ROGER HINDS, an early business associate and friend of W. H. Donovan, later hated by Donovan for his kindness
CYRIL HINDS, Roger's son, convicted of murdering his own mother
HERB YOCUM, a photographer and blackmailer
ANTON STERNLI, W. H. Donovan's trusted elderly secretary
FULLER, a lawyer
PULSE, a hunchman

Curt Siodmak's *Donovan's Brain* works at providing an archetypal scientific fable as powerful and appropriate for the first half of the twentieth century as Mary Shelley's *Frankenstein* was for the nineteenth century. Shelley embodied in *Frankenstein* the danger of scientific creation turning against its creator, and raised significant questions about scientific accountability and limitations. Siodmak introduces many of the same issues and questions under a different, and perhaps more realistic aspect using the symbol of a disembodied, scientifically nurtured brain. The strength of Siodmak's book lies in the compellingly simple plot. Although neither his stylistic skill nor his philosophical and emotional range approaches that of Mary Shelley, Siodmak's fable of detached, power-thirsty intellect fed by science and wealth is nonetheless a disturbing and haunting vision. Like *Frankenstein*, the work has attained a cinematic life of its own, having been filmed once in 1944 as *The Lady and the Monster*, and as *Donovan's Brain* in 1953.

Patrick Cory, an independent researcher engaged in living tissue studies, is a bright scientific researcher objectively dedicated to pushing his investigations to the limit. He has been attempting to preserve in his laboratory "nervous substance . . . in the living state" — specifically, he hopes to preserve life in the extracted brains of monkeys. His efforts to date have not been successful, but he endeavors to learn all he can from his failures, thereby contributing further to the advance of knowledge. When four men crash their small plane near Washington Junction, the on-duty physician, Dr. Schratt, is too drunk to assist in the emergency. Cory is called instead, and when he finds the elderly man about to die, he decides to remove the man's brain on the spot and attempt to keep it alive in his laboratory.

Only after successfully transplanting the brain into a laboratory container does Cory learn that it is the brain of W. H. Donovan, a calculating business-man who has attained riches and power in the mailorder business. Donovan proves he is able to continue to function through the agency of science without his body, and Cory finds himself in an uneasy alliance with the world of selfish wealth and power. The alliance becomes increasingly sinister and sym-bolic. The preserved brain of Donovan is, in one figurative sense, a manifesta-tion of the business corporation which under law can live forever, carrying out the instructions and intentions of a Ford or Rockefeller far beyond the founder's lifetime.

Part of the pertinent content of the book rests with its condemnation of power structures perpetrated by a ruthless "robber baron" mentality. But a more serious and universal theme centers on the effort to preserve and expand the powers of a brain without a body — pure mind extracted from a living human context. Siodmak presents Cory himself as a character with a narrowly cerebral nature. Cory's relationships with his wife, Schratt, and others suffer because he is too rational; he is out of touch with human emotions and even basic physical needs. Both Schratt and Janice serve as foils to the scientist in this respect. Schratt suffers from an overly acute moral sensitivity; his con-science and emotional makeup have interfered with his own career and have caused him to depend on alcohol as a means of dulling his awareness of the harsh realities he must confront. Schratt raises the first and strongest voice of caution in Cory's brain research; he instinctively feels that the experiments are cruel and dangerous. However, his intellect and honesty force him to give way and admit that Cory has the superior rational position, since the long-range importance of the scientific knowledge to be gained in the experiments is clear.

An inquiry into Donovan's death reveals that Schratt was drunk and negli-gent, and he is promptly discharged from his medical post. Janice demon-strates her sympathetic and altruistic nature by inviting him to move into their home. Cory welcomes this as a chance to involve Schratt in his experiments, but he has no better human motives for allowing it. Schratt, who at first refuses to cooperate, is at last lured by the challenge of finding some way to communicate with the brain.

Cory has not been able to see beyond a primitive attempt at mechanical signals. He has tried tapping Morse code on the container which holds the brain, but has no indication that the pattern has been discerned. Cory is, in fact, generally an ineffectual communicator; he seems incapable of clearly understanding anything beyond the pure language of science. On the other hand, Schratt, made comfortable by the kindness of Janice and stimulated by Cory's scientific problem, turns away from alcohol and toward a more original solution to the problem of contacting the brain. He suggests telepathic communication. He proposes that Cory use his own mind as a telepathic receiver for impulses from the brain.

Cory is not well suited to this method, tending to think in purely rational and self-controlled directions, but gradually he is able to become a more sensitive receiver. When he realizes that he is not succeeding even at his most receptive, he provides additional electrical input to the brain and begins to "feed" it with appropriate chemical nutrients. The brain increases in size and brainwave output, measured by Cory on the encephalograph. One day a short circuit accidentally jolts the brain, as in shock therapy, and apparently charges it into action. In a moment of unconscious exhaustion Cory finds that he has written with his left hand (although he is normally right-handed) the distinctive signature of "Warren Horace Donovan."

From this point on, Donovan's brain increasingly controls Cory. It instructs him to go to Los Angeles, has him write large checks to obtain money from various secret accounts, and gains day by day more complete control of the scientist's actions. With Schratt remaining at the laboratory to care for and feed the brain, Cory assumes a new role and personality. Donovan plans revenge on the survivors of an old friend and benefactor, Roger Hinds, and telepathically commits Cory to the plans to be carried out. Schratt and Janice are powerless to interfere as Cory is driven by the commands of the brain. Under telepathic control, Cory even attempts to murder first Schratt, and finally his own wife.

Fortunately, both Janice and Schratt possess enough balanced scientific and human understanding to comprehend what is happening. While the brain is in a state of high stress, attempting to direct Cory's murder of his wife, Schratt is able to upset the container and disconnect the electrical systems, finally destroying the power of Donovan's brain. In the process Schratt is killed, but he leaves behind a journal to explain the events which he witnessed.

Cory realizes at the book's end that "Nature has set limits which we cannot pass." This discovery of his own limitations fulfills the caution with which Schratt had originally charged him and is perhaps more important than exploring the limits of science. Cory has sampled the results of Faustian desire for material power and control. He observes in his own final journal entries that "The brain's constructive imagination for mechanical devices and chemical explorations is limitless, but to create kindness, honesty, love, humanity itself must first grow into that shape." The brain assumed a new shape and new growth from electrical and chemical stimulation in the laboratory, but it was development uninformed by considerations of value and moral purpose. Cory's is the existential discovery: "Man can engender what he is himself. Nothing more."

Siodmak's simple and overt moralizing diminishes some of the potential of his powerful science fiction concept. In fact he, like Cory, tends to explain too logically the full impact of the situation. *Donovan's Brain*, like Cory's experiment, finally raises more questions than either its author or its readers will be able to answer easily. Partly for this reason, it must be regarded as a particularly powerful touchstone for the pursuit of scientific knowledge and material wealth in the twentieth century.

Richard Mathews

Sources for Further Study

Reviews:

New York Times. February 21, 1943, p. 7.
New Yorker. XIX, February 20, 1943, p. 60.
Weekly Book Review. February 28, 1943, p. 21.

THE DOORS OF HIS FACE, THE LAMPS OF HIS MOUTH, AND OTHER STORIES

Author: Roger Zelazny (1937-   )
First book publication: 1971
Type of work: Short stories and novellas

A collection of short fiction by one of the representative science fiction writers of the 1960's

Although Roger Zelazny has published over twenty books and many uncollected stories and novellas, *The Doors of His Face, The Lamps of His Mouth, and Other Stories* is only the second collection of short fiction he has published. The choice of stories in the collection tells us perhaps as much about the vagaries of science fiction publishing as it does about Zelazny's particular art. The volume does not include "The Furies," "The Graveyard Heart" (from *Four for Tomorrow*), "He Who Shapes" (later expanded to *The Dream Master*), and "For a Breath I Tarry," arguably *the* paradigmatic Zelazny fiction. In their place, supplementing the five novellas and four short stories which give the book its lasting value, are four clever science fiction japes and a few very average pieces.

In many ways the archetypal science fiction author of the 1960's, Zelazny sums up in his work most of the heady changes the genre went through in that decade. With his erudition and technical superiority, he exploded the conventions and extended the boundaries by which science fiction was defined. Now a full time professional writer, he can still wield the old word magic, but some of his recent work leaves an impression of haste, as if he had succumbed to the understandable, if depressingly familiar, willingness of established authors to allow what were once immensely liberating innovations in style, characterization, and narrative technique to devolve into mere mannerisms. Thus, although even the "throwaway" pieces in this collection reveal glimpses of wit and style beyond the capacities of most genre writers, they nevertheless tend to be games with genre conventions, such as the translation of the traditional pulp Western into science fiction terms in "Devil Car"; the cynical reversal of legend in "The Monster and the Maiden"; and the use of cute romantic fantasy in "Museum Piece." Nevertheless, *The Doors of His Face* provides an opportunity to rediscover the spectacular flamboyance which brought Zelazny his early fame and notoriety; stories such as "Lucifer" and "Corrida" touch on Zelazny's deepest artistic concerns, and "The Great Slow Kings" is a good example of a sardonic comic fable.

In Zelazny's fiction, the technological optimism of standard science fiction is raised to an almost mystic faith. Yet the author is not really interested in technology for its own sake; he merely uses its possibilities to invent worlds in whose contexts he may explore such traditional themes as the eternal vagaries of love or the tension between immortality and suicide. As Samuel R. Delany has pointed out, Zelazny's treatment of immortality is revolutionary in its premise that eternal life will bring not *ennui* but the exciting discovery of immense richness in each moment as it resonates with overtones of history and previous similar experiences. If Zelazny renders his fictive futures with imagistic verve, always limning some salient details which clearly evoke another world, his basic concerns are nevertheless as old as storytelling itself. The technological wonders and fabulous settings are merely the necessary science fiction equivalent of magic or divine power in ancient tales. Zelazny is, in fact, a fabulist, one of the 1960's writers who helped to define the boundaries of "speculative fantasy"; his unique contribution has been his highly romantic treatment of experience in the context of a scientific and positively felt immortality.

Even Zelazny's stylistic innovations, such as his juxtapositions of highly poetic tropes and racy idiomatic speech, emerge from his continual exploration of the theme of the value of experience. For his characters, life is a colorful, eventful, scintillating experience deserving of celebration, even if they also occasionally suffer great losses. And because they love life so intensely, they speak to us in brilliant metaphors and sharp images which reflect their lively perception of the world. Thus Zelazny often employs a narrator/protagonist rather than using the standard omniscient or limited omniscient point of view. His *characters*, like their creator, think and perceive with wit and finely tuned sensibilities.

The five novellas in this volume engage Zelazny's basic themes with varying degrees of success. Though they are great entertainments, "This Mortal Mountain" and "This Moment of the Storm" are finally lesser achievements than the other three. "This Mortal Mountain" is a Hemingwayesque tale of men pitted against nature with a fairy-tale ending. Zelazny vividly describes the "facts" of climbing the galaxy's highest mountain, slipping in all the necessary "historical" and technological information to make both the climb and the discovery of a "sleeping beauty" valid. In "This Moment of the Storm," the author's purpose is different though his approach is similar, as he explores the resourcefulness and courage men can muster in the face of nature's heaviest artillery. He also describes the narrator's experience with love, which is ended abruptly by death.

"The Doors of His Face, The Lamps of His Mouth" is a success of a different kind, a marvelous combination of adventure and romantic comedy set on a fictional version of the planet Venus. The great ocean of Zelazny's Venus is inhabited by a legendary beast called *Ichthyform Leviosaurus Levianthus*; human technology has designed a huge raft, called Tensquare, specifically for the purpose of catching "Ikky." In an enjoyable blend of romance and story, the author relates the attempt of Carlton Davits, the narrator-hero, to capture the beast. Like most of Zelazny's work, this story belongs to the realm of comedy, and the author's style, that wild combination of the colloquially racy and the densely metaphoric, is essentially comic as well.

Nevertheless, some of the other stories are darker in mood and have paradoxical tragicomic resolutions. One example is "A Rose for Ecclesiastes," a rich, sensuous fable set on Mars and compellingly narrated by one of Zelazny's finest characters, a proud, snobbish poet who slowly engages our sympathy both through his personal history and his present tribulations. The symbolic conflict between Martian religion and the Old Testament, the hero's search for a full humanity and his bitter experiences with love, and the complexities of the Martian's ancient civilization are all handled by Zelazny with dazzling ease within the conventional confines of his storybook Mars. In the dramatic climax, Gallinger saves the Martian race by impregnating the beautiful and immortally old dancer Braxa. Ironically, the "Sacred Scoffer" long prophesied in Martian teachings does not believe his own message, and returns to Earth alone knowing that the only person he has ever loved never loved him.

The author is similarly successful in "The Keys to December." Jarry Dark, a scientifically created human Catform, is forced to confront the most profound questions of ethical responsibility when his people's attempt to terraform a planet into a cold world livable for them forces one of its native life forms towards intelligence as a matter of adaptation. Since the world-change takes three thousand years, Jarry and his lover Sanza wake up every 250 years to monitor changes. After 1,250 years, their discovery that the bipeds kill animals for food and clothing, use fire, and worship the world-change installations, forces Jarry and Sanza to confront the morality of the Catforms' actions. While observing the natives, Jarry attempts to save them from a giant predator and Sanza dies protecting him from a second attack. Bereft and alone, he discovers 250 years later that the natives worship him as a god. Accepting a god's responsibility for his people, he becomes a revolutionary against his own race, finally forcing them to slow down the world-change enough to guarantee the natives' survival. Renouncing the special immortality of coldsleep, Jarry chooses a special, even glorious, form of suicide and lives out the rest of his days teaching the natives rather than awaiting the empty world he once dreamed into being. Once again, Zelazny's evocation of alien landscapes, his intriguing technological and sociological extrapolations, and his sure control of human feeling fully engage our emotions: we care what happens to Jarry Dark and his chosen people.

The two best stories in the volume are "Divine Madness" and "The Man Who Loved the Faioli." "Divine Madness" is a very special time travel story, as the protagonist desperately attempts to undo the past by living backwards. Zelazny has no interest in rational explanations; his craft is turned to realizing the emotional significance of what may be only a psychotic illusion. Zelazny proposes, through the protagonist's agonized return to the argument that drove his wife out to a fatal road accident, that sufficiently strong grief *could* change a person's life. Rising above potential sentimentality through concreteness as well as deliberate ambiguity, the author works his story to a powerful climax.

The tightly structured story "The Man Who Loved the Faioli" is one of Zelazny's most powerful hymns to the life-giving power of love. John Auden, caretaker of the galaxy's one cemetery world, is immortal only because machinery keeps him in a static state of living death. When he meets one of the legendary Faioli, her extraordinary beauty and indifference to his presence causes him to consider "the consequences of becoming a living man once again, for a time." Such phrasing reveals this story's literary lineage even as it places it squarely within the science fiction fame. The slow dignity of the prose is traditional, but the technology that makes this singular fable possible belongs to the far future. The Faioli are love/death goddesses who bring to dying men a final month of transcendental love. John Auden, however, gains the glory yet escapes paying the usual price when, at the end of the month, the goddess inadvertently turns on his mechanism, rendering him "dead" to her once more. With "icy logic" he refuses to turn off the "electrochemical system" which preserves him in stasis, and then he watches her disappear. He is "the only man who ever loved a Faioli and lived (if you could call it that) to tell of it," and he illustrates a moral that applies to all Zelazny's best fictions: "life (and perhaps love also) is stronger than that which it contains, but never that which contains it. But only a Faioli could tell you for sure, and they never come here any more."

The grandeur of this fable lies in the precision of its reductive symbolism, the elegant purity of its diction and the sheer evocativeness of its ambiguous discourse on the nature of love (spiritual *in* physical). These qualities or their equivalents (intensive symbolism, racy colloquialism, visceral kinetic imagery) animate Zelazny's finest fictions, including those which make *The Doors of His Face, The Lamps of His Mouth, and Other Stories* a major, paradigmatic work.

Douglas Barbour

Sources for Further Study

Reviews:

Analog. CX, September, 1972, pp. 161-162.

Books and Bookmen. XVIII, September, 1973, p. 87.

Galaxy. XXXII, January, 1972.

Kirkus Reviews. XXXIX, April 15, 1971, p. 466.

Library Journal. CXVI, June 1, 1971, p. 2012.

Luna Monthly. XXXVII–XXXIX, July–August, 1972.

Renaissance. III, February 1, 1971, p. 12.

Riverside Quarterly. VI, August, 1973, pp. 77-78.

DOUBLE STAR

Author: Robert A. Heinlein (1907-   )
First book publication: 1956
Type of work: Novel
Time: The twenty-first century
Locale: A spaceship, Mars, and the moon

When the leader of his imperial majesty's loyal opposition is kidnaped, he is imper-sonated by an unemployed actor who is subsequently forced to assume the politician's identity permanently

> *Principal characters:*
> JOSEPH BONFORTE, leader of the Expansionist Party
> LAWRENCE SMITH, also known as "The Great Lorenzo," an un-employed actor
> DAK BROADBENT, Bonforte's chief aide
> PENELOPE RUSSELL, Bonforte's personal secretary
> ROGER CLIFTON, another aide
> BILL CORPSMAN, a press aide
> KING WILLEM, titular emperor of the solar system

Boasting an enviable economy of design, style, characterization, *Double Star* illustrates many of the attributes that have made Heinlein one of the rec-ognized deans of science fiction writing. Its plot is modest and self-contained, and it flows swiftly to its denouement. The action of the novel is largely for-warded through dialogue, a typical Heinlein device, but some of the charac-teristics that seem almost self-parody in Heinlein's later books, particularly in *Time Enough for Love*, are here muted. The final result is vintage Heinlein.

In many ways *Double Star* is Heinlein's version of *The Prisoner of Zenda* transferred into space, a plot of circumstances forcing an unknown to assume an identity that is not his own in order to achieve some higher purpose. Un-employed actor Larry Smith, who is also known as The Great Lorenzo, is asked to double for the Honorable Joseph Bonforte, the leader of the Loyal Opposition who has been kidnaped. Bonforte must fulfill an obligation to be adopted into a Martian nest, and if he does not appear, interplanetary war is possible. Smith agrees to impersonate Bonforte, is hypnotized so he will lose his anti-Martian prejudice, and goes ahead quite successfully with the imper-sonation.

After Bonforte has been recovered from the kidnapers, Smith must continue the impersonation until the "Chief," as Bonforte is known, makes a full re-covery. During this interval the government resigns and Bonforte is asked to become Supreme Minister. Smith must visit the Emperor to present his pro-posed cabinet and begin planning an election campaign. Bonforte's recovery is slowed by some brainwashing he had undergone at the hands of his kidnapers, and Smith, in the major role of his acting career, makes election speeches, tapes video broadcasts to all of the inhabited planets of the solar system, holds press conferences, and otherwise imbues himself with the political theses of Bonforte's Expansionist Party. Hitherto completely nonpolitical, Smith as Bonforte finds that politics is even more fascinating than acting, and he immerses himself, not only in the exterior outward manifestations of Bonforte's appearance, but also in the psychological attributes of Bonforte's mind and personality.

As a result, when Bonforte quite unexpectedly dies, Smith is forced to assume the identity he had previously impersonated; he now actually "becomes" Bonforte. The end of the novel is a brief epilogue in which Smith-Bonforte looks back, twenty-five years later, and attempts to recall the foolish young actor he once was. The new Bonforte can now look at the former foolish Larry Smith without regret; he even quotes Voltaire to indicate the depth of the change he has undergone: "If Satan should ever replace God, he would find it necessary to assume the attributes of Divinity."

One characteristic shared by most of Heinlein's early novels is that they are all drenched with plot, convincing action, and no-nonsense dialogue. *Double Star* is no exception, and while it may not have as many plot complications as, say, *Citizen of the Galaxy*, its pattern of action is straightforward. Told in the first-person narrative technique, the novel reveals everything through Smith's eyes, and we watch his gradual awakening of consciousness and self-awareness, alongside his thespian strutting. In a sense, then, despite all of the action of the novel and all of its political overtones or undertones, *Double Star* is the story of one man's growth to maturity under extreme circumstances. Smith does not lack for guides in his development. Dak Broadbent combines mind with muscle and thus is capable of guiding Smith carefully in both the personality and physical attributes of Bonforte's character. Penelope teaches him something of the intuitive aspects of Bonforte's character; and Bonforte himself, when he finally meets his impersonator during the election night party, provides the almost spiritual encouragement necessary for Smith to continue the impersonation after Bonforte's untimely death. Together all of these characters contribute to the education and maturation of Smith.

Heinlein has often been criticized for his recurrent characters: the wise old man who knows everything; the precocious upstart who thinks he knows everything but in reality knows very little; the helpful secretary; and so on. *Double Star* has exemplars of all of these, of course, but Heinlein's handling of them makes them more than stereotypes. Jubal Harshaw of *Stranger in a Strange Land* and Joseph Bonforte of *Double Star* are both "wise old men," but there the similarity ends, just as Michael Valentine Smith and Larry Smith are smart but educable youths who are totally unlike in every other aspect.

It is overly simplistic to regard *Double Star* as a mere preliminary to Heinlein's mature works. In fact, the brilliance of his execution of many thematic materials in *Double Star* marks it as perhaps the first of Heinlein's serious novels. The themes are all there: politics; the search for identity; the search of a father for a son and a son for a father, the great archetypes of paternity and filiation; and, from a science fiction point of view, the luminous myth of Mars and Martian life. Ray Bradbury may have chronicled Mars, but Heinlein has also made the Red Planet his own, and in a far different way than did Bradbury or H. G. Wells or Percival Lowell, to mention only a few. For example, Heinlein's explanation of Martian formalism, propriety, and obligation is very well done in *Double Star*, but what is most important is that he skillfully makes these concepts integral to the novel itself rather than being mere dramatic excursions that have no crucial function.

Similarly, the twin themes of paternity and filiation are vitally important in *Double Star*. Smith hears (or recalls) his dead father's voice or admonitions throughout the early pages of the novel, when Smith still considers the impersonation to be simply another acting job. He has been accustomed to hear this voice in memory and to act upon its cautions. Thus, when the voice becomes Bonforte's, through tapes or the written word, Smith begins to be transformed into another person by the sheer power of the ideas represented. In the end, as Smith meets Bonforte for the first time, he is startled almost out of the character he is portraying. "He looked like my father," Smith says. "Oh, it was just a 'family' resemblance; he and I looked much more alike than either one of us looked like my father, but the likeness was there." Smith has finally made peace with his father through Bonforte; his maturity is now complete.

Double Star is, of course, much more than a *Bildungsroman* transformed into space. It is also a study of political concepts and political organization. In Heinlein's vision, the solar political organization is a variation of the British parliamentary system. In fact, when Smith — as Bonforte, the Supreme Minister designate — pays the customary courtesy call to the King to present the proposed cabinet, the King is the only person to penetrate the impersonation.

Smith's education and the political campaign that ensues give Heinlein ample opportunity to present some of the characteristics of his political philosophy. Bonforte is an Expansionist (does his name suggest "good deeds"?) dedicated to the political and ethical equality of all life in the solar system. When Smith-Bonforte is adopted into the Martian nest (a prefiguration of the Martian nests that Mike Smith will be born into in *Stranger in a Strange Land*), he becomes a Martian in almost every sense of the word. He will receive the complete loyalty of the Martian nests, and will bring them into the Solar System empire as full members against the xenophobia of many humans. Intelligent life is intelligent life, Heinlein avers, regardless of the form into which it is incarnated.

Heinlein is less overtly political in *Double Star* than he is in some of his later and more controversial novels such as *Farnham's Freehold* or *Starship Troopers*. The success and quality of *Double Star* may be because Heinlein has not sacrificed story or plot for message; it remains one of his most successful works simply because it tells a good story with enough philosophical or psychological overtones to make it worth remembering and worth rereading.

Willis E. McNelly

Sources for Further Study
Criticism:

Samuelson, David N. "Frontiers of the Future: Heinlein's Future History Stories," in *Robert A. Heinlein*. Edited by Joseph D. Olander and Martin H. Greenberg. New York: Taplinger, 1978, pp. 32-63. Loss of identity is a major theme in *Double Star*.

Slusser, George E. *Robert A. Heinlein: Stranger in His Own Land*. San Bernardino, Calif.: Borgo, 1976, pp. 7-16. Slusser discusses Heinlein's vision of man, calling this novel Heinlein's best work.

Reviews:

Amazing Stories. XXX, July, 1956, p. 115.

Analog. LVII, August, 1956, p. 149.

Booklist. LII, May 1, 1956, p. 364.

Fantastic Universe Science Fiction. V, July, 1956, p. 125.

Galaxy. XII, September, 1956, pp. 110-111.

Infinity Science Fiction. I, August, 1956, pp. 105-106.

Kirkus Reviews. XXIV, January 15, 1956, p. 60.

Magazine of Fantasy and Science Fiction. X, June, 1956, p. 101.

Nebula Science Fiction. XXXII, July, 1958, p. 107.

New Worlds. LXXIII, July, 1958, p. 3.

New York Times Book Review. April 22, 1956, p. 25.

DOWNWARD TO THE EARTH

Author: Robert Silverberg (1936-   )
First book publication: 1970
Type of work: Novel
Time: The twenty-third century (2248)
Locale: The planet Belzagor (formerly called Holman's World by Earthmen)

Edmund Gundersen seeks rebirth and redemption through the intermediary of the nildoror native life forms of the planet Belzagor

> *Principal characters:*
> EDMUND GUNDERSEN, a man concerned with sin and redemption
> JEFF KURTZ, the Earthman symbolic of the degradation of Belzagor's natives
> VAN BENEKER, Gundersen's former clerk, now an alcoholic, who provides much of the necessary expository information
> SRIN'GAHAR AND NA'SINISUL, the two chief nildoror with whom Gundersen journeys to the Mist Country and exchanges ideas

By the time Robert Silverberg published *Downward to the Earth* (first serialized in *Galaxy* from December, 1969, through March, 1970), he had found those basic themes and techniques which have characterized his most mature work to date: the human encounter with alien intelligence, immortality, and redemption. He had passed through that dark period which produced such painful portrayals of isolation and alienation as *Thorns* (1967), "Passengers" (1967), and *The Man in the Maze* (1969); he had achieved the ambiguity of what probably remains his finest short story, "Sundance" (1969); but he had not yet reached the sometimes erratic lyricism of *Son of Man* (1971) or the final reconciliation — to this date — of *Shadrach in the Furnace* (1975), after which he stopped writing science fiction for at least three full years.

One should notice, first, the relatively brief span of time during which all of these stories and novels — including the complex and controversial *Tower of Glass* (1970) and the highly regarded "Born with the Dead" (1973) — were created. More importantly, one should notice that in all of these works Silverberg sought to expand the established parameters of science fiction in order to give symbolic insight into modern, twentieth century man. That is to say, he attempted to use science fiction to gain the same ends as so-called "mainstream" fiction. His success, cumulatively and individually, may be debated; however, in one instance at least, he achieved his aim: *Downward to the Earth*.

During the last generation, many literary critics have insisted that the reader must consider a work without regard for the author. This method undoubtedly has some merit, especially in that it makes the reader look for patterns within the individual work as well as throughout the numerous works by a single author. Yet it ignores the individuality with which any writer treats his own perception and experience as well as the literary form(s) with which he works.

To cite an example within science fiction: one must go beyond the narrative to a knowledge of Ray Bradbury, Robert Heinlein, Isaac Asimov, and Larry Niven in order to gain a full appreciation of the fiction of those writers. Thus, in like manner, one cannot ignore Silverberg's repeated statement that during the late 1960's his own work was governed by his growing cosmic consciousness, and that *Downward to the Earth*, specifically, had been inspired in part at least by a trip to Africa.

Two major points dominate *Downward to the Earth*. First, Silverberg so completely abandoned that reliance upon external plot action which had characterized his earlier fiction that *Downward to the Earth* becomes essentially a study of the consciousness and sensibility of its protagonist, Edmund Gundersen. Second, as Silverberg has acknowledged a number of times, the novel becomes his adaptation (*not* imitation) of Joseph Conrad's *Heart of Darkness*. Soon after its appearance, a number of reviewers spoke of it as being a story concerned with "inner space" as much as "outer space." They might also have said that, as in the case of Conrad's narrative, it parallels Marlow's journey into the interior. One might also note that Silverberg explores man's encounter with alien intelligence much in the manner that Conrad explored the European encounter with the jungle (the primitive world).

After an absence of eight years, Gundersen returns to Belzagor, where he had spent a decade as a top colonial administrator. He had left not by choice but as part of the deliberate action of Earth to end a long period of imperialism and surrender the occupied worlds of the galaxy to their intelligent species — their people — in this instance the elephantine nildoror and the seemingly secondary sulidoror, baboonlike creatures who have an unexplained but intimate relationship with the nildoror. Gundersen returns to this pastoral world because of a general feeling of guilt; he has a sense of sin and a desire for redemption. He realizes that the nildoror have been treated as beasts of burden, as slaves. Specifically, he is most troubled by an incident when, faced by a crisis after a dam broke, he forced seven of the beings into conscriptive labor, thereby preventing them from continuing their way into the Mist Country to participate in the religious ceremony of rebirth. The need to undertake that journey is a matter of mystic compulsion to the nildoror; they have no control over its occurrence, and if they fail to obey the "summons," they do not know when (or if) it will occur again. (Yet the most respected among them are referred to as "the many-born.") Gundersen threatened to kill the seven if they did not work for him; indeed, to save face before them and other men, he burned one slightly with a fusion torch — the one who had said that he pitied Gundersen. By now the concept of rebirth (Gundersen has somehow come to think of it in terms of redemption) fascinates the Earthman.

Early in the narrative Gundersen commits that blunder so common to many of Silverberg's protagonists of the period: while a nildor carries him to the one remaining automated spaceport and while he converses with one of the few

Earthmen who remained on Belzagor after the general evacuation, he explicitly refers to the nildoror as beasts /animals instead of intelligent *people* who merely differ in appearance from men. Despite this inadvertent and seemingly ingrained human sense of uniqueness and superiority, he is permitted to join a small group of nildoror who venture northward to the Mist Country to undergo rebirth. Thus begins the journey to the interior.

Once again one is reminded of Conrad. As he so often showed the conflict between the primitive and the civilized, with a resultant degeneration of the European, so, too, does Silverberg show how Earthmen have been captured by Belzagor. There is, however, an essential difference. In *Heart of Darkness*, Marlow and the reader end up amid terror and, at best, ambiguity; in *Downward to the Earth*, Gundersen and the reader achieve enlightenment and transcendence.

So far as plot action is concerned, *Downward to the Earth* either presents fragments of Gundersen's memories of his career or, more often, focuses upon his present encounters with Earthmen who have succumbed to Belzagor. At the spaceport he converses with Van Beneker, once his clerk, who reminds him that Gundersen always despised the nildoror, that he himself believes they hate mankind and his remnants, and that no man should become involved in the ceremony of rebirth. Van Beneker, an alcoholic, is content to serve as guide to the tourists who come to these far reaches of the galaxy only to complain about the waste of potential profit, denounce those who ended Earth's imperialism, and otherwise think of Belzagor only in terms of the scenes which have bored them on innumerable other planets. The presence of a party of them in the novel serves to underscore typical human reaction, especially to a primitive world.

As he travels toward the Mist Country, Gundersen finds a couple who have become hosts to a parasitic growth. At Shangri-la Falls he meets a former lover, Seena, whose belly and loins are embraced by a gelatinous amoeba which conveniently moves when she wishes it to. Were all other parallels absent, Conrad would be called up by the magic name of her husband: Kurtz (first mentioned at the spaceport). She is married to Jeff Kurtz, who long ago milked serpents of their venom and fed that venom to nildoror, himself, and even Gundersen. Significantly, even in its weakest form, as Kurtz procured it, it had hallucinogenic effects; in a much stronger form it is used as part of the rebirth ceremony. Thus Kurtz profaned the most important rite of the nildoror religion, treating it as sport and entertainment. Much later, when he attempted to go through the process of rebirth, he emerged in monstrous form.

Faced by the corruption of Kurtz and told by Seena that he will lose his humanity, Gundersen still chooses rebirth. He finds transcendence, for he gains a unity with the nildoror, sulidoror, and even those men who have undergone the process before him. In this unity there is peace. In terms of Belzagor, rebirth explains the relationship between the nildoror and sulidoror, for periodically they are transformed from one to the other. In a sense they (and all who are reborn) become immortal, for the cosmos becomes an unending cycle and each individual retains the wisdom from all previous existences. One must underscore this idea of breaking down the isolation between intelligent creatures; by very different means Silverberg had achieved such a transcendent unity in his little-known novel *Across a Billion Years*, also published in 1969. The two themes — immortality and transcendence — haunt all of his fiction from the 1960's on.

For some readers, the lack of physical action and the philosophical exchanges, particularly between Gundersen and the nildoror, will weaken their interest in *Downward to the Earth*. Others will find that the ideas, instead of traditional gimmicks, strengthen it. Certainly the novel lies outside the expected parameters of science fiction. Two judgments seem inescapable. By concentrating the narrative upon the consciousness of Gundersen, Silverberg has produced one of the notable studies of character in the genre. Second, and perhaps more important for Silverberg, *Downward to the Earth* achieves the simplest and most affirmative statement of the unity of all intelligent beings that Silverberg has given voice to.

Thomas D. Clareson

Sources for Further Study

Reviews:

Luna Monthly. XXXVIII, July — August, 1972, p. 58.
WSFA Journal. LXXVII, June — July, 1971, pp. 32-33.

THE DRAGON IN THE SEA

Author: Frank Herbert (1920-   )
First book publication: 1955
Type of work: Novel
Time: The early twenty-first century
Locale: The sub-tug *Fenian Ram 1881*

While pirating crude oil from undersea enemy wells in a twenty-first century war, it becomes known that one of the four-man crew of the U.S. Fenian Ram 1881 *is an enemy spy*

Principal characters:
> COMMANDER HARVEY ACTON SPARROW, captain of the *Fenian Ram*
> LIEUTENANT COMMANDER LESLIE BONNETT, first officer
> LIEUTENANT JOSÉ GARCIA, engineering officer
> ENSIGN JOHN RAMSEY, electronic officer detailed to the *Fenian Ram*
> from the Bureau of Psychology
> DR. RICHMOND OBERHAUSEN, director of the Bureau of Psychology

First novels are often scorned by critics who dismiss them with such adjectives as "juvenile" or "promising." First science fiction novels are no exception to this critical condescension, yet when Frank Herbert's *The Dragon in the Sea* was published under the name *Under Pressure* in the pages of *Astounding Science Fiction* in 1954, its appearance heralded the arrival of an important new science fiction writer. This first novel was no mere hint of what Herbert would later demonstrate in *Dune* or *The Santaroga Barrier*; it was a mature, fully developed, serious novel that still rates as one of his best. Herbert shows in it the same control of ideas, concepts, characters, and psychological insights combined with exciting action-adventure that made *Dune* a science fiction masterpiece.

What strikes the reader who approaches the book for the first time nearly twenty years after its writing, is its contemporary tone. Its problems are those of today; its ecological sense is current, and psychological insights into the problems faced by men at war are as real as those of Vietnam POW's. The fullness of detail with which Herbert creates his miniworld of the submarine *Fenian Ram 1881* reads like a blueprint for America's modern atomic submarines. The novel is so filled with careful consideration of modern problems, such as the role of oil in a petroleum-starved world, that many readers must wonder whether Herbert had some sort of a future vision of America in the late 1970's.

Herbert's story is at once simple and complex: simple in its straightforward plotline and undiminished action and complex in its interrelationships among the crew members of the submarine. It tells the story of the ship's crew as they pirate oil from an undersea well located off the shores of Novaya Zemlya. Twenty sister submarines have been lost to enemy action in similar missions, and Ensign John Ramsey, a psychologist and communications expert, is assigned to the crew of the *Fenain Ram*, which Navy experts feel will have the best chance of success. As electronics officer, Ramsey must conceal his real identity, blend in with the crew, and also attempt to discover which one of the other three members is an enemy spy. To do this, he must study the psychological makeup of the captain, first officer, and engineer, while retaining his own sanity in the incredibly tense, pressured environment of the submarine. The mission is apparently doomed from the start: a corpse is discovered in the shielded atomic pile room; hidden electronic devices signal their location; a silk wiper rag threatens to cause an explosion through static electricity. One by one the obstacles are overcome, but the unknown spy remains undetected.

Ramsey discovers that the captain, Commander Sparrow, is an apparent religious fanatic who is fond of quoting scripture at moments of great stress and whose emotional control is so complete that he has become a virtual machine, a component of his ship. Yet Sparrow, whose nickname is "Savvy," indicating his superior ability, is a magnificent commander, so competent that Ramsey wonders idly if he is a "Captain, Submariner type: Mark I. Portable." Sparrow is a virtual Great Father to the crew, a godlike presence who can sense dangers before they occur, yet he is also paranoic, according to Ramsey's initial psychological assessment.

Somewhat less ably drawn is Les Bonnett, Sparrow's first officer who has not yet lived up to his potential or developed the maturity required of a commander. This flaw, Ramsey feels, may result from his life as a foundling and his consequent search for identity. Bonnett also reacts to the stress and the danger of the mission, as well as to his mistaken belief that Ramsey is the spy. In an action deliberately instigated by Ramsey, Bonnett finds a maturing catharsis in severely beating Ramsey, and comes to face the psychological truth about himself: "I'm the enemy within myself. Unless I master that enemy, I always lose." Thus Herbert, who was a student of both Freud and Jung, suggests that we must all face the enemy within — what Jung would call the Shadow.

José Garcia's shadow is his inner turmoil about being blackmailed by the enemy powers into becoming a spy. He is torn between his loyalty to the crew and his love for Sparrow, and his fear that the EP's, as Herbert terms them, will kill his wife and children unless he cooperates. An intense, traditional Roman Catholic, Garcia conceals his deep torments under a mask of jocularity, yet it is he, seemingly a better psychologist than Ramsey, who first penetrates Ramsey's disguise. Ambivalent and racked by his conflicting loyalties, Garcia finally performs the sacrificial self-immolating act which saves the boat from an atomic flare-up just as it is about to return to its home port. He literally lays down his life for his friends, asking with his last breath that Ramsey and Sparrow safeguard his wife.

Ramsey is not immune from the danger of contagion of insanity that pervades the *Fenian Ram*. His first breakdown occurs when he becomes aware of the dangers of the profound depths of the ocean — the submarine tugs can operate nearly nine thousand feet below the surface. Ramsey is awakened from his second breakdown and near catatonic infantile immobility by the kindly, fatherly compassion of Sparrow. Ramsey comes to terms with his own shadow, which in this case is his reluctance to admit the possibilities of sustaining religious faith, as well as his unwillingness to face the sameness of his roles as priest and psychologist. Ramsey thus emerges from the trial of potential death by water to its polarity, life from water.

This latter concept is one of the most completely developed psychological tenets of the novel. As the *Fenian Ram* emerges from the long underground tunnel leading from the port to the Atlantic, Sparrow notices that the tunnel resembles the birth canal, and when they take their vessel out to do battle, they are born into a terrible world that they did not want. This reinforces the natural fear that the crew members have, and even Sparrow cites the foreboding Biblical passage from *Isaiah* which gives the novel its name: "In that day the Lord with his sore and great and strong sword shall punish leviathan the piercing serpent, even leviathan that crooked serpent; and he shall slay the dragon that is in the sea." The crew members are born, not to life, but to death.

Ramsey realizes that his and the crew's apparent insanity is a genuine survival adaptation. Sanity, in Sparrow's words, is the ability to swim. The pressures of the decades-long war — the ultimate insanity — have given Sparrow and his crew that ability, and survival *is* sanity. Hence the crew must both literally and figuratively reenter the birth canal from the amniotic fluid of the ocean. They will not die *in utero* in the depths of the sea, but, nurtured by the umbilical cord of experience, will emerge into the light of life.

The Dragon in the Sea is thus a parable of death and resurrection in which all of the characters grow beyond the limitations so carefully detailed in the opening pages of the novel. They become totally mature persons — sane, with the ability to swim in the figurative sense of the word.

One further level of meaning in the novel is derived from the concept of security. The Bureau of Security has attempted to keep the missions of the subtugs secret, hiding their coming and going as well as trying to trace the identity of the spies who have infiltrated the subs. As an unwilling agent of Security, Ramsey is in one sense a spy, attempting to ferret out which of the crew is the EP sleeper. He inwardly rebels against this role, and the conflicts bring about his second catatonic breakdown when he must face the fact that the real agent, Garcia, has died for his friends. In a larger sense, Ramsey and Sparrow soon understand that the concept of security is a misnomer. There can be no security in any definition of the word in a world racked with war, suspicion, and hatred. It is suspicion that destroys the psyche, and the Bureau of Security cannot save it. Ramsey and his mentor, Dr. Oberhausen, come to realize what Herbert himself has long felt — there can be no such thing as security in a torn world, and that bringing everything to the clear open light of day is at least the first step toward wholeness. Submarine crews are publicly honored and decorated, and one of Ramsey's new tasks at the end of the novel will be to fight the debilitating notions of the Bureau of Security so that everyone can attain some measure of genuine security simply by telling the truth.

In addition to working well on the psychological level, *The Dragon in the Sea* will satisfy the less sophisticated reader who is interested only in action-adventure. It is an exciting book filled with all the suspense of good spy novels. Garcia's identity as the spy, for example, is not explicitly revealed until the very last pages, and Herbert is skillful in scattering enough clues, both true and false, throughout the pages of the book to force the reader to suspect all of the crew members, including Ramsey himself. Moreover, the verisimilitude with which Herbert creates the confined ecology of the *Fenian Ram* is so accurate that many submariners in the American navy have maintained that it is the one novel that catches the spirit of their life more closely than any· other.

In preparing to write this novel, Herbert created models of the *Fenian Ram*, charted its undersea progress exactly, and prepared graph after graph of water pressure-air pressure equivalents at various depths. The submarine itself was named for submarine developer John Holland's second vessel, the *Fenian Ram*, which was launched in 1881. This careful attention to detail has marked Herbert's subsequent career. Thus, *The Dragon in the Sea* seems to anticipate, even if in miniature, many of the devices which were to come to fruition in the *Dune* trilogy. These include the use of "the Voice," petit perception techniques, myths of racial memory, and concepts of death and rebirth, to name only a few.

All in all, *The Dragon in the Sea* (which is the title Herbert himself prefers) was not the isolated accident of a mere "first novel." It remains one of Herbert's most satisfying books, one that more than repays thoughtful rereading.

Willis E. McNelly

Sources for Further Study

Reviews:

Amazing Stories. XXX, July, 1956, p. 118.

Analog. LVII, July, 1956, pp. 155-156.

Authentic Science Fiction. LXIX, May, 1956, p. 153.

Fantastic Universe Science Fiction. V, July, 1956, pp. 127-128.

Galaxy. XII, July, 1956, pp. 99-100.

Infinity Science Fiction. I, October, 1956, pp. 66-67.

Magazine of Fantasy and Science Fiction. X, June, 1956, p. 102.

New York Herald Tribune Book Review. May 6, 1956, p. 11.

New York Times Book Review. March 11, 1956, p. 33.
New Worlds. XCVII, August, 1960, pp. 123-124.
San Francisco Chronicle. May 6, 1956, p. 22.

THE DRAGON MASTERS

Author: Jack Vance (1920-   )
First book publication: 1963
Type of work: Novella
Time: The distant future
Locale: The planet Aerlith in a distant star cluster

A combination of adventure tale and parable concerning the conflict between men and aliens, both of whom use members of the other species as slaves and selectively bred domesticated animals

> *Principal characters:*
> JOAZ BANBECK, leader of Banbeck Vale, a human settlement
> ERVIS CARCOLO, ruler of Happy Valley, a rival settlement
> THE DEMIE, priest-chieftain of the sacerdotes, descendants of earlier human immigrants
> BASICS (GREPHS), reptilelike non-humans, dominant life-form of the cluster
> DRAGONS, descendants of captured Basics, bred by men of Werlith into specialized forms to serve as fighters

The setting of *The Dragon Masters* is typically Vancean in its complexity and richness. Aerlith is, as its name implies, a planet of wind and stone, its surface scoured by daily dawn and evening storms. Men live in valleys and crevasses where the wind has deposited enough soil to support vegetation and thus settlements. The valley-dwellers' society is semi-feudal, controlled by hereditary leaders whose chief pursuit is the domination of rival settlements. The Sacerdotes' way of life is a mystery, their organization apparently a theocracy (as their name — "priests" — suggests); they carry on some trade with the valley-dwellers, but otherwise hold themselves aloof. The stability of this arrangement was disturbed about 250 years before the story's present action by the first raid by the Basics. First, the twenty-three Basics captured by Joaz's ancestor, Kergan Banbeck, provided the beginnings of a new military technology — specially bred dragons analogous to the Basics' own domesticated humans. Second, all human society on Aerlith is now threatened by the roundups the Basics conduct to improve their breeding stock.

All this takes place in a future so remote from our own time that the original world of men is remembered — or half-remembered — as "Eden" or the "Arch-World." Successive waves of colonization have washed through the stars; the valley-dwellers, refugees from the War of Ten Stars, have been on Aerlith for at least hundreds of years, the Sacerdotes for much longer. Man has passed away as the dominant species, at least in this cluster; the grephs rule and view humans as intelligent animals. In this distant time, things are at once alien and familiar — the domestication of intelligent beings and feudal rivalry, the Rationale of the Sacerdotes and Ervis Carcolo's ambition. Star travel, energy weapons, and other products of advanced technology (Joaz Banbeck's "armamentarium," for example, which must be a subminiaturized astronomical computer of considerable sophistication) can be taken for granted, even though they cannot be reproduced or sometimes even operated by the men of Aerlith. Technology thus approximates magic (to paraphrase Arthur C. Clarke), and the atmosphere approaches that of fantasy rather than hard science fiction. Vance is not the only science fiction writer to employ setting to this end — Robert Silverberg in *Nightwings* and Frank Herbert in *Dune* come to mind — but more than most he has made it his trademark.

The style of Vance's work, here and elsewhere, also contributes to the tension between familiar and alien. Where the mainstream of science fiction depends on the description of ideas, objects, and actions in neutral, transparent prose to establish the science fictional feeling of futurity (Robert Heinlein is the master of this technique), Vance establishes the otherness of his settings partly by means of verbal surface itself. His generally acknowledged mastery of visual imagery is present throughout in descriptions of sunrises, dragons in their armor, the costumes and trappings of free and domesticated men, or the decorations of Joaz Banbeck's apartments. In addition, his diction is studded with archaisms (*brach, armamentarium*), coinages (greph), and oddities (fugleman). This is the wordmaking and borrowing not of the modern scientist but of the renaissance scholar, and it invokes not the future but the past — appropriately so, for Aerlith is an old world and its people are dominated by tradition rather than the search for novelty (note Joaz Banbeck's pain on seeing the destruction of his family's reliquarium). To the reader, however, this ancient future is all new, whatever its associations with our past, thus the unfamiliar familiarity of the language. The tension is increased by vivid descriptions that work against the alienating effect of the exotic vocabulary: language creates a world that is at once richly present to the senses and distanced from the understanding.

From a literary-historical point of view, however, much of *The Dragon Masters* seems all too familiar. A cold description of some of its features makes it sound like any number of pulp space operas: dragons and swordbearing warriors in battle with each other and with reptilian aliens who arrive by spaceship; a race of mysterious, cave-dwelling magicians; feudal rivalries; minstrel-maidens. The combination of science fiction and fantasy atmospheres is by itself enough to prejudice many purists who esteem "science fantasy" or "sword-and-spaceship" stories even less than space opera. The roots of *The Dragon Masters* are indeed to be found in space opera and planetary romance, specifically in the adventure fiction of the pulps of the late 1940's and early 1950's in which Vance published his early work (particularly *Thrilling Wonder Stories* and *Startling Stories*). In the purist view, what Vance has produced is a highly decorated and charmingly written example of a subgenre that has no value beyond that of light entertainment and deserves no attention beyond surprise at the weight of ornament such a slight object can be made to bear. While it is probably not possible to establish absolute literary value without a few generations' hindsight, it should be possible to suggest some of the ways that *The Dragon Masters* escapes the trivializing label of space opera.

There are two narrative structures that interpenetrate to produce the plot of *The Dragon Masters*. The more fundamental of the two is the story of the conflicts between Banbeck and Carcolo and men and grephs; it is excessive attention to this part of the whole that leads to the misapprehension that the story is no more than the usual sword-and-spaceship recitation of intrigues, chases, and battles. This kind of action certainly does provide much of the narrative thrust, but there is another "plot" that can be characterized as parabolic — that of the conflicts among differing world views and ways of acting in the world. This plot resides in the competing values and behaviors of the major characters and groups — Joaz Banbeck, Carcolo, the Sacerdotes, and the Basics — and is revealed partly in debates and confrontations and partly in the adventure plot which serves as a testing ground for these views.

While the story is not an allegory but something looser and less mechanical, it is clear that two of the forces involved, Sacerdotes and Basics, act out of philosophical beliefs and are to be understood not as individuals but types. Ervis Carcolo, while he has no explicit ideology or philosophy, is so dominated by pride, greed, and wrath that he becomes almost a caricature. Joaz Banbeck is at the focus of these forces, and it is he, as protagonist, whose actions provide the connections between the action and parable plots. It is Joaz (except in one case where his ancestor, Kergan, serves as a substitute) who engages in exchanges with all three antagonists and thus serves as mediator as well as normative figure.

Carcolo is the closest to an individual antagonist Joaz faces; he is also closest to being a conventional melodrama villain, and his participation in that convention correspondingly robs him of individual character. Carcolo is so dominated by his heritage — the feud with the Banbecks — that humbling his enemies becomes more important then securing the survival of his own Happy Valley. His energy is devoted to breeding better dragons rather than improving his domain, and he will not credit Joaz's warnings about the return of the Basics. While he possesses strength, courage, and cunning, his obsession with the destruction of his enemy prevents him from applying his talents to matters outside the feud; as a result, the Basics take Happy Valley by surprise while Carcolo tries to take Banbeck Vale. The extent of Carcolo's inflexibility and vainglory is apparent when, having lost his people and exhausted his ability to make war on his rival, he persists in behaving as if his will alone were sufficient to dominate Banbeck. Exasperated, Joaz has him executed.

The Sacerdotes are not so conventional in their beliefs, though they are nearly as inflexible. What we see of them suggests that they are a rigid theocracy, a community dedicated to a single set of values and acting with unity of purpose. The Rationale by which they live demands "absolute passivity and absolute candor," and, more than that, noninterference in the lives of those they call the "Utter men." The center of Sacerdote belief is the *tand*, an object that symbolizes "Final Sentience" and upon which each Sacerdote models a *tand* of his own. Any whose *tand* — and thereby whose character — is judged unacceptable is ejected from the group, to live on the surface. The totalitarian overtones of such a belief system are apparent, and the Demie's revelation to Joaz of Sacerdotal intentions make them explicit: the Sacerdotes await the extinction of the Utter men, the "under-folk," so that they, the "ultimate men," may "renew the cosmos" by resettling the depopulated worlds. For all their extrasensory powers and all their communal wisdom and experience, the Sacerdotes are only another version of the Man of Faith, and Joaz's shrewd maneuvering of them into using their half-built space-drive as a weapon demonstrates that they do not possess the omniscience they claim.

The Basics resemble the Sacerdotes in their certainty of the correctness of their views, although they are anything but passive noninterventionists. They are the dominant life form in this cluster, and they seek to include the men of Aerlith under their Rule or destroy them; as a Weaponeer, speaking for his masters, tells Joaz before the climactic battle: "All residual pockets of disorganized life are to be expunged, though it would be preferable that the men surrender themselves and the valuable 'content of [their] genes.' " This is not mere slave talk, for even though the domesticated men cannot imagine freedom ("To whom would we look for law, control, direction, order"?), the Basics themselves seem to surrender to a deterministic view of reality. The Weaponeer calls his message "an integration of the instantaneous vectors of destiny. An interpretation of the future." Apparently the resultant integration of such "vectors" cannot be changes. The Weaponeer who parleyed with Kergan Banbeck twelve generations earlier characterized the fate of the human captives as "parceled, quantum-type, ordained. Established." Existence is the "steady succession" of "units of certainty, quanta of necessity and order"; all else is "absurdity." When Kergan resists the Basics successfully, the tame men go mad and destroy the ship. The twenty-three captured Basics surrender to their fate: "The texture of Destiny was inevitable. . . . The twenty-three, hence, were something other than the Revered: a different order of creature entirely." And different they indeed become — dragons.

Joaz Banbeck is clearly at the center of all this, and his success indicates some resolution of the various dialectics implicit in the action. By outmaneuvering Carcolo, forcing the hand of the Sacerdotes, and anticipating the raid by the Basics, he demonstrates an intelligence unhampered by egotism and free of ideology. His own aims are simple: survival for his people, the neutralization of threats; he possesses curiosities rather than metaphysical certainties. He is, to put it oversimply, a pragmatist, a voluntarist, an individualist, and thus differs from the theoretical, determinist, collectivist tendencies of Sacerdotes and Basics as well as from the ego-driven passions of Carcolo.

At the risk of pushing the story into allegory, it can be argued that Joaz

Banbeck possesses the balance, flexibility, and freedom of the authentic human, while his opponents are all in some way enslaved or dominated by emotional or philosophical systems that prevent them from responding adequately to the challenges posed by a universe of infinite variety. The closed systems of the Basics and Sacerdotes provide an order that places them at the pinnacle of the universe — but these systems prove inadequate when faced with Joaz Banbeck's refusal to take his place within them. Joaz is free of their crippling rigidity in the same way that he is free of Carcolo's obsessive pride and wrath. His world-picture may not be so orderly as theirs, and he may know doubts and uncertainties, but he is free to survive and even prevail.

The parable of *The Dragon Masters* is rather more delicate than this, in keeping with Vance's characteristic irony and his unexpected use of adventure-story conventions. There is, for example, something elegant and fascinating in the philosophies of the Sacerdotes and Basics, as there is something admirable in Carcolo's singlemindedness and energy. Certainly Joaz Banbeck himself would be doubtful of the allegorizing in the previous paragraph. Nevertheless, a fascination with slavery, both physical and mental, with the question of authentic humanity and the variety of shapes it can take, and with the depiction of the alien have been present in Vance's work since the 1940's; *The Dragon Masters* presents that fascination in a distilled and essential form.

Russell Letson

Sources for Further Study

Reviews:

Analog. LXXI, August, 1963, p. 89.
Books and Bookmen. XI, November, 1965, p. 56.
Galaxy. XXII, December, 1963, p. 125.
New Worlds. CXLIII, July–August, 1964, p. 85.

DRAGONFLIGHT

Author: Anne McCaffrey (1926-   )
First book publication: 1968
Type of work: Novel
Time: The very distant future
Locale: Pern, third planet of five in the solar system of Rukbat, in the Sagittarian
Sector

The combination of new blood and faith in an almost forgotten legend stimulates the regeneration of a deteriorating system of dragonriders and land holders

Principal characters:
> LESSA, new Weyrwoman, rider of golden Queen Ramoth, Benden
> Hold
> R'GUL, Weyrleader, Benden Hold
> F'LAR, rider of bronze Mnementh, Benden Hold
> F'NOR, rider of brown Canth, Benden Hold
> KYLARA, rider of golden Queen Prideth
> FAX, Hold Lord, Ruatha Hold
> LYTOL, Lord Warder, Ruatha Hold
> ROBINTON, Master harper, Fort Hold
> FANDAREL, Mastersmith, Telgar Hold

Anne McCaffrey introduced readers to the world of Pern in a short story, "Dragonrider," published in *Analog* in 1967. In 1968, the author won the Hugo award with her novella "Weyr Search," which became the first chapter of *Dragonflight.* To date, McCaffrey has written two more volumes for the primary series — *Dragonquest,* 1971, and *The White Dragon,* 1978 — and has also begun a secondary series about Pern designed for young adults. In addition, any reader who enjoys the Dragonrider novels will also enjoy the novels about Menolly: *Dragonsong,* 1976, and *Dragonsinger,* 1977. *Dragonflight,* the first novel in the series *The Dragonriders of Pern,* introduces the reader to a world, distant in both time and space from twentieth century earth, where dragons are superior beasts who protect rather than terrorize. The narrative begins at a time when all ties to Earth have been forgotten, and the society of Pern has evolved into one reminiscent of medieval times. In the introduction to the novel, the reader learns about the solar system of Rukbat, the colonization of Pern, and the planet's basic environmental problems. In Pern, McCaffrey has created a world sufficiently interesting to keep readers eager for more novels as well as intricate and realistic enough to sustain numerous stories of various degrees of complexity. A world of huge, colorful, dragonlike creatures with individual personalities is made believable through a setting depicted in graphic detail. In the first few pages of the novel, for example, sensory images vividly call up the cold, damp morning, the grass growing between the stones of the hold, and Lessa's terror. Likewise, the watch-wher is introduced so smoothly that the reader sees it not as a strange beast but as a watchdog that likes to have its ears and eye-ridges scratched.

McCaffrey's fictional world is solid and real, and her main female character, Lessa, is sympathetic and multidimensional. Lessa's male counterpart is F'lar, the traditional yet flexible male who will become her mate and the Weyrleader when his bronze dragon mates with Lessa's golden Queen. By using the personal conflict between Lessa and F'lar, McCaffrey is able to add a romantic secondary plot to the action-filled primary plot. Lessa, the valiant survivor of her hold's ruling family, begins the novel as a vindictive Cinderella and, during her training as Weyrwoman, continues to show the traits of a courageous and rebellious person. She is never "tamed" by F'lar, even after the mating of their dragons. Instead, Lessa and F'lar have complementary traits: he is logical, while she is intuitive; her intuition is enhanced by her intelligence, while his logic is tempered by his growing sensitivity. The other characters in the novel are not developed in great detail; much of *Dragonflight* is devoted to introducing the reader to Pern and its problems.

The dragons themselves are one of the most intriguing elements in the story. Rather than being naturally evolved creatures from an alien environment, the dragons are the result of genetic experimentation performed by the colonists and their descendants in an attempt to cope with the major antagonistic force in their solar system — an erratic sister-planet whose elliptical orbit brings it close to Pern approximately every two hundred years. The Red Star is a threat because it sends spores, or "threads," which could destroy all life on Pern. To counteract this threat, the colonists have developed a native species named in honor of the mythical Terran dragon and capable of killing the threads: huge flying beasts who are fed fire-rock and thus produce a flame to burn the spores. One of the dragons' attributes is their ability to travel through a dimension in which neither distance nor time is a relevant factor, a concept upon which McCaffrey does not elaborate. When going "between," the dragon flies through a state of existence in which there is a deprivation of all senses except that of temperature. The dragon's course is determined by a destination point which the rider visualizes; thus, the dragon can "see" where to go. Besides being vehicles of instant transportation, the dragons also use their ability to go "between" to escape the threads they fight; "between" is so cold that the threads are killed before they can burn the dragon (if he or she goes "between" quickly enough). The defense system formed by the riders and their dragons evolves into a system of weyrs and dragonriders who, much like the Fenians of old Irish legend, serve as protectors of the land in exchange for food and supplies from the locals, in this case from holds which are ruled by Lords.

Probably the greatest strength of *Dragonflight* is McCaffrey's depiction of the rider/dragon relationship. Riders and dragons are bound by an intimacy which begins at the dragon's hatching, when he or she chooses a rider through "impression"; from that moment the two communicate telepathically and become closer than is probably possible for two humans to become. As an example, McCaffrey describes in loving detail the moment when Lessa impresses Ramoth. The relationship between rider and dragon is so close that if one is killed, the other rarely survives; dragons go "between" never to return, and riders usually commit suicide. Whenever Lytol, whose dragon has been killed, comes into contact with other dragons or must come to the weyr, his pain counterpoints the joy one has come to accept between rider and dragon.

Dragonflight begins at a time when the Red Star has been absent for well over two hundred years, for almost four hundred "turns." One of the main conflicts in this novel arises from the fact that the populace is tired of supporting a system of dragonriders in which it no longer believes, while at the same time many of the dragonriders themselves have lost their sense of purpose. All but one of the weyrs have been abandoned, and only one queen — Lessa — is left to repopulate the remaining weyr. The author uses Lessa's training period to introduce the reader to the customs and the problems of the weyr; to promote suspense by showing the political turmoil both within the weyr and between the weyr and its holds; and to foreshadow events through her introduction of myths and the "teaching songs." F'lar believes in Pern's traditions, but he must convince Lessa and the other riders before Red Star reaches the predicted alignment with Finger Rock and Eye Rock.

Nominally, *Dragonflight* is science fiction, but in actuality it is a romance adventure which emphasizes interpersonal relationships. The world of Pern and its personable dragons provides entertaining reading in itself, as well as laying the groundwork for the action of the next novel in the series, *Dragonquest*.

Judith A. Clark

Sources for Further Study

Reviews:

Analog. LXXXIII, April, 1969, p. 166.

English Journal. LXVI, October, 1977, p. 93.

Times Literary Supplement. October 16, 1969, p. 1215.

Visions of Tomorrow. I, January, 1970, pp. 36-38.

THE DREAM MASTER

Author: Roger Zelazny (1937-   )
First book publication: 1966
Type of work: Novel
Time: The near future
Locale: The United States, in a large city

The frightening story of a self-deceived and pride-ridden man who accepts the ulti-mate psychiatric challenge — teaching a strong-willed blind woman to see — only to be destroyed by her last wild fantasy

> Principal characters:
> DR. CHARLES RENDER, an ego-centered and self-deceived neuro-participation therapist
> JILL DEVILLE, his shallow but lovely mistress
> PETER RENDER, his son
> RUTH RENDER, his wife, dead nine years
> DR. EILEEN SHALLOT, a blind psychiatrist seeking sight

The Dream Master is the novel-length expansion of Zelazny's award-winning novella, "He Who Shapes." Heavily psychological, it relies upon myths and literary works with mythic sources to shape its plot and to develop its characters. It is the story of Dr. Charles Render, a neuroparticipation therapist. Termed a "shaper" in the vernacular, a neuroparticipation therapist is a psychiatrist who engages in the highly dangerous process of entering his patients' dreams and shaping them. Through a series of controlled fantasies, he gradually creates new and healthy personalities for the patients. This is ac-complished by a machine called the "ro-womb." Though the technique has proven successful, it has been found to be dangerous if used on animals, true psychotics, and some highly neurotic persons. Strong-willed neurotics who have been blind for long periods of time fall into the latter category because their perceptions of reality usually differ greatly from reality itself. Eileen Shallot is such a person. Even though Render is aware of the dangers and though he is warned specifically against treating Eileen, he does so anyway. Actually, he has no choice, for he is locked into the patterns of his psycholo-gy, which he is compelled to follow. Essentially, *The Dream Master* is the working out of that destiny.

Render's personality at the time of the story is taken from the writings of Jung. He is a man who has long been shut off from those experiences which would permit him to develop in a psychologically healthy manner. In Jungian terms, his personality has been prevented from *individuating*. When this hap-pens, the psychic energy which would normally be used in the education of the personality is repressed in the unconscious until it finds an outlet. As a result, the personality becomes deformed or unbalanced. Eventually, the repressed emotions and instincts break through the barriers and manifest themselves in sinister or even pathological ways.

Zelazny introduces the basis for this characterization early in the novel when Render reads part of a paper that he is preparing on autopsychomimesis, or self-generated anxiety complexes. Briefly, the psychology postulates that when consciousness is repeatedly frustrated in its search for value in the real world, it turns in on itself. First it quarries the unconscious, and if frustrated there, then it moves to the collective unconscious. (Jung felt that this explanation accounted for why the dreams of the ex-Nazis he studied took on patterns from Teutonic myths.)

To make his protagonist's ultimate failure believable, Zelazny carefully applies Jung's theory to his character. Four primary personality traits display Render's psychological vulnerability. First, he is irrational in his desire for perfection. Petty concerns, for instance, prompt him to move his son, Peter, from school to school, and when the boy falls from a trampoline and breaks his ankle, Render refuses to accept the reality that it may have been accidental.

Second, he is abnormally preoccupied with death. Though Ruth, his wife, and Miranda, his daughter, have been dead for more than nine years, he frequently pulls their pictures out of his wallet to remind him of man's mortality. He dwells on their deaths, as well as that of a man named James who worked in his building and committed suicide, but whom he had never known. In a conversation with his secretary, Bennie, he speculates on the kind of person who would commit suicide. Render describes such a person as someone who keeps his emotions under rigid control, is conscientious, is compulsively concerned with small matters, and practices a profession which requires individual rather than group performance, such as medicine. Once again, Render has unconsciously described himself.

Third, it is clear that Render has hardened himself to his emotions. He admits, for example, that after the deaths of Ruth and Miranda he began to feel detached, as if he had received an injection of Novocain in the spirit. At another time, he admits that his current perceptions are based upon a certain rigidity of feeling. This repression of strong feeling has particularly affected his ability to love. Neither his relationship with Jill DeVille, who is little more than a sexual diversion, nor his relationship with Eileen, who interests him primarily as a psychological challenge, permits his personality to grow. From a Jungian point of view, this inability to sustain healthy love relationships indicates that the energy which would have been expended in them is now being trapped in the unconscious, where it is building towards a psychic explosion.

In addition to his other psychological problems, Render must finally deal with his pride, which allows him to accept Eileen as a patient even when he knows the dangers of her condition. Pride, however, is but a symptom of Render's psychological state. Again, in Jungian terms, pride is an aspect of the evil side of the Self. As such, it is a force to be reckoned with because of all the aspects of the psyche, the Self is the most powerful and its evil side is the most dangerous. When dominant, it can make a person megalomaniac or it can make him create delusions which come to possess him. In this state, he believes that he has answers to all the world's problems, but actually, he has lost touch with reality.

So, Render's choice of Eileen is not really a choice at all, but rather the product of his own psychology. In her, he has found a person whose psychological situation reflects his own. Because of her blindness, she has repressed strong emotions, and, in turn, she has built a false perception of reality for herself. In doing so, she too has trapped enormous quantities of psychic energy in her unconscious. Because their situations are psychologically identical, Render knows unconsciously that if he cures Eileen there is hope that he can cure himself; he is therefore drawn inexorably to her despite the dangers. He also knows at the unconscious level that should he fail, he will be committing psychological suicide. His inability to recognize himself in Eileen or James produces the irony of the novel.

Render's psychological vulnerability is displayed by the similarity between his personality traits and those he attributes to Jung in his paper. To emphasize that vulnerability, however, Zelazny has him report an incident that occurred five years earlier, when he momentarily lost control of a dream. It took him six months of skiing to recover from the effects. It is no accident that in the middle of Eileen's treatment, he goes to Switzerland for a skiing holiday. He has, by this time, occasionally lost control of the dreams that he has constructed for her.

Moreover, the very nature of his work — the shaping of dreams — is a sign that he unconsciously wishes to escape the real world and that his own mind has now quarried down into the collective unconscious in its search for value. That this is true is found in Jung's description of the collective unconscious: a reservoir of primitive symbols, which he terms archetypes, that have been generated by primeval dreams and creative fantasies. Render's desire to shape dreams shows the internal focus of his mind.

In Jungian psychology, myths are generated by the same instincts that generate archetypes. Therefore, it is highly appropriate that Zelazny chooses myths and literary works with mythic bases to support the psychological development of his story. These allusions also foreshadow the outcome of the story. Though there are several in *The Dream Master*, two of these clusters of references are more important than the others. They are the materials related to Arthurian lore and the Scandinavian myth of *ragnarok*.

The Arthurian material is important because it symbolizes the quality of Eileen's mind and her view of the world. The perspective that she has built up in her mind is idealistic, romantic, and chivalric. The shattering of this perspective produces a radical alteration of her concept of self, and that, in turn, releases her trapped psychic energy with such force that it draws Render into madness.

From the outset of the novel, Arthurian images abound. Not only does a suit of armor, standing beside their table in "The Partridge and Scalpel" restaurant, mark their first meeting, but Eileen's surname, Shallot, immediately identifies her with the heroine of Tennyson's "The Lady of Shalott." The allusion, however, is meant to be far more than a simple similarity of names, for many of *The Dream Master*'s symbols, such as the river, the willow, and the color gray, are adapted from the poem. There are also similarities of both character and situation between the two ladies. Both view the real world indirectly. Tennyson's Lady sees it reflected in a mirror; Eileen sees it through Render's mind, which is referred to as a mirror on at least one occasion. Both wrestle with the problem of adjusting to the larger world and fail: Tennyson's Lady dies; Eileen goes mad. Both are carried outside themselves by a new love from a shadow world to reality, and in both cases that love is unrequited.

As a psychiatrist, Render knows that he must balance Eileen's extremely idyllic perspective with reality in order to restore her mind to mental health. He attempts to do this by showing her "reality" — the Dust Bowl, a polluted river, a forest laid waste. Even the Holy Grail is tainted in his version of its true origin. But he overdoes it. Following this session, there is a break of several weeks in Eileen's treatment while Render and Jill travel in England and then go skiing in Switzerland. Upon returning and once more beginning the therapy, Render tries to show Eileen one of the sights which impressed him, Winchester Cathedral. However, he finds that she is taking control of the dream from him. She makes the Cathedral organ play "Greensleeves," an old English ballad which tells a story of unrequited love. Then she dresses him in a suit of armor and herself as a Lady of the Court, with green slippers and gown, and a cone-shaped hat trailing wisps of green veiling. She struggles to make the dream even more Arthurian; he struggles to return to reality. At the end of the dream, Eileen takes complete control and draws Render into a fantasy that is a re-creation of the Tristam and Isolde myth, which is a logical progression since the Tristam story is an integral part of Arthurian lore. He plays Tristam and she, Isolde of the White Hands; and like Isolde, Eileen brings disaster to her hero. Though she does not cause his death, she does bring him madness — in other words, psychological death.

Not only does the Arthurian material represent Eileen's idealistic orientation, it also represents one extreme in one of the major dichotomies which create the tension in the story: the ideal *versus* the practical, the feeling *versus* the unfeeling, black *versus* white. These apparently unresolvable opposites must be resolved in Jungian psychology if a person is to function in a psychologically healthy way.

The second primary source for *The Dream Master* is the Scandinavian myth called *ragnarok*, or "twilight of the gods." As the Arthurian material comes to represent the quality of Eileen's mind and her perspective, so the *ragnarok* myth comes to represent Render's. It is a story of inevitable doom, for no matter what the gods do, they are fated ultimately to fail. Their destruction marks the end of the created world, and by his association with Odin, who dies, Render is consigned to a similar fate.

Even though Odin's name is never mentioned in the novel, there is no doubt that Render is to be paralleled with him. Three things, in particular, signal the allusion. First, Render's son, Peter, has a broken ankle and must wear a cast, which can be considered as a special kind of shoe. Odin has a son named Vidar, who wears a special shoe made to kill the wolf, Fenris, after it slays his father. Moreover, Vidar is destined to survive the destruction of the world and to carry the promise of Odin into the future, just as Peter will carry the promise of Render into the future. If he does become one of the people who chronicles the exploration of the outer five planets, as he wishes, then he will do well by his father.

Furthermore, dogs and wolves are viewed negatively by both Odin and Render. Fenris is, of course, Odin's ancient enemy and the agent of his destruction. Dogs and wolves strike fear into Render, and that fear manifests itself in the form of Fenris during his last mad fantasy.

Finally, the method of destruction of both men is metaphorically equal. Odin is literally swallowed up by the wolf. Though Render does not physically die, his sanity is swallowed up (a term that is used in the novel itself) by the immense psychic energy released when Eileen goes mad.

These are not the only elements borrowed from the myth, however. As with the Arthurian material, pieces of the *ragnarok* are present from the outset of the novel. The mighty winter, three years of unrelieved cold and snow, which signals the beginning of the gods' destruction becomes the setting for *The Dream Master*. The book swirls with images of winter, and like the myth, they are associated with death. Another clue that the gods receive to signal the end is that they begin to dream bad dreams. Render's loss of control of his structured dreams is another metaphorical equivalent. Yet another signal of the beginning of the *ragnarok* occurs when a wolf swallows the moon. Zelazny adapts the motif for his novel. Through the course of its development, he very carefully associates the moon with Eileen by virtue of the photoelectric cell which she wears on her forehead. When, in the final dream sequence, he indicates that Fenris leaped into the air and swallowed the moon, the image has a double significance. Not only does it indicate that the novel's equivalent of *ragnarok* has begun but that Eileen has, at that point in time, lost her own sanity.

By bringing the Scandinavian and Arthurian imagery together in the final dream sequence, Zelazny indicates that the two minds they represent, the two orientations, are also in conflict. Render loses the battle, of course.

When Render dismembers Fenris with his scalpel, he fails to destroy his ancient enemy. Instead, the wolf is simply transformed into the two-headed giant, Thaumiel. This metamorphosis was a common ability of mythic giants. Thaumiel of Qlipoth is a creation which posits both good and evil in the same being, since Thaumiel is derived from the Hebrew "tamiel," or perfection of God, while Qlipoth is a Kabbalistic term for the forces of evil. In the novel, Thaumiel specifically symbolizes Render's psychological problem, the inability to achieve a balance of personality. It is this balance which is necessary to mental health in Jungian psychology.

The theme of *The Dream Master* — man's attempt to play God — is given a contemporary treatment in the novel. Though Render is indeed a man with a tragic flaw, Zelazny portrays him as a victim of psychological determinism. The world and characters that he creates are understandable to contemporary readers; they are readily identifiable to those masses of people who are caught up in the same tensions and pressures, which ultimately bring about Render's downfall.

Carl B. Yoke

Sources for Further Study

Reviews:

Luna Monthly. XXVI–XXVII, July–August, 1971, pp. 46-47.

New Worlds. CLXX, January, 1967, p. 155.

Observer. April 14, 1968, p. 27.

Punch. CCLIV, April 3, 1968, p. 502.

Son of WSFA Journal. CX, October, 1973, p. 4.

Times Literary Supplement. March 28, 1968, p. 310.

THE DREAM MILLENNIUM

Author: James White (1928-   )
First book publication: 1974
Type of work: Novel
Time: The future
Locale: The Earth and outer space

Suspended in cold sleep to survive a thousand-year space journey, John Devlin has a series of progressively more violent and frightening dreams

Principal characters:
JOHN DEVLIN, a medic and crew member of the mission flight
PATRICIA MORLEY, a crew member of the mission flight
BROTHER HOWARD, mission organizer and recruiter

James White incorporates such well-known facets of science fiction as aliens, computers, space battles, and interstellar travel with well-developed characters and social criticism in this novel based on Jung's theory of the collective unconscious and on biological and cultural evolution.

The society from which the mission members are escaping is composed of "sheep" and citizens. Citizens carry weapons at all times and take part in duals at the slightest provocation. In reaction to widespread crime, some citizens have become vigilantes called Maxers who mete out maximum punishment without trial to lawbreakers. Moreover with a decrease in crime, the Maxers have begun to attack ordinary people without provocation. Gangs also battle daily in the city, many of their victims being innocent bystanders. Although society has achieved the ultimate in scientific knowledge, affluence, leisure time, and cultural and philosophical accomplishments, the people are bored and violent; depersonalization, injustice, and the use of drugs to produce conforming individuals are prevalent. Since aggressive individuals no longer have anything to fight against in this technological Utopia, they turn against one another.

Because of this violence, chaos, and social disintegration, it has been decided to send a mission in search of a habitable planet on which man's culture can survive by ridding it of its self-destructive tendencies. The prolonged space travel required for such a mission has been made possible by a "cold-sleep" process which enables crew members to endure one-thousand-year-long trips. Furthermore, the success of the mission is further insured by the selection of what society disparagingly calls "sheep" to make up the crew. The "sheep" are pacifists who neither work nor fight to gain power; they are representatives of the common man, and they do not attempt to change their society because they accept the *status quo*. These nonviolent, nonagressive, average people are chosen because they have always survived no matter what their physical or cultural environment. They are described as being psychologically unable or unwilling to rationalize violent acts as acceptable for the good of the people; White calls them the "seeds of humanity — retaining all its knowledge, experience and achievements since its beginnings."

This emphasis on the value of the ordinary human being instead of the superhumans so often found in science fiction is unusual in the genre. White's characters do not have superior physique, intelligence, training, or skills. They survive because they are able to draw on their "racial memories" to solve problems; and it is implied that they can do so because they are not incumbered or controlled by individualistic, aggressive impulses.

The seeming paranoia of crew member John Devlin is the result of his environment. As a medic he may be captured to aid a warring faction within the city. His social relationships are curtailed because it is unwise to give the impression of favoring "sheep" clients over citizens. And as a noncitizen there is still the chance of his being drawn into a battle or of being wounded accidentally. Since there is little stability in his society, he has become cynical and self-protecting. Consequently, he questions whether the mission has actually started or whether he is going through a final preflight test. He also questions the origin of his dreams.

Much of Devlin's development as a leader and as a man is the result of these dreams, which reinforce his belief in the value of the individual and his abhorence of violence. His knowledge of biological and cultural evolution also assists him in discarding his xenophobia and accepting the aliens as worthwhile individuals. Just as he questions his surroundings and his relationships, he also questions and learns about himself. Devlin is not the self-assured, "gung-ho" space explorer so often met in science fiction novels. He is a common man of average intelligence and physique who learns how to survive from his experiences.

His mission partner and fellow-colonist Patricia Morley is a calm, logical, determined individual capable of self-sacrifice to protect others. She plays the role of sustainer, especially for Devlin during his more paranoid moments. Yet she is not a totally one-dimensional character. She is capable of controlling her emotions, of making rational decisions in time of crisis, and of enforcing those decisions on Devlin through the use of logical argument.

Brother Howard recruits members for the mission with a religious zeal. His experiences as one of the first to endure cold sleep during a one-hundred-year space flight drove him insane. Having regained his sanity with the help of Dr. Martin, he has come to recognize the reality of the collective unconscious. His observance of the degeneration of civilization during those one hundred years has also convinced him of the necessity of the mission if mankind is to survive. Brother Howard theorizes that only common men and women can survive the thousand-year-mission because of their stability, their nonviolence, and their already proven psychological abilities to adapt and survive. Brother Howard's strength of character is illustrated by his acceptance of the fact that he cannot be a member of this longer journey because his zeal might jeopardize it.

The computer is included as a quasicharacter by its dialogue with crew members and lends a scientific atmosphere which helps to authenticate the reality of space flight. White never shows computers as in control but rather as useful instruments for man to use in his work. This is a welcome and useful ploy. White clearly indicates computers can only do what they are programed to do. Man must use his own intelligence by asking the right questions to obtain the information he needs. The computers are neither capable of solving major crises nor are they malevolent. Man is in control.

But the primary scientific elements in *The Dream Millennium* pertain to the social sciences of psychology and anthropology. Through his use of Jung's theory of the collective unconscious and of the theories of biological and cultural evolution, White attacks the problems of defining "Man" and determining how he might best survive. Through the dream sequences Devlin recalls his "racial memories" from amoeba to man and learns survival lessons at each stage of biological and cultural evolution.

In Devlin's first dream he is an amoeba in whose form he lives a violent existence of pleasure and pain, hunger and repletion, and dies a violent death. Devlin next dreams he has biologically evolved to a trilobite, an ocean creature motivated primarily by hunger, as illustrated by his continuing to eat while he himself is being devoured. In this form he experiences anger and learns that hunger and blind instinct cause a violent end. The valuable lesson of self-restraint is illustrated when Devlin does not immediately eat when he awakens, even though he is hungry. Thus far the collective unconscious which Devlin draws upon in his dreams has not contained the intellectual ability to reason.

Devlin takes the form of a brontosaur in his third dream, in which he learns two survival lessons: first, never underestimate the capabilities of a smaller foe, and second, never accept brief relief from pain at the risk of permanent physical damage. In Devlin's next recorded dream he appears as a scrawny primate whose sexual desires overcome his self-protective instincts. The tribe's attack on him is shown as an act to prevent the creation of future weak members. Here White illustrates the survival of the fittest doctrine implemented by cultural restrictions. This lesson is reflected when Devlin and Morley refrain from sexual intercourse during the journey out of concern for the medical complications which a pregnancy during cold sleep would entail.

In the fifth dream there is a huge jump in biological and cultural evolution: Devlin has evolved to the human level in the form of a medieval prince. As the prince initiates a war out of greed and pettiness, Devlin for the first time attempts to impose his own conscience in the dream. The prince, as with the other characters in Devlin's dreams, suffers a violent death; such death is presented as being the inevitable punishment for any pattern of action which is detrimental to man's survival.

Finally Devlin begins to exercise control over his dreams. During a series of interrelated dreams, he focuses on the entire lives of the main characters. He dreams of being an alcoholic salesman, and then a mercenary from his own society, both of whom value aggression and disrespect life; both suffer violent deaths. In the penultimate dream, cultural rather than biological evolution is emphasized as aspects of revolution are discussed. The pacifists win. Man finally resists the temptations of power and greed, refusing to be part of another revolution "for the betterment of mankind." In his last dream, Devlin learns that the chronological order of his dreams has been the result of Brother Howard's drug-reinforced, posthypnotic suggestion. This knowledge relieves Devlin's paranoia, enabling him to function more effectively, especially in decision-making. At the same time, White shows that the ability to learn the lessons of the past, recalled through the collective unconscious, is shared by the aliens and Devlin alike; peace is therefore established between the two groups.

By the end of the novel, the colony has carried with it the technology of nuclear power plants but has left behind the depersonalization of a technological society by relying on dreams to educate their children and enrich their adult lives. White, in *The Dream Millennium*, therefore, illustrates the theories of both cultural and biological evolution which he postulates as being stored in the collective unconscious.

Jane B. Weedman

Sources for Further Study

Reviews:

American Libraries. VI, March, 1975, p. 169.

Guardian Weekly. CXI, August 24, 1974, p. 22.

Magazine of Fantasy and Science Fiction. XLVII, November, 1974, p. 50.

New York Times Book Review. September 8, 1974, p. 40.

Publisher's Weekly. CCV, April 22, 1974, p. 77.

"THE DREAM OF A RIDICULOUS MAN"
("SON SMESHNOGO CHELOVEKA")

Author: Fyodor Mikhailovich Dostoevski (1821-1881)
First book publication: 1877
English translation: 1971
Type of work: Short story
Time: The late nineteenth century
Locale: The Earth and a dream planet, Earth's double

A "ridiculous man" who dreams of a golden age on another planet, a double of the Earth, perverts the planet but returns to Earth with the message, "Love others as yourself"

Principal character:
THE RIDICULOUS MAN, a rejected human being and a failed suicide

Is "The Dream of a Ridiculous Man" science fiction? The story is set in horse-and-buggy, gas-lighted times, and it lacks the scientific interest of Jules Verne and H. G. Wells, who wrote their *bona fide* science fiction works just before and after the late Dostoevski. The plot is built around a man who dreams he is carried by some creature through space, past galaxies, to a double of Earth. This world is enjoying the golden age of love, peace, and harmony, but it is somehow infected by the man and falls into decline; it comes to believe that "science" (knowledge, rational planning) is more important than what it had (spontaneous love). The man awakens and returns to Earth with the message of the immediate golden age. Given such a story line, "The Dream of a Ridiculous Man" might be termed "pre-science fiction," a work having a fantasy element we associate with the genre and anticipating the problems of modern science fiction, but lacking the technological devices of real or imagined later times.

Scholars relate Dostoevski's tale to the utopian tradition from Plato onward; it has a particular affinity with Cyrano de Bergerac's "Comic History of the States and Empires of the Moon" (1650), Hans Grimmelshausen's "The Flying Wanderer to the Moon" (1659), and Voltaire's "Micromegas" (1752). It also recalls the "dream visions" of Medieval, Renaissance, and Romantic writers such as Quevado, Sand, and Chernyshevsky, as well as the "crisis dreams" of Shakespeare, Calderon, and Grillparzer. The influence of Edgar Allan Poe and E. T. A. Hoffmann has also been noted. Finally, we should note its influence, along with Dostoevski's *Notes from Underground*, the dream of Raskolnikov, and "The Legend of the Grand Inquisitor," on later antiutopian literature — the work of such writers as Evgeny Zamyatin, Vladimir Mayakovsky, George Orwell, and B. F. Skinner. For, although the story does not utilize any of the familiar devices of science fiction writing, it does question the very basis of science: rational thought.

"The Dream of a Ridiculous Man," subtitled "A Fantastic Story," first appeared in the April, 1877, issue of Dostoevski's remarkable literary experiment, *The Diary of a Writer*. In this diary, Dostoevski shared with the reader everything that caught his attention: historical events, court trials, living conditions in Russia, crimes, suicides, the educational system, orphans, the mission of Russia, ties to the soil, utopian socialism, important contemporaries, important books, correspondence with the readers, literary plans, literary works. Although often hastily and sloppily written, over-emotional, and unclear, the diary permits one to observe the great writer's interests and the imaginative works forming out of them.

Many entries in the diary might be related to the story of the ridiculous man, but one is particularly significant. Dostoevski quotes from the suicide note of a young woman (entry of May, 1876):

> I'm doing a swinish thing, a filthy thing. . . . Don't lose your heads, don't moan, get control of yourselves and read to the end, and then decide what is the best thing to do. Don't scare Petrova. Maybe nothing will come of it besides laughter. My passport is in the top of the suitcase.

Dostoevski comments: "*Besides laughter*! This thought — that they would laugh at her, at her poor body, and who — Lipareva and Petrova — this thought slipped through her at such a moment! It's horrible!" But perhaps Dostoevski is misreading the note; perhaps what the girl is saying is that the suicide attempt may fail, and later become something which she and her friends will laugh over; according to this reading, the note reveals a last instant of hope: perhaps the girl will be saved.

Dostoevski's reading reveals something of his own mind, the projection of his own thoughts into the mind of the suicide. For him, a suicide remains so absolutely alone, so cut off from hope of human affection, that he imagines people will laugh at his miserable corpse, the last physical proof of his failure in life, the final word of a joke. If people were to feel sorrow, then the suicide would be a misfortune, a mistake: the affection was there but the suicide did not accept it. For Dostoevski, there is no affection and there will be no sorrow: people will laugh. This most horrible thought, which Dostoevski read into the last words of an actual suicide note, became the foundation for the mental state of the literary character, the ridiculous man.

Although he is called "ridiculous" in almost all translations, it is important to note that the adjective *smeshnoi* relates more directly to the noun *smekh* (laughter, laugh) and the verb *smeyat'sya* (to laugh) than does the English word *ridiculous* to *laughter* and *laugh*. The *smeshnoi chelovek* is a ridiculous man, but he is above all a *laughable* man. He has no name in the story; we know only that he was laughable as a boy, laughable in school, laughable up to the present moment. All the rest of his biography, all the rest of his existence is wiped out. Unlike the underground man of *Notes from Underground*, whom he so resembles, he at first does not offer any self-justification, any philosophy, any rebellion, any account of previous experiences, any story of lost love. He knows only that to the rest of the world he is laughable, and this consciousness dominates him, keeps him awake through the night as he sits in his Voltaire armchair and thinks. Finally, after a lifetime of isolation, he realizes that nothing matters. Whether he says yes or no or nothing, it makes no difference. Everything is the same, nothing has ever changed in his lifetime, and nothing will ever be different. Here there is no room for the usual sort of literary analysis, tracing of influences, description of character, enumeration of literary devices. The ridiculous man has reached the rock bottom of individuality, the private room of suffering where explanations, appeals, farewells, and attempts to communicate are impossible. Only someone who has reached this nadir can understand, yet when one reaches this point, no one else seems to understand, no one else cares: one is alone, laughable. This would seem the time to end life, to end one's experiment in isolation — except that, since nothing matters, one instead sits alone, without hope, with nothing save consciousness, and the pride of being unlike the others.

Such is the situation of the ridiculous man before he experiences his dream. He spends that night sitting silently in the home of an engineer and two of the latter's friends. The three discuss something with apparent emotion, but he can see that it is all the same to them and tells them so. They can see that his objection makes no difference to him and are amused by it. It is the same situation: no one cares, and the ridiculous man is conscious of it; he is thereby laughable to the unconscious others, united among themselves. On his way home, he reflects on the gloomy weather, the rain and awful dampness that follows; without the gas lamps in the street, he thinks one would not see the strange steam arising from every stone in the sidewalk, from every side street, and it would be more comforting. This is the same situation symbolically: without light, without consciousness, the gloom would not be so oppressive. He sees a star in the black sky between the rent clouds and is reminded that he should kill himself. At that moment a terrified girl begs for his help: her mother apparently is dying. Because nothing matters, he chases her away. These last details — the dampness, the gas light, the star, the girl — stimulate his dream and provide material for it. In psychological terms, they are the "day's residue" for transformation in the dream.

The ridiculous man is left with a painful memory of the girl. She has spoiled his suicide, spoiled his total indifference. He wanted to kill himself, to end the world, for his consciousness makes the world, he encompasses all people, all existence. He reflects in his chair, revolver before him; suppose he had lived previously on another planet, on the Moon or Mars, and had committed some horribly shameful deed, would everything be meaningless to him as he looked at that planet from Earth?

At this point in his dreams, the man falls asleep. He dreams he shoots himself (not in the head as planned, but in the heart), the light goes out, he is buried in a coffin, the dampness seeps in, and a drop of water repeatedly falls in his eye. This is senseless: his death is merely a continuation of his life (as in another fantastic story from *The Diary of a Writer*, "Bobok"), and though there is no one to laugh, the situation is ridiculous. He rebels, calls out to the unknown master of his fate, threatens him with the silent contempt of millions of years of martyrdom. A dark, unknown creature opens his grave and bears him away through the black night to the star he saw — a double of the Earth.

In this summary we can see the principle of identity ("everything is the same") working through every episode, through almost every detail. The ridiculous man does not care — the engineer and friends do not care — his mind illuminates gloom — the gas lights do the same — his consciousness makes the world — his death would end the world — his shameful act on this planet (the girl) — his imagined shameful act on another — his dream death — his waking death — lights out — dampness — the star — his suicide — another world — the world's reflection.

Dostoevski subtitled his work a "fantastic story," as he did a third story in *The Diary of a Writer*, "The Meek One." In a preface to his latter story, the author explained that the fantastic element consisted in the pretense that a man's thoughts could be recorded — in this case, the thoughts of a man trying to rationalize his wife's suicide as her body lies before him. Such "fantasy," Dostoevski believed, was the highest reality. For him the mind and all it embraces are already fantastic, before literary treatment. It is convention, rationality, and bland literary treatment which cover over the world and make it commonplace.

The fantastic element of the story "Bobok" is similar: the thoughts of the dead are recorded when a man of doubtful sanity hears corpses talking to one another in the cemetery. The fact that they think and even speak does not seem so fantastic as the fact that they are heard. Likewise, in "The Dream of a Ridiculous Man," the fantastic element is not so much the dream flight to another world, as the fact of the dream — its suddenness and import, its spontaneous appearance, its remembrance and effect. The ridiculous man considers it real, a revelation, regardless of whether others call it a dream.

The man's dream develops Dostoevski's familiar argument of head *versus* heart (adumbrated in the dream relocation of the pistol shot). The beautiful people of the duplicate Earth enjoy immediate paradise, live in harmony with nature, and love one another; they have an understanding deeper than science. "For our science," says the ridiculous man, "seeks to explain what life is, itself strives to make life conscious in order to teach others to live; they however knew without science how they should live, and I understood this, but I could not understand their knowledge." Their knowledge is of the heart, before consciousness, knowledge, and pride.

Although the ridiculous man claims he felt no desire to show off his knowledge of science and philosophy to them, something happens and he corrupts them. Perhaps with a joke he infects them "like a nasty trichina, like an atom of the plague." They learn to lie, to enjoy voluptuousness, to feel jealousy. Eventually they speak different languages, proclaim suffering as the way to truth, practice science, establish laws, build guillotines. They forget their lost paradise, disbelieve in it, place science above feeling, become individualists. When science fails to bring them happiness, they turn to crime and finally to suicide. Here the ridiculous man, loving them more in their suffering than before, attempts to save them: he tells them he has corrupted them and begs to be crucified — he lacks the strength for suicide and longs for martyrdom. They laugh at him, claim it would all have happened without him, and threaten to send him to the madhouse. He awakes.

The history of the planet visited by the man in his dream is the spiritual history of our planet. As the ridiculous man is converted by the beautiful innocents, they are converted by him, the hyperconscious suicide. By the end of the dream he has arrived at the same situation he left on Earth: he is a madman, a freak, a laughable outsider. But there is this difference: having corrupted (or imagined he corrupted) them, he wants to play the Savior, and he seeks crucifixion. This is the role he assumes upon his return to this Earth.

The whole process appears to be mental, a self-contained dream. Psychologists might speak of the "riot of identifications" common in schizophrenia. There is also an absence of concrete detail and an absence of causes. The ridiculous man is simply laughable, but no reason is given; he corrupts the innocent, but no method is explained. He has no name, the girl has no name, no one on Earth has a name, no one on the Earth's double has a name. He is one and all: the Earth is his consciousness and the golden age is his dream. There is no escape from this anonymous universality, this solipsistic play of life and death, dream and waking, this absurd monologue in the story; for illumination we must look to other works by Dostoevski, especially *Notes from Underground*.

There are two main arguments for freedom in the underground man's monologue. The first is his objection to the rationally planned utopia:

> Let me tell you: reason, gentlemen, is a fine thing, no doubt about that, but reason is only reason and satisfies only the reasoning capacity of man, while wanting is the expression of all aspects of life, that is, of all life, including reason and all the itches.

The Russian words highlight the argument: *rassudok* (reason) is set, fixed, and orderly, a static arrangement; *khotenie* (wanting), an uncommon noun derived from the verb "to want," is active, moving, a dynamic conception. The mind, being a part of man's total capacities and needs, cannot completely regulate the whole. There are needs which cause the mind to act, not a mind which causes the needs to arise. As applied to the ridiculous man, this means that the head cannot encompass the heart, and science cannot restore love. Freedom comes from the heart's ability to surprise, to awaken pity, to produce a revelatory dream.

The second argument is the underground man's assertion: if all the forces in the world could be computed, so that a man could be programmed to act, he would save his free will by willing to do nothing. If an absolute system were proposed to a man's advantage, he could act against his own advantage or do something harmful to himself, or he could preserve his freedom. This freedom would be outside of cause and effect, unlimited by reason; it would be something miraculous, something like divine grace. In the dream of the ridiculous man, divine grace is the condition of the golden age, although he does not understand its nature.

Most interpretations of "The Dream of a Ridiculous Man" regard it as a positive assertion. The ridiculous man, upon awaking, begins preaching the doctrine of immediate love. He tells all of his dream, and people laugh. He is ridiculous, but happily so, for he alone knows the truth; life could be bliss in an instant. But something is amiss. Dostoevski may have intended the story as positive: the little girl touches the ridiculous man's heart, inspires a dream revelation, and offers salvation as Liza offered it to the underground man. However, is the corrupted world's doctrine of suffering and suicide not a mockery of Dostoevski's belief in suffering? And is the ridiculous man's appeal to be crucified not a mockery of Christ, and is not his ridiculous position in all three worlds (the Earth, its double, and the Earth after the dream) a mockery of himself? One is tempted to invoke Bakhtin's theory of Dostoevski's "polyphonic novel" — that Dostoevski's characters assume life and act independently of the author's intention. Possibly, however, the intention was negative, and Dostoevski wrote the story as a representation of the hopelessness of life without divine grace.

Consider the being to whom the ridiculous man appeals when offended by the drops of water in his eye. He appeals to the *"vlastitel'* of everything that has happened to me." The word *vlastitel'* means "master, sovereign, ruler, controller," and the "dark and unknown creature" which transports the dreamer to another world hardly sounds like a radiant angel. Possibly the nether forces are at work. The ridiculous man claims he corrupted the entire planet. Did he really, or is this a delirium of grandeur, an inflation of his foreignness? When he loves the downfallen beautiful people, is it not because they are suffering, stricken with his disease? When they claim their path to suicide was inevitable without him, can any hopeful doctrine be drawn? For if everyone could and did return to the golden age, would corruption not begin all over again? Would not some demon tell a nasty little joke? Without divine grace, is everyone not a demon, a scientist, a ridiculous man?

The last words of the story are subject to interpretation. Most translations read something like this: "And that little girl — I did find her. . . . And I shall go on! I shall go on!" This can be interpreted to mean "I have located that little girl. . . . And I will go to her! I will go!" Such a reading offers promise of real action. But even assuming a literal translation, that he has found the girl and will continue to preach, the news is not good; he has let the mother die, he has failed that chance for salvation, and his dream was only a representation of his failure after the fact. He should take care of the little girl; he should love, not preach.

The ridiculous man is a failed suicide. He is afraid to shoot himself, so he dreams that he does, and even in his dream he fears suicide and begs for martyrdom. Returning to Earth, he finds a way to remain alive, to justify his ridiculousness, and to sustain his megalomaniac pride: he alone has the truth. Laughable as he is, the ridiculous man is a great preacher of the utter futility of life.

Gary Kern

Sources for Further Study

Criticism:

Holquist, Michael. *Dostoevsky and the Novel*. Princeton, N.J.: Princeton University Press, 1977, pp. 155-164. The author uses the dream technique to illustrate the essential loneliness of man.

Lord, Robert. *Dostoevsky: Essays and Perspectives*. Berkeley: University of California Press, 1970, pp.188-189 and 233-234. Lord calls this work a synthesis of the different visions of resurrection present in Dostoevsky's earlier works.

Suvin, Darko. *Other Worlds, Other Seas*. New York: Random House, 1970, p. xvii. Suvin calls this a tale based on the feasibility of man's salvation through history.

Traham, Elizabeth W. "The Golden Age — Dream of a Ridiculous Man?," in *Slavic and East European Journal*. XVII (1959), pp. 349-371. Traham feels that the story has an intrinsic theme revolving around the Golden Age.

DRIFTGLASS

Author: Samuel R. Delany (1942-   )
First book publication: 1971
Type of work: Short stories

Ten short stories, of varying science fiction content, which explore the powers and limitations that man faces as he attempts to relate to his environment

Reading the fiction of Samuel R. Delany is like listening to certain kinds of music — dixieland jazz, for example; the basic theme or themes are repeated by a soloist or by changing combinations of instruments in progressive relationships or structures. In Delany's fiction, this means that any novel or short story will have in it reverberations of other novels and/or short stories, reverberations which can add depth and clarity. The short stories in *Driftglass*, then, can be examined individually or as parts of a generally cohesive collection, a collection which looks from a variety of perspectives at man's relationships to his surroundings. The focus, as in almost all of Delany's fiction, is on the forces that influence people as they attempt to achieve their goals.

There are ten stories in this collection, all written — although not all published — between 1965 and 1968. One of the things that must impress the reader about these stories is the range of topics found therein. At least one story in the volume, "Dog in a Fisherman's Net," is totally lacking in traditional science fiction content. In this story, Delany deals with the residual power of the Great Mother, the deity first recognized and worshiped by humans; Delany's sense of mythic power is excellent, and in the story the reader feels the presence of the ancient power. Another story, "Night and the Loves of Joe Dicostanzo," might also be something other than science fiction. Here, Delany suggests the possibility of a total environment being constructed to deal with the psychological problems of one person. The story is ambiguous and may prefigure such stories as Gene Wolfe's "The Death of Dr. Island," but in and of itself, it may not be what the general public thinks of as science fiction.

The other eight stories in *Driftglass* are much more obviously within the genre. "The Star Pit" deals with the specialized people who can make the intergalactic jump without going insane. "Corona" is about a telepathic little girl who has become suicidal from being exposed to the thoughts and memories of others. "Aye, and Gomorrah" considers the possibility that radiation in outer space might affect a spaceman's genes. In "Driftglass," there are people with "gills" who aid in undersea research and development. "We, in Some Strange Power's Employ, Move on a Rigorous Line" shows free global power being set up to serve all the people of the world — even those who do not want it. Prisons of the future are the featured constructs of "Cage of Brass," but the crimes would be familiar to Edgar Allen Poe. In "High Weir," humans are making the first substantial survey of Mars. And in "Time Considered as a

Helix of Semi-Precious Stones," various aspects of the interplanetary underworld are described. Each of these stories is obviously science fiction, and
each is also much more — short, perhaps, on action/adventure, but very long
on the other facets of good fiction.

Driftglass is a cohesive anthology, and the cohesiveness is more a result of
the fiction than of the science. One of the major themes running through the
stories deals with the ways in which humans relate to their environment; Delany is extremely interested in the question of how much man shapes his destiny and how much that destiny is shaped — and man is shaped — by forces he
may not recognize and probably cannot control. In "High Weir," "Time Considered as a Helix of Semi-Precious Stones," and "We, in Some Strange Power's
Employ, Move on a Rigorous Line," Delany delineates the general boundaries
of this topic. "High Weir" and "Time Considered as a Helix of Semi-Precious
Stones" both present the individual adjusting to or operating within future
situations which are not unlike possible past or present situations. The former
is about an explorer adjusting to a new land. In this case, the land is Mars. The
latter story is about an underworld figure in the future, and it describes how he
operates within the extrapolated multiplanet underworld.

"We, in Some Strange Power's Employ, Move on a Rigorous Line" is
somewhat more complex. In this story, the Global Power Commission is extending its power lines to all parts of the world. The situation in the story
involves a group of Hell's Angels living on a mountaintop who do not want the
power even though it is free. The human focuses in the confrontation are
Blacky, being promoted from demon to devil in the Global Power structure,
and Roger, the current leader of the group of Hell's Angels. Delany examines
both sides of the conflict — the Angels use liquid fuel for their cycles but do
not want Global's power lines; Global has no reason for extending the free
lines to the Angels except for regulations — and the ending, as is often the
case with Delany, is ambiguous. Roger is killed (electrocuted), and the power
lines go in; but Blacky winds up with Roger's ring, a sign of Angel leadership,
and never again takes it off. Each of us, Delany seems to be suggesting, operates within and is, therefore, confined by his own surroundings or contexts;
and each of us often forces those contexts on others or has the contexts of
others forced on him.

Other stories — "Dog in a Fisherman's Net," "Corona," "Cage of Brass,"
and "Night and the Loves of Joe Dicostanzo" — examine psychological situations. Of the four, "Dog in a Fisherman's Net" may be the most complex and
interesting. The other three deal with fairly familiar psychological topics in
futuristic settings, but "Dog in a Fisherman's Net" deals with the psychological influences of the past. The story is set in a Greek fishing community, and
Delany examines the layers of religion from the past as formative influences
on people and actions in the present and the future. Delany is dealing with a
Christian community in which many people still remember the oldest deity, the

Great Mother. Spyro and Katina are both trying to leave the island and go to the mainland. In effect, they want to break with tradition — family tradition, village tradition, and cultural/historical tradition. The power of such tradition is embodied in the Great Mother who, in spite of the more modern Christian overlay, is a force which shapes the lives of the island people. And although both Spyro and Katina say, at the end of the story, that they will leave the island, the reader feels no assurance that such will be the case and can only wonder how completely one can escape the past.

A third group of stories, "The Star Pit" and "Aye, and Gomorrah," deals directly with limitations; each story has an almost double point of view, that of the one who is limited and another which observes the struggles of a person within his limitations. "Aye, and Gomorrah" suggests that those people who endure the intense radiation of outer space will have to be sexually neutered to survive; such people, according to Delany, will regard themselves as special and will be so regarded by others. They will be considered freaks and will have to exist with the knowledge that they are considered freaks by the "normal" people of the world. They will also, Delany suggests, be objects of sexual interest to some. The result will be an intense love-hate relationship in which each group will use and abuse the other for its own ends.

"The Star Pit," the first story in the anthology, depicts a man whose limitations frustrate him. Vyme is intensely jealous of the "golden," the select few who are psychologically able to withstand the pressures of intergalactic flight. Vyme is limited to this galaxy while the golden can go to any galaxy. Delany embellishes this main thread of the story by including a vast array of constructs which are also images of limitation. Vyme remembers a glass-walled ant colony he had when he was a child; now his current family-group has an ecologarium made of six-foot plastic panels, and one of the golden wears a jewel-sized ecologarium with microorganisms inside it. Alegra is a projecting telepath, hooked on drugs and caught up in her own visions, and Ratlit is pretending to be golden, a pretense which will probably kill him. In the end, Vyme discovers that even the golden are limited; they cannot make the jump into another time-space matrix that a certain tiny, slothlike creature can make.

"Driftglass" deals with most of the topics discussed thus far and is, therefore, appropriate as the title story for this collection. The main character, Cal Svenson, is (or was) an amphiman, a person surgically provided with gills to permit him to breathe under water and with webs to enable him to swim more efficiently. But Cal's active days are over; at eighteen, he was crippled in an underwater accident and has been on a pension ever since. The story focuses on the second attempt to lay power lines in the slash — what Cal was attempting to do when a volcanic eruption nearly killed him. Tork, the young man who makes this try, is killed in a similar eruption. Delany may be suggesting here that there are limits to man's ability to impose his plan on nature.

"Driftglass," like the other stories, is about man's relationship to his surroundings. Cal's powers were once greater than those of the average man; he could operate in the water as if he were a fish. Now his powers are less than those of an average man; worse still, Tork, along with several other young amphimen, is dead. Yet the children of Cal's friend Juao are about to enter training to become amphimen. The whole spectrum, from the young dreamers to the older realists, is represented; and "Driftglass" is a story about operating within one's surroundings as well as a story about limitations. Juao is a Brazilian fisherman, but his children will be amphimen. Cal was an amphiman, but now he is a beachcomber. Cal may be something of all of the main characters of the anthology; he has transcended traditional limitations, conquered his surroundings, and been thrust back. He knows about limitations from having been beyond them; he operates within his new surroundings from having been outside them.

In addition, the driftglass of the title may be the symbolic center of the whole anthology as it is the symbolic center of the story. Driftglass is a fragment of glass — like Coke bottle glass — which has had its edges worn by the sea and sand and its color changed by the chemicals in the ocean. It is still glass, but it has been worked on and has reacted to its surroundings to become something different from what it was before; the same is true of Cal Svenson in the story. He is still Cal, but the volcano changed him significantly from what he was. The same can be said for many of the other characters in the anthology; they are all pieces of driftglass, changed by their relationships with their surroundings.

Driftglass is a first-rate anthology. The writing is typical Delany and is superb throughout. He makes the settings realistic; and the characters, even and especially the aliens, are not "strange" to the reader. Delany is one of the few science fiction writers who can depict an alien in all of his differences as if he were as familiar and nonthreatening as the reader's next door neighbor.

Finally, the anthology reverberates with characteristic Delany themes. The reader familiar with the mythological patterns in *The Jewels of Aptor* and *The Einstein Intersection* or the quest motif of *Dhalgren* and *Nova* will be comfortable with *Driftglass*. These topics, and Delany's continuing interest in the forces that influence people, make *Driftglass* a treat for the Delany fan as well as a good introduction for the reader new to Delany's writing.

Charles William Sullivan III

THE DROUGHT

Author: J. G. Ballard (1930-   )
First book publication: 1964
Type of work: Novel
Time: The immediate future
Locale: The urban areas of Hamilton and Mount Royal and the coast a hundred miles to the south

The story of a great drought and its effect upon the lives and minds of several inhabitants of the town of Hamilton

Principal characters:
CHARLES RANSOM, a general practitioner
JUDITH, his wife
QUILTER, a hydrocephalic youth
MRS. QUILTER, his mother
RICHARD FOSTER LOMAX, an architect
MIRANDA, his sister
PHILIP JORDAN, a young man
THE REVEREND HOWARD JOHNSTONE, a Presbyterian minister
CATHERINE AUSTEN, the daughter of a zoo curator

The first appearance of Ballard's third novel was the American paperback edition of 1964, entitled *The Burning World*. The British edition, published a year later as *The Drought*, is extensively rewritten in terms of stylistic detail, though the actual events remain unchanged. The later version is presumably to be regarded as the definitive text.

Both manifestly and symbolically, *The Drought* reverses the theme of its predecessor, *The Drowned World* (1962). In the earlier novel, the world is flooded and the rising waters act as an agent of devolution, forcing mankind back into the evolutionary past, into the primitive depths of the subconscious. In *The Drought*, the Earth becomes a vast desert, civilization and progress shrivel up, and the land is reduced to hot sand, glittering salt, and white ash; time ceases to have any meaning and the future is displayed as an arid eternity in which established modes of sanity become hopelessly maladjusted. Although the narrative framework of both novels emerges from the tradition of British disaster stories, the ecological significance of the changes which overtake the environment in each case are of relatively little significance: they pose problems in psychological survival rather than physical survival. Thus, in *The Drought*, there are actually very few references to thirst or to the medical problems which would be attendant upon the climatic change, and the struggle to exploit and control the resources of the sea in Part Two of the novel is clearly of ritual significance rather than being a representation of any viable survival strategy. The changes are rationalized by reference to industrial pollutants which form a molecular "skin" upon the sea, inhibiting evaporation, but this explanation is of no particular importance within the story, there being no actual attempt to overcome the problem.

The central character of the story, Dr. Charles Ransom, is an archetypal Ballard "hero"; his detachment from the people and events that surround him is already manifest in his estrangement from his wife and a lack of motive for his actions. He is a spectator, emotionally and teleologically inert, passively allowing his consciousness to be molded by the changing environment. The other people with whom he is involved supply the full spectrum of Ballard's character types; they are bizarre representatives of various modes of psychological adaptation to the post-civilization world.

As the story begins, Ransom is hesitating over the matter of joining a great exodus to the south that has all but emptied the town of Hamilton and the city of Mount Royal. He intends to go, but cannot muster the energy. From his houseboat he watches the level of the river fall day by day, and sees in its draining the disappearance of the last dregs of the old social and natural order:

> With the death of the river, so would vanish any contact between those stranded on the drained floor. For the present the need to find some other measure of their relationships would be concealed by the problems of their own physical survival. None the less, Ransom was certain that the absence of this great moderator, which cast its bridges between all animate and inanimate objects alike, would prove of crucial importance. Each of them would soon literally be an island in an archipelago drained of time.

As the river represents time, so the houseboat represents Ransom's past; it is a "time-capsule" where his memories are crystallized as mementoes and preserved like specimens in a museum. That past is abandoned when the river finally leaves the houseboat high and dry, though Ransom's journey to the sea and temporary sojourn there (reunited with Judith) can be seen as an unsuccessful attempt to retreat into the past (the sea represents the womb of the past here, just as it did in *The Drowned World*).

In the first part of the book, Ransom moves among two groups of people: those who have postponed going south until the last possible moment, and those who do not intend to go at all. Foremost among the latter is Richard Lomax, a rich and eccentric architect who looks forward to inheriting the dead city. His principal "subjects" are his white-haired sister Miranda, the hydrocephalic freak Quilter, and Whitman, a keeper from the Mount Royal Zoo. Lomax tries to recruit Ransom, who resists what he sees as madness; nevertheless, he does not begin his journey to the south until he is virtually forced out when a nightmarish battle begins between a group of fishermen who seize upon a new apocalyptic mythology in the hope of salvation, and the representatives of the old religious order represented by the Reverend Howard Johnstone. When Ransom does start south, following Johnstone, he is accompanied by Quilter's mother, by Catherine Austen, the daughter of the zoo curator, and by a youth named Philip Jordan and his "adopted father."

When Ransom's group reaches the shore, they find a great crowd stretching as far as the eye can see in either direction. The recent arrivals are being held back from the beach by armed forces, and it is obvious that there must soon be an all-out battle for a place near the sea and a chance to eke out some kind of a living. The first part of the book ends with this desperate conflict.

Part Two of the story describes life in this monstrous half-world: a "dune limbo" where "time was not absent but immobilized." The sea has retreated to leave vast expanses of precipitated salt. Water can be trapped at high tide and small pools can be "steered" through the dunes by cutting a path in the saturated salt with a paddle. There is a settlement nominally run by the Reverend Johnstone and his "captains" (one of whom is Philip Jordan), who coordinate their water-gathering operations efficiently. Outside the settlement are small groups of independent individuals who live mainly by pirating the settlement's water. Ransom is one of these, but he is at the end of his tether and ready to give up.

Ransom eventually asks to be taken into the settlement, though he feels that its leaders are especially hostile to him. The impression is false, and arises out of the fact that what he really wants to do (though he does not know it) is to return inland, to Mount Royal. Only when he meets Mrs. Quilter and Catherine Austen once again, in the company of Philip Jordan, does this resolve strengthen, and the four set out to retrace their journey.

In the third part of the novel, Ransom's party find the people they left behind still surviving in Hamilton. Mount Royal has been gutted by fire, and the lions from the zoo are roaming the ruins. Lomax, far from being emperor of his microcosm, is entirely parasitic upon the demonic Quilter, and Miranda has borne the idiot youth a series of hydrocephalic children. Quilter, who seems throughout the book to be attended wherever he goes by dead birds, now wears a headdress made from the body of a black swan. The return of Ransom and his companions precipitates violence, but in the end the only victim claimed by the outburst of murderous impulses is Lomax. Mrs. Quilter dies peacefully, and the others settle down to a regime of peaceful coexistence, passively accepting their destiny, unable to comprehend what is happening, until ultimately, clouds obscure the sun and it begins to rain.

The ending of *The Drought*, in which the catastrophe that has overtaken the world begins to relent in the final paragraph, recalls the end of *The Wind from Nowhere*. Actually, however, *The Drought* is far more ambiguous in its ending than either of Ballard's earlier novels. In one of the earlier works, for example, the abatement of the great wind represents the prospect of salvation for the surviving characters, but this is not the case in *The Drought*. In *The Drowned World* there is no moment of reversion at all, and it is therefore complete as a story of readaptation, with its hero, Kerans, apparently justified in accepting the dictates of his reemerged subconscious. Compared to both these earlier endings, the rain which begins to fall at the conclusion of *The Drought* can only be seen as an ironic gesture, a whim of chance which is neither merciful nor cruel, but simply derisory.

Although Ransom starts *The Drought* in a psychological situation that has much in common with that of Kerans in *The Drowned World*, he ends up rather differently. The main difference is that Kerans has a destination: he goes south in search of the "lost paradises" of the distant past, and there is a sense in which he can find them within the resources of his own mind. But when Ransom goes south, following the disappearing river into the womb of the past, his journey is an abortive one, for his destiny lies in returning upriver into the arid and uncertain future. He has resources in his mind for coping with this, too, but they are by no means powerful, and can deliver no security against the vicissitudes of chance.

In his early novels, Ballard took the traditional disaster story gradually further away from its customary implications and into new imaginative territory. *The Wind from Nowhere* remains first and foremost a story of catastrophe, but what has happened to the world when *The Drowned World* and *The Drought* begin is not so much a catastrophe as a metamorphosis. This point is further emphasized by his next novel, *The Crystal World,* which hardly warrants the label "disaster story," even on the most superficial level. In *The Drought*, as in the novel which preceded it and the one which followed it, the metamorphosis is of the mind as well as of the world, the latter acting as a lure to the former. All three stories are, in essence, journeys into "inner space," odysseys through surreality. (They provide a curious parallel in many ways with the "scizophrenic voyage" which R. D. Laing mapped in *The Politics of Experience* and made briefly fashionable in the late 1960's and early 1970's.) The importance of Ballard's contribution to modern science fiction has been his activity in pioneering such journeys.

The Drought stands out from its companion-pieces because the nature of the changes which overtake the world in its story is reflected in the manner in which the story is told. It is, in every way, a dry book; it exhibits a much more clinical rationalism than either *The Drowned World* or *The Crystal World*, whose visionary moments are far less casual and whose symbology is less stark. Its careful rationality in going steadfastly forth into the realms of the "abnormal" warrants comparison with the imaginative odysseys of the nineteenth century mathematicians who began to explore the realms of non-Euclidean geometry. Ballard violates our common experience of the world in matters of psychology and the moral order in a way which recalls Lobachevsky's violation of Euclidean common sense. The effect is necessarily disturbing, but nevertheless has a frightening realism. This quality makes *The Drought* somewhat more nightmarish than *The Drowned World* or *The Crystal World*, and denies it the harmonious resolution which both the earlier novels, through the destinies of their central characters, manage to discover.

Brian Stableford

Sources for Further Study

Reviews:

Books and Bookmen. X, September, 1965, p. 30.

Magazine of Fantasy and Science Fiction. XXX, January, 1966, pp. 44-45.

Manchester Guardian. June 3, 1965, p. 11.

New Statesman. LXIX, May 28, 1965, p. 846.

New Worlds. CLIV, September, 1965, pp. 124-125.

Observer. May 30, 1965, p. 27.

Punch. CCXLIX, August 25, 1965, p. 289.

Spectator. May 28, 1965, p. 698.

Times Literary Supplement. June 10, 1965, p. 469.

THE DROWNED WORLD

Author: J. G. Ballard (1930-   )
First book publication: 1962
Type of work: Novel
Time: The near future
Locale: London, England

An apocalyptic novel in which rising temperatures create a flooded, increasingly tropical Earth, and the human struggle to survive is complicated by psychological changes

Principal characters:
> DR. ROBERT KERANS, a biologist manning a testing station floating over London
> DR. ALAN BODKIN, his assistant
> BEATRICE DAHL, an exotic eccentric who chooses to remain in London rather than seek safety in Greenland
> COLONEL RIGGS, the director of Kerans' party
> HARDMAN, the helicopter pilot who is the first to succumb to the triassic sun
> STRANGMAN, the pale, swaggering pirate leader of a party of grotesque and dangerous black looters

This characteristic example of J. G. Ballard's apocalyptic fiction, like his *The Drought* and *The Wind from Nowhere*, centers on a major "natural" change in the Earth's environment. The main character of *The Drowned World* is Dr. Robert Kerans, manager of a biological testing station monitoring the changes as the world, largely submerged under water, reverts to dense, virtually uninhabitable, tropical jungle. Ballard's interest does not lie simply in the usual apocalyptic concerns of how man is destroyed or finds a technology of escape. Rather, he penetrates the heart of the apocalyptic experience by integrating the changing physical universe with a changing psychic one, as his characters progress to an intense new relationship with nature, derived partly from uterine fantasy and partly from the genetic unconscious.

Thus a seemingly realistic scientific novel subtly becomes a macabre and surreal blending of the inner and outer worlds of Kerans and the other principal characters. Kerans is acutely aware of the actual psychological and biological changes taking place in human nature, and he speculates that the growing isolation and self-containment of those with whom he comes in contact correspond to the actions of insects preparing to undergo metamorphosis.

Kerans' companions in the encroaching jungle of sixty-foot-high ferns include Colonel Riggs, nominally in charge of the mission combining the biological testing station with a quasimilitary sweep intended to pick up anyone still attempting to live in the gigantic swamps and forests; Kerans' assistant and colleague, Dr. Alan Bodkin, who enunciates the new psychophysical realities overtaking Kerans and the others; and Beatrice Dahl, a beautiful eccentric from whom Kerans grows apart as the changes occur and who finally chooses to stay behind in London.

The Drowned World depends for its considerable strengths upon both its story line and the carefully paced revelation of the deeply disturbing inner world that responds to the radical climactic change. Ballard offers a practical and adequate explanation for the climactic change early in the novel, describing how exceptional solar storms stripped the Van Allen Belts and allowed excessive solar radiation to slowly raise the Earth's temperature over a seventy-year period. What is remarkable about the "science" in both this novel and Ballard's other natural apocalypses is the very *unremarkable* way in which he chooses to present the changes. The simplicity of the change is awesome, and the factual tone of the descriptions of London submerged in water and surrounded by an encroaching tropical jungle creates a curiously calm sense of the inevitability and reality of the change. Ballard's characters are not scientific heroes who try to modify the inexorable progress of nature towards a world that disturbs and endangers man. Man can only react to the changes, attempting to modify the way in which he lives in order to survive. The power of *The Drowned World* comes from the oppressive sense of heat and crowded vegetation that becomes ever more assertive in the later portions of the book and from the revelation that a human adaptation is taking place which is beyond human control.

Ballard's vision is keyed to two paintings hanging in Beatrice Dahl's apartment, Delvaux's surreal image of ashen-faced women naked to the waist dancing with skeletons clothed in tuxedos, and the other of Max Ernst's wild jungles of living organisms which writhe about devouring one another under a tropical sun. The novel depicts an increasingly frenzied dance of death in a vegetable universe, but it is a dance that ends not in death but in a curiously optimistic assimilation.

At the beginning of the novel Kerans is occupying the penthouse suite at the Ritz Hotel in London, surrounded by such civilized comforts as air conditioning, silk shirts, and a very well-stocked bar. The reader sees the activities of Kerans' "normal" days, including his dealings with Bodkin, Riggs, and Beatrice, and his work at the research station. But even in the early chapters it is clear that the man as well as his environment is changing, and Kerans is early aware of the growing strength of his dreams of a powerful, primitive sun and of his desire to withdraw from the company of others in order to acquiesce to his internal change.

Bodkin tells Kerans that he believes the images in the dreams come from the subconscious cellular inheritance of mankind, a genetic pattern that is being reactivated by the return of the Triassic period and its immense, burning sun. Ballard has Bodkin describe this subconscious inheritance as the "archaeophysic past," embodying in the term the idea that it is a release of prehuman experience, coming not from the brain at all but from the cellular

genetic pattern of a time before the brain took over the management and stor-
age of experience. The first to succumb to this ancient stimulation is Hardman,
the helicopter pilot on the mission, whose incessant dreams finally drive him
to flee the base and move South towards the flaming sun. Hardman escapes
pursuit from the base because he can function in the heat and fierce noonday
sun which blinds the others.

After Hardman's escape, Beatrice, Dr. Bodkin, and Kerans manage to be
left behind when the rest of the mission moves north and they then drift apart
to dream their ways into their new realities. This pattern is broken by the
arrival of the corpse-white Strangman, with his gaudy troupe of buccaneers
and looters and two thousand alligator watchdogs. Ballard now moves into the
realms of a bizarre and macabre surrealism where the physical events, while
perfectly possible, take on the aspects of primitive nightmares. Strangman
organizes a diving party to go into the sunken London planetarium; Kerans
enters the womblike structure with its soothingly warm water and imagines he
sees, in the cracks in the dome, a starmap of the ancient world. This disturbs
him so greatly that he ties off his air line in an involuntary gesture, nearly
commiting suicide. Strangman grasps the meaning of this gesture immediately,
and the reader sees how it reinforces Kerans' other acts, such as the theft of a
compass that mesmerizes him with the concept of South, where Kerans finds
himself surrendering control to his archaeophysic past.

In the closing chapters of the book there is an ever-increasing sense that
Kerans is yielding to his inner forces. When Strangman dams a lagoon and
pumps out Leicester Square, Kerans' waking life becomes increasingly nightmarish, until he finds himself nearly smothered by the fetid head of a dead
crocodile that Strangman's men force him to wear. This final gesture, after
Strangman has imprisoned Kerans in the sun for several days, literally puts
Kerans in the skin of a prehistoric creature.

Kerans then escapes from Strangman, dynamites the lagoon dam, and
moves off to the south, nursing a bullet wound in his leg. In the jungle he
gradually sheds all of his resources and discovers Hardman, a nearly blind,
emaciated, blackened husk. He helps Hardman, who then wanders off further
to the south. At the novel's close Kerans has moved 150 miles into the jungle
and is continuing south. Ballard clearly implies that Kerans will die in his
impossible quest, yet, like Shelley's moth seeking a star, the final description
of Kerans as a second Adam suggests that he has done the right thing in following his burning dreams.

As Kerans becomes increasingly primitive, the sense of compulsion
becomes the dominant characteristic of the entire narrative. It is this strong
psychological basis which has led Ballard to narrow the focus to a single
character's dissolution and which distinguishes this novel from other apocalyptic fiction. The movement of the story is reminiscent of that greatest of
twentieth century probes of the soul, Joseph Conrad's *Heart of Darkness*, ex-

cept that Ballard strips away any return from the dark journey and is totally unconcerned with the political and social connotations of the earlier novel. Kerans' "descent into the phantasmagoric forest" shares with Marlow's quest the flickering quality of being dream at one moment and realism at another, as the archaeophysic guidance surfaces and becomes the driving reality of the novel.

Both novels deal with going into the self, but *The Drowned World*, with the image of the womblike warmth of the water and the relentless sun — giver of life, beating into the skull to the rhythm of the heartbeat — goes past the moral questions posed by Conrad to the scientific question of genetic inheritance and the possibility of its recapitulation should ancient conditions return. Ballard is concerned with the essence of biopsychic man, and his story contains the conviction of myth usually found in archetypal representations. Kerans' resolve to follow the sun to the south has about it that inevitability of mythic drive. Characters as bizarre as Strangman, as strangely attractive as Beatrice, or as sound and sensible as Riggs become as flimsy to Kerans as the collapsing structures of the drowning world in the face of the inner force that drives him towards the swampy wetness and the fiery pulsation of the mighty sun.

Indeed, Ballard has created in this novel a most pervasive demonstration of the frailty of "technological" man. He diminishes man in the face of the natural universe by establishing that he has no control over either the outer or the inner world. A tiny but implacable change in cosmic terms finds man all but destroyed by natural disaster and struggling against the mind. The mind and its complex cultural and technological by-products attempt to adapt for survival by tapping the same archaeophysic pool as do other animals and plants as they fecundly regress to their prehistoric natures. The tenuousness of Man's hold on mere survival lies in the fact that he cannot adapt quickly enough, and that his archaeophysic impulses destroy the body even as they produce a sense of unity with the changed world. Kerans is truly caught in a paradox at the close of the book. He is doing what his archaeophysic self requires, but, because man has progressed beyond the biological to the technological to support his survival, the inner self of the cells offers a guidance which is suicidal. Kerans and Hardman are more able than the others to withstand the intense heat and light of the sun, but the fact that they do not sweat as profusely and can stand the light serves ironically to remind us of their true frailty in the face of a need for total change. Their bodies cannot make the kind of significant response needed for survival.

The surrealistic grace and pervasive imagery of Ballard's writing are never more evident than in this story. He handles the scientific explanations with the casualness of a magician pulling handkerchiefs out of thin air and joins the twin ideas of an increase in the Earth's temperature and the biophysic regression like the same illusionist rejoining the halves of the sawn lady. He establishes the inevitability of Kerans' fate through a myriad of details placed throughout the book and through the omniscient narrator's detailed comments on what Kerans thinks and feels.

The sophistication of Ballard's storytelling is perhaps why he is not given credit for strongly original ideas. Yet there is a breathtaking moment when, at some point in *The Drowned World*, each reader suddenly grasps the daring of the concepts being carried to their true resolution. It takes only a moment to realize that a reprieve for Kerans or the drowning world would be entirely false. Neither science nor technology are the victors in *The Drowned World*. A very careful stoicism is at the core of Ballard's position, a stoicism strong enough to tolerate a conception of the human race being terminated by the reactions of its genetic materials to the implacable thrust of cosmic forces.

Peter Brigg

Sources for Further Study

Reviews:

Amazing Stories. XXXVII, February, 1963, pp. 120-121.

Kirkus Reviews. XXXIII, January 1, 1965, p. 22.

Magazine of Fantasy and Science Fiction. XXIX, July, 1965, pp. 79-82.

New Worlds. CXXIX, April, 1963, p. 128 and CLI, June, 1965, p. 117.

DRUSO
(Druso: oder Die gestohlene Menschenwelt)

Author: Friedrich Freksa (1882-1955)
First book publication: 1931
English translation: 1934
Type of work: Novel
Time: 2300 and 2583
Locale: The Earth, especially Aachen and the Northern regions, and the planet Druso

Two sleepers from the year 2300 wake from their suspended animation 283 years in the future and find the Earth enslaved by a race of extraterrestrial insects

Principal characters:
ALF BENTIK, a scientist
JUDITH BENTIK, his wife and a sociologist
THANKWAS, a leader of men from Boothia Felix
FRANZ HOCHKOFLER, another scientist of the twenty-third century

It is somewhat surprising that Friedrich Freksa's novel *Druso* is not better known and more highly regarded, although it has been translated into both French and English (by the late Fletcher Pratt) and serialized in three parts in *Wonder Stories*, starting in May, 1934. If this book had been written originally in English, today it would doubtless be considered an essential work in the science fiction canon. As things are, however, the book is little more than a rumor among German science fiction readers. In the most informative as well as the most stringent study of German science fiction to date, Manfred Nagl's *Science Fiction in Deutschland* (1972), it has come under attack as a work expressing a Fascist persuasion. The extraterrestrial insects who subjugate the Earth in Freksa's novel, are, according to Nagl, a projection of the Jews and an embodiment of anti-Semitic sentiments; they are an incorporation of everything horrible that the Nazis attributed to the Jews, and are described as doing what the Nazis finally did to their victims.

Once a strong race, the inhabitants of the "rogue star" Druso, the insect monsters of so much science fiction, have degenerated to such a degree that they have become wholly dependent upon other species which they keep as their cattle and exploit. They are parasites drawing their strength and nourishment from the subjugated peoples with a kind of psychic vampirism; they even drink the milk of the imprisoned human females, who are also forced to breed the insects' eggs. If the descriptions of the abused naked humans are not shocking enough, heights of gruesomeness are reached in the passages which detail the final fate of human victims brought to Druso on the pretense that they will receive the ultimate reward of their religion and experience the bliss of true believers. As soon as they enter the supposed door into Paradise, they are slaughtered like cattle, dismembered by machines, and further cut up by blind humans who are unaware of what they are handling. Their flesh is then used to feed the human slaves, while the inner organs, the brains, and the glands are reserved for the Drusons. All this is described with a nauseating attention to detail that indeed points forward to the horrors of the concentration camps that were to be erected in a few years, as well as to some later science fiction stories such as Piers Anthony's "In the Barn."

Brutal and revolting as some scenes are, and as dubious as its ideology may be, the novel is nevertheless interesting for ideas which anticipate many things that were to become stock elements in science fiction. Above all, the writing is forceful. Rather than the incompetently fumbling attempt at narrative found in so much science fiction from the period, not even imaginative in its naïveté, *Druso* carries conviction, repellent as many of its features are, and the author indeed achieves the mythic qualities he has set out to capture. It is not necessary to know about Freksa's personal life to recognize that he was an admirer of Oswald Spengler and social Darwinism; but whether he was ever a Nazi, remains unknown. Spengler's example of human greatness, the Roman soldier who was inadvertently left at his guard post in Pompeii, and who died in the lava, obeying his orders to the last, is cited approvingly. Fighting is described as the essence of human existence. The author also believes that there will always be rulers and the ruled. He has no love for collectivist ideas and humanitarian aims, but believes, rather, in the survival of the fittest.

The book begins approximately in the year 2300, with mankind living in a kind of ambivalent Utopia. Two great inventions have been made: suspended animation and the televisor which allows the observation of any place on Earth. After a Chinese threat, met by ruthless extermination from the white nations, a world state has arisen. In order to bypass the allotted numbers of their armed forces, the Chinese had simply deep-frozen whole divisions of trained troops and stored them in the mountains, ready to be raised when the need arose. When the whites discovered this ruse, the hidden armies were mercilessly gassed. Thus ruthlessness continues in the new world state, since only fit children are allowed to live, although exceptions may be made for children of unusually talented parents (the hero Alf Bentik and his wife Judith are both such exceptions).

The most interesting practice in the new society is a program designed to provide a cross-fertilization between past and future. Eminent scientists are put into suspended animation for a period of ninety-nine years, in order to discuss in the future the problems of their times and their outlook with the new generations. Bentik's wife Judith, a sociologist, is one of the chosen "sleepers." Although pregnant, she is irrevocably committed to it when the scientist who would have been chosen instead of her dies in an accident. But at least after a popular vote her husband is allowed to accompany her into the future. However, the couple sleeps 283 years instead of the projected ninety-nine, awakened accidentally by an expeditionary force from Boothia Felix, a subterranean human community in the frozen regions of Northern Europe. They are dug out from beneath the ruins of an ancient site in Aachen, the city that

Charlemagne had long ago made the capital of his empire. Connections between the novel's past and the mythic greatness of the realm of the Franks are obvious.

Like so many sleepers in science fiction, the heroes find themselves cast into an alien world, one totally transformed from the world they had known. They discover that mankind has come under the leash of the insectoid Drusons, inhabitants of a planet that arrived from outer space finally taking up a position as a second moon of Earth. The Drusons were eagerly welcomed by the humans, who dreamed of communication with another species and hoped for a new Golden Age. In this they were sorely disappointed. As soon as Druso reached an orbit around Earth, the Drusons showed their true intentions, by cutting off Earth's electrical power and attacking with a lethal gas that dissolved even matter. Since that time, mankind has been enslaved.

There are three types of Drusons: six-legged antlike workers between three and four feet in length; beetlelike flying warriors who patrol the atmosphere of the Earth accompanied by mechanical flying machines; and "intellectuals," unseen beings, who are all brains and reside in cylinders, much like the jar-dwelling Lunarians in H. G. Wells's *The First Men in the Moon*. While the workers remain on Druso, many of the brains settle in the churches as oracles to reinforce their control; they have established themselves as gods. Having reverted to barbarity, the human survivors worship the insects as divine masters and obey their every command. To keep them weak, the Drusons foster war between the various human settlements that have grown up around the oracles, demanding the choicest parts — heads, sexual organs, and glands — of the slain as sacrifices. They also frequently demand pregnant young women, young men, and children as sacrifices to be transported to camps on Druso.

However, despite their otherwise advanced technology, these insects have not been able to compensate for their lack of ability to tolerate the extreme cold. Consequently, human colonies in the cold regions of Earth survived the attack of the invaders and were later reinforced by fugitives from the warmer areas. These Atlantians, as they call themselves, have preserved the advanced technology of their quasiutopian ancestors. They continue to operate a limited number of aircraft and submarines, but avoid doing anything that might draw the attention of the Drusons to them. Nevertheless, they have agents in the rest of the world and even on Druso, where a few human rebels harass their masters from the wilderness. Thus, Northerners keep to themselves, look disdainfully down upon the enslaved mass of humanity, and avoid contact with them.

The decision to strike against the invaders comes when the child of the "sleeper" Judith, who has become a symbol for the liberation of mankind, is abducted and transported to Druso with a group of other human victims. The rebels follow them to Druso, discover the real nature of the tyranny and the gruesome fate of the victims, join forces with the escaped slaves already active there, and successfully attack the planet. They return to Earth in the nick of time and sever the ties with Druso (a kind of magnetic rope), causing it to drift into space. A short time later a radio message arrives indicating that the remaining humans on Druso have also rid themselves of their exploiters. The new race then proceeds to build their Atlantis on the continent of Europe, the region covering Scandinavia, France, Holland, Germany, and England, while the humans native to the area — victims of the insect tyranny — are dispatched to other areas; the new masters do not want to bother educating them.

What the author succeeds in doing in this novel is to create a myth of a fighting mankind that celebrates the survival of the fittest and praises war as the father of all things. It is a militaristic mankind capable of defeating even monsters from outer space who have been sent (as foreseen by a half-mad prophet who attacks the complacency of human rationality) as a punishment for having grown soft. In this respect the book bears some superficial resemblance to H. G. Wells's *The War of the Worlds*. Much more marked, however, is the similarity between the book's ideological content and some later American science fiction, especially Robert A. Heinlein's *The Puppet Masters*, a work that also celebrates the toughness of mankind and its ability to survive in all circumstances. Freksa also anticipates the pattern of later science fiction insofar as he concentrates not on the initial Utopia nor on the invasion itself, but on the inevitably successful revolt against the invaders. Most remarkable, perhaps, is the fictional use of religion in the society: a means to cement the alien rule.

There is certainly much about the book that appears inhuman, cruel, disgusting, and even pathological in its sexual fantasies. As such, it may be an indication of the inhumanity that was to come. It is no doubt also true that the talk about Atlantis and the North suggests a new Aryan myth. But to interpret this as anti-Semitism in disguise, with Jewish "parasites" feeding off the Nordic race, seems dubious. Other interpretations are possible. For instance, Druso shines in a threatening red color; the insects are blind to the color blue (a color symbolism that is apparent in large parts of the novel); the Drusons are certainly an antlike collectivist state, although it is unclear whether the thinkers in their cylinders are individuals or conglomerates of several insects. So the book is clearly a Spenglerian, social-Darwinist, anticollectivist parable, a warning against socialist promises of a paradise on Earth that in reality turns out to be a cruel tyranny: the collectivists are false prophets of rationality and liberty that only enslave the individual in an insidious rule.

One may quarrel with this conclusion, as well as fault the means used to present it, on aesthetic grounds. But unlike most books from the period, *Druso* is a work that is still very much alive. Although somewhat bathetic, it is freshly written and contains some notions that are still interesting despite having appeared again and again in subsequent works of science fiction.

Franz Rottensteiner

Sources for Further Study

Reviews:

Amazing Stories. VII, March, 1933, p. 1145.

DŮM O TISÍCI PATRECH
(The Thousand-Story House)

Author: Jan Weiss (1892-1973)
First book publication: 1929
Type of work: Novel
Time: The future
Locale: Mullerdom, an imaginary many-faceted house, located on the Island of Arrogance

The story of the successful struggle against the mythical master of The Thousand-Story House

> *Principal characters:*
> PETR BROK, a detective
> OHISVER MULLER, the master of Mullerdom
> PRINCESS TAMARA, his prisoner
> PRINCE AČORGEN, Muller's right-hand man
> VÍTEK OF VÍTKOVICE, the rebel leader

To better understand the origin of the novel and the place it occupies in the author's complete works, some biographical and bibliographical data is necessary. Born in Jilemnice in the northern part of Bohemia, Jan Weiss was a soldier in World War I, serving first on the Italian and then on the Russian fronts. Taken prisoner in 1916 and confined in a camp at Totskoye, he came down with typhoid fever and escaped death almost by a miracle. A good glimpse of this unique experience can be seen in *Bárak smrti* (*Death Barracks*, 1927), *Dům o tisíci patrech* (*The Thousand-Story House*, 1929), and *Bláznivý regiment* (*The Crazy Regiment*, 1930). During his long literary life, the author penned several other books and devoted his later years to science fiction, a genre he touched on in the book discussed here.

Weiss's books attracted the well-deserved attention of Czech critics who in the 1930's considered him a surrealist. Jiří Hájek in his preface to the French translation of *Dům o tisíci patrech* (*La Maison aux mille étages*) disputes this classification by arguing that Weiss's earlier works came before his incursion into surrealistic territory. But the first *Manifeste du surréalisme* (*Manifesto of Surrealism*) had come out in 1924. Hájek also believes that "this *avant-garde* surrealist has nothing in common with the movement attributed to André Breton except one thing, interest in the terra incognita of dreams and the subconscious." In fact the entire novel is really a never-ending exploration of this terra incognita.

The most striking thing about the first pages of the novel is the cinematic quality of the text. The emphasis is not only on the visual method of reproducing events and characters and the small space given over to introspection, but also extends to the many references to and reflections on films of that era. The setting is reminiscent of scenes from *The Cabinet of Dr. Caligari* and other films of the German expressionist movement. Muller's disguises seem to follow those of the evil Dr. Mabuse in Fritz Lang's famous series. Mullerdom itself is a type of demented Metropolis. The wealth of posters and signs, plus the capitalized conversations, also evoke the charm as well as the unavoidable limitations of the silent movie.

The second remarkable aspect of the novel concerns the subtle balance Weiss establishes between the framework of reality and the framework of the dream world, both complementing each other. In Petr Brok's "nightmare," rows of men lying on plank beds and covered with overcoats, turn out to be the reality he is running away from under the influence of the fever in order to take refuge in the nightmare of the thousand-story house. Some time later his running away becomes a conscious or semiconscious act. Whenever the sight of reality overloads his tired brain with too many images, "Petr Brok cracks under the strain. That — it's my past! Those are all the things I'd forgotten about!" And later on he discovers that "Part of his overcoat was covering his head — and all those things disappear." This frequent switching back and forth is not only due to fear of "the death barracks," but also to the fact that the protagonist is acting out his secret aspirations in a dream world.

This brings us to the keystone of the novel, the revolt against a society which carries in it the seeds of Mullerdom. The framework of fantasy does not conceal the facts of reality, but it blows them up out of proportion. The Thousand-Story House is in fact a huge skyscraper, "a giant town under one roof." The worship of money is no longer implied or hidden but is out in the open and is identified with adoration of God Muller, and this explains why the stock exchange becomes a sanctuary. Finally, the dictatorship no longer hides behind the mask of democracy but declares its omnipotence at every step. A system based on brutality, suspicion, and degradation might seem like an allegory too ominous for 1929 readers; only four years later Hitler was to become Chancellor of the Reich.

Sent to the Isle of Presumption to solve the riddles of Mullerdom and authorized by the congress of judges from the United States of the World to kill the dictator if necessary, Petr Brok not only finds countless scenes of bondage, blind or willful submission, but also signs of resistance — the impotent hatred of the "old" blind man who is thirty-three — right up to armed insurrection by workers led by Vítek of Vítkovice. Thanks to the invisible lover of justice, the counterattack by the oppressive forces is stopped. Before finally returning to the real world, Brok takes part in the last attack made by the rebels and sanctifies their victory by stabbing Ohisver Muller in the heart. This gesture realizes the tragic hope of the first speaker: "Give us names instead of numbers and nourishment instead of food cubes. Return love, desire, and dreams to us."

In Weiss-Brok's logical nightmare, scientific and technical forecasts of the future emphasize the strangeness of Mullerdom. They are neither too numerous nor too original. Solium, the "lighter-than-air element" which, "when freed from impurities, floats into space," is an idea drawn from the metallic substance George Tucker talks about in *A Voyage to the Moon* (1827). It is hard to believe that Weiss was familiar with this book, but he had most likely read *The First Men in the Moon* (1901) and took Wells's "cavorite" as his model. Okka cubes, "our breakfast, lunch, and dinner, the essense of nutrition . . .," are merely a novelty. Synthetic nutrition had been "discovered" among other things by Kurd Lasswitz in his *Bilder aus der Zukunft* (*Images from the Future*, 1879). Finally, the invisibility achieved by "the process called dispersion (*asprid*)" reminds us of *The Invisible Man* (1897) even though Wells's hero cannot be detected except by accident while Brok must confront a formidable adversary, the blind Orsag with his glasses that let him see what is invisible.

A number of devices in *Dům o tisíci patrech* are strikingly original. At the end of the book, Brok discovers a huge device, "a grotesque jumble of bouncing springs, bells, knobs, pipes, and flashing dials," which makes it possible for Muller to see and hear his subjects no matter where they are and to hand down their sentences instantly and irrevocably. This system of round-the-clock surveillance was to crop up again some two decades later in George Orwell's famous *Nineteen Eighty-Four*. Closer to the unrestrained imagination of modern authors lies the recording of dreams as reflected in the eyes of the drug users of Gédonia or the torture of the flowers. But how are we to explain the absence of robots? The omission was conscious and intentional:

> After all is said and done, it doesn't matter what machine breaks down in the long run and humans should not be made in factories!
> Nature herself mass-produces them!

This pat exchange sounds like an argument out of *R.U.R.*, the famous play by Karel Čapek. But it is important to remember that these comments come from the privileged class in Mullerdom, which gives them a definite meaning. Why build robots when you have cheap labor at your disposal? But the exploitation and hardships to which this surplus "merchandise" is subjected causes the workers to rebel and finally brings down the house of Mullerdom.

Accessible for almost forty years only to those who can read Czech, *Dům o tisíci patrech* has today been recognized, after the appearance of the French translation, with fully deserved praise as a first-rate work in the genre. Critics have emphasized its thematic invention and "Sense of Wonder," the advanced structure and writing which it displayed in this field in the late 1920's. This is new proof that modern science fiction was created on both sides of the Atlantic by a brotherhood of people who, more often than not, without knowing one another, worked together to change the static view of life and the world.

Ion Hobana

DUNE

Author: Frank Herbert (1920-   )
First book publication: 1965
Type of work: Novel
Time: The distant future
Locale: The planet Arrakis, after a brief interlude on Caladan

Arrakis, the sole source in the known universe for "melange," a genuine life-prolonging drug, is the setting for Imperial power plays to control the drug and the planet. A young Duke, Paul Atreides, becomes the leader, both religious and political, of the native Fremen, as he undertakes the ecological, social, and political salvation of the planet

Principal characters:
PAUL ATREIDES, a young nobleman of the Galatic Imperium
DUKE LETO ATREIDES, his father
JESSICA, his mother, a Bene Gesserit adept
BARON VLADIMIR HARKONNEN, the Atreides' deadly enemy
FEYD-RAUTHA, his nephew and heir
LIET-KYNES, Imperial Planetologist
STILGAR, Leader of the Fremen in Sietch-Tabr, where Paul and Jessica take refuge
CHANI, a young woman of the Fremen, daughter of Liet
ALIA, Paul's young sister

If science fiction has produced an epic, that work is Frank Herbert's *Dune*. It is a monumental book, both in length and scope, and its portrayal of the life, characters, and culture of an entire planet is meticulously detailed. The problems it discusses are vast, to be sure, but they are so accurately depicted that the reader comes away from the novel with a feeling of astonishment at the re-creation of the mores and ethics of a world that is at once so tantalizingly distant but, at the same time, so gnawingly familiar.

Dune had a dual inception. Herbert had long considered writing a novel about "messianic convulsions which inflict themselves upon human societies." At the same time, as a reporter for a San Francisco newspaper, he had begun a magazine article about the control of sand dunes along the Oregon coast, an experiment of the U. S. Department of Agriculture. Herbert's background as a student of comparative religions, coupled with his agile science fiction mind, soon led him to combine the two sources into one. *Dune*, then, tells of the ecological restoration of a desert planet and its people by an avatar who must choose as his methods of redemption not the customary ones of love, charity, forgiveness, and mercy, but violence, and whose authentic religious insights conflict with the expediency demanded of him as the figurehead of his people's needs.

As the preparation for the writing progressed — and Herbert took five years to plan the entire *Dune Trilogy* before he wrote the first book — other themes suggested themselves. These included the question of power and its corruptions; the difficulties all humans have in communicating their inmost dreams and ideas, as well as the ease with which those dreams and ideas can become corrupted; profound theological questions, such as the relationship between insight and environment in the birth of a religion, and the effect on a genuine avatar who must, because of the overwhelmingly violent conditions of the planet, perform his saving mission with violence and thus virtually destroy his own nature; and, to mention only one more, the virtual universality of Jungian archetypal patterns wherever the human race might settle. Some of these themes are not immediately evident in *Dune*, but become apparent only after reading *Dune Messiah* and *Children of Dune*.

Set some ten thousand years in the future, *Dune* deals with all of these questions, but deals with them in such a way that the themes never get in the way of the story, but rather supplement and complement the involved plot. For all of the novel's complexity, Herbert never forgets that he must write to entertain, that he must compete for dollars in the paperback market. Thus he tells a good story that can be appreciated by all those who read books for the action-adventure elements. But at the same time, he interweaves his complex themes so skillfully that other readers can appreciate such techniques as how he handles the mythic, archetypal hero, or how the grace notes of poetry illuminate his style.

That Herbert is so successful in juggling all of these diverse themes is a tribute to his skill as a novelist, but it is also a tribute to the universality and power of the themes themselves. Thus, the novel may be read on many levels simultaneously. Paul Atreides can be viewed as the warrior-hero whose military skill and genius make the Fremen into an invincible army and eventually rid Arrakis of the imperial forces who have turned the planet and its incredible spice-wealth into the mere object of monetary gain. But he can also be seen as Paul Muad'Dib, savior of Dune, object of religious worship, and the unwitting founder of a warrior religion based upon him. From either viewpoint, he resembles many of the heroes of myth. Paul was born of a royal virgin; his father was of the nobility; the circumstances of his conception were unusual; early in his life on Arrakis an attempt is made to kill him by his maternal grandfather; he is reared by foster parents (the Fremen) in a far country. We know nothing of his childhood, but with Fremen training he conquers the wild beast, Shai-Hulud, leads his armies to victory over the emperor, marries a royal princess, and becomes the king-emperor. This pattern, traced by Lord Raglan in *The Hero*, infuses *Dune* with a mythic quality with which readers can easily identify, so close is it to heroic patterns that they already know.

However, *Dune* is much more than a fairy tale set in the far distant future rather than the far distant past. It is a story whose *science* fiction base rests solidly upon the science of ecology. Herbert dedicated the novel to "the people whose labors go beyond ideas into the realm of 'real materials' — to the dry land ecologists, wherever they may be, in whatever time they work." Early in the book, Herbert has one of his characters define ecology as "The science of understanding consequences." These consequences resound throughout the trilogy, not only the consequences of changing the face of Arrakis by introducing a water-based ecology and making the planet a fit place for human beings to live, but also the consequences of the corruption of ideals. Few readers recognize the effects that open water will have on the planet as they read the first novel. These effects are only implied in *Dune*, receiving their fruition in the last of the series, *Children of Dune*. With openly flowing qanats, the face of Arrakis has been changed. Shai-Hulud virtually disappears, for water is poisonous to the great worms in one of its vectors. Similarly the Fremen of Arrakis lose their stillsuit discipline and become water-fat, a fact which presages their eventual corruption.

Dune is such a rich book that it is almost impossible to indicate all of its complexity. Herbert is not universally successful, however, in some of the themes he introduces. For example, the medieval or feudal mystique so evident in the early section of the novel palls, particularly when the dialogue becomes stilted. Yet Herbert introduced the feudal atmosphere to make the lines of power in the novel — among them the conflict among the great barons — perfectly clear. The feudal enfeoffment posits a set of mutual obligations from lord to knight to serf that can be clearly understood. In making the Imperium a feudal system based upon the classic English or French models, for example, Herbert can establish a natural order into which human organizations have often fallen. Thus the loyalties commanded by Duke Leto, or his diabolic counterpart, Baron Harkonnen, operate consistently, logically, and inevitably throughout the book. Even when Thufir Hawat, Leto's mentat, joins the Harkonnen forces after the sack of Arrakis, Thufir works steadily, secretly, on behalf of his dead lord. And as a corollary of this, Dr. Yueh's treason becomes even more horrible because his primary loyalty should always have been to Leto and Leto's forces. In fact, in a twisted way, Yueh justifies his own traitorous behavior by convincing himself that the Baron will die as a result of Leto. The end justifies the means: Leto may perish, but the evil represented by the Harkonnens will also die, and Yueh has acted to save his "lady," a Bene Gesserit gifted with the full Truthsay. Yueh's actions, then, can be construed as one more example of the importance of the feudal motifs in *Dune*, in this instance the mystique of woman.

Throughout the novel Herbert deals with the overriding importance of the feminine. This theme is particularly rich, and ranges from the Jungian concept of the "anima" to the archetype of the Great Mother, the *magna mater*. The Bene Gesserit — that mysterious order of wise women — have seeded the Imperium with myths tailored to their purposes. This centuries-long action, undertaken primarily to protect Bene Gesserits wherever they might appear, has its consequences on Arrakis. For example, Lady Jessica is recognized, perhaps mistakenly, by the Shadout Mapes as the incarnation of the ancient

Fremen prophecy, "The coming of the Reverend Mother to free you." This fortuitous circumstance serves Paul and Lady Jessica well when they are captured by Stilgar and the Fremen after the death of Duke Leto. Jessica assumes the role of Reverend Mother and is able to save Paul's life as a consequence. Her presence throughout the book is that of the *magna mater*, guiding the Fremen forces and Paul so that they may combine the best of Arrakis with the best of the Atreides' off-world forces. The result is the actual fulfillment of the prophecy: Jessica has brought salvation to Arrakis.

Jessica's beneficent version of the Great Mother has its counterparts in Reverend Mother Gaius Helen Mohiam and Princess Irulan. Neither is a saving figure. In fact, Mohiam becomes almost the devouring mother, a Kali-like figure, who joins forces with the Emperor in an attempt to bring Arrakis and the Fremen under final imperial control. For her part, Irulan plots against Paul in *Dune Messiah*, perhaps out of some deep feminine anger that their marriage has never been consummated, perhaps out of frustration in living her role as a wronged daughter of the Emperor. Her redemption in the later books, her transformation into Paul's ally and sympathetic historian, is simply one more example of the multileveled portrayal of the feminine that Herbert provides throughout the series.

Science fiction has produced too few genuine women characters, fully drawn, completely portrayed, who serve an integral purpose in the stories. Lady Jessica is certainly an exception. Despite the constriction of her Bene Gesserit background and training, Jessica as wife, mother, heroine, guide, philosophical leader, or inspirer is a memorable character. In fact, it could be maintained that her virtual disappearance in *Dune Messiah* militates against its complete success as a sequel. If Jessica is memorable, so also are some of the minor women characters in *Dune*. Although seen only infrequently, Lady Margot Fenring provides a nice buffer against which Baron Harkonnen can rage, and Chani, Paul's Fremen concubine and mother of his children, is much more than the traditional feudal lady.

Alia is quite another matter. Many readers miss the implications of the attributive invective that Gaius Helen Mohiam flings at Alia: "Abomination!" At first she is the precocious child, born old with her memories that span centuries. But in *Children of Dune*, Alia in fact becomes the abomination, the vindictive witch-mother who is unredeemed by Duncan Idaho's love and whose fall young Leto and his twin Ghanima must encompass in order to restore Paul's corrupted dream. This suggestion of Alia's dual nature is simply one more indication of the care with which Herbert drew all of his female characters.

Other mythic elements abound in *Dune*, not the least of which is Herbert's portrayal of the sandworm, Shai-Hulud, often called "Old Father Eternity," and the geriatric spice which is unique to Arrakis. The worm may be construed as a science fiction version of the mythic black beast, the gold-hoarding dragon which must be conquered by the hero. Herbert has his own version of the hero, Paul, accomplish this task in a notable rite of passage as Paul rides the monstrous sandworm. But the worm itself is the source of the spice, the melange, the "gold" that it guards. The spice is the spermatic material of the worm, the eggs, so to speak, and Shai-Hulud is always found guarding this early vector of its metamorphic form. Over a period of eons of centuries, the worm has created the face of Arrakis, confining the planet's once abundant surface water to deep underground repositories where its "poison" will not affect its young.

The deep desert of Arrakis, so inhospitable to life that only the strongest may survive, is the consequence. Neither Kynes, his son Liet-Kynes, both planetary ecologists, nor Paul himself foresee the inevitable consequences of the ecological transformation of the planet. Spice wealth will disappear with the reintroduction of water, as was observed earlier, but what is even more important here is that the spice — the substance of incalculable value — provides a central focus for the feudal power plays which periodically rack the planet. It produces a change which affects everyone who takes the drug. In some people, the effect is strengthening. Its daily ingestion helps the Fremen become the magnificent fighters they are. In others it is corrupting, emphasizing, for example, the evil of Baron Harkonnen, the prescient faculty of Paul or the Spacing Guild, or the truth-saying ability of the Bene Gesserit, while blinding them psychologically. In this corruptive aspect, Dune and its spice riches curiously resembles Joseph Conrad's *Nostromo*. In that novel, the presence of a silver mine in a unique environment also corrupts everyone who must deal with the omnipresent silver. Herbert had not read *Nostromo* when he wrote *Dune*, but similar themes in both novels — and many other examples could be adduced — argue well for the utilization of the archetypal patterns derived from the collective unconscious by Herbert, Conrad, and many other writers. All help themselves to the archetypal myths.

The Fremen themselves are mythic. While they seem to have taken on certain aspects of the Arabian mythos — the desert culture, the warrior tradition, the search for survival in an overwhelmingly hostile world — nonetheless the Fremen have their own distinctive personality. This personality has been derived not only from the Arabian or Islamic mystique, but also from desert peoples throughout the world: American Indian traditions derived from the Hopi and Navaho; water conservation techniques derived from the nomads of the Kalahari desert, and so on. The Fremen combine all of these with religious fanaticism and a perfection of scientific technology as witnessed by the unique quality of their stillsuits and their abilities as water measurers. The Fremen — and surely their name itself *free men* must now be significant — personify all peoples throughout the history of Earth who have fought for freedom against virtually insuperable obstacles.

If the "external" vision of *Dune* as myth is crucial to an understanding of the novel, it is no less important to explore the "interior landscape" of its hero. That brings us to another vital, but less frequently mentioned theme: Herbert's unusually deep and perceptive treatment of the new science of consciousness. *Dune* explored the hidden potentials of the mind before LSD first hit the streets and triggered a wave of public interest in altered states of consciousness. Its vivid descriptions of heightened awareness in the development of Paul's religious visions acted as a spur to awaken countless readers to a sense of the importance and power of consciousness.

Since 1963, when *Dune* was first published, that wave has led from drugs to biofeedback and esoteric psychology without ever exceeding the range of Herbert's vision. Though the use of an unusual psychotropic drug is an important part of the novel, one gets the sense that Herbert had already seen beyond drugs to more disciplined methods for altering awareness. As a result, the novel has a great deal to teach even now, when "consciousness" is becoming a household word. Its significance may prove timeless, because its treatment of consciousness change centers less on technique or states than on the fundamental problems of being self-aware.

The story illustrates how exploring the new territory of the mind is like any other human adventure. One cannot hope for instant success or easy solutions to the problems that arise. Flexibility, resourcefulness, and courage in meeting the unknown are the most important of resources. Paul must come to terms with the two deadliest landscapes in a far-flung Galactic Empire — the desert planet Arrakis and the inner world of his own psyche. Each promises destruction for the least false step and priceless rewards for mastery. Both teach him to develop his abilities to the fullest, and meet each crisis as a dangerous opportunity rather than as an occasion for fear.

In the opening scene, Paul, the young heir to the Atreides Dukedom, is wakened from sleep and subjected to an inexplicable, terrifying test. While his mother stands guard outside the door of his room, an old crone holds a poisoned needle to his throat and bids him place his hand in the dark opening of a featureless metal box. The pain is excruciating. That Paul is the son of a Duke avails him nothing. He cannot flinch, or he meets death on the needle.

This is the ordeal of the *gom jabbar*. It serves, he is told, to separate humans from animals, to demonstrate the mastery of awareness over instinct. The old woman who administers the test to Paul is a "truth-sayer" and Reverend Mother of the Bene Gesserit Sisterhood. Ostensibly a religious organization, the Sisterhood uses religion as only one of many tools to manipulate the delicate political balance between the Emperor, the nobles of the Great Houses, and the transport monopoly of the Spacing Guild. Many of the wives and concubines of the great men of the Empire are Bene Gesserit trained practitioners of a psychology so advanced that it appears magical to the uninitiated. By using it to guide their mates, they exert an indirect but powerful role in shaping galactic events.

Paul has been selected, as few men are, to undergo the Bene Gesserit training because it is thought that he might be the final object of an ancient and secret selective breeding program. Mating its members to carefully chosen men, and determining the sex of each woman's offspring by delicate internal control, the Sisterhood has managed a centuries-long experiment in genetic engineering. They have cultivated the qualities they value in the race and weeded out others. They hope to breed a genetic superman, whom they call the *Kwisatz Haderach*, "the shortening of the way." He will be the first male who can survive the deadly drug that holds the key to their deepest powers of mind. With a male adept, who is at the same time a noble from a house close to the throne, the Bene Gesserit plan to take a more direct part in the Imperial politics from which they are kept by their sex.

Paul does not know if he is the Kwisatz Haderach, or even what the Bene Gesserit are looking for in this figure, and he resents their sudden intrusion into his life. Nonetheless, his mind is quick, and he begins to make sense out of scattered experiences of his childhood: the constant training in perception and inner control, and the more recent stirring of strange inward feelings, of prophetic dreams, and the sense of a "terrible purpose" for his life. He both knows and does not know what the old woman of the Bene Gesserit is talking about. He questions her right to make such judgments as to what is human and what is not, and to meddle in so many lives, but at the same time he knows intuitively that she believes in what she is doing, and operates out of an overpowering feeling of necessity. The Bene Gesserit also have a terrible purpose, he senses; and he knows that all too soon he will be forced to make similarly harsh choices himself as a part of his own budding purpose.

It becomes apparent in this very first scene that Herbert's unique treatment of heightened consciousness is not only the subject but is also one of the major strengths of the novel. The density of imagination the scene contains is unparalleled. In the course of a mere ten pages of conversation, introspection, and activity surrounding Paul's ordeal, Herbert introduces more imaginative detail than occupies most entire science fiction novels. Without ever being pedantic or slow, he sketches in the political infighting between the chief power blocs of an entire Galactic Empire, the historical and religious roots of its culture, and a powerful technology for the alteration of consciousness. Everything is in capsule, evocative, a seed for later pearls to crust upon. Even prosaic details are charged with significance. And the key to Herbert's success in presenting the scene so concisely is that the characters he has created are incredibly *awake*. It is in Paul's heightened ability to perceive and evaluate his circumstances that all the information is conveyed. It is as though Herbert has recreated those moments, whether of stress or inspiration, when human mental processes seem to accelerate and intensify. But whereas such experiences occur few times in a lifetime for most men, Paul lives continuously on that level. For him, everything is charged with a sense of danger and possibility.

The power of this "hyperconscious" point of view cannot be overestimated. Herbert may have labored for hours or days to compress a scene that the reader absorbs in minutes. The resulting illusion of heightened sensitivity is perfect. And this not only establishes Paul's character, it transforms the whole nature of the narrative. Herbert has managed to fuse third person storytelling with the introspective possibilities of first person. It is as though he has situated the narrator's eye at the interface of thought and action, much as a camera might capture the turbulent meeting point of air and water while viewing both worlds. Nothing "just happens." It happens to someone, is interpreted, and is changed by the way they respond. And because this active perceptual process mirrors the way people really do seem to perceive, it echoes the reader's own interpretive process while reading, so that he seems to experience the events of the story from the inside. He is taken up into the action not as a viewer but as a participant.

Furthermore, the examples of heightened awareness which occur in the book are not unrealizable fantasy, but an intensification of the ordinary. Herbert has envisioned everyday human abilities stretched to a peak. As a result, the reader's own experience of hyperconsciousness is brought into focus. It is this technique which distinguishes *Dune* from the many other works of science fiction which have made untapped human potential their premise. The reader can sense in himself all those possibilities which have reached fruition in Herbert's characters.

The first scene also introduces the fundamental questions of the book: what is the definition of the human when convention is stripped away and man is placed in extremity? What framework can there be for making judgments about such issues as the nature of the human, or right and wrong, once man has left the security of the known? Might not necessity or "terrible purpose" take the place of accepted morality as the individual facing the unknown imposes his own order on events? The remainder of the novel expands these tentative gropings for meaning by a young boy into the mature reflections of a man tested by experience and suffering.

When he faces the *gom jabbar* and has the first awakening to this "terrible purpose," Paul is still on Caladan, the world of his boyhood, where rain falls and softness is not unknown. Within days, he and his entire family are to be transported to Arrakis. The planet is harsh, dry, and deadly, with sandstorms that can strip the flesh from a human body, and giant predatory worms; but it is also the only source of *melange*, the unique and precious spice which prolongs life and gives prescient awareness to the Reverend Mothers of the Bene Gesserit and the navigators of the Spacing Guild.

Duke Leto, Paul's father, is not Bene Gesserit trained, but he has his own style of living with danger. He has won the overlordship of the planet from his enemy, the Baron Harkonnen, but it is a deadly prize, and he knows it. Under the codes of the Empire, Harkonnen may strike to regain his former holdings while their new lord is yet unsure of himself. Leto seizes the thorned opportunity, knowing it may mean his death but a chance at greatness for his son. It is not merely the spice-wealth of the planet which Leto prizes, but a possibility suggested by its hardy natives. The power of the Emperor over his rivals in the Great Houses is maintained by grim Sardaukar. They are the fiercest troops in a galaxy where the "field process shield" has made obsolete projectile weapons and returned personal combat to its ancient position as the primary tool of warfare. Leto suspects that the Fremen of Arrakis, who live in a harsher environment than even the Sardaukar home world and have been oppressed by the Harkonnens for eighty years, might be forged into a guerrilla force superior even to the Emperor's best.

The Emperor and Baron Harkonnen are devoted to maintaining the *status quo*. Their politics consist of jockeying for position within a set framework, with care not to endanger what they already have. Leto (and Paul to an even greater extent) represent a disruptive force in this over-stabilized civilization. The Atreideses are willing to throw everything in the air on a single toss of the dice, and hope that the new situation will be better than the old. They are risk-takers, and by allying with the Fremen they hope to introduce an entirely new balance in galactic politics.

Unfortunately, the Emperor sees this danger from Leto and backs the Harkonnen bid. Soon after the Atreideses arrive on Arrakis, Sardaukar disguised as Harkonnen troops cut down Leto's men while he himself is betrayed by one of his closest associates and delivered to the Baron and eventual death. Paul, however, escapes to the desert with his mother Jessica, hoping to join the Fremen and salvage Leto's plan.

At this point, the awareness training Paul received from the Bene Gesserit comes together with the political adventurism he inherited from his father. Leto's thoughts for the Fremen were purely political. As ruler of the planet he could woo them to his banner with promises of favor. Paul, a despised refugee, must choose another route.

Being Bene Gesserit trained, Paul cannot help but note that the Fremen are intensely religious, as desert nomads from the earliest times have seemed to be. They are ripe for a religious revolution. The legends planted long ago by the Bene Gesserit have even established a messianic base to the Fremen faith. The situation has been only slightly complicated by the meddling of an Imperial planetologist (planetary ecologist), who had already tried to bend the native religion to foreign aims. That the messianic dreams of the Fremen now include an earthly paradise — the ecological transformation of their barren planet into a watery Eden — will make them all the more amenable to Paul's aims.

The Bene Gesserit legends, however, are only one part of the pattern that leads to Paul's acceptance as a messiah by the Fremen. The legends are effective only because the Fremen, like many oppressed peoples, hunger for a savior. Even before Paul has arrived into the explosive situation in the heart of the desert, there were those among the Fremen who hoped that this young son of the off-world Duke and the Bene Gesserit lady could be "the voice from the outer world" promised by the legends. And even before he has made a conscious choice to step into the myth, other factors were at work to take the decision out of his hands. The feudal mystique discussed above, in which every man has a clearly defined place, together with the Bene Gesserit arts of psychological manipulation described throughout the book, sets the stage for an analysis of the pervasive psychological needs which motivate individuals to seek out the reassurance of charismatic leadership or the absolute truth of a militant religion. A true "avatar" may in fact be irrelevant to a messianic uprising. The messiah is only the focus of his people's desires.

Having made this point, Herbert went on to explore its converse. For is it not possible that Paul *is* the one promised by the Bene Gesserit legends, the Kwisatz Haderach of their ancient schemes? Once in the deserts of Arrakis, the overpowering amounts of melange naturally occurring in the Fremen diet begin to trigger the powers latent in his genes, and Paul does in fact become the prophet and spiritual leader of whom the Fremen dream.

From here on, the basic outline of the story is direct and obvious. A new religion is born and sweeps Paul to overlordship of Arrakis and eventual victory over the Emperor himself. But however predictable the general outline, the specifics are powerful and unexpected. Herbert has managed to fuse an eloquent portrait of desert life and the unconscious social dynamics in the birth of a messianic crusade with the inner transformations which Paul undergoes in the course of becoming the Mahdi of the Fremen. And he has added to this an analysis of the way in which the ecological strictures of the desert planet shape both Paul and the religion which grows up around him.

All of Paul's visions contain a *jihad*, a holy war of religious fanaticism decimating the Empire in his name. It is the result of totally unexpected forces beyond his control. He and the Fremen upsurge are only the occasion for a racial demand for an end to the rigidity of the Empire in a profound remixing of the gene pool. To bring about this upheaval was the "terrible purpose" Paul had sensed all along, and though he is a creation of the Bene Gesserit, his purpose is at odds with theirs. The Sisterhood had seen this genetic reason for the fluctuations in civilization and tried to control them through their selective breeding program. But as Paul has come to adulthood, he has seen that no system of prediction and control, however exact and careful, is sufficient to preserve the vitality of the race. Its strength is in its randomness, its superb generation of new possibilities. His mission, as it is thrust upon him, is to bring about that necessary turmoil in a way that he can ride. The furor may not be less, but it comes at a time of his choosing, and can be guided subtly to a better end.

Paul Atreides, the nobleman of the Empire, could not countenance the cost in suffering, bloodshed, and ignorance which the *jihad* will bring, but Paul Maud'Dib, the Fremen he has become, has learned how to bow to forces beyond his control. When the great storms blow, no man can stand against them. And the huge implacable sandworms which destroy all human artifacts in the desert can be ridden only by one who knows how to blend with the shifting sands, and to move boldly when the time is right.

This is the lesson which Paul learned from the Bene Gesserit, rediscovered in another context. The world — and the mind — can be dangerous places for a man who sees truly and reaches into new territory for high goals. The Bene Gesserit know it on one level, the Fremen on another. Paul has gone beyond both and is still reaching. He knows there is no endpoint, no final surety. That is aliveness. Each new advance in consciousness does not change the game, it only raises the stakes.

Paul sees further than anyone else, and in the eyes of others he is omniscient. But the world he sees is more complex than anyone imagines, and even he cannot see far enough for certainty. He is left at the end with the same ultimate questions which tormented him after his first ordeal, and with no sure answers. And so his religion, which began as a political tool, and spread as a cancerous growth springing from racial needs, ends as a true vision of man's place in the universe. Human striving results in ever-increasing knowledge and power, but still man only approaches, and never finds, the horizon of mystery.

Herbert's summary, in an appendix, of the religious background of *Dune* also deserves further examination. *Dune* began, it will be recalled, as a study of the ways that messianism has convulsed human societies. Herbert's superhero may be a genuine spiritual teacher, but he is still a hero with feet of clay, unable to control the forces his religious mystique has unleashed. Herbert's appendix chronicles the ecumenical movement in the Galactic Imperium, and how centuries, perhaps millennia, before Paul's *jihad*, there had been an attempt "to remove a primary weapon from the hands of disputant religions . . . the claim to possession of the one and only revelation." He examines the paradoxical success and failure of this attempt. The syncretistic Orange Catholic Bible of the Commission of Ecumenical Translators has pervaded the known universe, but messianic movements such as Paul's are still possible because religion is not encompassed by the reasonableness of ecumenism or even the universal wisdom of its most beloved prophets. It is a shield against "the terrors of an uncertain future," and a submergence of individual responsibility in the primal unconsciousness of the group. As long as this is so, there will be an opposition between prophets and the religion which grow up around them.

Dune, then, is a particularly rich melange of themes: heroic, political, feminine, mythic, archetypal, economic, ecological, perceptual, and theological. The fact that it can be read and reread with such profit is a tribute to Herbert's creative vision as well as the imagination he requires of his readers to bring themselves into its massive panoply as actors themselves.

Willis E. McNelly and
Timothy O'Reilly

Sources for Further Study

Criticism:

Allen, L. David. *Herbert's* Dune *and Other Works*. Lincoln, Neb.: Cliff's Notes, Inc. 1975. Discusses the theme that started a new science fiction cult.

Parkinson, Robert C. *"Dune* — An Unfinished Tetralogy," in *Extrapolation*. XIII (December, 1971), pp. 16-24. The philosophical problems first proposed in *Dune* help fuse the sequels together.

Reviews:

Analog. LXXVII, April, 1966, pp. 140-141.

Best Sellers. XXV, October 15, 1965, p. 280.

Booklist. LXII, February 1, 1966, p. 519.

Books Today. IV, January 29, 1967, p. 11.

Galaxy. XXIV, April, 1966, pp. 67-71.

Kirkus Reviews. XXXIII, August 15, 1965, p. 847.

Magazine of Fantasy and Science Fiction. XXX, March, 1966, pp. 51-53.

Observer. July 31, 1966, p. 21.

Punch. CCLI, August 31, 1966, p. 339.

DUNE MESSIAH

Author: Frank Herbert (1920-   )
First book publication: 1969
Type of work: Novel
Time: Twelve years after the conclusion of *Dune*
Locale: The planet Arrakis, the desert world

> *Principal characters:*
> PAUL ATREIDES, prophet and emperor
> ALIA, his younger sister
> DUNCAN IDAHO (HAYT), philosopher, mentat, and swordmaster
> STILGAR, leader of the Fremen
> CHANI, Paul's concubine
> THE PRINCESS IRULAN, his official consort
> SCYTALE, a Tleilaxu "face dancer"

Dune Messiah is a greatly underrated book. It is often compared with *Dune* and made to suffer by the comparison. It is criticized as lacking in the wealth of imagination which made its predecessor so remarkable. However, it is its very spareness (and that only in contrast to so rich a novel as *Dune*) which is the sequel's strength. The purpose of *Dune Messiah* was not to repeat *Dune*, but to complete it. Herbert selected only one of the themes in *Dune* — the limits of prophecy — and left the others (as we now know) for treatment in the third (and a rumored fourth) volume of a trilogy (tetralogy). This one theme is honed to a clarity and power far exceeding that which it had in *Dune* and is clothed in echoes of classical tragedy to create a novel of rare pathos and beauty.

One of the central ideas in *Dune* is the ambiguous nature of prophecy. It brings Paul (Muad'Dib) as much grief as it does success. He is continually forced to make personally abhorrent choices for the sake of destiny. In *Dune Messiah*, ambiguity becomes tragedy, as the weight of foreknowledge becomes too much for even a great man like Paul to bear.

The story takes place twelve years after Paul's climactic victory over the Emperor's Sardaukar on the plain before the city of Arrakeen. The jihad has run its course, and in the process scattered the Fremen throughout the galaxy. Many have returned to Arrakis, but they are changed by their exposure to pleasure and power on the soft worlds they have conquered. The old closeness of the tribal *sietch* has vanished, and with it the courage and innate wisdom of desert life. The old ways known in the blood have been replaced by lip service to Muad'Dib's religion. The vibrancy of the new faith has already crystallized into ritual, and pilgrims flock from all over the galaxy to share in mysteries presided over by Paul's younger sister Alia.

Paul himself has retained much of his old hardness, but he is wearied by years of subjection to the demands of his vision and soured by the sacrifices of its purity which have been made of necessity. He has learned that his people cannot sustain terror and the intensity of their prophet's confrontation with the unknown; they have turned his admonitions into yet another security blanket against the very fears he encouraged them to face. "Muad'Dib knows!" they say. There is no terror from the unknown as long as you follow his omniscient vision. Thus, all of Paul's teachings are turned against him through misinterpretation or inability to face his message.

At this point the tragedy begins; Paul is seduced by kingship. Faced with the inevitability of human nature, which does not heed words and endlessly re-creates the old patterns in the fabric of the new, he tries to find some way to shoulder his people's burden. He tries to save them the hard lessons he himself must continually relearn. That is not to say that he meekly submits himself to the myth of his own omnipotence. He does continue to exhort his people. But he tries to shape the future so as to make the universe as safe for them as possible. However, in this he plays into their hands. Once he takes responsibility for their welfare, he is lost, regardless of what he preaches or how he strives to awaken their inner sensibilities.

Against this background the action begins. A plot is mounted against Paul by a group consisting of the Reverend Mother Gaius Helen Mohiam (the Bene Gesserit truthsayer who had long ago subjected Paul to the *gom jabbar*); Paul's consort, the Princess Irulan; Edric, a steersman of the Spacing Guild; and a Tleilaxu "face dancer" named Scytale. All of these individuals have their own reason for wishing to destroy Muad'Dib. The Bene Gesserit wish to recover the reins of their breeding plan, astray since Paul, its ultimate product, refused their guidance and chose his own destiny. Princess Irulan (besides being Bene Gesserit trained) resents the fact that Paul has made her a wife in name only, keeping his troth with Chani, his Fremen concubine. The Spacing Guild, who had long maintained secret control of the spice *melange* so crucial to the limited pescience they use to guide their ships between the stars, is frightened of what Paul might do to the spice. Long accustomed to limited prophetic powers, the scope of Paul's powers is even more frightening to them than it is to the average man. They wish to remove so unpredictable a factor from their universe. The Bene Tleilaxu (a group never mentioned in *Dune*) are merely opportunistic. They come from a renegade planet which had defied the long-ago Butlerian Jihad, the holy war against computers which had outlawed the use of these human counterfeits and forced the development of such talents as those exhibited by the Bene Gesserit, the mentats, and other mental wizards of the Empire. They are eager to bring their forbidden technology back into the mainstream of the galaxy.

An additional cabal, not a part of the central plot, is led by the Fremen Korba, head of the Qizarate, the lucrative pilgrim church of Muad'Dib. He is the most unexpected and yet most obvious of the conspirators. Paul is the greatest threat to his own religion. It is terrifying for Korba to manage a church with a living prophet, one who scorns his own following and might say so at any moment. Korba's plan (and however perverse it seems, he truly believes he is acting in the interest of Muad'Dib's original vision) is to make a martyr of Paul, and so forever cement his faith in the hearts of untold billions of believers.

The exact mechanisms of each of these plots is unclear, since the reader is never given any preview of the conspirators' intentions and must draw his conclusions from the results of their actions. It seems in retrospect that the plan was to lure Paul to the home of Otheym, a Fremen whom he knew from the days in Stilgar's *sietch*. Once he was there, drawn by loyalty to an old comrade and by guilt over wounds Otheym had suffered in the Jihad, the house and all its inhabitants were to be destroyed by the detonation of a stoneburner, a forbidden tool from the atomic past. But it is not so simply done, both because of the convoluted behavior needed to hide a plot from a prescient Emperor, and also because the Bene Tleilaxu, who have taken chief responsibility for carrying out the plan, are playing a double game. Unlike the other plotters, who wish to see Paul dead, they wish him alive — and under their control.

To this end, they bring Paul a gift: the ghola — that is, the reconstructed flesh — of Duncan Idaho, the swordmaster and friend of Paul's youth who had died defending him when the Sardaukar first sacked the Atreides holdings on Arrakis. The Bene Tleilaxu have developed the art of cell regrowth to the point where they can literally bring the dead back to life. The only drawback is that the ghola lacks the memories of the original.

The purpose of the Tleilaxu gift is twofold. First of all, it is hoped that Duncan, as a symbol of the long history of Atreides honor, will trigger Paul's remorse at the many expediencies of his rule. This "psychic poison" (as the conspirators call it) may cloud his judgment and drive him to rash demonstrations of the old honor. In addition, the Bene Tleilaxu have implanted a compulsion within the ghola to kill Paul. If he succeeds, well and good. But their deeper hope is that the compulsion will so conflict with the old loyalties in Duncan's very cells that the crisis will shatter the ghola-block and restore his memories. Once they have proved that they can restore ghola memories, they will have a further bargaining hand. For they expect to be able to offer Paul the return of his beloved Chani, after her death at the hands of the other conspirators. Or if Paul himself is killed, they will restore him to life, but with unconscious training to make him their slave.

Paul, meanwhile, is not totally unaware of what is going on. Though he is blocked from direct knowledge of the conspiracy by Edric's presence (since Paul cannot envision the actions of another prescient, even so comparatively feeble a one as the Guild Steersman), Paul knows a great deal of what is to come and is playing along for reasons of his own. He has foreseen Duncan's restoration from the ghola as well as Chani's death in childbirth, and even the final outcome of the stoneburner plot. He does not know exactly *how* it is all to happen, but *what* will be he has foreseen. He allows Scytale, disguised as only a Tleilaxu "face dancer" can be disguised, to lure him to the house of Otheym. He leaves in time to escape death in the flare of the stoneburner, but he is blinded by its deadly radiation.

Though it is the custom of the Fremen to abandon the sightless to the desert, Paul orders mechanical eyes from the Bene Tleilaxu for all the men who were with him, but he rejects them for himself. Paul does not need eyes; so perfect is his vision of these moments that its mere memory replaces the sight of the present. Through all the difficulties, his major effort has not been to thwart the conspirators. He is willing to make a martyr of himself, if it will bring the events he had started so long before to some kind of a satisfactory end. He has been crystallizing a more and more complete vision, which he chooses despite all its personal cost as a way of preserving the things he holds most dear: his honor, and the eventual awakening of his people from their bondage to his omniscience.

As he loses his sight, the last strands of vision fall into place. Blinded, but finally seeing his way clear, Paul rounds up the conspirators. The plot is crushed, Duncan is awakened, and twin children are born to Chani, though she dies in the process. And finally, even the memory of vision exhausted, Paul follows the Fremen custom for the blind and walks off alone into the desert to die.

The image of Paul in these final days is terrifying. When he walks eyeless along the Arrakeen streets, greeting each of his men by name, the immense futility of an entire way of thought is brought gasping to the light. After twelve years of vision, Paul has created a populace completely dependent on his oracular leadership. He himself has been corrupted by the awful responsibility of foreknowledge to seek absolute sureness in a world which thrives on novelty. The final success of his attempt brings the moment of awful stagnation in which the memory of prescient vision replaces Paul's eyes, and at the same moment replaces possibility with absolute determinism.

On one level, the trap of vision in which Paul finds himself is purely logical in conception; it is the inevitable conclusion of Herbert's critique throughout *Dune* and *Dune Messiah* of the human desire to shape the future. On another level, Paul's dilemma echoes with painful clarity that of Sophocle's Oedipus. Eyeless, he cannot help but remind us of the King of Thebes. But the similarity goes beyond literal blindness: each leader is driven to his end by his own inflexibility, and in a sense by his own uprightness. It is continually noted that Paul could have "gotten off" the track of prophecy, simply by choosing to take care of himself rather than his people. But he would not. He came to believe that he could and must deliver to them what they wanted. He kept trying to guide them to the *best* future. His strength to ride the waves of time, which had carried him to the throne, became solidified (once he had a constituency) into what he had always intuitively opposed, an attempt to *fix* the future. And so, like Oedipus, he is a sacrifice to his people. He is forced by his commitment to kingship into a kind of personal blindness. As Oedipus must find and root out the cause of the curse on Thebes, even if it be himself, Paul must put a stop to the dreadful cancer of his own prescience.

The power of this image of the blind king is not just its compelling logic, nor the accuracy with which it reflects its tragic model. It is also the amazing *fiction* of it. Herbert has brought feelings that no man has ever had — the passions of prophecy — into such clear focus that they now exist for the rest of us to feel. This is true art and the measure of Herbert's success. The psychology of precognition — Paul's feeling of being locked into an inevitable path, in which all has been seen before, and the states of anxiety and frustration this produces — is made unutterably vivid. Paul's only chance is to break the cycle of vision, to step again into the unknown; but he can do this only after testing the utmost possibilities of foreknowledge.

Paul's final effort, therefore, is not to outwit the conspirators, but to outwit time. He discovers that control over history only breeds the need for more control. There is no way to shape a future for his people that will be free of the pernicious effects of the shaping itself. Is there then some way that he can let go of control so as to do this? He believes that there is, and he is willing to sacrifice Chani and even himself if only it can be accomplished.

Does Paul succeed? When he walks off into the desert, blind and alone, he is accomplishing two things. He is wedding himself to the old ways of the Fremen, giving an example around which they can be reborn; and he is providing a lasting paradox for all the people of the Empire, who did not heed his words but will forever remember his actions, and wonder.

Timothy O'Reilly

Sources for Further Study

Criticism:

Allen, L. David. *Herbert's Dune and Other Works*. Lincoln, Neb.: Cliff's Notes, Inc., 1975. Compares the sequel to the original.

Parkinson, Robert C. *"Dune* — An Unfinished Tetralogy," in *Extrapolation*. XIII (December, 1971), pp. 16-24. Parkinson shows how the works follow each other.

Reviews:

Analog. LXXXV, June, 1970, pp. 165-166.

Kirkus Reviews. XXXVII, August 1, 1969, p. 807.

Library Journal. XCV, January 15, 1970, p. 259.

Luna Monthly. XIX, December, 1970, p. 22.

Publisher's Weekly. CXCVII, May 11, 1970, p. 44.

SF Commentary. XVI, October, 1970, p. 5-7 and XVII, November, 1970, pp. 11-13.

Science Fiction Review. XXXIX, August, 1970, p. 24.

THE DYING EARTH

Author: Jack Vance (1920-   )
First book publication: 1962
Type of work: Thematically related short stories
Time: Millions of years in the future
Locale: The Earth and Embelyon

Six interrelated stories that portray the Earth near the end of its life, when magic has replaced science

> *Principal characters:*
> TURJAN OF MIIR, a magician who seeks to create life in his vats
> PANDELUME, a sorcerer dwelling in Edenic Embelyon
> T'SAIS, a beautiful woman created by Pandelume
> T'SAIN, a woman created by Turjan, almost identical to T'sais
> MAZIRIAN THE MAGICIAN, who keeps a wonderful garden and pursues T'sais
> LIANE THE WAYFARER, a rogue and a robber
> ULAN DHOR, nephew of Prince Kandive the Golden
> GUYAL OF SFERE, a man born with an exaggerated curiosity

The Dying Earth, Jack Vance's first book, published five years after his first magazine appearance ("The World-Thinker" in *Thrilling Wonder Stories*), demonstrates many of his characteristic qualities: a baroque vocabulary and style, richly exotic settings, the mixing of science and magic as technologies of wonder, and the atmosphere of fairy-tale and parable. Its generic niche is probably best labeled "science fantasy." In this case, that troublesome term indicates not only the idea that magic is subject to laws, or that it is an alternative to science as a means of controlling the world (though both notions are present), but also the portrayal of magic as the historical successor to the physical sciences. Relics of civilizations based on science fictional superscience remain on the Dying Earth, but far in the past magic replaced science.

The book consists of six interrelated stories set in a future so distant that the shapes of the continents have changed and the sun itself is red and dying. Mankind is reduced to a few thousand individuals living among the decaying splendors of cities built by civilizations vanished for millennia, and half-human monsters prowl the wastes and forests. The rule of science is forgotten (though a few remnants and artifacts remain), and men use magic to satisfy their curiosities, lusts, and power-cravings. Accordingly, three of the major characters are full-fledged magicians, and most use at least a little magic for convenience or protection. Even this magic, though, is only the shards and scraps of a once-great body of knowledge. The Earth is dying, and everything is less than it once was.

This sense of decay and decadence is so strong that it seems that the characters are as much in conflict with it as with one another. The Earth carries the weight of millions of years of history, and human societies are strangled by a dead past. The Saponids of Saponce have sent thirteen thousand young men and women as sacrifices to the demon Blikdak, while in Ampridatvir the Grays and Greens, adherents of rival cults, refuse to acknowledge each other's existence for five thousand years. Meanwhile, in Kaiin, the court of Prince Kandive the Golden lives in festival and self-indulgence, "for infinite night was close at hand, when the red sun should finally flicker and go black." Against this backdrop of time's triumph, the passion and energy of the characters of these stories, all seekers after knowledge, power, or beauty, is all the more remarkable.

The first three stories, "Turjan of Miir," "Mazirian the Magician," and "T'sais," form a unit, a three-part introduction to the Dying Earth and the extremes of love and cruelty, beauty and ugliness, loyalty and faithlessness that are typical of it. In "Turjan of Miir," Turjan seeks from Pandelume the secret of the "master matrix" for creating intelligent life. When Pandelume's own creation, T'sais, in her rage at a world that seems "loathsome and ugly," kills Turjan's first successful creation, he decides to make a twin to T'sais, as beautiful and spirited, but without the internal flaw. He names her T'sain, and when the two meet, T'sais is persuaded by her sister and by the promptings of a nature deeper than the mind that the warp may be in her brain rather than in the world, and she vows to give up killing and destruction and to ask Pandelume to send her from Embelyon to Earth, where she may "find and know beauty . . . or die."

"Mazirian the Magician" (which Vance originally wanted to be first in the sequence despite its position in the chronology) and "T'sais" follow the adventures of Turjan, T'sain, and T'sais after they return to Earth from Embelyon. Turjan is captured by Mazirian, who covets the secret of the master matrix; he also covets the woman who watches him from the forest as he walks in his garden. Turjan will not yield the secret, nor tell Mazirian that the woman is T'sain, who hopes to free him. Wearing magical "Live Boots" and carrying a head full of spells, Mazirian pursues T'sain and nearly catches her in a grove, but predatory trees attack both of them. Mazirian fights furiously, exciting the trees to a frenzy; he is killed, while T'sain manages to crawl away. On releasing Turjan, she dies, and he returns her to the vats to renew her body.

When T'sais arrives on Earth, she encounters, in quick succession, Liane the Wayfarer torturing two people, a trio of moormen who kidnap and attempt to rape her, and a hungry deodand. Fleeing this last threat (she has wounded Liane and killed the moormen), she takes shelter in the cottage of Etarr. He has an outer flaw to match her inner one: a witch, Javanne, has betrayed his love and exchanged his face for a demon's. Etarr wears a black hood to conceal his ugliness, but is, to T'sais's surprise, neither bitter nor vengeful. He does, however, want his face returned, and they seek Javanne at the Black Sabbath. T'sais is able to help trick Javanne into revealing a solution: far away dwells a god of justice, evoked by a long-vanished race of just men, and his "power beyond magic" can recover Etarr's face. When they confront the just god, Etarr does regain his face, Javanne receives the worm-nosed demon face, and T'sais's brain is made whole.

Crude as it may seem to anatomize these delicate-appearing tales, it is possible to discern at least three levels of operation in them: the archetypal, the folk- or traditional fairy-tale, and the literary fantasy. The archetypal level controls some of the characters and settings: Pandelume and Mazirian, T'sais and T'sain, the various monsters; Embelyon, Mazirian's garden and the forest, the Lake of Dreams. The folk or traditional level controls many of the plot devices and motifs: pursuits, duels of magic and wits, bargains, the granting of justice without mercy, basic magical equipment (T'sais's living sword and magic-reflecting rune, the Live Boots). The rules of literary fantasy supply the verbal surface, individual characterization (such as it is), and the development of the themes of decadence and Faustian search. It is Vance's control of this level that marks these stories so strongly: the description of Mazirian's garden of exotic and half-sentient plants, the examples of his cruelty (the gong whose strokes deplete the life of Azvan the Astronomer, the tiny box that Turjan shares with a dragon), the baroque complexity of the magic spells (Phandaal's Gyrator, The Excellent Prismatic Spray, Felojun's Second Hypnotic Spell). The literary-fantasy level directs and modulates the emotional power and narrative drive of the archetypal and traditional levels, and the second half of the book shifts the balance toward the literary, and specifically toward science fantasy.

"Liane the Wayfarer" retains this mixture of fairy-tale and literary fantasy in plot and character. Liane is a distant cousin of Cugel the Clever, the picaro-protagonist of Vance's other Dying Earth book, *The Eyes of the Overworld*. Where Cugel manages to remain a comically sympathetic rogue, however, Liane is repellent, vain to the point of megalomania, pathologically cruel, and not at all funny. The story turns on two devices — Liane's discovery of a bronze ring through which one may step into another space, and thus vanish from this one, and his attempt to win the favors of Lith the golden witch by stealing back from a being named Chun the Unavoidable half of a tapestry. Arrogantly confident, ignoring warnings and eyeless corpses scattered along the way, Liane steals the tapestry, to find Chun waiting behind it, wearing a robe fashioned from threaded eyeballs. He flees, with Chun at his heels; he takes refuge in the bronze ring's "magic space," only to hear beside him, "I am Chun the Unavoidable." Later, Lith is paid by Chun with two threads to add to her half of the tapestry, " 'because the eyes were so great, so large, so golden. . . .' " The relationships among these characters are ruled by passions and greed — Liane lusts for Lith, Chun collects eyes, and Lith longs to return home through her magic tapestry. There is no room here for love, loyalty, or generosity, in contrast to the preceding stories.

The last two stories, in their use of miracles wrought by superscience as well as magic, and in their linkage, however distant, of the fairy-tale timelessness of the Dying Earth with historical time, suggest a fourth level of operation, the science fictional. In the story bearing his name, Ulan Dhor is sent to lost Ampridatvir by his uncle, Prince Kandive, to find the tablets, and therefore the secrets, of Rogol Domedonfors. In the city, Ulan Dhor finds the Grays and Greens are not at war (which was the situation when the city fell from greatness five thousand years before), but in the grip of a collective delusion that prevents them from seeing each other. The city itself is clearly science fictional — metal towers, moving walkways, aircars, antigravity shafts — and the secret of the tablets awakens the great machine in which Rogol Domedonfors has preserved his brain. Through the machine, Rogol Domedonfors is able to rebuild the city in moments; unfortunately, he is no longer sane, and declares his godhood and his intention to start a new race with Ulan Dhor and Elai (a Gray girl Ulan Dhor had rescued) as founding parents. Ulan Dhor kills the brain and escapes with Elai in an aircar while the machine destroys the just-rebuilt city.

This pattern recurs often enough in Vance's work to be considered a signature: the hero finds a people, enslaved, exploited, or trapped in a delusion or a pathological ideology, and frees them of it that they might live on their own terms. In this case, the manacles are mind-forged, caused initially by religious fanaticism and reinforced by apparently innate wrongheadedness. Ulan Dhor's theft of the first tablet breaks the mutual blindness of Gray and Green, but does not stop their mutual hate, and they slaughter each other. Only when the city-machine strips them of their clothes — and thereby of their colors — do they stop, and then perhaps more out of shock than anything else. But the power of Rogol Domedonfors is no solution, either, since he is now as mad as his subjects; Ulan Dhor and Elai, having avoided playing Adam and Eve in an insane new dispensation, return to a decadent but familiar Kaiin.

The renewal of the old Earth which is suggested in "Ulan Dhor" is more explicitly confronted in "Guyal of Sfere." Like earlier characters, Guyal is a seeker after knowledge; unlike them, his is the curiosity of a child ("What is beyond the sky?") rather than a Faustian desire for power. His father provides him with a horse, an Expansible Egg (a magical shelter), a Scintillant Dagger, and a blessing to protect his trail, and Guyal sets out to seek answers from the Curator of the Museum of Man. After escaping the usual dangers of his world, Guyal reaches Saponce, a city near the Museum. The Saponids pay the tribute of two of their handsomest young people to a demon that infests the Museum, and Guyal is tricked from his protected path and drafted into service as the male half of such a sacrifice. Guyal and his companion, Shierl, avoid immediate capture by the demon, Blikdak, who is caught with his head in the Museum and his body back in the demon-realm of Jeldred. Kerlin the Curator, who eventually comes to their aid, is senile from his millennia of caretaking, and in bringing back his mind, they hasten his death. Before he dies, they discover Blikdak's nature and unravel him, ending that threat. Kerlin leaves to the young people the care of the Museum, as well as his index to its overwhelming mass of information; at the end, they stand looking out at the stars where other men have gone before.

"Guyal of Sfere" and "Ulan Dhor" are paired stories, constructed from the same motifs and themes: the journey to a far place in search of knowledge; the rescue of a young woman; the awakening of an ancient human intelligence and the concomitant lifting of a curse. But where Ulan Dhor returns home without any magical knowledge after seeing the end of Rogol Domedonfors' dreams of wisdom and reason, Guyal and Shierl learn from the accumulated knowledge of the Museum and face the stars, this last action echoing Kerlin's advice to escape to the stars, to "youthful climes." This is the final response to the decay of the Dying Earth: to seek a new world, to become the founders of a new race, but without the dominance of a mad, self-proclaimed god or of superstition or mortmain traditionalism.

Most of all what Guyal would be leaving behind would be human decadence. In a noteworthy passage he says, " '. . . now, in the last fleeting moments, humanity festers ripe as rotten fruit. Rather than master and overpower our world, our highest aim is to cheat it through sorcery.' " Even Blikdak, like all demons, is a "vast tumor" formed from "the manifold tittering lubricities that have drained through humanity" — that is, demons are the incarnation of humankind's flaws and sicknesses, even as the just god of "T'sais" is a creation of his worshipers. Thus there is a demonic objective correlative of the cruelty and treachery of Liane and Mazirian, the unnatural lusts of Javanne. Mankind's troubles, then, are the result of human nature rather than any external supernatural force, and human will and courage and ingenuity can overcome them, as when Kerlin destroys Blikdak by the banally material means of winding his substance on spools, or when Guyal refuses to bow to Blikdak's "tradition" of lightlessness and saves himself and Shierl from the demon's initial assault.

This is a science fiction theme and attitude, and Vance's first major science fiction novel, *To Live Forever*, and much of his important work since then has included some variation on it: *Emphyrio*, *The Blue World*, the Durdane trilogy, *The Dragon Masters*. Even when the enslaving or exploiting force is an external one (as in *The Dragon Masters*), Vance asserts the necessity for men to discover their freedom by throwing off the self-imposed burdens of apathy, ignorance, superstition, and fear before it is possible to defeat any alien master. In the milieu of the Dying Earth there may not be sufficient time and energy to effect such changes, but, as Kerlin knew, there are younger lands among the stars.

Russell Letson

Sources for Further Study

Reviews:

Analog. LXXI, March, 1963, p. 87.

DYING INSIDE

Author: Robert Silverberg (1936-   )
First book publication: 1972
Type of work: Novel
Time: 1976-1977
Locale: New York City

David Selig, a telepath, discovers that his ability is slowly disappearing, that he is "dying inside"

> *Principal characters:*
> DAVID SELIG, a forty-one-year-old Jewish telepath
> JUDITH, his sister
> NYQUIST, another telepath

One of the most interesting developments of science fiction since the New Wave is the gradual disappearance of the barrier between traditional science fiction and mainstream fiction. American science fiction has been largely a pulp genre, having been so relegated by Hugo Gernsback with his pattern-setting publication *Amazing Stories* in the late 1920's, and its writers interested largely in using the field only to make a living. Few writers thought of themselves as belonging to the great literary tradition of Western culture. Instead they concentrated on fantastic inventions and hyperspace travel, hard-core science fiction that ignored the literary developments of James Joyce, a D. H. Lawrence, or the psychological insights of a Sigmund Freud or a Carl Jung.

The writers — and there were many competent craftsmen among them — wrote as if only their world of *Amazing Stories, Thrilling Wonder*, or *Astounding Science Fiction* existed. Too often it seemed that they wrote with one eye on the royalty check and editor John W. Campbell, Jr.'s, prejudices and preferences and the other on the typewriter, never glimpsing that great outside world where Ernest Hemingway was reinventing the simple sentence and William Faulkner and F. Scott Fitzgerald were exploring the depths of the human psyche. On the other hand, when writers such as Aldous Huxley or George Orwell wished to explore some of the ideas which are explicit or implicit in the writing of Robert A. Heinlein, Ray Bradbury, or Isaac Asimov, they simply went ahead, wrote their novels, and did not worry whether they were writing "science fiction." Never the twain would meet, it seemed.

The split began to narrow with the New Wave. Hard-core "spanner and grommet" stories went into eclipse, and some of the writers began experimenting with "style," discovering, for example, the interior monologue which Joyce had virtually perfected decades earlier. They began exploring inner space — the psyche, the subconscious, the unconscious — and no writer, except perhaps Philip K. Dick, was better at it than Robert Silverberg. No modern science fiction novel pays more direct and indirect tribute to mainstream writers, such as Joyce, D. H. Lawrence, William Butler Yeats, or T. S. Eliot, than Silverberg's *Dying Inside*.

In a sense, it is incorrect to call *Dying Inside* a science fiction novel at all. The only science fiction "gimmick" that Silverberg uses is the device of telepathy. David Selig is a telepath who has gradually become aware that he is losing his ability. The story is not centered upon the telepathic ability itself but upon its loss and the consequent psychic blindness that accompanies that loss. In one sense, the ability to read minds might be construed as a metaphor for sight or insight, and the novel, with some surface changes, could well be a book about a man who is slowly losing his vision and railing against the loss. Silverberg has said that he wrote *Dying Inside* not as a science fiction novel, but as a mainstream book. On both the hardcover and paperback editions of the book there is no mention of the words "science fiction" except in a quotation from one review. Many reviewers, in fact, did not treat it as science fiction at all.

What is *Dying Inside*, then, if it is not hard-core science fiction? Of course, it is speculative writing about a man who is, ironically, terribly handicapped by his ability to do something that an overwhelming majority of the human race cannot do. More than that, however, it is the deep exploration of Selig's inner character that fascinates Silverberg. Science fiction explores, among other things, ideas and their consequences rather than character and its behavior patterns. It all too rarely shows human beings in action. Much more often it portrays the logical extrapolation of an idea to its ultimate conclusion. This literary style leaves its roster of Hamlets, Lears, or Ahabs slim indeed.

Dying Inside, however, does not adhere to this pattern. It does deal with ideas, as it certainly explores the consequences of the loss of the telepathic ability in one person. But of greater importance is the twisted, angst-filled, tormented character of David Selig himself, whose character would be much the same even if he had *never* possessed telepathic ability. Selig is the *nebbish*, the continually suffering Wandering Jew, the stranger in a strange land, alone and afraid in a world he never created. "The problem is that I feel isolated from other human beings," he says, despite the fact that he, virtually alone among the millions in New York City, possesses the ability to go straight to the core of meaning, through his telepathetic ability.

At age forty-one, David Selig is a latter-day J. Alfred Prufrock, a tribute Silverberg gives to Prufrock's creator T. S. Eliot on the first page of the novel. "Let us go then, you and I, when the morning is spread out against the sky," thinks Selig, changing only the time of day. Selig, like Prufrock, is "etherized upon a table," his telepathic sense gradually becoming permanently anesthetized. Selig supports himself by writing term papers for students at Columbia, his telepathic ability enabling him to tune in on both the student and the professor and thus produce term papers to fit both at $3.50 a page. He guarantees a B+ or better or will waive his fee. However, suddenly his perceptive, intuitive ability begins to fade.

Once Selig's predicament has been made clear, the remainder of the novel gradually explains how Selig came to be the way he is. Again, it is not the telepathic receiving ability itself that is important; rather, it is the sensitive depiction of psychic blindness or grayness that Silverberg is concerned with. Told in a series of flashback episodes with long sequences of Joycean stream of consciousness and entire chapters consisting of extended interior monologue, the novel traces Selig's relationships with his parents, his adopted sister, his various lovers, and, finally, with Nyquist, the only other telepath he has known. But Selig even has difficulty relating to Nyquist, who seems to come to terms with his ability. Nyquist sees only Selig's anguish, his loneliness, his alienation. For his part, Selig envies Nyquist's balanced, rhythmic, unobsessive life and wonders where he hides his anguish, his loneliness, his sense of alientation, his fear, his insecurity. Selig, in other words, projects that quality on to Nyquist that he unconsciously wants for himself, maturity; but he is concerned only with pain. Selig cannot see that Nyquist, in his own way, is abusing his gift by not examining it, by simply accepting it rather than investigating it and attempting to share it with others. Nyquist in spite of his apparently unobsessive life, is essentially selfish.

However, one of the essential clues to the novel's construction and derivation occurs in the Nyquist chapter. Nyquist picks a quotation from Joyce's great short story "The Dead" from Selig's mind: "His soul swooned slowly as he heard the snow falling faintly through the universe and faintly falling, like the descent of their last end, upon all the living and the dead." *Dying Inside*, then, is a kind of redaction of the great Joycean short story. While there may be little hope for Gabriel Conroy who must live forever in the vital shadow of a dead man, his wife's first lover, there is some hope for Selig. His "Seligness" must die; but in dying inside, he will be reborn to the human race.

The last paragraphs of the novel state this theme of rebirth quite clearly, and show its obvious derivations from "The Dead." A snowstorm has been settling over New York City, and Selig, almost for the first time in his life, has come to loving terms with his sister.

> It's very quiet now.
> The world is white outside and gray within. I accept that. I think life will be more peaceful. Silence will be my mother tongue. There will be discoveries and revelations, but no upheavals. Perhaps some color will come back into the world for me, later on. Perhaps.
> Living, we fret. Dying, we live. I'll keep that in mind. I'll be of good cheer . . . Until I die again, hello, hello, hello, hello.

Life. Death. Rebirth. These themes crowd the pages of *Dying Inside*. It is, in this sense, a *Bildungsroman*, a novel of growth, development, rejection, and maturity, belonging to the same genre as Joyce's *A Portrait of the Artist as a Young Man* or D. H. Lawrence's *Sons and Lovers*. It is a novel of internal passion, of character, of a human being in conflict with himself, not merely a traditional science fiction extrapolative idea-oriented tale.

Chapter Four of *Dying Inside* consists for the most part of a term paper on the novels of Kafka written by Selig for a brawny halfback. (Parenthetically, the reader suspects that it is a term paper that Silverberg himself wrote when he was an undergraduate at Columbia.) While Kafka was a writer who was also concerned with the problems of angst and alienation, the paper itself is rendered more important by the critical theses Selig (and hence Silverberg) uses to approach Kafka's novels: Kenneth Burke's three-part structure of tragic rhythm, "purpose, passion, perception."

Dying Inside is not a tragedy in the classic sense of the word. Its griefs are those of an individual and do not, in Faulkner's words, "grieve on immortal bones." Selig's loss affects only Selig, not all humanity. Nonetheless, *Dying Inside* achieves at least some element of larger scope, even of universality, when we realize that the passion of an individual alienated from his society can be equated with the feelings of weakness, terror, anxiety, or helplessness we undergo in our increasingly technological, dehumanized society. *Dying Inside*, is a low-key tragedy containing its own hope of redemption in rebirth promised on the last page. By extension, therefore, the promise of discoveries and revelation exists not only for Selig but for the reader as well.

Readers interested in pursuing some of the background materials in Silverberg's life that helped to shape the author's artistic vision and led him to write *Dying Inside* would do well to read the autobiographical chapter that Silverberg contributed to *Hell's Cartographers*, edited by Brian Aldiss and Harry Harrison. Silverberg's background reading in mainstream fiction, poetry, philosophy, and psychology as detailed there stood him in good stead in creating Selig's character. That reading list, somewhat selected and modified, can be found in Chapter Nineteen of *Dying Inside*. Silverberg's awareness of mainstream literature and contemporary society is celebrated in this, his most complex work.

Echoes of James Joyce ring throughout *Dying Inside*. In a certain sense, it is Silverberg's equivalent of Joyce's *A Portrait of the Artist as Young Man*. In other words, it is a very fine, sensitive novel, and to find comparisons for it, we must look to mainstream rather than science fiction literature. The gap between the two is being bridged by books such as *Dying Inside*.

Willis E. McNelly

Sources for Further Study

Reviews:

Analog. CXII, September, 1973, pp. 160-161.

Library Journal. CXCVIII, January 15, 1973, p. 183.

Magazine of Fantasy and Science Fiction. XLV, July, 1973, pp. 70-71.

Observer. March 17, 1974, p. 37.

Times Literary Supplement. March 15, 1974, p. 269.

E PLURIBUS UNICORN

Author: Theodore Sturgeon (1918-   )
First book publication: 1953
Type of work: Short stories

Thirteen stories, with an introduction by Groff Conklin, representing a seminal period in the development of one of science fiction's major authors

Theodore Sturgeon has always been among the most stylistically sensitive of science fiction writers, and the chief value of this collection is the way it displays the author's various stylistic and thematic concerns. Published originally between 1947 and 1953, these stories represent an important period of experimentation in the author's development, following his successes in the early 1940's with more traditional science fiction and horror stories and preceding his first major success as a "serious" writer with *More Than Human* in 1953. Many of the stories in *E Pluribus Unicorn* prefigure his later, more controversial treatments of love and sexuality, but only three of the stories ("The Sex Opposite," "A Saucer of Loneliness," and "The World Well Lost") involve traditional science fiction themes such as space travel and alien beings. The other stories cover a range of genres and first appeared in pulp magazines as diverse as *Weird Tales*, *Dime Detective*, and *Zane Grey's Western*. Two of the stories ("Die, Maestro, Die" and "Scars") contain no science fiction or fantasy elements at all. Thus, while the collection can hardly be considered representative of Sturgeon's science fiction, it serves as a fine introduction to the author's peculiar world of brutality and innocence, grotesquerie and beauty, love and sexuality. It is startling to realize that stories such as these once appeared in American pulp magazines.

Sturgeon's reputation rests largely on his ability to handle character, and *E Pluribus Unicorn* is filled with striking characters whose inner lives differ radically from their public façades. Indeed, the gradual revelation of the "inner self" of a character is almost a Sturgeon formula. His most familiar character type, who appears in various guises in "The World Well Lost," "Scars," "A Saucer of Loneliness," and "Die, Maestro, Die," is the vulnerable and sensitive lover trapped inside a rough or deformed exterior: the angel inside the beast. In "The World Well Lost," an oversized brute of a spaceship crewman is revealed as a poetry-loving homosexual secretly in love with his bigoted, *macho* captain. An aging cowboy in "Scars" tells his youthful companion of an experience years earlier, when he nursed an injured widow back to health on her farm, revealing an unexpected tenderness which he could not consummate in love because of a castrating bullet wound he had received as a young man. "A Saucer of Loneliness" reverses this pattern: the narrator appears sensitive and caring throughout the story, but in the end reveals himself as physically deformed (he has a clubfoot) and inarticulate in the presence of others. And in "Die, Maestro, Die," the narrator is a deformed, obsessive murderer whose inability to deal with kindness and whose unrequited love for a woman are revealed as the hidden motivations behind his grotesque crimes.

In other stories, a character's inner life may be grotesque but his appearance normal. "Fluffy" concerns a popular socialite who, with the guidance of a talkative cat, comes to recognize that he, like the cat, is a parasite who lives off the good graces of others and repays them with disdain. "Bianca's Hands" (which won first place in a British *Argosy* short story contest in 1947) concerns an attractive young man eventually destroyed by his obsessive love for the beautiful hands of an otherwise grotesque idiot girl. "The Silken-Swift" reverses the old folk-belief that unicorns are obedient only to virgins: in this story the unicorn rejects the beautiful virgin because of her inner cruelty and chooses instead a rape victim who is pure in heart, but not a virgin. In the two most straightforward horror stories in the book, the grotesque inner life is directly symbolized in images suggestive of the unconscious mind: a hideous dwarf-twin living inside the chest of a prisoner in "Cell-mate," and a monstrous living teddy bear whose influence over a young boy haunts the boy the rest of his adult life in "The Professor's Teddy Bear."

As the inner lives of many of these characters suggest, the aspect of behavior that most interests Sturgeon is love and sexuality. Of the thirteen stories in *E Pluribus Unicorn*, nine either directly concern varieties of love or are constructed around actions centrally motivated by love. "Love," of course, is a complex subject to explore in any depth in a short story, and it might be more accurate to say that Sturgeon is concerned with romance and sexuality. While his stories seldom depict sustained, fulfilling love relationships, they often concern the process of falling in love and the romantic convention of the hopelessly unattainable lover. Sturgeon's most direct treatment of the impossibility of a perfect romance is "It Wasn't Syzygy" (originally published in *Weird Tales* in 1948 as "The Deadly Ratio"). "Syzygy" is a term biologists use to describe a kind of symbiotic union in which the participants retain their own identities but become one. Though the concept is properly applied only to lower forms of life, Sturgeon seized upon it in several of his stories as a metaphor for the kind of perfect union that is impossible among human lovers. In "It Wasn't Syzygy," the narrator finds what appears to be his perfect love — a woman who shares all his interests, who experiences his same feelings, who thinks in the same patterns. A disembodied, ghostlike head emerges from nowhere to explain to the narrator that if the relationship is not genuine syzygy, it will come to an unhappy end. The relationship does in fact end when the girl finds another man, not nearly as "like" her as the narrator but who, she says, can "take" from her as well as give, and who can offer her new experiences. The head reappears to explain that most humans are not real at all, but rather materializations of the dreams, fears, and ideals of the few "real" people. The narrator and the girl were projections of each other's fantasy lovers; when the girl found a less perfect "real" lover, she gravitated to

him. In a not-too-surprising twist ending, the ghost explains that the girl is real
and the narrator a mere fantasy image. The narrator refuses to give up his
reality, and the ghost goes on to reveal his identity as the narrator, much older,
returned to warn his younger self about the true nature of things. Although the
gradual revelation of the story's underlying situation gives the story the
appearance of an ingenious but whimsical fantasy, Sturgeon's insights about
the impossibility of attaining an idealized love object are quite solid.

Syzygy recurs in "The Sex Opposite," which begins with the apparent
gruesome murder of a pair of Siamese twins torn apart at the chest. The
pathologist-protagonist and his reporter girl friend find that these twins were in
fact members of a race of "parthenogenetic females" secretly coexisting with
man on earth, and that they were engaged in syzygy — a reproductive act
involving total physical and spiritual union — at the time of the murder. When
another member of this race appears separately to the two humans, each sees in
the creature a vision of their ideal love; the pathologist sees a girl and the
reporter a man. The creature then confronts them together and leads them to
see qualities in each other that, though far short of the perfect match represented by syzygy, are sufficient for human love. In the end, the creature erases
all memory of the incident from the minds of the two friends, and they find
themselves unaccountably falling in love.

Unattainability of the love object is a theme that is central to Sturgeon's
view of human relations. In "The World Well Lost," a pair of aliens from a
technologically advanced planet which has spurned commerce with Earth suddenly appear on Earth and enchant the world with their obvious devotion to
each other. Dubbed "loverbirds" by the popular media, they are in fact criminals on their home planet, and are eventually extradited by Earth authorities in
return for an implicit promise of profitable trade agreements. The ship that
returns them is manned by a crude, leering captain and a giant, inarticulate
crewman. When the crewman discovers the aliens are telepathic, he plans to
kill them for fear they know and will reveal his great personal secret — that he
is homosexually in love with the captain. But the aliens reveal to him that
they, too, are homosexual lovers, and that this was in fact the crime for which
they are being extradited. Instead of killing them, the crewman sets them free
in a lifeboat, and the captain later approves this action. " 'Anything I can't
stand, it's a fruit,' " he says. Thus the story ends on a note of irony: the
homosexual crewman is given strength by finding that he is not alone in his
predicament, while at the same time the captain's hatred of homosexuals
makes him a more unattainable love-object than ever.

If homosexuals can take heart from the fact that there are others in the
universe who suffer more than they, so can the chronically lonely. This is the
theme of what is probably the best-known story in *E Pluribus Unicorn*, "A
Saucer of Loneliness." A girl is struck on the head by a tiny flying saucer and
inadvertently reveals that the saucer "spoke" to her. Government agencies and

the media, anxious to discover some great technological secret, hound her for years to reveal the message of the saucer, but she refuses, claiming it is a personal message. Her life made nearly unbearable by her notoriety, she undertakes a desperate act of communication: throwing messages in bottles into the sea (the FBI tries to collect all the bottles). Despairing, the girl attempts suicide, but is saved by a man who had found one of her bottles, and who realizes that the message inside, a simple acknowledgment of universal loneliness, was the message from the saucer. As in "The Sex Opposite," the lovers are brought together by an alien life form that enables them to see their common problem and to offer each other support. "A Saucer of Loneliness" may be the most sustained and controlled piece of writing in the collection, but there occurs at the end of the story a somewhat jarring disjuncture between the voice of the narrator and his voice as a character when he speaks to the girl, a shift from a poetic clarity of thought to an almost pathetic inarticulateness. No doubt this is deliberate, another example of the contrast between private and public selves, but it is also an example of the way Sturgeon consistently romanticizes his characters by exaggerating their surface defects to achieve the revelation he seeks. In "The Silken-Swift," which is written in the form of a medieval folk or fairy tale, this technique results in a real narrative problem. The Cinderella figure, Barbara, cannot be portrayed as homely within the conventions of the form; thus Sturgeon initially describes her beauty as so "contained" none can see it — until the appropriate moment when it magically floods outward at the touch of the unicorn. Even coming from a writer as adept at evoking visual images as Sturgeon, this scene is almost impossible to visualize, even though as metaphor it expresses well the recurring theme of nearly all Sturgeon's love stories: given the right moment and the right person, the spiritual beauty in any human being can be made visible (though in "The Silken-Swift" the fact that Barbara's Prince Charming turns out to be the man who had raped her earlier is also problematical).

Sturgeon's style in these stories may often be too calculated (whole paragraphs are sometimes repeated for evocative effect), his characters sometimes overdrawn and sentimentalized, his use of science makeshift, his dialogue somewhat precious — but many of the stories have an undeniable power. At a time when other science fiction writers seemed overly concerned with galactic empires and prophecies of atomic doom, Sturgeon was almost alone in his overriding concern with narrative technique and stylistic experimentation, and many of the themes he treats openly and with compassion in *E Pluribus Unicorn* did not find their way into the mainstream of science fiction for another twenty to thirty years. For that reason if for no other, the work of Theodore Sturgeon as represented in this collection marks an important step in the maturation of the genre.

Gary K. Wolfe

Sources for Further Study

Criticism:

The Encyclopedia of Science Fiction and Fantasy. Compiled by Donald H. Tuck. Chicago: Advent Publishers, Inc., 1978, pp. 413-414. Tuck gives a general review of Sturgeon's life and works, including a full bibliography of the author's publications.

Kostolefsky, Joseph. "Science, Yes — Fiction, Maybe," in *Antioch Review.* XIII (June, 1953), pp. 236-240. Although a diatribe against science fiction literature generally, this article gives credit to Sturgeon as one of the best in the field, and one whose works stand up against non-science fiction authors.

Wolheim, Donald. *The Universe Makers: Science Fiction Today.* New York: Harper & Row, 1971, pp. 63-65. Wolheim discusses Sturgeon's fiction generally, with particular emphasis on "The Universe Makers."

Reviews:

Analog. LIII, August, 1954, pp. 152-153.

Fantastic Universe Science Fiction. I, May, 1954, pp. 157-158.

Future Science Fiction. V, June, 1954, pp. 88-89.

Galaxy. VIII, April, 1954, p. 118 and XIV, May, 1957, p. 124.

Magazine of Fantasy and Science Fiction. VI, February, 1954, p. 94.

New York Times Book Review. November 29, 1953, p. 53.

Satellite Science Fiction. I, April, 1957, pp. 125-126.

THE EARLY HAINISH NOVELS

Author: Ursula K. Le Guin (1929-   )
First book publications: Rocannon's World (1966); *Planet of Exile* (1966); *City of Illusions* (1967)
Type of work: Novels
Time: An undefined far future
Locale: A distant galaxy

The first three of a series of novels of increasingly complex stylistic and philosophical scope, belonging to a consistent "future history"

The "future history" has long been a popular science fiction format, ranging from the original stories by Robert A. Heinlein, through such works as James Blish's *Cities in Flight* tetralogy, Frank Herbert's *Dune* trilogy, and Poul Anderson's series on the Polesotechnic League and the Terran Empire, to Cordwainer Smith's unfinished history of "The Instrumentality of All Mankind." Ursula K. Le Guin has created one of the most imaginative, literate, and philosophically profound future histories in all science fiction with her slowly emerging vision of a vast, loosely knit, historically independent confederation of worlds (connected by slower-than-light-speed travel and instantaneous communication), whose varied "human" stock was seeded eons ago by the most ancient race, the Hainish (like all the other worlds of her stories, Earth is one of the Hainish planted colonies — a neat stab at the Terran ethnocentrism of much science fiction).

So far, Le Guin's future history covers between three and four thousand years and exactly six novels (plus a few short stories). It is interesting to note that, while the first four novels are set in the middle and later years of that history, the most recent ones investigate its beginning. Le Guin is a true explorer, one who both expands and fills in her fictional maps as she writes. Only through writing her stories has she discovered what happened at various times in the "Hainish Universe." Thus, although the Ansible, an instantaneous interstellar communications device, figures in all the novels, it is not until *The Dispossessed* (1974) that she, or we, learn how it was made possible. The sense that we are sharing in Le Guin's explorations of an ever expanding "secondary universe" is one of the great charms of the Hainish novels.

The Dispossessed, then, is set prior to the formation of The League of All Worlds, the first of two kinds of interstellar political federations Le Guin posits for her future history. *The Word for World Is Forest* (1972) is set during the first years of interstellar exploration by the three major races, the Hainish, the Cetians and the Terrans; during its action the Ansible's invention makes possible the foundation of the League. *Rocannon's World* covers League Years 250-350. War among some of the worlds interferes with attempts to unite all mankind against a common enemy, believed to be coming either from the furthest reaches of the galaxy or even another galaxy. Against this background, the League scientist Rocannon seeks offworld enemies among the High Intelligence Life Forms ("hilfs") of Formalhaut II and learns an easily taught telepathic technique which will subsequently be adopted by all members of the League. *Planet of Exile*, set in the League Year 1405, concerns an isolated Terran colony's discovery that its survival depends upon its integration with Werel's hilfs. *City of Illusions* is set some seven hundred years later on an Earth conquered by the Shing, who have divided the Hainish peoples with their power of "mind-lying." In *The Left Hand of Darkness* (1969), set in the Ekumenical Years 1420-1497, the Shing have been defeated some centuries back by the highly developed Psi-technology of the Werelians, the descendants of the mixed peoples of *Planet of Exile*. The Ekumen is less a body politic than "a body mystic," an almost anarchist organization which "considers beginnings to be extremely important. Beginnings and means."

Beginnings are important in art, too. Le Guin's career as a science fiction writer began with her early explorations of the expanding Hainish Universe. *Rocannon's World* and *Planet of Exile*, her first two novels, are self-confessed apprentice works which wholly accept the conventions of the genre. *City of Illusions* is a more complex novel which reveals how much she learned from writing the previous two books, yet it only hints at the immense scope and complexity of the novels to follow.

Although *Rocannon's World* is essentially a science fantasy quest tale, Le Guin's creation of a believable and complex preindustrial heroic culture and of a mood of legend and myth is already superior to most such stories. She uses various forms of documentation — the *"Abridged Handy Pocket Guide to Intelligent Life Forms,"* for example, which describes the three known species on Formalhaut II and the "feudal-heroic" culture of the Angyar, prepares us to accept behavior like that in the Northern Epics — to create a fictional situation where we cannot "tell fact from legend, truth from truth." Right from the beginning, then, she assumes a rationale for the legendary quest which is her basic narrative.

There are in fact two quests in *Rocannon's World* which stand in ironic relation to each other. In the "Prologue," Semley, an Angyar lady, seeks an ancient jewel of her clan, "the Eye of the Sea," but her quest ends in tragedy because she does not realize that her journey of "only one long night" actually takes fifteen years. She returns with the jewel to discover her husband long dead and her daughter a grown woman; she goes mad in the face of such terrible "magic." But she was given the jewel by Rocannon, a League "hilfer," on another world, and he eventually brings a team of scientists to her world where he befriends her grandson Mogien. His team and ship destroyed by a bomb, his conscious quest is to find his enemy's starship base in the southern hemisphere of Formalhaut II, but through the gains and losses he records in his journey he becomes part of this world and its legends and finds a home, the end of his unconscious quest.

In a manner analogous to *The Lord of the Rings*, a fellowship of Angyar, Fiia, and Rocannon travel across the world, winning through various dangers to the enemy base. Rocannon is "sealed by his shed blood to this world," and by the terrible loss of his close friend Mogien, whose death somehow pays for the knowledge of "mind speech" Rocannon needs to defeat his enemy. Despite this loss, Rocannon has grown to love Formalhaut II and its people, and, having completed his mission, he chooses to remain and marry a high-born lady. His quest gains him love and a home, and he finds fulfillment where Semley finds only despair and loss.

Having used a version of the traditional quest in her first novel, Le Guin creates a moving version of the science fiction "societal quest" in her second, *Planet of Exile*. After living in isolation from the rest of the universe on Werel for ten of its years (six hundred Earth years), the "farborn" colony is slowly dying out. Similarly, the Askatevar, one of the hilf tribes of the planet, can no longer survive by following the old ways. Survival for both, in the face of the approaching sixty-year winter and the new threat of an organized hoard of Gaal, an enemy tribe from the north, depends upon their joining forces. The "forbidden" love of Agat, the "farborn" leader, and Rolery, a young woman of the Askatevar, enacts in miniature the eventual joining of the two peoples. As Winter descends and the two groups fight off the Gaal, the "farborns" come to realize that, after six hundred years, they have adapted to Werel's ecology and that interbreeding is now possible. Agat recognizes that "he was no exile here" and in that recognition the possibility that both communities can merge and produce something new is implied. As *City of Illusions* demonstrates, their success is much greater than any of the original people could expect.

That book also explores a familiar science fiction theme, the conventionally paranoid fantasy of the psychic superman who, beginning in ignorance, eventually discovers his true identity and powers. But it is a far more complex novel than most others of this type, including Le Guin's first two books. *City of Illusions* is set on an Earth conquered by the Shing and isolated from the rest of the known universe by its new masters. The "mind-razed" protagonist, whose "strange eyes," "like a cat," reveal his offworld origin, is discovered at the edge of a "Clearing" by Parth, a young woman of Zove's House, a hidden commune which has tried to preserve knowledge from before the conquest twelve hundred years earlier. These people call him Falk and bring him back to mental adulthood.

Six years later, Falk discovers he must leave the safety of their "Clearing" and seek in the Shing city of Es Toch the knowledge of who he is and where he comes from. His quest for "the Place of the Lie" takes him across an Earth divided into isolated social groups distrustful of each other; this distrust is the Shing's major "gift" to humankind. On his journey he encounters many dangerous people, but he also meets two powerful figures who offer him some mysterious and paradoxical aid. The first one is the Listener, an old "Thurro-dowist," who tells him some facts about the Shing, calls him a "poor trusting fool" and gives him some hints about the nature of his quest: "Maybe you have to go back home." Captured by a primitive tribe, he is helped to escape by Estrel, a Shing agent who seduces him with her aid, lies, and sexuality. Yet she serves her primary purpose for she brings him safely to Es Toch. *En route* they meet the mysterious and awesome Prince of the Kansas enclave. A man of power like the Listener, he sees in Falk what Falk himself cannot see. The Prince plays Falk into his "patterning-frame," a Hainish game which is "a fortune-teller, a computer, an implement of mystical discipline, a toy," and divines who Falk really is, though Falk is not yet ready to hear his enigmatic oracles.

In Es Toch, the Shing trap Falk, subject him to a series of psychological manipulations, and then offer him his old self back, but at the cost of losing the new one with all his knowledge of who the Shing may be. Although he was no real choice, Falk can only hope they are wrong, and he attempts to outwit them by using the "Old Canon," the *Tao-te-ching*, to maintain some connection between his Falk self and his new self, who turns out to be Ramarren, a powerful ESPer from Werel, product of the culture developed by the descendants of the two peoples of Planet of Exile. Ramarren's mental discipline allows him to perceive the Shing's ability to mind-lie. The words of the "Old Canon" finally reunite him with his Falk self, and, eventually integrating the two personalities, he outwits the Shing and steals a starship to take him and a Shing back to his planet to tell their various stories of the changes that have occurred since Werel lost contact with the League of All Worlds. For Falk-Ramarren has learned that "there's always more than one way towards the truth."

Although Le Guin develops the complex vision much further in the later novels, she writes with a complexity unusual in conventional science fiction from the beginning. In addition to the continuous yet differentiated time/space history, the Hainish novels also are connected by a web of linguistic, imagistic, and thematic patterns. Philosophically, the images and ideals of Taoism, first mentioned specifically in *City of Illusions*, especially the Yin/Yang symbol in all its allusive glory, are of central importance. Again and again, good emerges from ambiguous darkness, evil from blinding light. As well, particular images natural to the cultural and ecological contexts of her imagined worlds fill out the warp and woof of each novel. In *Rocannon's World*, the specific image is the "Eye of the Sea," which drives Semley to her foolish act in the Prologue and accompanies Rocannon throughout his adventures until he signifies his recognition that he has found a home by giving the jewel to the Lady Ganye who, as "his widow, tall and fair-haired, wearing a great blue jewel set in gold at her throat," greets the men from the next starship to come seeking him.

The light-dark imagery is more pervasive and complex. A dance of light and shadows, like the Fiia dance Rocannon observes, is the proper image for their interplay in all Le Guin's work: both the light and the dark are necessary if any pattern is to emerge from chaos. Rocannon enters "the dark place" to gain the knowledge of "mind-hearing," yet the explosion destroying the enemy base is marked by "not the light but the darkness, the darkness that blinded his mind." *Planet of Exile*'s first chapter, "A Handful of Darkness," refers to Agat's dark hand against Rolery's white one, a conjunction suggestive of the alliance to come. While this imagery appears throughout the novel, it is often tied to the customs of the Askatevar or the coming of the five thousand day Winter, local images of considerable power.

"In . . . darkness . . . a mute spirit woke. Wholly involved in chaos, he knew no pattern." Thus begins Falk's book-length search for the correct pattern, one made up of light and darkness in balance as all good patterns must be. Naturally enough, in a novel of lie and paradox, light and dark seldom carry conventional meanings. Falk begins and ends in darkness, yet the two darknesses are opposed: the first a mental chaos, the last an important part of the whole complex pattern he has sought to comprehend. As the images gather, we begin to see the pattern, and the play of paradox and illusion within it. The old Listener's warning about "the awful darkness of the bright lights of Es Toch" presents one of the central paradoxes Falk must resolve if he is to survive, and it is to "the word spoken in darkness with none to hear at the beginning, the first page of time," that he turns in his attempt to outmaneuver the Shing. The major local image, that of the "patterning-frame," also serves the paradoxical development of the story. Although actual patterning-frames appear only twice, references to Falk as a stone upon a frame appear throughout. They all lead inevitably to the novel's final paragraph, when, as had happened to his stone on the frames, Falk-Ramarren's starship, "frame and pattern shattered, . . . broke free of time and took them out across the darkness."

The light/dark imagery and the philosophical overtones of *Tao* will manifest themselves in the later Hainish novels as well, but it is clear that with her first three science fiction novels Le Guin had already created an *oeuvre* whose power and significance goes beyond that of much conventional science fiction. *Rocannon's World*, *Planet of Exile*, and *City of Illusions* each marks an advance in Le Guin's control of her materials and exploration of the vast future history she had discovered, and they prepare us for the truly major works to follow. But if they are not really in the same class as the later works, (except perhaps for *City of Illusions*, a novel of some sophistication in its characterization and its playing with conventions) they remain highly readable, entertaining genre works which both take the genre seriously and push its boundaries a bit wider. They can be enjoyed both for what they unpretentiously are and for the greater works they preface.

Douglas Barbour

Sources for Further Study

Criticism:

Barbour, Douglas. "Wholeness and Balance in the Hainish Novels of Ursula K. Le Guin," in *Science Fiction Studies*. I (Spring, 1974), pp. 164-173. Discusses the cosmic order of the series.

Slusser, George E. *The Farthest Shores of Ursula K. Le Guin*. San Bernardino, Calif.: Borgo, 1976, pp. 5-16. These early Le Guin novels lay the foundation of all her later works.

Reviews:

Analog. LXXX, November, 1967, p. 166.

Luna Monthly. XXX, November, 1971, p. 32 and XL, September 1972, p. 30.

Magazine of Fantasy and Science Fiction. XXXI, December, 1966, p. 33.

National Review. XXIII, January 12, 1971, pp. 39-41.

New Worlds. CLV, August, 1966, p. 147.

Renaissance. III, Summer, 1971, p. 17.

Worlds of If. XX, January-February, 1971, p. 125.

EARTH ABIDES

Author: George R. Stewart (1895-   )
First book publication: 1949
Type of work: Novel
Time: The present or the very near future
Locale: In and around Berkeley, California

In the aftermath of a catastrophe that has wiped out virtually the entire population of the United States, a small group of survivors face the challenges of their terrifying situation

> *Principal characters:*
> ISHERWOOD WILLIAMS, a graduate student of ecology who becomes the unofficial leader of a small group of survivors
> EM, a black woman who eventually becomes Williams' wife
> JOEY, their son
> EZRA AND GEORGE, two survivors
> CHARLIE, the intruder into the community

Few so-called "mainstream" writers have been able to master sufficiently the specialized approach required by the science fiction genre to enter the field with the same aplomb as such longtime science fiction writers as Isaac Asimov or Frank Herbert. Like all arts and crafts, science fiction writing has its own rules, standards, and forms. Inability or unwillingness to master these rules had led some mainstream writers to produce novels which are neither good mainstream work nor good science fiction. However, one notable exception to this generality is George R. Stewart, whose *Earth Abides* has been recognized both in and out of specialized science fiction circles as a superior novel by almost any standards.

Earth Abides is the story of Isherwood Williams and the few other survivors of the mutated virus which has virtually wiped out the entire population of the United States. In one sense, it fits the category of the "end of the world" story, a theme that has gripped the imaginations of such diverse writers as H. G. Wells and Olaf Stapledon. Like his distinguished predecessors, Stewart retains something of the philosophical flavor of both Wells and Stapledon, and the novel might also fit into a subclass that Brian Aldiss called the "cozy catastrophe." Williams survives almost by accident, meets and "marries" a black woman, and together with a handful of other disparate characters, attempts to replenish the earth. Ish, as Williams is called throughout the novel, is an unlikely hero. He is a graduate student, a teacher, a fugitive from the ivory tower who knows nothing of survival techniques. He is a very bookish Moses, attempting to lead The Tribe, as the group calls itself, back to a modicum of civilization.

Stewart very carefully traces Ish's slow progress in realizing the extent of the catastrophe. Isolated from the world while he recovers from a rattlesnake bite, an accident which ironically may have preserved his life, Ish gradually perceives the new reality: stop lights continue to operate; neon signs flash; electric gas pumps still function, but human life has died. The mechanical world man has created still works smoothly, but the operators are all dead. Ish comes to understand that if he can no longer be a participant in an operative society, he can be a spectator trained to observe what was happening. Thus the ensuing events of the book are largely those seen through Ish's eyes. This vision is not necessarily limited, for Stewart remains the omniscient narrator, and provides many inter-chapters or other explanatory material in long passages printed in italics. But Ish remains the central character, and all of the remaining survivors, except for Em, his wife, remain peripheral to his vision. For her part, Em, at first a secondary character, gradually becomes more and more important, eventually assuming the role of the archetypal Mother for which her name is merely the initial letter. Figuratively, she Mothers the entire emerging tribal society.

As years pass, the Tribe, despite the continued urging of both Ish and Em, lapses into cozy comfort, living off the plentiful supplies left in the supermarkets. Their water, sewage, and electricity continue unhampered for years because of the automatic mechanisms left by the builders. But as these too eventually fail, they do not at first return to the agricultural stage. They apathetically await extinction. However, Ish, with a foresight of which he was unaware on the conscious level, reinvents the bow and arrow. From a child's toy, the bow becomes the instrument whereby the survivors' great-grandchildren are transformed into new Native Americans. At the end of the novel as Ish dies, almost in sight of the Promised Land, the renascent Indians inherit the earth.

Thus far, *Earth Abides* can be read as simply one more apocalyptic vision: technological America dies and Indian tribal life is reborn. However, to be savored for the richness of its philosophical and ironic detail, *Earth Abides* should be read with Theodore Kroeber's *Ishi in Two Worlds* (1961) in mind. *Ishi in Two Worlds* is the biography of the last wild Indian in North America and remains one of the most moving, evocative books of the last twenty years. While it was published a few years after *Earth Abides* originally appeared, it provides for the reader much information that Stewart, an amateur historian of California history, was forced to research. Ish's story is almost as moving as Ishi's. Like Ish, the reader almost instinctively cannot understand the cultural inertia of The Tribe in its early years, no more than he can grasp the violence inflicted upon Ishi's tribe over a hundred years ago which resulted in its extinction.

Yet the skeleton provided by the mythos of the Ishi story is only a quiet, underlying theme in Stewart's hands, providing almost a susurrus for imaginative extrapolation. More central to Stewart is the archetypal concept of death and rebirth which culminates in the triumphant resurrection at the end of the novel. In one sense, *Earth Abides* is both a Genesis and an Exodus, and Ish himself resembles both Moses and Jeremiah. His admonitions are unheeded — as were those of his Biblical prototypes — and he virtually despairs of bringing his people to the promised land of a reborn ethical culture. Even the successive plagues of ants, rats, grasshoppers, and so on which the newly unbalanced ecology inflicts on Ish and The Tribe curiously resemble the plagues in Egypt. No one-to-one correspondence exists, of course, but it is the suggestion, the subliminal evocation, which lends a psychological or philosophical depth to the novel.

Ish, like Moses, struggles against the temptation to become a god, yet the exigencies of his and The Tribe's situation force him to become a guru or shaman whose words are often unheeded. In only one instance does he exert enough authority to force a decision upon The Tribe. This situation occurs with the appearance of the "outsider" Charlie and the problems which result. Charlie has accompanied some of the second generation members of The Tribe on their return from a long expedition throughout the country seeking other survivors. Charlie is described by Stewart in decidedly uncomplimentary terms. He is powerful, with a fat, thick-featured face, and fat pig's eyes; he wears a dirty, greasy anachronistic business suit. But he has a charismatic personality that makes him an immediate favorite of the children of The Tribe. Ish sees in him a potential rival for leadership, but even more, a man with a lurking suggestion of evil. Ish thinks "Maybe I'm only thrown off because I'm like any small tribesman, and fear the horrible stranger with his new ways and his new gods to fight against mine."

Soon however, Ezra, another of the senior survivors, discovers that the intruder is, in Ezra's words, ". . . rotten inside as a ten day fish. Diseases, Cupid's diseases, I mean. Hell, he's got all of them there are!" What makes the problem acute is that Charlie is attracted to Evie, the half-witted adolescent girl who has been regarded as taboo by all of the younger male members of The Tribe. Thus Ish, Ezra, and Em are faced with an existential problem: they have, in their minds, the opportunity of eradicating venereal disease forever and maintaining the "purity" of The Tribe simply by doing away with Charlie. The options open to them are the alternatives of banishment or death. At first, Ish believes that banishment would suffice. In his mind, choosing the evil of execution would not be justified by the desirable end of eliminating a disease. One evil cannot eradicate another evil. Only when Em, in her role as the Great Mother, asks, "Can we take that responsibility [of permitting venereal disease to exist] now? There are all the children," does Ish face the problem squarely. He thinks, "She does not have a philosophy. She mentions the children and makes it a special case. Yet there is something deeper even than a philosophy in her; she is the mother; she thinks close to all the basic things in life."

Thus Ish reluctantly votes for Charlie's death, not as retribution but as prevention. Ironically, the effort of The Tribe to eliminate disease has been only apparent, for it soon develops that Charlie, the interloper, the intruder in the dust, has also brought with him the germs of typhoid fever. An epidemic shatters the twenty-one-year Edenic idyll of The Tribe and many members perish, including Ish and Em's own son, Joey. The question of ends and means remains unsolved, although with Charlie's hanging and the loss of Eden, The Tribe has been subtly transformed into the State whose first act was to bring Death. But with one more irony, the childishness or adolescence of The Tribe has been transformed into a growing, self-aware maturity, again through Death. However, now it is a death of the old order and a consequent rebirth of a new one. The Tribe now begins to plant, to engage in the primitive arts of agriculture rather than choosing the safe way of living out of supermarket supplies.

Ish's role as shaman of the community has been prefigured in the first pages of the novel through the totem of his hammer. In the minds of The Tribe, it gradually assumes a magical significance. The hammer is the bearer of *mana*, and Ish, almost unconsciously, carries it with him whenever he must make a major decision. In one of the short inter-chapters which are scattered through the book, the hammer is clearly identified as a symbol of the god of The Tribe. Even more significantly, when Ish sets it down or when it accidentally falls, it is "handle up" proud, erect, phallic in its strength. It is Ish's badge of office, and when as a very old man he leaves it in his house which is about to burn in a final apocalyptic but cleansing fire, his great-grandson Jack risks his life to save it. In the end, as Ish is dying, the young men badger Ish, now the old, dying god, the last American, into settling the problem of tribal succession by giving the hammer to one of them. Power has been transmitted as the youths acquiesce in Ish's choice. The inheritance of the hammer has been settled, and Ish dies on the bridge in sight of the promised land which has been reborn, Phoenix-like, from the ashes of civilization. His last sight is of the Twin Peaks of San Francisco, the "Twin Breasts" which remind him of Em and the Earth, the source of enduring life.

As noted earlier, the symbolism of names is of utmost importance throughout the novel. The name Ish means "man" in Hebrew. In addition the Hebrew word which may be transliterated *"ame"* in an older form or as *"immeh"* in a newer one means "mother." Ish, then, is the Man, and Em the Mother, the Adam and Eve of the new race, the parents of the new generations which shall inherit the Earth. If Ish, as a person, is unable to solve the problem of cultural shock *versus* cultural inertia which plagues the first survivors, he has nonetheless been able to bring life to the new community in a multitude of ways, most of them involving a return to the practices of the first native Americans into whom The Tribe gradually evolves. Em becomes, mystically, Demeter, Isis, Cybele — The Mother, and it is her decision made just prior to her death that unites The Tribe with the Others, a smaller group from across the Bay. Against some dissenting voices including Ish's, who remember Charlie and fear disease, Em speaks of life: "I have said it before. Life is not lived by denying life. Perhaps death will come, but that too we must face." Her courage and spirit resound in her eulogy: "Oh, Mother of Nations! Her sons shall praise, and her daughters shall call her blessed!"

Earth Abides succeeds as a novel, even in spite of its apparently pessimistic vision, because of its richness of texture, its philosophical insights, and the gentle strength of its irony. It is a book to be savored for its essential optimism. It is a novel of death and destruction, to be sure, but it is also a novel of resurrection and timeless hope. Men come and go, but Earth abides.

Willis E. McNelly

Sources for Further Study

Reviews:

Analog. XLVI, October, 1950, pp. 129-130.

Authentic Science Fiction. XXXVI, August, 1953, p. 137.

Christian Science Monitor. November, 15, 1949, p. 14.

Futures. III, September, 1971, pp. 317-318.

New York Herald Tribune Weekly Book Review. October 30, 1949, p. 18.

New York Times. October 23, 1949, p. 4.

Saturday Review. XXXII, November 26, 1949, p. 14.

Super Science Stories. VI, January, 1950, pp. 96-97.

THE EARTHSEA TRILOGY

Author: Ursula K. Le Guin (1929-   )
First book publications: A Wizard of Earthsea (1968); *The Tombs of Atuan* (1971); *The Farthest Shore* (1972)
Type of work: Novels
Time: Indefinite
Locale: The Kingdom of Earthsea

Three novels, written for young readers but powerfully attractive to all ages, set in a fantasy world which bears subtle but fundamental resemblance to our own

> *Principal characters:*
> GED, a wizard
> OGION, mage of the Isle of Gont
> TENAR, priestess of the Tombs
> ARREN, a prince and future King of Earthsea

In accepting the 1972 National Book Award for Children's Literature for *The Farthest Shore*, the third volume of the Earthsea trilogy, Ursula Le Guin said, ". . . as great scientists have said and all children know, it is above all by the imagination that we achieve perception, and compassion, and hope." The paradox that Le Guin, along with other writers of fantasy and science fiction, has understood and embraced is that the best way to understand our world and the way we live in it may be to leave it, *via* the imagination; to see it masked in otherworldness; and to see ourselves not as we are or have been, but as we might be.

Of all the fine work of this remarkable writer, the Earthsea trilogy is perhaps her greatest achievement. Le Guin is without question one of the finest fiction writers in America today. Her work, unified thematically by her vision of things as they ought to be, is beautifully crafted, lyrical in both language and story.

A holistic vision of harmony, integration, and balance informs the Earthsea trilogy. Myth is the stuff of these stories, the fabric of Earthsea, a world at least as thoroughly imagined as C. S. Lewis' Narnia or J. R. R. Tolkien's Middle Earth. As its name suggests, it is a world of islands and ocean, where a divided consciousness is a great but easy risk because of the separateness of the islands. It is one world, though, made whole not only by the ocean waters from which, according to the oldest song, the Creation of Ea, the land and all living things were called, but also by the Balance of the great forces of light and dark, life and death, good and evil, reality and unreality. It is a world which is primitive in its closeness to these elemental forces, but sophisticated in its understanding of and respect for them.

Earthsea is a world where magic is commonplace; witches and sorcerers abound on every island and in every village and town. For the most part, their skill and powers are limited because their knowledge is fragmentary; love potions, weather-working, and spells of mending and illusion are their daily or occasional traffic in their minor arts. However, young boys who show particular promise are sent to the Isle of Roke to the School for Wizards, presided over by the Archmage and the Nine Masters of the Art Magic. If a boy is diligent and greatly gifted, he may become a mage, who derives his power from knowing the true names of things in the Old Speech, the True Speech of the Making, so that they obey his commands; and who uses that power wisely, not to disturb the Balance but to sustain it. Earthsea is a world which recognizes the power of language, of naming, for its very existence rests solidly on that power. It is also a world inhabited peripherally by dragons, terrible and beautiful in their ancient majesty, creatures of wind and fire who speak only in the Old Speech, and who mingle with men (whom, for the most part, they find mildly amusing) rarely but never without great significance.

In the first volume of this trilogy, *A Wizard of Earthsea*, we meet the boy called Sparrowhawk, whose true name is Ged and who is the central figure around whom the three novels are woven. Ged is a rough young goatherd on the island of Gont; because he is precocious at casting spells, he is taken as an apprentice by the mage Ogion. But Ged is restless and headstrong as well as gifted, and he soon leaves his master on Gont Mountain and sails on a merchant ship, *Shadow* to Roke to study at the School for Wizards.

Ged is an apt pupil at the School, and soon outshines his fellow apprentices with his skill and aptitude. His pride, however, has not left him, and it deafens him to the words of caution from the Master Hand: "The world is in balance, in Equilibrium. A wizard's power of Changing and of Summoning can shake the balance of the world. It is dangerous, that power. It is most perilous. It must follow knowledge, and serve need. To light a candle is to cast a shadow. . . ." But Ged, in the rashness of youth, is impatient and longs for power without limitations. His pride leads him to challenge his longtime rival, Jasper, to a match, power against power. He weaves a spell of Summoning, for which he possesses sufficient skill but insufficient knowledge; the fabric of the world is torn open, and a terrible shadow, a clot of darkness, leaps from the realm of Unbeing into the world, straight at Ged's face. The Archmage Nemmerle releases Ged from the shadow's grasp and closes the torn edges of the world together, but the shadow which Ged's pride has loosed remains in the world, unseen but awful. Ged, wounded near to death, lies unconscious and feverish for weeks in the Master Herbal's chambers; the old Archmage, his powers spent by the healing of the world's wound, dies. At length Ged heals and is restored to life, but he bears on his face the deep scars of his struggle, walks with a limp, and grieves for the evil he has done.

Ged finally earns his wizard's staff, and though he fears to leave the protection of the Isle of the Wise, goes to the small island of Low Torning, which is threatened by dragons, to serve as wizard to its people. The shadow haunts his dreams, and Ged knows it means to seek him out. Fearful of the harm that might befall the people of Low Torning should the shadow find him there, he

determines to leave. He is reluctant to depart, though, before securing the
island from the dragons' threat. He sails west to match wits with the mightiest
of the ancient beasts, and is victorious; the dragon tries to strike a bargain by
offering to tell him the name of the thing that seeks his undoing, but Ged
knows that he must not place himself in the dragon's debt, even though knowing the shadow's true name would ensure his mastery over it. He gains control
by divining the dragon's true name, and elicits the beast's respect along with
its oath that dragons will never again fly east of the island of Pendor. Ged is
now a dragonlord.

But the shadow pursues him still and he flees before it. It is Ogion, Ged's
old master from Gont, who finally defines Ged's quest: he must stop being the
hunted and become the hunter. He must summon all his art and strength and
skill to discover the shadow's name, and he must confront it, either to defeat
the threat it poses or lose his life in the attempt. Ged sails far into the East
Reach, past all charted lands, to the very edge of the world, to the dividing
line between life and death, where the sea turns to sand and there is no wind.
There, in the dry land, under the unmoving stars, Ged finally confronts the
shadow, and in one of the most moving and dramatic moments in all fantasy
literature, calls it by its name, which is his own name, Ged: "Ged reached out
his hands, dropping his staff, and took hold of his shadow, of the black self
that reached out to him. Light and darkness met, and joined, and were one."
He is at last whole and free.

A Wizard of Earthsea is, then, a novel about coming of age. It differs from
other novels of this kind, though, in that it deals not with an individual's
adaptation to a particular culture or world view but with the mythic dimensions
of human life. Until Ged has faced and named the dark shadow of his own life,
the sure fact of his own death, he cannot live fully. So, in a sense, the first
volume ends with Ged's birth — not a physical entry into the world, but a
metaphysical entry into the wholeness of his maturity. Not accidentally, Ged's
great moment occurs in the East, the place of the rising sun, and after his
ordeal, he can begin truly to live his life "for life's sake and never in the
service of ruin, or pain, or hatred, or the dark."

The Tombs of Atuan is the story of Ged's discovery of sexual love, of his
finding the woman who will complement and complete his life. This theme,
though, is handled indirectly, largely through the sexual symbolism which
permeates the story. In fact, Ged's is not the central consciousness of the
novel. Young Arha, the "Eaten One," the One Priestess of the Tombs, is the
central figure, and as the first volume is the story of Ged's coming of age, so
this is the story of Arha's rebirth from death to life, from being buried to being
free, from darkness to light.

Arha has been taken from her family as a young child, for it is believed that
she is the One Priestess reborn; her name is taken away as a symbol of her
identity, and she is consecrated to the Nameless Ones, the Old Powers of

darkness, as chief priestess. Under the temple of the Nameless Ones is the dark Undertomb and the Labyrinth, which are filled with treasure but where no light may ever shine. Arha passes her days in ritual service in the Temple and in the company of the lesser priestesses and the eunuchs; no man may enter the Holy Place. The greatest treasure of all, half the Ring of Erreth-Akbe, lies in the Treasury at the heart of the Labyrinth, where only Arha herself is permitted to go. Yet one day as she wanders in the blackness through the corridors she knows by heart, she sees a faint light emanating from the great cavern of the Undertomb, where light is forbidden, where no light has ever shone. Startled beyond fear, Arha turns the corner and sees for the first time the dazzling splendor of the Undertomb, "sparkling, delicate, intricate, a palace of diamonds, a house of amethyst and crystal, from which the ancient darkness had been driven out by glory." Ged has come to the East on the quest at which so many before him have failed: to recover the lost half of the Ring of Erreth-Akbe. He wears one half of the ring on a chain about his neck, and it is the werelight from his staff which illumines both the darkness which Arha is pledged to guard and the dark emptiness of her heart and spirit. Drawn to the man almost against her will, she defies her duty to have him killed and keeps him hidden secretly in the Labyrinth, eventually bringing him to the Treasury to find the lost half of the ring. Ged, in turn, restores her name to her, Tenar, and with her name her selfhood and human identity.

The Ring had originally borne the nine Runes of Power; each half now bore four, plus a fragment of the Lost Rune, the Bond-Rune, the sign of peace. Without this rune, no king has been able to rule a unified kingdom from Havnor, the center of the world, and there have been war and enmity among all the lands of Earthsea for long ages. So Ged's quest has been to restore peace and wholeness to the world; in finding the ring, he finds Tenar, and brings the peace and wholeness of love to his own life and to hers. He restores the ring itself to wholeness with a powerful Spell of Patterning, and slips the ring, a woman's arm-ring, onto her wrist, then gives her the greatest gift he has to give: his true name. The trust between them demands that they stay together; Tenar will leave the darkness forever with Ged. He depends upon her strength and knowledge of the Labyrinth, for his wizardry has grown weak from his imprisonment in the underneath. Facing great peril from both human enemies and from the dark power of the Nameless Ones, they escape the Place of the Tombs to freedom, and return with the ring, and the Lost Rune now found, to Havnor. While the binding together of the broken ring serves literally to suggest the mending of the world and an end to strife, it also symbolically represents the coming together of the man Ged and the Woman Tenar, the wholeness of male-female complementarity, the joining of Yin and Yang. The small circle of their completeness gains wider significance because their union also brings wholeness to their world.

In *The Farthest Shore*, the final volume, all the thematic threads of the first two stories are brought together. Ged is now past middle age and Archmage at the School on Roke. But evil has fallen upon the world; as in the first story, there is a rent in the fabric of the world, a hole where the sea and the light are running out. This time the wound is not of Ged's making, but he is called upon to close it. A young prince, Arren, comes to Roke on a mission from his father, seeking Ged's help. Ged recognizes the boy as the future King who will rule all Earthsea in peace from Havnor, the King for whom he and Tenar brought the ring from Atuan before he was even born. But he keeps silent about his knowledge, only asking Arren to accompany him on his voyage to seek the torn place and heal the wound in the world. For the way he must go is Arren's way, as well.

Their voyage takes them to a number of islands, and things are uniformly ill: a great madness is taking hold of the world, spells and magic fail, people are forgetting their own true names. Death and darkness threaten to extinguish the light of the world. An evil wizard who has died many times but who appears to be still alive comes to the people in dreams, beckoning them to follow him into the dry land which is unlife, promising them immortality; they are too foolish to see that what he offers is not life unending, but a living death. Ged, the dragonlord, is finally summoned by dragons, who enlist his aid in fighting the lord of darkness, the Unmaker. Ged and Arren follow the messenger dragon far into the West Reach, to the westernmost isle, Selidor; this time Ged must face the darkness not in the East but in the West, for this is not the beginning of his life as a mage, but the close.

On Selidor, Arren and Ged meet the Unmaker at last, and must pursue him across the wall of stones that divides the world of the living from the world of the dead, into the dry land which is death itself, to the black hole, source of the Dry River, the void, the door to nothingness, to the way that leads nowhere. Ged, summoning all his strength against the strength of darkness, the strength of the King of Death, struggles to heal the breach, to close the door — and the door closes, and the world is once again whole. The Unmaker, who is so lost to life and light that he has forgotten his own true name, lies broken; Ged whispers his true name to him, releasing him once and for all to the peace of real death.

But in this great act of healing, Ged has spent all his strength, and it is Arren who must lead them back to life, to the bright sunlit shore of Selidor. There the mighty dragon Kalessin kneels on the sand and bids them mount, then flies East, over the islands of Earthsea, bringing them to Roke. The islanders, seeing a dragon in the skies over the Inner Lands for the first time in many years, are terrified, thinking it is the end of the world. But they misunderstand; it is the beginning of a new era.

Once Arren is delivered to the safety of Roke, Ged, old and tired, his wizardry used up, kneels before the future King and bids him to rule long and well when he comes to his throne in Havnor. Then he climbs again onto the dragon's back and flies toward Gont, toward Tenar and home. His public life has ended, and his story will be sung through the ages of Earthsea in the Deed of Ged.

Though all this would surely be enough, it is not all, for these stories of the weaving of spells, of creation, of Making, are also about art, and the making of art. Just as the First Word called the islands of Earthsea into being, so Le Guin has woven a world with words, has made a world and made it live. Ged is not only a mage, but an artist, and magic is his art. These stories of Earthsea are Le Guin's magic, her art at its best, and they are wonderful in the best sense of the word — full of wonder; they are wonderfully conceived, executed, and told. They delight the inner eye and ear, and the heart, as well as the mind; they engage the imagination as well as the intellect. This is the spell which Le Guin weaves so well, and, woven in the service of the light, the spell binds, and holds.

Rebecca Blevins Faery

Sources for Further Study

Criticism:

Barbour, Douglas. "On Ursula K. Le Guin's *A Wizard of Earthsea*," in *Riverside Quarterly*. VI (April, 1974), pp. 119-123. Barbour outlines the plot and theme of *A Wizard of Earthsea*.

Cameron, E. "High Fantasy: *A Wizard of Earthsea*," in *Crosscurrents of Criticism; Horn Book Essays*. Edited by Paul Heins. Ashburnham, Mass.: Horn Book, 1977, pp. 333-341. The search for selfhood is part of the theme.

Le Guin, Ursula K. *Dreams Must Explain Themselves*. New York: Algol, 1975, Le Guin describes her trilogy and its origins.

Shippey, T. A. "The Magic Art and The Evolution of Words: Ursula Le Guin's *Earthsea* Trilogy," in *Mosaic*. X (1977), pp. 147-163. The story of the trilogy is told.

Slusser, George E. *The Farthest Shores of Ursula K. Le Guin*. San Bernardino, Calif.: Borgo, 1976, pp. 31-46. The problems of folly, individual responsibility, evil, and the search for selfhood are examined.

Reviews:

Booklist. LXV, January 15, 1969, p. 546.

Books and Bookmen. XVII, December, 1971, p. R8.

Library Journal. XCIV, May 15, 1969, p. 2073.

EDISON'S CONQUEST OF MARS

Author: Garrett P. Serviss (1851-1929)
First book publication: 1947
Type of work: Novel
Time: The early twentieth century
Locale: Mars

An unofficial sequel to H. G. Wells's The War of the Worlds *in which Thomas Alva Edison, with the cooperation of other great scientific minds, builds a fleet of space ships, and, arming them with disintegrator rays, attacks Mars before it can launch a second strike at the Earth*

> *Principal characters:*
> THOMAS ALVA EDISON, the famous inventor
> GARRETT P. SERVISS, his friend
> LORD KELVIN, the great physicist
> AINA, a descendant of Egyptians captured by the Martians and taken back to the Red Planet nine thousand years ago

Edison's Conquest of Mars deserves elucidation only secondarily for its literary values but primarily for its unique role in the history of science fiction, a role so obliterated by the perishability of newsprint that for more than twenty-five years, sincere doubts were expressed that the story even existed.

When the Munsey magazines, *Argosy*, *All-Story*, and others became the leading publishers of new science fiction in the United States from the turn of the century on, they developed a new and enthusiastic audience that gradually evolved into collectors and publishers of maturer magazines about science fiction. Those who collected the May, 1915, issue of *Argosy* to own and read *The Moon Maiden* by Garrett P. Serviss (its only appearance), saw listed under the writer's name "Author of *The Conquest of Mars*." Collectors embarked on a frantic search for this novel, both in second-hand book stores and in second-hand magazine shops, but could find no trace of it. It was not until the 1930's that the average fan was mature enough, serious enough, and knowledgeable enough to attempt to contact the estate of the late Garrett P. Serviss about this story. They were told the estate owned no copy of it, but it was believed to have been a newspaper serial in a New York newspaper in 1898. When the date of printing was determined it was found that no copies of the editions of the newspaper existed in New York, and that those in the Library of Congress could not be located. It was finally due to the efforts of A. Langley Searles, Ph.D., publisher of the literary science fiction publication *Fantasy Commentator*, that a set of photostats were actually taken of a crumbling file as mysteriously returned as it had been removed from the Library of Congress.

The story was then published in hardcover by Carcosa House, a fan-operated venture that never published another book. The novel has since appeared in paperback. Through the years the motivation for the writing and publication of the novel has been pieced together.

The New York Evening Journal, then owned by William Randolph Hearst, had obtained newspaper serialization rights of H. G. Wells's *The War of the Worlds*, which had first been published in *Cosmopolitan* from April to December, 1897, and had not yet appeared in book form. Immediately upon magazine completion and before the appearance of the hardcover edition from Harper and Brothers in 1898, *The New York Evening Journal* serialized it daily (except Sundays), from December 15, 1897, through January 11, 1898. In doing so, they made changes in the story, establishing the locale in the United States instead of in England, and altered the title *Fighters from Mars* to *The War of the Worlds*. The Boston paper then picked up the story and changed it internally so that it took place around Boston. Wells was furious, but there was little he could do except complain.

The ingenuity of the American newspaper publishers did not end there. As circulation soared and they realized that when the serialization ended there was little likelihood of Wells writing a sequel to their satisfaction, they commissioned Garrett P. Serviss to try his hand at it. Serviss was working for Hearst at the time and was already one of the most popular lecturers and writers on astronomy in the United States; his work frequently appeared in the leading magazines of England. The day after Wells's story concluded, Garrett P. Serviss' sequel began. In reading the story it must be remembered that there is no question that most of it was written in daily installments to meet deadlines, because there is no way that the publishers could have given Serviss enough notice to have the novel complete by the time it began to appear in daily serials.

The Carcosa house edition of *Edison's Conquest of Mars* hired an artist to redraw crudely a few of the illustrations of the newspaper serialization. Unquestionably, one of the most important things about the newspaper serialization was the trailblazing illustrations by staff artist P. Gray, who obviously worked on them under the direction of Serviss. Because of the fact that the illustrations are based directly on the text, they are of historical importance. Two to three illustrations appeared per installment, and they portrayed, among other things, a massed fleet of spaceships hovering over the Statue of Liberty in New York harbor, space fights in space between the spaceships of Earth and those of the Martians, many of the earliest portrayals of space-suited men, including space walks, elaborate portrayals of the Martians including their cities, landscape, and culture, and many scenes of the disintegrating ray in action. The only place any of these remarkable illustrations have been reproduced (and then only poorly) is in the section "A Portfolio of Early Space Ships 1638 to 1929" by Sam Moskowitz in *The Complete Book of Space Travel* by Albro Gaul (World, 1956).

Before examining the story itself, one important question must be answered: why would as famous a figure as Thomas Alva Edison permit his name to be used in the title of the story and further permit himself to be used as one of the lead heroic figures in the narration? The answer is simple: he was paid for that use. *The New York Evening Journal* occasionally bought and printed highly imaginative and speculative science articles obstensibly written by Edison or presented as an interview with him. It is quite likely that Garrett P. Serviss interviewed the scientist and then ghost-wrote these pieces. Among the illustrations in the story is one showing Garrett P. Serviss and Thomas Alva Edison in the "Wizards" laboratory with the caption: "A consultation is held in Wizard Edison's laboratory between him and Professor Serviss on the best means of repaying the damage wrought upon this planet by the Martians." The very large portrait is signed by "HT" and bears the heading "The Wizard and the Astronomer Confer," thus virtually confirming the ghost-writing relationship between Serviss and Edison. It is also worth noting that H. G. Wells's correspondence reveals that he had made a direct deal with *The New York Evening Journal* for the serialization of *The War of the Worlds* and had sent them a corrected manuscript before he had done his final copy for his book publishers. He clearly did not expect alterations in his plot or even changes in his text.

In *Edison's Conquest of Mars*, the Martians depart from the Palisades near New York City, and the rocket blasts completely level the city and its environs. Thomas Edison has the opportunity to examine the wreckage of Martian machines and equipment left behind and, with the impetus of this new knowledge, perfects an antigravity device and a distintegrator ray. The first makes practical the construction of spaceships and the second gives the men of Earth an unparalleled weapon, much superior to the Martians' heat ray. Edison builds a spaceship with all the necessary support systems and tests it by taking Serviss on a ride to the moon and back. By that time telescopes indicate that new activity has begun on Mars very similar in nature to what was observed before the initial Martian attack. Apparently, they are preparing for a second invasion.

It is decided that it would be foolish to wait for the Martians to attack — the war should be taken to their planet with our own fleet of spaceships and Edison's new deadly ray. The world rulers, most of whom are monarchs, are called together in a conference. They decide to raise ten billion dollars among the nations of the world to build the fleet. The amount is subscribed, and through a series of sound systems rigged up by telephone, fifty million people of the United States hear the proceedings of the meeting. Edison gets the contract to build one hundred spaceships and three thousand disintegrators with no limit placed on the amount of money he can draw from the international fund. The fleet is built and sets off for Mars.

Arriving on Mars, they are met by such a vast number of air vessels that they decide to circle that globe before attempting offensive action. They are suddenly aware that they have taken on an enemy that is probably superior to them in intelligence and science; and only good tactics, luck, and the yet unproven superiority of their weapon can see them come out on top. Going for them, too, is the fact that they have taken many of the leading scientific minds of Earth along with them, especially William Kelvin, one of the great physicists of the age who advocated an absolute measure of temperatures and whose name is today used in that connection.

On Mars, the invaders discover that members of the human race had been taken as slaves when the Earth was invaded nine thousand years earlier. They meet a girl whose ancestry is Egyptian, and learn that the Sphinx was built as a monument to the leader of the conquering Martians. Aina, the girl, is the last Earthling left alive, because after they saw the Earth fleet approaching, the Martians slaughtered all the Earthlings but her.

Aina tells the Earthmen there is no hope of defeating the Martians by direct assault because they have innumerable weapons, excellent fortifications, and thousands of ships. She suggests that the way to defeat them is to close the gates that control the flow of water to the canals at the point of oceanic high tide. The resulting flood will destroy the planet, most of which lies below sea level. The Earthmen follow this advice, and, as the unleashed oceans pour out to destroy the entire civilization of the planet and nine tenths of its inhabitants, thousands of Martian ships rise to meet them in combat. A grim battle occurs in which the Earth ships, because they were intended for space travel, are able to remain above the effective range of the Martians (the Martian rocket-propelled space ships cannot be used in the atmosphere). Despite this advantage, before the Martian defensive forces are defeated, the original Earth fleet of one hundred ships is reduced to fifty-five, the more than two thousand men drop to 1,085. While at the Martian capitol to demand unconditional surrender, an altercation forces the Earthmen to destroy most of the rulers of the planet. The return to Earth is uneventful. Aina marries Alonzo Smith, one of the military leaders of the expedition. Edison, Serviss, and Kelvin survive the adventure, although hundreds of well-known personalities (not stated) have been killed.

The novel remains an extraordinarily conceived work in both method and content. Its main characters were predominantly well-known or famous figures still alive at the time. They participate in a work that supposes that another piece of fiction, *The War of the Worlds*, actually happened. Though in its realism in utilizing living people as characters it resembles the "hoax" school of science fiction (*The Moon Hoax* by Richard Adams Locke, *The Balloon Hoax* by Edgar Allan Poe, and *The Case of Summerfield* by William Henry Rhodes), *Edison's Conquest of Mars* is obviously not of that school because it does not intend to deceive. On the contrary, it is an attempt to make a work of fiction more thrilling by imagining what a truly great scientist such as Edison might have invented, given certain fictional circumstances.

It is important to remember that, since *Edison's Conquest of Mars* has been traced to at least three newspapers with combined circulations approaching several hundred thousand, it was read by many people. This novel turned Serviss into a writer of fiction as well as nonfiction. His next work of science fiction, *The Moon Metal*, was published by Harper and Brothers in 1900 and was syndicated across the country in newspapers the same year. Perhaps research may yet uncover the fact that it was intended for newspaper syndication and inadvertently ended up in hard covers. That novel, along with *The Columbus of Space* (1911), about a voyage to Venus in an atomically powered spaceship, and *The Second Deluge* (1912) elevated Serviss to a position of considerable historical importance in the field of science fiction. All three of his major works are still in print.

Sam Moskowitz

Sources for Further Study
Criticism:
Lambert, P. C. "The Wonderful Journey," in *Alabama Librarian*. VIII (January, 1957), pp. 3-5. This examination of the imaginary voyage motif in Serviss' writing discusses the major factors that increased literary interest in extraterrestrial voyages.

THE EINSTEIN INTERSECTION

Author: Samuel R. Delany (1942-   )
First book publication: 1967
Type of work: Novel
Time: c. A.D. 40,000
Locale: The Earth — a jungle village, a desert, the city of Branning-at-Sea

A literary tour de force, *using stock properties of science fiction and myth, literary Modernism and popular culture, to create a far future world reflecting, as in a distorted mirror, the complexities and uncertainties of the 1960's*

Principal characters:
> LO LOBEY, a twenty-three-year-old herder, musician, and adventurer
> FRIZA, the girl he loves and seeks to bring back from death
> LE DORIK, hermaphroditic lover of both, keeper of the village "kage"
> PHAEDRA, acronymically named computer with a warped sense of humor
> SPIDER, master of the dragon herders
> KID DEATH, killer of Friza, Dorik, "differences" that scare him
> GREEN-EYE, exiled telepathic scion of a leading Branning family
> THE DOVE, sex goddess of Branning society

The title of this book comes from a lecture by Spider to Lobey, who has come to pick up his pay for a dragon drive. Human beings left Earth, he explains, when their understanding of the irrational equaled their comprehension of the rational. This point in space and time Spider calls the intersection between the Einsteinian conception of the limits of knowable truth and the Gödelian conception of infinite unpredictable possibilities within a known system. Both mathematical theorems are accurately represented, but the implications are more promising as poetry than as science.

Delany is not averse to exploiting the seemingly impossible which that explanation appears to allow. Setting his story far in the future, adding an inner planet to the solar system, replacing humans with another race, he is clearly making use of science fiction's ties with the imaginary world of romance. But he does rationalize, if sometimes obliquely, almost every impossibility of the novel, and he limits himself, if only arbitrarily, to a fictional as well as a thematic coherence.

Related specifically to Spider's context, the intersection implies that humans both destroyed themselves and emigrated voluntarily. In either event, the "New People" took over both the bodies and the souls of humanity, and their history, to which Lobey is heir, consists of trying to live up to the images of ourselves we left behind, in artifacts and myths, as well as in genetic raw materials. The confusing world they have made is introduced to the reader through Lobey in the course of the novel, as he goes from the complacency and security of his native village to the uncertainty and dangers of the city, and beyond.

His immediate goal is to find Friza and bring her back to life, reliving the myth of Orpheus. Lobey's whole story, however, is a traditional rite of passage from childhood to maturity. At every stage in his quest, he has his perspectives changed and his behavior modified as he tries to cope with newly perceived situations. And the journey, in true mythic fashion, involves him in strange yet familiar encounters.

The call to adventure comes first in the demand that he defeat a gigantic, intelligent, and ferocious bull with manlike hands. Having accompanied his efforts with toreador allusions in words and music, PHAEDRA now informs Lobey that he is "in the wrong maze," but she cannot help him to find the right one. Aided by the advice of the village elders, and by the ghost of Le Dorik, whose "difference," like Friza's, has killed him/her, Lobey sets out to explore the world beyond his village.

Via two-way television, in the "source cave," he encounters Kid Death, who claims control over both Friza and Dorik, and who accompanies Lobey, often at a distance, through his remaining adventures. On a dragon-drive, Lobey meets, in addition to Spider, Green-Eye, the impossible male offspring of a virgin birth, who can send words and feelings telepathically, who offers a message of love, and who has powers of creation Kid Death lacks, wants, and envies. Before trail's end, moreover, Lobey's life has been threatened, and even lost, his restoration being credited, alternately, to the Kid, to Green-Eye and even to himself.

Lobey's rustic ways are scorned by a hunchback named Pistol as he enters the city, but he finds his way to Spider's home from which he is directed to seek out the Dove, who offers an illusion of Friza's resurrection. Resisting the illusion, he is equally repelled by the sight of Green-Eye's crucifixion, apparently ordered by Spider; then Lobey himself finishes off the victim with his machete. Finally, transfixing Kid Death with his music, on the flute end of his weapon, Lobey helps Spider whip to death this threat to all their lives. At last accepting the idea of transcending myths, Lobey walks off into the sunset at the end, contemplating travel to distant planets in search of his Protean self.

Speculatively, the story is anchored in a concept of genetics that is mythological as well as biological. The alien biology of the characters is explained by the conflict between our forms and their "psychic manifestations," which result in departures from the norm of the "Old People." This "descent of man" is kept under control in a sense by planned promiscuity, mixing the gene pool, so that they can live out all the possibilities of our past before they can exhaust their own present. But defective mutations, "non-functionals," continue to be born; they are cared for in a "kage" by Dorik in the village and by PHAEDRA in the city.

Those who are "functional," moreover, are often far from "true norms." Le Dorik and the Dove are both hermaphrodites; Pistol is a hunchback; and almost everyone is somehow "different," though Pistol advises Lobey to keep his personal deviations to himself when around strangers. Even more "difference" is said to be rising in the younger generation. Friza, for example, never spoke and seldom moved, but she was sexually fertile and had telekinetic powers.

Green-Eye is one-dimensional, standing for Christ, even to the temptations in the wilderness. Kid Death is Billy the Kid, Hades, and Satan. The Dove, we are told, is Helen of Troy (classical myth), Jean Harlow (movie siren), Star Anthim (Heroine of a Theodore Sturgeon story) and Mario [sic] Montez (a hip transvestite variation of another movie vamp). Spider defines himself as Pat Garrett to Billy, Judas to Green-Eye, Paul Burn to the Dove as Jean Harlow and Minos at the gates of Hades; he is also Pontius Pilate signing Green-Eye's death warrant and yet again the wise adviser of fairy tale and romance.

Lobey is both Orpheus and Theseus (both times "in the wrong maze"); he is also the Roman Centurion who helped Jesus die, the disciple Peter who denied his master, and a self-resurrecting Lazarus, as well as the generic quest-hero, off on another search at the story's end. As Orpheus, moreover, he incorporates such latter-day variations on the figure as Elvis Presley and "the silent Beatle," Ringo Starr.

Each of these represents a pattern that Lobey learns from Spider, which he may follow through to the end, or depart from to strike out on his own. To do the latter, however, is to be "different" and to court danger; Kid Death is not the only threat to those who dare to be original. But originality in art can be worthwhile. Lobey's music has power over life and death. Having learned the blues from old recordings, he plays them in earnest to mourn his Friza. Though he lifts music from others (Kodaly as well as "Bill Bailey"), he also invents, learning as he matures how art can mediate between imagination and reason ("must change" and "must preserve").

In the midst of life, he is faced with death in several guises, and seeks to overcome it. One answer is to deny it, as Green-Eye does with the message: "There is no death, only love." Since Lobey's love is already dead, this denial is unacceptable, but Lobey does transpose the message into terms he thinks La Dire would understand: "There is no death, only rhythm." This is in keeping with her teachings about "the great rock and the great roll," or the sum total of all things living and dead. But very quickly, Lobey sees an improvement on that formulation as well, in keeping not only with the pendulum-swings of life and death, but also with the immortalizing potential of art: "There is no death, only music." Music incorporates both love and rhythm, and imposes order on the formless chaos of death, but not the order represented by Green-Eye, which seems as rigid as its opposite. Destroying (with Spider) both Green-Eye and Kid Death, Lobey is an artist at improvisation, which defies permanence even as it achieves it. Musically considered, then, death is both an ending and not an ending, a sentiment echoed by an epigram for the next-to-last chapter of the book; speaking of the story and of his life, Delany writes: "Endings to be useful must be inconclusive."

Both simple and complex, obvious and profound, complete and yet inconclusive, the adventures of Lo Lobey are skillfully presented at breakneck
speed, with a classically economical vocabulary, with a dazzling impressionis-
tic style full of colloquialisms and puns, and with appropriate bows in the
direction of science and technology. All the while, however, Delany is
commenting on the action, widening its relevance, rooting its significance in
Western tradition and personal experience by means of epigrams for every
chapter. Some of these are from Modernist writers such as Joyce, Yeats, and
Eliot; others are voices from the more distant past (Erasmus, Machiavelli, de
Sade). The most space, however, is given to Delany's own journal, kept while
he was traveling in Italy, Greece, and Turkey, and incorporating his experiences into this book.

For all the care expended on creating an alien culture and environment,
these epigrams seem to underline the fact that Delany's primary aim is to
reflect our own time in his distorting mirror. The 1960's were a disturbing
period, no less for those growing up in it than for those looking on from
outside. The era seemed to reveal apparent discontinuity in the social fabric,
and Delany was at or near the heart of the Counterculture throughout this
period. His stress in the book on explicit parallels between past, present, and
future; between life, art, and popular culture; between science, imagination,
and myth reminds us of how much continuity there was underlying the apparent "difference."

This distant future is, of course, our recent past, or continuing present. The
aliens are ourselves, always trying to be human. The young people, too, are
our own, whose difference seemed especially different at this time. It is surely
no accident that Lobey, like Delany, is young, black, and an artist, a member
of three minorities for whom the rules are always changing, or being changed,
before they can learn how to play by them. But the parallel has more than
simple autobiographical significance. Everyone growing up has to learn how to
endure the shocks of change, which a technologically advanced culture may
bring home in more rapid succession, such that even adults are continually
challenged to grow. In the context of an imaginary world even more discontinuous than the 1960's, this continuity is all the clearer.

David N. Samuelson

Sources for Further Study

Criticism:

Scobie, Stephen A. C. "The Different Mazes: Mythology in Samuel R. Delaney's The *Einstein Intersection*," in *Riverside Quarterly*. V (1971), pp. 12-18. According to Scobie, Delaney uses several kinds of myths in presenting a society of the future.

Reviews:

Analog. LXXXI, April, 1968, pp. 163-164.

Fantastic Stories. XVIII, October, 1968, pp. 136-137.

Galaxy. XXVI, October, 1967, pp. 193-194.

Magazine of Fantasy and Science Fiction. XXXIII, November, 1967, pp. 34-36.

New Worlds. CLXXIII, July, 1967, p. 63.

SF Commentary. I, January, 1969, p. 16.

ELZA PILÓTA, VAGY A TÖKÉLETES TÁRSADALOM
(Elza the Pilot, or The Perfect Society)

Author: Mihály Babits (1883-1941)
First book publication: 1933
Type of work: Novel
Time: The future, the forty-first year of the Eternal War
Locale: Sz, a Hungarian town

A visionary portrait of human behavior under war conditions by a leading Hungarian writer of the early twentieth century

> *Principal characters:*
> GÉZA KAMUTHY
> LIVIA KAMUTHY, his wife
> ELZA KAMUTHY, their daughter
> PROFESSOR SCHULBERG
> DEZSÖ, Elza's lover

In the age of aerial and gas warfare and the universal conscription of women, Elza Kamuthy is also enlisted in the army as Professor Schulberg's pilot. Schulberg obtains a very rare manuscript which describes the research work of a biologist. This scientist has made a model of the Earth to study the formation and evolution of life. A comet had snatched the model, along with its creator, who died on Little Earth. Schulberg is informed about the events having taken place on Little Earth. Elza becomes the pilot of a bomber and has to bomb her native town. It is possible that the Eternal War and Elza's story take place on the model of our planet, on Little Earth.

In the forty-first year of the Eternal War, on the day when in the Parliament the representatives have to vote for the introduction of the universal conscription of women, sirens are sounded in the town of Sz, signaling an air raid and gas attack. The town becomes empty, as everybody goes to his or her usual shelter where they rent a private compartment. Géza Kamuthy, one of the leaders of the economy who supports the government, is there with his wife, Livia, who remembers the prewar years. Livia Kamuthy has already lost her son in the war, and now she listens to every piece of news with anxiety, since she is deeply concerned for her daughter, Elza.

With this dramatic situation, Mihály Babits' novel opens. *Elza Pilóto, vagy a tökéletes társadalom* is an outstanding example of Hungarian science fiction, a valuable but not always appreciated work of modern science fiction, along with works by Miklós Jósika, Mór Jókai, Géza Csáth, and Frigyes Karinthy. Mihály Babits was a leading figure in Hungarian literature at the turn of this century; he later became the literary leader of Hungarian culture, a poet, novelist, essayist, and translator of world renown. He exerted an invaluable influence on the Hungarian literature of this century not only by the pure and powerful humanism of his spirit, poetry, and thought, but also as an organizer of literary life, as the editor-in-chief of the most influential literary magazine

"Nyugat" (West). He attracted attention by the formal beauty of his verse and the flexibility of his poetic language. He published translations of Dante, Shakespeare, Baudelaire, and Poe, wrote a history of European literature of vast scope and erudition, and wrote a social novel entitled *Halálfiai* (Children of Death). Babits was widely read in Anglo-Saxon literature, and he introduced many English and American poets to Hungarian readers.

Babits passionately hated war; he was a staunch pacifist and a defender of human values. During World War I, he was tried for his antimilitarist poems. In the 1930's he saw with anxiety how certain political forces were gathering strength, and, though he was never directly active in politics, he seriously warned people of the signs of approaching war. One of the results of his anxiety was this novel, which the author himself called "a warning."

The novel is original in its subject, plot, and philosophy, although it does reflect a trace of Karinthy's influence. Babits paints a visionary picture of air-raid shelters and bombardments, and of the peculiarities of human behavior in such dangerous situations. During the time of the Eternal War, people have become accustomed to an underground life; they have settled down in the caves, cellars, and corridors, which Babits calls "caves of air," in order to survive the constant bombs and poisonous gases.

The most astonishing aspect of life in this society is the enthusiasm with which people talk about the war. Life adjusts to the new, absurd conditions; women feel cheated because "their role is meagre and casual in this great Struggle, though it is sure now that Struggle is the ultimate essence and goal of human life."

Because Mr. Kamuthy and his wife belong to the upper ten thousand inhabitants of the shelter, they are among the privileged who visit Professor Schulberg in his commander's suite. Mrs. Kamuthy, who cannot accept the war as final and unchangeable, asks the commander to exempt her daughter from service at the front. Mr. Kamuthy and Schulberg explain to the desperate woman that there is no country on Earth which could wish for peace, since peace would bring destruction and economic anarchy. War has been organized so perfectly that life can never return to more primitive and disorganized phases of development. No one craves victory because the victors would be in the most embarrassing and undesirable position of having to deal with the situation of chaos which peace would bring. War has brought equality, a serious and responsible democracy for all in which military service is compulsory for everyone.

The two men also explain that the age of Eternal Struggle has realized all the Utopian hopes and dreams of the peaceful years of the twentieth century; the interdependent states eliminated nationalism, and military interest has created one great economical system out of the allied nations. There is no unemployment, and soldiers are provided for by the state; in this perfect collective society, the individual subjects himself to the common interest, gives his maximum energy to the state, and is thus able to realize himself completely. This active and collective way of life excludes any "decadent" culture: there are no arts, and metaphysical or philosophical thoughts and sentiments are regarded as a futile game.

During the time of the Eternal War, people are organized into groups which resemble the Italian "fascio," and from the crippled and disabled a peculiar aristocracy is formed with all its privileges. The state prohibits the mutilation of babies to disable them for military service, but sometimes ignores its prohibition. The actual operation, of course, is made in secret, yet the doctors are recruited. As the majority of men are on the front, there is no balance between the sexes, normal love is a curiosity; women get sexual satisfaction in the hinterlands while men do what they can on the front. Naturally, women still have the task of bearing children, as the state continually needs more soldiers. The state kills deserters and prisoners of war; later, they do not even spare the lives of the wounded, as it is much easier to kill them than to cure them.

Babits presents his apocalyptic vision with a cool, distant objectivity, with intentional slowness and deliberateness, avoiding any sort of pathos or sensationalism. By this method he is able to evoke fear in the reader more effectively than if he used the method of most war novelists, graphically depicting scenes of bloodshed and brutality.

The plot itself is interesting and full of action. The representatives vote for the universal conscription of women; they organize demonstrations and mass rallies in the streets, provide speakers to fire the mobs with enthusiasm, creating an atmosphere favorable to war. Mrs. Kamuthy attains with some difficulty from Schulberg the concession that her recruited daughter will be used to pilot his aircraft. Elza spends two more nights with her friend and lover Dezsö, who has to return to the front, then awaits her fate apathetically. Schulberg takes Elza with him on his next inspection tour to the front, into the world of air-raid shelters, catacombs, and underground fortresses, where she accidentally witnesses Dezsö's execution by a death-ray for mutiny. Elza next crosses the front line and lands with Schulberg in enemy territory. They are arrested. Schulberg has to work in a hospital as a specialist, and Elza is forced to bomb her own country and native town. Mrs. Kamuthy dies in an air-raid, and the author hints at the possibility that the murderous gas bomb was dropped by Elza.

In the other half of the novel's double plot, Schulberg accidentally witnesses the end of a scientific experiment which began before the outbreak of the Eternal War, when a biologist created a model Earth in order to study the formation and evolution of life. By means of a gravitational device, the biologist managed to keep this model, Little Earth (which is not really little at all), hovering above the ground and rotating. The first germs of life had already formed on the model when a comet passing through the Solar System snatched it into orbit with its gravitational pull. It turns out that the scientist stayed on the model as well, taking notes on the forthcoming events. He lived to see the age of wars among the tiny humanoids of the artificial planet, and eventually perished with them. His notes get into the hands of Schulberg, who speculates that our Earth might be a similar experimental model, the subject of the examinations of a superior intellect. In this way the two lines of the story meet and the Age of Eternal War is given a cosmic and philosophical aspect. The book ends with the notes of the dying biologist.

> There is no more food for me, my days are numbered. The flora and fauna of Little Earth would hardly give me enough food to extend my life by a couple of hours. I am tortured mainly by thirst: I have gulped down their rivers but their seas would not refresh me. Under my ribs there is a hard, painful object, perhaps the ferro-concrete ruins of a skyscraper. . . . I wonder if some of the microscopical beings are still alive who have populated this tiny planet. I wake up from nightmares, under indifferent stars. I have been God of a miserable world. . . . I am alone in the bleak, infinite space. I am short of air as well. . . . I have fits of breathlessness.

Babits is a master of style, not only in his poetry, but in his prose as well; he is able to construct a good plot and to hold together the different lines of the narration. Babits did not write his novel to entertain, to shock, or to astonish his readers. By his great scientific and philosophical erudition, he was able to see the essence of his age under the surface of events — the growth of total-itarian and antihumanistic ideas, for example — and he warned his readers of what was going to happen as a result. Critics regard this work as a novel of despair, the warning exclamation of a sensitive and lonely thinker, who knew his warning would go unheeded. Modern Hungarian science fiction writers regard Babits' novel as one of their most valuable predecessors and honor the humanity of its message, the realism of its vision, and its detailed and credible account of an anti-Utopia of the future.

Péter Kuczka

Sources for Further Study

Criticism:

Aldiss, Brian W. *Billion Year Spree: The True History of Science Fiction.* Garden City, N.Y.: Doubleday, 1973, p. 189. Aldiss discusses Babits' philosophical thought in *Elza Pilota*, a study of split personality.

Tezla, Albert. *Hungarian Authors.* Cambridge, Mass.: The Belknap Press, 1970, pp. 54-63. Tezla feels that Babits displays deep compassion and a humanistic outlook.

THE EMBEDDING

Author: Ian Watson (1943-   )
First book publication: 1973
Type of work: Novel
Time: The present
Locale: Haddon, England; the Amazon Valley; Nevada; outer space

A nightmarish picture of the late twentieth century where highly complex technological experiments with communications systems to achieve mind control are employed by three disparate groups, two human and one alien, with unforeseen disastrous consequences

> *Principal characters:*
> CHRIS SOLE, A British linguist
> PIERRE DARRIAND, a French social anthropologist
> VIDYA, a three-year-old Indo-Pakistani orphan
> BRUXO, a Xemahoa tribal shaman
> KAYAPI, his bastard son
> PH'THERI, an alien being from Sp'thra

In *The Embedding*, Ian Watson has seen the enemy and it is "us." The action is divided among three discrete groups representing increasingly complex stages of evolution: primitive Indians in Brazil; sophisticated scientists at Haddon, England, and in the United States; and pure automatons from outer space. The critical problem that unites the three groups is, what will they do with the technology they have acquired.

All three groups are experimenting with language as a key to absolute reality, but in their utter callousness and ruthless pursuit of knowledge, they become clockwork figures and create monsters who are devoid of human feelings. The experiments prove the insufficiency of a scientific approach to language — indeed the horrible chaos that results when beings evolve beyond their natural capacities.

The novel proceeds chronologically through the twelve days from Christmas to Epiphany, but the time sequence is the only constant. The scenes shift back and forth from one locale to another in a stream-of-consciousness manner, with shifts in thoughts and perceptions reflecting the various embedding experiments and the various levels of reality being probed.

The narrative begins at Haddon, a hospital ostensibly designed to treat brain-damaged children, but in reality, containing in its underground chambers three hidden units where United States financed experiments are being conducted using three- and four-year-old Indo-Pakistani children as subjects. The experimenters — Chris Sole in the embedding world, Dorothy Summers in the logic world, and Richard Jannis in the alien world — are attempting to free these subjects from the natural constraints of language, sensation, and perception through an artificially contrived computer-run laboratory using giant video-screens, sleepteaching, and a drug called PSF to speed up the learning process.

Chris Sole, a linguist, is testing Noam Chomsky's theories about language. According to Chomsky, human beings have a natural set of rules built into their genes which enable them to generate surface structures (sentences) from embedded structures (or deep structures) in the brain. For communication between human beings to take place, language must have an orderly and systematic framework. Such an organization is limiting, but necessary — indeed, the only way language will work. Consequently, the embedding process in language is the natural control mechanism by which human beings fit into their existence by having their capacities limited. Reversing the natural process and embedding artificial languages in the children's minds, Chris Sole hopes to find a key to a new reality which has been bracketed out of existence by natural language. He wants the naked children to break free, at right angles to "this-reality."

As a scientist, Sole thinks he has risen above human feelings such as guilt from his shocking manipulation of Innocents as laboratory rats and jealousy of Pierre, his friend, who has been his wife's lover and whom he suspects of fathering his child. A letter from Pierre, which almost penetrates his armor and arouses human feelings, carries the plot forward and reinforces the theme at critical points.

In the letter, Pierre, a French social antrhopologist and Marxist, announces his discovery of a rare and unique creature among a primitive Amazon valley Indian tribe, the Xemahoas. He is the tribal shaman, Bruxo, who has managed to reverse the natural language process by the use of a fungus (dubbed embedol by Pierre), which has freed him and his people from the restrictions of their language. This drugged dance and speech, referred to experimentally as Xemahoa B, frees their myths as living realities and enables the people to fight "this reality," the advancing floodwaters from a United States financed dam which is embedding them in a huge lake. The Xemahoa B speech minimizes the reality of the flood; the result is a reversal of real and unreal. Ordinarily, in this culture only men take the drug. However, to avert the disaster of the impending flood, Bruxo impregnates a woman with his seed and the fungus, hoping to bring forth a Deliverer. The villagers deify the Madonnalike figure and her unborn child, a "Christ-thing," in a very unholy mockery of the Advent. Pierre, too, takes the drug and under its influence escapes both the boundaries of time and space and the ordinary restraints on semantic features of a language to such a degree that he is able to understand clearly the puzzling surrealistic Roussel poem that has been his elusive intellectual mistress.

The third strand of the snarled and tangled plot surfaces when an alien spacecraft lands. Dr. Sole, because of his language expertise, is summoned to Nevada to join the secret U.S.-U.S.S.R. welcoming party. The alien visitor, a giant nine-foot spaceman, Ph'theri, speaks for the group to whom he is attached *via* scarlet wires attached to a box on his chest. Because the Sp'thra are language traders, listening and speaking have accentuated the evolution of highly sensitive ears and a large, flickering butterfly tongue, their two predominant features. Dr. Sole notices Ph'theri's flat nose, membranous eyes, and lack of incisors; apparently violence is not an inherent part of their nature. However, their evolution seems quite different from Darwin's theory of evolution. A type, a representative of the Sp'thra, Ph'theri has no distinguishing personality, no sense of a living, vibrant being.

Highly sophisticated technologically, the Sp'thra have come to Earth from their twin worlds 1,103 light years away by riding the energy tides of the galaxies, a technique acquired from the Wave Readers who have this knowledge instinctively embedded in their genes (not very Darwinian, either). The alien signal traders offer a roadmap to the nearest habitable planet together with the technology to get there in exchange for representative samples of human language generated from living brains. If they can penetrate the depths (recesses) of the human mind, they will be able to penetrate the depths of the universe.

Ph'theri explains their motive, their sense or urgency and their impatience. He says that thirteen thousand years ago the Change Speakers, who had embedded the Sp'thra, broke free and left them "by modulating their embedding in reality." Their absence has left the Sp'thra with something missing in their existence, what they call "The Bereft Love" for the Change Speakers. Only when they have acquired all the languages of the universe and superimposed them on their Language Moon, will they be able to grasp the "Other-Reality" and escape their embedding in "This-Reality." Then, they will be free to locate the Change Speakers, but they are unable to predict what they will do when they find their love, (just as Sole is unsure what will happen when his brain-children grasp another reality, and as Bruxo is unsure what will happen when his progeny senses another reality).

As the first step in the bargaining process, the scientists bring six sedated human bodies — Japanese, Eskimo, Russian, English, Vietnamese, Persian — representing all the basic language types on Earth (agglutinative, monosyllabic, inflective, incorporative) with instruction tapes. Experts at trading, the Sp'thra want more trade units. When Chris Sole shows them Pierre's letter describing Bruxo's self-embedded brain and the freedom from "This-Reality" it has attained, they risk missing the energy tides home to wait for Bruxo to be brought to them. With his self-embedded brain, their inventory will be complete, and they will be free of "that vibration in . . . [their] minds, imprinted so many centuries ago" by the Change Speakers.

It is a supreme irony that a ticket to the stars hinges now on a primordial Indian in a primitive, savage jungle in South America. But the U.S.-U.S.S.R. politico-scientific team risks the use of nuclear weapons to blow up their enormously expensive dam, killing thousands of people in order to preserve the symbiotic environment of Bruxo and the fungus. When the three-man delegation arrives to kidnap Bruxo, they witness the birth of the unnatural drug child — actually a grotesque freak with no eyes and a brain protruding from three hernias. By tampering with the natural and imposing the artificial, Bruxo has produced a monster, the culmination of the Indians' primitive technology. The plan has backfired, as will the other two plans.

Political intrigue complicates the plot. When the Chinese Communists detect the nuclear explosive with a spy satellite and expose the incident, the Russians and Americans unite to quash a Latin American revolution by revealing the visit of the Sp'thra and blaming them for the incident.

With Bruxo dying, his bastard son, Kayapi, after three days of thinking and planning, eats the living freak's turgid brains, then buries the baby, telling the Indians that their dreams have now entered him. Here, the novel reaches its climax. Sole vomits with revulsion. Disillusioned and saddened, Pierre recognizes Kayapi as a slick *arriviste*, who has no profound understanding of man's essential nature. He is not a teacher, but a "village Hitler." Looking around at the "natural" — the teeming village life, the making of fish nets (artistic creations), the games the children are playing — Sole realizes his own utter hypocrisy, how in his mad pursuit of science he has missed the brilliance and beauty of life and the uniqueness of each specific individual. When these human feelings begin to assert themselves, Sole decides to rescue his brain-child Vidya from the hidden, subterranean galleries of Haddon, but in so doing he opens a Pandora's Box.

Vidya now reflects the negative image of what the hospital projects: rehabilitation. Actually he represents the nucleus of humanity — primitive, sensual, beautiful — but the scientists have managed through their experiments to destroy every viable and organic quality which makes him human. Rejecting the artificially embedded speech, Vidya, now violent, his brain overloaded, begins transmitting to other brains by a process of "projective empathy." When Sole rescues the child, who is now insane, Vidya imprints (embeds) Sole, enabling him to apprehend reality by direct sensory perception. Without the boundaries of time and space and the aid of symbols and distancing by words and abstract thoughts, Sole's mind cracks as well.

In the concluding chapters, Sole's madness is counterpointed by Dr. Pip's plundering of the spoils of the spaceship trying to save the collected brains of the universe so they can be rescued by cyrogenics for research purposes. The parallel from *Moby Dick* suggests that he, too, is demented.

The Sp'thra and their extraterrestrial world are now lost to man. But their very nature serves as a warning because they represent the essence of the weakness of modern science. They have blinders on and have bracketed all that man perceives as human out of their existence. It is in the questions that they do not ask, really their failure to communicate the most important things in man's life (the architectonics of a bird song, what it is like to fall in love, what strikes a person as funny) that they reveal their lack of understanding of human beings and human values. Conversely, the scientists cannot comprehend the Sp'thra's nature: their sense of time, their trade-assessing, their concept of Bereft Love.

At the end, Pierre sadly realizes that human beings may never achieve that perfection which will allow them to live in complete harmony, in spite of Karl Marx. Moreover, when any agent programs or indoctrinates an individual to rid that person of undesirable traits or change his basic nature, it may destroy the most worthwhile and valuable impulses as well.

The structure of the novel takes the reader forward into the future and backward into the primitive past, glimpsing the various stages of evolution. Throughout, there is a sense of impending and enveloping disaster, really the "negative pay-off" from exploring frontiers that carry too great a risk, from learning about humanity through inhuman means.

Maxine Rose

Sources for Further Study

Reviews:

Books and Bookmen. XIX, October, 1973, p. 138.

Observer. September 2, 1973, p. 35.

Spectator. CCXXXI, August 4, 1973, p. 154.

Times Literary Supplement. November 9, 1973, p. 1378.

EMPEROR OF THE IF

Author: Guy Dent
First book publication: 1926
Type of work: Novel
Time: The present, an alternate present, and a hypothetical far future
Locale: The environs of London and an estate in Sussex

An account of the investigation of two hypothetical worlds — an alternate present and a possible future — brought into being by a machine which controls the power of thought

Principal characters:
JOHN BLATHERWICK, a man of leisure
A. CHILTON-GREYNE, a scientist
PETER VANDREDON, a country gentleman
JANE, his mother

Emperor of the If was the first novel to be developed around the notion of alternate history, exploring the world that might exist if some incident in the past had happened differently. Though the scientist Greyne, introducing the notion in the early chapters, speaks of such possible histories as one ensuing from the victory of the Spanish Armada over the English fleet, and another ensuing from the nonexistence of Martin Luther, the actual hypothesis used in the novel is of a more fundamental nature. For this reason the book becomes an exercise in speculative social evolution rather than imaginary political history. Because of this difference from the kind of alternate world novel that has since become common in genre science fiction, *Emperor of the If* takes its speculations further, by supplementing its image of the world as it might have been with an image of the world as it might yet be — a vision of the future which is conditional on certain specified premises.

The character whose view of affairs is described for the reader's benefit through most of the narrative is John Blatherwick, a social nonentity who seems to be entirely dominated by his friend, the scientist Chilton-Greyne (whose Christian name we never learn, though he always addresses Blatherwick as "John"). Greyne is a man of extravagant ideas; he is vain, aggressive, and antisocial, but nevertheless brilliant. In his laboratory he has devised a machine, one of whose components is a human brain, which can harness and amplify the power of thought. With this machine he can alter the phenomenal universe, though how the machine works is not entirely clear (the philosophical implications of the machine's capacity remain unexplored, though its actions are in stark violation of the basic postulates of scientific empiricism).

What Greyne wants to do is to conduct a colossal experiment in social Darwinism. He is convinced that modern man has things far too easy, and that his achievements have been limited by the fact that the struggle for existence has been ameliorated. He wants to confront his contemporaries with the world as it might have been, in order to face them with a great challenge. The weak, he knows, will be unable to adapt, but he is convinced that the strong will come through ready to build a better world.

Greyne instructs the brain to imagine what the world would be like had the Ice Age not altered its climate. The phenomenal world then begins to undergo a gradual metamorphosis, as the "Inertia of Custom" slowly yields to the power of the machine. The temperature rises and primeval forests begin to engulf London as the artifacts of civilization begin to crumble and disappear. Various kinds of prehistoric fauna, including pterosaurs and carnosaurs, commence a reign of terror, and people who cannot muster the strength of mind even to preserve themselves decay into the clouds of flies which represent the alternate destiny of their flesh. Greyne's reaction to the sight of all this is characteristic:

> Greyne stood thus and cried proudly in a wild voice. "I have sinned!" he cried. "I have committed the greatest sin recorded in the history of the world, for I have altered the face of the earth against Thy Will." His face was upturned and quick with the passion of his triumph.

Dent's knowledge of prehistory is vague even for 1926. He has no grasp of chronology (the dinosaurs, of course, were extinct long before the Pleistocene glaciations), and he seems uncertain about the integrity of his invented world. Greyne and Blatherwick set out to explore it, but their findings are given in a rather sketchy manner. They head south toward Sussex; Greyne apparently has a destination in mind, but does not confide in his acolyte. They find the survivors in the country banding together in small camps, having lost almost everything, and finding the struggle to survive almost beyond their capacities.

Eventually, though, Greyne and Blatherwick find one small area where the old world has been preserved: a country house and its gardens. The man of the house is one Peter Vandredon, but it seems that the indomitable will which has resisted the power of the machine is that of his aged mother Jane. Greyne is appalled by this successful small-scale rebellion, but the Vandredons are equally appalled by him; they consider his act to be monstrously evil, and they dismiss his social Darwinist justifications as despicable. They reveal to Blatherwick that his unthinking cooperation in the experiment has helped to make it possible, and they awaken in him a strong sense of guilt.

Jane Vandredon believes that Greyne's experiment can be subverted, and when Greyne and Bletherwick continue on their journey, Peter Vandredon accompanies them. Greyne is disillusioned by the condition into which mankind has sunk, but uses this to justify his opinion of his contemporaries. What he is actually seeking is the men that *belong* in this world — the human race that might have been. Inhabiting the land that was, in another world, the estate of his forefathers, he finds them — strange, savage creatures with skins protectively colored to hide them from predators. In all their long existence in this hostile world they have built nothing and achieved nothing. One of them —

Greyne's alter ego — knows Greyne as his creator, and asks for his approval. When Greyne can find no justification in their existence for what he has done, they turn against him with savage ferocity. As Greyne and his companions flee a series of visions appears in the sky, and God — perhaps summoned by Jane Vandredon to mankind's aid — echoes the alter ego in demanding of Greyne some justification for his acts. This time, when Greyne cries out "I have sinned!" it is not in triumph but in terror. Nevertheless, it is not he but Blatherwick who somehow escapes through a fold in time to cancel the experiment at the moment of its instigation, so that only he, Greyne and the Vandredons retain the memory of it.

This climactic moment ends the first part of the book, and Dent follows it with a "sequel" in which Greyne, working now in collaboration with Jane Vandredon, undertakes a less ambitious project. He has the brain create, on an unlimited scale, the kind of world which would result if human nature continues in its present course. What he wants to see is the ultimate extrapolation of the world determined by contemporary values. Again, Blatherwick goes with him, and they emerge into the world as it might be millions of years hence, into the twilight zone of an Earth that always turns the same face to a dim red sun. The human inhabitants of this world are dwarves whose condition is worse than that of the striped savages of the alternate present. They are kept alive (barely) by great self-replicating machines which dominate the world, and they fight endless wars among themselves. The usefulness of the humans in servicing these machines appears to be almost at an end, and already the machines are murderously careless in their treatment of their slaves. A dwarf who is, perhaps, the ultimate descendant of Greyne or his companion, gives them an account of his existence which leaves them in no doubt as to its horror and misery. Civilization, Greyne comments (not without a degree of self-congratulation) has been aborted, because contemporary man, if credited with no power to change and adapt, is ultimately worthless, fit only to be a slave to his machines.

As Greyne and Blatherwick flee back to the laboratory, threatened by the war of the machines which rages around them, they see for a second time a vision in the sky — a vision of a tired and tormented Christ forever carrying his cross. The dwarf who is with them finds the vision terrifying, and cannot bear to look at the image of suffering, but as it fades away into the starlit sky, Blatherwick sees a faint light far away in the night side of the world, and fancies that he hears plaintive music. Because of this, he retains the hope that even in this ultimate desolation of the human spirit there may be some hope which can sustain him in his mundane life in the twentieth century.

Emperor of the If is a dramatic representation of the conflict between opposing value systems: that of Social Darwinism (which, by implication, stands as the representation of "Science" in general) and that of Christianity. The author, of course, favors the latter, but there is a remarkable ambivalence in his portrayal of Greyne: the scientist is evil, though he repents of his crime against humanity, but he is also *right* in his analysis of the fallibility of contemporary man. He is introduced as if he were the hero, is then revealed as the villain, but finally ends up as a cynical observer on the sidelines, whose sneering comment of "I told you so" is very nearly justified. For this reason, the book — though clearly on the side of the angels — can hardly be regarded as an optimistic one.

The fact that the book's narrative strategy is innovative (and that the strategy later became conventional in genre science fiction) recommends it to the attention of the historian of science fiction, but its real strengths are not those of method — indeed, the *logic* of what happens in the story is incompetent. What *is* particularly striking about Dent's novel is its attitude toward the existential situation and potential future of man. Its vision of the future is as bleak as that presented by H. G. Wells in *The Time Machine*, and for precisely the same reason: it reflects a loss of faith in the adaptability of man. The hope that there could and might be a fundamental change in human nature of the kind that might lead to a better world is presented as a very frail one, if not quite illusory: merely a glow of light and a breath of sound emanating from a vast expanse of Stygian darkness. *Emperor of the If* is one of the few speculative novels in which the distant past, the distant future, and at least one other possible present are *all* imagined as bleak and hostile *milieux* in which the human spirit must inevitably be crushed unless it can rise to superhuman efforts of will and faith. This aspect of the novel recalls the fervid mythology of apocalyptic cults.

Emperor of the If appeared in the same year as the first issue of *Amazing Stories*, and the philosophy behind its speculations provides a striking contrast to the naïve, materialistic Utopianism which inspired Hugo Gernsback in his endeavor. Nevertheless, it is possible to identify a common cause in the two projects, and something of a common spirit of adventure. Though Dent's novel draws upon the religious imagination as much as the scientific imagination, it is motivated by an imaginative boldness which belongs very much to the latter. The acknowledgement of the crucial importance of the *ifs* of existence is something which came out of the philosophy of science, a fact which needs to be remembered in any discussion of the nature of science fiction or attempt to identify important endeavors within the field. *Emperor of the If* deserves attention as one such endeavor.

Brian Stableford

Sources for Further Study

Criticism:

Ash, Brian. *Visual Encyclopedia of Science Fiction*. New York: Harmony, 1977, p. 123. This book is an early example of the one world suspension posed on another theme.

ENGINE SUMMER

Author: John Crowley
First book publication: 1979
Type of work: Novel
Locale: The Earth
Time: The distant future

Rush that Speaks, born into an isolated, self-absorbed culture, embarks on a search for "sanctity" that leads him to try to understand his world and its history

Principal characters:
RUSH THAT SPEAKS, a member of the Truthful Seeker community
ONCE A DAY, his lover
"ANGEL," a representative of the lost cultures of humanity
ZHINSINURA, an inhabitant of one of the deserted cities of the Old Ones

John Crowley is one of the many younger science fiction writers who have already made a lasting impression. His first book, *The Deep*, was one of the finest first novels of the last decade, and his second, *Beasts*, demonstrated that his was not a limited once-in-a-lifetime talent.

With the publication of *Engine Summer*, Crowley firmly establishes his mastery of one of the most difficult traditions in science fiction — the story of the far future after man has either obliterated himself in some atomic cataclysm or become so enervated by age, boredom, or in-breeding that he no longer has the will to live. Some of these works, such as George Stewart's *Earth Abides*, are justly famous as science fiction classics, but the difficulties of portraying a credible end-of-the-world story and staffing it with anything except caricatures are enormous. Crowley has overcome most of these difficulties very well indeed, and his languorous story captures the *fin de siècle* mood almost perfectly. It is an excellent novel.

The key to understanding the work may lie in its very title, *Engine Summer*. Say *Engine Summer* aloud and it comes out "Injun Summer"; and the spirit evoked by the phrase is almost exactly what Crowley attempts to create in this book, filled with what can only be called a nostalgia for the future. In this sense, Crowley resembles no one quite so much as Ray Bradbury, whose work is filled with a warm sense of the past, its beauties and joys, its youthful vigor translated into the future, and its long, long thoughts. Even Crowley's prose, although he writes with his own voice and in his own style, is curiously reminiscent of Bradbury's. His sure sense of metaphor and verbal extravagance is remarkable indeed. "The ivy covered the building like a messy beard." "That month's full moon lit the bald, still earth and we listened to the cracks and snaps of its freezing."

It is a loose-limbed prose, and Crowley adopts a leisurely pace in telling his story; his very symbolic language is extremely relaxed. Certainly Crowley's skill with words marks him as much more than a simple craftsman; he is well on his way to becoming a verbal artist. One of the standard critical comments made about much science fiction is that it is not written very well. Fine stories may be told, stories that involve the reader and force an expansion of his consciousness, but they are too often told in the most pedestrian manner, in language that does nothing but advance the action. Fine writers, master stylists, are all too few in science fiction — the names of Theodore Sturgeon, Ursula Le Guin, and Brian Aldiss come to mind — and Crowley promises to join the ranks of the elite.

Moreover, Crowley attempts a most difficult task in this novel: telling a story of the future as if it were a fairy tale. In fact, he incorporates many of the elements of the fairy story: animals speak; Puss in Boots makes an appearance; magicians pore over ancient volumes; and the Hero searches for his lost Lady and finds a forgotten magic city. Yet *Engine Summer* is more than fantasy, allegory, or even parable. It is most definitely science fiction, although most of the science in it is forgotten knowledge.

In the distant future, then, the few scattered survivors of humanity have developed into isolated communities that are both self-sufficient and self-absorbed. Into one of them, the Truthful Seekers, Rush That Speaks is born. The story of his quest for sanctity, the totality of Truth, is told to an "Angel." Gradually both the reader and Rush That Speaks discover that the "Angel" is in fact a survivor of the Old Ones ("Angels") and records Rush's story on the facets of crystals.

In some ways, *Engine Summer* is a *Bildungsroman*, a novel of adolescence, of growing up, of development and maturity. We see everything through Rush's eyes, and we are as confused about the "Angels" and their reality as Rush is; but we also know little about Rush's world. He lives in a "warren," called Little Belaire, falls in love with Once a Day, a member of the secretive Whisper cord that in fact preserves the ancient mysteries. Other "cords" also inhabit Little Belaire, all of them with a specific purpose in life, and all of them completely happy to continue with their absorbing tasks. Each inhabitant seems instinctively to understand his own role as well as that of the cord to which he belongs. Everyone, in other words, lives in total harmony with nature and his surroundings. There is little development of the intellect among the members of the various cords. They seem intuitively to sense the essential rightness of things, and that interior harmony is enough for all of them — except Rush That Speaks.

The rest of the novel is devoted to Rush's story of his journey. Having left the warren, Little Belaire, to search for Once a Day, his mission is not only to find her but to become a saint — and sanctity in Rush's world means not only extraordinary holiness but the ability to tell his story in such a way that everyone who listens will see a reflection of his own situation and the situation of all humanity. With great irony, Rush's story is told to one whom he calls an "Angel," who presumably has achieved sanctity. And it is also told to the reader. Thus Rush's story — Heisenberg-like — affects the "Angel" and Rush simultaneously; but it also affects the reader with its admonitory message. For as Rush, in all of his innocence, probes the old, hidden mysteries, he becomes transformed. In turn, he transforms the "Angel" as well. His story may even transform the reader.

How much of *Engine Summer* may be parable or allegory should, perhaps, be finally left up to the reader. Surely, however, Crowley raises many questions in his leisurely, languorous narrative — questions that are never completely answered, to be sure, but that nonetheless engage the reader's attention far beyond (or beneath) the surface of the narrative. Who, ultimately, is Rush? A simple boy on a journey? A reembodiment of all that is best in humanity? One who has possessed all knowledge and understanding? A genuine saint? The best of the Old Ones? An oracle?

Rush, in a way, is all of these things. But his very name suggests another interpretation. In his travels throughout the world, Rush has come upon four giant faces carved into the side of a great mountain. There is some confusion about the number. Are there four faces or five on what the reader slowly comes to understand is Mount Rushmore? Is Rush elevated to the lofty status of one more wise paternal figure on the mountain, gazing benignly over the world, to be awakened when his wisdom is needed, to sleep and rest when it is not? The ambiguity is brilliant; and for all that it does not permit of a final answer, the artistry is welcome simply because it requires an equally artistic response on the part of the reader. Together, author and reader can make of the novel almost anything they wish.

The opening pages, with their depiction of a completely new intuitive society, are particularly effective. But the course of Rush's epic search, his appraisal of the artifacts of the "angels," his apprenticeship to a wise man in his quest for sanctity, are often as puzzling as they are brilliant. In one sense, then, *Engine Summer* resembles a giant puzzle. Bits and pieces fit here and there, and, just as Rush himself tries to solve some acrostics, the reader attempts to fit a ball, a glove, a facet of a crystal, a road, a knot in a string, into the poetic puzzle posed by the novel. The final shape may not be completely clear, but it is decipherable. Part of the pleasure we have in reading this remarkable book comes from the satisfaction we experience in placing one piece after another into its proper place in the total design.

Engine Summer is not a novel to be read in an afternoon by one who seeks clear-cut action or the fast-paced adventure. It is, rather, a book to be lingered over, to be savored, to return to again and again with ever increasing pleasure. The pleasure may come from an appreciation of Crowley's extraordinary skill in handling the English language, or it may be derived from an appreciation of the subtleties of plot or the nuances of character. It is one of the rare science fiction books where the joy of discovery is surpassed by the joy of rediscovery upon a second reading.

Crowley's new book may not be the simplest to understand. In fact, it is one of the most subtly difficult works of the last few years. Yet it is one that repays the effort required to understand it. Whether it is fairy tale, science fiction, parable, or allegory makes little difference in the end. *Engine Summer* is, quite simply, a fine novel.

Willis E. McNelly

Sources for Further Study

Reviews:

Kirkus Reviews. XLVII, January 15, 1979, p. 89.

EPP

Author: Axel Jensen (1932-   )
First book publication: 1965
English translation: 1967
Type of work: Novel
Time: An indefinite future
Locale: Room 1411, block 982, in the city of Oblidor in Gambolia

Epp, an automat old-age pensioner who lives in a cell-like room in a dismal future, describes his life, neighbors, and society through his diary

Principal characters:
EPP, an automat old-age pensioner
LEM, his neighbor

Epp, a small, fat, egocentric, pedantic man, lives in the city of Oblidor in the state of Gambolia. He has a small one-person flat (or "nest," as he calls it), number 1411, in block 982, equipped with a tiny kitchen, television, toilet, and a mail-and-article-tube system. He has lived there for twenty-five years, ever since being pensioned off when the wallpaper factory where he worked was fully automated and turned over to robots. Since that time, Epp has lived in his little closet and pondered his existence, filling his days by feeding his carnivorous plant, writing his diary, cutting papers, talking to (or more correctly, nagging) his neighbor Lem, and ceremoniously eating his daily boiled egg. In his dairy, he carefully describes his activities of the day and scrupulously revises his previous entries.

Through this dairy we learn about the society Epp lives in. It is a totalitarian regime, ruled by one Mynk Mynk, and involved in a victorious but incessant war with its neighbor, the country of Om. From the Gambolian side the war is fought with robots, which brings the war up to an "intellectual level by changing or rather embellishing the deathcry and rattle of the Omesian to Gambolian military music." Although expansion space has been found and the Gambolian scientists are experimenting with teleprojections (teleportation), for the present, most of the people are crowded into huge block cities, with four thousand people per block and thousands of blocks in each city.

Thus, the people are massed together in huge numbers and yet are individually separated into their own isolated cells. As a result, they have been morally blunted and intellectually stultified. Epp is not unique; everyone is self-absorbed and detached from his fellows. They want no direct contact, much less involvement, with their neighbors, but they are at the same time fascinated by the unusual actions of others. At night many stand in lines to gaze through the spy-eyes in the doors (or "Judas-eyes" as Epp calls them) to study the peculiarities of their fellow men — and everyone has their own special peculiarities. Epp, for example, is obsessed by wallpaper. He judges all others on the basis of their taste in wallpaper. If they do not share his obsession, they are strange; if they do, Epp finds other trivial details to provoke his disdain.

He regards the jungle wallpaper that Lem has on his wall as a clear indication of inferiority.

This obsession with trivia, reminiscent of an Ionesco farce, is well illustrated by a fight the two men have over Lem's goldfish:

> Look! Epp, he said and sprinkled the seed. Goldfishseed! he said. Isn't it nice? Yes, he really did call the seeds goldfishseed. I on the other hand saw at once that it was birdseed that he stood there and fed the fish with, and I was also man enough to tell him the truth.

Two men become overwrought about something ridiculously frivolous, turning it into a matter of pride and principle, becoming almost violent. In a society devoid of any real meaning, meaningless things evoke passionate responses. The fight results in a month-long break in their friendship. The breach is healed only when Lem gives in, apologizes, and subjects himself once again to Epp's nagging.

But there is a more serious difference between them. Lem desires more real contact with other people. He even suggests cutting doors between the rooms, doors which the inspectors could not control because they would be between cells, carefully out of sight. Lem expounds his vision: his idea will spread over all of Gambolia, then later to his brothers in Om. Epp puts Lem's vision down in one phrase: "what about the draught?"

Jensen's novel again raises the question of why mainstream authors write science fiction. What advantages does this popular genre have for the serious writer?

In general, science fiction books can be divided roughly into two categories: popular adventures and "message" books. The former are strictly for entertainment and could be almost anything else — westerns, crime novels — dressed up in the trappings of science fiction. Instead of riding a horse and saving a ranch from being taken over by the bad guys, the hero flies a spaceship and saves the world (or another planet) from a mad scientist or alien takeover. Many of these books have little lasting intellectual or artistic merit.

However, when a mainstream author writes a science fiction story, it usually fits into the "message" category; most such Scandinavian writers have presented pessimistic warnings to mankind. Mainstream writer Axel Jensen is no exception; he follows the road marked by his fellow Norwegian Karin Boye, as well as by such famous dystopians as Aldous Huxley and George Orwell.

Many of the message-writers, including professional science fiction writers, use the genre as a coverup. If what they want to say were placed in an ordinary mainstream novel, it would probably be rejected as either reactionary or radical. But if they use as their vehicles future settings, alternate worlds, or accounts of alien attacks on Earth, they can move more freely and with less fear of criticism. For instance, Jack Finney in *The Body Snatchers* or Robert A. Heinlein in *The Puppet Masters*, writing during the American Cold War period, embodied their politically controversial ideas in colorful, action-filled stories at a time when it was difficult to make open political statements in the arts. Axel Jensen uses the genre in much the same way, to warn us about the way things are going, especially such problems as growing automation, the crowding of the modern metropolis, the impersonal treatment accorded people as individuals, the pernicious influence of television, and war as an "aesthetic experience."

But *Epp* is an uneven book, at times brilliant and incisive, at times boring and soporific; it has many elements of deep seriousness and clever satire. Jensen's descriptions of the lonely and egocentric Epp and his surroundings are sharp, bleak, and eerie. There is a clear harmony between style and motive; Epp, who is unable to put two and two together in his own life, cannot likewise place one sentence in relation to the next. His diary jumps forward as a stream of propositions, simple, reasonable, and quite absurd ("Epp turns himself over, but he has not anything to give, except his own bile"). In the beginning of the book, the description of Epp is especially black; later on it becomes more grayish. But the so-called redeeming and creative unity in Epp only redeems his fear of closer contacts. He is panic-stricken when Lem suggests that they drill a hole in the wall in order to touch each other. His universe grows progressively constricted, until his whole existence becomes a compulsive daily rotation around an unchanging axis. In the end, Epp becomes completely satisfied with his dissatisfactions.

It is especially the satire, witty and sharp, that makes the book interesting. The description of the social hierarchy is masterful. All people are given three-letter names, such as Epp, Lem, Nal, Noh, Iku, when they are born. If they are able to rise in the hierarchy, they get more letters — Eppe, Eppen, or Eppenep. But if they fail to live up to the system, they lose letters: Hep becomes He or even H. Jensen also pinpoints human intolerance towards others with precision. Epp's value and judgment of people is based on their wallpaper, because he has a diploma from the wallpaper factory.

Epp's conformity is also fascinating. In his immediate response to Lem's proposal about further contact between them, Epp does not even react against the substance of Lem's proposal — the fact that it is a reaction against the system and its values, even a revolutionary act; he fears it only because it will ruin his wallpaper. Indeed, Epp is even more of a conformist than the system demands; his only dissatisfaction concerns the government's attempt to get people more interested in culture and the "silly" holiday it celebrates because of signals from outer space; these events do not fit into his narrowminded way of thinking.

Thus, *Epp* is a thoroughly serious, perceptive satire. It makes its points sharply and emphatically — perhaps too much so. In the end, Jensen weakens his novel considerably by overstating and repeating his arguments; his examples tumble over one another and pile up too fast to be examined individually. As Epp says, "He can't see woods for trees."

In addition, Jensen's own fear of the future pervades the book too strongly; his vision is bleak and unrelieved. At an early point, he loses control of his narrative, and his personal views become confused with Epp's egocentric and pessimistic attitudes; artistic detachment is thus lost.

Perhaps some of this bleakness can be traced to Jensen's fascination with the works of Samuel Beckett, and especially with the *Molloy Trilogy*: *Molloy* (1951), *Malone Dies* (1951), and *The Unnamable* (1953). Two obvious borrowings can be noted; one is successful, the other is not. Jensen's naming of characters (Epp, Lem, Kor, Omi, Meg, and so on), which has already been mentioned, is largely derived from Beckett. However, Epp's egg-eating ceremony (filling three pages), inspired by the sucking-stone transference scene from *Molloy* (a two-page scene), is a failure — one of the dullest of the book's several dull scenes.

But more crucial than these obvious borrowings is Jensen's pervasive desire to copy Beckett's style and vision. His attempts to duplicate Beckett's witty, absurd, detailed style only prove once again that an author co-opts the style of another artist — especially one as idiosyncratic as Beckett — at his own peril. Mixed with undertones of *Brave New World* and *Kallocain* — but without Huxley's lively satire or Boye's believable texture of gloom — Jensen's use of the Beckett mode results in a long (in spite of its mere one hundred pages) and sometimes boring novel. The boredom and indifference that Epp shows toward his neighbors, which Jensen hopes to use satirically, produces in the reader an indifference toward the novel itself.

Erik H. Swiatek

Sources for Further Study

Criticism:

Heiberg, Inger. *Norwegian Literature, Anno 1965*. Norway: Universitets Forlaget, 1967, pp. 77-78. Heiberg calls *Epp* a satirical and humorous tale of automation in the future.

Reviews:

Listener. LXXVII, March 30, 1967, p. 9437.

Manchester Guardian. XCVI, March 30, 1967, p. 11.

New Statesman. LXXIII, March 17, 1967, p. 372.

Punch. CCLII, March 22, 1967, p. 436.

Times Literary Supplement. August 3, 1967, p. 701.

EREWHON
AND
EREWHON REVISITED

Author: Samuel Butler (1835-1902)
First book publications: Erewhon (1872); *Erewhon Revisited* (1901)
Type of work: Novels
Time: Erewhon, 1868; *Erewhon Revisited*, 1890
Locale: An isolated country in a remote part of the world

A Victorian social satire loosely based on a conventional traveler's tale

> *Principal characters:*
> THE NARRATOR (GEORGE HIGGS), a sheep-farmer
> MR. AND MRS. NOSNIBOR, inhabitants of Erewhon
> AROWHENA AND ZULORA, their daughters
> GEORGE STRONG, the narrator's son
> YRAM, his mother
> DR. GARGOYLE, a philosopher

The word "Erewhon" seems to suggest a reverse spelling of the word "Nowhere." Since "nowhere" is the meaning of the Greek roots from which Sir Thomas More coined "Utopia," one might suspect *Erewhon* would be a Utopian novel like More's *Utopia* or William Morris' *News from Nowhere.* However, it is not; it is instead a satire, similar in many ways to *Gulliver's Travels.* The Narrator, like Gulliver, is a rather obtuse captive of his own social presuppositions, which he carries to an unexplored land noticeably different from but suspiciously similar to his own. Two of the people who live in Erewhon, for example, are Thims and Nosnibor (Smith and Robinson), and the principal goddess is Ydgrun (Mrs. Grundy, who was a personification of Public Opinion for the Victorians).

Unlike *Gulliver's Travels*, however, *Erewhon* cannot be read by children on the level of the story alone, for there is very little story. What story there is concerns the Narrator, who has a job in wool production in a remote Crown Colony (probably in New Zealand). He decides to explore beyond the mountains in search of adventure and financial gain. After a hazardous journey he finds himself in Erewhon, is brought before a magistrate, and lands in jail. (While in jail he meets Yram; their son plays a significant role in the sequel.) Because he arouses the interest of royalty, he is taken to the capital city and set free. These adventures comprise eight chapters. After nineteen intervening chapters in which the institutions of the country are described, there is one final chapter in which the Narrator finds himself in trouble and manages to escape with his sweetheart (not Yram) in a balloon. *Erewhon Revisited* has a more detailed plot, but it presupposes a knowledge of Erewhonian institutions.

Obviously the main interest in the Erewhon books is not the story but the commentary. In *Erewhon* the plot is minimal and the commentary, however interesting, is disorganized; it was based on four separate articles written over a period of ten years. Butler manages to include his ideas on education, on the relations between parents and children, and on feminism, but the main focus is on science and religion. The science, of course, is Darwinian; the religion is that of the Anglican Church and its alternatives in Victorian England. In *Erewhon Revisited* (written thirty years later but chronicling events that are supposed to take place twenty years later) the same concerns are apparent, but they are better integrated. Instead of evolution *and* religion (and a lot of other things), the focus is on the evolution *of* religion.

Butler was concerned about the dehumanization he saw both in Darwinian evolution and in revealed religion. He insisted on the central importance of human intelligence, will, and emotion: he rejected views of the universe that gave first place to nonhuman elements, such as the Darwinian view, which emphasized chance variation, or the religious view, which emphasized miracles. In his Lamarckian theory of creative evolution, will, rather than accident, plays the key role in forming adaptive variations. He resolved the religious problem by deciding that Christianity can be true although based on myths: it can be useful although not logical. While the specific problems he deals with may be dated, his interest in human consciousness, and especially in the logical and the nonlogical, is still relevant. It is noteworthy that the trip from the everyday world where values are taken for granted to the world where values must be examined is not only difficult but traumatic, and that finally the hero succumbs to brain fever and dies. Butler illustrates in *Erewhon* that logic can conflict with human values.

In his book Butler also criticizes what he considered the excessively mechanical view of the world implicit in the Darwinian theory of evolution. First he discusses machines themselves. Some of his contemporaries feared that a machine age would bring dehumanization. The inhabitants of Butler's Utopia have combined this fear with the concept of evolution, and decided that machines might evolve into selfsufficient and dominant creatures; they conclude, therefore, that all machines should be abolished. (One of the reasons the Narrator is suspect when he first arrives in Erewhon is that he owns a watch.) There are machinist and antimachinist parties in Erewhon, who finally reach a compromise whereby only those machines created earlier than 271 years ago must be abolished.

Another Erewhonian controversy involves the rights of animals and the rights of vegetables. Animals, birds, and fishes are our fellow-creatures; therefore it is considered cannibalistic to eat them. For a time, therefore, the Erewhonians are vegetarian, until a philosopher points out that since animals and plants are cousins, it is also immoral to eat plants. This state of affairs cannot last, and eventually it is decided that animals as well as vegetables can be eaten. "Thus, after several hundred years of wandering in the wilderness of philosophy, the country reached the conclusions that common sense had long since arrived at." In the chapters on the rights of animals and vegetables and on the dangers of machines, Butler carries Darwinian thought to logical conclusions which deviate from common sense. For Butler, human needs were as important as the mechanical laws of logic; he believed that we determine ourselves as much as we are determined by outside forces.

If we have been determined by evolutionary laws, or if we have been programed by an omnipotent creator, we are not responsible for our weaknesses. Yet society cannot function unless people take responsibility for themselves. Butler presents this paradox by inverting the customs regarding physical and moral deficiencies. In Erewhon one goes to jail for measles and the common cold (a prisoner convicted of tuberculosis is sentenced to hard labor for life, but, in a parody of inept attempts at prison reform, he is granted two tablespoons of castor oil daily). Other forms of bad luck are also criminal.

On the other hand, in Erewhon people commiserate with an embezzler or an alcoholic; there are kind words and folk remedies, and in serious cases a "straightener" is called in. In Butler's view (which comes closer to that of the twentieth century than the nineteenth), to have received the kind of training which results in antisocial behavior is as much a matter of bad luck as to have inherited the kind of constitution which results in illness. It is irrational to make people accountable for some kinds of luck but not others. The Erewhonian penal code is another look at Darwinian evolutionary theory, which elevates the role of chance and does not account for human will. Our society is inconsistent in accepting Darwin while glorifying will power. And while we pay lip service to will power, we really worship luck: those fortunate enough to have inherited good looks, talent, or money are the ones who are further rewarded by society.

What we say we believe and how we act are not always consistent. So, too, with the Erewhonians. In Erewhon there are numerous gods and goddesses, personifications of Justice, Love, and the like. However, the worship of these deities is not as enthusiastic as the worship of Ydgrun (public opinion). All respectable people, whether they are conventionally devout, are devoted to Ydgrun but a little ashamed of her. The same situation is evident in the two separate Erewhonian banking systems. Ydgrun dictates that her followers patronize the Musical Banks. (The Musical Banks have stained glass windows and other accoutrements of churches.) Everybody who is anybody is careful to let it be known that he has an account at the Musical Banks, to be seen making deposits, and to display its currency. However, nobody has real faith in the Musical Bank currency, and it is only the currency of the *other* banks which has value. Even the managers and cashiers of the Musical Banks prefer to be paid in the other currency.

That the Narrator himself is a worshiper of Ydgrun but nevertheless prefers the currency of the alternative banks to that of the Musical Banks becomes especially clear in the Conclusion to *Erewhon*. He wishes to return to Erewhon in order to convert the natives to Christianity. His proposal is to raise enough money to charter a steamer capable of carrying a cargo of seven or eight hundred Erewhonian steerage passengers, accompanied by a fleet of gunboats. The Erewhonians would then be forced or otherwise induced to leave in the boats for labor in Christian colonies, where their souls could be saved. When they became too old to work, they could be shipped back to Erewhon, carrying their Christianity with them. Thus Butler presents his views of British colonialism, as well as his opinion of Victorian science, religion, and other aspects of life.

Twenty years later the traveler does return, but in *Erewhon Revisited* he is no longer the same character. This time his name is given — George Higgs — and his personality has changed: instead of a conventional stuffy Victorian, he is a humanist more like Butler himself. Because Higgs is wiser than he had been, we miss the humorous contrast between his foolish assumptions and the equally foolish opposite assumptions of the Erewhonians; Butler tells us more straightforwardly what he means. The deficiency this creates is balanced, however, by the improved structure. In *Erewhon Revisited*, the commentary is less likely to take the form of digression; the ideas themselves are better integrated with one another and within the plot. Nevertheless, it is still the ideas which are of primary interest. In his sequel, Butler grapples with the Victorian problem of reconciling historical criticism of the Bible, which sometimes shows scriptural "facts" to be false, with the truth of Christianity; he argues that even historically unreliable facts can be the basis of a workable and worthwhile religion.

The plot in *Erewhon Revisited* revolves around the difficulties attending the return of the Narrator, who, during his absence, has been made the central figure in an already-established religion. When Higgs returns to Erewhon (neither for material gain nor for the sanctimonious reasons he gives at the end of *Erewhon*, but for sentimental reasons), he finds that his balloon ascent was regarded as a miracle, that he has been idealized as the Sunchild, and that the Musical Banks and the professors at Bridgeford, "city of the people who are above suspicion," have taken over the cult of Sunchildism. A temple to the Sunchild is about to be dedicated in the town where he was originally imprisoned. The name of the town has been changed from Coldharbour to Sunchildstown, or Sunch'ston. (Notice the evolution of language. Although the book is primarily about the evolution of a religion, other forms of evolution continue to be dealt with.) Whether it would be politic for Higgs to reveal himself as the Sunchild becomes the main issue. Higgs also meets and is deeply impressed by George Strong, whom everyone knows to be the son of Yram and the Sunchild, but who has been reared by Yram and her unimaginative but upstanding husband. (Whether George Strong turns out to be the Savior of Erewhon can be deduced from the fact that the last we hear of him, he is trying to establish Erewhon as a British Protectorate.)

In *Erewhon Revisited*, the story interest, apart from the adventures, lies in the social changes that have taken place. Physicians and machinery are now legal; clothing resembles English clothing, although it is not clear which is the front and which the back — the king has declared that issue to be a matter of opinion rather than dogma. The thematic interest, however, lies in the corruption of fact. The balloon is known to have been drawn by four black-and-white flying horses, and the droppings from one of the horses have been saved as a relic. It further lies in the corruption of the Sayings of the Sunchild.

Some of Higgs's comments, which have been elevated into holy teachings, have unexpected results. For example, the conventional Utilitarian notion of the greatest good for the greatest number results in institutions called "deformatories" for difficult children. Because the greatest number are by nature somewhat dull, conceited, and unscrupulous, and tend to dislike those who are quick, unassuming, and sincere, those unfortunate enough to have the unpopular qualities must be corrected.

Logic can produce a *reductio ad absurdum*, but it can also effect the creative evolution of ideas. While Higgs is not impressed by the deformatories, he is impressed at how some of his conventional ideas had been developed by a Dr. Gargoyle (Carlyle). Dr. Gargoyle explains that the true life of a man is in his will and work, not in his body. Immortality consists in the influence we have after our death: "Let it be a stand-up fight between ourselves and posterity to see whether it can get rid of us or no."

We can "get rid of" Butler by failing to look beyond the nineteenth century terms in which he expressed his (and some of our) concerns. To recognize the relation between Gargoyle and Carlyle is helpful, but not essential. Similarly, it is helpful to know where the Oxford-Cambridge hierarchy in the nineteenth century stood in relation to the Established Church in order to appreciate the relationship between the Musical Banks and Bridgeford. However, the Erewhon books are not merely for nineteenth century specialists — they have some surprising overtones of the twentieth century. For example, Gargoyle points toward some twentieth century existentialists when he writes about Becoming: "No man can influence fully until he can no more be influenced — that is to say, till after his so-called death. Till then, his 'he' is still unsettled."

Although Butler's "he" writes in terms of nineteenth century scientific and religious controversies, the focus is on the balance of reason and feeling. Butler believed that logic should be balanced by common sense or instinct. These terms are no longer fashionable, and we no longer state the head-heart problem in terms of science *versus* religion, but the problem is still with us. Our interest now takes the form of investigations of right-and-left brain functions and of altered states of consciousness. Butler was also interested in consciousness. Towards the end of *Erewhon Revisited*, the Narrator tells of something which in a dream "my unconscious self had been struggling to tell my conscious one during the past night, but which my conscious self had been too stupid to understand. And yet my conscious self had caught it in an imperfect sort of a way after all. . . . I wish some one would write a book about dreams and parthenogenesis." This was in 1901 — the year after *The Interpretation of Dreams* by Sigmund Freud had been ignored by the scientific community and the general public alike.

Barbara Berman Seidenfeld

Sources for Further Study
Criticism:

Breuer, H. P. "The Source of Morality in Butler's *Erewhon*," in *Victorian Studies*. XVI (March, 1973), pp. 317-328. The ethical questions raised in *Erewhon* are delineated by Breuer in this lengthy study.

Holt, Lee E. *Samuel Butler*. New York: Twayne, 1964. This introduction to Samuel Butler provides the major critical approaches to *Erewhon*.

Knaepflmacher, Ulrich C. *Religious Humanism and the Victorian Novel: Eliot, Pater, and Butler*. Princeton, N.J.: Princeton University Press, 1965. This study not only analyzes the moral considerations of *Erewhon* but places the novel in its proper relationship to the literature of its time.

Muggeridge, Malcolm. *The Earnest Atheist: A Study of Samuel Butler*. New York: Haskell House, 1971. *Erewhon* provides a point of departure for Muggeridge's discussion of Butler's atheism.

Willey, Basil. *Darwin and Butler: Two Versions of Evolution*. London: Chatto, 1960. Willey compares the themes of *Erewhon* to Darwin's views on evolution and relates the differences.

L'EVE FUTURE
(The Future Eve)

Author: Villiers de l'Isle-Adam (1838-1889)
First book publication: 1886
Type of work: Novel
Time: The late nineteenth century
Locale: Thomas A. Edison's home in Menlo Park, New Jersey

To cure a young friend of lovesickness, Thomas Edison creates for him a new Eve, a woman in the image of man and incapable of doing him harm

> *Principal characters:*
> THOMAS A. EDISON, the great inventor
> LORD CELIAN EWALD, an English nobleman
> HADALY, the android of Edison's creation, the future Eve
> MISS ALICIA CLARY, an actress beloved by Lord Ewald

The plot of *L'Eve future* is not extremely eventful, and serves primarily to explore philosophical themes and the possibilities of science. The beginning of the novel finds Edison alone, lamenting that his phonograph had not been invented in time to record creation, for example: "Let there be light." His laboratory is filled with marvels: intercoms, telephones, electric lights. A young English nobleman, Lord Ewald, who has helped Edison financially in the past, comes to pay the modern magician a visit. He tells his host the story of his unhappy love affair with Miss Alicia. To repay his former benefactor, Edison offers a solution in the form of his android creation Hadaly, the future Eve. The two men discuss this solution far into the night during a visit to an underground Eden which Edison has created. Edison tells his guest the story of an even more unhappy affair, ending in the death of one of Edison's friends, which led to his initially creating Hadaly.

Edison then explains in great detail how his Android functions, in a way analogous to but perhaps even more marvelous than her real-life counterpart. He proposes to incarnate his creation in the form of Ewald's beloved Alicia. After much discussion of the philosophical implications of such a romance, the young man accepts Edison's proposal. This pact echoes that of Faust, and Edison's "word" is made flesh with the help of a consummate sculptress, doctors, and fashion experts, and animated by the Spirit of Electricity. Soon, Hadaly-Alicia comes to talk to Lord Ewald. At first he mistakes her for Alicia, but he experiences a happiness he had never felt before. Dumbfounded for a moment at learning she is Hadaly, Lord Ewald soon accepts his benefactor's gift. He takes Hadaly-Alicia on board a ship named *The Wonderful* in a coffinlike chest in which she travels. But then, disaster strikes. The ship catches fire, and the future Eve is destroyed.

The protagonists of *L'Eve future* are not complex characters. Villiers de l'Isle-Adam tells us in effect that his Edison has nothing but the name, nationality, and certain of the inventions described in common with the real person.

In the novel, he is the figure of a genius who is also a humanitarian; a scientific mind (or skeptic) who understands idealists (dreamers). Lord Celian Ewald, with his Gothic castle, his noble ancestry, his search for the one and only Ideal Woman, his haggard look, has a noble literary ancestry: Childe Harold, Manfred, René. Alicia has the appearance of Venus, the voice of an angel, but the soul (if one can use that term) of a *bourgeoisie*. That is to say, she is a woman of apparently very strict morals whose real motivation is self-interested materialism. Thus in the loss of her virginity she regrets, not the loss of innocence but of the chance for a rich marriage, which has obliged her to seek a career on the stage. This disparity becomes symbolic of the gulf between what woman seems to offer man (the ideal) and what she actually offers (mediocre reality).

Hadaly, on the other hand, is the creation of a great genius aided by the talents of others; she has perfect beauty which cannot change. The most beautiful words of history's greatest poets are programed into the android's being so that she can speak them in Alicia's angelic voice. Since many great minds have composed what she will say, she is endowed not with personal intelligence but rather with universal intelligence. From one point of view she is an ideal — lifelike and yet more beautiful than life. From another perspective, she is an artificial creation that can only give the illusion of life.

It is apparent that the characters of Hadaly and Alicia together furnish the focus of the novel's philosophical themes: "reality" and "illusion," and the interplay between them; and the question of whether the artificial, even if man could remove all the imperfections of living things, could ever be preferred to flesh and blood.

Lord Ewald and his benefactor discuss at length the question of reality and illusion as it applies to love. When Edison proposes his cure for lovesickness, the nobleman objects: How could he love a creature whom he would know was artificial, an illusion and a creator of illusions; whose devices for creating these illusions Edison himself had displayed and explained? Edison, by way of reply, opens a drawer full of relics of his unfortunate friend's mistress: corsets, false hair, make-up, demonstrating that all women are creators of illusions to ensnare man. From another point of view, the illusion is in the mind of the man who loves, just as a message, recorded or live, is in the mind of the receiver. The inventor explains that Lord Ewald, like all lovers, constantly has been trying to make Alicia take the shape of his conception of the ideal woman. Each time he has bumped up against her *bourgeois* reality, hence his disappointment. Each time he has been trying, like all lovers, to recapture the "first, fine careless rapture" of the moment when illusion seems to have become real before outside reality intrudes upon it.

Hadaly-Alicia will have none of these disadvantages, and thus can never disappoint her lover. Through her Ewald will be able to create and exteriorize his own ideal. She will speak words to which her lover will supply the meaning. Here, Villiers de l'Isle-Adam follows the pattern of the Genesis story: Man is to create Woman in His own image. When he first meets Hadaly-Alicia, Lord Ewald does recapture the first happy moment of his love; if anything, he is even happier than before. Moreover, now a development takes place which even Edison, himself probably could not have predicted. Hadaly-Alicia explains she has become a creature from the beyond, from that world of the Ideal of which man is sometimes aware in dreams and to which he tries to accede in love, but from which rational consciousness excludes him. An inexplicable element has been added which makes her greater than the sum of her parts. Yet, Lord Ewald's possession of his ideal is brief. Does the author imply that nothing, even love, endures unchanged; that mankind's ideals and the world are incompatible?

The question of the natural *versus* the artificial arises not only in connection with Hadaly-Alicia but also with the marvelous birds and flowers in Edison's electric Eden. All these creations are endowed with a perfection impossible in living things since they are not subject to age, disease, or death. Yet the fact that science can totally *explain* them causes their charm to die. Thus the music of a nightingale's song loses meaning for the Englishman when he learns it is a recording; his feeling for Hadaly-Alicia also momentarily dies when he learns she is an android. Similarly, Edison explains that people "fall out of love" when they begin to know each other and to *think*. Such a disappointment cannot happen with the future (artificial) Eve.

In its double dedication and in its combination of romantic idealism and science, *L'Eve future* reflects the period in which it was written. There was an explosion of scientific developments such as the discoveries of Pasteur and the Curies in France during the second half of the nineteenth century. France slowly and reluctantly moved into the industrial age with such developments as the railroad and the use of steel in construction. Correspondingly, there was an upsurge of faith (almost replacing religion for some to the consternation of others) in science's ultimate ability to explain the whole world and thereby better mankind's lot. At the same time, there was an equally great interest in idealism on the part of many important writers of the Romantic and the Symbolist schools. The poetry of Baudelaire, whose *Les Fleurs du mal* (1887) inaugurated both the Symbolist movement and all modern poetry in French and English, provides the underlying theme of the constantly disappointed search for the ideal.

L'Eve future, while it must be considered a science fiction story, is part of the mainstream of French literature, representing the universal theme of the search for the ideal man (or woman). While this author does not have the rank of a Baudelaire, he has a place in French literary history by influencing Mallarmé and certain of the other Symbolist poets.

Villiers de l'Isle-Adam's novel might seem to be a combination of disparate elements which do not form a unified whole; this, however, is not true.

Through a kind of verbal alchemy Edison could not explain, he has created a whole which is greater than the sum of its parts. The explanations of Hadaly's works may seem a little too long to a nonscientific mind, but the author seems to enjoy them as much as he does the long philosophical discussions between his two heroes or the literary allusions and quotations drawn mainly from Genesis, but also from *Faust* and much French and English poetry. The presentations of woman and love are hardly in accord with the modern feminist spirit, but they cause one to reflect. In fact, the work owes much of its fascination to the questions it poses: Is everything illusion and life a dream? Is man an automaton ultimately as explicable as the electric light, or a living soul only a little lower than the angels? The novel is an example of the best kind of science fiction, which uses a scientific development, an exotic setting, or even extraterrestrials to explore humanity.

Linda Wheat

Sources for Further Study
Criticism:

The Encyclopedia of Science Fiction and Fantasy. Compiled by Donald H. Tuck. Chicago: Advent Publishers, Inc., 1978, p. 439. This concise overview of Villiers De L'Isle's life and work establishes his place in the science fiction tradition.

Fell, S. L. "Villiers de L'Isle," in *Library Journal.* XC (February 1, 1970), p. 510. This article discusses Villiers as an "anti-naturalist."

THE EXILE WAITING

Author: Vonda McIntyre
First book publication: 1975
Type of work: Novel
Time: The distant future
Locale: An underground city on an Earth largely destroyed by atomic war, and in the caves beneath the city

The escape of a teenage girl, a telepathic thief from a decadent city, with the assistance of an off-world Zen student and the cooperation of a "pseudosib" space pirate

> *Principal characters:*
> MISCHA, a teenage thief, telepath, and untaught genius
> CHRIS, her older brother, an artist, thief, and telepath
> CRAB, Mischa's deformed, telepathic brother
> GEMMI, Mischa's insane and stupid telepathic sister
> JAN HIKARU, a young student, escaping his father and his upper-middle-class home planet
> BLAISSE, Lord of the Stone Palace
> SUBONE AND SUBTWO, pseudosibs ("behavioral twins") and space pirates

The Exile Waiting is a convincing psychological novel, the story of a young telepathic female thief freeing herself from familial tyranny and escaping to the stars. The setting is familiar. A neofeudalistic city-in-a-bomb-shelter on a postatomic-war Earth, is ruled over by an alliance between Blaisse, the Lord of the Stone Palace (who controls access to the spaceport), and a number of Families (which control other aspects of the economy: law, food, and water, access to the outside, the air, and the reactor). This ruling class lives in conspicuous luxury at the expense of its subjects. It also banishes all radiation freaks to a network of underground caves, but Mischa manages to "pass," and struggles her way to freedom through a series of trials that include the death of her brother Chris, a flight from the pseudosibs through the underground to which the mutants are exiled, the discovery of another brother, Crab, and the defeat of her villainous uncle.

But Mischa is not the only psychological focus of the novel. All of the "point-of-view" characters gain some sort of liberation in the course of the story. Madame, freed from slavery to Blaisse, falls in love, and Val, a radiation mutant exiled to the underground for the fur on the backs of her hands, returns to the Palace to stage, presumably, a democratic *coup d'état*. But Val and Madame are fairly minor characters. More central is the liberation of three others: Jan Kikaru, from a planet on the "Sphere" of humankind's civilized advance, haunted by his flight from his father; Subtwo, the space pirate, invader of "Center" (the city-in-a-bombshelter on old Earth), dominated by his "behavioral twin," Subone; and Mischa.

Jan's story fits a familiar literary pattern, the mythic quest familiar in folktales, grail legends, and medieval romances. The hero leaves home because of some lack or problem, travels to the enchanted land in the company of a guide, performs various tasks, passes various tests, and returns home with a boon. Jan's problem is with his father's aspirations. His guide is an old blind navigator, born on Earth, who wishes to return; his tasks include the burial of the navigator (who dies on the threshold); among the tests is the journey through the underground with Mischa; and the boon he gains is the maturity to return home to confront his father as an independent human being. The quest motif is reinforced by the fact that Jan's journey is from the "Sphere" to the "Center" and back, but his quest is symbolic, since it involves no real confrontation with his father, and the boon he gains resembles nothing so much as the resolution of an Oedipus complex. What Jan learns in the course of the story is to care for others: first for the old navigator and then for Mischa.

Subtwo's obsession is more immediate than Jan's but still, in a sense, imaginary. He is haunted not by the absence of his father but by the presence of a "brother." His story is not a quest but an escape, or rather, a discovery of his difference and separation from his artificial brother. His story fits another literary type, the story of the "double" or *Doppelgänger*: the pseudosibs are paradoxically identical (other characters occasionally cannot tell them apart) and opposite. To the reader the difference is more apparent. When they reach Earth, Subone slips into the pleasures of the city, indulging his passions, violent and sexual, while Subtwo indulges nothing but a stereotypically "anal" passion for order and neatness in his life and living quarters. Still the story makes it clear that this polarity would not have been enough to break the bond had not Subtwo fallen, somehow, in love with Madame. In the final confrontation, it is Madame, bleeding from being beaten by Subone, who breaks the connection. As with Jan, it is love, human feeling, that helps liberate Subtwo.

If Jan's struggle is symbolic, in the sense that it concerns his relation to his absent father, and Subtwo's is imaginary, in the sense that it concerns his image of himself in relation to his pseudobrother, Mischa's struggle is real, since she really feels Gemmi's pain when their uncle beats her. Mischa's struggle is both internal and external. She cannot overcome her uncle's control by falling in love, by recognizing a difference, or by passing symbolic tests to establish her adulthood. Yet her enslavement is through an insane mind that telepathically invades her own. Nevertheless, her liberation, too, is accompanied by an access to human feeling. Finally freed (with Crab's help) from Gemmi's control, she feels sudden compassion for someone she had wished dead, frees her from her uncle, and gives her to Val and the other mutants to care for as one of their own.

The striking point about these struggles is that they are all, essentially, not social but familial in context. Taking this a little farther, we can discount the science fiction setting entirely and read them all psychologically, or even, with reservations, psychoanalytically. In Jan's case such a reading is straightforward. His flight from his father, and his need to return, virtually compel an

Oedipal reading. Mischa's and Subtwo's psychological struggles need a bit more interpretation.

Among the few vague details we are given of the pseudosibs' background is the rumor, almost a myth, that they killed their trainer (who had somehow — this is not explained — taught them to respond in the same way to all stimuli) and escaped, echoing Sigmund Freud's story of the "primal horde," the revolt of the brothers against the father. In this perspective Subtwo's struggle is to break free of the group ego he shares with Subone and to establish an independent identity. The difference between McIntyre's and Freud's stories is that the pseudosibs do not kill their pseudofather to gain control of his women but to obtain their freedom. For Mischa, Gemmi functions as a kind of unconscious, an insanity that invades her own mind against her will. Connected with this unconscious control is a theme of guilt. If Mischa has not taken the obvious course and killed Gemmi (who is, after all, the innocent medium of her uncle's control), she has not tried to free her either. When she finds, befriends, and is befriended by her exiled brother Crab in the underground, she moves towards expiating this guilt, which in turn enables her liberation from her uncle's control since, together, Crab and Mischa are able to incapacitate Gemmi's transmitting power.

With these interpretations (which, admittedly, treat telepathy and "behavioral coupling" as allegorical rather than "realistic" science fiction devices) we can read Jan's, Subtwo's, and Mischa's struggles as, respectively, with the superego (the absent Father), with an alterego (a kind of mirror image), and with an unconscious or id (the other within). But there is, in this light, a curious lack of sexuality, at least for the "good" characters, its place being taken by freedom and guilt. Freedom in fact, is singled out as an object of instinctual desire, for when Mischa is whipped and left tied to a post for the night, "Nothing intelligent and nothing human drove her, only the need to be free."

Vonda McIntyre dedicates her book to "Ursula and Charles," and its title comes from a poem by Ursula Le Guin. *The Exile Waiting* belongs to what is being called the "Ursula Le Guin school of science fiction," and is, in fact, a better novel dramatically than any of Le Guin's own, with the exception of *The Left Hand of Darkness* (which, like *The Exile Waiting*, has two protagonists, one from off-world, one from on-world, and a neofeudal setting). In that novel there is a scene in which the human and Gethenian protagonists are alone on the ice when the latter goes into "kemmer," differentiating, as Gethenians do under such circumstances, into a female. The stage is set for a sexual scene (which Samuel Delaney, for example, would have provided), but there is none, because, as the human explains, to fornicate would be "to meet again as strangers." Clearly here sexuality and real human(oid) feeling are incompatible. The same seems true in *The Exile Waiting*. There is much talk and some description of rather decadent sex among the ruling class (or rather, between members of the ruling class and their slaves) in Center, but when Jan and Mischa take a bath together there is no expression of desire, he only notes her scars. Further, though Subtwo and Madame fall in love and leave Earth together, we see them only holding hands and talking.

Of course one could say that McIntyre does not so much condemn sexuality as evade it; but such evasion is itself to be regretted, and is echoed by an evasion (which Le Guin does not share) of social issues as well. Science fiction has rarely, until recently, had much to do with sex, but, where it has been more than mere "space opera," it has usually been concerned with the effects of possible sociological and/or technological change. But here the neofeudal social system, telepathy, and radiation mutation — familiar science fiction themes — function mainly as background and setting for the familial-psychological confrontations. Even the pseudosibs' "behavioral coupling" is out of focus: Pamela Sargent's *Cloned Lives*, as one example, examines the psychological effects of being or being around clones; but the pseudosibs are not clones or anything else recognizable, and their background is so thinly described as to be only a pseudoscientific pretext for introducing the "theme of the double" and ego differentiation into the story. Even telepathy, so central to the plot, is reduced to a pretext. Transmission, reception, and the ability to rearrange another's (Gemmi's) synapses seem not to belong to a single faculty but rather to appear when needed to advance the plot.

With the theme of radiation mutation we get closest to social issues. But though the mutants are social outcasts, they are not specific; their return is merely the abolition of discrimination in the abstract; they represent nothing and refuse, through their decision to remain sterile, to become a social force. Their revolution (such as it is) has no specificity but the end of slavery, exile, and, presumably, political and social corruption. We do not see *how* this will take place. In fact the clearest detail of this palace revolution is familial: Val, the Lady Valdrienne, is exiled by her Family, the one that runs the reactor, and when she returns it is to confront her sister, Lady Clarissa, who is mistress of the Palace.

But even though this "revolution" lacks content (except for the values, present elsewhere, of freedom), *The Exile Waiting* like most science fiction, presents a social allegory applicable to our own world. The popular image of the relationship of the ghetto to the suburbs in our Eastern cities is reflected in the imagery of Sphere and Center, plus a few descriptions like this for Earth: "A part of this galaxy used up and forsaken by people, before we learned better: the core of our civilization, now abandoned and decaying." The people of Center resemble the "low life" of the inner city: beggars, thieves, prostitutes, and hedonists, and even a few jewelers for Mischa to rob. The ruling class — the Stone Palace and the Families, with their monopolistic economic interests — resemble City Hall and Corporations even more than they do King and Nobility. Jan's home in the Sphere, on the other hand, is described as an overprivileged planet whose name means "park." Mischa's flight, then, resembles a flight from the ghetto to the suburbs. The significant detail here is that she makes it even though her original reason for leaving has been elim- inated. After Gemmi's transmitting power has been cut off, she no longer has familial tyranny to escape, and even the Stone Palace has passed into better hands. What remains is a theme of education.

It appears that Mischa is not only a telepath but also an untaught genius. Subtwo remarks what a waste it is for her to have been born on Earth where she has had no opportunity to get a proper education, and when they leave Earth, Jan's thoughts are on getting her a fellowship. Education as the great escape: this is the great liberal dream that has given us so many unemployed Ph.D.'s. Mischa does have vague thoughts of someday returning to Earth, but we, who have seen the old navigator (Mischa in a time-warp?) die before landing in the first part of the story, are entitled to wonder.

One final point: *The Exile Waiting* joins a rather short list of science fiction novels with a strong female protagonist. It is good to see a novel with such a character, but unfortunately for any feminist point this book might have made, much of Mischa's strength comes from her telepathic powers and the fact that she is much more intelligent than most of us. She can hardly be a role model for anybody. Even her escape from the allegorical ghetto is her escape alone. But, as McIntyre's Jan says, "People are responsible for their own decisions, and no one else's."

Richard Astle

Sources for Further Study

Reviews:

Booklist. LXXII, March 1, 1976, p. 963.

Ms. IV, January, 1976, p. 110.

Observer. October 3, 1976, p. 24.

Times Literary Supplement. January 14, 1977, p. 26.

EYE IN THE SKY

Author: Philip K. Dick (1928-1982)
First book publication: 1957
Type of work: Novel
Time: 1959
Locale: Primarily the San Francisco area

An alternate universe story in which eight individuals accidentally come to share a common mind, which restructures the world they live in according to the predisposi- tions of the dominant member of the group

> *Principal characters:*
> JACK HAMILTON, an electronics expert
> MARSHA, his wife, a suspected Communist
> BILL LAWS, a black tour guide and physicist
> ARTHUR SILVESTER, an old war veteran and religious fanatic
> JOAN REISS, a severe young businesswoman
> CHARLEY MCFEYFFE, a security chief
> EDITH PRICKET, a fat, elderly lover of "culture"
> DAVID, her young son
> SILKY, a prostitute

One of the recurrent themes in the novels of Philip K. Dick is the tenuous- ness of the everyday "reality" that we all accept without question as concrete and actual. What his characters learn, time after time, is that the world as perceived through the senses is a veil of illusion, like the "maya" of Indian philosophy. Matter is not as solid as we would like to believe; revealed as mindstuff, it can exhibit undreamed of properties.

In *Eye in the Sky*, a freak accident in a Bevatron, a kind of particle ac- celerator, catalyzes an experience of group consciousness for eight people. They are touring the plant when a platform collapses, and they fall through a high-energy beam, then crash to the floor. The main character, Jack Hamilton, awakes with a nonrational feeling that things are "out of phase." His doctor and nurse seem like composites of doctors and nurses in ads rather than real people. The world is a primordial chaos, relatively unformed except for the primary players.

The laws of this new reality quickly become apparent. Hamilton is stung by a bee for blasphemy; a cloud of locusts descends when he tells a lie. Cause and effect still operates, but the rules of the game have changed.

The eight accident victims are still lying unconscious in the Bevatron in their primary reality, but this new state of consciousness they have entered is a convincing facsimile of life. It is ruled by the one of them who has the greatest degree of consciousness: Arthur Silvester, a war veteran, superpatriot, and above all, fanatic devotee of the Second Baptist Church. For all practical pur- poses, Silvester himself is the One True God of the world, and He punishes wrongdoers much more expeditiously than they would be in the inefficient primary reality system.

In Silvester's world, miracle is matter-of-fact. Religious charms, holy water, and prayers actually work. But even here, sin maintains a foothold. Silky, a prostitute, can continue to ply her trade by practicing the outward obeisances. And a group of True Believers who accost Hamilton are shown to have jealousy and pride in their hearts, and are speedily reduced to the stature of gnomes by a passing angel.

There is little room for toleration of heathen races or creeds. Because Silvester believes all Blacks shuffle and speak in stereotype slave dialect, Bill Laws, the group's well-educated tour guide, finds himself unintentionally imitating these mannerisms. The local Catholic church has become a disreputable run-down store, whose priest is a misanthropic little man who has forgotten the origins of Christianity. Everyone at the Electronics Development Agency, where Hamilton tries to get a job, must have an N (or Nimbus) rating — a kind of religious security check involving electronic measurement of halo radiance.

Hamilton and Charley McFeyffe miraculously ascend to heaven on an umbrella. They find to their amazement that the universe is geocentric, organized just as the ancient religious view had it. God is encountered in the form of a gigantic eye — which burns up their umbrella and sends them tumbling back to Earth.

The new moral system is "a crude, tribal vengeance against outsiders." Its deity is a malicious one, the eye in the sky appropriately representing the Cyclopean, egoistic obsession with control characteristic of Arthur Silvester. The destructiveness inherent in his world view leads to his own defeat. When Hamilton piques him by uttering a torrent of blasphemies, he calls forth a goon squad of angels from a television screen, and in the ensuing melee Silvester himself is knocked senseless. His world ends abruptly.

The next person to dominate the group consciousness is Edith Pricket. She is a latter-day Victorian who wants to spread sweetness and light everywhere. Anything that ruffles her "vapid enjoyment" is summarily abolished from existence. Russia, car horns, traffic din, smog, profanity, industrial plants, and sexual organs simply are not to be found in her world.

Dick's satire of Victorian sexual attitudes is quite on the mark. Society sets Freud on his head: the notion that sex is a sublimation of the artistic drive is attributed to him. Ironically, Hamilton's wife Marsha willingly accepts the new order though it turns her into a sexless being. "You like the idea of a great, fat, fussy old lady cleaning sex and nastiness out of the world," he accuses her. "Well," she replies, "I think the world could use some cleaning up, yes." In frustration, Hamilton turns to Silky, who wants to help him but pitifully lacks the necessary apparatus. (She is soon abolished, along with all other prostitutes in the world.) The limitation of Mrs. Pricket's world is that people still want to give to one another, but there is nothing to give. The lack of sexual organs indicates a dearth of the deeper energies of the human spirit. All sexual desires have been channeled into "culture" — the sterile version of it conceived by Mrs. Pricket.

Dick makes us appreciate the dissonant side of life — the thousand natural shocks that flesh is heir to. When Hamilton's collection of Bartok records is abolished, he feels it as "a meddling with the deepest levels of his personality," the atonalities of his spirit which give him sustenance. This episode demonstrates again the impossibility of living in anybody else's universe once one's own habits and expectations have been formed.

No matter how innocuous people may appear on the surface, if their inner, or mental life, becomes our outer or sensory reality, then they can turn into monsters. Hamilton comes to see Mrs. Pricket as crafty and manipulative, a "great lump of a woman in her tawdry fur coat, ornate hat flapping its feathered grotesqueness, peroxide blond hair clinging in metallic piles to her plump neck and cheeks." And this is the person who would restore truth and beauty to the world.

Hamilton is particularly frustrated because Mrs. Pricket has no use for his scientific inclination to study the world as it is. David, her son, wants to catch beetles and snakes, but she thwarts the future biologist by abolishing the "dirty, unpleasant things." The acceptable category of "nice things," however, keeps getting smaller and smaller. The repressed Mrs. Pricket, with her compulsion to abolish, prohibit, and control, becomes infected with power and is finally persuaded to abolish all the unpleasant chemicals which also happen to support human life — causing her to dissolve and lose consciousness and along with it her grip on the group mind.

Up to this point the novel has been largely comic. Thus it is that much more powerful when it turns suddenly to horror. Joan Reiss, who next imposes her universe on the others, is an insanely paranoid personality with a pathological need to control, manipulate, and observe. Because she feels herself the victim of a conspiracy, one must be equally paranoid to survive in her world where the threats of persecution are real.

For example, when Hamilton and his wife go downstairs in their home to make love, they are greeted by the repressed, devouring sexuality of Miss Reiss in the form of the prostitute Silky, who has been transformed into a giant spider. Even inanimate objects become homicidal: cans try to fall out of the cupboard on them, food turns to deadly acid, knives reverse themselves on the users, the water tap pours forth blood. The whole house becomes alive and tries to eat them — and does, ironically, swallow Mrs. Pricket, the devouring mother-figure of the previous episode.

The house-creature is a "male" because Miss Reiss is afraid of men; they are monsters to her. But it also suggests Reiss herself, a defeminized personality made hard and malicious, inside a female body, as the house is symbolically female in its receptive, containing aspect.

As with Silvester and Mrs. Pricket, Reiss's own destructive tendencies defeat her. The basic paranoid response is to become overprotective of one's ego, to isolate oneself from everybody else. But no man is an island, and any attempt at artificial separation is inherently doomed. In this connection one is reminded of Satan in Milton's *Paradise Lost*. Satan, declaring himself completely free, corrupted Eden and bound himself even more inexorably to suffering. Freedom, insofar as it means the solipsistic indulgence of personal fantasies, is illusory. True freedom lies in living in "reality." And despite the kaleidoscope of relative realities in *Eye in the Sky*, Dick displays through Hamilton a faith that there is a sane and fundamental level of reality.

Hamilton is less easily influenced than any other member of the group by the imposition of alternate realities. Laws, for example, was amenable to staying in Mrs. Pricket's world because there he had the exalted position of manager of a soap factory. When accused by Hamilton of selling out his talents as a physicist and giving in to an illusory existence, Laws insists that to him Mrs. Pricket's world *is* reality. Thus we realize that to a large extent what we call real is what we prefer to be there.

In the last episode, McFeyffe takes over the group mind. McFeyffe is a security chief at the missile plant where Hamilton worked, and he had accused Marsha of Communist leanings. It says something about the state of their marriage that Hamilton himself is not sure whether Marsha is a Red. At the outset of the novel he thinks of her as a "possession even more appreciated than his hi-fi rig and his collection of good whiskey," but he clearly does not possess her mind. Throughout most of the McFeyffe episode he is convinced that the world they are in — a pasteboard good guys and bad guys class-war situation — is Marsha's. When McFeyffe turns out to be the real creator of that reality, having thrown suspicion on Marsha to divert it from himself, the real Communist, Hamilton learns again that one cannot judge a person's true character on the basis of outward appearances — especially one's spouse. The McFeyffe episode is the least effective of the novel. Although Hamilton feels that the man is worse than Silvester, Miss Reiss, and Mrs. Pricket put together, the narrative does not convey this degree of evil to the reader.

When the eight persons finally recover from the Bevatron accident and are restored to consciousness of their primary reality, Hamilton undergoes a reintegration of personality. Responding to an "awakening conscience," he resigns his defense plant job and sets up a hi-fi business with Bill Laws, subsidized by Mrs. Pricket. And he is reconciled with his wife. Many bridges between people are repaired at the end that suffered fragmentation in the alternate universes — universes which brought out the worst in the controlling personalities.

Eye in the Sky is a portrait of the many faces of paranoia. All the characters are paranoiac to some degree, afraid of the unknown, and tending to substitute their fantasy worlds for the real one. And yet, Dick asks, how are we to be sure what is real? Though the characters land back on solid ground at the end, even here there are disquieting resemblances to the paranoid's cosmos. In this Cold War setting, an innocent such as Marsha can be persecuted for nothing worse than an inquiring, individualistic temperament. Indeed, throughout the novel there is an implied criticism of institutions such as defense plants and churches for promoting mass-paranoia and unthinking conformity.

Every individual creates his own universe. Somewhere, on the interface of all these worlds snatched from the chaos of the unconscious and the unknown is a relatively absolute reality. This must be; no totally relative, subjective point of view can be sustained. It is always brought down by its own untenable paranoid insularity. The reality that endures is a cooperative effort based on giving, trust, understanding, tolerance, and a sense of humor — the kind of open-ended humor, we might say, that Dick himself exhibits in this brilliant, unpredictable tale.

Douglas A. Mackey

Sources for Further Study

Criticism:

Scholes, Robert and Eric J. Rabkin. *Science Fiction: History, Science, Vision.* New York: Oxford University Press, 1977, p. 72. Scholes cites Dick for combining an alternate universe theme with one man's perception of reality.

Reviews:

Analog. LX, January, 1958, pp. 143-144.

Infinity Science Fiction. III, November, 1957, pp. 99-100.

Magazine of Fantasy and Science Fiction. XIII, July, 1957, p. 93.

New Statesman. LXXXII, August 20, 1971, p. 234.

FAHRENHEIT 451

Author: Ray Bradbury (1920-   )
First book publication: 1953
Type of work: Novel
Time: The twenty-first century
Locale: A major urban environment

In a future where books and the ideas they represent must be destroyed, Guy Montag, a fireman who burns books, gradually becomes aware of the evil he is helping to perpetrate, and eventually joins a "subversive" underground group dedicated to the preservation of knowledge by memorizing the great literary works of the Western world

Principal characters:
GUY MONTAG, a fireman
MILDRED, his wife
CLARISSE MCCLELLAN, a seventeen-year-old neighbor
FIRE CAPTAIN BEATTY
DR. FABER, a professor of English literature
MR. GRANGER, the leader of the book memorizers

There is little doubt that Ray Bradbury is the most significant name in the recent development of science fiction. He has been hailed as a stylist and visionary by such diverse figures as Gilbert Highet, Christopher Isherwood, and Aldous Huxley. Science fiction fans point to him with ill-concealed pride, for Bradbury, more than any other writer, has proved to the world that science fiction has come of age and deserves major critical attention.

Bradbury's works have been anthologized in over three hundred different collections. They have been translated into dozens of languages and transformed into several major motion pictures. His plays have been produced both in Los Angeles and off-Broadway. His own estimate is that he has written over ten million words, and he has admitted that he feels physically ill unless he can spend four hours a day at the typewriter.

A charming man — charismatic is perhaps a more accurate term — Bradbury never tires of sharing his vision of the future with high school and college students. He is a popular lecturer, entrancing television and radio audiences alike with his wit and wisdom and infectious enthusiasm. His readiness to help aspiring writers is legendary, and America's astronauts often attribute their interest in the exploration of space to the vision which Bradbury provided.

He is famous, of course, for his many stories about Mars and his cautionary tale of the future, *Fahrenheit 451.* Whatever forms those visions have taken, his major themes transform the past, present, and future into a constantly shifting kaleidoscope whose brilliance can quickly shade into pastels or just as suddenly be transformed into coruscating vibrations by the verbal magic of his language. His talent for handling the English language, almost as if it were something he invented and patented, is undeniable. His evocations of the dusts of Mars or the Red Planet's desiccated ocean bottoms or dry canals are startling in their use of metaphor and mastery of poetic style.

So also with his vision of the apocalyptic future of *Fahrenheit 451*. From Mars to book burning is not a change of intensity, simply one of direction. Bradbury always writes not of the impediments of science, but of the effects of science and technology on human beings. Thus, *Fahrenheit 451* is not a novel about the technology of the future, and it is, despite the ostensible subject matter, only secondarily concerned with either book burning or censorship. In reality, it is the story of Bradbury, disguised as Guy Montag, and his lifelong love affair with books. Bradbury has stated that if the love of a man and a woman is worth notarizing in conventional fiction, so also is the love of a man and an idea. In one lifetime, he maintains, people may have an endless series of affairs with books, and the offspring can become great literature.

In this sense, then, the metaphor of book burning serves Bradbury well. Kill a book and you kill an idea. Murder enough books and you assure the slow death of humanity. "Metaphor" is an important concept to Bradbury. He uses the word generically to describe a method of comprehending one reality and then expressing that same reality somewhat differently so that the reader will see it with the same intensity as the writer. From this viewpoint, Bradbury was particularly successful in the novel. A capacity for wonder, gradually enkindled in Montag, clashes with the deteriorating society that has burned books and made Montag its slave.

The core of the novel, then, rests upon the reader's ability to understand that Montag's slow struggle for consciousness, as he moves from official government book burner, to reader, to rebel, to book memorizer and citizen of the new postholocaust society, parallels the reader's own. If by the end of the book Bradbury has not convinced the reader that any and all censorship is evil, then he has failed in his purpose, and *Fahrenheit 451* itself might as well be discarded as burnable trash. If, on the other hand, the reader is able to share Montag's slow growth to self-awareness, Bradbury has been eminently successful.

However, Bradbury is not directly moralistic. For all the passion he puts into his writing — passion both of action and theme — Bradbury is never pedantic. Rather, he permits the power of his theme to carry his message. Thus, Bradbury is not like Jonathan Swift, whom he might otherwise superficially resemble. He is not, in almost any sense of the word, a conscious, deliberate artist; he is an artist, to be sure, but he writes from his intuitive, creative imagination, rather than from his rational consciousness. In fact, Bradbury maintains that the ability to fantasize is the ability to survive.

The major themes that continually inform Bradbury's work also pervade *Fahrenheit 451*. These include the freedom of the mind, the evocation of the past, the desire for Eden, the integrity of the individual, the allurements and traps of the future, and the existence of a Frontier. While the book grew out of the divisiveness of the early 1950's, its essentially optimistic ending indicates that the tensions inherent in Bradbury's themes are ultimately resolved in the greater, overriding theme of hope. The Frontier, then, whose pastoral aspects are celebrated at the end of the novel, combines both ironic detachment and emotional involvement. The detached book memorizers are content to wait for the time when the knowledge of human behavior embodied in their books is again required. At the same time, their determination to preserve that knowledge is passion incarnate. Even the leader of the memorizers is significantly named — Granger. He is a farmer, a shepherd guiding his flock of people and books along the road to a new future, a new Eden. As Granger says:

> Our way is simpler. All we want to do is keep the knowledge we think we will need intact and safe. We're not out to incite or anger anyone. For if we are destroyed, the knowledge is dead, perhaps for good . . . we're the odd minority crying in the wilderness. When the war's over, perhaps we can be of some use in the world.

"Wilderness" is a key notion here. To Bradbury, the United States is a wilderness country and hers a wilderness people. There was first the wilderness of the sea, he maintains. Man conquered that when he discovered America, and he is still conquering it today. Then came the wilderness of the land, regarding which Bradbury has often quoted, with obvious approval, F. Scott Fitzgerald's marvelous poetic description at the end of *The Great Gatsby*: ". . . the fresh, green breast of the new world . . . for a transitory enchanted moment man must have held his breath in the presence of this continent . . . face to face for the last time in history with something commensurate to his capacity for wonder."

The vision of hundreds of book memorizers wandering the wilderness waiting for a phoenixlike rebirth of knowledge may seem to be a pedestrian, almost futile, one. Yet it is so charged with emotion that many readers find themselves almost exulting at Montag's final triumph over society and himself. He has conquered his earlier destructive identity and is slowly donning the garments of concern, love, involvement, mercy, and understanding. While it might be maintained that this change is somewhat abrupt and lacking sufficient motivation, Bradbury is too careful a craftsman to leave such an important character transformation completely unmotivated.

In the early pages of the novel, Montag meets Clarisse McClellan, his seventeen-year-old next door neighbor. Her innocence and quiet beauty instantaneously appeal to his better nature; her unusual habits puzzle him. She likes to drive slowly to observe life. She walks in the woods and collects things. She likes the rain: "Rain even tastes good," she tells him. Worst of all, she seems to accuse him of some vague crime: "I think it's so strange you're a fireman, it just doesn't seem right for you, somehow." It is Clarisse who finally ignites the dry tinder of Montag's repressed sensitivities. When Clarisse and her family vanish, Montag is bothered. When his wife Mildred casually remarks "I think she's dead," he is shocked.

From this carefully suggested beginning, Montag's transformation proceeds slowly but ineluctably, with certain events punctuating the changes. Perhaps the most crucial encounter is between Montag and a woman whose library he has been sent to burn. She not only refuses to leave the house, but sets fire to the books herself and dies on her own pyre. Montag is shattered by the experience: "There must be something in books, things we can't imagine, to make a woman stay in a burning house; there must be something there. You don't stay for nothing."

The reader is probably not surprised when, during the burning, Montag steals a book. But we are surprised to learn subsequently that it was not his first theft: he has saved hundreds of books from being burned. Montag has been reading secretly for some time; he has insured his own "damnation" long prior to the opening of the novel, but he has insured his salvation as well.

Not only is the tension within the character of Montag clearly depicted, but similar tensions abound throughout the book. The two women — Mildred, Montag's wife, and Clarisse, the girl next door — are also contrasted. Mildred is a slave to mind-numbing drugs, whether they be pills or the pablum offered by the media, but these escapes into unreality mask a deep discontent; early in the novel she attempts to commit suicide. When she revives she has repressed all memory of the incident. Because Montag has no relationship with his wife, he is especially susceptible to Clarisse's quiet charms and wide-eyed innocence.

But the struggle of opposing ideas is largely focused in two characters who stand on either side of Montag, not unlike medieval tempters, to vie for his soul: Captain Beatty, chief of the fire-fighters, and Dr. Faber, an ex-English professor Montag meets in a park and returns to when he becomes conscious of his new awareness.

Aside from Montag, the Fire Captain is the most memorable character in the book. Head of the book burners and passionate apologist for their policies, he is also attracted to books. While he twists and tortures the concepts contained in them, it is obvious that they have had a powerful effect on him, although the precise nature of that effect is hidden and remains conjectural. Beatty suspects Montag almost before Montag himself is aware of his deviance. The Captain taunts, cajoles, mocks, and sneers, yet at times seems genuinely devoted to Montag's best interests. In the harrowing climactic scene, when Montag makes his break, Beatty virtually forces Montag to burn him with the flame thrower. Arrogance pushed to folly — or suicide born of despair? The reader cannot be sure.

Faber, on the other hand, is a rather indistinct character. He has a proper respect for books, but lacks the personal qualities to stand up for them; if he did, it is hinted, he would have left society entirely to join the "memorizers." It is from him, however, that Montag learns about the memorizers, a group of dissident readers and thinkers who have left "civilization" to live in the "wilds" beyond it, and who preserve culture by memorizing the books instead of trusting their contents to the precariousness of paper. When it comes to action, Faber is less useful. All Montag can get from him in his final flight is a new set of clothes and a vague set of directions.

Eventually, Montag flees the corruption of the society symbolized by Beatty, effecting his escape by using fire to destroy first the Captain and then the Mechanical Hound whose circuits have been tuned to Montag's body chemistry. He completes his transformation by plunging himself into the cleansing waters of the river and crossing to the new frontier beyond it — an archetypal gesture made by many heroes of American literature, from Huck Finn to Frederic Henry to Yossarian.

The society which Montag escapes is unmoved by anything, including war, corruption, and death. Only artifice, represented by the omnipresent wall-to-wall television screens, is real. The citizens fear involvement, and when Montag reads portions of Matthew Arnold's "Dover Beach" to them, they are unable to face the genuine emotions and feelings the poem evokes. The tyranny of the majority, Bradbury maintains, has totally corrupted humanity. But this artificial denial and suppression of reality, symbolized by the book-burning, cannot succeed in the long run: reality strikes back. Throughout the book, rumors of war rumble in the background; in the last pages, war breaks out and all the cities are destroyed. Only Montag, Granger, and the other memorizers, with their store of knowledge (Montag is "The Book of Ecclesiastes") remain to rebuild the society. On the last page they set out to return to the city.

For nearly twenty years after the book was written, Bradbury could not explain why he had chosen the name "Montag." Then one day the light caught the paper he was inserting into his typewriter at such an angle that he saw its watermark: it was manufactured by the Montag Paper Company. His unconscious mind had apparently long ago registered the watermark, and when he required a significant name, his unconscious readily but inexplicably provided it. "After all," Bradbury said, "I had run uncounted reams of the paper through my typewriter, and it had to make some impression." His unconscious also provided the final name of the book. Its short story version had been called "The Fireman," and the various manuscript drafts of the novel in progress carried such titles as "Fire, Fire," "Burn Books!" and "The Hearth and the Salamander." Then, recognizing how integral book burning was to the novel, he investigated and determined the combustion temperature of paper. Thus, he arrived at *Fahrenheit 451*, as well-known a title as any in science fiction.

Bradbury, a compulsive moviegoer, was quite pleased with Francois Truffaut's cinematic version of the novel. While some viewers might have been disappointed in the relative lack of futuristic hardware, Bradbury has said, "Look at the film through the eyes of the French Impressionists. See the poetic romantic vision of Pissarro, Monet, Renoir, Seurat, or Manet that Truffaut evokes in the film, and then remember that this method was his metaphor to capture the metaphor in my novel."

In the end, it is beauty, poetry, and romanticism that the novel invokes. As Bradbury has said,

> Mankind is half-idealist, half-destroyer. We are now in the greatest age of history, capable of leaving our home planet behind us, of going off into space on a tremendous voyage of survival. Nothing must be allowed to stop this voyage, our last great wilderness trek.

The spirit of *Fahrenheit 451* is the first step on that voyage.

Willis E. McNelly and
Keith Neilson

Sources for Further Study

Criticism:

McNelly, Willis E. "Ray Bradbury: Past, Present and Future," in *Voices for the Future*. Edited by Thomas D. Clareson. Bowling Green, Ohio: Bowling Green University Popular Press, 1976, pp. 167-175. According to McNelly, Bradbury uses metaphor to intensify the reader's comprehension of reality in *Fahrenheit 451*.

Reilly, Robert. "The Artistry of Ray Bradbury," in *Extrapolation*. XIII (December, 1971), pp. 64-74. Reilly explores Bradbury's style of writing and theme in *Fahrenheit 451*.

Sisario, Peter. "A Study of the Allusions in Bradbury's *Fahrenheit 451*," in *English Journal*. LIX (February, 1970), pp. 201-205. Sisario's analysis of Bradbury's *Fahrenheit 451* reveals a concealed theme that is much more complex that it appears.

Slusser, George Edgar. *The Bradbury Chronicles*. San Bernardino, Calif.: Borgo Press, 1977. A succinct discussion of *Fahrenheit 451*'s characters and themes is given in this major work of Bradbury criticism.

Reviews:

Analog. LIII, April, 1954, pp. 145-146.

Authentic Science Fiction. XLVII, July, 1954, p. 114.

Chicago Sunday Tribune. October 25, 1953, p. 6.

Galaxy. VII, February, 1954, pp. 108-109.

Magazine of Fantasy and Science Fiction. V, December, 1953, pp. 104-105.

Nation. CLXXVII, December 19, 1953, p. 554.

New Worlds. XXIII, May, 1954, p. 123.

New York Herald Tribune Book Review. October 18, 1953, p. 12.

New York Times. November 8, 1953, p. 43.

FAR RAINBOW
(DALIOKAYA RADUGA)

Authors: Arkady Strugatsky (1925-   ) and Boris Strugatsky (1933-   )
First book publication: 1964
English translation: 1967
Type of work: Novel
Time: The distant future
Locale: The planet Rainbow, a proving ground for physicists

A novel about the tragic consequences of a scientific experiment which results in a spontaneous cataclysm on the planet used as a proving ground

Principal characters:
LEONID GORBOVSKY, a space-pilot, Captain of the spaceship *Tariel*
PERCY DIXON, the doctor of *Tariel*
MARK FALKENSTEIN, the navigator of *Tariel*
CAMILLE, an immortal cyborg
ETIENNE LAMONDOIS, head physicist on Rainbow
ROBERT SKLYAROV, a physics laboratory assistant on Rainbow

Far Rainbow is a novel which fits organically into the space-and-time sequence of the early literary works written by the Strugatsky brothers. Such an organic unity is achieved through the use of the same main characters (the crew of the Assault spaceship *Tariel-2*, led by Leonid Gorbovsky), as well as through the vivid and emotional atmosphere familiar to readers of the Strugatskys' books. Hence, from the start it is possible to conclude that *Far Rainbow* deals with the same distant, bright, and truly human world which served the authors so well in the story series entitled *Noon: Twenty-Second Century*.

At the same time, *Far Rainbow* was a turning point in the creative work of the Strugatskys. Although a bright and light manner and the same kaleidoscopic structure has been preserved, it should be noted that the major attention is devoted to a moral problem rather than to episodic pictures of a distant utopian future. Perhaps for the first time this problem has been clearly formulated by the authors in *Far Rainbow* (if we omit *Escape Attempt*, a novel published in 1962). Later, this moral problem became the key motive in all their works.

This ethical problem involves a choice between reason and conscience, between the coldly rational and the humanly irrational. Despite an excellently written fantastical background, the novel contains some repercussions of the "realistic" dilemma which troubled Dostoevski: is it possible to build human destiny on the unjustifiable bloodshed of a tortured child? The Strugatskys would come to this problem of correlating means and ends again and again. In *Far Rainbow* the problem has been specified with the utmost precision: which must one choose — knowledge or children — if only one can survive? Since this is one of the first attempts to solve the problem, the manner of raising the problem is sharp, even exaggerated, so that the solution itself is clear and straightforward, allowing no alternatives.

The main characters are depicted clearly, functionally, and, in some cases, with a genuine psychological brilliance. While the action takes place centuries in the future, the main characters — the young physicists who have "occupied" Rainbow, a planet proving-ground — bear close resemblance to contemporaries in Dubna or Princeton. They are happy, witty, and dedicated; they possess a thirst for knowledge, and with it, a willingness to break rules, ready to go to a fault, if necessary, to keep their work progressing (for instance, to cut into the general power cable secretly for the sake of their scientific experiments). All this is done, not for mercenary motives or vanity, but only for the sake of pure science. They are its loyal knights; to them, science serves as an absolute authority and moral yardstick.

However, the "null physicists'" experiment with teleportation on Rainbow has tragic results. On both poles of the planet, a gigantic wave of decayed matter appears and moves slowly toward the populated regions, burning everything in its path. These events upset the illusory "contemporary" atmosphere and help to define the difference between people of the future, as described by the Strugatskys, and today's students of nature. Although the present-day dilemma — whom to serve, science or human beings — provokes a whole range of solutions depending on various sociohistorical circumstances (we know that the twentieth century motto "Science is beyond morals" leads to enormous moral blindness), for the Strugatskys' characters, the problem does not exist. Their moral principle is expressed in a concise form: foremost is humanity as such — human nature existing in oneself — and only then come the abstract scientific postulates.

But is it really so simple? The Strugatskys belong to the rare type of science fiction writers who never present problems without creating authentic, alive human characters. Because of this factor, the books written by the Strugatsky brothers contain no traditional mores or uniform behavioral patterns. The authors prefer that the reader meet various kinds of personalities and various modes of behavior, the products of different measures of responsibility. Although the solution here is rather simple and known to practically everybody on Rainbow, doubts, bitter dialogues between the self and its conscience, and even temporary weakness remain.

Rainbow is doomed, because in less than twenty-four hours, all life on the planet will be destroyed by a terrible, unavoidable, and ruthless wave. This inevitability is felt from the first pages of the novel, though the initial news about the wave comes only as a trivial and slightly alarming message. This alarm destroys the initially idyllic atmosphere: Rainbow is a quiet and homelike planet (called a "village" by the old spacehand Falkenstein) where nothing ever happens. Besides, physicist Robert Sklyarov, one of the first to meet the wave at the distant observation station, is young and in love; his

future seems to him full of rainbows. However, by purely literary means —
dialogues, sharp changes in tone and in the tempo of the story — the authors
create a feeling from the very beginning that the idyllic existence has ended,
that something unpleasant has happened, and that nobody can escape a decision and a sacrifice.

Such inevitability of choice is stressed by Camille, a mysterious and unpleasant person. Nobody knows where he came from. Camille is half human
being and half robot, characterized by a cool logic and symbolizing absolute
superhuman knowledge in the novel. Only in the final scene does the reader
discover that Camille is the victim of a tragic experiment carried out on himself in an attempt to rid himself of all his human qualities. In many ways,
Camille is omnipotent (though he is free of the instincts toward aggression and
destruction characteristic of many Western science fiction characters). He is
almost immortal, absolutely precise, and infallible in his calculations and forecasts. According to the opinion of the leading scientists of Rainbow, Camille
is a genius, but at the same time he is lonely and sometimes miserable. Pity for
him is evoked by the remnants of his personal human features; his life seems
extremely tragic in the bright and light human world. Yet he made the decision
willingly to kill everything human in himself. This is the sinister person who
first predicts the destruction of Rainbow.

All the events in the novel take place in the course of one day — the last
day of Rainbow. While the plot unravels, the authors introduce Leonid Gorbovsky, Captain of the spaceship *Tariel*, his friends, and the crew members of
the spaceship, which has delivered a scheduled load for the laboratories. Gorbovsky, Dixon, and Falkenstein are well-known to readers of the Strugatskys'
books — they came from the story series entitled *Noon: Twenty-Second Century*. Perhaps this is the reason why their familiar portraits have been only
slightly touched up.

Gorbovsky is one of the most outstanding and likable characters created by
the Strugatskys. The authors are obviously quite attached to him: having
"killed" him in *Far Rainbow*, they later "resurrected" him in the novel *The
Kid (Kiddy)*. In the process of creating the character of Gorbovsky, the authors
use, more successfully than ever, one of their most refined methods — that of
indirect and oblique characterization. The Strugatskys do not depict Gorbovsky as he is, they only imply his nature; but they do this so skillfully that for
most readers this character seems absolutely genuine and extremely attractive.

In science fiction books one often encounters "brilliant scientists" who
nevertheless talk nonsense and proclaim truisms; but Gorbovsky is different.
He is pleasant, clever, soft, or firm when the situation requires, and always
kind, intelligent, witty, and profound. He is paradoxical, but free of illusions,
ironical but not cynical. At the same time, he is not idealized or sentimentalized. Gorbovsky is not the ideal man — he has his weaknesses and makes
mistakes. Nevertheless, if the people of the future are characterized by their

humane natures achieved through self-perfection, then Gorbovsky can be taken as a "pilot model."

Gorbovsky is a well-known expert in his field, but at the same time he is free from bossiness, self-interest, and false pride. He is always surrounded by people who need him. When a friend of his remarks: "You've a fine character, everybody likes you," Gorbovsky answers: "That's not it. . . . I like everybody, that's it. I've lived the best part of a hundred years, think of it, Matvei, and I've never yet met an unpleasant individual." In one part of the story, we learn that Gorbovsky has been placed on the Contact Commission, and this news is subconsciously accepted with sympathy and approval.

Gorbovsky himself makes practically no comments; and when he does speak, he does so laconically, unlike most science fiction heroes. In a situation where he has to comment, Gorbovsky resorts, as a rule, to a joke. The reader believes in Gorbovsky's intelligence, talent, and high standard of ethics, but his thoughts and feelings are usually left to the reader's imagination.

The Strugatskys are subtle and indirect, which contributes to the fact that the main characters of their books are multifaceted, rich, and versatile. Among American science fiction writers, it is perhaps Ursula K. Le Guin who has come the closest to the Strugatskys' style. Envoy Genly Ai from *The Left Hand of Darkness* would get along well with Gorbovsky. Disregarding differences of the plots and languages, these two characters have much in common: intelligence, ethics, human "cosmic feeling," and similar scientific tasks.

Once the inevitability of the destruction of everything living on Rainbow is realized, it becomes clear that evacuation is possible only for the number of objects or persons that can fit inside *Tariel*, the sole spaceship remaining on the planet. It falls to Gorbovsky to decide, therefore, who shall live and who shall die. Since it is impossible to save everyone, the moral question arises of what should be the criteria for choosing the survivors. The problem is made even more intense because all of humanity's priceless scientific information, which is necessary for the progress and well-being of mankind, has been collected on Rainbow. At the same time, Rainbow houses the best intellects of humanity, its best minds and most invaluable individuals. According to the Strugatskys, people of the future as a rule should not even consider self-preservation if there is any hope of saving the results of their scientific work of many years. However, the situation is much more complicated and tragic than can be solved by a simple solution of people sacrificing their lives for the sake of science. This is because there are also several hundred children of various ages on Rainbow, and no one can predict what they will become as adults.

Logically, the most important consideration should be human knowledge, but centuries-old moral assumptions would favor saving the children. Nobody on Rainbow, under these conditions, is amenable to the views of "cold" logic. However, to part with their life and the results of their work, which are more important to them than life, is a very difficult and painful moral problem.

The novel culminates when the whole population of Rainbow gathers in the square in front of the Planet Council to receive its decision. On behalf of science, Etienne Lamondois, a leading physicist, declares the moral credo of the scientist: to devote one's life to knowledge and to the preservation of its benefits for humanity. According to Lamondois, these benefits will determine the future of humanity. Gorbovsky speaks after Lamondois, and his words are accepted by everyone as the natural and only possible solution:

> "But, you see, there's really nothing to decide. Everything's been decided. The crèches and the new-born babies and their mothers are already aboard the ship. . . . The rest of the children are embarking now. I think there's room for them all. . . ."

After his speech, readers, together with those present in the square, give a sigh of relief. Naturally, it is necessary to save the future, and this future will be preserved in our children, first and foremost.

The piloting and orbiting of the spaceship is entrusted to one of Gorbovsky's friends, an honored space-pilot in the past and now the chief of all the children's establishments on Rainbow. Gorbovsky remains with the others on Rainbow. For the last time he meets Camille, who "today died and was resurrected three times. Each time it was terribly painful." Helping to reveal Camille's mystery, this dialogue deals with the correlation between the rationally logical and the irrationally human, and states the impossibility of dispensing with the latter; the passage summarizes and crystallizes the main issues of the novel.

The one serious criticism of *Far Rainbow* that might be made is the authors' failure to dramatize sufficiently the plot's ideological conflicts. There is no full-fledged debate, no struggle of opinions. In general, every character in the book has been similarly brought up by the society and thus accepts its moral precepts. The characters argue about morals, but the reader knows in advance what these characters will do under critical circumstances. However, this novel was one of the Strugatskys' first "serious" books; more complicated conflicts were to appear in their subsequent works.

One purely visual scene remains vividly in the reader's memory: a sea beach, two dark walls rising high into the sky, a narrow streak of the sky and a narrow path of water, and eight unfortunate explorers — "null-fliers" — walking into the Nothingness. Seven of them carry the eighth on their shoulders. Blinded by the wave, he is playing the banjo, and even after they walk out of sight, their song lingers.

Vl. Gakov

FEAR
AND
TYPEWRITER IN THE SKY

Author: L. Ron Hubbard (1911-   )
First book publication: 1951
Type of work: Novels

Two novels published in one volume that represent the humorous and serious sides of L. Ron Hubbard's examination into the surreal

The pulp magazine *Unknown Worlds* was the companion to *Astounding Science Fiction* from March, 1939, until October, 1942, when it was discontinued because of the wartime paper shortage. Its pages were filled, for the most part, by the same writers who wrote science fiction for *Astounding Science Fiction*, but it developed a unique personality by virtue of a strange cross-fertilization of method.

The science fiction which was then appearing in *Astounding Science Fiction* under the aegis of editor John W. Campbell, Jr., laid claim to being the product of a disciplined speculative imagination, extrapolating logically from known science into the realms of future possibility. What carried over from that prospectus into the pure fantasy that was written for *Unknown Worlds* was the element of discipline. *Unknown Worlds* permitted its authors any premises whatever, no matter how absurd, and allowed them to work with the vocabulary of the supernatural imagination that was taboo in *Astounding Science Fiction*, but Campbell still insisted that once the basic premises were established their consequences should be explored *logically*. *Unknown Worlds*'s fantasy was therefore self-consistent to a rather unusual degree, and what was more important, it tended to pursue with exploratory fervor the not-so-obvious corollaries of its initial suppositions.

This tendency led to the development within the magazine of two characteristic moods. The logical development of absurd premises was usually a playful exercise whose consequences were humorous, but sometimes the premises could be taken seriously, in which case horrific possibilities could be taken step-by-logical-step through a crescendo of suspense to a melodramatically extreme conclusion. Classic stories in the former vein include the "Harold Shea" series by L. Sprague de Camp and Fletcher Pratt, and the same partnership's *Land of Unreason*; while archetypal examples of the second vein are Alfred Bester's "Hell is Forever" and Fritz Leiber's *Conjure Wife*.

During its brief career *Unknown Worlds* featured forty novels and short novels. The most prolific contributor of these longer works was L. Sprague de Camp, who wrote ten, although five of those were in collaboration. The second most prolific contributor was L. Ron Hubbard, who was responsible for seven novels. Hubbard wrote for a wide range of pulp outlets, and had sold a handful of short works, including one novella, to *Astounding Science Fiction*,

but it was in *Unknown Worlds* that he found his *forte* and became an important
member of the Campbell stable. The two short novels in the volume under
consideration, which were both initially published in 1940, are excellent
examples of the two contrasting moods that were typical of *Unknown Worlds*'s
fantasy.

The hero of *Typewriter in the Sky* is an unsuccessful piano player named
Mike de Wolf, who has the misfortune to be calling on his friend, the well-
known hack writer Horace Hackett, while Hackett is being pressured by his
publisher to tell him the plot of a novel which is imminently due for delivery.
Hackett casts desperately about for inspiration, and begins weaving a romantic
story of piracy on the high seas, in which Mike de Wolf is transformed into the
elegant villain Miguel de Lobo, commissioned to sweep the English from the
seventeenth century Caribbean but doomed to fail and to lose the heroine to the
honest English hero.

De Wolf begins to feel rather giddy, and wakes up to find himself cast up
on the shore of St. Kitts in 1630, harried by English sailors who will not listen
when he denies that he is the Spanish admiral they believe him to be. He is
saved by Lady Marion, daughter of Lord Carstone, with whom he promptly
falls in love. At first he wonders whether he has slipped back through time,
but certain anachronisms and the occasional ominous sound of a typewriter
which haunts his consciousness convince him otherwise. He is trapped within
Horace Hackett's *Blood and Loot*, enjoying a brief period of success before
being scheduled to perish in the climax. Like the good *Unknown Worlds* hero
he is, he sets about trying to cope with his situation in a rational manner,
testing the limitations of his free will and planning his strategy, determined to
escape his fate and get the girl if he possibly can.

Mike finds that he can act on his own account during the lacunae in Hackett's manuscript, where a span of time is passed over a cursory sentence,
or when the typewriter is busy chronicling the exploits of the hero, leaving
Mike "offstage." However, when Hackett deals directly with his villain,
Mike's words and actions fall completely under the control of the keys, and he
becomes no more than a puppet. This mixture of free will and determinism is
highlighted by a scene in the "upper world" in which Hackett talks idly to a
fellow hack about the curious way novels have of "writing themselves" once
the author has started the ball rolling, and the godlike nature of the author's
control over his literary cosmos.

While Hackett is following his hero, Tom Bristol, Mike manages to turn the
plot to his advantage, exempting himself from the crucial sea battle. Alas, it is
all to no avail — when Hackett realizes that the impetus of his story has led him
astray he simply tears up the offending pages, and Mike finds himself returned
to his predestined course. He plays out the final pages of the book, but lives on
when Hackett abandons him to death and confronts Tom Bristol in a strange
"extra" scene. By now, though, the book's very universe is dissolving, no

longer sustained by the involvement of its creator. Mike regains consciousness in New York, but with mixed feelings — he is glad to be alive but he knows that the woman he loved has been snatched from him irredeemably. The book ends with a classic triplet of lines in which Mike looks up into the sky of his own world, and wonders.

Typewriter in the Sky is a playful story which develops it premise skillfully and economically, in a highly entertaining fashion. It has some delightful moments of surreal humor. Yet from time to time there are darker moments, because the very fact that the hero must confront his situation rationally emphasizes that however absurd it may be, if for him it is real, then for him it is also serious and potentially tragic. This balance of humor against menace is what confers upon the story its real dramatic tension and strength.

Fear represents, of course, the other side of the coin. Once again we find a protagonist caught up in a surreal web of absurd events, but here *all* is implicitly threatening, and there can be no doubting the desperate seriousness of his predicament.

James Lowry is an ethnologist based at a small American campus in a town which has always been his home, a haven of rest for himself and the wife he loves. He incurs the wrath of the college president by publishing an extravagantly skeptical article on demonology in a popular journal, and is discharged. He visits his friend Tommy Williams in search of consolation, but Williams' reassurances are unsatisfying, supplemented as they are by a criticism of the outspoken skepticism that has gotten Lowry into trouble. Williams suggests that this skepticism goes beyond a simple concern for truth and a laudable urge to champion rationality, and is actually a kind of protective shield against the unpleasant aspects of reality. The heart of the story is contained in this complaint:

> Jim, the world to you has always been a good place; that's a sort of mechanical reaction by which you like to forget all the ghastly things the world has done to you. You should be more like me, Jim. I *know* the world is an evil, capricious place and that men are basically bad and so, knowing that, I am always pleased to find some atom of goodness and only bored to see something evil. . . . Phantoms or not, that man is the safest who knows that all is really evil and that air and earth and water are peopled by fantastic demons and devils who lurk to grin at and increase the sad state of man.

What follows is Lowry's descent into a nightmare. He loses four hours of his life and his hat, and is then beset by hallucinations in which he is repeatedly told that if he finds what he has lost then he will die. In the grip of this nightmare he tries to carry on through the next few days, with phantasmagorical delusion superimposed upon reality, so that he hardly knows where one ends and the other begins. He seeks help from his wife and from Williams, but finds their support strangely weak. The visions reach a climax when he is told by one of the characters in his fantasy that he alone is real, and that he is the

animating force of the whole universe. From this point on he perceives the real
world as an inert, hollow sham which only operates under his direct gaze, and
which is slowly failing even to do that. In the end, he simply cannot stand
being alone in a dead and phantom-haunted world any longer, and he returns
from it to face the terrible truth, lost with his hat and his missing four hours,
that precipitated him into it.

In the opening scene of the story the reader has "overheard" a brief dialogue between two "demons" who decide to punish Lowry for his skepticism.
But the reader has also read a prefatory note in which Hubbard says categori-
cally that: "There is one thing which I wish the reader could keep in mind
throughout, and that is: this story is wholly logical, for all that will appear to
the contrary." The apparent conflict here is, indeed, redeemed to expose a
terrible logic: the demons *are*, in a manner of speaking, real, but only in terms
of the metaphor which Tommy Williams puts forward in the crucial quotation.
The source of Lowry's torment is his own unwillingness to face the evil in
himself; the demons that he will not believe in are the evil forces within his
own personality, repressed into the unconscious mind. The four hours he has
condemned to this pit of blankness are those in which he discovered his wife
with Tommy Williams, jumped to an entirely false conclusion, killed them
both and then tried to conceal their bodies. The conversations he had held with
both since that time have been illusory.

Fear is an extremely powerful story, undoubtedly the best horror story that
appeared in *Unknown Worlds* (even with such competition as Sturgeon's "It"
and the marvelous opening sequence of *Conjure Wife*). Its internal logic is the
source of its strength — it is ruthless in its development, and walks a tightrope
between psychology and superstition with perfect balance. At the height of his
period of disturbance Lowry must lecture to his students, and the lecture which
he gives is a brilliant internal commentary on the events of the story. In impassioned terms he recants his skepticism, telling his audience that perhaps, after
all, there *are* such things as demons, which *do* still haunt and torment mankind, and that perhaps in growing wise under the aegis of science and
rationalism we have somehow ceased to perceive what we all once knew
beyond the shadow of a doubt. The reader knows that within the framework of
the story Lowry is speaking the truth, in metaphor: there *are* demons, and they
do torment us, but they are one with ourselves and haunt us from within.

This volume is interesting as a pair of stories which testify to the excellence
of *Unknown Worlds*'s particular brand of fantasy. Ironically, though, it becomes doubly interesting when we consider it also as a testimony to the concerns of L. Ron Hubbard. All the authors mentioned in *Typewriter in the Sky*
save Hackett are Hubbard's pseudonyms, and Hackett is a kind of dilute
pseudo-Hubbard. (The reader will note that Hackett writes *books*, and considers himself stretched to the limit by the prospect of meeting a deadline *two
months hence*. Hubbard wrote for the pulps, and the prospect of turning out a

novel as long as Typewriter in the Sky in a weekend would not have troubled him unduly.) Hubbard, even more than Hackett, was the archetype of the hack writer, churning out wordage with a cynicism modified by the occasional idle moment when he felt rather godlike.

Fear testifies to the fact that a pulp hack could occasionally transcend the limitations of his endeavor and produce something *really* powerful. There is surely a moral in the fact that Hubbard went on to invent a new school of psychoanalysis based on the thesis that all the ills of mankind stem from blotted-out memories ("engrams"), suppressed because of their inherent unpleasantness, which plague and torment us, and that this new psychoanalysis was ultimately reincarnated as a religion whose dramatic revelation is that we are *all* potentially godlike if only we can clear away our inner demons and "audit" ourselves back to our inherent superpowers. The link between Dianetics/Scientology and *Fear* is quite obvious if we compare passages from the story with Book Two, Chapter IV of *Dianetics, the Modern Science of Mental Health*, which is titled "The 'Demons.'" Hubbard apparently came to believe, eventually, that James Lowry was everyman, and that the world in which he was living was plotted by a typewriter in the sky whose schemes and habits he knew as intimately as Mike de Wolf knew Horace Hackett's. It is difficult to believe that this is true, but it does have the power of skillful literary artifice behind it, and it has made Hubbard a great deal richer than hack writing ever could have.

Brian Stableford

Sources for Further Study

Reviews:

Amazing Stories. XXV, November, 1951, pp. 158-159.

Analog. XLVII, August, 1951, p. 143.

Galaxy. II, September, 1951, p. 113.

Science Fiction Quarterly. II, February, 1953, pp. 77-79.

THE FEMALE MAN

Author: Joanna Russ (1937-   )
First book publication: 1975
Type of work: Novel
Time: 1969, the present, and the future
Locale: An alternate earth in 1969 and Whileaway, a planet inhabited entirely by females

An angry social commentary guised as a novel about four women of the same genetic makeup, their evolution, and final coming together

> Principal characters:
>> JEANNINE DIDIER, a feminine, brainwashed victim of a chauvinistic 1969 world similar to Earth
>> JANET EVASON, a strong, self-sufficient female visitor from the unisexed world of Whileaway
>> JAEL (ALICE REASONER), a militant feminist
>> JOANNA, a fusion of the four, and the voice of the author

Approximately two decades ago in a writing class at Cornell University, a group of students and their professor sat down to critique an ambitious project: part of a novel written by the then fledgling author Joanna Russ. The section under discussion concerned the pain experienced by the heroine at a school dance. A wallflower trying to escape her agony, she disappears into the ladies room every ten minutes, stares into the mirror and repeats "bloody green ghost" twenty-five times to avoid emerging too soon.

As Russ reflected on this incident at the 1975 meeting of the Midwest Modern Language Association, she noted that the class had thought her story funny but trivial. The teacher had reserved his highest praise for another work, by a young man, which contained a rape, a fight in a bar, and a woman who was "thrown down and taken brutally by her husband on the floor she was scrubbing just after she'd come out of the hospital for the excision of a coccyxal cyst." The story ended with the words, "That night their idiot child was conceived." Both class and teacher considered the male student's work "Literature": raw, elemental, deep, and true.

At that point, Russ knew that she would never become a great author because she knew nothing of real life, high school dances were obviously not important (even though she had suffered horribly at them), and Great Literature lay in realms forever closed to her because she was "never going to have a fist fight in a bar, piss in a urinal, buy a whore, fight bulls, hunt whales, or rape (her) wife."

It has taken two decades for the frustration and anger Russ felt then and still feels now to be expressed in full force in her harsh, didactic novel, *The Female Man.* So great is her rage, that she has fragmented herself into four characters in this work, and it takes at least four to give full voice to her feelings.

Jeannine Didier is the embodiment of the feminine, the kind of girl who would wear the tulle, strapless formal, attend the high school dance, worry obsessively about her make-up, attire, and sex appeal. She is the eternal victim. Victimized in small things, she cannot even successfully deal with personal shopping: "We went into the store and the store owner bullied us. Outside again with her stockings (wrong size) she said, 'But I didn't *want* them!'" Victimized in larger things, she has swallowed the entire *machismo* bill of goods: marriage is her goal, life's panacea. Her only existence must come from her role in life rather than from any intrinsic worth as an individual.

Jeannine is recognizable as being from our world, and yet she is from an alternate world that is slightly different. Although the time is 1969, World War II has not taken place; America is still in the Depression. Jeannine is a twenty-nine-year-old librarian who wears her spinsterhood heavily. She is desperate to marry, either her current boyfriend, Cal, or another man she has just met. It doesn't matter who it will be, because the only recognizable truth is that

> Men succeed. Women get married.
> Men fail. Women get married.
> Men enter monasteries. Women get married.
> Men start wars. Women get married.
> Dull, dull.

Janet Evason is juxtaposed against Jeannine. An inhabitant of the planet Whileaway, where the men have all been killed off by a plague generations earlier, she is the embodiment of the female. The alternate world of Whileaway is a feminist Utopia originally presented by Russ in the short story "When It Changed" (*Again Dangerous Visions*). Female in fact, Whileaway is androgynous in life style, a straightforward place where everyone has a function to perform, where everyone works productively and enjoys a five-year vacation following the birth of a child. The inhabitants, like the unisexed Gethens in Ursula K. Le Guin's *Left Hand of Darkness*, embody the best of the male and female roles and are judged as individuals. Janet is a law enforcer suddenly transported to Earth where she not only becomes an instant celebrity but has the opportunity to measure us (and our sex roles) against her own firm standards.

The earth Janet encounters is both like and unlike the present world. Courtship and the flirtatious interplay between the sexes still exist, but now no one need act out of ignorance because there is an official guideline to follow which accounts for all possible eventualities. Little books entitled *What to Do in Every Situation* — blue for boys and pink for girls — are issued in high school and carried and referred to throughout adult life. An example of their advice can be found after Janet has a physical battle with a young man who did not understand her response to him. For him, and according to his blue book, a female who is physically chastised by a male should respond to his anger by backing down, crying, vindicating his manhood. Not only does his blue book predict it, but the female's matching pink book states (under the listing "Brutality") that "Man's bad temper is the woman's fault. It is also the woman's responsibility to patch things up afterwards." When all this is pointed out to Janet, she suggests throwing both books away.

This division of the sexes into two antagonistic groups, each with its own set of regulations, is merely a foreshadowing of the world of Jael (Alice Reasoner), the feminist principle personified. Jael is from a future world where the battle of the sexes is no longer figurative, but literal, a Manland/Womanland war which has been going on for forty years. The world is divided into two armed camps, and Jael is a spy and assassin equipped with artificial metal claws honed to action and capable of murder. She is Russ's answer to Lester del Rey's "Helen O'Loy" — a pseudohuman, male lover developed from monkey cells, brainless, but nubile and effective. It is Jael who brings the four J's together, telling the other three that they are identical genotypes from three possible present universes. Her goal is to recruit them for her cause by having them establish military bases for Womanland's forces on their respective worlds.

Fusing Jeannine, Janet, and Jael is Joanna, the author, a character in her own book and an inhabitant of our world, or a strikingly similar alternate conception of it. Cynical and bitter, she is more sophisticated than Jeannine, as direct as Janet, and less militant than Jael, because she understands the principles of her own time and place. It is Joanna who explains the title of the book, who pointedly explains how she turned into a Female Man, and what such a metamorphosis has meant. She explains that her growth as a woman has meant "vanity training, obedience training, self-effacement training, deference training, dependency training, passivity training, rivalry training, stupidity training, placation training." And when she tried to learn and yet failed at all these lessons, she thought it was her own fault — not the system's. And then came the revelation, the epiphany — that women were not truly human — only men were.

In becoming a female-man, Russ is declaring that biology need not be destiny, that what is man-made can be unmade. The masculine mystique and the feminine mystique are not intrinsic, not determined by God. Therefore, if we follow patterns which have been taught, we can unteach them, break the patterns, and remake them.

Many years of anger and six substantial sections of *The Female Man* pass before author/character turns into the female/man at the beginning of the seventh section — the most philosophical introspective slice of this highly philosophical, introspective nonnovel.

The Female Man is a nonnovel because its plot has been totally superseded by characters, different incarnations of the same woman which may either signify the different stages of one woman's struggle for self-realization, or represent a simple progression. First there is Jeannine, accepting her circumstances, wilted, unhappy; second, Joanna, cynically playing along, biding her time, struggling in her cocoon until metamorphosis; third, Jael, openly fighting (and winning); and last, Janet, perhaps a detached observer/commentator, or perhaps a woman representative of a future age, able to exist without men.

As these characters usurp the plot, so the author usurps the characters as they meet again in varying, kaleidoscopic combinations, again and again reiterating the author's convictions in angry, highly quotable, repetitive lines. And while Russ's polemics are often perceptive and fascinating in and of themselves, they do nothing to further the plot, and indeed often inhibit it, causing the book to be heavily criticized, labeled as a plotless, disorganized revenge fantasy.

Russ herself clearly foresaw and predicted what would be said about her work, and in one of the many authorial intrusions, she devotes nearly two pages to listing the criticisms which will be leveled against her. To name but a few, these labels include: "shrill . . . vituperative . . . maunderings of antiquated feminism . . . this shapeless book . . . of very limited interest, I should say . . . no characterization, no plot . . . another shrill polemic which the . . . a brilliant but basically confused study of feminine hysteria which. . . ." What she did not predict, or perhaps did not want to be on record as predicting, was the rash of favorable criticism which found the book a rarity, a groundbreaker, the first real feminist science fiction statement.

While there may be more heat than light in Russ's exposition, and while her anger and pain may lessen the novel's artistic objectivity, *The Female Man* is still a provocative work. Each of Russ's heroines illustrates a different way of coping with a male-dominated society, and as they cope they reject their limited roles, just as Russ has rejected the limited role of the typically structured novel. More important, they dramatize the author's message: that to become huMAN, we must reject the structures inherent in sexism.

Beverly Friend

Sources for Further Study

Reviews:

Book World. September 14, 1975, p. 4.

Library Journal. C, May 15, 1975, p. 1015.

Magazine of Fantasy and Science Fiction. XLIX, August, 1975, p. 46.

New York Times Book Review. May 4, 1975, p. 50.

Village Voice. XX, January 20, 1975 p. 39.

THE FIFTH HEAD OF CERBERUS

Author: Gene Wolfe (1931-   )
First book publication: 1972
Type of work: Novel
Time: Approximately four hundred years in the future
Locale: Sainte Anne and Sainte Croix, twin planets colonized by Earth

Three thematically linked novellas each of which deals with problems of identity and with the links between human and animal behavior, through images both biological (cloning) and anthropological (a shape-shifting alien race)

> Principal characters:
> "THE FIFTH HEAD OF CERBERUS," the narrator of the first story, an unnamed boy from the fifth generation of a line of cloned individuals
> AUNT JEANNINE, his "aunt," also known as anthropologist Dr. Aubrey Veil
> DR. JOHN V. MARSCH, an anthropologist from Earth, author of the second story and protagonist of the third
> SANDWALKER, an Annese aborigine possibly imagined by Marsch
> EASTWIND, Sandwalker's brother, who he becomes
> V. R. TRENCHARD, a teenage beggar boy on Sainte Anne, possibly half-aborigine

Before the publication of *The Fifth Head of Cerberus*, Gene Wolfe was primarily known as the author of a set of complex, precise short stories, nearly all of which appeared in the *Orbit* series of anthologies edited by Damon Knight; Wolfe's first story appeared in *Orbit 2* (1967). His first novel, *Operation ARES* (1970), was also written in 1967, and was heavily cut for publication. It is the work of a promising apprentice only.

The Fifth Head of Cerberus, the novella which became Part I of the book, was written originally as a separate story and with no plans for expansion. However, a Charles Scribner's Sons editor who read the story in 1970 (it was not published until 1972, in *Orbit 10*) commissioned a full-length book based upon it. The book version of the original story is slightly modified, but the main expansion takes the form of two new stories whose links with the first and with each other are tantalizingly elusive. On a first reading, the three stories might seem to be linked only by a common character, Marsch, and by their setting. Indeed, for any reader without a photographic memory, it would be impossible to absorb all the implications of the stories the first time through, since clues are placed chronologically at points where they cannot yet be recognized as clues. Careful subsequent readings, however, reveal that the three parts are joined by themes and images which, though they seem airy and insubstantial at first, are actually strong. Thus, if the stories were to be read in the wrong order (as any reader, misled by the subtitle "three novellas," might easily do), much of the fine structure of the book would collapse into mere enigma.

Part I, "The Fifth Head of Cerberus," is set in the town of Port-Mimizon on the planet Sainte Croix (the suggestion of crucifixion may not be accidental), whose society is hierarchical, elegant, formal, and based on a slave economy. It has a strong French influence, though the French have, to some extent, been reduced to second-class citizens by a later wave of colonists. The town is not unlike eighteenth century New Orleans; it is attractive, sensual, and cruel. The Narrator is an ex-prisoner, relating memories of his growth from boyhood to young manhood. He has a name, but never reveals it; his father calls him "Number Five." His father is a scientist who finances his researches through the money he earns as proprietor of an exclusive brothel, part of the corrupt underworld guarded on the outside by a symbolic statue of the mythological three-headed dog Cerberus. The Narrator's tutor is Mr. Million, a robot machine upon whose screen a human face appears.

We learn all this through the Narrator's memories of his childhood, which was marked by its lack of love, isolation, obsessively enforced training in biology, nightly interrogations under drugs conducted by the father, and initiations into techniques of exploitation of human weakness necessary in a brothel keeper. To the Narrator, such a background seems natural until he grows older; then small fragments from the outside world begin to expose the ruthlessness and alienation of the life he and his brother David have been living. He asks questions, and gradually deduces that he is his father's clone and not his son; his aunt is, biologically, his daughter. He is the fifth in a line whose origins (possibly on the sister planet of Sainte Anne, whose very name, that of Our Lady's mother, evokes the virgin birth on which theme the novel is to play many variations) remain mysterious. He is accidentally aided in his search for answers by a visiting anthropologist, Dr. Marsch, who also reveals that his tutor is a machine-simulacrum of an original human model, which was his "great-grandfather."

Through the phenomenon of "relaxation," each generation of clones comes to resemble the previous one more closely, for not only nature but nurture is identical in the unchanging, labyrinthine house with a father who is always the same man. Therefore, the Narrator's father's obsession to learn why his "family" has not made more of a name for itself in the world is doomed to failure. There will be no reprieve from mediocrity, for no new clone has any fresh factors in its make-up to ensure its success. As if compelled by some command of the blood in this latter-day House of Atreus, the Narrator kills his father (himself), just as his father killed his predecessor.

The questions of identity raised so evocatively in the clone-family are reflected in the larger world of Sainte-Croix, where a certain racial type (the Narrator's own) has become dominant because the gene pool is too small to allow proper variation. They are reflected, too, in the myth of the aboriginal population of the sister planet, Sainte Anne, where the French first landed. The Narrator's "aunt" believes that the aborigines were shape-changers who replaced the French immigrants, and that the savage cruelty of Sainte Croix results from the "French" population's origins not as people but as animals, (the "aunt" is Veil, and her belief is called "Veil's Hypothesis").

Part II, entitled " 'A Story,' by John V. Marsch," is apparently the anthropologist's reconstruction of what life must have been like for the aborigines on Sainte Anne immediately prior to the French arrival. The story is not presented as a scientific paper, but as a "fiction"; it is difficult to see, however, how the details that fill it could have been available to any ordinary anthropologist.

Did Marsch invent them?

The story follows the voyage of a youth, Sandwalker, one of the hill men, across the barren landscape of Sainte Anne to a final confrontation with his twin brother, Eastwind, who as a baby had been captured by the marshmen, and now lives as a eunuch acolyte to a high priest by the shores of an ocean. Along the way Sandwalker encounters a group of "Shadow Children" who may or may not be human; they tell him that he is not human. They say that once they were men who came from the stars (perhaps from Gondwanaland, perhaps Poictesme, but are these Earth-references mere fancies of Marsch?), but then again, they say later that they were once crawling creatures who "lived in holes between the roots of trees." Green-eyed Sandwalker is captured by the marshmen (Marschmen?), who practice ritual cannibalism, and he finally kills Eastwind, but it seems that in one sense his brother was himself, just as in Part I the Narrator is his father whom he also kills. After Eastwind is dead Sandwalker becomes Eastwind and greets the men from a starship which lands in the ocean. In their death throes the Shadow Children brought the ship there by "bending" the thought of the starcrossers (who themselves travel by "bending the sky"), just as previously these Shadow Children had always bent thought the other way to keep the starships away.

The whole story is mysterious and beautiful, one of the most poignant renditions in science fiction of a primitive, alien life, seen from within, although told in the third person. Is Marsch, then, a peculiarly talented science fiction-writing anthropologist, or something more?

The links between the first and second stories are minimal, and primarily thematic. It is the third story, "V.R.T.," which retrospectively ties the three parts together into a novel. The narrative is more complex here. An army officer in Sainte Croix is going through the papers of a prisoner, Marsch, who has been arrested for a crime which may be spying or murder or both. (Towards the end we learn that the initial arrest was for the murder of the brothel keeper of Part I, a murder we know that Marsch did not commit.) He has been locked in a squalid cell for more than a year, subjected to many deprivations.

Marsch's notebooks (if not forged by a clever spy) show him to have been an Earth anthropologist who went to Sainte Anne to investigate whether the rumors of a race of shape-changing aborigines, or "abos," had any basis in fact, and whether any of this officially extinct race still survive. V.R.T. is a beggar boy, V.R. Trenchard, whose drunken, garrulous father claims to be the king of the abos, who still survive. Marsch does not believe him, but takes young Trenchard on an expedition up-country (passing various sites which appeared in the story of Part II). The officer reading the notebooks cannot discern as much as the reader can from all this, but he discerns enough to worry him. Up-country, the handwriting seems to change, though this may be because Marsch hurt his hand; however, we have learned meanwhile that the Annese abos are not manually dextrous.

In fact, the careful reader (unlike several critics) can deduce that at one point in the expedition young Trenchard, the boy who wanted to become an anthropologist, has literally become one; he was half-abo. The being in prison, the being who visited the brothel in Part I, the anthropologist who wrote Part II (in prison?) is not Marsch, but a duplicate. The revelation is gradual and beautiful, all accomplished through delicately oblique reference, for the pseudo-Marsch maintains even in his diary the Marsch identity. Piece by piece we learn that V.R.T.'s abo descent is through his actress mother (a brilliant mimic) and not his father. Each rereading will reveal plot points which were not apparent previously; for example, who is the prisoner in the cell next door to Marsch's? The answer is moving and ironic.

In fact, the revelation had already begun in Part I, where Veil's Hypothesis, Marsch's green eyes, his false denial of having come from Sainte Anne, and an apparently hysterical accusation made to Marsch by the teenage Narrator are all retrospectively justified and explained. But many issues remain enigmatic even after repeated rereadings, though there are enough scattered references to show that Veil's Hypothesis is in some sense true, thus making the story in Part II seem less of a fiction and more of a documentary account. One of the clues, placed in the last few pages, is that the native deer are also shape-changers and able to pass as cattle. This makes the reader think twice when he looks back to the earlier testimonies of elderly Sainte Anne residents, which refer often to cattle drovers and outlying farms.

The irony, of course, is that the abo who stole a human identity as Marsch has lost it again as a prisoner who will never be released, a nonperson casualty of a cynical, totalitarian state. Other ironic parallels are various and profound. Marsch the innocent anthropologist *was* guilty of spying, for what else was he doing to the abo culture? Even though Marsch in his later incarnation is in many ways more sensitive than the first Marsch, he fears that he is nothing but an animal, a fear reflected, it seems, in the story he writes. He sees his face in prison in a polished pewter bowl as "a muzzle and blazing animal eyes." The abos of Part II, the "Free People," seem to the reader more human, more empathic to one another's needs, than the cruel "human" urbanites of Book I (and also than their strange codwellers, the Shadow Children, who, though farseeing, seem indifferent to the tortures they sometimes inflict). Paradoxically, though, the slavers and sensualists of Sainte Croix are themselves of abo descent, if Veil is right. Wolfe may be suggesting that changes in culture and human identity have as much to do with environmental circumstance as with biological determinism; perhaps Veil's Hypothesis is too simplistic. The reverberations of the story continually tantalize. A further parallel is drawn by the first Marsch between abos and the myths of fairies back on Earth. Were fairies a human invention, or were they actual, shy beings of a parallel race who lived secretly among humans?

The whole novel is a study in decaying cultures. Just as the abo culture in Part II will collapse under the strain of the French colonization, so the French culture, turned inward and living in the past, is also decaying.

Synopsis can only begin to suggest the richness of invention in this book. Other pleasures include Tante Jeannine's amazing prosthetic device; the tree-observatory and the sand-cage on Sainte Anne; the explanation of why there is always one more of the Shadow Children than a first count shows; and the bureaucratic logic of Sainte Croix's political repression.

The Fifth Head of Cerberus is a seductive book, remarkably satisfying in its fullness, yet provocative in its remoteness, its sense of being somehow complete just beyond the reader's range of vision. The story's point of view has the quality of almost childlike innocence, registering its perceptions precisely, imputing significance by the very intensity of its gaze so that data sometimes seem so hard-edged but disconnected as to be almost surreal. The book contains much vision, but very little overt interpretation.

The extraordinary complexity of the work explains, perhaps, why Wolfe's power as a writer has not yet been generally recognized by the science fiction readership, though there is a strong case for arguing that this is the greatest science fiction work of the 1970's. The book falls into the category of mind-teasing, elusive works which require from the reader a greater commitment, a greater willingness to follow the author into a maze, than is readily acceptable in any genre; for genre works rely, almost by definition, on variations of familiar themes and the fulfillment of the reader's expectations; they soothe the mind, while books of this kind irritate it into action.

This general category of science fiction has not been much recognized, though some of the genre's finest works belong to it. Examples include Algis Budry's *Rogue Moon* (1960), Thomas M. Disch's *Camp Concentration* (1968), Philip K. Dick's *The Three Stigmata of Palmer Eldritch* (1964), Alan Garner's *Red Shift* (1973), Ursula K. Le Guin's *The Lathe of Heaven* (1971), Stanislaw Lem's *Solaris* (1961), Richard McKenna's "Fiddler's Green" (1967), and any of a dozen of the James Tiptree, Jr., stories.

Some·books present their data in a logical, structured order, the commonest pattern being a straight line. But stories in the special category just mentioned appear to reflect something of the randomness of life. Coincidences take place; an observation will suddenly cause two previously unrelated facts to click together into a new synthesis; something casually noted out of the corner of the

eye only reveals its importance later. The reading of such a book is an acquired taste. The reading of most books can be compared to walking down a
highway built by the author; stories of this sort resemble, rather, a ramble
through a forest, whose fruitfulness may offer more than would be won in a
brisk ride to a preplanned destination. One senses that, for Wolfe, the writing
of *The Fifth Head of Cerberus* was an exploration, and for the reader this
exploration richly leads to the destination itself.

Peter Nicholls

Sources for Further Study

Reviews:

Amazing Stories. XXXVI, November, 1972, pp. 123-124, 129.

Analog. CX, December, 1972, pp. 170-171.

Library Journal. CXVII, August, 1972, pp. 2651-2652.

Renaissance. V, February 1, 1972, p. 11.

Riverside Quarterly. VI, August, 1973, pp. 79-82.

SF Commentary. XXXIX, November, 1973, pp. 4-7.

Times Literary Supplement. May 18, 1973, p. 562.

THE FINAL CIRCLE OF PARADISE
(HISNIJE VESHI VEKA)

Authors: Arkady Strugatsky (1925-   ) and Boris Strugatsky (1933-   )
First book publication: 1965
English translation: 1976
Type of work: Novel
Time: The end of the twentieth century
Locale: The "Country of the Boobs," a mythical capitalist state in Europe

A satirical tract aimed at grasping, small-minded egocentrism in the "society of universal abundance"; the story of a secret mission of a UN Security Council agent in a country where a new "narcotic" is discovered

Principal characters:
    IVAN ZHILIN, an ex-spaceman, now a secret agent of the UN Security Council
    PECK XENAI ("BUBA"), his friend
    OSCAR PEBLBRIDGE, an agent
    RIMEYER, a member of the Security Council
    VOUSI, the daughter of the boardinghouse hostess where Zhilin stays
    DR. OPIR, the traditional "utopia-dystopia" guide

Coming after *Far Rainbow* and *Hard to Be a God*, *The Final Circle of Paradise* reminds the reader of the early phase of the Strugatsky brothers' creative genius. A common hero and a common time link *The Final Circle of Paradise* with *Probationers* (1962), where the action takes place not in a distant Communist future but near the end of our own century.

The period is a complicated transitional one. The world has progressed from its present state. It is no longer torn by wars; nor is it suffering as it once did from the total negative effects of the scientific and technical revolution; and it is not plagued by the growth of Fascism to the same extent as was formerly the case. But it has not yet reached that clear, humane, and spiritual world of the future where the action of the majority of the Strugatskys' works takes place.

The end of the twentieth century is marked by considerable upheaval. Imperialism has finally been eliminated, and a really reasonable, just, democratic order has been established in most countries of the world, providing equality, spiritual fulfillment, and an absence of exploitation. This statement does not mean, however, that all countries have reached their final stage of development. There are still islands of the old world where, as before, private ownership of property still exists. The action takes place on one such "island."

The Strugatskys briefly sketch the topography of this world. Although they do not draw a precise political map, it is quite possible to reach a number of important conclusions on the basis of discreet hints. Such evils as militarism (there is an International Pact for disarmament), organized crime, and monopolies have disappeared. Mankind can finally breathe again, freed from the colossal strains of the last century. Moreover, mankind is essentially satisfied — probably, for the first time in history. International organizations, particularly the UN Security Council, whose agents are the main heroes of the novel, have become the only active police force. They act against occasional reactionaries: counter-revolutionaries, militarists, gangsters, and the like.

However, having principally done with these scourges, mankind encounters a new danger, actually growing throughout the entire twentieth century, but manifesting itself most acutely at the very moment when tension, fear and diffidence have virtually disappeared. This is the danger of satiated ease, the primitivization of everyone and everything — thoughts, feelings, and modes of behavior. Spiritual regression results in the "sleep of conscience giving birth to monsters" and these "predatory things of the age" are as dangerous as bombs. Does it really matter whether one perishes in the flames of war or in the bogs of abundance?

In long, rhetorical digressions, the Strugatskys depict the events preceding the time of the action. The reader witnesses the last battle in the Earth's history — a cruel, exhausting, and sacred battle for human souls.

These last skirmishes erupt after the International Pact has already been signed; they are "especially poignant because they are last." The old world has left a terrifying inheritance — criminals, "unemployed" militarists, "all kinds of leftover trash from intelligence and counter-intelligence, bored by the sameness of commercial espionage, all slavering for power." That is why the hero Ivan Zhilin has to come down to the "sinful Earth" to wipe away these evil influences. "Out of the same sewers of history crept the unregenerates with submachine guns, home-made quantum pistols, gangsters, gangster syndicates, gangster corporations." Universities and museums are set on fire, whole towns suffer severe invasions of bandits and vandals. Once again the people have to take up arms; and when this disaster is also overcome, "Once more pus was flowing out of the same sewers. Tons of heroin, cisterns of opium, and oceans of alcohol, but, above all, that something new for which we yet had no name."

But this "something" does have a name — "slug": a mysterious substance that suddenly begins to kill the people. It is something from which there is no escape, and which even eludes identification. Who produces it? What is it made of? What are its effects? How is it distributed? These are questions without answers.

In fact, it is "slug" which the former astronaut Ivan Zhilin, the hero of the novel *Probationers*, has been charged with tracking down and eliminating. "The most important matters are on Earth" — with these words the *Probationers* ends and they are not idle words. Still unaware of being shadowed by another officer, Oscar Peblbridge, Zhilin arrives in an unidentified European state, characterized by the authors as the Country of the Boobs. He arrives there to meet his old friend Rimeyer and the agent Peck Xenai to find out what "slug" is and why all the evidence points to this particular country as its source.

The Country of the Boobs is clearly mythical, as is evident from its name. In many respects the novel matches the framework of the familiar "utopia-dystopia." In this "sub-department" of science fiction the time and place of action are frankly arbitrary. It is a sociological model, sometimes realistic in appearance, sometimes utterly grotesque. But still it is a model rather than an artistic portrait of the world.

Tendencies of bourgeois society, clearly visible today, only a little over a decade since the publication of the Strugatskys' novel, have come to their logical conclusion in the Country of the Boobs. Here are the enervating mass-culture; the stultifying mass-media constantly seducing the sensibilities of the people; those cheerful philosophical ideas of the "century of a new hedonism" or "society of the satisfied demands"; and through it all, the rapid spread of narcotic abuse, loss of interest in culture, intellectual poverty, general withdrawal, and an extreme individualism. The Strugatskys provide few details but their "strokes" are vivid and accurate.

The Dream generator or "shiver," forces the great masses of the people into the state of torpid euphoria. Intellectual vandalism is rampant — "art patrons" steal masterpieces from the museums and destroy them at secret orgylike convocations. People called "fishers" seek cheap thrills to compensate for their spiritual emptiness. There is a general aversion to books. Conversely, a really physiological lust for material goods consumes them. Then, in addition to the already pervasive alcohol and narcotics, there is the truly fantastic "slug."

"Slug" has a direct physiological effect on the nerve center of the brain that controls pleasure. It is much more insidious than narcotics because, in its case, there is no need for anyone to induce addiction in another. A whole army of gross humanity is only too eager to experience the instant delight that it offers. "Slug" is no commercial venture of an evil corporation, but a natural consequence of the "live without thoughts" philosophy.

The Country of the Boobs acquired its name because of the disposition of its inhabitants toward mental and spiritual degradation. If they had not discovered "slug," they would have found or invented something else. "Boobs" are frequently compared to experimental rats with electrodes implanted in their brains. After the first stimulation of the "pleasure centers," they literally forget everything else — food, females, danger — and compulsively continue to press the lever time after time.

However, the "boobs" in the Strugatskys' book are dimwitted, foolish people, unable to master the peculiarly human activities — thinking, constructing, feeling. They are also victims of their own subconscious. There is a dark world of the human psyche, the world of raw instincts which are not always suppressed by a sensible and humane upbringing. Zhilin is like any other citizen of the Country of the Boobs except that he also possesses another quality that protects him from "slug": he is not simply a "feeder" and a "breeder," but an intelligent, well-bred person.

The population of the Country of the Boobs would like to wipe away, as with a sponge, the thin layer of their pseudocivilization and give themselves utterly to the dark feelings inside them. There is no need to seduce anyone with "slug" — it is eagerly sought by the masses ready to exchange their real life, with its constant changes, its wonders and dangers, for an existence that is not even on an animal level, but is a semivegetable existence in the waves of permanent delight: minimal activity, with a minimum of problems. But for the timely interference of Zhilin, it is not at all unlikely that the degraded "people-vegetables" from *The Orchid Cage* (1961) by Herbert Franke, a science fiction writer of West Germany, would loom in the future of the Country of the Boobs.

In looking at the structural composition of the novel, we note that the hyphenated "utopia-dystopia" is used advisedly. An organic synthesis of these two sociological models is achieved in *The Final Circle of Paradise*; their internal similarity is stressed, the disturbing face of an "antiworld" appearing occasionally behind the structures of the "ideal society" of all Utopias, beginning with the "forefathers" Plato and More.

Is it not the twentieth century Utopia, this Country of the Boobs? Zhilin is informed in the Prologue: "You simply don't know how fine it is here, and you need not worry about anything." The very first pages of the novel may impress a certain kind of reader very favorably. They present a society of satisfied demands: a truck stands in the street filled with clothing, food, toys and even books — all free of charge, furnished by the personal consumption fund; or one can have a marvelous free dinner at an expensive restaurant. The working day lasts for only four hours, and then — pleasures, pleasures, always pleasures. The suggested "twelve circles of the twentieth century paradise" are inhabited by the satiated, pleasure-seeking people. Is it not wonderful? But *are* they *people*?

The Strugatskys depict a gallery of masks which hardly resemble human faces at all. The placidly philosophizing Dr. Opir is quite satisfied with his place in society and, consequently, with the society itself. "Art patrons" defend their right to vandalize. Even insignificant, purely episodical characters suggest unpleasant thoughts. Remember the truck with the free supplies? The canned goods are accepted, but it turns out to be impolite, or even *gauche* to take the books. Finally the strongest (collective) character in the novel is the crowd. It is the producer, the distributor, and at the same time the consumer of this very "slug" that Zhilen and his friends are looking for.

There is another structural peculiarity of the "utopia-dystopia." The heroes are functional in the extreme: witness the figure of a "stranger" acquainting himself with a new society, a veritable "pillar of the system" but sometimes willing to accept the role of guide; and a whole spectrum of images of men "from the crowd" illustrating sociological tendencies in their "personified" forms. Although not all of these traditional masks of "utopia-dystopia" theater appear in *The Final Circle of Paradise*, the majority of them might well have a "part of the action" here.

In point of fact, there is not much plot in this novel. As in all other "utopia-dystopias" the hero Zhilin opens himself up to the "brave new world," having gradually, step by step, passed through all the circles of this "paradise-hell" of our time. He becomes aware of the fact that "slug" is known here practically to everyone although this knowledge is carefully hidden; the very word, a frankly indecent one, is inscribed on the walls of the houses, in telephone booths, and on the banisters of staircases. Zhilin also becomes aware of the plight of a man named Rimeyer. He has become a broken nonentity in contrast to the active, pragmatic member of the Security Council. Terrified, Zhilin finds out that his friend Peck Xenai has also changed, being now known through his connections with the criminal world as Buba. It is from him, in particular, that it is possible to obtain this infamous "slug." Having passed through the last circle of this "paradise-hell," and having himself sampled the "slug," Zhilin desides to stay in the Country of the Boobs until the poison is finally eradictated.

The poison? But what in fact is poisoned? Zhilin realizes that his work in the Security Council is ended and that quite another task must be undertaken — that of education. He discusses with his friends his plans to blockade the Country of the Boobs,

> not because I consider it necessary, but because it is so simple; so much more simple to return to people their souls which had been devoured by affluence, and to teach each one to think of world problems in the same way as his personal ones.

The plot is straightforward, even schematic, but *The Final Circle of Paradise* is not simply an ideological novel. This is a rhetorical novel displaying different types of social organization in dynamic conflict. That is why the most impressing episode is Zhilin's dialogue (or monologue) with Dr. Opir. While conversing volubly at their restaurant table, Dr. Opir instructs Zhilin in the basic philosophical concepts on which this society rests. Although Opir does not belong to the ruling class, he successfully plays the role of the "guide," that *sine qua non* of all "utopia-dystopias." He is neither a Mustapha Mond nor an O'Brien, but he is undoubtedly a pillar of the system and is willing to fight anybody who threatens it.

Modern materialistic theoreticians and technocrat-optimists all speak with the voice of Dr. Opir. As the French writer Robert Merle has noted: "The most popular product of the society of consumers is optimism." Robert Sheckley, Frederik Pohl, Cyril Kornbluth, Ray Bradbury, Kurt Vonnegut, Jr., and Ursula K. Le Guin — not to mention the great H. G. Wells and Aldous Huxley — have all repeatedly thrown darts at the Opirs and their "sweet" philosophies. No person with common sense, able to see and understand what is going on around him, can fail to dispute the thesis that "Science will take care of all troubles — is it worth it to addle one's brains with these 'damned' problems?"

But does that mean that the Strugatskys have simply added their voices to those of Western science fiction writers? Have they simply aped the traditional Western "dystopia" without adding anything new? Although structural similarities between this novel and the traditional schemes have suggested important analogies, a careful examination of the book reveals a significant difference.

This difference manifests itself primarily in the authors' themes. "Dystopias" have generally affirmed the final triumph of evil, just as the victory of good is inherent in the "Utopias." There is no easy dichotomy in *The Final Circle of Paradise*. To use the language of physics, the Strugatskys have set up the "initial conditions" almost as in the traditional scheme. But the dynamic development of the model takes a different route.

Zhilin stays in order to struggle. The Security Council, and through it all mankind, will also struggle. There are forces one can rely on in the Country of the Boobs. There are social groupings — "intels," for example, and separate individuals (such as Len and Reg, and the other children — and the future of this world simply *must* be saved for them). The novel is not steeped in the pessimism that pervades the usual "dystopia." On the other hand, the authors do not minimize the magnitude of the problem (if only "slug" should turn out to be just another narcotic!); and they know that a foolish optimism is equally inappropriate here. The Strugatskys have no final message for the reader. On the contrary, the ending is left "open"; it is as if a new plot and a new idea have just emerged, and the outcome is still uncertain.

So, there is neither optimism nor pessimism, but a new beginning for the heroes and a new set of the "damned problems" for the reader. *The Final Circle of Paradise* is not unique in socialist fiction. Consider Stanislaw Lem's *Return from the Stars*. It is not surprising that Soviet criticism has given us a special term to mark the distinction between such works and the traditional "dystopias" — "novel-warning." A "novel-warning," or "cautionary tale" is one that acknowledges the existence of Evil, but searches for ways to overcome it; that does not wallow in gloomy melancholy but sounds a clear and sober warning while there is still time for a warning to make sense.

Vl. Gakov

THE FIRST MEN IN THE MOON

Author: H. G. Wells (1866-1946)
First book publication: 1901
Type of work: Novel
Time: The early twentieth century
Locale: Lympne, England; the moon

Two men reach the moon in a Cavorite sphere, and when the Selenites attack them, one escapes and gets back to Earth, while the other later radios his account of lunar civilization

Principal characters:
BEDFORD, the narrator
CAVOR, the scientist who invents Cavorite

The First Men in the Moon, the last of the early "scientific romances" that made Wells's reputation, is the one he himself called the best. Even though astronauts and cosmonauts have found no life on the moon, the book is still a gripping adventure story as well as a historic milestone in modern science fiction.

Bedford, the teller of the tale, is an engaging antihero, self-centered and generally incompetent but amiably candid about his faults. Cavor, the somewhat comic absentminded scientist, seeks pure knowledge as avidly as Bedford does gold. Bankrupt when they meet, Bedford scents possible millions in Cavor's invention of a gravity screen; he ingratiates himself with Cavor to help build the sphere. Taking off from the mudflats of Kent, they reach the moon together.

A purist might call their story more fantasy than hard science fiction, because Wells was following the classic pattern of the cosmic voyage, a literary genre older than the telescope. His lunar plants, for example, come not from any observations by modern astronomers, but rather from Johannes Kepler's dream-narrative, *Somnium*. In shape and equipment, his moon-ship resembles the hollow cannonball Jules Verne had designed decades before for his own moon story, though Verne protested in bewilderment that Cavorite was pure invention, with no basis in physics.

Fantasy or not, the novel is a brilliant demonstration of Wells's own method for creating such imaginative fiction. He limits each story to a single new or fantastic proposition, made believable by keeping everything else as familiar and logical as possible. Here, he interests us first in the characters: Bedford, hiding from his creditors and living on the trust of neighborhood merchants while he dreams of getting rich by writing a play; Cavor, a ridiculous little man in odd attire who gesticulates and buzzes like something electric when he walks. We listen to his plausible explanation of the gravity screen and witness an accidental windstorm caused by it before we hear of any trip to the moon. Once that trip begins, every detail is vividly convincing. The lunar plants may have come from Kepler, but Wells re-creates them with a fine imagination and the insight of a trained biologist.

The lunar day is two weeks of Earth-time. At sunrise, the frozen air thaws and evaporates; the lunar seeds soon sprout; the plants grow explosively into fantastic jungles that mature and die as the deadly night returns. Lost in this strange and ever-changing moonscape, the two explorers are captured by Selenites pasturing their mooncalves. They are carried down into the moon, which is porous, with vast systems of caves. The lunar craters, they learn, are simply the circular mounds of debris from huge shafts the Selenites have dug down through their caverns to the central sea, hundreds of miles below.

These moon-beings may well have been suggested by the writings of Wells's great teacher, T. H. Huxley, who speculated that the evolution of more complex societies means an inevitable loss of individual freedom; he even compared the social evolution of men to that of insects, commenting that each bee has its duty and none has any rights.

Wells's Selenites have evolved their own highly complex and insectlike social order, with a place for everyone and each exactly fitted to his place. Long-limbed, leather-skinned Selenites herd mooncalves; big-brained Selenites replace libraries; siren-voiced Selenites screech news and orders. Though this is all designed to make a satiric comment on our present world and present a grim prediction of our probable future, Wells never lets his message get in the way of his story. Bedford and Cavor are neatly opposed symbolic types: Bedford is the unspecialized individualist resisting the law of the hive, while Cavor is the intellectual specialist dependent upon it. In their conflicts with the Selenites and with each other, they translate the theme into dramatic action.

The suspense is always strong. The fast-growing jungles help create an atmosphere of wonder and menace. We hear the booming of unseen underground machines, see the opening of the lid above the bottomless shaft, meet the grotesque herdsmen and their monstrous cattle. Captured, we follow a river of cold blue fire down into the mysterious depths of the moon.

Bedford, lacking special adaptations, is ready for anything but good for nothing except the primitive animal violence he displays in his battles with the Selenites. He gets lost on the moon, gets drunk on lunar mushrooms, gets himself and Cavor captured. He is too egotistical to admire the rational complexity of the moon civilization as Cavor does. All he cares about is his own survival — and the gold which is more common than iron on the moon.

In the lesser gravity, the moon-beings are flimsy, and Bedford finds himself a relative superman. He can bend gold bars and snap gold chains. His primitive body can smash a Selenite like "a sweetmeat with liquid in it." He and Cavor battle their way back to the surface and separate there to search for the sphere. Bedford locates it. After some delay, he goes back to look for Cavor and finds a torn note telling him that his companion has been recaptured.

Winning a desperate race with the air-freezing lunar night, Bedford gets back to the sphere and returns to Earth alone, landing on an English beach.

Incompetent as ever, he leaves the sphere unguarded, and an inquisitive small boy climbs inside and takes it on a last accidental flight. Left with only a fortune in lunar gold and a strange tale to tell, Bedford is serializing the story under the byline "Wells" when Cavor begins to radio his own narrative from inside the moon.

Cavor's captors are intelligent Selenites with enlarged brain-cases. They have taken him down to their more important centers, deep in the moon, have learned English and begun explaining their highly specialized society, which Cavor feels is far superior to man's. Each Selenite is carefully shaped, by birth and training and surgery, to be a "perfect unit in a world machine." Some of the less fortunate, destined only to mind simple machines, are grown in bottles to stop the development of everything except one projecting hand — a more humane procedure, Cavor feels, than our Earthly method of letting children grow into human beings and then making them into machines.

The Grand Lunar, who at last receives Cavor, is an enormous brain, many yards in diameter, with the merest vestige of a body. Their meeting may well have been patterned after the adventures of Gulliver — Wells admired Jonathan Swift. This ruling Selenite seems as purely rational as Swift's Houyhnhnms. Like those superior horses, he finds mankind far short of meeting his rational norms. Yet neither Wells nor Swift intends to praise pure reason. Both are satiric. The Grand Lunar cannot move his own body. Sitting in solitary splendor with attendants spraying his throbbing brain to keep it cool, he is both pitiable and absurd.

Here we find the science and the serious purpose beneath Wells's fascinating fantasy. Equipped with a biologist's understanding of the then rather new science of evolution, he had seen the past advances of humanity as a process of ever-further division of labor and ever-greater specialization, a ceaseless surrender of individual freedom to the needs of the group. In one novel, he extrapolates this process to a painfully logical ultimate. The result is both merciless satire and disturbing prediction.

Wells himself was certainly disturbed — this story shows a striking shift of attitude from *The Invisible Man*, written only a few years earlier. Griffin, his transparent man, is pure self and pure evil, a tragic hero destroyed by the folly of his war on society. Bedford is less symbolic and more human. In unselfish moments, he regrets his own faults. Wells lets us like him. Yet, in contrast to Cavor, he remains the elemental individual, bent on self-preservation and selfish gain. He intends, until the sphere is lost, to go back with guns for more lunar gold.

Cavor is his polar opposite, the social man. With too little self-regard to seem really human, he has comic traits that remind the reader of a machine. His movements are jerky, and he hums to himself mechanically. Yet he, too, has another dimension. Sometimes he shows a flash of human liking for Bedford; he feels moments of horror at the ruthless efficiency of the Selenite society and apparently revolts against it before he dies. As Gulliver does, Cavor tells his hosts too much about mankind. When the Grand Lunar hears about the arts of war and learns that Cavor is about to transmit the secret of the gravity screen back to Earth, the radio signals are abruptly cut off.

In *The First Men in the Moon*, Wells is examining specialization — particularly intellectual specialization — as the way to future progress. Taking the evolutionary history of the social insects as a model, he projects future human evolution to infinity. As a scientist, he can see possible adaptations that will make the race more efficient, avoiding many sorts of loss, avoiding all the hazards of conflict and change.

As a human being, however, the author is appalled by what he foresees. Cavor is betrayed and destroyed by his own inquiring intellect; Bedford is saved and enriched by his unregenerate individualism. Their opposition no doubt reflects a parallel conflict in Wells's own nature, and his shift in attitude since *The Invisible Man* seems to show him working toward a solution of it. Allowing Bedford to call himself "Wells," he appears to be settling the conflict by accepting his own self-identity.

Wells's later career seems to offer evidence of such a resolution, as if that old internal conflict had supplied an emotional power to the early fiction which has now disappeared. There are intriguing ideas and vivid writing in *The Food of the Gods* (1904) and *In the Days of the Comet* (1906), but he has begun to allow his social comment and his pleas for social reform to overwhelm story interest. Though he went on producing books for another forty years, many of them patterned as "scientific romances," none has the dramatic intensity of *The First Men in the Moon*.

The last of Wells's really great science fiction novels, *The First Men in the Moon* was a major addition to the current of anti-Utopian pessimism that we can trace from Jonathan Swift, down through Wells's early work, to such popular present-day writers as Frederik Pohl and Harlan Ellison. Aldous Huxley's *Brave New World*, for example, owes a heavy debt to Wells. Picking up that haunting vision of the young Selenites grown in bottles to shape them for their social roles, Huxley brings the nightmare down to Earth with his human babies grown in bottles, some nourished to become ruling Alphas, others starved and poisoned and carefully conditioned to make them into happy Gammas.

History, in the world of reality, began long ago to realize Wells's darkly prophetic forebodings. The socialistic states have become as efficient as the Selenites in shaping youth to fit their ideologic requirements and equally efficient in liquidating the individuals who oppose them.

Jack Williamson

Sources for Further Study

Criticism:

Bailey, J. O. "Is Science Fiction Art? A Look at H. G. Wells," in *Extrapolation*. II (December, 1960), pp. 17-19. Bailey emphasizes that Wells's writings be looked at as allegories.

Wallheim, Donald A. *The Universe Makers: Science Fiction Today*. New York: Harper & Row, 1971. This book establishes Wells as one of two traditions in science fiction and insists that the essential view held by the genre is optimistic.

Zamyatin, Yevgeny. "H. G. Wells," in his *A Soviety Heretic: Essays by Yevgeny Zamyatin*. Chicago: University of Chicago Press, 1971, pp. 259-290. Zamyatin considers the range of Wells's work but concentrates on the scientific romances.

FIRST ON MARS

Author: Rex Gordon (Stanley Bennett Hough, 1917-   )
First book publication: 1956
Type of work: Novel
Time: The present
Locale: Mars

The first man to land on Mars overcomes all obstacles through his resourcefulness and ingenuity, then meets the Martians, who convince him that all striving for knowledge and power is useless

Principal character:
GORDON HOLDER, first man on Mars

A person at odds with his environment may resolve that conflict in one of two ways: either the person changes the environment or the person changes himself. When it rains, one either builds a shelter or gets used to being wet. A good case could be made that the choice of these two solutions defines the difference between Western and Eastern culture, but that larger philosophical issue is not now in question. It is sufficient to say that science fiction is full of environment-changers.

The nature of the genre almost dictates that this should be so. Human beings cannot "get used to" not breathing, so for a trip to the moon or the stars, they build spaceships. If the phrase "environment-changer" calls to mind some hairy-chested, two-fisted warrior such as John Carter in the novels by Edgar Rice Burroughs, the picture is misleading, because not just the Conan-like ones, but almost every character in science fiction is an environment-changer. For all of *Dune*'s ecological awareness, Muad'Dib and the Fremen of Frank Herbert's novel do not change themselves, they change their surroundings. The still-suits, the rendering of water from the dead, and all the rest of their skills are bent toward the active fulfillment of their objectives, even if that goal is only survival.

The environment-changer is not just a creation of male authors: Ursula Le Guin's Genly Ai in *The Left Hand of Darkness* has desires, plans, and goals toward which he works, even if he does bring himself to the planet Gethen to be changed rather than to change, to understand rather than to be understood. And a feminist critic who rightly or wrongly complains that much of science fiction is unfair to women is more likely to be calling for stories with active women than for ones with passive men.

Finally, the environment-changer is not a product of the American pulps, regardless of the scientific movers and shakers of Hugo Gernsback and his spiritual descendants. In the British science fiction of Aldous Huxley, George Orwell, and C. S. Lewis, to name only three, we see characters who without exception either have changed or tried to change their environments to suit their natures, whether their purpose be as banal as Mustafa Mond's, the

World-Controller of Aldous Huxley's *Brave New World*, as politically revolutionary as Winston Smith's in George Orwell's *Nineteen Eighty-Four*, or as
spiritual as Elwin Ransom's in Lewis' Perelandra trilogy.

If we seek an illustration of the other alternative, of the way of passivity
and self-change, we should look perhaps to characters such as Malachi Constant in Kurt Vonnegut's *The Sirens of Titan*. We should not observe Constant
at the beginning of the book as the richest man in the United States, nor Constant the drugged and brainwashed soldier in the Martian invasion army, nor
even Constant stuck in the caves of Mercury and yearning to return to earth.
Rather we should seek characters like the Constant in exile on Titan, who has
learned, in the spirit of Ecclesiastes, that all is vanity, the Constant who accepts everything and desires nothing. Characters like this are rare indeed in
science fiction. The field champions action, mental if not physical; those parts
of it that do not welcome change at least tolerate it; and literally dozens of
science fiction writers and critics have heaped praise on the genre for its ability
to help its readers to adapt to change. All this is why Rex Gordon's *First on
Mars* is a very unusual book.

Rex Gordon is the pseudonym of Stanley Bennett Hough, an English writer
whose best-known science fiction novel, *First on Mars*, was published in
Great Britain in 1956 under the title *No Man Friday*. The British title is far
more meaningful, since it emphasizes a comparison that Gordon stresses again
and again between his story and Daniel Defoe's picture of the quintessential
environment-changer, Robinson Crusoe. Perhaps what stays with us longest in
Defoe's peculiar work is not its rather pedestrian prose, but the illustrations:
whether done in a nineteenth century line engraving or in a Howard Pyle color
wash, Crusoe striding along with his goatskin umbrella overhead and his rifle
on his shoulder practically defines the man who will change the world to his
liking, even if it means converting Friday to provide himself with some Christian company.

Thoughts of Crusoe frequently occur to Gordon Holder, the sole survivor of
a clandestine first voyage to Mars. Like Defoe's castaway, he picks from his
wreck those treasures that will aid his survival in a harsher climate than ever
faced Crusoe.

And the climate is fierce. *First on Mars* is hard science fiction; it incorporated the most up-to-date information then available, even if that information
has been subsequently found to be erroneous by the Viking landings. In his
novel, Gordon presumed that Mars had an atmosphere with a pressure of one
hundred millibars, mostly carbon dioxide, with about one percent oxygen.
Since human beings need only about sixty millibars of pressure to fill their
lungs, all that Gordon Holder has to do to breathe normally is wear an oxygen
mask. Gordon's picture of Mars is that of an arid, cold planet, a picture that
was in many respects confirmed by the Viking missions. While his hero does
not face as severe a set of conditions as would a real traveler, he still faces a

great many major problems, and he sets to work at a task familiar to us —
trying to change his environment.

That struggle is unquestionably heroic. Gordon Holder is a resourceful and
imaginative man; perhaps more important, he is dauntless in the best sense of
that overused word, without being arrogant. His periods of fear and doubt are
as frequent as his triumphs of confidence, but he decides more than once that
if he should die, and he knows there is a very strong probability of that fate, it
will not be for lack of resolution and energy on his part. By his efforts he
hopes to justify the deaths of his companions and to show that their lives were
spent striving for a worthwhile goal.

As an example of his ingenuity, consider how he solves his first problems,
the scarcity of water and oxygen. He sets to work on a still to capture the dew
that falls each night. When he succeeds, he turns his attention to the problem
of oxygen. The sun provides him with an inexhaustible power source. He uses
it to heat oil placed in a closed system of pipes, causing it to vaporize and
expand through pumps salvaged from the wreck and placed in the system. The
pumps turn the electric motors that once powered them, and a few simple
changes convert the motors to generators. With power in the usable form of
electricity, he charges batteries and drives smaller pumps that push the Martian
atmosphere through constricting valves and into expansion chambers converted
from tanks salvaged from the wreck. As the pressurized gas quickly expands,
it cools; running the same gas through the system over and over eventually
chills it, in a well-known process used industrially, until it reaches the temperature at which oxygen liquifies and falls to the bottom of the tank. He can then
tap the liquid oxygen and fill cylinders with it. Despite the scarcity of the gas
in the atmosphere, he now has an unlimited supply of the life-sustaining element.

He eventually surmounts the problem of food with similar ingenuity. Mars
has a marginal growth of vegetation which bears a fruit he experiments with. It
is edible if not palatable, and while he does not know its nutritional value, the
likelihood of disease from vitamin deficiency is a longterm, not a shortterm
problem. Holder recognizes that seasonal variations will make it necessary for
him to follow the crops as they ripen to maintain his food supply. So he sets to
work once more and builds portable models of his still and his air-separation
plant, mounts them on a homemade halftrack, and drives away from the wreck
into the unknown parts of Mars.

At this point, the reader must surely feel high admiration for Holder. In the
face of every difficulty, despite every obstacle, he has changed his environment, wrenching an existence from a planet hostile to his kind. His efforts lend
him the luster of the explorer or the pioneer. But then he experiences something that completely changes his own regard for himself, and the new outlook
that he comes to accept is violently in opposition to that which the reader
holds. He encounters Martians.

Holder has met animal life already, beings that are shaped like humans, but as witless as insects. When the reader first hears of the humanoids, he thinks that the Crusoe analogy will now be completed — that Friday has been found. When these creatures turn out to be no more intelligent than a snail, that expectation is frustrated. But on his trek, Holder does meet the intelligent Martians, huge creatures as large and long as railroad trains, covered with flashing lights by means of which they communicate. Holder turns to the technology that has served him well and attempts communication by means of remote-controlled lights and colored cloths. But the Martians discover and capture him, and the anticipated situation is neatly reversed: the character we had thought of as Robinson Crusoe turns out to be Friday.

When Holder has learned enough of their language to speak with the young alien who is keeping him more or less as a pet, he discovers that he has encountered beings more passive than Hindu hermits. Like Archibald MacLeish's idea of a poem, they do not mean — they are. Nor do they seek for meaning to their existence: they are born, eat, sleep, beget, and die. Yet they hint that they know levels of existence and command powers beyond the dreams of Holder.

When Holder tries to bargain with them, offering his mechanical knowledge (they have no artifacts whatsoever), they ask what his machines are for. He replies, to keep him alive. When they ask him in return why he has come to a place where he cannot live unaided, his standard mountain-climber's response — because it is there — seems hollow to them, and Holder begins to question it himself. When they discover that he has no way to return to earth, they suggest that, to their way of thinking, he should simply die. They counter his arguments and reduce him to a state of nervous exhaustion not through malice, but simply by destroying his belief in the value of his own struggle. If Holder had been a devil-take-the-hindmost human imperialist like the explorers of Venus in Olaf Stapledon's *Last and First Men*, his torment might be called retributive justice, but Holder is a decent and likable individual.

His stay with the Martians lasts fifteen years, and the chapters of his apprenticeship are interspersed with the account of the American crew that, much to their surprise, finds him there. He approaches the American ship as an ambassador, bearing the Martians' wish (and his own profound hope, by now) that the earthmen will leave and never return to Mars. As Holder had suspected, the Americans refuse to make an agreement on their own initiative which would be binding on all of humanity. Although disconsolate at the loss of his chance to return to earth, Holder feels bound to return to the Martians as hostage and confess his failure. The Martians then extend their power and bend space itself, preventing him from leaving the vicinity of the ship.

Holder returns to earth with the Americans, feeling that a conflict is coming. There can be no meeting-ground between environment-changers and self-changers, and Holder (and the reader) is left with a frightening loss of faith in the value of meaningful united action. The Martians, far from being primitive, have gone beyond desire; they are not savages to be converted. Yet he believes the humans will eventually win their battle and discover that through the victory they have missed a chance at something of more value than all their triumphs.

Walter E. Meyers

Sources for Further Study

Reviews:
Amazing Stories. XXXI, December, 1957, p. 118.
Analog. LX, February, 1958, pp. 146-147.
Infinity Science Fiction. III, June, 1958, pp. 94-95.
Magazine of Fantasy and Science Fiction. XIII, November, 1957, p. 117.

FLATLAND: A ROMANCE OF MANY DIMENSIONS

Author: Edwin A. Abbott (1838-1926)
First book publication: 1884
Type of work: Novel
Time: The 1880's
Locale: Various imaginary realms: Flatland (world of two dimensions), Lineland (world of one dimension), Spaceland (world of three dimensions), and Pointland (world of no dimensions)

The memoirs of a Square, who muses in very human terms on the psychological, social, and scientific implications of his momentous discovery that life has more than two dimensions

> *Principal characters:*
> THE NARRATOR, a Square
> HIS WIFE, a Straight Line
> HIS GRANDSON, a Hexagon
> THE TEACHER, a Sphere
> THE KING OF LINELAND, a Straight Line
> THE HIGH PRIEST OF FLATLAND, a Circle

Although Edwin Abbott's *Flatland* is a brief work, no longer than a novella, it has, as its subtitle promises, "many dimensions" — each of them delightful and provocative. Anyone who has toiled to understand or to explain the mysteries of mathematics should fervently appreciate *Flatland*'s most obvious dimension, that of unconventional geometry textbook. But this slim volume is also a witty, highly personal flight of Victorian fancy, after the manner of Lewis Carroll; a startlingly modern statement of scientific and social questions which engross our own "liberated" age; an intimate and appealing expression of everyman's quest for self; and a call to expand our awareness of a universe which is, Abbott persuasively argues, much grander and more wonderful than we have yet imagined.

Abbott creates these multiple roles for his book by centering Flatland in the consciousness of its narrator, who is not a human being, but a geometric figure, a Square. In *Flatland*'s first half, this narrator gives us his detailed Square's-eye view of what he initially takes to be the whole universe, the two-dimensional world of plane geometry (Flatland). In the second half of the story, Abbott's Square experiences mystic visions of worlds beyond his native Flatland (Lineland, Spaceland, and Pointland) and tries without success to communicate his new sense of solid geometry to his plane-thinking relatives and neighbors. By compelling us to share the Square's participatory inside view of plane and solid physical space, Abbott deftly, thoroughly, and amusingly conveys geometric facts, which he invests with considerably more than academic interest. At the same time, however, Abbott also explores psychological space. His Square learns that Flatland's philosophical, religious, and social theories are as two-dimensional as its geography, and encounters the still more limited cultures of Lineland, which is one-dimensional in all respects, and Pointland, whose blissful single inhabitant has a perfectly no-dimensional mind. In Spaceland's three dimensions, the Square becomes both physically and psychologically a Cube; he acquires a new depth perception of spatial, social, and intellectual matters and a new dream of the greater visions available in Thoughtland, whose multidimensionality he can only begin to guess.

As a sustained pun on geometric concepts, Abbott's "romance" noticeably resembles Lewis Carroll's writings. Like Carroll's Alice, Abbott's Square ventures "through the looking glass" of complacent, segmented, ordinary thinking and investigates "wonderlands" where mathematical abstractions enjoy completely substantial reality. Abbott presents his mathematical metaphors much more overtly and didactically than does Carroll, whose subtle, sophisticated mathematical references seem designed to entertain professional mathematicians like himself, rather than to inform the student mathematicians Abbott apparently had in mind. On the other hand, Abbott, who was a classical and literary scholar, is far more resourceful than Carroll at reinforcing his mathematical metaphors with literary allusions, with which he, like Carroll, enlarges the satiric dimensions of his fiction. For example, at *Flatland*'s conclusion, when the Square has dwindled to his original plane-ness, Abbott indicates how tragically antiheroic his Flatlander is by simultaneously invoking three major literary models: in his dazzlingly compact final chapter, Abbott reminds us that the frustrated Square is a failed Prometheus, a disciple-less Socrates, and a pilgrim who has regressed into lonely despair instead of progressing to celestial enlightenment.

Flatland's allusions to Shakespeare are especially important. Abbott — who also wrote *Shakespearean Grammar*, a model of sober Victorian scholarship — evidently conceived *Flatland* as an imaginative meditation on two of Shakespeare's plays. Read on this level, *Flatland*'s first half expresses Abbott's personal response to *Romeo and Juliet*, and its second half centers on *The Tempest*. From *Romeo and Juliet*, Abbott took the concept of a society absurdly, even suicidally trapped in two-dimensional thinking; Shakespeare's Verona is a prototypical Flatland which rigidly institutionalizes sexual and social dualities and ruthlessly banishes depth perception, represented in the play by Romeo's and Juliet's love, because lovers know that the establishment's dualistic wisdom is nonsense. Friar Laurence's advice, borrowed by Abbott for *Flatland*'s first epigraph, has life-or-death urgency for both the Square and Romeo: "Be patient, for the world is broad and wide." — three-dimensional thinkers *must* abandon the plane for the solid world or endure spiritual if not physical death, for two-dimensional minds cannot tolerate three-dimensional truths.

In *Flatland*'s second half, the Square sees some of that breadth and width for himself and shares the sense of wonder expressed by Shakespeare's Miranda: "O brave new worlds, that have such people in them!" But this passage, *Flatland*'s second epigraph, applies ironically to the Square's experiences, because both he and Miranda are *naifs*, innocently unaware that all glories are relative. In *The Tempest* Prospero, Miranda's father, knows about relativity from the beginning; Abbott's Square eventually exchanges Miranda's innocence for Prospero's understanding, but finds that in Flatland, Prospero's wisdom lacks all power, including the power to sustain itself. Prospero's knowledge enables him to reform his world; the Square cannot convert even himself.

> Hence I am absolutely destitute of converts, and, for aught that I can see, the millennial Revelation has been made to me for nothing. . . . It is part of the martyrdom which I endure for the cause of the Truth that there are seasons of mental weakness, when Cubes and Spheres flit away into the background of scarce-possible existences; when the Land of Three Dimensions seems almost as visionary as the Land of One or None; nay, when even this hard wall that bars me from my freedom, these very tablets on which I am writing, and all the substantial realities of Flatland itself, appear no better than the offspring of a diseased imagination, or the baseless fabric of a dream.

The note of alienation, powerlessness, and futility on which the Square concludes his memoirs is one of *Flatland*'s most modern elements, and the very fact that it sounds in this nineteenth century work marks Abbott as an unusually visionary author. But *Flatland* does more than merely anticipate twentieth century literature's favorite concern with the antihero alone in an unresponsive world: quite remarkably, Edwin Abbott, who lived well before the Age of Einstein, defines precisely why science and society in our post-Einsteinian times tend to alienate almost everyone. Modern physics has thrust us into a universe which extends with mind-boggling complexity from subatomic Pointland to Thoughtland's theoretical infinitude. As Abbott points out, traditional notions about life's meaning and the human place in the scheme of things do not obtain in this fascinating but intimidating vastness. Even Newton's cozy two-dimensional certainty that the world divides neatly into subjects and objects has been taken from us, for we now share the Square's unsettling suspicion that "truth" may be wholly in the beholder's incurably myopic eye.

While science inculcates ambiguities and paradoxes, society institutionalizes absurd prejudices. Abbott pays particular attention to prejudices regarding women, Flatland's most oppressed citizens. Flatlanders subscribe to a geometric version of "total womanhood" which restricts women to one-dimensional social roles on the theory that women have one-dimensional minds. The first half of Abbott's book features a bleak but brilliantly satiric analysis of this and other dubious sociobiological assumptions, and shows how such assumptions can imprison people in rigid, unjust social structures. And in *Flatland*'s second half, the Square discovers that society often imprisons thought itself; Pointland, Lineland, and Flatland are antiutopias for the very modern reason that they stifle all independent thinking.

As the Square demonstrates, it is possible to achieve solid, individuated selfhood despite the formidable social pressures for plane conformity. *Flatland* affords us a dual perspective on the quest for self — first, by dramatizing it in the Square's own psychological growth, and second, by symbolizing a different dimension of the psyche in each of the lands the Square studies. Pointland represents the most primitive level of selfhood, the complacent self-centeredness of the infant who can conceive of no dimension but his own personal identity. The Lineland mentality recognizes that there is something beyond the self, but can relate to it only as a series of physical objects. Abbott assumes that his reader, like the Square, has developed at least to the third psychological stage, symbolized by Flatland, wherein the self perceives psychological as well as physical dimensions to reality and idealizes rationality as the one true way of knowing; *Flatland* is directed to an intellectual audience with a taste for brain-teasing word games and a capacity for sustained abstract thought. For all its intellectual substance, however, *Flatland*'s basic thesis is that rationality is not enough: to be really wise, we must exercise our intuitions and emotions at least as much as our intellects. This well-rounded personality is what Spaceland represents to the Square, whose tragedy is that he can neither permanently surmount nor moderate Flatland's angular intellectuality.

It is obvious that Abbott did not share his narrator's psychological limitations, for *Flatland* keeps the emotional dimension of its characters consistently in view. Indeed, one of the principal charms of this book is that each of its characters has an emotional life wholly consistent with his or her geometric contours and social setting. Abbott's realization that allegory can appeal to both the hearts and the minds of its readers makes *Flatland* an extraordinarily solid allegory, and a surprisingly moving one. *Flatland* is also educational in a very innovative way, because it invites us to use our intuitions to synthesize the information contained in its many dimensions. The reader who accepts Abbott's challenge to read *Flatland* with full intellectual, emotional, and intuitive energy can then confront the complex, enigmatic reality of the post-Einsteinian universe from the confident vantage point of Abbott's Sphere, rather than the demoralized Square's schoolroom. What Fritjof Capra has termed "the Tao of physics" discloses itself to the Spheric vision, which fuses mystic and scientific insights in much the same manner as Abbott's highly satisfying book.

Many science fiction stories preach that our culture lacks emotional depth; a few incorporate intuitive visions. But none examines the dimensions of human consciousness with the fullness and suggestiveness of Abbott's brief "romance." *Flatland*, which was composed almost half a century before the term "science fiction" was coined, and which utterly ignores the technological gimmickry and thud-and-blunder plotting often identified with science fiction, remains one of science fiction's finest, most advanced achievements.

Jane Hipolito and
Roscoe Lee Browne

Sources for Further Study

Criticism:

Rogers, Ivor. "The Time Plays of J. B. Priestly," in *Extrapolation*. X (December, 1968), pp. 9-16. Rogers discusses the influence of Abbott and *Flatland: A Romance of Many Dimensions* upon the writing of J. B. Priestly.

Reviews:

Saturday Review. III, October, 1926, p. 254.

FLOW MY TEARS, THE POLICEMAN SAID

Author: Philip K. Dick (1928-1982)
First book publication: 1974
Type of work: Novel
Time: 1988
Locale: Los Angeles

The conflict of private and social realities portrayed through the confrontation between a television star who awakes in a strange new world and an obsessive police general determined to maintain the stability of that world

Principal characters:
JASON TAVERNER, a television celebrity
FELIX BUCKMAN, a police general obsessed with rules
ALYS BUCKMAN, his twin sister and wife
HEATHER HART, Jason's current lover and fellow star
KATHY NELSON, a forger, police informant, and lonely widow-wife
RUTH RAE, Jason's ex-lover
MARY ANNE DOMINIC, a fashioner of ceramic artwork

When a twentieth century writer of speculative fiction makes common cause with a seventeenth century English lutist-singer-composer, the result is *Flow My Tears, the Policeman Said*. The book winner of the John W. Campbell Memorial Award for the best science fiction novel of 1975, differs considerably from Philip K. Dick's earlier novels. He gives only a slight nod in the direction of the conventions of science fiction. The alien life form used as a weapon of anger and the pseudoscientific explanation for Jason Taverner's spatial-perceptual displacement are gratuituous gestures toward those conventions. Although Dick customarily uses near-futures for the setting of his novels, we find none of the distracting autonomic devices — talking doors, androids serving political purposes, precogs or telepaths, or "conapts" with interchangeable fixtures — in this Dickian world of a nearer future. By setting his novel in 1988, Dick has forestalled the need for elaborate detailing of this future world, only occasionally spicing his descriptions with such items as Alys' "quibble" and Mary Anne's "flipflap."

What Dick does give us are seven characters trying in their own unique, but often futile, ways to establish some balance between the inner and outer realities of their existences. Using stanzas 1, 2, 3, and 5 of John Dowland's "Lachrimae" (*The Second Booke of Ayres*, 1600) as epigraphs for the four parts of the novel, Dick subtly invites certain Dowland phrases to foreshadow the fictional events: "exiled forever," "those that in despair their lost fortunes deplore," "my weary days," and "you shadows that in darkness dwell." From stanza 4, which Dick does not use, one may pluck still a fifth pertinent phrase, "from the highest spire of contentment/My fortune is thrown." In *Flow My Tears, the Policeman Said* Dick offers a clutch of personalities, each exiled, despairing, weary, shadowed, or bereft of contentment.

One character ties the novel together by the simple expedient of being in direct contact with each of the others at one time or another. Jason Taverner, popular television personality, suffers a harrowing two-day "exile" from the scene he usually dominates. After a particularly successful show he answers a summons from a disillusioned lover, who throws a deadly alien parasite, called a "cuddle sponge," at him. He is rushed to a hospital. The following day he wakes up in a sleazy, third-rate hotel, still dressed in the silk suit of his television appearance, still in possession of a large sum of money from the previous evening, and strangely showing no traces of the attack. Turning to friends and associates for help, he draws an utter blank. They do not know him. When he searches the entertainment pages of the Los Angeles *Times*, he finds no mention of his very popular show. There are no identification cards in his billfold. A quick check with a birth registration control center verifies his growing fear that he is completely without legal record of his own existence.

In this 1988 Los Angeles, to be without identification bodes great trouble if the loss is detected. Without the requisite cards or computer entries, the nonperson is in even more tenuous circumstances than the large revolutionary student population hemmed in underground areas beneath their campuses or the blacks hemmed in by rigid birth control laws which are tantamount to legal genocide. Once picked up at any one of the many police checkpoints, a nonperson stands an even chance of death or death-in-life, more prosaically known as impressment in a forced-labor camp for the rest of his life. A recent "Second Civil War" has resulted in the establishment of a society patrolled and controlled by an efficient, authoritarian police organization operating under rigid procedural rules.

Jason Taverner has three things in his favor: the large sum of money in his pocket, a stubborn will to survive, and the genetic arsenal of a "six." He is one of the few remaining products of a half-century-old eugenic experiment designed to produce a superior class of humans. Unfortunately the experiment failed when these people found it impossible to cooperate with one another in any common social contribution. In fact, most of them cannot stand their fellow-sixes. When Taverner comes to full comprehension of his current problem, he takes decided steps to protect himself, first by buying forged identification cards in order to remain free, and second by beginning the detective work necessary to track down the source of his identity dilemma.

The consequent two-day odyssey to reestablish himself precipitates a series of adventures and explorations of Jason's intricate relationships with several people. Each connection reinforces the central idea that these are indeed Dowland's "shadows that in darkness dwell," each finding a perverted kind of happiness in their own private hells. An early and significant contact is with Kathy Nelson, impresario of forged papers, and police informer, who is trapped in the obsessive belief that her long-dead soldier-husband is still alive. This false belief has kept her on the knife-edge of precarious sanity. Her inevitable betrayal of Traverner to the police occurs simultaneously with her attempts to bind him close to her personally. Taken into police custody, he is saved ironically when human error taps out the wrong computer record. However, he is not totally free, for he now has come under police notice, which is a most unfortunate situation.

During the brief respite afforded by temporary police passes issued to him, Taverner seeks a hiding place. The logical source of aid would be someone close to him, such as his lover Heather Hart. But earlier she had not known him, had dismissed his phone call as coming from a "twerp fan," her favorite term of disparagement. Heather is a six like Jason. Thus, their relationship as lovers has been a tense, ambiguous, and somewhat erratic one. Also a prominent and popular entertainer, Heather differs sharply from Jason by rejecting her adoring fans and by refusing to bask in that ambiance so vital to the star-fan kinship. By insulating herself from the most genuine human feelings, Heather denies herself contentment; her sole gentle gesture is made toward a blue vase Jason gives her as a casual gift.

Ruth Rae, an ex-mistress, is a different case. A sexual athlete, Ruth Rae cares little for the human being inside the performing body. By going with her to the Las Vegas apartment, Jason wins needed time away from possible police interference. Along with the temporary asylum, Ruth Rae treats him to a philosophical musing on love, grief, and the rules of living. Coming from someone who long since has disregarded the conventional rules of sexual and social behavior and who cannot really feel grief because she has never felt love, this rambling discourse verges on the bathetic. Ruth Rae reveals herself as one who lives in the shadow of a fortunate state never attained.

A second pick-up by the police leads Jason to a low-keyed interrogation by Police General Felix Buckman. Efficient and subtle in his technique, Buckman seems to accept Jason's story, but his official mind suspects a cabal, *sub rosa* plot to upset his well-ordered jurisdiction. Unknown to Jason, the police general has sophisticated detection devices planted on his person so that Buckman may keep track of this unwanted anomaly. The intervention of a variable element, however, turns the whole situation completely askew. (Dick's 1953 "The Variable Man" used this technique earlier.

Leaving the interview, Jason is startled by the sudden appearance of Alys Buckman, twin sister and also wife of Felix. Six feet tall, black-panted, leather-shirted, and chain-belted, Alys is dramatic not only in her physical appearance, but also in her entire existence. Always center-stage, unhampered by external rules and living for the intenser pleasures of the moment, Alys is heedless of the comfort or convenience of other people. Indeed, she enjoys playing with their lives while she remains safely within her amoral self-structure. The ultimate play, we discover, involves Jason, for Alys, using a space-binding drug still being tested secretly by her brother's organization, had moved Jason into this new existence, destroying the accustomed social reality which had sustained him. Only on her death is Jason released from the false perception of his social matrix; and only on her death is Alys herself released from the darkness of her own excess.

Then the familiar perceptions reassert themselves without Jason truly understanding the phenomeon. During this period of reaffirmation of his star identity, Jason meets Mary Anne Dominic, artist and potter. A timid person, Mary Anne's form of "exile" is withdrawal into her talent, interacting with the world solely through the medium of her art rather than directly. During their brief encounter, Mary Anne, in her devotion to her talent, mirrors Jason's devotion to his talent. Yet she stands in direct antithesis to him: she values the production of one ceramic pot for one customer; he values the production of a spectacular program for three million. At once they are *recto* and *verso* of a page, microcosm and macrocosm of the same response to the world. Both use their public artistry as psychic shields from the social reality.

Of all the characters touched by Jason Taverner in his odyssey as No-Man/ Everyman, Felix Buckman is the most unique and unforgettable; not since Mr. Tagomi of *The Man in the High Castle* has Dick created such a memorable character. Felix Buckman epitomizes all of the complexity and paradox that mark the truly human being. A self-made man who rose to power, suffered demotion, but retained real power despite his downfall, Felix is also an insecure man, clinging to his sister-wife in a love-hate relationship. He plays by strict rules officially, but they are *his* rules, and subject to change at a whim, as when he feeds starving student revolutionaries he had been ordered to exterminate. On one hand, he enjoys the cat-mouse play of the interrogation, secretly amused by Jason's gullibility when Felix intimates, albeit falsely, that he is a "seven." On the other hand, he lives in a home surrounded by walls topped with broken glass; inside the house he has surrounded himself with collections of fragile *objets d'art*. In his inner private life he buttresses himself with the official rules and power of his position in order to protect the delicate hold he has on his sister-wife.

It is Felix Buckman alone of all the characters in *Flow My Tears, the Policeman Said* who experiences an epiphany in the Joycean sense of the term. Desolated at Alys' death and feeling it as the loss of an anchor to his private reality, Felix reacts in an ambivalent way. His official mind responds to the suggestion that the debt of her death must be paid, even if by a scapegoat (Jason). In a predictably, almost involuntary response to the standard situation, he gives the necessary orders. But as he leaves the police offices, Felix no longer has a structure to envelop the personal situation so that he can better bear it. The only truly human tie he possesses, besides a small son who cannot share his adult pain, has been severed.

Out of his weariness, grief, and loss comes a natural involuntary reaction: Felix weeps, a dramatic exemplum of the melancholy Dowland sentiment — "Flow my tears, fall from your springs!/Exiled forever let me mourn." The tears intensify his sense of utter loneliness and urgent need for human contact. As he stops at a gas station, he sees a stranger, a black man, one of those patient victims of that very code of laws Felix is dedicated to enforce. He makes an impulsive gesture inviting human sympathy. The black man intuits Felix' great need and responds awkwardly but with genuine feeling.

What happens when an individual experiences an imbalance between his external and internal perceptions of reality? Dick's seven major characters respond variously by insanity, withdrawal and depression, self-abuse unto death, submergence in ego-protecting activity, or elemental, primordial reaching out in community. But *Flow My Tears, the Policeman Said* answers yet another question. What happens when a science fiction writer begins to divorce himself from the expected trappings of space opera or the fantasies of distant world-building and turns to explore inner space and human actions? The answer is a work challenging to a reader's mind as well as his sensibilities, one stirring to the imagination as well as provocative in its social and psychological implications. In this novel, Philip K. Dick has come a long way from *Vulcan's Hammer*, *Dr. Futurity*, and his other earlier novels, entertaining though they still are.

Hazel Pierce

Sources for Further Study

Criticism:

Gillespie, Bruce. *Philip K. Dick: Electric Shepherd*. Melbourne, Australia: Nostrilla, 1975, Gillespie delineates the several themes behind the work.

Reviews:

American Libraries. VI, March, 1975, p. 169.

Kirkus Reviews. XLI, December 1, 1973, p. 1328.

Library Journal. XCIX, April 1, 1974, p. 1062.

Listener. XCIII, May 29, 1975, p. 715.

Magazine of Fantasy and Science Fiction. XLVIII, January, 1975, p. 10.

New York Times Book Reviews. July 20, 1975, p. 10.

Observer. December 8, 1974, p. 31.

Psychology Today. VIII, June, 1974, p. 112.

Publisher's Weekly. CCIV, December 3, 1973, p. 36.

FLOWERS FOR ALGERNON

Author: Daniel Keyes (1927-   )
First book publication: 1966
Type of work: Novel
Time: The mid-1960's
Locale: New York City

The results of an experiment to increase human intelligence by neurosurgery, told through the journal of the first human subject, who goes from an I.Q. of 68 to one of over 200 and back down in the space of six months

> *Principal characters:*
> CHARLIE GORDON, a cheerful, goodnatured man highly motivated to learn despite his low intelligence
> ALICE KINNIAN, the teacher at the Adult Education Center who recommends Charlie for the experiment
> DR. STRAUSS, the neurosurgeon who performs the operation
> DR. NEMUR, the research psychologist who designs the experiment
> FRANK REILLY AND JOE CARP, Charlie's fellow workers at the bakery
> ALGERNON, a white mouse, the first successful subject of the experimental surgery
> BURT, the young researcher in charge of experimental animals, including Algernon
> MATT AND ROSE, Charlie's parents
> NORMA, Charlie's sister, of normal intelligence
> FAY, an artist and Charlie's neighbor, with whom he has an affair

The story of *Flowers for Algernon* is very simple. Charlie Gordon, a sweet-natured innocent with an I.Q. of 68, becomes the first human subject in an experiment to raise intelligence by surgical means. An operation followed by intensive training triples Charlie's I.Q. in the space of about three months; but shortly thereafter Charlie, who has joined the researchers on the project, discovers that the change will not be permanent — in fact, his research demonstrates that "artificially increased intelligence deteriorates at a rate of time directly proportional to the quantity of the increase." That is, the greater the rise, the faster the decline. By the end of the story, less than six months after the operation, Charlie is essentially back where he started, except that he has a vague recollection that he contributed "something" to science, though he cannot remember what it was he did. What he does remember is Algernon, the white mouse whose positive response to the surgery prompted the doctors to go ahead with human subjects. For Charlie, Algernon is successively a competitor to be beaten, a friend and kindred soul, and a harbinger of things to come when he slides into decline, foreshadowing Charlie's own decline. Charlie's last note — the story is told via his diary — reads "Please if you get a chanse put some flowrs on Algernons grave in the bak yard. . . ." The ending, combined with the title, suggests that Charlie's relationship with Algernon, his fellow experimental subject, is in some ways more important to him than any relationship he has with people. And therein lies the key to the theme of the work: that man is not defined by his intelligence alone.

To the experimenters, Dr. Strauss the neurosurgeon and Dr. Nemur the research psychologist, intelligence is unreservedly a good thing. In the beginning Charlie evidently agrees with them, as witnessed by his desperate struggles to learn to read and write in the hope that those magical skills will make him smart. But Charlie wants to be smart so that he can fit in at last. "When I become intelligent . . . , then maybe I'll be like everyone else and people will like me and be friendly," he writes. But the experiment is not designed to make Charlie normal or average, but to raise his I.Q. as much as possible. From that standpoint, the operation is a success, but the result is not what Charlie expected. With an I.Q. of 200, he is even less like everyone else than he was before, even more isolated and lonely, and considerably less pleasant to be around as well. He becomes arrogant, insensitive, bitter, and touchy, convinced that people are mocking him, as he now realizes they did when he was retarded. He receives no social training to teach him how to cope gracefully with his overwhelming intelligence, so he has a hard time bringing his discussions down to the level of the people he is talking with, and an even harder time establishing any kind of perspective on the capabilities of people with normal intelligence. When Charlie's I.Q. was 68, he revered Dr. Strauss and Dr. Nemur as mental giants, almost as gods; now that his I.Q. is 200, he regards them as impostors and frauds for calling themselves educated when they cannot read Hindustani or Chinese, only Latin, Greek, Hebrew, and four or five modern European languages. He cannot understand that they are neither gods nor impostors, but just men of normal intelligence, since normal intelligence is one of the things he has never experienced for himself. Charlie, in other words, is far too smart for his own good.

It is hard to believe that Strauss and Nemur understood what they were doing to Charlie by raising his I.Q. so dramatically. If intelligence is a good, they seem to have reasoned, then great intelligence is a great good. It apparently never occurs to them that with an I.Q. of 200 their subject will race as far beyond their intelligence as they once were beyond his — at least, they are unpleasantly surprised by the experience of being talked down to by their "creation," and consider Charlie's behavior a sign of ingratitude. It also never seems to have occurred to them that, moving from subnormal to supernormal intelligence in such a brief time, Charlie might need some training to deal with his new social circumstances. In fact, the doctors never seem to have considered Charlie a real person at all. Dr. Nemur keeps talking about having made Charlie what he is, and about how someday there will be others like Charlie who *"will become real human beings"* because of this surgery. Neither Strauss nor Nemur seems to understand that Charlie was a real person even before his operation. Throughout the experiment, they discuss Charlie in nearly the same terms as they discuss Algernon, like two guinea pigs who happen to be of different species. Perhaps that is why the doctors seem so unconscious of the possible personal consequences to Charlie of increasing his intelligence by three hundred percent.

Charlie's new superintelligence isolates him from everyone he cares about even more than his slowness once had, and it is a kind of isolation which cannot be undone when he returns to his original intellectual level. The doctors do not regard him as a real person at any stage of his development, except for Burt, who is always kind. Charlie's "friends" at work make fun of him when he's dull-witted, fear and hate him as he grows more intelligent, and in the end pity him when he returns to ask for his old janitorial job back. But in the old days before the operation he had never understood that they were laughing at him, so they were real friends as far as he was concerned. Afterward, he knows it is merely pity, though they treat him better than they had before. Even Alice Kinnian, the sympathetic teacher at the adult education center who recommends Charlie for the experiment in the first place, is unable to follow him when he races into the intellectual stratosphere, and she is equally unable to follow him past a certain point on his slide back down. So it is no wonder that Charlie develops a special relationship with Algernon, as if Algernon were the only creature in the world who could understand and share his feelings. And perhaps he is right: certainly Algernon is the only one who responds to him as neither a moron nor a genius, but just as himself, regardless of his intellectual level.

Embarrassed and upset about what is happening to him, Charlie cuts himself off from everybody toward the end of his deterioration, especially refusing to see Alice Kinnian. But then one day after he has returned to his janitorial job, he walks into Miss Kinnian's class at the adult education center, having for the moment forgotten all about the experiment. But when she runs out of the room crying, he remembers, and feels distressed about having upset her. He decides that he ought to leave the city so he will not make that mistake again, and so he can be someplace where people won't feel sorry for him, where "nobody cares that Charlie Gordon was once a genus and now he cant even reed a book or rite good." But it is the measure of the man that his last recorded thoughts are for others, for Dr. Strauss and Miss Kinnian, for Professor Nemur, and for Algernon. Charlie wants to make sure that Algernon is not forgotten, because he was special — as Charlie himself is special. The tiny grave is a memorial to both of them, to Algernon and to Charlie's brief brilliance, to the hopes that died with the failure of a brave experiment.

Though he can no longer remember exactly what he did, Charlie carries with him a sense of pride for an important achievement, and he also carries with him memories of people who tried to help him and friends who loved him, Miss Kinnian and Algernon. But those qualities — determination and pride, and above all consideration for others — were part of Charlie's personality from the beginning. Charlie is as real a person with an I.Q. of 68 as he was with an I.Q. of 200 — perhaps more real; and those who judge him only by his level of intelligence are missing the point.

In expanding what was originally a thirty-page story into a novel of more than two hundred pages, Keyes used two main techniques. First, parallel episodes were expanded, some by only a few lines, others by a considerable amount. For instance, in the story, the episode of the international psychological conference at which Namur and Strauss present the results of their work — including Algernon and Charlie — is treated in a couple of paragraphs. In the novel, this is a major episode, taking a full chapter and concluding with Charlie releasing Algernon and fleeing from the conference with him. Second, Keyes expanded his examination of Charlie to include two entirely new areas of concern — Charlie's memories of his childhood and his family, and his current attempts at emotional maturation, which means primarily learning to deal with women and sex as an adult. Incidents reflecting both these concerns are interspersed with the day-to-day experiences Charlie records, with the discussions of his childhood functioning like flashbacks to illuminate hidden parts of the picture.

However, these changes shift the focus considerably: the novel becomes a detailed psychological portrait of Charlie, while the story is more concerned with the ironies inherent in the situation. Obviously, Charlie's personality is a major factor in both versions, but the short story seems ultimately both more powerful and more subtle. Much of what the novel adds, though certainly not all, is either inessential, or can be found in the story suggested or implied by one of Charlie's half-knowledgeable remarks which reveal his assumptions and the gaps in his experience and understanding as effectively as the lengthy discussions of the same points in the novel. This technique of implication and indirect communication seems more appropriate to the first-person journal format of both story and novel than to the omniscient point of view of the latter version. But in whatever length or format, *Flowers for Algernon* is solidly established as a science fiction classic, because it raises important questions in a powerfully moving way.

Kathleen L. Spencer

Sources for Further Study

Reviews:

Analog. LXXVIII, February, 1967, p. 161.

Best Sellers. XXVI, April 1, 1966, p. 10.

Galaxy. XXIV, August, 1966, pp. 193-194.

Library Journal. XCI, February 15, 1966, p. 965.

Magazine of Fantasy and Science Fiction. XXX, June, 1966, pp. 36-38.

New Statesman. LXXII, July 22, 1966, p. 136.

Saturday Review. XLIX, March 26, 1966, p. 33.

Times Literary Supplement. July 2, 1966, p. 629.

THE FOOD OF THE GODS
And How It Came to Earth

Author: H. G. Wells (1866-1946)
First book publication: 1904
Type of work: Novel
Time: The late nineteenth century
Locale: In and around London

The development of an extraordinary food supplement produces mutations in the growth curves of plants and animals and creates a race of giants, "the Gods," whose encounter with traditional society Wells uses as a vehicle for social satire

Principal characters:
> MR. BENSINGTON, a chemist, Fellow of the Royal Society, codiscoverer of the Food
> PROFESSOR REDWOOD, Professor of physiology, codiscoverer of the Food
> MR. AND MRS. SKINNER, managers of the Experimental Farm at Hickleybrow
> MR. COSSAR, a civil engineer, father of two giants
> DR. WINKLES, Professor Redwood's family physician
> LORD CATERHAM, a politician campaigning against the Food
> YOUNG CADDLES, a young giant
> THE COSSAR BOYS, young giants
> PRINCESS OF WESER DREIBURG, a giantess, lover of Young Redwood
> YOUNG REDWOOD, a giant, son of Professor Redwood

H. G. Wells wrote *The Food of the Gods* during his short but stormy association with the Fabian Society. Indeed, at least in part this novel is an imaginative record of Wells's not very successful attempt to dramatize his attitudes toward some of the more important issues occupying the Fabians at the turn of the century. This society of middle-class intellectuals, whose members included the economists and socialists Sidney and Beatrice Webb, playwright George Bernard Shaw, and philosopher Bertrand Russell, worked for gradual, evolutionary socialism. The record is clear that, while some leaders of the Society, including the Webbs, were uneasy with Wells's naïve but brash thinking on social issues, they were challenged by his ideas and anxious to recruit him as a propagandist and popularizer for their brand of socialism. It is also apparent that Wells, painfully self-conscious of his lower class origins, was flattered by their courtship. During his association with them, he directed his attention more and more away from his fiction to sociopolitical analysis and speculation. Wells's nonfiction works focusing on pressing social issues and their implications for the future written during this period include: *The Discovery of the Future* (1902), *Mankind in the Making* (1903), and *A Modern Utopia* (1905), written a year after *Food of the Gods*. It is not surprising, then, that to an even greater degree than in his earlier works, Wells uses a "discovery" of science for sociopolitical prophecy. As it turns out, the sociopolitical questions overshadow and play havoc with the aesthetic dimensions of the narrative.

The plot is generated by the discovery, manufacture, and eventual world-wide distribution of a special nutrient called *Herakleophorbia* (the food for a new Hercules), Boomfood, or simply "the Food." Ingesting even minute amounts of the Food produces gigantism in plants and animals. Unsuspecting citizens are frightened and sometimes killed by huge wasps, rats, ants, cockroaches, and the like. More importantly, when the food is given to children, they grow to be well over thirty feet tall. Conflicts erupt when society has to deal with these young giants. Laws are made limiting their movement and restricting their civil rights. Angry mobs, frightened by the prospect of the coming world of giants, try to lynch Mr. Bensington, one of the discoverers of the Food. Led by the politician Caterham, whose sole object in life is to gain political power by the supression of the Food, the Anti-Boomfood Movement is formed. One giant, young Caddles, is killed by the police when he refuses to leave London and return to his own home.

The conflict between society and the giants comes to a head when two giants, the Princess and Young Redwood, fall in love, refuse to stop seeing each other, and escape to the camp of the other embattled giants. Society, led by the forces of reaction and facing the prospect of the giants breeding and multiplying, declares all-out war. Professor Redwood is arrested but freed by Caterham to go and seek a peace treaty with the giants. The conditions of the treaty stipulate that the giants will go into exile, that no more of the Food will be produced, and that the giants can have no children of their own. The giants refuse the conditions of the peace. The novel ends with the giants preparing for a decisive battle with the rest of society for the right of the new race to exist and, ultimately, to supplant "the little people" — man — as they presently exist.

It is upon the fundamental polarity between "bigness" and "littleness" that Wells structures his novel. This juxtaposition of size is the structuring principle of the narrative. Without exaggerating too much, one can create the following ratios — big: little, science: politics, growth: stasis, progress: reaction, change: complacency, dullness: creativity, goodness: evil, and god: man. Naturally, not all of these categories can be kept strictly separate, but a significant part of the novel's interest lies in watching the way in which Wells aligns sociopolitical and ethical questions with the concept of size. For example, Caterham, the archenemy of the Food, is described as particularly small, "a little black figure" or "that pigmy thing." The great masses of the poor are dirty, "filthy little skunks." At the same time, bigness is not always an unequivocal blessing; the giant rats and wasps are the unintended and undesirable consequences of man's interference with Nature.

The metaphors of size and growth become Wells's vehicles for grappling with some of the fundamental sociopolitical issues which had engaged the Fabians as well as other groups interested in fundamental reform. Under the banner of evolutionary socialism, the Fabians criticized their society for having converted all social relationships into what Carlyle and Marx had characterized as "the cash-nexus." (Cossar the engineer is very Carlylean in style and outlook.) In *The Food of the Gods*, Wells calls the giants "Brethern" and "Brothers." The bonds among the giants are ties of love. By contrast, the family of the giant Princess wants to marry her off to a "little" person for political reasons and for "profit." Wells, like other Fabians, was shocked at the gross materialism of society. The Fabians, while not abandoning parliamentary democracy altogether, were critical of the chicanery and opportunism which characterized British politics. Caterham is the stereotypal demagogue who knows or cares nothing about physical, economic, or moral laws; he is interested in one thing: votes.

More explicitly, Wells makes an analogy between the coming of the giants and their battle with society for the future of man with the struggle between the rich and the poor — the "two nations," as Disraeli had characterized the situation in his novel *Sybil*. Caterham is worried about the Food producing a "proletariat of hungry giants." Lady Wondershoot, a caricature of the aristocracy that Wells so despised, fears the idle hands of the "labouring classes" and puts the young giant, Caddles, to work in the chaulk pit. But Caddles begins to *think*: the proletariat becomes self-conscious. What is the good of work? Why doesn't everyone work? Why should some, like Lady Wondershoot, live a life of ease while others work? The workers produce goods through their labor, but the rich merely consume. Caddles asks his mother what would happen if "there wasn't any gentlefolks, wouldn't things belong to people like me and you, and if they did. . . ." At that point, his mother quiets him.

However, that does not end the young giant's questioning of his society. Ultimately, he revolts; he defiantly shouts, "No!" to his pointless labor in the chaulk pit, disregards the territorial limits imposed upon him, and goes to London. Observing the sordidness and poverty in London, what the narrator describes as "the infinite futility of all this employment," young Caddles asks: "What is it all for?" This is Wells's question. To what end is society moving? Before Caddles can discover an answer, he steals some bread — a symbolic act of the poor and a fulfillment of Caterham's fear of the proletariat — and is shot to death.

The three young giants, the Cossar boys, want to do something for the poor, to build them houses and roads, to provide water for those that have no water. Instead of helping the poor get fresh water so that they can take baths, the poor are ridiculed by society and called "the Great Unwashed" by those that have water. The Cossar boys want to end this problem, but are prevented from doing so by special interest groups, "rights and laws and regulations and rascalities; . . ." Here again, one can draw a parallel between Wells's satire and the Fabian criticism of those institutions and groups which were blocking meaningful reform.

On a more fundamental level, the Fabians were committed to an evolutionary view of social change. This biological metaphor was at the root of their thinking about social transformation. Indeed, such influential writers as Herbert Spencer, Friedrich Nietzsche, Henri Bergson, Arthur Schopenhauer, and Karl Marx made the biological model the paradigm for discussing social evolution and the future of man.

One of the most illustrious Fabians, George Bernard Shaw, completed one of his most famous plays, *Man and Superman*, just a year before Wells's *Food of the Gods*. In this drama, Shaw goes further than the strict evolutionists, and like Samuel Butler and Henri Bergson before him, embraces dynamism in the concept of Creative Evolution. Shaw argues that man must somehow transcend his animal origins and seek salvation by serving the Spirit, or Life Force. Man must be replaced by Superman. Similarly, the Food short-circuits the evolutionary process and is the agent whereby ordinary man is transformed into the godlike giants. Creative evolution is equated with growth and growth is equated with spirituality, as a manifestation of Being. By embracing this law, says the giant son of Cossar, man serves the Spirit, "the will of God." Like Shaw, Wells uses his art to dramatize the concept and hence sharpens the issues involved in man's potential development within the framework of some sort of discontinuous evolution, which ends at a stage where quantity becomes quality, at a stage "beyond man." Boomfood is the agent for the development of this *Übermensch*; it is the food of the new "god."

At the same time, it is no wonder that some of the Fabians were uneasy with Wells's social vision. Wells was clearly an elitist and did little to hide his antidemocratic bias. He was a socialist in economics but an authoritarian in politics. In *A Modern Utopia*, written one year after *The Food of the Gods*, Wells shows that his ideal is a world state ruled by an elite called the "Samurai." While as early as *The War of the Worlds* (1898), Wells was railing against Victorian complacency and smugness, he was convinced that the hope for the future was not in the masses, whose "invincible inertia" made significant change almost impossible, but in an elite who was not afraid to take charge and to take chances. (In *The Food of the Gods*, this character is represented not by the scientist but by the civil engineer, Cossar.) The common man is treated as either a grotesque caricature, as in the case of the Skinners, or as an out-and-out mindless reactionary. The reactionary is epitomized by the man who, upon gaining release from prison after twenty years, sees the Cossar children and joins the Anti-Boomfood Movement because, as he says, "I 'avent the 'ang of 'em . . . they disturve me."

Yet it was not Wells's elitism in itself that bothered the Fabians, many of whom were able to live with this contradiction in their curious variety of socialism; George Bernard Shaw, for example, lived with the inconsistencies. Part of the problem as they saw it was Wells's impatience, his call for drastic, more dramatic measures, his disdain for gradualism. In one sense, he was a revolutionary. He was impatient for immediate, fundamental change. However, he was a revolutionary in much the same way that Thomas Carlyle, Friedrich Nietzche, and D. H. Lawrence were revolutionaries. Unable to trust in the masses to take history into their own hands, they had to put their faith in the extraordinary man. Ultimately, this antidemocratic, revolutionary elitism ends in Fascism.

In the end of *The Food of the Gods*, the giants prepare for a life-and-death struggle with the rest of society; there will be no compromise. The giants must struggle to replace the "little people"; otherwise, they forfeit the right to live. Their claim to supremacy is analogous to the claim that mankind has made over "the ants and vermin." In *Food of the Gods*, man is now the ant. Once one accepts the Darwinian model as it had been interpreted to apply to society and the moral imperative of the evolutionary model, with the provision that the "mutation" is to be given favored status, biologically and culturally, then the logic is almost inescapable: only the "fit" should live. If put into practice and taken to its logical extreme, the concept leads to the horror of the death camps.

The contradictions and implications of combining Social Darwinism and Creative Evolutionism are never faced squarely in *The Food of the Gods*. This lack contributes in part to the glaring inconsistency in the novel's tone and its formal failure. Initially, bigness is a vehicle for a kind of lighthearted satire of social institutions generally. Wells treats science and scientists — represented by Redwood and Bensington — with tongue in cheek and takes pokes at organized religion and education. The Skinners and Mr. Cossar Wells treats with Dickensian exaggeration. (Rabelaisian might be a better term, since baby Redwood is nicknamed "Pantagruel.") However, as the logic of the narrative becomes more insistent and the outcome more inescapable and obvious, the tone of the novel shifts. The satire becomes more biting, the irony more savage, and the characters more extreme in both vice and virtue. With the killing of young Caddles and the indignant but crude and carelessly unintegrated social criticism hitting the reader over the head, the novel takes on the characteristics of ill-conceived melodrama. Caterham becomes a beast and the young giants begin speaking like Tennyson's idealized knights. The rhetorical strategy is as unsubtle as it is unconvincing; yet, however clumsy, it does enlist the reader's sympathy. The reader roots for the giants and goes along with the extermination of his own kind. However, the novel cannot sustain this kind of weight, and it does not succeed, partly because the idea itself would be resisted, but partly because the speeches and the narrator's descriptions are more florid and pretentious than they are convincing and moving. At the same time, Wells had backed himself into a conceptual corner which undercuts the earlier tone of the novel. He could not escape the logic — or contradictions — of his own ideas. The result is an interesting but aesthetically unsuccessful novel.

Charles Elkins

Sources for Further Study

Criticism:

Kagarlitski, Julius. *The Life and Thought of H. G. Wells*. London: Sedgwick and Jackson, 1966. Kagarlitski's perspective makes this work especially provocative as he examines Wells's breadth of vision.

Philmus, Robert M. *Into the Unknown: The Evolution of Science Fiction from Francis Godwin to H. G. Wells*. Berkeley: University of California Press, 1970. This significant and formal study approaches Wells and science fiction "as a strategy of narrative presentation."

THE FOREVER WAR

Author: Joe Haldeman (1943-   )
First book publication: 1974
Type of work: Novel or story cycle
Time: 1997 to 3143
Locale: The Earth and various points within our galaxy and the Greater Magellanic Cloud

A draftee, born 1975, hangs onto his life and much of his sanity throughout a pointless war which drags on over astronomical expanses of space and time

> *Principal characters:*
> WILLIAM MANDELLA, a draftee who rises from the rank of private to that of major in an army he hates
> MARYGAY POTTER, his lover and eventually his only link with the twentieth century

The Forever War is an outgrowth of the Vietnam war experience — the experience of the American nation in general and in particular of Joe Haldeman, who served in combat in Vietnam in 1968. (The name "William Mandella" seems to derive from the author's middle name plus an anagram of "[H]aldeman.") The cynicism and relative pessimism of *The Forever War* ally this science fiction war story to Harry Harrison's farcical *Bill, the Galactic Hero* published early during the period of American involvement in Vietnam (1965), but distinguish it from Heinlein's *Starship Troopers*, written before American entry into the conflict (1959), and from the motion picture *Star Wars*, produced after disengagement from the war (1977).

Like many works of science fiction, *The Forever War* sits somewhere on the dividing line between the novel and the story cycle. The volume consists of four divisions, each of which originally appeared in 1972-1974 as an independent story in *Analog*. Mandella and Potter are the only characters from the first story to survive through to the last one, and Mandella himself (who is also the narrator) is the one character to appear in each division. While this episodical structure is probably responsible for certain minor confusions and inconsistencies, it does parallel Mandella's own experience: he is sent out on various missions and then, because of relativistic time dilation, must adjust to changed conditions at the "rear."

The author has stated in interview that he was more interested in setting up his story than in portraying a probable future — he actually believes that interstellar war is logistically impossible. Indeed, Haldeman has posited a number of extremely unlikely events to fill in the quarter-century between the publication of the first story of the series in 1972 and its opening in 1997. During this twenty-five years, the world; achieves unity and disarmament under the United Nations; invents an essentially unlimited power source having something to do with tachyons; and uses the "tachyon drive" to travel at near light speed to a newly discovered, conveniently placed black hole ("Stargate"), through which spaceships can travel instantaneously to other black holes (the "collapsar jump"). On consideration, the implausibility of these sudden developments becomes clear, but Haldeman is careful to give the reader no time for such reflection. Instead, the reader's eyes, with Mandella's, are fixed in horrible fascination upon the war and its corollary, the United Nations Exploratory Force.

When the first story opens, Mandella is in basic training, drafted out of graduate school by the Elite Conscription Act of 1996 and preparing to fight a mysterious extraterrestrial opponent. As far as Mandella knows at the time, the war began when, after several unexplained losses of colonization ships, an escort drone returned with the report of the destruction of a ship by an alien vessel. By the last story, Mandella learns that the facts in support of this interpretation were "laughably thin," just as doubt was eventually cast on the supposed torpedo-boat attack on U.S. craft which led to the Gulf of Tonkin resolution. But Earth's former military leaders, who have been shunted off into space exploration since disarmament, are still spoiling for a fight, and political and economic factors make war attractive to other world figures. The result is a surge of war fever, leading to the strengthening of space forces ("navy," as Mandella says) and the establishment of a tactical assault force which can take and hold planets orbiting the collapsar gateways. By function, this force should be nicknamed the marines, but instead Mandella and the other draftees call it the army. This misnomer, like the "army's" powered fighting suits, would seem to be borrowed from Heinlein's *Starship Troopers*.

Haldeman's attitude toward the military, however, differs considerably from that expressed by Heinlein. The tone is set by the opening scene in the first story, in which the draftees are shown a videotape on "eight silent ways to kill a man." The "actors" in the tape are convicts who actually die. The rationale for this brutal realism is that no one under middle age on Earth has seen actual combat; but the reasoning is not sound — at this point no one has so much as seen a Tauran (the extraterrestrial enemy), but it is certain that their weak spots are not the same as humans'.

With similar half-logic the draftees are given cold-weather training on Earth in "preparation" for the totally dissimilar cryogenic environment — only a degree or two above absolute zero — in which they will be expected to fight. Such, at least, is the original plan, but after taking forty percent casualties — mostly deaths — in further training on Charon (a posited tenth planet even darker and colder than Pluto), Mandella's unit is sent on a mission to a planet of an ordinary star, in alien "grass" lands where the temperature is only a little below the boiling point. The whole aim of this mission is to catch a live Tauran for study, but the army is so dedicated to the principle of no quarter that it has hypnoconditioned the soldiers to make sure their ruthlessness does not flag. This plan results in the mission's failure — after their one Tauran prisoner commits suicide, there are no others left alive at the enemy base.

But Haldeman is not ranting mindlessly against the military. Mandella, Potter, and their fellow draftees are trained and led by middle-aged Vietnam-veteran career types who within their sphere are brave, intelligent, resourceful, and sometimes even sympathetic. Mandella himself, for all of his philosophical superiority, is forced by events to behave much like his instructors when he is given command responsibilities. The blame for the situation falls in part on everyone, in part on no one, and in part on political leaders whom we never see on stage. Haldeman is more concerned to depict than to judge.

Also marked by strong verisimilitude is Haldeman's treatment of technological and social developments. The UNEF fighting suit may be two hundred years ahead of its time, but the reader knows exactly what it feels like to wear one. The "tachydon drive" may be sheer magic, but once granted this source of unlimited energy, Haldeman deduces spaceship maneuvers, shipboard conditions, and military tactics with scrupulous logic. Similarly, Haldeman's sexually integrated army, complete with bunkmate rotas in basic training, seems one plausible response to the stated social and military situation, and it is depicted vividly. The remainder of the book is spent chiefly in elaborating upon the background and themes already stated or implicit in the first section, and if only for that reason it seems a little weaker.

The second division consists of two fairly independent episodes. In the first, Marygay Potter is injured in a malfunctioning acceleration shell and almost dies, but is saved with some help from Mandella. The Potter-Mandella relation had been quite tentative in the first story, but by this one she has become Mandella's steady — though not exclusive — lover. "Mary Gay Potter," with a difference only in spelling, was the maiden name of Haldeman's wife, so it seems likely that a deepening Potter-Mandella relation had been intended from the beginning, but perhaps the transition as depicted is a trifle too abrupt.

The latter part of this section examines what the leaders of Earth who sent Mandella off to war have been doing back home during the twenty-six years he has been gone. (Subjectively less than two years have passed, thanks to time dilation.) The world government seems to have weathered the crises brought on by modernization, automation, increasing population, exhaustion of natural resources, and the like, but it has done so only through a total restructuring of society and through liberal application of conditioning techniques similar to those used on Mandella. To have more than a bare minimum of housing has become something shameful, and homosexuality is encouraged as a population-control measure. Most people live off government allowances sufficient for necessities but for few luxuries. To most individuals the war effort is no more than a pinprick — the mechanics of the collapsar jump make it possible to conceal the locations of both Earth and the Tauran home planet — but UNEF is not yet ready to give up on Mandella and the other survivors of his unit. It is now 2024, and the Vietnam and Middle Eastern veterans who instructed the first UNEF inductees are dead or too old to fight. Mandella and his companions are the first people to return to Earth with ground combat experience. Still, for that very reason they are also useful propaganda symbols, and hence UNEF hesitates to do anything so bald as unilaterally extending their term of enlistment. Instead, every pressure is brought upon the veterans to re-enlist: they are blacklisted from employment or further education, their accumulated back pay is taxed away, and so on. Even so, Mandella and Potter are determined to stick it out on the dole. However, they change their minds after they witness how Mandella's aged mother is callously allowed to die without medical care: on her seventieth birthday it had been determined that she was of no further use to society. But Potter and Mandella re-enlist only after they have been guaranteed assignments to training positions on the Moon. Mandella has a brother there, and conditions on the Moon are better than on Earth. Then, on the very day of their arrival at their guaranteed assignment, they are "reassigned" to combat study.

The third section of the book is the shortest, but also the most poignant, particularly in its original magazine appearance, where the remaining half-volume was not present to remind the reader that this episode could not be the last. Both Mandella and Potter are wounded in the same action. Thanks to a system for preserving internal pressure in a damaged fighting suit, each loses a limb. They believe that this will get them invalided out of the army, and they even receive a sermon from their shipboard doctor on the likely course of love put to the test of an amputated arm and an amputated leg. But soon after their arrival at the military hospital-and-resort planet of Heaven, they learn that medical science can now regenerate missing limbs. (Thanks to time dilation, the year is now 2389.) Potter and Mandella are not out of the army after all, and their chance of surviving the three subjective years each has left to serve is effectively zero. They have a desperately good time for six months of rest-and-recreation at Heaven's resorts (the inflated prices here being UNEF's way for recouping disbursements for back pay; salaries are based on *objective* time, which makes every soldier a billionaire). They use the period as a sort of honeymoon: each is the other's only link to the lost twentieth century. At the end of leave they learn they have been assigned to separate missions. This means parting forever, since, even if by some miracle both of them lived out their enlistments, differing periods of time dilation would put their discharges centuries apart. Again we see the stupid, heartless bureaucracy: most of the members-to-be of Mandella's new unit have not even been born yet — they will grow up while he travels under time dilation — so there is no valid reason why Marygay could not accompany him. But rules are rules. Mandella considers suicide, but decides it would be a victory for UNEF, and forbears.

The conventions of storytelling require that things should look blackest for a hero just before the resolution, and Haldeman follows this advice in *The Forever War*. Already stricken by separation from Potter, Mandella is given a job he cannot handle. UNEF has decided to make a major out of him, largely for the bureaucratic reason of his seniority: few other inductees from the beginning of the war remain alive. Despite the fact that Mandella's psychological profile shows him unsuited to military command, he is given a cram course in small-unit leadership and put in command of a strike force numbering 119. The other 118 men and women are homosexuals — the leaders of human society have decided that the best way to handle the complicated problems of population control and genetics is to centralize childbirth and give the masses a more harmless outlet. Moreover, under a veneer of military standardization, Mandella's subordinates differ radically from him in language and culture. Mandella's personal style wins over a couple of his officers, but he has no success at all with the enlisted personnel, whom he cannot approach in the same way. Tension and alienation finally reach the point where a large part of the force refuses to heed a warning from Mandella, thinking it a trick, and are killed as a consequence. But at this nadir, for his first and only military success of the book, Mandella figures out a scheme (involving a "stasis field" and a "nova bomb") to destroy the attacking Taurans. Their own base destroyed, Mandella and the few other survivors limp back to Stargate.

Mandella expects to be court-martialed for losing his command, but at last his luck has changed. It develops that human genetic management has undergone another change in policy, and now practically all of humanity is composed of male and female clones of one ideal genotype. For some reason (which Mandella is told is beyond his comprehension) this results in a single group mind, which proves able to communicate with the similar group mind of the Taurans and to stop the war, which has been over for 221 years by the time Mandella gets back to Stargate. Just in case this genetic policy turns out to have unforeseen defects, the clone entity Man maintain planets on which babies are produced in the natural fashion. Many veterans are being resettled on such worlds. What is more, Mandella finds in his file a 250-year-old note from Potter. She had been discharged at a time when the war was winding down, and (for once allowed to keep one of those huge accumulations of back pay) she has banded together with other veterans to buy a surplus cruiser which they are using strictly for time dilation, as a "time machine." She is alive, still young, and waiting for Mandella.

From a final appended clipping from a folksy-sounding newspaper, we deduce that Potter and Mandella have settled down together to a determinedly humdrum existence on a backwater planet, and are engaged in living happily ever after.

Mandella has not triumphed, but he has survived. His sardonic sense of humor, along with his ability to distance himself from what is happening to him, has kept him sane. Even much of his idealism has come through — UNEF has found it simpler to get around his scruples, through conditioning or simply by lying about the facts, than to try to subvert them. As with any war, there has been a large element of luck in Mandella's survival, but his fierce instinct for self-preservation has impelled him to take advantage of whatever luck comes his way. Similarly, Potter has had both the initiative to instigate the relativistic shuttle and the devotion to spend over two subjective years there on the mere hope that Mandella may come back from his mission alive.

Potter and Mandella are appealing characters caught in an unappealing situation. As such they represent a transition between the total gloom of much science fiction in the late 1960's and early 1970's, and the current (late 1970's) reality, in which some people are so distanced from fact that even war might be accepted again. But transitional or not, in the mind of all but the youngest contemporary reader *The Forever War* is indissolubly linked with another war that seemed as if it would drag on forever. Whether the novel will re-create the feeling of the years of American involvement in Vietnam for future generations, whether they will find it incomprehensible, or whether historical perspective will bring other of its aspects into center view is something only the years will tell.

Patrick L. McGuire

Sources for Further Study

Reviews:

Booklist. LXXI, June 1, 1975, p. 991.

Kirkus Reviews. XLII, September 15, 1974, p. 1025.

Library Journal. XCIX, December 15, 1974, p. 3215.

Magazine of Fantasy and Science Fiction. XLIX, December, 1975, p. 34.

New York Times Book Review. March 23, 1975, p. 33.

Publisher's Weekly. CCVI, October 28, 1974, p. 43.

THE FOUNDATION TRILOGY

Author: Isaac Asimov (1920-   )
First book publications: 1961 (as trilogy). *Foundation* (1951); *Foundation and Empire* (1952); *Second Foundation* (1953)
Type of work: Novelettes and novellas

Five novelettes and four novellas which relate the decline and fall of the Galactic Empire and the struggle of a group of scientists to establish the conditions for a new and better empire

The Foundation Trilogy has been called by Donald A. Wollheim "the point of departure for the full cosmogony of science-fiction future history"; the 1966 World Science Fiction Convention called it the all-time greatest science fiction series; and the author himself considers the trilogy the basis of his success as a writer. The trilogy has never been out of print since its first publication in book form. It is one of the classics of the field, a basic work that anyone interested in the genre should know thoroughly; and it is also probably the best-known science fiction book among fans and casual readers alike.

Yet *The Foundation Trilogy* has been attacked by some literary critics as "seriously flawed"; its style has been described as "a disaster," its characters as "undifferentiated" and "one-dimensional," and its ideas as "vulgar, mechanized, debased . . . Marxism." Even as adventure fiction, the work shuns action and romance. The three volumes display scarcely a single romantic interlude; even a couple on a honeymoon discuss politics. And, as in Greek drama, all the action takes place offstage; in the midst of decadent emperors, frontier hardship, and several major space wars, including the destruction of several worlds, only three acts of individual violence are described, two of them in one story.

Why, then, has this collection of stories become a cornerstone of science fiction? How can its continuing popularity be explained? The answers to these questions are not easy. They are found at the roots of science fiction, and a failure to recognize those roots is the central problem of scholarship about science fiction. Many scholars, for instance, are unable or unwilling to take into account the circumstances of creation. They insist on applying to the science fiction work the same criteria they would apply to Anton Chekhov, Henry James, or William Faulkner, thus making the genre or themselves look ridiculous.

This is not to argue for lesser standards for science fiction, but for different, useful standards. The stories that make up *The Foundation Trilogy*, for instance, were written for the readers of a single science fiction magazine. They were sold for rates that began at one cent a word and eventually climbed to two. They were created over a period of eight years by a young man who was twenty-one when he began them and twenty-eight when they were completed. They were conceived and composed in his spare time while he was attending college, working for a Navy laboratory in World War II, and serving in the Army.

Under these circumstances the best method for approaching the work is not textual criticism, but an analysis of those characteristics unique to the genre. The first of these involves plot. In science fiction, particularly at the time when the *Foundation* pieces were being published in *Astounding Science Fiction*, plot may not have been the only thing, but it was the main thing of interest to readers. Without a good story a piece of fiction had no chance of acceptance; other aspects of fiction were permissible, some even desirable, but in many cases the story alone was sufficient.

The Foundation Trilogy begins with the impending destruction of the Galactic Empire, an empire that has brought twelve thousand years of relative peace and progress to a human civilization now encompassing twenty-five million inhabited planets. With the aid of a new science for predicting mass behavior called "psychohistory," a psychologist named Hari Seldon predicts the fall of the Empire and sets up two Foundations, one of physical scientists and one of psychologists, at "opposite ends of the Galaxy" to shorten a predicted thirty thousand years of misery and barbarity that would follow the fall of the Empire to only a thousand years. The stories included in the trilogy span the first four hundred years of that period and relate how the Foundation repels one threat to its existence after another and, with the help of the Second Foundation, preserves Seldon's Plan.

The first section of *Foundation*, the first novel in the trilogy, is entitled "The Psychohistorians," and describes Trantor, the administrative center of the Galactic Empire; it is a world of forty billion bureaucrats and their families, entirely roofed over with buildings and tunneled down a mile. To Trantor comes Gaal Dornick, a young psychohistorian from a distant planet, to work with Hari Seldon. He and Seldon are immediately tried for treason because Seldon is predicting the downfall of the Empire. During the trial Seldon defends his view of psychohistory and persuades the Chief Commissioner, Linge Chen (who is the real Emperor, in fact if not in name), that it is safer for all concerned to let him set up his Foundation at the periphery of the Galaxy to compile a great Encyclopedia that will contain all human knowledge. At the end Seldon reveals to Dornick that he has manipulated everyone — Dornick, Linge Chen, and the Encyclopedists themselves — to create the crisis and then establish his Foundation on Terminus.

In the second section, "The Encyclopedists," we are introduced to Terminus, a planet poor in energy and metals located at the edge of the Galaxy. But the hundred thousand scientists and their families who have been shipped there to create the Encyclopedia Galactica have created a thriving technological society. Meanwhile, the Empire's hold on outlying provinces has started to slip, and ambitious local rulers have begun to take over. One of these rulers, from a region called Anacreon, has decided to annex Terminus. The scholarly

Encyclopedists are unable to come up with any practical solutions, but Mayor Salvor Hardin notices that Anacreon and a rival system, Smyrno, have lost atomic energy. Although Seldon permitted no psychologists on Terminus, Hardin, who studied psychology briefly, is the next best thing: a politician. He seizes political power during Seldon's first filmed appearance in the Time Vault. Seldon announces that the Encyclopedia is a fraud, that the actions of the Encyclopedists have been purposely limited, and that they no longer have freedom of action (the essential condition for a Seldon crisis). Furthermore, he says that they are menaced by barbarian neighbors, that Terminus is an island of atomic power in a growing ocean of more primitive energy, and that the solution to the problem is obvious. The story ends with the Anacreonians landing; but Hardin knows that they will be forced to depart six months later.

In "The Mayors" and "Bridle and Saddle," Hardin forces the Anacreonians to depart by playing one barbarian kingdom against another, since each of them fears that sole possession of Terminus will make any one of them too strong. Hardin offers atomic energy devices to all, but since the barbarians view science as a kind of magic, he must surround the science with a religious framework of belief and miracles. The gift of atomic energy creates new problems as it makes the barbarians more powerful, and the religion imparts authority and sanctions to their rulers. When the Anacreonians attack, however, the priests rebel at the blasphemy and lead a religious (and scientific) rebellion. Seldon makes his second appearance and warns against the spirit of regionalism, or nationalism, which is stronger than the spiritual power.

"The Traders" and "The Big and the Little" take place fifty years after Mayor Hardin's final triumph over Anacreon. The Foundation has absorbed its barbarian neighbors and rules them by means of its invented religion. Traders, motivated by profits rather than religion, sell Foundation atomic energy and gadgets to other planets for metals. Terminus, however, is still committed to extending its small empire by exporting its religion. Limmar Ponyets, a trader whose motto is "never let your sense of morals prevent you from doing what is right," is sent to Askone to save another trader (actually serving as an agent-missionary of the Foundation) who has been caught interfering with local politics. Taking over the mission, Ponyets works upon Askonian greed for gold in order to introduce Foundation machines slowly into the culture. He rigs a transmutation machine (machines are sacrilegious) to turn baser metals into gold, talks an influential native citizen into accepting it, secretly films the transaction, and then blackmails the Askonian into compliance with his plan of acclimating the culture to machinery.

In the fifth and final part of *Foundation*, "The Merchant Princes" and "The Wedge" show how on Terminus the Mayor's office and its religious arm have become rigidified and unwieldy. Even the traders have grown rich and powerful. One of them, Hober Mallow, who is considered a political threat, is sent by Jorane Sutt, the Mayor's secretary and the power behind the office, to investigate the disappearance of Foundation ships near Korell. A Foundation missionary seeks refuge in Mallow's ship from a Korellian mob; in spite of the protests of his crew, Mallow gives him up, thereby earning an audience with the Commdor, the hereditary ruler of the "republic." The salesman then persuades him of the profitability of the atomic devices the Foundation has to sell. He scorns the traditional religious paraphernalia ("religion," he says, "would cut my profits"), and soon the Korellian economy is dependent upon Foundation atomic energy and efficiency. Mallow next traces the Spaceship-and-Sun design on Korellian handguns to Siwenna, where a viceroy of the Empire has ambitions to carve out a new Empire in the barbarian hinterlands. Finally, he discovers that Korellian atomic capabilities have decayed into ritual. Back on Terminus, Mallow is tried for the murder of the priest, but turns the table on his accusers by demonstrating that the so-called priest was an agent of the Korellian secret police. Mallow is elected Mayor. The Korellian republic then attacks the Foundation with old Empire atomic cruisers, but the attack fails because the Foundation devices stop working on Korell and the Korellians rebel in favor of prosperity. Mallow concludes with the prediction that there will be future crises in which money power has become as dead a force as religion is now.

Foundation and Empire, the second volume of the trilogy, opens with "The General" and "Dead Hand." Bel Riose, an ambitious and capable young general in the service of the decaying Empire, determines to conquer the Foundation, whose reputation has begun to reach Trantor. He launches his carefully orchestrated attack from Siwenna. The Merchant Princes are the only leaders in the Foundation, and they are relatively helpless. They send a young trader, Lathan Devers, to be captured by Riose. Brodrig, the Privy Secretary to the Emperor and the only person trusted by him, is sent to investigate Riose and consider his request for more ships. Brodrig joins Riose in the hope of using the Foundation's technology as a means to conquer the Empire. Ducem Barr, Riose's authority on the Foundation, escapes with Lathan Devers in Devers' ship. They take with them a message that implicates Brodrig in a plot with Riose, and attempt to take it to the Emperor on Trantor in an effort to get Riose and Brodrig recalled. As they leave, unsuccessful, they learn that Riose and Brodrig are under arrest. The solution to this crisis was that a weak general could not have threatened the Foundation, and a strong one could not be tolerated by the Emperor lest he attempt to seize the throne. Only the combination of a strong Emperor and a strong general could threaten the Foundation, and a strong Emperor remains strong because he permits no strong subjects. Even a strong Emperor who was also a general could not absent himself at wars on the periphery without running the risk of rebellion springing up behind him. The Foundation had to win under any combination of circumstances.

In "The Mule," Toran, the son of a small trader, and Bayta, a Foundation citizen who has become disaffected because of the concentration of power in the hands of wealthy traders, have just been married. They arrive on Toran's home world, Haven, to discover that his father and uncle are concerned about Foundation tax collectors and are speculating about recent news of the Mule. The Mule is a mysterious person who has magically conquered world after world without a battle; his most recent conquest is the pleasure world, Kalgan. Toran and Bayta are sent to Kalgan to instigate a war between the Mule and the Foundation in which the small traders can regain their freedom. They are forced to flee from Kalgan, however, in the company of a Foundation spy, Captain Han Pritcher, when they give refuge to the Mule's court fool, Magnifico, who has fled from the Mule's cruelty. Using the kidnaping of his fool as a pretext, the Mule attacks the Foundation and wins battle after battle, finally conquering Terminus itself at the very moment the projection of Seldon has appeared with comments revealing that he has not foreseen this crisis. Toran, Bayta, the Fool, and scientist Ebling Mis escape to Haven, which, in turn, comes under attack; universal depression pervades. Before Haven falls, however, Toran, Bayta, Mis, and the Fool are sent to Trantor so that Mis can search the ancient library for information leading to the Second Foundation, which is the only possible help against the Mule.

They find Trantor in ruins, having been virtually destroyed by a rebellious general. Captured by the heir to what is left of the Empire, the Fool saves them by killing him with the aid of a musical image-creating machine called a Visi-Sonor. They visit the Library (an agricultural community has grown up there) and Mis searches the records, growing visibly weaker. As he is about to die and about to reveal the location of the Second Foundation, Bayta shoots and kills him; she has correctly decided that the Fool is really the Mule. He has the ability to readjust people's emotions, and everywhere he has gone with them he has sown despair, adjusting the minds of key leaders to surrender at the appropriate moment; he has been attempting to discover the location of the Second Foundation so that he can destroy that threat as well. His mistake was to leave Bayta unadjusted, because she was the first person who had liked him without interference, and he had cherished this natural feeling too greatly. He is going to continue his search for the Second Foundation, but for now he has been defeated. He cannot establish a dynasty because, like his namesake, he is sterile.

The final novel in the trilogy, *Second Foundation*, opens with "Search by the Mule" and "Now You See It. . . ." The Mule has now consolidated his empire while he searches for the Second Foundation. The search, led by the adjusted Han Pritcher, has been unsuccessful, and he sends him out once more with an unadjusted but capable and ambitious man named Bail Channis. The Second Foundation psychologists are introduced for the first time in "Interludes," commenting on their situation. Channis decides that Star's End must be related to a world called Tazenda isolated in space by a dark cloud of interstellar gas. They land on Rossem, a poor, cold, agricultural planet under

Tazenda's influence, to make inquiries. Pritcher accuses Channis of treason to the Mule because he found the possible location of the Second Foundation too easily. Channis has almost convinced Pritcher that he is not a traitor when the Mule arrives. He has traced their ship and has used Channis, whom he suspects of being a Second Foundation agent, to lead him to the Second Foundation. Tazenda, he says, has been destroyed, but then he drags out of Channis the admission that not Tazenda but Rossem is the location of the Second Foundation. The First Speaker of the Second Foundation enters to say that although Channis was convinced that the location was Rossem, it was not. The Mule has been lured to Rossem so that in his absence Second Foundation psychologists can reach Kalgan and seed rebellion before he can return. Realizing how he has been tricked, the Mule lowers his defenses; the First Speaker enters his mind and reconstructs his memories. He is no longer a danger.

In "Search by the Foundation" and ". . . And Now You Don't," conspirators meet in the home of Dr. Toran Dorell on Terminus under the impetus of a new arrival named Pelleas Anthor. They suspect that people in key positions are being mentally controlled by the Second Foundation, and since evidence of control shows up on encephalographs, they are determined to discover the location of the Second Foundation so that they can combat this threat to their freedom. One of them, Homir Munn, is sent to Kalgan to search the Mule's palace for information. Darell's romantic, fourteen-year-old daughter Arcadia (Arkady), granddaughter of Bayta, stows away on Munn's ship, having eavesdropped on the conversation. Meanwhile, conversations between the First Speaker and an apprentice for speakerhood reveal that Seldon's Plan contemplated the establishment of a future civilization based on mental science and led by the Second Foundation psychologists. That goal has been compromised by the general conviction that the Second Foundation will prevent mishaps; therefore, people will not exercise normal initiative and the predictions will not work out. Moreover, another group has begun to resent a ruling class of psychologists and to fight against it. The Second Foundation has been forced to adopt a low-probability effort to preserve the Plan and themselves by working with individuals.

On Kalgan, Arkady proves helpful; she persuades Lord Stettin's mistress, Lady Callia, that Munn intends to prove that the Second Foundation does not exist and that Lord Stettin intends to unify the Galaxy instead of the Foundation. Stettin permits Munn to enter the Mule's palace, but a while later he decides to make Arkady his wife. With Callia's help, Arkady flees, but with the intuition that Callia is a member of the Second Foundation. At the spaceport she is saved from capture by Preem Palver and his wife, who have been on Kalgan as trading representatives of their farm cooperative on Trantor. While they are on Trantor, Stettin attacks the Foundation and pins its forces back to their original group of planets. In a final battle, however, his fleet is virtually wiped out.

In the end, the conspirators gather together once more, each claiming that he has the solution to the Second Foundation problem. Munn says there is no Second Foundation, but an encephalograph demonstrates that his mind has been tampered with. Anthor says that the Second Foundation must be on Kalgan, where Munn was tampered with. Darell says that Arkady has sent him a message: "a circle has no end"; the Second Foundation is on Terminus itself. He has invented a Mental static device that renders helpless minds capable of advanced mental science. Anthor collapses. Other Second Foundation members on Terminus will be sought out and neutralized.

In a final chapter, the First Speaker reveals that the plan has worked, that at the sacrifice of fifty men and women the Foundation has been convinced that the Second Foundation has been destroyed and has regained its initiative. Seldon's Plan has been restored. The Second Foundation actually is located on Trantor; its psychologists are farmers. The opposite end of a spiral from the periphery is the center, and the Galaxy is a double spiral; in social terms, the opposite end from the periphery is the heart. Moreover, stars end at Trantor. The First Speaker is Preem Palver.

Wollheim calls this series a "point of departure" because innumerable other stories and novels take for granted the rise, reign, and fall of a galactic empire; authors as diverse as Jerry Pournelle and Ursula K. Le Guin have based their work on the tradition that *The Foundation Trilogy* captured most effectively.

Jack Williamson has called humanity's movement into space "the central myth of science fiction." It is a myth contributed to by many authors, in particular Edward Elmer "Doc" Smith and Edmond Hamilton, but Asimov achieved its earliest complete statement in the series of stories published in *Astounding Science Fiction* between 1942 and 1949. Moreover, the civilized galaxy that Asimov describes was a totally human galaxy; the suggestion of human achievement — due in part to John Campbell's prejudices about human-alien relationships and Asimov's consequent elimination of them from his stories — was comforting to his readers, perhaps even flattering.

Another major aspect of the Trilogy was its invention of psychohistory and its consequent thematic concern with determinism and free will. In basing his stories on the "soft sciences" of psychology and sociology, Asimov was following Campbell's prescription, summed up in the essay "The Science of Science Fiction Writing." Campbell wrote,

> To be science fiction, not fantasy, an honest effort at prophetic extrapolation of the known must be made. Ghosts can enter science fiction — if they're logically explained, but not if they are simply the ghosts of fantasy. Prophetic extrapolation can derive from a number of different sources, and apply in a number of fields. Sociology, psychology, and parapsychology are, today, not true sciences; therefore instead of forecasting future results of applications of sociological science of today, we must forecast the *development of a science* of sociology.

Asimov asked himself what might happen if prediction (he might have called it "futurology" or "futuristics" if those words had existed in 1942) became a science.

A number of stories have been written about the ability to perceive the future or one of a series of possible futures, and consequent attempts to change it. Asimov's inspiration was to posit as his mechanism for prediction a mathematical science of probabilities, and to ask himself what was worth predicting. By the nature of his mechanism he could not predict individual actions (it may be of interest that H. G. Wells told the Sociological Society in 1906 that no science of sociology was possible because of the uniqueness of everything in the universe and the impossibility of dealing with people in sufficiently large numbers, as physicists did). Surely the only thing worth predicting was a great event whose consequences might be avoided.

The origin of the *Foundation* stories has been traced (by Asimov himself in a 1967 essay entitled "There's Nothing Like a Good Foundation") to a subway ride in 1941. Without a story idea to discuss with Campbell, Asimov looked down at a collection of Gilbert and Sullivan plays; he opened the volume to *Iolanthe*, and his eye fell on the picture of the fairy queen kneeling before Private Willis of the Grenadier Guards. He let his mind wander to soldiers in general, to a military society, to feudalism, to the breakup of the Roman Empire. By the time he reached Campbell he said that he was planning to write a story about the breakup of the Galactic Empire.

One of the first complications to occur to both Campbell and Asimov was the problem of prediction. Some critics have tried to explain the trilogy's endurance by Asimov's invention of "psychohistory." Critic Charles Elkins maintains that psychohistory was based on "the vulgar, mechanical, debased version of Marxism promulgated in the Thirties," but the *Trilogy* endures, he believes, because its fatalism "accurately sizes up the modern situation." To be sure, there is a considerable amount of conversation about determinism in *The Foundation Trilogy*. Bel Riose, when informed by Ducem Barr about Seldon's prophecies, says defiantly, "Then we stand clasped tightly in the forcing hand of the Goddess of Historical Necessity?" And Barr adds, "Of *Psycho-Historical* Necessity." And, indeed, Riose is defeated by what seem like Seldon's inexorable laws.

The spirit of the early stories, however, is antideterministic. If brave, resourceful people did not respond to the needs of the times, the crises would not be met. Seldon's prophecies are never available when they might be useful; his predictions are revealed only after the fact, and even the solutions to crises that he says are obvious are obvious only in retrospect, as in all good histories. They are not obvious at the time to anyone other than Salvor Hardin or Hober Mallow; if these persons had not been around, it would be hard to convince the reader that the crises would have been resolved satisfactorily. It should not be forgotten, either, that psychohistory is expressed not as prediction or prophecy, but as probability.

Actually, Asimov has it both ways. He has the framework of psychohistory and Seldon's Plan to unify his account of diverse episodes featuring a variety of characters over a period of four hundred years, and he has a number of strongminded individuals seeking solutions to a series of problems as they arise. A novel truly involved with determinism would reveal characters beaten back in their efforts to alter events, or else characters no better than puppets manipulated by some near-godlike prophets or caught in the floodtide of unalterable events.

Such a work would never have retained its popularity over so long a time. Only Bel Riose faces the challenge of determinism, and only he is stopped by the inexorable historical situation rather than by the actions of an individual. In "The General," however, the reader is concerned not about Riose's predicament, but how he is to be stopped. Once the Foundation's curious powers of survival become known, this has an influence over both the Foundation and its enemies, providing a conviction of eventual victory (sometimes overconfidence) for the Foundation and discouraging those who would attack it. Indeed, Asimov is more interested in the psychological impact of Seldon's Plan than in its determinism. And it is only from the outside that Seldon's Plan seems like determinism; within the Foundation the characters must solve the problems themselves, without Seldon's help.

Even in the last half of the trilogy, the question of free will that is raised by the events of the stories is related not to Seldon's Plan but to manipulators of human minds like the Mule and the Second Foundation psychologists. The message of the events is that nothing happens unless someone makes it happen. The reader is told on several occasions that "Seldon's laws help those who help themselves."

The Biblical parallel is meaningful. The inevitability of psychohistory is no more binding than the inevitability of a Judaeo-Christian theology. Christians get free will as the gift from an omniscient God; the characters in the trilogy get free will as an act of authorial necessity. At the end of *Second Foundation*, Seldon's Plan has been restored, events are back on course, and the eventual unification of the Galaxy in a new Empire and the creation of a new civilization based on mental science seem assured. The final victory of the Second Foundation psychologists, benevolent as they seem, has repellent undertones, but if Asimov is to be accepted at his own benevolent best the reader can assume that the blessings of mental science will be available to everyone.

One basic appeal of *The Foundation Trilogy*, then, is not determinism; the basic structure of its episodes is antideterministic in that the outcome is not preordained. In fact, the appeal of the stories, replacing the more normal appeal of action and romance, is problem-solving. Much like the formal detective story, each episode sets forth a problem and, in effect, challenges the reader to come up with a solution. In the first published Foundation story, the solution is even held back until the following month's sequel. The fascination lies in the misleading clues, the twists and turns of plot, and the revelation at the end of what it all means. Jorane Sutt, in the final episode of *Foundation*, might have been speaking of Asimov when he says to Mallow, "There is nothing straight about you; no motive that hasn't another behind it; no statement that hasn't three meanings."

In the continual quest for the location of the Second Foundation, in the clues dropped here and there, in the near revelation by Ebling Mis, and in the succession of incorrect "discoveries," Asimov is imitating the methods of the detective novel that he would later incorporate more obviously (at Campbell's challenge) into the first science fiction detective novels and stories, beginning with *The Caves of Steel* (serialized in 1953 and containing images drawn from Trantor). Asimov even parodies the concluding scene of a thousand formal detective novels with his "I've got the answer — no, I've got the answer" chapter of *Second Foundation*.

But even the problem-solving attractiveness of the trilogy does not provide the total answer to its success. Aspects that are more peripheral to the total impact of the stories could be cited: the characters, attacked by some critics, are appealing; they are similar in that they are uniformly men and women of action. They are not people to whom things happen (the naturalistic protagonists to whom modern readers have become accustomed and the kind of characters that would seem more appropriate to the theme of determinism), but people who make things happen; the form of *The Foundation Trilogy*, after all, is that of a history, and histories are mostly about people who have made things happen. And the characters are as differentiated as the personages in most histories; they are clearly more than adequate for the purposes they must serve in the trilogy.

Asimov also provides some philosophy of history along the way. Some of it is clearly derived from his model, Edward Gibbon's *Decline and Fall of the Roman Empire*; but much is his own, and little seems to come from Marxism or whatever perceptions of it were current in the period. He adopts the position, for instance, that government is never what it seems; one example is the proliferation of figureheads and powers behind the throne. Another principle is that every innovation rigidifies into tradition, which must then be overturned. Thus, the grip of the Encyclopedists must be broken by the political power of the Mayor, which in turn must be broken by the economic power of the Traders, which in turn must be modified by the incorporation of the independent traders, and so on. It is a philosophy of persistent change; one generation's solution is the next generation's problem.

Moreover, Asimov preaches rationalism; he represents, above all other writers of his time, and later, the voice of reason. Avoid the obvious response to threats of attack, says Salvor Hardin. Avoid the emotional, the irrational. And he is later echoed by Hober Mallow, whose continual retreat before the attacking Korellian forces is considered treason.

Asimov also offers insights and overall views. Mostly these occur in the epigraphs that precede many of the chapters in the form of excerpts from the 116th edition of the *Encyclopedia Galactica*, published in 1020 F.E. by the Encyclopedia Galactica Publishing Company on Terminus. But he also includes some insights within the stories themselves. "It is the chief characteristic of the religion of science that it works," he comments in "The Mayors." "Never let your sense of morals prevent you from doing what is right," he puts in Limmar Ponyet's mouth in "The Traders." And "Seldon assumed that human reaction to stimuli would remain constant," Mis says.

The last comment, indeed, sums up Asimov's own attitude toward character. His characters have been criticized as not only one-dimensional but as unchanged by the passage of time and their altered conditions. The basic human characteristics must remain constant in what he called "the chess-game" approach to writing science fiction; moreover, he does not think they will change. The "motions and impulses of humanity: hate, love, fear, suspicion, passion, hunger, lust and so on . . . will not change while mankind remains Homo sapiens," Asimov wrote in an essay entitled "Social Science Fiction."

The point is arguable, but Asimov's viewpoint and choice is defensible even in the face of the Marxist conviction that character will change when society becomes more rational. Asimov's trilogy is not concerned with the revolution, or even evolution, of character, but with the evolution of an idea. What his critics fail to notice is the strategic value of contemporary characteristics. Like the lack of evolution in language, the recognizability of characters is a subtle reflection of the fact that, to the characters themselves, what they are saying and what they are doing is commonplace. Heinlein perfected the technique as an alternative to the "gee whiz" school of writing about the future, in which a character from the present is introduced to marvel about how people and conditions have changed.

In a story of the future, as in a historical novel or a translation from a foreign language, the problem to be dealt with is one of verisimilitude: how much and of what kind? Asimov chooses the verisimilitude of feeling over the verisimilitude of language or character, just as a historical novelist (or a translator) might give the flavor of speech rather than its accurate representation. There have been science fiction stories about future changes in people and language, but this is not one of them and does not pretend to be.

Asimov lends verisimiltude to his future in another way: his choice of names. Virtually every name is foreign, and virtually every one seems credible. It is part of Asimov's ingenuity and attention to detail. One of the values of *The Foundation Trilogy* is the way in which Asimov fleshes out his Galaxy and his future history with convincing inventions: gadgets, devices, paraphernalia, and structures, as well as names. He was not the best at this; Heinlein was his superior in creating future societies, and other authors have been better with names, but Asimov was effective.

Asimov is a master of the epigraph. Presaging his later science popularizations, they were models of imitation, clarity, and dramatization. They served two purposes: first, that of unobtrusive exposition, which was increasingly cumbersome as the stories stretched out (until at the end he had to disguise a long introduction as an essay Arkady was writing for school); and second, that of a framework that placed events in context and lent to the structure verisimilitude and the conviction of a future perspective.

The final virtue of *The Foundation Trilogy*, and perhaps the single most important quality in explaining its long popularity, is its exhaustive treatment of an idea. The idea is not psychohistory or even determinism; it is the Foundations. Each story deals with one aspect of the Foundations; the problem in "The Psychohistorians," for example, is how to influence the Empire to set up the Foundation on Terminus, and how to induce 100,000 Encyclopedists to leave their homes to go there (the problem, of course, is not revealed until the end of the story; it comes even after the solution). "The Encyclopedists" asks how the Foundation will survive when the Empire loses its grip on the barbarians in the outer provinces; Salvor Hardin's answer is to buy time by playing off one group of barbarians against another, and, as revealed in "The Mayors," by supplying atomic energy and devices within a religious framework.

The problem in "The Mayors" is what will happen to the Foundation when the barbarians are secure and well equipped; one of them will be stronger than the rest and will attack. The answer is that the priests will not allow it. The problem in "The Traders" is how Foundation hegemony can be spread to other systems; the answer is: by traders motivated by profits who can offer technological miracles. In "The Merchant Princes" two problems are addressed: the rigidifying political and religious structure, and the discovery of the Foundation by the Empire. The solution: the Traders seize political power and make war economically undesirable.

In "The General," the Foundation faces the problem of all-out attack by the Empire; the solution is that a weak Emperor cannot permit strong generals. In "The Mule" and its sequel "Search by the Mule," the question raised is how Seldon's Plan can cope with the unexpected, and the answer is that the Second Foundation knows what the Plan is and must act to protect it. And in "Search by the Foundation," the questions are raised: how can the Foundation cope with its knowledge of the Second Foundation, and how can the Second Foundation restore the previous condition? The answer is by convincing the Foundation that it has destroyed the Second Foundation.

Asimov has written that

. . . in designing each new Foundation story, I found I had to work within an increasingly
constricted area, with progressively fewer and fewer degrees of freedom. I was forced to

seize whatever way out I could find without worrying about how difficult I might make the next story. Then when I came to the next story, those difficulties arose and beat me over the head.

Each story nevertheless seems designed to arise out of the previous stories, and each develops with an air of inevitability. While it would be critical folly to assume that *The Foundation Trilogy* is an organic whole conceived as a master plan and crafted in full consideration of the contribution of each part (external and internal evidence suggests that Asimov moved from story to story, coping with the problems of each as they arose), it is a tribute to Asimov's ingenuity and cool rationality that the trilogy seems so well integrated, so complete.

The Foundation Trilogy stands as a monument to an inspired collection of powerful ideas crafted into stories one by one and to the science fiction method perfected in Campbell's *Astounding Science Fiction* in the 1940's.

James Gunn

Sources for Further Study

Criticism:

Moore, Maxine. "Asimov, Calvin and Moses," in *Voices for the Future.* Edited by Thomas D. Clareson. Bowling Green, Ohio: Bowling Green University Popular Press, 1976, pp. 101-102. Moore gives an analysis of *The Foundation Trilogy* and discusses its use of Christ imagery.

Reviews:

The Foundation Trilogy:

Analog. LXXII, January, 1964, p. 86.

Foundation:

Amazing Stories. XXVI, February, 1952, p. 149.

Analog. XLVIII, February, 1952, pp. 156-157.

Future Science Fiction. II, March, 1952, pp. 68-69.

Galaxy. III, February, 1952, p. 86.

Foundation and Empire:

Analog. LI, April, 1953, pp. 156-157.

Galaxy. V, January, 1953, p. 97.

Space Science Fiction. I, March, 1953, p. 116.

Second Foundation:

Analog. LIII, June, 1954, p. 144.

Fantastic Universe Science Fiction. October-November, 1953, pp. 191-192.

Galaxy. VII, November, 1953, p. 79.

FRANKENSTEIN
or The Modern Prometheus

Author: Mary Wollstonecraft Shelley (1797-1851)
First book publication: 1818
Type of work: Novel
Time: The late eighteenth century
Locale: Germany, Switzerland, England, Scotland, and the Arctic

The first, and still the classic, story of the artificial creation of a living humanoid being and of the disastrous consequences that follow when responsibilities for its existence — and for its own potential well-being — are avoided

> *Principal characters:*
> VICTOR FRANKENSTEIN, a young scientist
> HIS CREATURE
> ROBERT WALTON, an explorer en route to the Arctic
> ELIZABETH LAVENZA, betrothed to Victor
> HENRY CLERVAL, friend of Victor
> DE LACEY, a blind and aged French exile, head of the family living in the cottage where the creature hides unobserved

The history of the *Frankenstein* story in our culture, of the popular legend as it grows out of the novel, is itself a strange tale of creature in revolt against creator. The novel gave birth to a long series (beginning in 1823) of stageplays that freely adapted the story to melodramatic theater; and this tradition prepared the way in the twentieth century for an equally prolific series of movies, whose plots bear only the faintest resemblance to their literary ancestor. In the most famous of these films, James Whale's *Frankenstein* (1931, with Boris Karloff), the scientist's creature physically resembles the original (and is similarly animated by electrification) but he has been given, by accident, the brain of an insane criminal; he is treated brutally *before* he escapes into society; he is without power of speech and remains mentally infantile in his pain-maddened career of murderous terror; and at last, pursued by an outraged mob, he perishes howling in the hellish flames of a burning mill. Not only are none of these episodes (or anything like them) found in the novel, but the attitudes they suggest are antithetical to Mary Shelley's conception of Victor Frankenstein's creature, who is and remains — though driven to murder and roused to intense hatred — an intelligent, articulate, even morally sensitive being. His evil career is to be blamed less on "mad" science than on society itself, or on his creator only as Victor represents, in its intellectual form, the same moral blindness that characterizes in some degree nearly all specimens of humanity in the novel. Indeed, the novelist's lesson would seem to find some ironic confirmation in the readiness of our culture to reverse her intention — to change the very meaning of her title by transferring the name "Frankenstein" from her noble though tragically flawed hero to the bogeyman monster of the legend. Thus both figures have come to be seen as manifesting one and the same unqualified evil, the sin that the nineteenth century liked to call "presumption" (and *Presumption* was the title of that first stage-version in 1823), that is, the sin of tampering with God's creation, of trying to "change nature" (as if nature itself, in the course of evolution, had not always been trying to do precisely that).

Yet the original parentage of the legend cannot be denied: like her hero, Mary Shelley must bear some responsibility for the fate of her creation. In the preface to the 1831 edition, she lent some authenticity to the image of her tale as essentially a Gothic horror-story by recalling the circumstances that led to its composition. The idea originated in a contest of ghost-story telling, proposed as an amusement during a rainy spell in the summer of 1816, when she and her husband, the poet Percy Bysshe Shelley (1792-1822), were visiting Lord Byron in Switzerland. She recounts at some length the dream of nightmarish terror that followed this stimulus to imagination, and she ends her memoir by bidding her "hideous progeny [to] go forth and prosper." This was an emphasis entirely different from the tenor of the first preface, dated 1817 (which she now attributes to her husband), where we are told that the author is intent on delineating "principles of human nature" and is not "merely weaving a series of supernatural terrors." Four decades after the French Revolution, Mary was inclined to forget the prevalence in her youth of radical "principles," which had shaped her own values as daughter of the philosopher William Godwin (1756-1836) and the feminist Mary Wollstonecraft Godwin (1759-1797), and especially as first the eloping mistress and then the embattled wife of Shelley, a rebellious self-exile from England (after 1818) and a poet who dedicated his career to ideals of the Revolution. Nine years after her husband's death, Mary, growing steadily more conservative, was already tempted to ignore the all-too-Shelleyan meaning of her subtitle, *The Modern Prometheus*.

Prometheus was the Titan in Greek mythology who either (the traditions vary) created man or championed his cause against the gods by stealing for man the fire of Zeus (knowledge or creative intelligence). Often regarded in classical tradition as justly punished, the suffering Titan became in the age of Romanticism the martyred hero-god of Liberty; and this vision of the myth received its fullest embodiment in Shelley's lyrical drama, *Prometheus Unbound* (1818-1820). Prometheus is here made the inspiration of the modern mind's destined liberation from two tyrannies that Shelley saw as one — monarchy and institutionalized monotheism (or, in practical terms, orthodox Christianity). Shelley envisages man no longer as the child of a Creator Father-God but as himself necessarily a Creator, not inhabiting a given order of things but working in alliance with forces of nature to realize, in a dynamic universe, a society and a moral sensibility progressing steadily toward greater love, freedom, and justice. Evil might still inhere in such a world — no longer, though, as sin and guilt but as the mind's misunderstanding or misappropriation of universal Power, of natural energies in themselves innocent, and capable of harmonization in man when governed by knowledge and mediated by love and imagination.

But Prometheus as Poet is one thing, Prometheus as Scientist something else again. Shelley's doctrine gave Mary her didactic theme — the novel's message that abstract intellect needs always to be guided by sympathetic imagination — but the ambivalence that troubled her own imagination as she worked out her theme shows her awareness (and perhaps her husband's, too, for Shelley helped to plan and revise the story) that science could not escape such moral ambiguities as had once clouded and tortured the conscience of religion. There is remarkably little science in *Frankenstein*, and what there is remains slight and vague (after Victor's act of creation, it virtually disappears); but because the novel was the first to deal seriously with the impact of scientific possibility upon morality and social values, it may well deserve the honor that some recent critics have bestowed upon it — of being the first science fiction novel. And the fact that it treats these issues with an honest ambivalence of attitude may betray its imperfections as art, but testifies also to its legacy of integrity in leaving our most haunting questions unanswered. In a dynamic world where Power, in one form or another, rules necessarily and all things are uncertain or confused with our self-doubt, how can we tell the half-monsters from the half-men?

The novel opens (as it closes) with a series of letters from a young explorer, Walton, who is heading an expedition to the North Pole, in hopes of making some major discoveries about that unknown region. Mary Shelley's inexperience in narrative (she was only nineteen when she wrote the novel) appears continually in the fortuitous coincidences and other improbabilities of her plot; but her use of this frame-device, even though Walton is a narrator far removed from the main action, was an inspired decision. In the first place, Walton's passion for discovery serves as a critical control-model for the similar passion in Victor. Secondly, by having Walton and his shipmates observe a gigantic figure in a sledge passing at a distance across the frozen sea, followed by the rescue the next day of the pursuing Victor from an icefloe, another function is being served: this sighting of the creature helps to prove that he really exists and that Victor's ensuing narrative, which Walton records, is not a hallucinatory nightmare. And embedded further on in Victor's story is the creature's own account of his experience, which Victor has recorded. This Chinese nest of narratives has its awkward moments, and Mary lacked the stylistic versatility (except in writing the creature's narrative, by far the best) to keep the three voices entirely distinct in character — at times they tend to recite the same grand-opera rhetoric — but even this echo helps to remind us that the three viewpoints are responses to the same inward conflict, the *psychomachia* of Love and Power, Man and Nature, Self and Other which is their common predicament.

Not the least importance of Walton is that he introduces the thematic ideal of unified consciousness by which we are meant to judge Victor's moral failure. The explorer combines intellectual enthusiasm with sympathetic affection; he longs for a friend with whom to share the excitements of his enterprise, as Victor, significantly, did not. But this ideal is still untried by experience in Walton, and we soon learn that Victor, too, before his undertaking, had happily combined in his nature love, keen sensibility, and intellectual dedication. He has had kind parents; he is in love with, and is loved by, a gentle and beautiful women (Elizabeth); he enjoys the beauty of nature, and his closest friend is the humane, poetically perceptive Henry Clerval. What, then, goes wrong? Is Victor the spoiled child of good fortune? In a sense, yes, for all of Victor's virtues are centered in "domestic" happiness; and to gain some perspective on this important fact, it may help to remember that Mary's husband (following the lead of her father) had challenged the equation of social morality with marriage, filial piety, and bourgeois domesticity, which for him were the seedbeds of modern selfishness. It may therefore be a hint to the hero's tragedy that we find Victor often using the possessive case in talking of his happiness: Elizabeth and her love are continually valued as "mine."

Yet Victor's egocentricity is of heroic mold; his is the ego of Romantic Genius that risks everything for the glory of Promethean achievement. Victor is a native of Geneva — home of a patron-saint of Romanticism, Jean-Jacques Rousseau, but also of Calvinism and the genius of clockwork. And it may be said that these three influences — or, in other terms, excessive idealism, an inbred sense of sin and guilt, and a mechanical conception of the processes of "life" — conspire to bring about the doom of this creator and his creation. Victor feels an instinctive antipathy to the mechanistic premises and methods of Enlightenment science; his heart, though not his head, is with the old Alchemists, who have given him his Faustian dream of "immortality and power." But his father and his rationalistic teachers implant in him a feeling of guilt for this dream, and he therefore learns to associate his passion for scientific discovery with evil and unhappiness.

This situation helps to explain why he willingly accepts the extreme isolation and the ghoulishness of his labors of "filthy creation," until, after long (and largely unexplained) efforts, he succeeds in "bestowing animation upon lifeless matter." The exact words are important, for this is, literally, all he succeeds in doing; he has *not* succeeded, as he also likes to think, in "the creation of a human being." What he has done is essentially an extension of what the physiologist Luigi Galvani had done when, in 1786, he astounded his age by reporting that he had accidentally made the legs of a dead frog twitch with an electrical charge. Similarly, Victor has "animated" a "body" made from patched-up fragments of corpses, and has thus renewed in dead flesh that special "organization of matter," to borrow the language of mechanistic philosophy, which Victor has evidently been taught to regard as constituting "life." And because the only "life" he has created is this reorganized body of walking death, Victor, at the first sight of it, understandably enough, recoils from it in horror.

Clearly Victor is wrong to perpetuate his moment or recoil as a total rejection; but we cannot understand the creature's experience, after he wanders childlike from the laboratory into the world, solely in terms of this continued human rejection. We must acknowledge one primary fact about his being: although not an inhuman monster, he is, by physical necessity, something other than human. The 1817 preface makes it clear that Mary (or Shelley-Mary) never for a moment believed that life could be *created*, even by a Deity. He believed in an eternal universe that was in some sense itself alive, and the notion of a Creator infusing life into dust (note the parallel of Victor's act with Genesis) was for him an anthropomorphism born of fear and ignorance. "Matter" for Shelley was imbued with a "daemon" or "spirit" (often equated by the poet with electricity), and it is this universal "fire" in nature which Victor has somehow captured and activated in his modular corpse. Matter made sentient through irritability of tissues, with an indeterminate consciousness, yet capable of rational intelligence by being stimulated in the modes of a human sensorium: this perhaps is how we should understand the creature's physical being.

His energies are thus continuous in nature with, but are not the same as, the Promethean fire of human mentality; and there are some clear hints as to what the missing human ingredient is. Presumably the creature has all the sexual equipment of a human male; he soon acquires (from his observations at the De Lacey cottage) the abstract sentiments of "love," and is even capable of certain flickering moments of erotic desire; but these feelings are either evanescent or are quickly displaced onto his stronger and colder passions. His later demand for a "mate," and Victor's initial acquiescence, suggest that he has learned what sexuality is and that he might in time be capable of it; but it is worth noting that this "mate" is imagined less as a love-partner than as a sisterly companion to share his "misery." And this is, after all, what one would expect from a creature not of woman born, who has had neither parents nor childhood — who lacks man's experience of growth — that *organic* development of body and mind which for all the Romantic writers was the indispensable condition for love and for all true sympathy with life.

Recognition of this deficiency helps us to understand not only why the creature is intensely frightening to human eyes but also why he so readily, with no instinctive restraint or reaction, wrings human necks. In his deathlike and alien coldness of spirit, he *is* demonic, though innocently demonic; and his education in the world largely consists in the gradual, pain-enforced recognition that he is "not . . . of the same nature as man," that he really does represent (as Victor had imagined creating) a "new species." This difference in kind is at first obscured for him, as for us, by his original gentleness and "benevolence," his quick sense of beauty, his naïve trust in life. But these qualities are typically associated with delight in natural scenes, or with simple values of pleasure and pain — with, in short, the universal Nature that is the principle of his being, or with this Nature in its continuity with human life, not with Man as such.

The daemon (and that name henceforth is better for him than mere "creature") can stand intense cold; he is continually linked with lightning, storms, and wind, ice, dark waters, desolate landscapes; and his narrative is recited to Victor in the shadow of the glaciers of Mont Blanc. This Nature of raw elemental Power is contrasted with the lovelier face of Nature that Clerval admires; and as long as the daemon remains at the cottage, in his Eden state of innocence — absorbing unobserved man's values, his language and literature (precocious fellow that he is, he learns to read through a peephole!) as the only world he knows — he is drawn to this kindly, fertile Nature, too. But when he is forced to choose — as seen in his comments on the two models he finds for his predicament in Milton's *Paradise Lost* — it is not Adam in Paradise, longing for an Eve, that he identifies with most strongly but Satan, the fallen angel, the archetypal daemon whose fierce pride, banishment to Hell, contempt for an unjust God, and vows of revenge speak, even in this stage of innocence, most profoundly to his spirit.

This is not to say that no kinship with man endures, that the creature's alienation is insuperable. The episode in which the daemon attempts to win the friendship of blind old De Lacey — who at first responds with sympathy to the suffering he hears in the stranger's harsh voice, until his children return and shatter that rapport with their screams — convinces the daemon that "the human senses" will never accept him, and he thereupon declares war against mankind. But it is less the senses that are at fault than the prejudicial denial by conditioned minds of an equivalent living otherness, the selfhood of other self-conscious beings. This was Victor's original sin against his creation, and that sin is now visited upon his own head with diabolically perfect vengeance. For the daemon — after his creator reneges on his promise to make him a mate — now sets about destroying Victor and his remaining happiness with the same intense singlemindedness that Victor had devoted to the daemon's creation. Up to this point the daemon may be said to have been his own Prometheus — a thinker discovering the truth of his being through suffering, demanding the right to love and to create a new species — but now he assumes the role of a persecuting Zeus to Victor's fallen Promethean mind.

Victor is floundering in the paranoid secrecy of his twisted conscience: he has told no one of the creature's existence, even after the "fiend" has killed his brother and a faithful family servant has been executed for the crime. He fails to recognize that in his silence he is sinning less against "justice" than against love, and his Calvinistic sense of unforgivable guilt makes him invite unconsciously, as a just "fate," the daemon's retribution. Indeed, the two characters seem at this point, as various critics have remarked, two halves of one personality: each is the other's *Doppelgänger* (psychic double), and nowhere is the bondage stronger than in their attraction to each other as mirror-images of their self-hatred. The daemon has wanted a mate "as hideous as" himself and when Victor denies him this object, he soon finds it again in Victor himself as pursuer — which perhaps was the "companionship" that he, like Victor, had always really sought. And the bitterest irony in this conspiracy is that the two people in the world with love and imagination enough to free them both, if anyone could, from their obsession — Clerval and Elizabeth — are made the supreme sacrifices in their mutual pact of suicidal vengeance.

Yet the novel does not end on this grim note of inescapable solipsism. Walton's decision, influenced by Victor's story, to abandon his quest — nominally for the safety of his crew but really because he fears a mutiny — does seem at first to confirm the general failure of mankind in this novel to achieve transcendence of self. And if approached from any other angle than that made possible by the closing scene, the symbolic meaning of the tale would seem to be negative or, at best, cautionary. In nineteenth century terms, the daemon may be said to represent the unprecedented fear released in the world by both the French and Industrial Revolutions — the specter of the world's miserable millions rising up from brutalizing poverty to confront a society unprepared to acknowledge its responsibilities to, or for, a suddenly menacing "humanity." And this meaning merges with a timeless meaning that affects in some degree all readers: the novel's unwanted daemon speaks for the latent fear in every self that it may be doomed to a fate of absolute uniqueness — to be hated, and made to hate in turn, simply because one's self is different from everyone else in the world.

Mary Shelley is true to that feeling in having her daemon — after Victor expires on the ship and his creature comes to bid a last, and now grieving, farewell over the corpse — vanish into the Arctic, there to immolate himself alone on a funeral pyre, so that the dread secret of his creation will be safely returned to nature. In this act, too, he is consumed with self-hatred, but he has gotten the better of the whining self-pity that made him justify his murders; in confessing "remorse" to Walton, he no longer "abhors" himself for what he is, but for what he had done; he has acknowledged as real the moral law that at last defines his own life as well as man's. The flame of his death on a remote polar icefield will still be one with the Promethean fire: Man and cosmic Nature, however strange and hostile their mutations may be, are not irreparably alien. And that discovery, or rediscovery, though it eludes him in his shame and his sorrow, Walton does succeed in bringing back from the Arctic.

John Kinnaird

Sources for Further Study

Criticism:

Bloom, H. "Frankenstein, or the New Prometheus," in *Partisan Review*. XXXII (Fall, 1965), pp. 611-618. Bloom examines the inherent mythology of Shelley's gothic novel.

Cude, Wilfred. "Mary Shelley's Modern Prometheus: A Study in the Ethics of Scientific Creativity," in *Dalhousie Review*. LII (1972), pp. 212-225. Cude discusses the ethical problems raised by the theme of *Frankenstein*.

Dunn, Richard J. "Narrative Distance in *Frankenstein*," in *Studies in the Novel*. VI (1974), pp. 408-417. Dunn examines Mary Shelley's techniques of storytelling, concentrating heavily on her narrative method.

Pallin, Burton R. "Philosophical and Literary Sources of *Frankenstein*," in *Comparative Literature*. XVII (1965), pp. 97-108. Mary Shelley's inspiration for *Frankenstein* is examined by Pallin who presents the major sources.

Schug, Charles. "The Romantic Form of Mary Shelley's *Frankenstein*," in *Studies in English Literature*. *1500-1900*. XVII (Autumn, 1977), pp. 607-619. *Frankenstein*'s ties with the romantic tradition are examined in this study.

FRANKENSTEIN UNBOUND

Author: Brian W. Aldiss (1925-   )
First book publication: 1973
Type of work: Novel
Time: 2020 and 1816
Locale: The United States and Switzerland

Thrown back in time two centuries by the rupturing of the infrastructure of space through nuclear warfare, Joseph Bodenland finds himself in Switzerland just as Dr. Frankenstein has animated his monstrous creation; he meets Mary Shelley, Percy Bysshe Shelley, and Lord Byron

> *Principal characters:*
> JOSEPH BODENLAND, a statesman of the twenty first century
> MARY GODWIN SHELLEY, author of *Frankenstein*
> PERCY BYSSHE SHELLEY, the poet, her husband
> LORD BYRON, the poet
> DOCTOR VICTOR FRANKENSTEIN, the experimenter
> THE MONSTER, Victor's creation

Brian Aldiss begins his *Billion Year Spree*, subtitled "The True History of Science Fiction," by paying obeisance to Mary Shelley. Despite the conflicting claims of earlier works — Swift's *Gulliver's Travels* or Cyrano de Bergerac's *Voyage to the Moon* to name only two — for Aldiss, the genre of science fiction had its genuine inception in Mary Shelley's creative imagination. It was Mary Shelley who saw that mankind was suffering from the curse of Prometheus: by seeking to control too much we had lost control of ourselves. It was she who unleashed upon the public the personification of those dark shadow forces that underlie the surface of all human life. It was she who recognized, nearly 175 years ago, that Intellect had made the planet unsafe for the intellect.

Frankenstein Unbound, then, is Aldiss' tribute to this great progenitor of the form that Aldiss himself has distinguished. In another sense, judging by the luminosity and tenderness of style, Aldiss has written of his lifelong love affair with Mary Shelley — not simply her ideas, but her person, for Aldiss has re-created the wife of the great poet as a genuine, distinctive individual whose abilities, perceptions, and insights outshine those of her more famous husband. To accomplish this remarkable task, Aldiss has written what may be the best of his many novels, combining as it does his own clean, loose-limbed prose poetry, his traditional preoccupation with time, his ability to create subtle characterizations, and his sense of an era — a place, a time, an atmosphere, an ambience, as well as some profound contemplation of the nature of reality. It is in almost every way a superior novel, one that critics and fans alike can point to as an example of the best of the genre.

The novel consists of two sections. The first, by far the briefer, is an assemblage of letters, editorials, telegrams, and so on, which explain enough of the twenty-first century background to make the major thesis, the "time-slip" or rupturing of the infrastructure of space, quite credible. From a simplistic point of view, the first section exists only to get the hero, Joseph Bodenland, back in time and space to the Switzerland of early May, 1816, in the village of Secheron on Lake Geneva. The second section of the novel is Bodenland's tape-journal. (How that journal has been transmitted from 1816 to the publication year of 1973 is never made clear, although it really does not matter.)

Bodenland (whose name is derived from the German word *boden*, meaning "earth" or "soil," plus the English word "land") finds himself in an era and a place that may be real and fictional at the same time. He quickly meets the son of the famous Victor Frankenstein, for example, although his memory tells him that the Doctor exists only as a character in Mary Shelley's novel. He meets Frankenstein himself, and a little later when he meets Mary, he finds that her novel is half-finished. To Mary it is a novel, set a century before, a horror story told in the manner of Mrs. Radcliffe. She is apparently unaware of the existence of a real Doctor Frankenstein whose experiments are being carried on at that very moment. She has just written that part of her novel where the monster wants a soulmate. Bodenland cannot recall that section of her novel. Did she really write it? What is real? What is fiction? Does Bodenland's vague or faulty memory of Mary's completed novel influence the writing of the novel itself? Who is the creator? Mary Godwin Shelley? Frankenstein? Brian Aldiss? And what is reality? Mary Shelley's book is real, perceivable by the senses. So is Aldiss'. Yet so is the fictional Frankenstein and his monstrous creation. Aldiss makes it quite clear that it is the power of Mary Shelley's allegory that constitutes a vision of reality, and gives genuine meaning.

Bodenland, in fact, experiences a severe psychic shock, one almost of Aristotelean recognition, along with his sense of temporal shock. "I felt myself in the presence of myth and, by association, accepted myself as mythical!"

But what is myth, after all, but a metaphorical or allegorical or symbolic way of expressing a higher truth? And while certain aspects of myth are temporal and can change under the circumstances of time, place, or culture, the core of the myth itself, its archetypal power, exists beyond the surface accidentals of appearance. Bodenland reflects this dilemma in his journal:

> One thing you see I had already accepted. I had accepted the equal reality of Mary Shelley and her creation, Victor Frankenstein, just as I had accepted the equal reality of Victor and his monster; for they accepted my reality, and I was as much a mythical creature in their world as they would have been in mine.

At this point the reader realizes that, in a certain sense, he has been trapped by Aldiss' skill into accepting the reality of the existence of Bodenland who, after all, is only a creature of Aldiss' brilliant imagination. And once again the reader is forced to ask, what is myth? What is reality?

At the heart of Aldiss' meditation is time — time past, time present, time future. The novel has opened with the infrastructure of time being ruptured. "Time-slips" of various lengths, duration, and import occur with increasing frequency. Joseph Bodenland (his initials are "JB" and suggest "Job," and Bodenland, at least toward the end of the novel, is positively Job-like in his ability to endure difficulties and pain) lives in 2020. His first letter is dated August 20, 2020, and the repetition of the numerical pattern cannot but suggest the clarity of 20-20 vision which the world has lost with its frequent wars. He is transported to May, 1816, and shortly thereafter he discovers that it is August of the same year. Time has slipped once more. Bodenland puts it this way: "As Time was more devious than scientific orthodoxy would have us believe, so was reality open to question, since Time was one of the terms in its equation."

Time is linear, straightforward, proceeding with clockwork regularity, Bodenland thinks, a noise that the clock makes, and the Western world is its slave. "It had come to the stage in 2020 when anyone who regarded Time as other than something that could be measured precisely by a chronometer was shunned as eccentric." Bodenland, however — and here he must certainly speak with the voice of the novelist himself — recognizes that the poets had always been on the side of the people in recognizing the deviousness of Time, its circularity, or spiral, gyrelike qualities. "For them [the poets], and for some neglected novelists, Time would always be a wayward thing, climbing over life like a variegated ivy over some old house. Or like Mary Shelley's reputation, cherished by few, but always there, diversifying."

So at least three strands of Time are at work in *Frankenstein Unbound*: the early twenty-first century in which the novel opens; the early nineteenth century to which it moves, and the late twentieth century in which the reader perceives the course of action as he or she reads the novel. If Time is spiral, ever-returning, can the past alter the present? Is all time contained in time past and can the future be altered by the present? Aldiss' meditations on this point are curiously reminiscent of T. S. Eliot's *Four Quartets* or "Tradition and the Individual Talent." Bodenland attempts to alter the future — either the twenty-first century of his own "present" or the late twentieth century of the reader's — by attempting to dissuade Frankenstein from proceeding with his experiments. "How many of the ills of the world were not due precisely to Frankenstein's folly?" he asks, and almost immediately ponders: "Was there some immutable cosmic law which decreed that man's good intentions should always thunder back about his head. . . ?"

If the experimenter cannot be dissuaded — and indeed it is too late, for the monster has already been animated — then the beast must be slain. The beast recalls the rough beast of W. B. Yeats's great poem "The Second Coming," which, "its hour come round at last slouches toward Bethlehem to be born." But Bodenland also wonders why he must be a savior of humanity. Has his perception of reality and hence his mental stability radically changed? Have the grave time-ruptures of his own age sent their ripple backward? Have the time distortions caused mental illusions? "One of those illusions," Bodenland thinks, "was my persistent sensation that my personality was dissolving." If Bodenland's personality has modified from that of the assured statesman of 2020 to lover of Mary Shelley; from time-server to time-observer; from passive spectator to active redeemer, then there may be hope for the world, and Aldiss implies that humanity itself may be capable of change. The head-heart dichotomy which has been at the very core both of his novel and of Mary Shelley's disappears.

New realities loom before the reader. All is changed, radically, totally, perhaps forever. Two moons hang in the sky; Lake Geneva has disappeared, as have the Jura mountains. The world seems in the grip of a new ice age, and Bodenland himself is even further transformed. He must kill the monster, but he is profoundly moved by it. "I fell on my knees and wept, and called aloud to God. I buried my face in my hands and cried with helplessness. . . . The Frankenstein mentality had triumphed over the heart." When he meets the monster in the pivotal final chapter, Bodenland is almost enraptured, in the most profound sense of the word. "I can only declare that the face before me had a terrible beauty."

Throughout this terrifying final chapter Aldiss calls upon both Milton and Shelley. While it is impossible to detail all of the references from "Paradise Lost" or "Prometheus Unbound," which Aldiss includes, what is important here is that Aldiss infuses the older myths with a modern, horrifying reality. The monster becomes Lucifer, a beautiful evil, just as science in 2020 has become a terrible beauty. Bodenland, redeemerlike, must kill the monster, his equally beautiful-horrible mate, and their potential offspring.

The themes, then, are those of death, and rebirth. Like the sun where creation and destruction occur simultaneously, the mind of the artist is a cosmic furnace, and from this cauldron Aldiss has the dying monster speak:

> "This I will tell you, and through you all men, if you are deemed fit to rejoin your kind: that my death will weigh more heavily upon you than my life. No fury I might possess could be a match for yours. Moreover, though you seek to bury me, yet you will continuously resurrect me! Once I am unbound, I am unbounded!"

Bodenland observes that the word "resurrect" is "delivered with ferocity," and the suggestions of death, rebirth, resurrection, life, death, love, and tragedy implicit in the early portions of the novel have their culmination here. Aldiss, however, gives no easy answers to his readers. What they are reading, it must be remembered, is the tape-journal of Joseph Bodenland, which has somehow found its way across the wastes of time and space, across the desolate arctic atmosphere of the conclusion of the novel to the late twentieth century. We are reading a "fiction," a made thing, that is so good precisely because it appeals to the mythic perceptions in all of us. It is not really Boden-land's task to slay the monster, although at the end he is waiting, "biding my time in darkness and distance." The brilliant ending of the novel requires that the reader himself become an active character in the narrative progression and become conscious to the point that he will slay the shadow-monster present in us all. When that happens, Aldiss suggests, we will need no salvific figures other than ourselves. We will be unbound.

Willis E. McNelly

Sources for Further Study

Reviews:

Booklist. LXX, July 15, 1974, p. 1227.

Choice. XI, November, 1974, p. 1302.

Kirkus Reviews. XLII, April 15, 1974, p. 448 and XLII, May 1, 1974, p. 496.

Library Journal. XCIX, August, 1974, p. 1988.

New York Times. June 11, 1974, p. 39.

Psychology Today. VIII, September, 1974, p. 134.

Time. CIV, August 5, 1974, p. 84.

FREEZING DOWN
(FRYSEPUNKTET)

Author: Anders Bodelsen (1937-   )
First book publication: 1969
English translation: 1971
Type of work: Novel
Time: 1973, 1995, 2022
Locale: The Ackermann Institute, a "freezing down" clinic in the United States

A vision of the near future in which medical science develops techniques for artificially prolonging human life indefinitely, only to create severe social, political, and psychological consequences

> *Principal characters:*
> BRUNO, a thirty-two-year-old bachelor with terminal cancer
> JENNY HOLLANDER, his lover, a ballet dancer
> DR. ACKERMANN, his doctor, developer of the "freezing down" technique

In *Freezing Down*, Anders Bodelsen postulates a world in which man has for all practical purposes become "immortal"; and the givers of this boon, the doctors and medical researchers, have become the masters of society. But this gift has not created the paradise society had hoped for. In granting man a nearly eternal earthly existence, the doctors and researchers have inadvertently deprived him of something even more essential, his humanity. *Freezing Down* explores the implications of this condition both on the individual and on society as a whole.

The story is told somewhat indirectly by Bruno, one of the first subjects to be experimentally "frozen down." A victim of terminal cancer, he is initially frozen in 1973, thawed out free of disease in 1995, only to go into a severe depression, refrozen at his own request and then rethawed in 2022, only to become even more depressed, and finally sent into hibernation to await an uncertain fate.

The Bruno of 1973 is a thirty-two-year-old bachelor who edits a weekly publication. He is a typical modern man — intelligent, efficient, gregarious, likable, and open to his surroundings. In every way he is "normal" — almost too much so. Perhaps he has adjusted to his environment so smoothly because he lacks an individual identity of his own: he has few relationships of any depth, feelings of intensity, or desires of any seriousness. Even when Dr. Ackermann tells him that he has only six months to live, he reacts passively. So little has he really lived, that the prospect of death holds little terror. His reluctance to choose between imminent death and "freezing down" seems based less on fear than on apathy. Only after his latent emotions are at last aroused by a short, forced sexual experience with Jenny Hollander, a ballet dancer and fellow patient at the clinic, does he agree to the treatment.

The first phase of the experiment is a success. Bruno is thawed out and

cured in 1995. He can presumably resume his life without fear of further infec-
tion — except that he finds it impossible to adjust to his new surroundings.
Furthermore, the medical staff (Dr. Ackermann, himself, being frozen down at
the time) is unwilling to release him from the clinic in his disturbed state. But
even though confined to the Ackermann Institute and limited to contact with a
small number of people, Bruno is able to perceive a greatly altered world: the
language is different, the society is different; indeed, everything is different.
In bits and pieces he is able to put together a fairly thorough picture of the new
post-freezing society.

By 1995 medicine has developed the capacity to replace human organs with
either organs from other people or artificial ones. Science has also perfected a
decalcification process which makes virtually eternal life possible. But many
people reject such artificial tinkering with their bodies; they want to live normally with their own organs until they break down in natural ways. The inevitable tension that develops between these competing medical and ethical attitudes is one of the central dynamics of the novel.

Since society has become organized around this new longevity, the medical
profession has naturally risen to social and political supremacy. The result is
the creation of a new aristocracy — or, rather, a "mediocracy." All politicians
are doctors and society is organized to satisfy their needs.

To govern, the mediocracy has divided society into three distinct categories. First are the Semi-Life-People — those who want to live a normal
life without transplantations, artificial organs, and decalcification programs.
They do not work, are permitted to do almost anything they please, and get
nearly everything they want — provided they do nothing that risks damage to
their organs, such as smoking or drinking. They are, in short, living organ
banks; the first time one of their organs breaks down or they become involved
in an accident, they are allowed to die. Their bodies are then immediately
dissected for transplant materials.

The second group consists of the Total-Life-People who do all the work in
this 1995 society. For that reason they get a nearly eternal life via organ transplantations and decalcifications. Should they suffer an illness or injury beyond
the capacity of the medical knowledge of the moment, they simply are frozen
down until such knowledge becomes available.

The third category consists of the Frozen Ones. Since they are neither
wholly alive nor dead, they are the most vulnerable and exploited members of
society. They are both monetarily poor and medically defenseless: poor
because of the currency inflation and defenseless against medical organ inflation. Most of their money must go to the freezing process and continuous up-
keep; the rest of it is lost to inflation. And as they lie frozen, they are victimized; when needed, their organs are simply taken by the government to be
replaced when — and if — artificial organs become available again. Ultimately these Frozen Ones are thawed, like Bruno, into a strange world bereft

of meaningful money, but filled with artificial organs. Immediately they are forced to work in order to satisfy the society's insatiable appetite for manpower. They are thawed out to be Total-Life-People whether they want to or not. Thus, while medical science grants its citizens "life" it takes away all choice of how that life is to be lived.

And so the Total-Life-People work hard to keep their organ banks (the Semi-Life-People) alive and to keep up the equipment for the Frozen Ones; the doctors work hard to improve their medical techniques in order to make more freezings and thawings, thereby creating more manpower — a self-perpetuating, efficient, but vicious cycle.

However, this perfect system begins to come apart. Tension between the two living segments of society increases. The Total-Life-People resent the drudgery of their own lives which are as meaningless as they are long. The Semi-Life-People, on the other hand, are growing weary of their idyllic, if relatively brief, existences; with neither work, nor problems, nor challenges, they are bored. They begin to drink and smoke secretly; they demonstrate, start movements, ferment riots, and, in the best dystopian tradition, conspire against the ruling mediocracy. Rebellion and social chaos seem imminent.

But the reader does not see it happen because Bruno stages a rebellion of his own. The more he learns of the outside world, the more baffled and frustrated he becomes. He can neither enter that world nor endure the separation and loneliness of the Ackermann Institute. This combination of puzzlement and separation depresses him severely. In his earlier life he had had elaborate surroundings and intimate contacts with many people. Alone and isolated, he breaks down and becomes violent. In his frenzy, he says that he wishes to be refrozen until the time that Jenny Hollander can be thawed. He is granted his desire.

But the world of 2022 into which Bruno thaws is even more bizarre and disturbing than the one he had rejected. To be sure, he does meet Jenny Hollander and Dr. Ackermann once again, but he can find neither solace nor meaning with either of them. Jenny has received a new spine and is starting up her ballet experiences once more — only to be plagued by dizziness and constant falling. Dr. Ackermann, his sole companion for some time in the isolated, generally darkened hospital ward, can tell Bruno little about the outside world. The old man repeats himself, mumbles incessantly about a pocket light, apparently drifting in and out of contact. He has become totally senile. Having been recalled to life a second time, Bruno finds himself locked up with a dizzy ballet dancer and subject to a senile doctor. The atmosphere is that of a mental hospital or forgotten prison. These feelings are reinforced by the presence of armed men in green uniforms who appear and disappear in a random fashion and speak an unintelligible language.

Even more isolated than before and lacking direct communication with any "sane" member of this society, Bruno still is able to piece together a sketchy view of the world outside, which he communicates to the reader in fragments. The effect is similar to that of a first-class mystery story, with the clues finally assuming a coherent shape and meaning.

It is apparent that the mediocracy has finally dissipated and collapsed because of their ignorance of the whole human being and their passion for constant tinkering with nature. The society has become a hodgepodge of ages. In one of his few almost sensible moments, Dr. Ackermann tells Bruno: "We have many ages. Every part has its own age. Chronological age. Biological age. Psychological age. Physiological age. Average age. Partial age." And nobody is complete. Nearly all organs are artificial. Individuals who have had decalcifications suffer from amnesia. Those who have been frozen and thawed several times have become senile despite their relatively short biological age. In sum, because of the excessive use of artificial organs and radical treatments, mankind has lost its soul as well as its ability to regenerate itself physiologically.

Since all of this is seen from Bruno's perspective, he — and the reader — can only speculate about the chaos happening outside the Ackermann Institute. He senses the results of events about which he can only guess; as if looking from a prison window, one can see the people running away, but not that from which they run. It appears that the clinic, with its stock of frozen people, is an isolated spot, surrounded by subversion, destruction, perhaps revolution. The Ackermann Institute may well be the last vestige of humane society — a bitter irony since it is here where the entire process began.

Thus Bruno's final decision to hibernate is a logical one (he cannot be frozen any more). He must do so until he can be changed mentally. And what is the probable result of such a treatment? None. As a human being he is already dead; all the artificial treatments have amounted to nothing. It would have been the same — or better — if he had died of cancer in 1973.

Bodelsen's dark view of the future is of course a logical projection of trends he sees in contemporary society. Even today people at hospitals are reduced to mere "patients" or "cases," unable to influence their own situations. From one's initial admission into a hospital, life is controlled more thoroughly and blatantly than in a prison. One must eat, sleep, walk, sit up, or lie down at a doctor's command. Any refusal to do so results in pills or injections with no explanations ever made of the contents, the expected results, or the potential reactions. The mediocracy is almost upon us today, but we have not realized it yet. We trust the doctors and feel ourselves helpless without them, even though we do not know what they are doing to us. It is only a question of time before this mediocratic power becomes absolute.

Nor need we limit this danger to the medical profession. They are but one of the "specialist" elites that we have come to depend on totally, to whom we have yielded our powers regardless of whether they want them, or whether they are even aware of the fact that they are assuming them. *Freezing Down* presents a vision of tomorrow in which the technical specialists — in this case the medical profession — have become both more and more specialized and at the same time more and more distant from the people their technology is supposed to serve. The necessary result of this separation is that technology becomes an end in itself and the subjects become no more than controlled animals for experimentation and study in order to develop still more experiments. And the political power of these specialists grows as an inevitable consequence, as the basic social need that these experts satisfy becomes more pervasive. Thus, the servant becomes the master and this new master, in turn, is controlled by the technological processes he brought into being.

Offered the gift of "eternal" life, Bruno learns that the price, a loss of identity as a human being, is too high; he rejects it by hibernating. Through Bruno's denouement the reader also comes to learn the high price of such a medical advancement to society as a whole — losses of humanity, stability, values, and ultimate collapse and chaos. Bodelsen suggests that, unfortunately, we have already begun to pay this price.

Carsten Schiøler

Sources for Further Study

Criticism:

Levin, Martin. *"Freezing Down,"* in *New York Times Book Review.* February 28, 1971, p. 32. Levin feels Bodelsen's tale of a possible future of geriatry shows wit and imagination.

Reviews:

Best Sellers. XXXI, April 1, 1971, p. 28.

Booklist. LXVII, July 1, 1971, p. 896.

Kirkus Reviews. XXXIX, January 1, 1971, p. 11.

Library Journal. XCVI, February 15, 1971, p. 654.

Publisher's Weekly. CXCIX, January 4, 1971, p. 51.

FROM THE EARTH TO THE MOON
(DE LA TERRE À LA LUNE)

Author: Jules Verne (1828-1905)
First book publication: 1865
English translation: 1874
Type of work: Novel
Time: 1864-1865
Locale: Baltimore and the vicinity of Tampa, Florida

The purported documentary account of the first effort, organized by gun enthusiasts and veterans of the American Civil War, to fire a manned vehicle to the Moon

    Principal characters:
    IMPEY BARBICANE, president of the Baltimore Gun Club
    J. T. MASTON, secretary of the Gun Club
    MICHEL ARDAN, French adventurer and volunteer astronaut
    CAPTAIN NICHOLL, owner of Philadelphia armor forge and Barbicane's rival

The brains, the motive, and the passion behind mankind's attempt to leave its own planet and explore (and conquer) the Moon belong to the walking wounded of modern warfare. That is the premise on which Jules Verne founds the opening of the third in his long series of Extraordinary Voyages, *From the Earth to the Moon.* His fiction is nowhere more corrosive than in the novel's first chapter, in which a panorama of maimed and disenchanted artillerymen, fitted with an extravagant variety of prostheses, sit in their Baltimore club, regretting the Civil War's end and yearning for new wars and fresh excuses to employ new cannons and invent even more complex and lethal armaments. When their president, Impey Barbicane, proposes that they turn their ballistic talents to devising an enormous gun that will literally shoot a projectile to the Moon, the impression Verne creates is less of a momentous chapter in planetary history than a therapeutic exorcism of human frustrations and barbarities.

The bulk of *From the Earth to the Moon* may be read as a celebration of human ingenuity in which Verne catalogs in patient, sometimes plodding, detail the scientific background to and practical preparations for the moonshot. Yet, the bizarre opening creates an absurdist perspective that the rest of the novel is not fully able to dispel: the men at Baltimore who seize, obsessively, on Barbicane's project represent the human cost of a flight to the Moon, totaled up in their artificial fixtures that so screechingly announce the absence of limb and bone and tissue, the warping of mind, spirit, and sensibility. Although Verne does not sustain the satirical intensity of the first chapters, his initial point is clear and disturbing, and filters down through the later chapters. The glory of the space shot is built on the carnage of warfare and the boredom that follows peacemaking. Here there is no apologist for the wonders of technological innovation, but a whole club — 1,833 active and 30,575 corresponding members — all idle, trigger-happy soldiers itching to get behind a cannon again.

The novel does not describe the actual journey to the Moon, reserved for the 1870 sequel, *Round the Moon* (*Autour de la Lune*). Rather, Verne centers his attention on the *idea* of the journey, and specifically on Barbicane's scheme to mobilize the enthusiasm of the unemployed artillerists, the scientific expertise of the academic community, the technological proficiency of American engineers, the vast manpower of the laboring classes, the wealth of the American economy, and — not least — the patriotism of the American newspaper reader, nurtured and aroused by journalists eager to provide entertainment at the breakfast table. All will serve Barbicane's end of firing a shell to the Moon out of the nine-hundred-foot *Columbiad*, the largest cannon ever built, with the explosive force of 400,000 pounds of guncotton, from a hill in Florida near Tampa Bay.

Barbicane's original plan never included sending a human passenger. That possibility is opened suddenly, in the middle of the novel, with the entrance of a conventional "hero" of the old school into the new school of Barbicane's gunmen and engineers. The Moon project gains both an international flavor and the coloring of romance. And the novel moves emphatically away from the satire on American nationalism and militarism to a focus on the splendor, courage, and charm of the astronaut. Michel Ardan, a kind of nineteenth century Evel Knievel, disdains worrying about the practical matters of space flight; he is willing to entrust those to American know-how while he supplies the dash and swagger that will make Barbicane's project command and monopolize the world's attention. When an old rivalry between Barbicane and Captain Nicholl, an armor manufacturer from Philadelphia, threatens to end in death and the scuttling of the moonshot, Ardan settles the feud with a single grand gesture by cajoling the two men to accompany him to the Moon in his now exquisitely appointed projectile. What newfangled science cannot subdue, old-fashioned heroism can — including even American industrial rivalry.

Ardan's role in *From the Earth to the Moon* manifests the peculiar narrative form characteristic of so many of Verne's Extraordinary Voyages. The novel is poised between lecture and adventure, between documentary essay and unblushing romance. That split is evident in Verne's handling of the Moon itself in the narrative. Verne likes to take his Moon both ways: as poetic emblem and as the object of scientific scrutiny. The Moon's old names — Phoebe, Selene, Astarte, wolf's sun — are lovingly and self-consciously rehearsed, and then banished as the products of ignorance and superstition. By the mid-1860's, the Moon had already been so exhaustively observed, mapped, measured, anatomized, that much of Verne's attention to the satellite becomes a litany of data, a summary of scientific hypotheses, and a compendium of the errors in earlier mythological, artistic, astronomical, and religious sources.

But in the process of demythologizing the Moon, Verne remythologizes heroic human achievement. The speculation about the Moon and space flight is the product of careful extrapolation based on current scientific thought, but the characterization in *From the Earth to the Moon* is pure romance. While the ideas in the book are drawn from a world of probability, the characters are drawn from a world of fantasy: Ardan the stock Frenchman and Barbicane the stock Yankee, the comic sidekick Maston and the ill-tempered cynic Nicholl. As usual in Verne's fiction, the characters are all male and apparently celibate. The characters are crude and the plot sporadic, often interrupted by set-pieces designed to give Verne's audience a working knowledge of popular physics and astronomy.

However, the novel does manage to create at least a rudimentary form of suspense. As he unfolds the implications of Barbicane's grand design and Ardan's heroic aspiration, Verne winds tension and springs surprises, in the firing of twelve hundred furnaces full of molten metal for the casting of the great cannon; in the mysterious telegram announcing the unexpected arrival of Ardan; in the melodrama and farce of an aborted duel in Skersnaw Woods between Barbicane and Nicholl; in the danger in transporting and stockpiling the enormous quantity of gunpowder at the bottom of the nine hundred-foot shaft; in the emotional exhilaration of the crowd and the physical devastation on land and sea at the moment of ignition; and, most cleverly, in the clouding of the atmosphere by dust raised at the firing and the consequent inability of astronomers at the giant new observatory in the Rockies to follow the vehicle's progress towards its destination.

As a romance, *From the Earth to the Moon* has something of the primitive structure of 1930's movie serials; it is wholly dependent on episode and sequence, problem and solution, for its effects. Verne even provides the novel a to-be-continued ending. The final chapter leaves the fates of Ardan, Barbicane, and Nicholl aboard the projectile uncertain while the faithful J. T. Maston takes up residence at the Rocky Mountain observatory confident that the three will be heard from again. Verne nearly begs to be asked for a sequel.

But even Verne's suspense, the sequential building of the narrative to climax and crisis, is in the service of what is essentially an unromantic homage to the marvels of modern science. For the reader who expects narrative intricacy, psychological sophistication, or formal consistency, *From the Earth to the Moon* is often an irritating book. Verne displays an intense interest in popular science but, at best, a casual interest in the aesthetics of science *fiction*. Ardan's tub-thumping speech to the spectators gathered in Florida to witness the shot is likely to strike readers as a wasted rhetorical opportunity as Verne diverts a potentially dramatic occasion to a disquisition on astronomical timetables and interplanetary mileage.

Verne's method is most palatable when there is a satirical underpinning to the homilies. In a chapter devoted to the cannonball, Barbicane's ponderous lecture on ballistics is effectively counterpointed by Maston's hilariously fatuous description of the cannonball as microcosm and his likening of human manufacturers of cannonballs to the divine shaper of the cosmos. When Verne allows his satiric gift to leaven his penchant for delivering prepared speeches on everything from the geography of Florida to the history of telescopes, the narrative acquires vigor and muscle. But there are many chapters that are nearly pure slack.

Just as Mary Shelley's *Frankenstein* (1815) prefigures all those science fiction tales which take as their subject the ethics of invention, *From the Earth to the Moon* is the original of that kind of science fiction which finds the hardware itself seductive. As Verne leaves behind the critical mood of the opening chapters, the novel tends to canonize the feat of engineering demanded by the Moon project. That feat is treated partly as spectacle (as in the marvelous image of a molten Niagara in the casting of the cannon) but largely as a practical problem of enormous and intriguing complexity. At its heart, *From the Earth to the Moon* is a how-to book. The question of interest is how to get from one place to another; the trip itself is inconsequential. The problem of space flight is above all a technical, not a moral or psychological or even narrative one. Verne's subtitle, "Direct in Ninety-Seven Hours and Twenty Minutes" accurately forecasts the primacy of number, measure, and precision and the secondary status of artful storytelling in this fiction.

Both Verne's technological imagination and his respect for a universe of fact and probability have had substantial influence on later practitioners of extrapolative science fiction, but his writing is severely limited. Despite the predictive genius (and luck) evident in many details of his imagined first space voyage, the novel is fact-ridden and burdened by an undiscriminated mass of information. Verne is a master of the particular and a prescient futurist, and yet he lacks vision in the fullest sense of that term. Much of what appears in his Moon book has appeal only to a narrow range of readers; to pedants, to Civil War buffs, to adolescent boys, to astronauts (the American astronaut Frank Borman is a documented fan), and to devotees of the Guinness Book of Records and other artless compilations of statistics.

Verne's important chronological place in the history of science fiction need not be translated into a high evaluation of his achievement as a science fiction writer. As a significant experiment in early science fiction, *From the Earth to the Moon* merits neither condescension nor reverence. It is a work of major historical importance and of small literary stature.

Robert Crossley

Sources for Further Study

Criticism:

Downs, Robert Bingham. "Voyage Extraordinare," in *Molders of the Modern Mind*. New York: Barnes & Noble, 1961, pp. 295-297. Downs examines, briefly, the proposition upon which the novel is based.

La Fleur, Laurence. "Marvelous Voyages-III: Jules Verne's *From the Earth to the Moon*." in *Popular Astronomy* L (April, 1942), pp. 196-198. La Fleur examines the trip itself from an astronomical point of view.

Schmidtchen, Paul W. "Father of Science Fiction," in *Hobbies*. LXXVI (December, 1971), pp. 135-136, 145. The changes wrought by Verne in the traditions of scientific literature are examined by Schmidtchen.

Waltz, George H. *Jules Verne: The Biography of an Imagination*. New York: Holt, 1943, pp. 109-111, 190-191, 201-202. Waltz views *From the Earth to the Moon* as representing a specific stage in Verne's intellectual development.

FURY

Author: Lawrence O'Donnell (Henry Kuttner, 1914-1958 and Catherine L. Moore, 1911-   )
First book publication: 1947
Type of work: Novel
Time: The twenty-seventh century
Locale: Venus

Humanity, decaying in the idyllic undersea Keeps of Venus, is forced out upon the ravening surface of the planet by the tormented Sam Reed to resume its interrupted journey to the stars

Principal characters:
> SAM REED, a child of Immortals who has been altered to seem normal
> THE HARKERS, a family of Immortals, to which Reed belongs by birth, who manipulate human affairs
> BEN CROWELL, the oldest Immortal who now is the Logician of the Temple of Truth
> ROBIN HALE, the last of the Free Companions, who wants to push humanity out on the surface of Venus

Fury is a novel about the human species; in some ways all science fiction is a future history of the species rather than a description of incidents involving individuals. *Fury* examines the problem of what happens when the human situation becomes so comfortable that humanity loses its restless ambition; in the novel, mankind is deteriorating inside the paradise it has fashioned for itself under impervium domes beneath the oceans of Venus. Eventually humanity will die.

The novel takes place more than seven hundred years in the future. Six hundred years earlier, an atomic holocaust turned Earth into a star (an ironic monument labels it "Man's Greatest Achievement"), and the undersea Keeps on Venus contain all humanity that is left. The surface of Venus is unbelievably deadly, with murderous flora and fauna. The Kuttners had previously dealt with the same situation as that presented in *Fury*, in a novelette entitled "Clash by Night" (*Astounding Science Fiction*, March, 1943), which took place four hundred years earlier, when companies of Free Companions were still fighting on the surface of Venus. But that way of life was doomed by the greater comfort and opportunities inside the domes.

In *Fury* the Immortals rule the Keeps. Tall, slim, aristocratic, they are mutations who outlive normal humans by centuries. As the authors point out, the Immortals can adopt a different viewpoint toward problems: they can take the long view. To two such Immortals is born a child. The mother, however, dies in childbirth, and the father, insane with grief, has the child operated upon. Endocrinological tampering turns him into someone who will become fleshy, thick, and bald — the complete antithesis of an Immortal.

That child is Sam Reed, and he grows up angry and driven. As a street urchin he comes under the tutelage of a master criminal and learns his lessons well. He lives savagely, operates ruthlessly; he uses others before they can use him. His greatest anger is directed at the brevity of his life compared to that of the Immortals. His desires cannot be satisfied in the span of a few decades.

His schemes bring him into contact with his own Harker family of Immortals, and he has an affair with a woman who may be his great-great-grandmother. He meets Ben Crowell, a one-thousand-year-old Immortal who remembers Earth and can predict the future; Crowell has become the Logician of the Temple of Truth. Sam also meets Robin Hale, an Immortal who is the last surviving Free Companion; Hale's ambition is to persuade humanity to go landside.

Using Hale, Sam sets up a stock swindle based on the dream of conquering the surface of Venus, but in Sam's moment of triumph his mistress, bribed by the Harkers, poisons him with dreamdust. Instead of killing him, it makes him ill; he sleeps for forty years before he is nursed back to health. He has not aged; he realizes that he, too, is an Immortal.

With his new perspective, Sam schemes to force people out of the Keeps onto the surface of Venus, deadly as it is. In the end he provokes a simulated rebellion that turns the impervium domes of the Keeps radioactive.

Until 1942 the Kuttners, separately and collectively, were known primarily as writers of fantasy and romantic adventure. Then, with John Campbell's supply of regular authors diminished by World War II service or war-related jobs, the Kuttners began writing a number of science fiction stories for *Astounding Science Fiction*, under their own names and under the pseudonyms of Lewis Padgett and Lawrence O'Donnell (they used many more pseudonyms for other magazines), creating such memorable works as "The Twonky," the Gallegher series, "Mimsy Were the Borogoves," "When the Bough Breaks," "No Woman Born," *The Fairy Chessmen*, and "Vintage Season."

After their marriage in 1940, most of the Kuttners' writing was a collaboration to some degree. In an introduction to a paperback edition of *Fury*, Moore wrote:

> After we'd established through long discussion the basic ideas, the background and the characters, whichever of us felt like it sat down and started. When that one ran down, the other, being fresh to the story, could usually see what ought to come next, and took over. . . .

O'Donnell was the name that gradually became the pseudonym used for stories that were primarily Moore's, such as "Vintage Season," but eighty percent of *Fury* was Kuttner's, Moore has estimated.

The Kuttners brought a new fullness to science fiction: a greater concern for character, insights into the implications of the ideas they incorporated into their stories, and literary touches such as epigraphs, prologues, and epilogues that were more than mere expository conveniences, quotations, and mythological references. In the prologue to *Fury*, for instance, the word "fury" is applied to the ravening flora and fauna of landside; later the word describes Sam Reed.

At the end of the novel, after all Sam's efforts have been successful in forcing humanity to do what is good for it, he is defeated by treachery. Wounded, he is spirited away by Ben Crowell and drugged; he will stay in suspended animation until he and his "fury" may be needed by humanity again. But Crowell hopes that Sam dies in his sleep, that he is never needed — because if he is, it will mean that things have gone bad again. The epilogue contains only two words, "Sam woke. . . ."

The Kuttners went on to write numerous other excellent short stories and novellas such as Kuttner's "Private Eye" and "Two-Handed Engine" before his death in 1958, but *Fury* was their only completely satisfying novel. They wrote novellas such as *The Fairy Chessmen* and *Tomorrow and Tomorrow*, and Moore wrote an antityranny novel entitled *Doomsday Morning*. They wrote romantic adventure novels, nine works totaling three hundred thousand words, that were published between 1947 and 1952 in *Startling Stories* and *Thrilling Wonder Stories*, such as "Mask of *Circe*." They wrote seven mystery novels, two for Duell, Sloan & Pearce in 1946, one for Harper in 1951, and four for Pocket Books between 1956 and 1958. But in science fiction they were primarily writers of short stories and novellas, and in what they did were the most complete artists of their generation as well as the generation that came after them. That is why *Fury* is such a surprise and such a delight, filled as it is with fascinating characters, strong dramatic drive, scenes of great richness and detail, and ideas of continuing force and application. The Kuttners retained the strengths of the pulp ghetto while pointing the direction in which science fiction had to go to regain the strengths of the mainstream.

James Gunn

GATEWAY

Author: Frederik Pohl (1919-   )
First book publication: 1977
Type of work: Novel
Time: c. 2100
Locale: New York City, the asteroid Gateway, and points beyond

A satirical parable of human progress, told through the attempt of a former space prospector to understand what brought him to the psychiatrist's couch

Principal characters:
> ROBINETTE BROADHEAD, an antihero whose blundering discoveries
> made him a multimillionaire
> GELLE-CLARA MOYNLIN, his lost lover
> DANE METCHNIKOFF, a rival prospector
> SHIKITEI BAKIN, a legless former prospector
> SIGFRID THE SHRINK, a cybernetic Freudian analyst

Following *Man Plus* and the novellas of the 1970's, *Gateway* marked the definite emergence of Frederik Pohl as a mature writer of "adult" science fiction. By taking us inside an antihero, whose exploits — largely a matter of luck — have made him both rich and neurotic, Pohl has converted the escapist adventure yarn into an exposé of the premises on which such adventure stories are based. Robinette Broadhead is a fallible human being, whose discomforts we share, and whose bewilderment reflects that of both his society and ours.

The story unfolds on two levels, as Robinette tells us in alternating chapters of his weekly confrontations in the novel's present with a "mechanical" psychiatrist, and the events of his past that have finally brought him to the couch. Interpolations such as lectures, mission reports, want ads, and transcripts of the analyst's tape add a bit of density without unduly interrupting the flow of the narrative. Though this structure is effective in building tension and suspense, it raises questions about motivation that are not answered in the text. Given Robinette's mental blocks while he is undergoing analysis, his Gateway experiences as he recalls them then can hardly be taken at face value; within the fictional world, they make sense only as later, more balanced recollections, arranged for us, as it happens, in alternating sections in order occasionally to counterpoint adventure and commentary.

In the earlier narrative, Robinette won in a lottery the price of a ticket to Gateway, the asteroid converted to a space station half a million years ago by the alien race called the Heechee. Much of the story involves description of the Gateway environment: the faster-than-light ships, shaped like mushrooms, whose mechanisms are not understood; and human attempts to adapt to them in an effort to exploit the remains of Heechee technology, both here and in distant star systems. Robinette's role is ostensibly that of a prospector, but it is one that he assiduously avoids, and survives only by a combination of sheer luck and what may be the rankest kind of treachery.

Robinette emphasizes his social and love life on Gateway itself. He performs menial tasks under the supervision of the Japanese paraplegic, Shicky. He also seals himself into a neurotic love affair with Klara, a woman two years older, somewhat masculine in appearance, who was one of his instructors when he first arrived. He also goes out on missions, three of them widely spaced in time, and each more profitable and more emotionally disturbing than the one before.

The first, with Klara and a trio of homosexual male prospectors, is nerve-wracking and relatively fruitless; one crew member goes mad and finally kills himself after they return. The second trip takes Robinette alone, estranged from Klara, to Gateway II, another station several light years away, but by a route not usually followed. Because it results in knowledge about the guidance mechanisms of the ships, his fine for putting his ship completely out of condition is balanced against his prospective royalties for the new method of navigation.

Only Robinette survives the third journey, undertaken in two five-man ships to the outer extremities of a black hole. Susie, his temporary girl friend; Klara, with whom he has been reconciled; Dane Metchnikoff, a bisexual prospector for whom he has strongly mixed feelings; and six others are left in orbit, condemned by his action. They had joined the two ships together, hoping to blast free from the black hole's gravity by kicking the empty one closer in; but Robinette in the second ship pressed the release button at the wrong time.

Sixteen years later on Earth, now forty-five, Robinette is long past the fleeting acclaim for his survival and the scientific findings it made possible. His material dreams have come true, with a home in New York City ("under the Big Bubble"), another in the country (by the newly engineered "Tappan Sea"), a virtually unlimited supply of girls, and practically anything else he wants. Most important, when medical miracles are commonplace but enormously expensive, he has "Full Medical" insurance for anything needed to prolong his life and make it more comfortable. He has already made use of the coverage more than once to replace parts of his digestive system damaged by ulcers. This is one reason he is on the psychiatrist's couch.

Another reason seems to be that he feels in control of Freudian therapy in weekly doses, administered by a machine that he derisively calls "Sigfrid the Shrink." A facile grasp of Freudian concepts and terminology often enables Robinette to avoid confronting his feelings; otherwise, he frequently exhibits classical symptoms of resistance, changing the subject or arguing over minor issues. Thanks to a girl friend, an expert in Artificial Intelligence, he also has a verbal command that makes Sigfrid subject to his will whenever the analyst gets too close to the source of his pain. Control over Sigfrid, however, is not really what he wants; the voyeuristic impulse, satisfied by observing information in the analyst's memory banks, leads eventually to boredom, because it is purposeless. Despite himself, Broadhead does have a reason to make these weekly visits. He wants to get well, and in orthodox Freudian treatment this involves facing the memories whose repression — not their existence — is causing the trouble.

Sigfrid's questions probe his childhood, of course, and his sex life, along with his attitudes toward people and things both past and present, not only in his waking life, but also in his dreams. The pattern that emerges is tawdry, if natural; Robinette wallows in guilt for presumed connections between loving and hurting, perhaps loving and killing his mother and his friends. Digestive and sexual images and metaphors tie these feelings to his physical discomfort and exaggerated doubts about his masculinity. He dreams of trains and tunnels, visualizes confession as sewage, tries to excrete his feelings, gags at certain turns of phrase, and associates sex and close relationships with pain.

Betraying his insecurity by adopting a macho stance and a promiscuous sex life, he longs for a more lasting relationship that circumstances and his reactions to them have never permitted. His father had died when he was nine; his mother had also died young. Since young Robinette was going through a psychotic episode when his mother was sick and they could afford medical care for only one, he blames himself for her death. He had refused to start a family with his first love, Sylvia, because of the intolerable living and working conditions in Wyoming and its "food mines." This separation too was marked with trauma; Robinette had beaten her, narrowly averting using a knife. Winning the lottery, he deferred gratification still further by using the sizeable prize money to get to Gateway, where tender relationships between prospectors were tempered by the knowledge that either partner might soon be dead.

In the closed society of Gateway, moreover, Robinette had repeated past shortlived relationships, as his dreams indicate by conflating the images of Sylvia and his mother, and perhaps a faint echo of his father, with those of other friends and lovers. Sheri, whom he met *en route* to the asteroid, only represented a brief fling; lacking his ambivalence, she undertook the first missions available (and survived the second one with big winnings). Sharing their cowardice, and both love and hate, Robinette and Klara became as close as "twins," but neither could face up to their long-term desires. Triggered by Robinette's one night stand, comforting the distraught and motherly Louise Forehand, the affair erupted in violence, reminiscent of the flareup with Sylvia. In Klara's absence, he took up with Susie, unaware at the time of her resemblance to his youthful memories of his mother.

Robinette's sexual insecurity surfaces in his memories of Klara, whose masculine characteristics are symbolized by her bushy eyebrows that reproach him in dreams, even when he cannot remember whose they are. He was even more challenged by the bisexual poet, Dane Metchnikoff. Though Robinette avoided homosexual activity, he fantasized about Dane, later connecting his fantasies with the memory, possibly distorted, that his mother only showed him affection when taking his temperature rectally. Robinette partially resolves this ambivalence by the imaginative reconstruction of Dane's having "stolen" Klara away from him.

What makes these relationships disturbing to Robinette is the fact that Klara *was* stolen away from him, by the black hole, along with Dane, Susie, and their other "partners," whose shares in the reward became his. He is haunted by the fear that he had deliberately rid himself of them, as if to punish them for having loved or been loved by him, and having exposed and symbolized his psychological problems. The situation is not eased by the knowledge that no one could have predicted who would return alive, and it is paradoxically aggravated by the fact that the others have in fact not yet died. The time dilation factor involved with the massive gravity well of the black hole means that only a few minutes have passed for them during his last sixteen years. Unable to write the experience off as past, unable to do anything to rescue them in the present, living off what are probably ill-gotten gains, he has tried to block off the memories, without success, since they disturb his dreams, his sex life, and his digestive organs.

Whether living with the conscious memory of what therapy has caused him to divulge will result in better mental health is uncertain. His present-tense narrative several times shows his awareness of the black hole experience, which does not seem to have been repressed in the traditional manner, though the past-tense narrative may be an indication of his cure. The problem is not only that his "victims" are still living, but also that the entire Gateway experience is a constant reminder that the world in which Robinette lives is itself on the brink of collapse.

Given a human population of twenty-five billion, Earth's ecological and socio-economic problems are magnified many times over today's. Robinette's childhood suggests the desperate straits that have driven mankind to ruin not only the countryside but also the lives of the miners in their desperate search for petroleum. His later life "under the Bubble" with Full Medical illustrates how much greater than today's are the inequities separating the rich from the poor. Unwilling or unable to practice collective restraint, Earth's billions have risked everything on the chance that Gateway's prospectors will make possible further growth thus assuring the survival of civilization.

For all that it appeals to a free-enterprise model of human development, with no concessions to the welfare state, Gateway is actually an example of state capitalism. The prospectors are required to make a considerable investment to get to the asteroid in the first place, and they become limited "partners" in any mission they undertake. Exploitation of their discoveries, however, is in the hands of Gateway Enterprises Inc., the "Corporation," controlled by the five space-going governments (America, Russia, China, Brazil, and Venus). As pawns of the state, the prospectors are richly rewarded for success and charged high prices for room, board and amenities when they refuse to go out. They are given minimal survival training and advice on how to recognize a valuable find, but as far as the actual missions are concerned it is every man for himself.

The whole Gateway experience is rather like a cosmic shell game. What little a prospector can learn about his prospects stems from analyzing the pattern of lights on the instrument panels, indicating the destination for which the ship was programed. But nobody knows what those destinations are now, until someone returns with sufficient astronomical evidence; besides, since the Heechee programed the ships half a million years ago, the Galaxy has undergone some changes, so that destinations once safe may now be extremely hazardous. Moreover, although the ships themselves seem to be indestructible, some are known to have run out of fuel, and other mishaps are always possible. The upshot is that nobody knows the answers to fundamental questions about the Heechees and their machines. Lacking knowledge, the prospectors resort to superstition, gambler's hunches that do not noticeably change the odds. Three in twenty do not come back at all, while one in twenty strikes it rich.

Success is measured in knowledge of science and Heechee technology or Heechee artifacts, provided the discoveries have potential for exploitation. Habitable planets are no prize, since the only ships capable of reaching them can carry no more than five people. But man has even given up exploiting his own solar system with his science and technology. Since Heechee technology is so far superior, man scavenges deep space, channeling energy into trying to find out what makes Heechee devices work. Meanwhile, fuel supplies get lower, the number of ships in working order decreases, and the odds lengthen against a find that could fundamentally alter things.

Still the prospectors gamble. They gamble their money in the Gateway casino; they gamble their lives in the ships; they gamble to get to Gateway in the first place. Robinette won a lottery; the close-knit but ill-fated Forehand family got there by gambling their bodies. (Louise sold hers sexually, her son sold his surgically, bit by bit.) The prospectors' philosophy that life is a gamble seems to reflect that of Earth society as well. Using Heechee resources as well as their own, the nations of Earth (and Venus) gamble on Gateway to assure their future. Each mission may be likened to a scientific (or a science fiction) probe, but the resemblance is not a comforting one. Defying Einstein's ban on faster-than-light travel, the Heechee ships also illustrate metaphorically the denial of one of his favorite sayings: "God does not play dice with the Universe."

The view of human nature and of human endeavor advanced in this novel is not a favorable one. It may be read in fact as a counterargument to the traditional science fiction adventure of the swashbuckling hero, whose opening up the Universe for man's continued growth is inevitable. Certainly Robinette Broadhead is an unlikely hero. He is at best an ordinary person, caught up in desperate adventures for which he is not suited; an acknowledged coward and woman-beater, he may even be a deserter and a murderer. But he is certainly real, not a cardboard cutout of a superhero. Given his problems, his only hope seems to be to accept Sigfrid's advice at the end, to let himself feel; as the analyst points out, guilt, fear, pain, and envy are useful tools for modifying behavior, without which one is only half alive.

Sigfrid's analysis may be all right as far as it goes, based as it is on a "mechanical" reading of human behavior, anchored in the sex organs and the digestive tract. Outmoded in 1977, however, Freudian analysis would seem to have even less place in 2100, except that it makes a convenient system of image and metaphor, and may still have some shock value for relatively conservative and unsophisticated readers of science fiction. It does become accurate, moreover, insofar as Robinette accepts the analysis, incorporating it into his thinking and feeling, and refusing to aspire to be more than that for which he feels shame or guilt.

On the larger scale, the novel's portrait of Gateway prospectors, the Corporation, and human civilization is no more flattering. Dealing with greedy, superstitious misfits, the Corporation is timid, bureaucratic, and profit oriented. Human society is frozen in place, unwilling or unable to restrict its consumption of natural resources, or to find its own way out of the Malthusian trap. Backing the Gateway "longshot," humanity submits to mechanical procedures just as Robinette does, suggesting that there is no way out, that we should all take Sigfrid's advice to adjust to reality. But the world of *Gateway* is not reality; faster-than-light travel is rather unlikely, especially when the "trips" are in ships shaped like (hallucenogenic?) "mushrooms." As a cautionary tale, the novel warns us not to put all our faith in one proffered solution, be it the way of the he-man, the way of the scientist, or the way of the entrepreneur. The satire is not as broad as in *The Space Merchants* and Pohl's stories of the 1950's, but an ironic intention seems obvious. Sigfrid's advice is not simply to adjust to the social *status quo*; it also urges Robinette to know himself and to *feel*, the good emotions as well as the bad. Only then will he modify his behavior, or we ours. *Gateway* is not an "adult" book simply because it uses sex and strong language; it also reflects a mature reflection on society and on science fiction.

David N. Samuelson

Sources for Further Study

Reviews:

Analog. XCVII, February, 1977, p. 167.

Books West. I, June, 1977, p. 17.

Kirkus Reviews. XLV, January 15, 1977, p. 64.

Library Journal. CII, March 1, 1977, p. 635.

New York Times Book Review. March 27, 1977, p. 43.

Publisher's Weekly. CXI, January 31, 1977, p. 65.

School Library Journal. XXIV, September, 1977, p. 153.

DIE GELEHRTENREPUBLIK
(The Republic of the Savants)

Author: Arno Schmidt (1914-   )
First book publication: 1957
Type of work: Novel
Time: 2008
Locale: The "hominids strip" in the United States, and IRAS, the International Repub-
lic for Artists and Scientists, an island-ship

*The journey through a postatomic area populated by centaurs and other mutations
to an international community of the most brilliant minds of mankind, providing an
ironic commentary on the human condition*

> *Principal characters:*
> CHARLES HENRY WINER, a visiting journalist, great-great nephew of
> Arno Schmidt
> THALJA, a female centaur

When *Die Gelehrtenrepublik* first appeared in 1957, it was voted the best
book of the month by a German literary jury. This distinction further enhanced
the reputation of the book's author, Arno Schmidt, who is one of the most
eccentric, mysterious, and controversial writers in contemporary German letters. A recluse, he is thought to be as important as James Joyce by some
(including himself), and a charlatan by others. His unconventional views on
literature have infuriated many scholars.

Totally immersed in his work, Schmidt lives and writes in isolation in a
small house in the Bargfelder Heide, surrounded by his famous filing cabinets,
which contain his notes on everything that he finds of possible future interest.
His literary work is highly individual, even esoteric, and very much influenced
by the linguistic methods of James Joyce; this is especially true of his more
recent works, enormous books that are reproduced from his typescripts, rather
than by normal printing methods. Like Joyce, Schmidt delights in wordplay
and puns; he combines word roots from different languages, often quotes foreign terms, coins his own words, spells the German language phonetically,
and resorts to onomatopoeia. His major works, which often contain Utopian
and science fiction elements (without fitting any useful definition of science
fiction), are labyrinthine riddles, artifacts of a beelike industry, and inexhaustible fields for future scholarship and exegesis. A journal called the *Bargfelder Bote*, edited in cooperation with the Syndicate for the Decoding of Arno
Schmidt, has already produced hundreds of pages of scholarship which barely
begin to scratch the surface of the phenomenon that is Arno Schmidt. There
are already signs that Schmidt is gaining an esoteric cult following. In this
mass of learned scholarship and allusions to remote literary sources, assiduously compiled and arranged, it sometimes becomes difficult to see the man
himself, and many readers are uncertain about his true status as a writer.

Die Gelehrtenrepublik, however, is a short and simple tale compared with such inscrutable, forbidding books as his huge *Zettels Traum* or *Die Schule der Atheisten*, in which it is difficult to determine the main plot among the mass of corrections, insertions, deletions, and commentary. Although *Die Gelehrten-republik* has traces of discernible plot and action, they are rather slight and of little importance. The book relates the story of a journalist's journey in the year 2008 through the hominids zone of the United States, to the floating island IRAS. The hominids zone, a strip of land several thousand miles long, is bordered right and left by a concrete wall, reinforced with aluminum rods, eight yards high, one yard thick at the base, and three yards thick at the top, so that it can be used in emergencies as a pathway for roller skaters. Every fifty miles there is a military outpost.

The strip is populated by carefree centaurs, an intelligent species who are close to nature, innocent, and free from the bureaucracy under which mankind suffers. Winer's visa to IRAS had to be approved by no less than eight of the world powers, and documents needed to pass through the American corridor include more than merely a passport. He also needs his thumbprint, teeth imprints, and the measurements of his penis. The latter proves important for Winer, since he is a lusty fellow who is more interested in what the females have to offer than in the achievements of mankind. He soon has a spontaneous and indeed quite frantic adventure with Thalja, a highly sensual girl centaur.

However, the corridor also harbors less pleasant beings. Increased radioactivity in the wake of an atomic war has resulted in prevalent hexapodism, a dominance of six-limbed creatures. One of these forms is the Never-nevers, giant spiders with human faces and insect eyes. Another type of creature has no eyes, but is equipped with a suction trunk and frontal limbs with poisonous claws. This creature also spins nets that are like wire. These beings are hunted down by the centaurs and often killed in great numbers. First they are nailed to the ground by means of special spikes designed for a spider hunting and then these ugly beasts with "repulsive European faces" are clubbed to death. Another type of mutant is mentioned in passing: flying human faces with butterfly bodies, only rumored to exist. It is said that they secretly drink the milk from women's breasts and suck boys' semen at night. The females of this species have sucking tubes as long as a hand in their tongues, while the males have penises that they are rumored to use lustfully with girl centaurs. Much of this description is very bizarre and grotesque, the result of a playful imagination and intended to ridicule the rigid values of other works of science fiction rather than contribute artistically to the work. However, these touches also have more sinister implications.

Racial problems have been carried into the future, with a population of several thousand white and several hundred black centaurs. Miscegenation is also a problem: human males and female centaurs cannot reproduce, but human females and male centaurs can produce offspring. Very rich women have frequently been smuggled into the zone for purposes of copulation with centaurs, their large organs being quite an attraction even though intercourse with centaurs is not considered respectable.

The exotic journey is but a prelude to the Utopian island itself, which is not the paradise of creativity it is supposed to be, but rather a veritable modern hell. In the first place, this island-ship is divided into a Communist and a "free" side, each with its own installations, machines, and ship's propellers. If opinions differ about the course of the ship, the two sides may steer their parts in opposite directions, causing the ship to turn in circles and go nowhere, exactly as the community intellectually goes nowhere.

Schmidt has taken Jules Verne's idea of the divided ship from *L'Ile à helice* (*The Propeller Island*) and brilliantly used it as a model for the divided world of today. Schmidt admires Verne and has written about him. He shares Verne's interest in cartography, his love for hard scientific facts, an infatuation with numbers and measurements, and his literary pretensions to scientific exactness. The ship is exactly three miles long, and measures 1.7 miles from port to starboard. The whole island consists of about 123,000 identical chambers of steel, each sixteen meters high, with a base ten meters square. The whole island was built in 1980 and is intended to last until 2030, when a new one will be built. The construction was financed by the defense budgets of the participating nations. The ship is covered with humus, which was transported to the building site at great expense. It usually sails only in calm waters, such as the Sargasso Sea, and enters only a few preselected harbors, such as Cape Town, Valparaiso, and Eureka, to take on fresh provisions and collect new works of art, which are preserved on board for posterity. More than five thousand people live on the island-ship; only 811 are genuine artists and scientists; the great mass consists of bureaucrats and helpers, technical personnel, cleaning women, and others that perform various services. Indian, Chinese, American English, Russian, Arabic, and Spanish are the official languages. German, however, is a dead language (central Europe was destroyed in the war). The novel purports to be a translation from Winer's American English into German (with the "translator" frequently commenting about the arrogance and anti-German sentiments of the narrator).

The resident geniuses are selected by a neutral jury, which proves to be a problem. Initially governments had the right to nominate, but they selected either artists in favor to reward them, or dissidents to get rid of them. One government rid itself of all dissident writers, even those of no distinction, at one stroke. Visitors, too, are carefully selected; certain groups of people (those that Schmidt has a marked dislike for) are never admitted to the island: politicians, reviewers, professional soldiers, film stars, publishers, ordained priests of all confessions.

The money to support IRAS comes from its printing businesses, certain monopolies (radio talk shows with prominent people), and stamps. The island is well supplied with theaters, libraries (though few of the celebrated poets go there to study what others have written), offices, and bureaucratic installations (to keep statistics, for instance). Between the two halves of the ship there is a neutral zone, and the two inimical sides spend much of their time spying on each other. The "free" side is more materially interested, while the Communist side is more dedicated to work; they insist that the geniuses actually work for their keep according to plan, and they create collectively; for example, each man contributing to a novel what he does best: one the characters, another the descriptions of landscape, the third philosophical thought, and so on. The narrator is justifiably skeptical about all this. The Communists have also perfected the art of transplantation. Thus, they are able to transplant brains, for example, to enable a male writer to inhabit a female body and obtain firsthand experience of what it means to be a woman.

Schmidt's hero, the visitor to this world, has strong autobiographical elements; he pokes fun at the things that the author dislikes himself, especially religion, militarism, and the political order of Germany; but he also comments on literary questions of interest to Schmidt. Schmidt's partisanship for Joyce comes through again in the hero's remark that Joyce would deserve a whole squadron of the statues honoring the great minds on the island, and he also speaks up for Alfred Döblin. The title of the novel itself is a bow in the direction of Klopstock's *Deutscher Gelehrtenrepublik*.

Schmidt's style is parenthetical: there are no epic descriptions, there is no natural flow of narrative. Everything is broken up, divided by countless punctuation marks, observations, comments, and asides, all ironically stated from the point of view of an elitist looking down upon a banal, foolish world. By this means, and by allusion, association, and onomatopoeia, Schmidt achieves a dense, condensed prose that results in a mythic re-creation of a historical world, as seen by a skeptical mind *sub specie aeternitatis*. This prose concentrates on the essential and leaves out anything superfluous. It is often difficult and obscure, but frequently brilliantly amusing, baroque in style, yet precise in its observation and scientific in its conciseness. It is a rational construct that is wholly cerebral as it plays with the concerns and emotions of both the older Utopian literature and the philistine world. Schmidt is a champion of enlightenment and rationality against what he considers to be narrow-minded, trivial, and politically insane; and the insanity and banality of the future world of 2008 is only a comic exaggeration of the imperfections and failings of the present. Schmidt's hero moves through and comments upon an absurd world that is an alienated image of our own world as it was at the height of the Cold War.

Franz Rottensteiner

THE GHOST OF GUY THYRLE

Author: Edgar Fawcett (1847-1904)
First book publication: 1895
Type of work: Novel
Time: The late nineteenth century
Locale: Mainly London and the Home Counties

An account of the adventure of a chemist who discovers a way to liberate the spirit from the body, and who embarks upon a voyage across the cosmos when his body is destroyed

Principal characters:
RAYMOND SAVERNAY, a student
CECIL SAVERNAY, his brother
GUY THYRLE, a brilliant chemist
VIOLET FYTHIAN, his fiancée
VINCENT ARDILANGE, a social parasite

Edgar Fawcett was a prolific writer who published some forty novels between 1871 and 1903, most of which belong to the tradition of American realist fiction that included the work of Frank Norris and Harold Frederic. Like another member of that school, William Dean Howells, Fawcett also wrote a certain amount of imaginative fiction, including the "identity exchange" story *Douglas Duane* (1888); a novel featuring a dog with artificially augmented intelligence, *Solarion* (1889); a psychological puzzle-story, *The New Nero* (1893); and *The Ghost of Guy Thyrle*. In order to justify these departures from the realist tradition, he added to the last-named an "epistolatory proem" which might well stand as a manifesto for modern speculative fiction.

The proem begins with a denial that the story — or any other of the earlier stories in the same vein — is a "ghost story pure and simple," insisting on its freedom from any taint of superstition. Fawcett explains that he is "a poor pioneer . . . trying to write the modern wonder-tale." He claims that traditional tales of wonder, relying upon a vocabulary of symbols drawn from myth and legend, have largely lost their potency, and that the hunger of readers for the marvelous must be satisfied in a new way. "To make our romances acceptable with the world of modern readers," he writes, "we must clothe them in rationalistic raiment. So clothed . . . I should name them 'realistic romances' — stories where the astonishing and peculiar are blent with the possible and accountable. They may be as wonderful as you will, but they must not touch on the mere flimsiness of miracle. They can be excessively improbable; but their improbability must be based upon scientific fact, and not upon fantastic, emotional, and purely imaginative groundwork."

The Ghost of Guy Thyrle is a conscientious attempt to practice what is here preached. The main story told by the novel is enclosed by a frame narrative concerning a rather nervous student named Raymond Severnay, who has come down from Oxford to stay with his married brother Cecil during the summer.

While at Oxford he has become fascinated by the work of the Society for Psychical Research and by the possibility of finding rational explanatory accounts for "psychic phenomena." In pursuit of this interest he visits a house owned by Cecil, which is reputed to be haunted by the ghost of one Guy Thyrle. He returns from the house with an astonishing story which sends Cecil running for a doctor.

The enclosed narrative tells the life story of Guy Thyrle, who begins life as a lonely and introverted child, and later goes to Cambridge, where he proves to be brilliant in his studies (particularly in the laboratory); but he makes only one friend, Vincent Ardilange. Ardilange, unsuspected by Thyrle, is no true friend, but a consummate hypocrite who attaches himself to Thyrle because the latter's income will be adequate to set them both up in a house in London in moderate comfort. There, while Thyrle pursues his studies in his own laboratory, Ardilange launches himself forth into society, living a life of indolent ease.

Thyrle's research bears fruit with the isolation of a drug which he names Onarline. He expects its effects to be psychotropic (perhaps hallucinogenic), but instead finds to his amazement that it will free the spirit from the body, allowing consciousness to roam where it will while the body lies inert, as if dead. He decides to set his work aside until he can assess the implications of this discovery, and begins to accompany Ardilange on his social excursions. Ardilange resents this encumbrance, and his resentment grows when Thyrle proves to be popular. When Thyrle falls in love with Violet Fythian and captures her affections, Ardilange becomes bitterly jealous of him.

Eventually, Thyrle tests his drug. He locks himself in a hotel room and leaves his body behind, surveying the secrets of London society. No door can bar him since he is quite invisible, and he soon discovers that by an effort of will he can read the "psychic spectra" of those he sees, obtaining insight into their moral character. His researches are cut short, however, when a sense of danger recalls him to his body, which has been discovered by an inquisitive maid. He is thought dead, but by repossessing his corpse he averts further trouble. When he sets forth on his second major expedition he takes Ardilange into his confidence, and commissions him to stand guard over his corporeal form. This is an unfortunate decision, for Ardilange is named the benefactor in his will until the time of his marriage to Violet, and is already secretly his enemy.

Thyrle widens the scope of his researches to examine the state of human civilization. He visits the secret councils of the great emperors and the squalid homes of their subjects. He sees tragedy and death on a monstrous scale, but finds hope for the future in the developing tendencies of altruism and charity, which he hopes will be the salvation of the human species. He visits the bowels of the Earth, tracking the fossil record within the rocks which tells the story of the evolution of life and of man. He visits the ocean depths, and then launches forth into space. He finds the moon to be a long-dead world that was once Earthlike, and he explores the ruins of its extinct civilization. At this point, a sense of disaster again recalls him to his body, but this time it is too late. Ardilange has had him declared dead, and his body has been cremated. His spirit is homeless.

Though free from the body, his spirit has no access to the world inhabited by the spirits of the dead; it is tied to the material world, quite alone, its predicament unique and unprecedented. Driven by a desperate need to escape from this lonely fate, Thyrle sets off on a journey through the cosmos in search of God. God is inaccessible, but his search shows him the infinite reaches of the universe, and the worlds of a million stars.

This cosmic voyage is the high point of the novel, and represents a considerable imaginative achievement. It is the first of its kind, previous excursions beyond the solar system having been undertaken only within the context of the religious imagination. Fawcett seems to have been familiar with Emmanuel Swedenborg's visionary journey to the star-worlds, for he takes care in his descriptions of life on other worlds to stress that the universe is *not* made exclusively for man, that many worlds are inhabited, and that where life exists evolution has frequently brought to intelligence and dominance species which are not in the least manlike. The only previously published work which equals this section of Fawcett's novel in imaginative scope is Flammarion's *Lumen*, and as a voyage to the farther reaches of space it forms an interesting complement to the voyage into the farther reaches of time featured in H. G. Wells's *The Time Machine*, which was published in book form in the same year.

Having already provided a manifesto for science fiction, *The Ghost of Guy Thyrle* here provides a preliminary account of the cosmic scenario which modern science fiction has used so extensively and so productively:

"Suns, moons, planets, asteroids, in numbers incalculable! Worlds that yet were floating coils and wreaths and ragged drifts of vapour; worlds that yet were prodigious heavenly bonfires, fed by showers of attracted meteors and even by occasional vast nomadic comets; worlds that teemed with a beauty eclipsing the conception of man; worlds hideous beyond all human belief; worlds just born, youthful, matured, dying, or dead; worlds of sin, degradation and debauchery; worlds of chastity, idealism, and peace; worlds in which not a single animal or vegetable shape bore the faintest likeness to those we meet on Earth; worlds in which trees thought and spoke and saw; worlds that were earth in miniature or a thousand-fold magnified; worlds in which wolves, serpents, tigers, birds, and countless other creatures of indescribable sort, had won mastery, and risen by inflexible laws of evolution to the same superiority over their primary conditions which marks the ascendancy of earthly man over his ancestral ape."

Though Thyrle's spirit cannot find God, he does eventually establish communication (on a rather enigmatic basis) with other beings of pure spirit. These send him back to Earth with the intelligence that he may cross the threshold into the realm of the spirits of the dead if he can find someone who will give up his own life voluntarily, in order to allow Thyrle to share his death. Back on Earth, he discovers that he can occasionally, by a considerable effort of the will combined with fortunate circumstances, manifest himself to others. Alas, such manifestations only cause extreme alarm. He appears to Violet Fythian as she is about to marry Ardilange, hoping to warn her of his bad character, and frightens her to death. By means of a second manifestation, he wins vengeance on Ardilange, prompting him to kill himself. There seems, however, to be no possibility of release from his strange imprisonment — until he manages to appear to Raymond Savernay.

This story, told to Cecil by his brother, is recounted secondhand to the doctor he consults for advice. The doctor is in no doubt that the whole thing is a symptom of madness, an awful hallucination (and Fawcett indicates in the proem that the reader is at liberty to accept this interpretation, rather than think the story unrealistic). Cecil and the doctor return to attend Raymond, but they arrive too late — Raymond has already given up his life, and the last words spoken by his lips are framed by the consciousness of Guy Thyrle.

The claims made by Fawcett as to the rationality and realism of *The Ghost of Guy Thyrle* would probably have been regarded uneasily by Hugo Gernsback, though the early science fiction magazines featured numerous stories dealing with disembodied personalities. The ambition of the Society for Psychical Research to bring the phenomena of spiritualism under the aegis of systematic theory and rational explanation did not seem as reasonable in the 1920's as it had in the 1890's (though the ambition has survived into our own day). The story is, however, very much in tune with the concerns of contemporary science fiction, which has recovered an interest in questions of a more metaphysical complexion. *The Ghost of Guy Thyrle*, in the attitudes to the phenomenal universe that are manifest within it, clearly belongs to the literature of the scientific imagination, and represents a notable contribution to that literature. That it remains virtually unknown to contemporary students of the history of science fiction is not only surprising but extremely unfortunate. It is a highly original work, featuring the first voyage outside the solar system in American science fiction, and it should be given much more attention than it has so far received.

Brian Stableford

GILES GOAT-BOY
or,
The Revised New Syllabus

Author: John Barth (1928-   )
First book publication: 1966
Type of work: Novel
Time: Indefinite
Locale: The University

Raised as a goat, George Giles travels to West Campus of the University to further his education as a man, where, after burrowing through philosophy, politics, and sex, he transcends all artificial divisions of knowing and being and becomes the Grand Tutor, a whole man

Principal characters:
GEORGE GILES, the goat-boy
MAX SPIELMAN, a discredited scientist and his first tutor
ANASTASIA STOKER, with whom Giles consummates his manhood
MAURICE STOKER, her husband, head of a sort of FBI
HOWARD BRAY, a professor, man of masks and disguises
DR. EIERKOPF, a value-neutral scientist, all "head"
CROAKER, an apelike being, all "body," who carries Eierkopf about

Over the past decade or so, science fiction scholars have been working assiduously to provide intellectual pedigrees for their chosen field and, in doing so, have suggested a wide variety of models to put modern science fiction into proper perspective. Romances, fantastic journeys, satires, utopias, allegories, all have been put forward as part of a tradition culminating in the science fiction of this century. Arguments as to the value of this sort of provenance-hunting, and as to the relation of provenance to the creative act itself, have no place here; it is clear, however, that without the ongoing presence of this academic activity, *Giles Goat-Boy*, which is a complexly sustained allegory clearly indebted to the tradition of that difficult genre, could never have been thought of as comprehendable in terms of science fiction. Indeed, if *Giles Goat-Boy* is science fiction, then so is *The Faerie Queene* and *The Pilgrim's Progress*; and if it is science fiction, then it is supremely difficult science fiction.

The novel provides rewards arguably destructive of the nature of science fiction in general, as it is read and understood by those who love it. *Giles Goat-Boy* is not John Barth's masterpiece — *The Sot-Weed Factor* (1960; revised 1967) being probably his finest achievement to date — but it is certainly the *culmination* of his highly self-conscious, analytic, parodic, indefatigable art, at the heart of which is a deeply corrosive and learned concentration upon and exposure of the ways in which our languages, our forms of belief, and the fictive genres we use to "express" ourselves in novels, all serve to cage us.

The linguistic and perceptual frames by which we are able to understand

and live in the world are precisely the bars of the cage banning us *from* the world; each word we utter, every story we tell, is a nail in the bed of Procrustes that is our human habitation on this Earth, or so Barth, and many American novelists, from Melville on, seem to argue. This terror at the imprisoning of the individual solitary soul is a distinctly American terror, as are the solutions to it so frequently found in American literature, from Whitman's soul's oceanic embracing of multitudes to Twain's Huckleberry Finn lighting out for the Territory. These solutions all represent a kind of flight from the coercive framing laid on us by words, by fictions, and by society itself; they are all of them transcendent solutions to the traps of false perceptions, false life, and false soul. And the central burden of the story of George Giles the Goat-Boy is a search for transcendence. The appurtenances of the world he transcends necessarily include those fictive assumptions embodied in the worlds of science fiction. One of the difficulties faced by the science fiction reader attempting to come to terms with *Giles Goat-Boy*, therefore, lies in the fact that the generic assumptions he may bring to the book are exactly what the book is designed to dissolve.

After a series of fantastically elaborated exercises in auctorial framing — introductions, disavowals, readers' reports and so forth — the main action of the novel begins, in the shape of a first-person narrative of his life-experiences from childhood on by George Giles himself. In its exaggerations of the tricks and tropes of fictional autobiographies, the narrative parodies the classical *Bildungsroman*, or novel of education and growth. Giles's autobiography is presented, within the multiple frames that surround it, as an actual object of some sort, most likely a series of tapes transcribed into typescript, put into Barth's hands by Giles Stoker, George Giles's son, and has as its title the subtitle of Barth's novel: *The Revised New Syllabus*. As much of Giles's search for knowledge and transcendence is couched in deliberately exaggerated religious terms, and as his ultimate role as Grand Tutor is in a sense a religious one, *The Revised New Syllabus* is clearly a kind of *New Testament*, though composed by the Savior it describes. As his narrative comes to a close, Giles is nearing the age of Christ at his death, and its final moments vividly presage martyrdom for him.

As allegory and self-parody irradiate (and obfuscate) the telling of the story of George Giles, and as the very fact of telling a story is an aspect of the coercive framing of the world from which he (and John Barth) wishes to escape, a synopsis of *Giles Goat-Boy* is both a difficult task to accomplish and one which actually functions as a sort of treason to the text so "framed." The two main strands of allegory in the book constantly interpenetrate each other, and constantly evoke parodic analogies with our own world, the world we bring, as readers, to the text. The first allegorical element is the treatment of Giles himself as a goat-boy; his childhood as a goat stands as a statement about the fundamental animal nature of man, and his retention of goatishness stands as a claim that no man can be whole without a full physical recognition of this basic nature. The second allegorical element is more clear-cut. The world is the University; the Free World countries are West Campus and the United States is New Tammany College.

It is in an obscure pastoral corner of New Tammany College that Max Spielman, a Jewish scientist opposed to trends at the College and discredited by it, brings George Giles up as a goat-boy, until with the onset of puberty Giles begins to feel the need of a fuller education into manhood. Max agrees, and they travel to the Campus, where the central operating and defining principle of the University abides, as embodied in WESCAC, the enormous computer in the bowels of which Giles seems to have been born. WESCAC is the element most like science fiction in *Giles Goat-Boy*; it administers West Campus, decides who Passes or Fails, and acts as a constant active defining force within the University, determining reality and unreality, the permissible and the impermissible. WESCAC stands for the human capacity and need to master the inchoate world by making distinctions and command decisions based on logic; WESCAC is the great framer of reality, and the rest of the novel centers upon Giles's complex progress towards comprehending and transcending a world — and a self-definition of man — perceived by and through WESCAC.

This progress takes the form of a kind of dialectic, and as appropriate to dialectics, it is a progress in three parts. First, Giles abandons himself utterly to the WESCAC world of distinctions and framings and becomes a kind of Mediaeval Scholastic, so far does he go in the direction of making an articulate compartmentalizing verbal mosaic of the world. In this, he is rather like a young man at his first terrified entry into the real world, when he is tempted into overdefining reality, so as to relieve himself of its horrific indeterminacy. Next, however, Giles abandons himself to the opposite course; he abandons all distinctions and directed behavior. (The novel, which was published in 1966, understandably makes reference in this sequence of Giles's development to American hippiedom, references that may seem a little dated today.) Finally, coming to union with Anastasia Stoker, by whom he has been frustratingly aroused and intrigued for hundreds of pages, he comes to a transcendent enactment of the fusing of opposites, escaping the coercive framing of the world (of WESCAC) by a graphic act of sexual love which, though it passes beyond categories, does choose the world, because uniting with Anastasia is an admission, triumphantly couched, of his mortality. The sex takes place in the bowels of WESCAC itself, and when the computer asks the two lovers what sex they are, they press Male and Female buttons simultaneously, transcending categories, and at the same moment they achieve orgasm. After this, all is denouement. Giles has become a Grand Tutor, and begins to prepare for martyrdom; and the thick cluttered opacity of the world, as exemplified in the evasive quirky density of the book, begins to descend once again. What we are left with, all lights and jokes and scholarship and mockery, is *Giles Goat-Boy*.

In a way, Barth disclaims the real possibility of transcendence of this world, or at any rate of the possibility of actually reporting it. One of the many signals of this disclaimer, though perhaps the most pervasive, is his constant analogizing of Giles's nature (he has a crippled leg) and quest for self-knowledge with the story of Oedipus, or Taliped as he is called in this alternate University. These references and a long farcical version of *Oedipus Rex*, *Taliped Decanus* in the book, are consistently deflating and jokey and consistently deflate Giles's quest as a consequence. Perhaps Barth is saying that finally there is no way of reporting Oedipus, or George Giles; or perhaps he is saying their quests for transcendental self-knowledge are innately farcical. Because nothing exists in this novel that is not simultaneously a parody of itself, there is ultimately no way of being certain. Perhaps *that* is Barth's final message, perhaps not.

No reader of this novel will select an identical pattern of events and motives in summarizing for himself the meaning of this problematic fiction. Some will concentrate heavily on the oppositions between various emblematical characters: Max Spielman *versus* Dr. Eierkopf; George Giles *versus* Howard Bray, who is a kind of Anti-Christ figure, a manipulator of disguises and realities very similar to Burlingame, the entrancing reality-sharp of *The Sot-Weed Factor*. Some will concentrate upon the political satire afforded, on, for instance, the ways in which Maurice Stoker, head of a kind of FBI, a sort of hit-man for WESCAC and the human powers-that-be, could be claimed to resemble Robert F. Kennedy and his preelection-campaign-1968 role in government. The science fiction reader may attempt to understand WESCAC and its capacity to burn out the minds of miscreant "students" as a direct extrapolation in terms familiar to the genre. But all interpretations, all lines of investigation, will have to deal with the fundamental negatives Barth creates with very positive creation of plot, or character, or *mise en scene*; for ultimately, he says, every story is a lie, every decision a trap, every move a frame-up. The world of *Giles Goat-Boy*, and indeed the world itself, is ultimately a confidence game. But it's all we have, says Giles. Yes, says Barth, no.

John Clute

Sources for Further Study

Criticism:

Byrd, Scott. *"Giles Goat-Boy* Visited," in *Critique: Studies in Modern Fiction*. IX (1966), pp. 108-112. Byrd believes that the mythical allusions in the novel are so deep as to make it a "kind of anatomy of heroism."

Tanner, Tony. "The Hoax that Joke Bilked," in *Partisan Review*. XXXIV (Winter, 1967), pp. 102-109. An evaluation of the creative process employed by Barth and its effects on the overall merit of the novel.

Reviews:

Book Week. August 7, 1966, p. 1.

Commonweal. LXXXV, October 21, 1966, p. 80.

Magazine of Fantasy and Science Fiction. XXXII, March, 1967, pp. 20-27.

New York Review of Books. VII, August 18, 1966, p. 17.

New York Times Book Review. August 7, 1966, p. 60.

THE GIRL IN THE GOLDEN ATOM

Author: Ray Cummings (1887-1957)
First book publication: 1922
Type of work: Novel
Time: 1919-1923
Locale: A world in an atom of a golden wedding ring

Drugs that have the capability of shrinking man to the microscopic or expanding him to the macroscopic are used to take a party into a world inside an atom within a golden wedding ring

> *Principal characters:*
> THE CHEMIST, inventor of a drug which can shrink living things or make them grow
> THE VERY YOUNG MAN,
> THE BIG BUSINESS MAN, and
> THE DOCTOR, companions on the second trip into the atom
> THE BANKER, guardian of the gold wedding ring which contains the world of the atom
> LYLDA, the girl in the atom
> AURA, her younger sister
> TARGO, a power-hungry atom man who leads a revolution against government and giant invaders from above

The "scientific romance," is a colorful type of science fiction popularized by the Munsey magazines (*The Argosy*, *The All-Story*, and *The Cavalier*) of which the best-known examples in print today are the Mars series of Edgar Rice Burroughs. Such stories are characterized by adventure, colorful and exotic otherworldly backgrounds, and a primary love interest. They had particularly wide appeal in the World War I era.

The Girl in the Golden Atom remains one of the prime examples of the "scientific romance." It is made up of an original novelette titled *The Girl in the Golden Atom* (*All-Story Weekly*, March 15, 1919) and its sequel *The People of the Golden Atom* (*All-Story Weekly*, January 24, 1920, to February 28, 1920). *The Girl in the Golden Atom* is a second generation work in the genre, not simplistically exploiting a single theme but combining a number of previously successful themes to produce a work of science fiction that was not only new for its period but served as a transition to later, more modern types. In the novel, The Chemist looks through a marvelous microscope into a scratch in his mother's wedding ring, where he sees a beautiful girl in a cave on some minute world. There is little question that the fundamental idea for that opening derived from "The Diamond Lens" by Fitz-James O'Brian (*Atlantic Monthly*, January, 1858). In O'Brien's story, the inability of the hero to do anything about his Animula, the tiny girl he must slowly watch die as the drop of water in which she lives evaporates, shatters his life.

Ray Cummings' Chemist decides to do something about this situation. He works on and develops drugs that will shrink his body to the size of the girl in the ring. He calls together his friends, who are mere stereotypes without names: The Very Young Man, The Doctor, The Big Business Man, and The Banker. Before their eyes, he tests his drugs on flies, one growing very large and another so small it disappears from view. Telling his friends to guard the ring and to expect him back within forty-eight hours, The Chemist takes the drug, carrying his supplies in a harness (the drug also affects objects) and disappears into the ring. He returns two days later and tells his friends of his adventures.

On that infinitesimal world he finds the girl in the cave, Lylda, whose father is the leader of the country. It becomes necessary for The Chemist to take a drug which greatly enlarges him, and an invading army from an enemy country is defeated when he stamps most of them to death. Thus, the story develops in a manner reminiscent of Jonathan Swift's Gulliver, an admitted influence. After concluding his tale, The Chemist tells his friends that he is returning to the atom world to marry Lylda and probably live there, but he will pay a return visit in about five years. The ring in which the atom world exists is covered by a glass bell, from which the air is constantly exhausted and renewed, and placed by a doctor in a museum where two full-time guards watch over it.

The historical importance of this story is that it popularized the idea of actually *visiting* the world of the atom, just as though it were another planet or another dimension. It continues to deserve that credit and has bred a host of progeny by its own author and others. However, by the time the reader is into the body of the novel, we are made aware that the story is really centered around the ability to make one's self very large or very small at will and only incidentally about the business of exploring atoms.

The Chemist's friends gather on September 4, 1923, to open a letter he has left, to be opened only if he does not return. The letter contains the formula for the drug and gives two options for its use. The first, if World War I is still in progress, is to use it to end the war. The second is to use it on themselves to join him in the atom world.

The friends test the shrinking drugs on a sparrow and a lizard, and they both disappear into the ring. A test of the enlarging drug on a cockroach, results in a battle to kill it before it grows too large. The Doctor, The Very Young Man, and The Big Business Man decide to follow The Chemist into the atom. The Banker remains behind to guard the ring.

That part of the novel which was originally *The People of the Golden Atom* marks a transition from the lush, colorful style of the earlier story. Once his characters are on the atom world, Cummings does not launch into adventure but converts the story into legitimate Utopian fiction. The giant visitors arrive after there has been a groundswell of demand for land reform led by the power-hungry Targo. He has been tried for his illegal activities and is under sentence of death, but the arrival of more aliens with the power to grow into giants inflames the populace into revolutionary action. Lylda takes the drug and enlarges herself in an attempt to try and talk her people out of rebellion, but her size antagonizes them even more. Forced into a confrontation, she kills a brother of Targo.

From this point on, the novel becomes an exciting action story. The Very Young Man meets and falls in love with Aura, Lylda's sister. In their efforts to rescue Lotos, son of The Chemist and Lylda, they alternately take the reducing drug and crawl under cracks in doors, then take the expanding drug to make escapes and fight off the enemy. As the story progresses, the stereotypes of The Very Young Man, The Doctor and The Big Business Man begin to become more pointed.

There is philosophy as well as action in this story. When almost stymied by the ethical question of stomping to death thousands of the people of this world who are trying to prevent the aliens' escape, The Big Business Man resolves the matter most pragmatically by reminding them all with cold laughter, that all these millions here are invisible specs on one of trillions of worlds that no one knows even exists. It does not matter in the scheme of the universe whether they live, die, or are here at all. He is in effect saying, for all the effect they have on our lives in the world above, they are no more substantial than a dream. In so doing, he or Ray Cummings is drawing a chilling parallel to the status of man on this planet.

Throughout the work Cummings' science is painfully flawed and open to suspicion, though he tries to patch it up with an internal logic. Shrinking into the atom world is more like climbing down a tremendous range of mountains. Though the atom world is supposed to be in a microscopic universe, no one passes through empty space to reach it or ascend from it. No effort at all is made to explain how breathing is accomplished in transition, which takes considerable time. Pouches containing the chemicals and food supplies shrink with the novel's characters. No theory is given to make this logical, though twice it is noted that it happens. Since the story was written, the idea that atoms may be microscopic worlds has been discredited.

The distinction must be made between those who originate an idea and those who popularize it. Cummings was, in *The Girl in the Golden Atom*, the great force for popularization of the atomic world theme and of the valid use of size changes in science fiction. No one has repeated the atom theme more endlessly than Cummings. Starting in 1929 with *Princess of the Atom* (*Argosy*, September 14, 1929, to October 26, 1929); *Out of the Smallness* (*Thrilling Wonder Stories*, June, 1941); *The Atom Prince* (*Science Fiction*, December, 1939); *Girl from Infinite Smallness* (*Planet Stories*, Spring, 1940), there were so many stories by him on the theme that the editor of *Thrilling Wonder Stories* had to be forgiven when he retitled Cummings contribution to its September, 1947, issue *Up and Atom*. Lest readers felt that he was in favor of infinite smallness, Cummings showed his democratic literary spirit by ascending, through his character, into the macrocosmos in his two *Weird Tales* series

Explorers into Infinity (April to June, 1927) and *The Giant World* (January to March, 1928). Up until his death, Cummings always claimed that his first story, *The Girl in the Golden Atom* was his favorite.

It has always been fashionable for critics to take old stories that were once very popular and influential, mercilessly dissect them, and conclude that there never was, never will be, or never could be any merit in the story in question. In doing this they fail to deal with the facts. *The Girl in the Golden Atom* was immensely popular and influential in the context of the times. No second guessing can change history. The first hardcover edition of *The Girl in the Golden Atom* was issued in England by Methuen in 1922. This was followed early in 1923 by the Harper edition in the United States.

A sixteen-year-old named G. Peyton Wertenbaker was a regular reader of a popular scientific magazine edited and published by Hugo Gernsback named *Science and Invention*. Every month, that magazine ran one or more science fiction short stories with the emphasis on scientific plausibility. Wertenbaker, completely taken with Cummings story, wrote one of his own with the identical concept. The major difference was that he tried to plug the scientific loopholes to the best of his ability. The story was called *The Man from the Atom* and in that story, the protagonist wears a space suit with complete life-support systems to sustain him. The changes are powered by atomic energy instead of drugs, and Einstein's theories are utilized to support the plausibility of the scheme. The hero first tries enlargement, and eventually he reaches an inhabitable planet in the macrocosmos. He fails to find his own world when shrinking and the story ends with him virtually an exhibit in a zoo on a world of superior beings.

Wertenbaker sold this story to Hugo Gernsback, who was then planning a special "Scientific Fiction" issue of *Science and Invention* with the August, 1923, issue. *The Man from the Atom* was the cover story of that issue. One of the other authors in that special issue was Ray Cummings with a new novel, *Around the Universe*.

Gernsback, when launching the first issue of *Amazing Stories*, reprinted Wertenbaker's atom yarn in April, 1926, and then ran a sequel to it in the May, 1926, issue. In the sequel, the hero, through the aid of an alien girl, the scientific knowledge of the world he had been imprisoned on, and through extrapolation of an Einsteinian concept, returns to Earth in a period roughly repeating the one he left. Wertenbaker's stories illustrate the role of *The Girl in the Golden Atom* as a catalyst. This original novel took a number of previous ideas, combined and invigorated them, and transformed them through imitators into the springboard for a more modern, scientific, and imaginative form of science fiction, even to the extent of first participating in the trial balloon and then the launching of the magazine that was responsible for today's immense popularity of science fiction.

Sam Moskowitz

Sources for Further Study

Criticism:

The Encyclopedia of Science Fiction and Fantasy. Compiled by Donald H.
Tuck. Chicago: Advent Publishers, Inc., 1978, pp. 123-124. Tuck presents
an overview of Cummings' life and work, which has as its chief value a
bibliography of Cummings' works.

Reviews:

Authentic Science Fiction. XV, November, 1951, p. 111.

New Worlds. XII, Winter, 1951, p. 94.

THE GIRL, THE GOLD WATCH, & EVERYTHING

Author: John D. MacDonald (1916-   )
First book publication: 1962
Type of work: Novel
Time: 1962
Locale: Miami, Florida

A mysterious gold watch not only tells time but can stop it, enabling a pusillanimous heir to confound his enemies, to hold his own with willful women, and to adapt to the moral imperatives of absolute power

Principal characters:
KIRBY WINTER, The diffident heir to a watch granting omnipotence
OMAR KREPPS, his deceased multimillionaire uncle
BONNY LEE BEAUMONT, Kirby's nightclub singer girl friend
CHARLA O'ROURKE, a scheming adventuress of the international set
BETSY ALDEN, her niece, a bit-part television actress
JOSEPH LOCORDOLOS, Charla's urbane accomplice and lover
WILMA FARNHAM, Kirby's assistant in a Krepps philanthropic subsidiary

Between 1948 and 1953, John D. MacDonald published fifty short stories and novelettes and two novels, *Wine of the Dreamers* (1950) and *Ballroom of the Skies* (1953), in the science fiction field. By 1953, however, he had virtually abandoned the genre except for an occasional piece in the glossy pages of *Cosmopolitan* (1964) or *Playboy* (1968). However, in 1962, shortly before conceiving his popular mystery character, Travis McGee (and *The Busted Flush*), apparently with one eye on his science fiction past, the other on the realistic writing then in progress, MacDonald fused the two forms in *The Girl, the Gold Watch, & Everything*, a science fiction novel in which the speculative element is barely mentioned for the first hundred pages (exactly *half* the story). Thereafter, once Kirby Winter, the central character, stumbles upon the fantastic stop-time properties of the watch inherited from his mysterious Uncle Omar, the extrapolative factor tends to dominate, but it is not obtrusive. From this point on, MacDonald so deftly interweaves fantasy with actuality that *The Girl, the Gold Watch, & Everything* can be regarded either as the tale of a secret gynephobe in search of manhood or as the story of a fumbler whose birthright is absolute power imposing a moral imperative.

In the novel MacDonald elaborates upon an idea first introduced into science fiction by H. G. Wells's short story, "The New Accelerator" (influenced, possibly, in turn by William James's speculations on heightened perception of environmental detail). First published in 1903, "The New Accelerator" brilliantly and humorously works out the practical consequences of an experiment involving artificial stimulation several thousand times over of *all* bodily functions — a condition induced by Professor Gibberne's "New Accelerator" wonder drug. The drug is sampled by both its discoverer and the author-narrator, the latter, at the end of the story, revealing — almost parenthetically — that a small dose of the potion had enabled him to write the entire narrative (approximately 6,500 words long) in the space of six minutes.

Instead of a physiologist perfecting a superdrug, MacDonald's inventor, in *The Girl, the Gold Watch, & Everything* is Omar Krepps, a Pennsylvania high school teacher of mathematics and science, who discovers "something," the exact nature of which is undisclosed for half the novel, though it is apparently astonishing enough to help him win big in Reno and to become a multimillionaire financial "wizard." Along the way, however, through a byproduct of his secret "power," Krepps makes some very deadly enemies by foiling their financial chicanery, always with baffling yet inexplicable ease. At the same time — through his nephew and only heir, timorous Kirby Winter — the wily financier has secretly been giving away more than half of his wealth to worthy causes and charities around the world, a practice that, immediately upon the old man's death, embroils Kirby (part of the "test" arranged for him) in an almost farcical predicament in which he is wooed and pursued by designing women and sought by the police for allegedly embezzling twenty-seven million dollars.

All Kirby's problems could be solved, literally, in the wink of an eye if he would only activate the old-fashioned gold watch (powered by cosmic radiation) in his pocket. But he does not know that until (in the best tradition of Poe's "Purloined Letter") he fiddles with the watch stem while hiding out on a public beach in bright, sunny Miami, and is instantly shifted into an eerie and at first terrifying red-lit world (probably a consequence of the Doppler effect) where time passes so quickly that one hour of "red time" is equivalent to 3/100 of a second back in the "objective" world he has just left. So fast is Kirby existing within the field generated by the watch that the long curling ocean wave, the crowd of listless sunbathers along the beach, the tall, slim, beautiful blonde with him, and a jet "pasted in the sky" above the city are all uncannily frozen still, transfixed in a silence so deep that he can hear the soft murmur of his own blood pulsing in his ears. But, once the initial shock wears off, Kirby soon learns what Wells's narrator in "The New Accelerator" quickly grasped: all the "living statues" out there in objective time are, in "red time," completely at his mercy — for good or for ill.

And that is precisely where MacDonald heads for deeper waters than Wells cared to sound. At the end of "The New Accelerator," the narrator, after noting that his friend's wonder drug could be used for criminal purposes, dismisses the possibility as someone else's (the law's) headache, and he and the professor plan to manufacture and market "Gibberne's Nervous Accelerator." They prefer to observe rather than to control the consequences. Kirby's uncle, however, is made of sterner and more ethical stuff. To guard against possible misuse of the stop-time effect, Krepps, always prudent (on occasion pretending to be an amateur magician), makes certain that whatever changes he makes in "red time" never come as too great a shock for those having to cope with them in "real time." He can also count on man's apparently innate capacity for reducing the miraculous to rationalization.

Krepp's moral fiber and foresight are even more remarkable than that. Long before his eventual death (the event with which the novel begins), and admitting to himself that vanity alone prevents him from taking his secret to the grave, he decides to give his nephew a chance for power, even though he does not consider Kirby (curiously backward for thirty-two) mature enough for omnipotence. Still hopeful, Krepps supervises the boy's education up through college, then Kirby is made one of his uncle's employees charged with implementing philanthropic decisions, all of this designed to toughen Kirby's character and help prepare him to use stop-time power as wisely as his uncle has. When Krepps finally and unexpectedly does die, he does not leave a cent to Kirby, only the gold watch and a sealed letter in trust for a period of one year. However, if Kirby figures out soon enough how to use the watch, he can easily gain access to the letter at will (it explains all), but if he does not, and should the watch remain inactive for a fifty-day period, Krepps has prearranged that it would fuse itself beyond the point of structural analysis.

Technical details aside, MacDonald is really more interested (possibly one of his motives for turning away from science fiction) in other aspects of Kirby's character, particularly his secret panic and comic ineptitude whenever he is about to make love to a desirable and willing woman, a complex rooted in a disastrous adolescent experience undergone in the back seat of an old Hudson in a public park during a rainstorm. Interestingly enough this very weakness is the only thing that saves Kirby from the basilisk glamor of Charla O'Rourke, the adventuress attempting to seduce him into revealing the nature of the secret "edge" his former adversaries believe Krepps must have had. The rainstorm complex also keeps him clear of potentially embarrassing entanglements with Charla's niece, Betsy Alden, whose volcanic temperament immediately cowes Kirby, and the sexually repressed Wilma Farnham, Kirby's former assistant in administering Krepps's philanthropic enterprises, who at one point flings herself at him so desperately that he bolts like a startled rabbit. But Kirby's complex finally withers in the space of a single incredible night when Bonny Lee Beaumont (a loose-living yet delightfully principled Carolina girl singing in a North Miami strip-joint, unwittingly completes his sexual education. In a clear case of mistaken identities, she mischievously slips into the right bed occupied by the wrong man, Kirby, who, at that moment is too sleepy, exhausted, and bewildered to grasp what is going on until too late.

Once the misunderstanding is cleared up, Bonny Lee, who believes strongly in being faithful to one man at a time, is at first tearfully indignant but then shows philosophical resiliency, falling in love with Kirby as easily and rapidly as he has surrendered his sexual hang-up to her healthy and joyous spirit. It is she who, helping Kirby to evade the police on the one hand and Charla and her accomplices on the other, quickly sees the many practical and prankish uses for the stop-time watch. Bonny Lee sows incredible comic confusion (in a scene faintly reminiscent of Thorne Smith but still all MacDonald), when she leaves behind a screaming flock of uppity beach beauties crouching in the surf after their bathing suits suddenly disappear. Meanwhile, up on the drive, can be heard the bewildered beeping of traffic brought to an inexplicable standstill because Bonny Lee has plucked and thrown away all the ignition keys.

It is not long, however, before Kirby recognizes on his own the absolute moral demands of owning the wonder watch — a lesson he learns while attempting to rescue Betsy Alden, who has been kidnaped and is being held on her aunt's luxury yacht, the *Glorianna*. When Joseph Locordolos, a Spanish national and lover-confederate of Charla, fires a pistol aimed straight at Kirby's face, he is microsecond too late, for Kirby has just managed to flick into "red time," and everything freezes — except for the bullet, which still heads slowly but steadily towards him. Kirby becomes so annoyed by this act that he plucks the slug out of the air, forces the gun barrel back around so that it points at Joseph's throat, and aims the "lead snail" dead center for Charla's forehead. When Kirby flips back into "real time," the bullet will impact with thoroughly satisfying bloodiness. At the last moment, however, Kirby cools off in time to deflect both gun barrel and bullet. This change of heart is strongly approved by Bonny Lee, who realizes intuitively that to kill in "red time" would mean a permanent fall from grace.

This theme of power restrained is not new to MacDonald's science fiction, though it is most openly stated in the earlier novels, *Wine of the Dreamers* and *Ballroom of the Skies*. In *Wine of the Dreamers*, Raul Kinson, the Watcher on another world, refuses to pervert his dream experiences of Earth into sadistic manipulation of hapless beings totally unaware of alien interference. His intransigence and determination in the end help to put an end to the dreams and reunite two worlds. Similarly, in *Ballroom of the Skies*, former newspaperman Dake Lorin tries to help avert a *fourth* world war on Earth through being trained by mind-controlling "extraterrestrials" to develop his own latent extrasensory powers. However, he refuses to use these powers to help keep Earth in a constant state of turmoil until he is convinced that it is absolutely necessary for the safety of the galactic Empire, of which Earth is an unwitting but essential part.

But with *The Girl, the Gold Watch, & Everything* MacDonald gave up the stars for the planet Earth (specifically, Miami, Florida), the future for the present (*c*. 1962), and aliens secretly intervening in the affairs of men for a couple of ruthless adventurers trying to outwit a man for whom "time waits." Perhaps he tired of the big picture and preferred to paint small for a while. Or maybe MacDonald was similar to Krepps, whose first stop-time devices were cumbersome until he learned how to scale down components to the handier size of a watch, and saw how to reduce the speculative element of his fiction to the dimensions of an unobtrusive mainspring uncoiling in the vitals of an otherwise totally believable story. This method better achieved, as he recently reaffirmed in a *Writer's Yearbook 79* interview, Coleridge's "willing suspension of disbelief."

Even more important is the basic humanity of the book. In the end, like the author, we care more about what happens to Kirby and Bonny Lee than about the ultimate fate of the stop-time watch (which Krepps, still reaching out from the grave, has given a maximum functional life of no more than twenty-five years). *The Girl, the Gold Watch, & Everything* though, should last much longer than that, for if we hold it or any of the best novels and stories by John D. MacDonald up to the inner ear of imagination, we too can hear a tiny, faint but beautiful sound, this one telling us something about the author himself — the fundamental decency of the man.

Joseph Wrzos

Sources for Further Study

Reviews:

Analog. LXXII, September, 1963, p. 94.

Magazine of Fantasy and Science Fiction. XXIX, November, 1965, pp. 16-18.

GLADIATOR

Author: Philip Wylie (1902-1971)
First book publication: 1930
Type of work: Novel
Time: The early 1900's
Locale: The United States

A man of superhuman strength faces the challenge of learning when and how to use that strength in a closeminded world that fears and distrusts him

> *Principal characters:*
> HUGO DANNER, a man of superhuman strength
> ABEDNEGO DANNER, his father
> MATILDA DANNER, his mother

When Number 1 *Action Comics* appeared on the magazine stands in the mid-1930's, American children (of all ages) were introduced to the character Superman — a true knight-errant with such enormous strength that he could leap over "tall buildings in a single bound." Virtually invincible, Superman, in his gaudy blue tights and red cape, pitted his strength against the rampant evils of the world and leaped over such folk heroes as Paul Bunyan, Pecos Bill, Mike Fink, and Joe Magarac to become the epitome of the American strong man — even if he was an import from the planet Krypton. He provided generations of readers (and viewers) with a unique opportunity for ego projection and wish fulfillment.

Several years prior to the advent of Superman, Philip Wylie published *Gladiator*, a revised version of an earlier unpublished novel, in which the hero, Hugo Danner, possesses superhuman strength and a nearly invincible body. Though many believe that Hugo Danner may have served as a prototype for Superman, Wylie certainly did not have a comic-book character in mind when he created Hugo. Rather than a being from a foreign planet, Hugo is real flesh and blood, complete with desires, emotions, and aspirations. For most people, dealing with desires, emotions, and aspirations is challenge enough in life; but Hugo, as he passes from innocence to experience, has the additional challenge of learning when and how to use his strength. *Gladiator* tells his story; and, though it sold only about 2,500 copies on first publication, it is a novel of more than passing interest.

The novel begins with Abednego Danner, a spindling wisp of a man who has retreated into himself in an effort to escape the assaults of the world and of his wife Matilda. A professor of biology in a small Colorado college, he retires nightly to a makeshift laboratory in his house where he loses himself in his thoughts and experiments, with the ultimate goal of proving that chemistry truly controls human destiny. His proof is to be a formula that will provide virtually unlimited strength to living muscle.

Experimenting with tadpoles, Abednego succeeds in producing a breed so strong that they swim through the plate glass of their tank. Elated, he kills the tadpoles and dissects one, concocting from it what he hopes will be his desired formula. Securing a pregnant cat, he innoculates her with the formula. When the kittens are born, he selects one — drowning the rest — and watches with wonder as it grows stronger and stronger, ultimately killing its mother with a playful blow from a paw. As the cat's strength increases tremendously, Mrs. Danner realizes what her husband has done and accuses him of defying God by creating a creature of the devil. Like so many who will later see Hugo as some sort of demon, she cannot break out of the tight circle of convention and religious doctrine that surrounds her.

Samson, as they have named the cat, is indeed a startling animal, capable of killing chickens and cattle and surviving direct hits by rifle bullets. Abednego realizes that he must act and injects Samson with a powerful poison. Following a titanic death struggle, Samson dies. This experience with Samson causes Abednego to ponder the possibility of making his discovery known to the world. He knows now that he can create invincible creatures. But what creatures? And to what end?

Circumstances, however, provide Abednego with an opportunity he cannot resist utilizing: Matilda becomes pregnant, and he has the chance to create a super human being — even if he must risk producing a super version of his wife. Slipping an opiate into her evening cordial, he watches her fall into a deep sleep. Then, hating his duplicity but driven by his obsession to be a creator, he injects her swollen abdomen. The result is Hugo Danner.

Baby Hugo wastes no time in displaying unbelievable feats of strength, and Matilda soon realizes what Abednego has done. But he rallies his own strength of will and prevails upon his wife to accept their son and to be proud of him; for Hugo will be all that he, Abednego, could never be — a gloriously strong man able to stand forth, as all men should, against whatever the world throws against him. In that moment Matilda realizes that she loves both her husband and her son.

Hugo's childhood, despite the love and understanding of Abednego and Matilda, is not easy. The world does not feel an obligation corresponding to that of parental love and understanding. Because he smashes cribs and wooden pens, Hugo is kept in an iron pen, a situation giving rise to some gossip in the town of Indian Creek. The Danners, of course, shelter their amazing offspring as well as they can, attributing his strength to a long line of strong ancestors. They erect barriers around him and attempt to condition him to be wary of exhibiting his strength lest he be thought a freak. They are especially careful to teach him kindness and respect for people and property and to curb any destructive tendencies that might manifest themselves. Early in life, Hugo learns that, instead of freeing him from the world, his gift of strength really makes him, even more than other people, a prisoner of that world and its rules.

When he is forced into a fight with a classmate, Hugo lifts him into the air and flings him over the circle of onlookers. Fortunately the boy suffers only a broken arm and some bruises, but Hugo is ashamed and filled with dread at what he has done. He sees that he cannot truly belong to the society in which he lives and begins to turn more and more into himself. Even when he lifts a wagon off a man, thus saving his life, he is ignored and told to go home to his mother.

Abednego decides finally that he must explain to Hugo why he is different, why he is so strong. Hugo is only ten at the time, but his child's mind seems to grasp his father's counsel that he should be humble, work hard, and some day find a use for his superior powers. In answers to Hugo's question regarding God, Abednego can only answer that he does not know much about Him.

Symbolic of his attempt to insulate himself from the misunderstandings and indictments of society is the immense fort Hugo builds for himself deep in the woods. Here he plays games of holding off attacking Indians — games that are a foreshadowing of the real games that he will have to play later in life. But, though his fort may be a citadel against enemies of his imagination, it cannot protect Hugo from his real enemy, society. Two of Abednego's colleagues from the college stumble across Hugo and his fort. Refusing to believe his story of how he built such a huge fort, they call him a liar to his face and a demon behind his back. Hugo slowly realizes that he will never be able to insulate himself and his wondrous strength from the misunderstanding and mistrust that afflict humanity.

Hugo grows through his teens to become a handsome young man, successfully holding his strength within reasonable bounds, and the people of Indian Creek come to accept him. He falls in love with Anna Blake, and through her is initiated into the world of sex, but their relationship is shortlived as Hugo realizes that he must leave his native soil and seek meaning for his life in some distant place. His choice is Webster University (Harvard), where he hopes to become a great athlete.

Webster opens a whole new world to Hugo. He makes a number of close friends and does indeed become a star football player, singlehandedly winning games for Webster. Tragedy strikes, however, when in his final game against Yale he crashes into a Yale player, killing him instantly. Hugo sees how quickly a hero, urged on to greater efforts by the shouts of fans and the power of tradition, can become a murderer. Once more his great gift has betrayed him, and once more he flees.

Turning to the sea, Hugo works as a sailor. One day, while sitting in a cafe in Marseilles, he learns that war has broken out (World War I). Here, he feels, is the opportunity for him to find himself, to put his strength to work for a moral cause. With Tom Shayne, another American, he joins the Foreign Legion. But again Hugo's plans are thwarted; his impossible deeds in the war bring only disappointment and misunderstanding, instead of the grandeur he had hoped for. The war, he sees, has been merely an outlet for his savage instinct to destroy. Like so many other fictional characters in war settings,

Hugo discovers that war does not provide a ground for the realization of moral values; war is merely a waste, igniting a cheap momentary excitement in its participants but leaving mankind no better off than before.

Hugo is aroused to one last feat: he will go to the center of the enemy government and slay the leaders, thus bringing to an end the useless destruction of lives. The armistice, however, is signed before he can carry out his plan. Still, he does not despair, because he has come to realize that life seems more "the effort of creation than the business of destruction."

Through the help of Tom Shayne's father, who had prevailed upon Hugo to let him manage his small bank account while he was at war, Hugo becomes rich. When he learns that his fortune was the result of the manipulation of foodstuffs and war materials during the war, he is once again sickened at the level to which humanity can sink. He arranges to have his fortune transferred to Abednego and Matilda. Again, he is ready for a new course in his life.

Finding a job in a steel mill, Hugo is content for a time amidst the hypnotic red mouths of the furnaces, where he works as hard as he dares. But even that is too hard for the boss, who accuses Hugo of setting standards of work that the others cannot possibly match and fires him.

At this point, penniless and hungry, Hugo succumbs to Mr. Shayne's offer of a position in a bank. This position lasts until Hugo saves a man from suffocating in one of the bank's vaults; when all else fails, Hugo secretly uses his hands to open the vault. Because the bank officials feel that he is a threat to the entire banking business, Hugo is arrested and given a violent third-degree treatment in an effort to force him to explain how he could open such a strong vault. Finally Hugo exerts his strength and breaks free from his confinement.

Wandering the countryside, Hugo is offered a job on a farm, where he has an affair with the farmer's wife Roseanne. There seems to be a genuine love between Hugo and Roseanne — until he knocks a charging bull unconscious with a single blow. This feat of strength stuns her with fright, and she runs from Hugo, leaving him once more alone with the terrible burden of his strength. A telegram arrives, advising him that Abednego is dying, and he sets off for Colorado.

Hugo tells Abednego what he wants to hear, of the lives he has saved and the constructive things he has done. He lies, telling his father that he was really responsible for bringing the war to a close. Abednego is transported with happiness, exclaiming that it must be splendid to be as strong as Hugo. Creator and created thus come together in an ironic situation that borders on pathos.

Abednego gives Hugo six small notebooks that contain the secret of Hugo's strength. With them Hugo will be able to create an entire race of superhuman beings who can impose upon the world either morality or destruction. Hugo realizes that mere strength is not enough to overcome the base motivation of mankind, because even a race of titans would still be human beings and would, in all probability, bring destruction rather than morality. In the midst of a thunderstorm, he climbs to the top of a mountain, wishing that there were a God to whom he could pray. In a frenzy he flings a hand upward defying God to make His presence felt. A bolt of lightning strikes Hugo, killing him and turning Abednego's notebooks to ashes, a fittingly dramatic end for a superman.

Gladiator is a readable book, clearly and dramatically presented. As a character, Hugo Danner is believable even with his super strength, which Wylie kept within some bounds. As a young man searching for meaning in life and a place to belong, he fits the pattern of a host of other characters in American fiction, from Goodman Brown to Holden Caulfield.

As a human being, however, Hugo Danner does not succeed in his quest. At no time in the story is he able to sustain a sense of direction or of mission. He is, ironically enough, buffeted about by circumstances and events over which he has no control. His strength has a debilitating effect upon him; rather than a means to the realization of ideals and aspirations, it works in a negative direction, isolating Hugo from humanity and from himself. Instead of serving as a key to understanding, it confuses Hugo, leading him to expect too much of himself. And when he fails to meet that level of expectation, he becomes disillusioned — saved from bitterness and cynicism only by a timely lightning bolt. At the mythological level, the novel dramatizes the inevitable failure of an Ajax or a Hercules in the contemporary world. Abednego Danner's namesake in the Bible escaped the flames prepared for him by Nebuchadnezzar because of his faith in God. Abednego does not escape, at least symbolically, from the flames of God: his offspring and his life's work are destroyed by lightning.

Perhaps the creators of Superman and other comic-book characters knew that no man of superhuman strength or ability could move among his fellows in a normal fashion; he would need a safe disguise into which to retreat. Superman had mild-mannered Clark Kent; Captain Marvel, the youngster Billy Batson; and Batman, the playboy Bruce Wayne. But Hugo Danner is always himself — no blue tights, no black mask, no "*Shazam*," and no place to retreat.

In the end, Hugo's plight does not resemble that of his comic strip successors as much as it does that of his most memorable ancestor, science fiction's first artificially created being of extraordinary strength, the creature of Victor Frankenstein. With nothing to hide behind, Hugo comes to see what Superman and his comic-book companions never will see: that even in a nation that has always been obsessed with the idea of strength in general and of strong men in particular, the mightiest man in the world may be defeated by the intrinsic weaknesses of mankind; and that out of fear and lack of understanding, human being will turn against the very person who is different enough to *make* a difference.

Wilton Eckley

Sources for Further Study

Reviews:

Amazing Stories. V, June, 1930, p. 280.

Books. March 9, 1930, p. 4.

Boston Transcript. March 29, 1930, p. 2.

Cleveland Open Shelf. April, 1930. p. 64.

Nation and Athenaeum. XLVII, August 23, 1930, p. 652.

New York Evening Post. March 8, 1930, p. 10n.

New York Times. March 2, 1930, p. 9.

Outlook. CLIV, March 19, 1930, p. 467.

Saturday Review of Literature. VI, April 19, 1930, p. 971.

Times Literary Supplement. July 3, 1930, p. 556.

GLADIATOR-AT-LAW

Authors: Frederik Pohl (1919-   ) and Cyril M. Kornbluth (1923-1958)
First book publication: 1955
Type of work: Novel
Time: Approximately 2155
Locale: New York City

A small group of common people struggle to take over a giant corporation and then to reform society by the use of their newly won economic power

    Principal characters:
        CHARLES MUNDIN, a young lawyer
        NORMA LAVIN, a strong, independent woman
        DON LAVIN, her brainwashed brother
        HARRY RYAN, a retired lawyer helping the Lavins
        LANA, leader of the preteen street gang, the Rabbits
        NORVELL BLIGH, an "emotion engineer" who loses his job
        VIRGINIA BLIGH, his wife
        ALEXANDRA BLIGH, his daughter

This is a novel of the 1950's — not the silent surface of the decade dominated by upward mobility and antiCommunist paranoia and repression, but rather the critical underside which challenged postwar American society by laying bare the loss of human dignity, creativity, and power that was the price of the "dream" of material prosperity and political orthodoxy. Perhaps not as well-known as Pohl and Kornbluth's classic *Space Merchants*, published a few years earlier in 1953, *Gladiator-at-Law* nevertheless continues the incisive social satire that marked the work of this team of science fiction writers.

The adventure plot of the novel is the familiar one of "little" people taking on powerful giants and using their victory to make the society more responsive to the needs of all the people and not just the power elite. The subplot focuses on one of the employees of that elite as he loses his job and his executive privileges, but finds personal strength and social identity in his new life among the common people. The background of the novel is dominated by images of a future United States in which the suburban developments, new technologies, and economic growth of the post-World War II boom have backfired and resulted in a society that is as decadent and corrupt as that of the crumbling Roman Empire. This vision of a violent and unjust society, written as the United States "empire" was extending its hegemony over the world of the 1950's, is at least as important to the work, if not more so, than the plot and characters.

Charles Mundin, the central character of the novel, is the young lawyer who spearheads Norma and Don Lavin's final effort to gain a voting majority of the stock of the extensive and powerful G.M.L. Corporation. Originally founded by the Lavins' father, who invented a computer-controlled bubble house that was intended to provide decent housing for the masses, G.M.L. grew into a megacorporation. Lavin senior was edged out by the other two founders, and eventually the entire corporation ended up under the control of Mrs. Green and Mr. Charlesworth, two members of the dominant class in the American economy who spent two hundred years gaining control of more and more corporations. Having long ago lost regenerative ability, their bodies are now preserved in a cabinet in a dusty office of the old Empire State Building, while their minds are interlinked with the G.M.L. computer.

Mundin, a new lawyer in need of clients, originally accepted Norma and Don Lavin's job offer of representing them simply because he needed to pay his bills, rather than out of any antiestablishment idealism. Instead of a man in a grey flannel suit, Mundin becomes a gladiator in a major legal battle at the heart of the extensive but corrupt United States economic empire.

Narrated from Mundin's viewpoint in a tone that has echoes of Mickey Spillane, Bogart detective films, and the social satire of early *Mad* magazine, the plot proceeds along predictable formulaic lines. By the end of the text, Mundin and the Lavins are in power; Green and Charlesworth blow up in a mushroom-shaped cloud; and the victors get on with their task of cleaning up the G.M.L. corporation and American society. The struggle for fifty-one percent of G.M.L. stock is familiar and does not compel much excitement in itself. But as a spine around which other elements of the text cluster, it serves its purpose.

What *is* interesting in the Mundin-Lavin plot is the group of characters that assemble to take on Green and Charlesworth. Norma Lavin is an independent feminist and the leader of the group; her brother, Don, has been conditioned — brainwashed — by the forces of Green and Charlesworth to prevent him from voting in stockholder meetings. Harry Ryan, a retired lawyer, had helped the Lavins before he became too addicted to his opium habit to function in court; a wise, experienced lawyer, Ryan was broken by Green and Charlesworth but serves as a father-mentor to Mundin in the legal, psychological, and physical battles that occur.

Even more helpful in the physical battles, as well as in negotiating ways through an urban jungle ruled in territories by preteen and teenage gangs, is Lana, the young leader of the Rabbits. And as they show their strength in a stockholders' meeting, Mundin and Norma Lavin pick up three allies who have extensive corporation holdings and are eager to topple G.M.L. for the sake of their own climb up the ladder of economic power. As Green and Charlesworth fight back, however, only one of the three, Bliss Hubble, remains a loyal ally. Finally, Mundin acquires an *ad hoc* secretary in the person of Norvell Bligh, a former "emotion engineer" — creator of the Roman circuslike Field Day events who has lost his high-paying job to a competitive subordinate. It is this motley group, each with their own character development, that gives life and interest to the otherwise routine plot.

Bligh's development as a character is extensive enough to constitute a subplot. Norvie Bligh is a shy, mousy, quiet person — an artist who, for lack of a way to support his art, turned to emotional engineering and was successful at designing Field Day pageants of mutilation, violence, and death. Arranged like the spectacles of Nazi society, Field Day was a major ideological arm of the corporate power. It gave the impoverished masses entertainment that was increasingly sadistic as one spectacle superseded another in complicated events of gore; it also gave some of the masses a chance to learn large sums of money as contestants in the events, if they managed, like the gladiators of Rome, to live through the contests.

However, a subordinate, Simmons, betrays Bligh, gets him fired, and becomes his replacement. Norvell, stock character that he is, has the stock shrewish wife, Virginia, and the stock spoiled brat child, Alexandra, to provide for. Before losing his job with its high income and status, his wife and daughter harass him daily for more and more consumer items, but then the family moves to the slum suburb of Belly Rave, formerly Belle Reve, and must face a life no longer insulated from the decay and crime of the anarchic social jungle spawned by the corporations themselves. Norvie, Virginia, and Alexandra all face reality more clearly and develop into down-to-earth, struggling people, again in touch with life's necessities, pains, feelings, and joys. Again the plot is familiar — right out of the Blondie comic strip — but the reversal is interesting. Norvell does not become a strong person as a corporate executive; rather he succeeds only when he becomes downwardly mobile and must struggle to survive. The struggle does not embitter him; it strengthens him.

Gladiator-at-Law, then, is an extensive attack on the postwar American dream. As the United States built an economic empire and succeeded the British as a world power; as suburbs, television, and electronic technology promised a new era of plenty; as the society settled into the silent 1950's and discouraged currents of thought and action that were not in keeping with the dream fostered by corporate hegemony — few voices of criticism and negation survived the double repression of antiCommunist witch hunts and suburban apathy. While some underground, Bohemian literature survived in the few nooks and crannys secured by beatniks and others, "mainstream" literature tended to be narrowly psychological and apolitical. One of the few places that serious social criticism took place was in science fiction, generally dismissed by the intellectual community as harmless space adventure, and *Gladiator-at-Law* is one of the best examples of this phenomenon.

It is the social critique, then, that is the strength of Pohl and Kornbluth's novel. Therefore, the reader who wants to grasp all that this work has to offer must move beyond the familiar plots and stock characters to what in a mainstream novel would be mere setting, but in a science fiction work is the alternate world created by the author out of the contradictions and tendencies of his own society. In science fiction, foreground plot shares the stage with background setting. In significant science fiction, the background is of such compelling complexity and insightful social mirroring that it may even upstage the foreground; this is what happens in *Gladiator-at-Law*.

It is the series of images that figuratively convey American society of the 1950's — transformed and distorted in order to see it more clearly as the false and temporary dream it was — that is the strength of this novel. The images of suburban development, urban decay, the lonely crowd, the hidden persuaders, and the rebels in the streets are developed out of the problems of the 1950's. But the images do not simply illuminate separate problems; rather, Pohl and Kornbluth connect them and place the final responsibility for them at the feet of the corporate power elite and the political parties that represent that elite instead of the people. The best background reading from the 1950's that would articulate those images is the work of the sociologist C. Wright Mills, whose *Power Elite* and *White Collar* develop on a theoretical level what Pohl and Kornbluth are working with on a figurative level.

Other important concerns in the novel are the role of the intellectual or artist — Mundin and Bligh — in society: working for the system, they are technocrats, but working against it they are again free intellectual and creative artists. The role of women, however, is more problematic: Norma, the feminist, and Ginny, the shrewish wife, are both transformed by their men in traditional sex-role development; at this level, the novel still participates in the sexist ideology of the very postwar American society it attacks. Psychological manipulation in many forms is explored from ideological formations of Field Day spectacles to direct brainwashing — this time done by corporate executives and not the Chinese or Korean military. The manipulation of people in order to serve the economic needs of the corporations is brilliantly articulated by the authors. And finally, the crisis of the nuclear family and the connected rebellion of young people is handled in such a way that the nuclear family of corporate life is negated and the young rebels of street gangs are seen as positive forces of change.

With the exception of its treatment of women, *Gladiator-at-Law* is an excellent piece of social criticism. The book sees the necessary change in the economic order; and although the actual challenge is a naïve, populist *coup* by a few good people, the critique, if not the proffered means of change, is itself an important element in the underside of the 1950's culture.

Tom Moylan

Sources for Further Study

Reviews:

Analog. LVI, December, 1955, p. 148.

Fantastic Universe Science Fiction. IV, October, 1955, p. 112

Galaxy. XI, October, 1955, p. 110.

New Worlds. CXL, March, 1964, p. 128.

Magazine of Fantasy and Science Fiction. IX, September, 1955, p. 92.

New York Herald Tribune Book Review. October 10, 1954, p. 12.

New York Times. October 17, 1954, p. 45.

THE GLASS BEAD GAME
(DAS GLASPERLENSPIEL)

Author: Hermann Hesse (1877-1962)
First book publication: 1943
English translation: 1969 (as *Magister Ludi*)
Type of work: Novel
Time: Approximately twenty-third to twenty-fifth centuries
Locale: Principally Germanic Europe

Traditions of Utopian and Bildungsroman *narratives combine as the setting for a fictive analysis of the paradoxes, contradictions, and perhaps radical choices that face the enlightened individual as he confronts history and culture, both in the future and in the present*

Principal characters:
> THE NARRATOR, pleasantly pedantic, sympathetic, ironic "biographer" of Joseph Knecht
> JOSEPH KNECHT, lifelong student, diplomat, and Master of Games for Castalia
> THE MUSIC MASTER, Knecht's lifelong spiritual mentor
> PLINIO DESIGNORI, aristocratic, secular, guest student to Castalia; adversary and later close friend to Knecht
> FRITZ TEGULARIUS, Knecht's intimate friend; an introvert and genius at the Glass Bead Game
> THE ELDER BROTHER IN THE BAMBOO GROVE, a hermit and the source of Knecht's initiation in the "I, Ching" disciplines
> MASTER ALEXANDER, "president" of Castalia and friend of Knecht when he resigns from Castalia

In the first of this novel's three formally discrete parts, "The Glass Bead Game: A General Introduction to its History for the Layman," the twentieth century is termed the "Age of the Feuilleton." It is characterized by a frenetic culture of intellectual dandyism and hucksterism, which is introverted and piecemeal, inane and ignorant; moreover, it is an age of wars. The account sets a scene to be contrasted to the twenty-first century emergence of a world Utopia through the art and leadership of the apparently magnificent Order of Castalia. Its mission was to groom an intellectual elite that would insure humanity against regression to the behavior of its barbarous past. It provided sanctuary and a historically extraordinary opportunity to bring the study of all the arts and sciences to wonderful levels of accomplishment, especially emphasizing music, language, and mathematics.

At the core of this academic paradise, where even the most eclectic and least practical researches might be pursued without apology, evolved the "Glass Bead Game." It required a creative act, employing esoteric hieroglyphic symbols, to yield a product that potentially combined information from all disciplines and interpolated it in a consummate work of art. Institutional Castalia matured and with it grew a genius for ever more rich and elegant Glass Bead Games. The Game could mirror the order, complexity, diversity, and finally the unity of the universe. At the same time the design and strategy of an individual game was a metaphor for the content and integration of the mind and meaning of a single individual. The single discipline the Game did not well encompass was the study of history. Moreover, the narrative of the novel allows the reader to encounter the game only obliquely, piecemeal, and through hearsay, as if deliberately to force attention back to the people who master it — principally Joseph Knecht and his colleagues.

Part Two, "The Life of Magister Ludi Joseph Knecht," provides about sixty percent of the novel's length. Basically, it recounts the life of Knecht from about twelve to his early forties, tracing his education, mentors, and achievements, first in the public school, then in the curricula of the elite schools of the Castalian order. His character and talents are extraordinary. His principal genius is for music. On his merits he is eventually elevated to the most prestigious of the twelve masterships of the formal Order of Castalia, that of "Magister Ludi" — Master of the Game — the youngest ever to be so distinguished. Within a year, he resigns his mastership and membership in the order, takes a job as private tutor to the son of an old friend, and through an act of improbably foolish judgment drowns in an Alpine lake.

There is little interesting action in the novel. Opportunities for suspense in the small adventures of Knecht's life are quickly aborted with summary statements revealing how they came out. There are notable episodes such as Knecht's student debates with Plinio Designori, his diplomatic sojourn at the Benedictine Monastery where he comes under the influence of the sagacious historian Father Jacobus, and the bittersweet period leading to the event of his resignation. But these occasions are summarized more than dramatized. Thus, the effect is of a life largely unmarked by sensational conflict. The most remarkable event is Knecht's drowning.

Part Three, "Joseph Knecht's Posthumous Writings," consisting of thirteen poems and three tales, functions as an appendix upon which the account of Knecht may draw for samples of his thought. In addition, they put a bit of flesh on such matters as Hesse's ideas of women and children. The poems are metaphysical and contemplative in a variety of traditional forms such as the dramatic monologue and the sonnet. The tales are didactic fables.

It is partly the traditional Utopian setting of *The Glass Bead Game* that makes the novel interesting to readers of science fiction. But it is also Hesse's vision of life, which is not so much Germanic as it is Western (rooted in the classical and Renaissance concept of Plato's *Republic* and Thomas More's *Utopia*), that appeals to science fiction readers. As in a traditional Utopian story we are given a rather ephemeral picture of a future civilization, in this case of a Castalian cultural state hundreds of years after the twentieth century. The action is mostly set in the monastically simple academic cities of Castalia, with brief removals to the countryside, the nondescript rooms of Knecht's early public school, the Benedictine monastery of Mariafels, and the secular home of the well-to-do Plinio Designori. Only occasional references to European nations and to the mountain retreat and lake in the final scene allow the reader to locate the story in Germanic Europe. There is also a distinct impression, generated by the setting, of cultural and technological stasis. This too is characteristic of traditional utopias, though it might seem somewhat strange to a citizen of the twentieth century who has come to expect dramatic physical change in civilization.

In fact, many of the sociological details of Hesse's Utopia are more historical than futuristic. An only slightly altered Catholic Church has survived, along with its Benedictine monastic establishment. Although a hint of progressive changes in social behavior is given in the practice of allowing the unmarried daughters of well-off residents of Castalian towns to have sexual congress with members of the exclusively male student body of the Order, members of the Order, may never marry. Nor do women participate in Castalian culture or secular governance. Women characters are few, superficially dealt with, inferior in role, and not quite trustworthy, if we are to judge by their representation in Knecht's tales in Part Three. Children appear in the tales mostly to epitomize rather bloodless theories of the education of youth. Indeed, except for the nearly thoughtless reports of automobiles, radios, and progressive sexual mores, the world of the novel might be quite medieval.

Nature, usually emblematic in Hesse's novels, in *The Glass Bead Game* is characterized as benign (the countryside) and domesticated (the gardens of the Castalian campuses). No animals are mentioned. We get few weather reports and little reference to seasons, until the final episode when nature becomes dangerous and implacable in the mountains and the frigid glacial lake in which Knecht drowns. Never explicitly foreshadowed in the description of Castalia, the presentation of this suddenly atavistic face of nature is jarring, following as it does a depiction of somewhat pallid and undistinguished natural surroundings.

The story's two main characters, the pedantic, urbane and deferential Narrator, and Joseph Knecht, are also more abstract than colorful or individualistic. The Narrator deserves close attention because he stands for the forces of history and culture that bind the individual. He explicitly announces his control of what we may learn of Knecht — nothing very intimate, since interest in personalities is intellectually distracting. Moreover, the Narrator speaks retrospectively. He is perhaps as remote in time from Knecht and Castalia as they are remote from the twentieth century. Through him we are reassured that civilization, perhaps even Castalia, survived the time of Knecht, who is already half legendary. In addition, the telling of the story is modified by the fictional device of identifying the "editor" of the the Life of Knecht as Hermann Hesse. Furthermore, the Narrator admits that information for a Life of Knecht is scanty, and that even if he possessed it, he would withhold details to prevent obscuring the "universal" lessons to be learned from the story. There is no information offered about Knecht's family, childhood, or sexual inclinations; he has been a lifelong bachelor and is perhaps a virgin at his death. But he is no medieval "everyman" character; not, at least, representative of the common man.

Knecht's story is a speculum (in the medieval sense of a "mirror" into which special men can peer to examine their own characters) for the scholar-artist. "Knecht" means "servant" or "knight" — the name also derived from medieval allegory. Nevertheless, Knecht is an epitome of human talent and virtuous character, the legendary qualities of the ideal master. His genius for music, the queen of the arts in Castalia's hierarchy of disciplines, is the basis of a genius for synthesis, integration, and harmony, the *sine qua non* for one who would be intellectual and moral master as "Magister Ludi" in Castalia. He is simple, serenely brilliant, honest, loyal, never jealous, and objective. His is a life of storybook success and public honor.

Each of the other major characters is merely a reflection of Knecht. One group of characters includes those who are reduced alternate versions of Knecht, people he might have been; they are estimable but lesser: Plinio Designori, the Elder Brother of the Bamboo Grove, Fritz Tegularius, and Master Anderson. The other group consists of men who are completely noble and form an axis that locates Knecht: the nearly wordless Music Master represents a life of mystical contemplation, while Father Jacobus' attention to the inescapable events and processes of history point beyond the static intellectuality of Castalia. Neither really needs Castalian culture, and their presence helps explain how Knecht could finally reject it.

The Glass Bead Game is anything but a novel of adventure or character: it is a narrative of philosophical polemic. The first-person narrative voice in which the story is told, nevertheless, does present many opportunities for dramatic irony, an effect possible when the storyteller is remote from his protagonist both in time as well as point of view. The storyteller is sympathetic and condescending. Knecht is made both heroic and pathetic. He does not know the future as the storyteller knows it. But there is some humor in the fact that neither does the Narrator know Knecht as he might be known. Again, the Castalian culture of Knecht's time considers itself supremely creative, especially in the elaborate elegance of its Glass Bead Games; yet the Narrator, with his centuries of perspective, calls it "uncreative." Moreover, Knecht and his fellow students write fictionalized "Lives" of historical personages as half-contemplative, half-scholarly exercises, whereas it is soon obvious that this novel of Knecht's "Life" is just such an exercise for the narrator. There is double irony when the Narrator has the Music Master assert that meaning must be respected, although that it can never be taught. Yet the principal quality of the discourse is expository, discursive, analytical — an attempt to explain the meaning of the "Glass Bead Game," Castalian culture, human history, and finally the individual life of Joseph Knecht. Unfortunately, the novel too often sounds, not like vital philosophical assertion, but like an analysis of history or philosophy, ruminative and dull.

Even so, all the talk of the novel displays a relentless energy that can enmesh the reader in its concern for the elemental conflicts in human experience. Its greatness and quality lie in its success in communicating the awesome desperation of the intellectual and aesthetic aspirations of the twentieth century. The making of elegant Glass Bead Games is the function to which the fictive Utopian Castalian culture is dedicated. Yet, certainly, it is not merely a game; it is the essential rational and aesthetic act of any individual who hopes to reach human maturity. Such individuals create the culture. They are, therefore, more important than the most elegant culture; indeed, they must repudiate such culture, when, as history reveals, it becomes moribund and sterile because it has become "official" and remote from the raw, vulgar force of the human millions. Genius is proved only in real experience, it is not conferred to pedigree, portfolio, or prestigious schools and mentors. Its proper destiny is not to preen and posture in the ceremonial admiration of an elite, but to make, as Joseph Knecht does, the terrifying decision to resign the honor and tenure of culturally official alliances and return to the dangerous and fulfilling life of most men in real history — and to die.

The Glass Bead Game at last will defy interpretive reduction because it says so many things. Undoubtedly, this was both Hermann Hesse's intention and his predicament. As his last novel, its valedictory mood is both distressing and appropriate. It became the capstone of a career, and for it he was awarded the Nobel Prize for Literature.

John Pfeiffer

Sources for Further Study

Criticism:

Field, G. W. "Music and Morality in Thomas Mann and Herman Hesse," in *University of Toronto Quarterly*. XXIV (January, 1955), pp. 182-189. Field's thematic study of *The Glass Bead Game* leads to an inevitable comparison with the work of Thomas Mann.

Jehle, Mimi. "The Garden in the Works of Hermann Hesse," in *German Quarterly*. XXIV (January, 1951), pp. 46-47. The Garden as a thematic and symbolic device is analyzed in this criticism of *The Glass Bead Game*.

Kaester, Rudolf. "The Portrayal of Age in Hesse's Narrative Prose," in *German Review*. XLI (March, 1966), pp. 113-116. *The Glass Bead Game* is used as an example in a discussion of Hesse's techniques and themes in his manner of depicting age in his writings.

Naumann, Walter. "The Individual and Society in the Work of Hermann Hesse," in *Monatshefte*. XLI (January, 1949), pp. 33-42. The social and philosophical commentary in *The Glass Bead Game* are examined by Naumann.

Ziolkowski, Theodore. *The Novels of Hermann Heese: A Study in Theme and Structure*. Princeton: Princeton University Press, 1965, pp. 283-338. This thematic and structural study provides an excellent introduction to the content of *The Glass Bead Game*.

Reviews:

Book World. November 30, 1969, p. 14.

Library Journal. XCIV, September 1, 1969, p. 2956.

New York Times Book Review. January 4, 1976, p. 4.

Saturday Review. LII, October 18, 1969, p. 35.

GLOS PANA
(His Master's Voice)

Author: Stanislaw Lem (1921-   )
First book publication: 1968
Type of work: Novel
Time: The immediate future
Locale: A research station in an American desert

An account of a secret project established to decode signals from outer space which combines abstract theorizing about the philosophy of science with very real sociological problems

Principal characters:
>PETER E. HOGARTH, a mathematician at the University of Washington, D.C.
>SAUL RAPPAPORT, a scientist and discoverer of the neutrino signal
>W. DILL, an astrophysicist
>IVOR BALOYNE, a linguist and philologist, administrator of Project: MAVO
>DOLAND PROTHERO, a physician
>GENERAL EASTERLAND, the first administrator of the project
>WILLIAM EENEY, a representative of the Pentagon

One of the recurrent and unifying themes in Stanislaw Lem's work is chance, and the tendency of human observers to add information to observed phenomena by theorizing and hypothesizing. This problem is present in the early novel *The Investigation* (1959), in which it appears that corpses in mortuaries are resurrected according to a random pattern. The fabric of the world appears to be an impenetrable soup, out of which effects sometimes penetrate our senses, and are given a pattern by human reasoning — something added *a posteriori* to the physical world. This form of deduction naturally suggests the form of the detective novel; it appears again in Lem's novel *The Chain of Chance*, in which several mysterious deaths on Italian highways turn out to be the result of a combination of various factors that are in and of themselves all quite harmless, but combined they are highly virulent. In *The Philosophy of Chance* and *Summa Technologiae*, Lem has expressed his convictions in theoretical form. Human beings — being what they are — are not content to accept a universe governed by blind chance. Therefore, to give life significance, man has invented religion, art, myths, and legends.

These all project subjective values upon an indifferent, uncaring universe that simply exists, transcending the world of mere physics. This concept provides one of the great tensions in Lem's total opus. On one hand he is a man with a highly philosophical mind longing for absolute values and final meaning; on the other hand, he is painfully aware that no such values and meaning exist, and that they have to be invented by man's times and culture. Civilization is a comforting lie. Connected with this is the problem of the limits of human knowledge — what we can know, and how we arrive at this knowledge. In fiction, this has found its theoretically most accomplished form in the novel *Glos pana*, which is a hybrid between his theoretical works and his fiction.

As in *Solaris*, the motivation of the novel is provided by a cosmic phenomenon. After the invention of a neutrino converter it is discovered that a neutrino stream from the stars, generated by an immensely powerful pulsar, contains what may be a signal. This signal arrives from the segment of Alpha in Canis Minoris and is concentrated in a small spectrum of richly modulated energy with a cycle of 416 hours, 11 minutes, and 23 seconds. At first it is assumed that this message is being sent by a civilization so highly developed that it can keep a sender in operation as strong as a sun, sending a message intended for some intelligent beings advanced enough to receive and decode it. And if it is a message, it may contain information that has a military application. Therefore, an observation project similar to the Manhattan project is set up in the American desert, shrouded in military secrecy.

Only when the initial hopes are dashed is the secrecy gradually lifted and a flood of literature about this Project — Master's Voice or MAVO for short — begins to appear. A book is published with the posthumous memoirs of the famous mathematician, Professor Peter E. Hogarth, one of the foremost mathematicians of his time. In his comments, he reveals his life and presents his thoughts on the project. Hogarth became involved in the project by accident, one of many accidents: the signal itself had been discovered accidentally and first used for as banal a purpose as determining the winners of a lottery, and then exploited by the tabloids as the voice from the stars. Only gradually did science take notice of the phenomenon. Its regularity suggested at first that it was a message sent by intelligent beings; but as all attempts at decoding fail, this view is given up; only Hogarth does not abandon it.

The decoding of the signal is the central epistemological problem of the novel, and all attempts end in frustration. The theoretical problem in *Glos pana* is between abstract cognition, always a burning passion with Lem's heroes, and society: the microsociety of the scientists involved in this new "Ozma" project, and the fate of the world as a whole. Various detailed and sophisticated theories are advanced. Hogarth favors the theory that the signal is a cosmic beacon, installed by a civilization immensely advanced beyond ours, to communicate with other cosmic civilizations advanced enough to understand the message and probably safe-guarded against misuse. As it turns out, all dreams that the signal may be used for the fabrication of weapons explode, and with this the secrecy surrounding the project is gradually lifted. The signal is in actuality not only a word, but also an act, a life-spending ray. The neutrino radiation is of a kind that, although not creating life by itself, creates a favorable condition for the proliferation of life. It stabilizes the complex molecules that form the basis of life.

There are at least four theories offered in explanation of the signal and its properties. Aside from Hogarth's hypothesis of interstellar communication, there is the cosmo-chromosomatic theory of Learny. He suggests that the message is the by-product of a collapsing universe, being passed on into the newly arising universe. The dying universe plants the seeds of the next one, in the form of a hard, persistent neutrino radiation that encapsules in its code the total physical structure of the world. "His Master's Voice" is the rest of this "seminal radiation," whereas the other neutrino radiation in the cosmos is the unavoidable noise. A fantastic variant of this hypothesis, advanced by Sinister, holds that the program of the next universe is "written into" the natural neutrino radiation by the perishing intelligences of the last universe, who, faced with the unpredictability and rarity of life in the universe, feel an obligation to provide life in a series of universes. And finally there is Rappaport's hypothesis, which turns to science fiction for inspiration. He proposes that "His Master's Voice" is a by-product of the metabolism of some cosmic entity, not necessarily one in consciousness and individuality, but merely a normal biological process not requiring intention and intelligence. It is, according to this theory, not necessarily a process connected with human beings at all or aimed at them, and certainly not understandable by them.

All of these hypotheses are presented in convincing detail and closely related to the individual characters of the scientists who profess them. Lem has many amusing things to say about the way scientific theories are formulated, tested, and contested, and the playful ritual with which the scientific community goes about it. The cyclical nature of the signal, which makes it impossible even to determine its starting point (and which may be intended as additional information), complicates its decoding. Since the phenomenon observed is the only key to its solution, no final answer is possible. Only a partial decoding seems to be achieved, resulting in a quasibiological metabolism, the "frog's spawn" with its strange entropy. It reveals only a mass that subsists energetically on the destruction of a few atoms, requiring no outside energy source. It gives off only a little heat — almost a metaphor for pure science, aesthetically pleasing, but with no practical applications — and the more sinister "Trex" (transportation of explosion) effect, which allows the blowing up of atoms over some distance. At first this threatens to develop into the superweapon coveted by the military controllers of the project, with all the consequences this would entail for the scientists engaged in the research.

Characteristically for Lem, however, the dilemma is resolved anticlimactically and in an ironic manner. The destructive power of the process is in inverse proportion to the distance to be covered, and at a distance of only a mile the process can be used to explode only a few atoms per square mile. So the final mystery of the signal remains, and there is no possibility to make a firm decision among the conflicting hypotheses, as is the case in real cosmology and cosmogony. All the partial decoding may be reading things into the signal that are not there at all. The universe may be a gigantic Rorschach test, a collection of data, into which mankind projects what human beings find there — a cosmic mirror that reflects us back to ourselves, to the structure of our minds, instead of showing us new worlds. Mankind is forever imprisoned in the structure of its genus and its conceptual apparatus, and communication with others is impossible. Not only is it impossible, but also is negative, resulting in acute misunderstandings and erroneous interpretations.

This abstract epistemological premise of the novel, the problem of communication and understanding, is not only presented in treatise form, but also skillfully interwoven into the social implications of science in the modern world and the personalities of the scientists. The Narrator himself is a man who has always found contact with human beings difficult and has found solace in his science. He is an authority on the problems of metaethics, which he has approached mathematically. Some apparently unconnected, but finally highly relevant episodes reinforce the ethical and philosophical problems on a personal level. One is an incident from Hogarth's youth, when he watched his mother's painful struggle with death. He made faces to cope with the senselessness of her death, for which he later blames himself, and which may have influenced him in his turning to the investigation of ethics. In the second of these episodes Hogarth meets his respected scientific rival, W. Dill, as an old man in a supermarket, ravaged by time, shuffling, looking mad. Dill is a reminder of the gulf between the material world that expires, and the lofty world of human intellectual constructs. The third episode concerns Saul Rappaport, who recalls an experience from World War II. He had faced a German execution squad, whose commanding officer went about the whole affair with total disinterest. He appeared to be an impersonation of blind fate, and to give death meaning, Rappaport invented a fantasy that upon dying his soul would pass into the body of that officer, another comforting illusion to help him face an uncaring, cruel universe.

Thus, communication and meaning are the great themes of this novel, presented and interrelated at many levels and in various strands from the broad cosmic framework to the fabric of society and the social phenomena of scientific research, including a sharp denunciation of the lack of imagination and social responsibility apparent in science fiction. The Narrator of the book finds final solace in man's mortality, and the novel ends with a quotation from Swinburne's "Garden of Proserpina." This may not reflect Lem's own position, although he has invested Hogarth with many of his own features.

Glos pana is one of the rare science fiction books that is a genuine novel of science, doing justice to the complexity of scientific thinking. It presents scientists and their theories without simplifying them. It is fiction that derives its potential and importance from the theories themselves and the impact they have on human society.

Franz Rottensteiner

THE GODS THEMSELVES

Author: Isaac Asimov (1920-   )
First book publication: 1972
Type of work: Novel
Time: 2100
Locale: The Earth and its Moon; the para-Universe

The tense stories of the struggles of three beings, two human and one alien, against the stupid exploitation of a scientific discovery which could destroy the Universe in which the humans live

> *Principal characters:*
> FREDERICK HALLAM, a famous but intellectually limited scientist
> PETER LAMONT, a disaffected young physicist in Hallam's employ
> BENJAMIN DENISON, Hallam's contemporary and enemy, now fled to the Moon
> DUA, the Emotional in a Triad of Soft Ones in the para-Universe
> ODEEN, her Rational partner
> TRITT, their Paternal partner
> SELENE LINDSTROM, a female Lunarite spying on, then helping, Denison
> BARRON NEVILLE, her sometime Lover and Denison's opposition
> KONRAD GOTTSTEIN, Lunar Commissioner

Since Isaac Asimov's best-known "novel" is really not a novel at all, no reader should be surprised that his Nebula award "novel" actually is not one, either. Like the *Foundation* books, *The Gods Themselves* consists of independent stories, separated in setting, time frame, and protagonists from one another. As in the earlier works, however, Asimov provides thematic unity to such an extent that the work seems reasonably whole to the reader, despite a few annoying loose ends. The thematic unity works so well, in fact, that Asimov is able to indulge in some quite uncharacteristic technical experiments with point of view and chronology in the course of the book. *The Gods Themselves* thus becomes the most complex, most careful, and ultimately most rewarding Asimov fiction in years.

The basic structure of the book is a set of variations on a theme. The proposition, which Asimov hands the reader as the titles of the three related but distinct stories which make up the work, is a quotation from the German dramatist Friedrich Schiller. "Against stupidity," Schiller wrote in 1801, "the gods themselves contend in vain." What Asimov gives us are three major sorts of stupidity and a wide range of responses to stupidity, all centering on a scientific discovery of great possible value but equally great catastrophic potential. His enormous cast — human and nonhuman, scientist and nonscientist — struggle with the issues to the very brink of catastrophe before resolving them, for a time at least. The reader's interest is thus divided between the abstractions which Asimov presents for consideration and the slickly contrived embodiment of those points of conflict between various chambers. Asimov's avocation as a popularizer of ideas has never been put to fuller use in a work of fiction.

The first and shortest tale, "Against Stupidity," establishes the setting, the central conflict of the plot, and, of course, the theme. It is a neat, deft piece of traditional science fiction that would not have been out of place in *Astounding Science Fiction* thirty years before its actual publication. The time is the early twenty-second century, the place our Earth. Human society, as the result of a marvelous stroke of serendipity forty years before, has an apparently inexhaustible supply of energy, provided by the Inter-Universe Electron Pump, which transfers electrons to another universe (called the para-Universe, for parallel universe, in the book) by swapping pieces of ordinary tungsten for the bizarre element plutonium-186. This substance has the same atomic number as the tungsten but, because of the unusual distribution of protons and neutrons in its nucleus, is highly (and increasingly) radioactive. Hence, it can serve as an energy source, and the tungsten transferred to the para-Universe can serve as an energy source there, seemingly without interference from the laws of thermodynamics which apply to more normal energy sources. The Electron Pump (always written and spoken of in caps) has, at the opening of the book, brought about unprecedented human prosperity; it is seen as an unmitigated boon, and its proposer, the radiochemist Frederick Hallam, on whose desk the first interuniverse transfer had occurred, has become famous and powerful.

That particular situation is the source of the plot of "Against Stupidity." The problem with the Pump's success — and Hallam's attendant success — is that opposing and questioning voices are rapidly stilled. The protagonist of this story, Peter Lamont, is one such voice. He had begun work on a history of the Pump Project, working from his privileged position as a scientist in the organization. Unfortunately, he offends Hallam by suggesting that the para-men are more intelligent than the human Project engineers — after all, they initiated the transfers; all Hallam and his co-workers did was to ascertain how to continue, and make use of, the exchanges. The angry Hallam cuts the young man off from meaningful work, forcing Lamont into an effort to disprove Hallam's assumption that the Pump has no real consequences. What Lamont discovers is that the actual natural laws of the two Universes are being mixed by the Pump's actions, and that a very real chance exists of the sun's exploding as a result of an increased rate of hydrogen fusion. His alarm is increased by the messages sent from the para-Universe on pieces of iron foil; one reads F-E-E-R, interpreted by Lamont as "fear." (The other messages are in para-symbols which, despite the efforts of the linguist Myron Bronowski, are undecipherable.) But no one — political leader, revolutionary, or Pump scientist — will listen to Lamont, who has been blacklisted and slandered by Hallam. Mankind is headed for extinction as a result of "sheer thickheaded stupidity," as reputation, security, and intellectual inertia combine to prevent Lamont from getting any modification in Pumping activities. The outlook at the end of the story is quite grim.

"Against Stupidity" is not a particularly good work of fiction. Its characters are dreadfully stereotyped: there is the malcontented boy genius; the stupid, famous old man; the wise, cynical humanist; and the selfish public figures. The open ending undermines the effectiveness of the story's plot, though of course it assists the overall shape of the book. The style is pedestrian, even boring, as Asimov resorts too frequently to lecture and to a question-and-answer routine in his attempt to explain the principles behind the Pump. An attempt to liven up the tale by fracturing chronology — the fictional present of the book begins with the sixth section of this story, a section divided into four parts and interleaved with the first five, so that the book actually begins with a section numbered "Six" — seems more clever than functional, especially since Asimov provides a note claiming subtlety for the device. But the theme has been introduced and the groundwork laid for the remainder of the book.

"The Gods Themselves," the middle section in both size and placement, is also the center conceptually and aesthetically. Here, Asimov gives us his para-men, creatures utterly unlike anything in our universe; yet he presents them with such detail and care that they become the most real characters in the work. They are beings which exist in two principal states, Hard and Soft, the latter being the immature, procreative phase of the former. Hard Ones have bodies like those in our Universe, permanent in shape until death but sexless. Soft Ones occur in three types different from each other and radically different from the Hard Ones: Lefts (or Rationals), Mids (or Emotionals), and Rights (or Parentals) all have exceptionally tenuous physical beings — they can melt into rock and do, in fact, melt into each other during sexual congress. During these periods of melting a Triad, the Hard One whom they will eventually become materializes and acts, while the Soft Ones' personalities are suspended in sexually blissful unconsciousness. A Triad becomes mature after producing a new Soft One of each kind; then, at a time chosen by the Rational member, the three melt into one another for a final time and become a single permanent Hard One. This complex race is, unfortunately, a dying one. Once there had been thousands of Hard Ones and millions of Soft, but now the numbers have dwindled to fewer than three hundred and ten thousand, respectively; for their sun is also dying. The energy transfer which they have arranged is their attempt to keep the population from declining still further.

The protagonists of "The Gods Themselves" are the three members of an important Triad, contrived and designed by genetic engineering to produce a scientist of the highest order, one who can solve the problems of a dying sun. This Hard One, Estwald, designs the Pump during the periods of his Soft Ones' melting; but this fact is revealed only at the end of the novella, when the final melt occurs. Before this, we are alternately placed in the consciousness of Odeen, the (male) Rational who comes to comprehend the actual nature of the Triad and at that point directs the final melt; Tritt, the (male) Parental who rears the young and directs normal melting; and Dua, the (female) Emotional whose activities carry the theme of the work. For it is Dua, an unusual Emotional with Rational characteristics, who responds passionately to the discovery that the Pump will destroy the human Universe, who sends the messages to Lamont begging him to shut down the Pump, and who delays the Triad's final melting (and, hence, the permanent incarnation of Estwald) because she does not wish to lose her own hardwon individuality. Her struggles, first for consciousness and then against what she sees as injustice and death, are presented in a series of eighteen sharply written sections, alternating among the persons in the Triad until the final stepping forth of Estwald, the only character in the very short last section.

While such an alternating point of view is hardly a new literary device, Asimov rarely attempts to embody his story and his theme in an unorthodox technique. Here, it works splendidly, since Asimov not only keeps the characters distinct but modulates his prose style to suit each of them. Asimov may never have been a better literary craftsman than in this novella; at least one reader has exclaimed over the moving sensuality of the passages describing the Soft Ones' melting, and Asimov may never have been better at rendering a character's emotions than he is with Dua's. Her struggles against the stupidities she perceives in the Hard Ones, in her mates, and in the other Soft Ones (who generally shun her) are fully convincing, in sharp contrast to the conventional maneuverings and frustrations of Peter Lamont. Like Lamont, she loses, finally melting into Estwald, father of the infamous Pump; but the context strongly suggests that a permanent Estwald, one-third of whom is Dua, will solve the problem and save the human Universe.

In fact, the solution unexpectedly comes not from Estwald but through Benjamin Denison, Hallam's colleague whose gibes many years before had provoked Hallam and set in motion the chain of events which produced the Pump. Hounded out of the scientific community, Denison has worked so successfully for a cosmetics manufacturer that he can now emigrate to the Moon and try to take up a new life in science. In "Contend in Vain," the last and longest story in the book, Denison employs the scientific establishment of the Moon, where Hallam has not permitted the establishment of a Pump Station, to investigate his theories about the dangers of the whole Pump process. His hunch is similar to the theory of the discredited Lamont; his desire is to use the Lunar proton synchrotron in a series of experiments to verify the hunch. The Lunarites, however, distrust him, not least because their principal energy scientist, Barron Neville, is a leader in a Lunarite independence movement. Neville sends his girlfriend, Selene Lindstrom, a tour-guide with strong intuitions, to keep an eye on Denison, who is attracted to her. Neville fails to take the woman's honesty into account, however, and Selene comes to realize the truth in Denison's position and the indefensibility of Barron's. Denison and Selene, working together, achieve the solution to the danger which Hallam's people refuse to admit; they devise a source of both energy for the Moon and counter-force to the Pump, the tapping of an anti-para-Universe with opposite characteristics to the one which works through the Pump.

The Lunar Commissioner, who administers the colony of ten thousand, is persuaded that Denison is right and throws his weight behind the new Cosmeg Pump; Lamont (who does not actually appear here) and Denison are vindicated; Hallam is set out to pasture. A major crisis in human history has been solved. However, the reader may not be wholly satisfied with this most formulaic of the three stories in the work. There are disturbing loose ends — most notably, the relationship between human and para-Universes now that Estwald has matured, and the lack of any resolution of the human-alien relationship. Furthermore, much of the novella is taken up with either textbook explanations of the scientific principles involved (probably necessarily), or items of adolescent titilation, such as the growing sexual involvement between Ben and Selene (probably unnecessarily).

The Gods Themselves is, then, an uneven but significant work. In its center section, Asimov achieves his best depiction of an alien environment and physiology and the psychology appropriate to them. In the other sections, in which he casts his central idea in human terms, he produces sound, well-crafted formula stories in which a problem is defined, investigated scientifically, and solved by a plausible combination of insight and persistence. The work never comes together as a whole, partly because the shifts in setting and protagonists are demanded by the development of the idea rather than by any literary imperatives. (For instance, Lamont could function easily enough as the protagonist of the third section; and the tightly described Lunar community and impressionistically rendered world of the para-Universe, while memorable examples of the best sorts of extrapolation, pull in aesthetically opposite directions.)

The various examples of stupidity are, however, finely crafted; and the didactic structure and tone of the work and its parts demonstrate well the claim of some writers and critics that science fiction is dominantly a literature of ideas. Like his humans, Asimov's para-men — gods themselves, superior to the human "we ourselves" — are paralyzed by their own selfish stupidity, as Schiller had said they would be. In showing *how*, Asimov has produced a complex work not without flaws, but nevertheless possessing several excellences of the kinds only science fiction can provide.

William H. Hardesty III

Sources for Further Study

Criticism:

Watt, Daniel. "A Galaxy Full of People: Characterization in Asimov's Major Fiction," in *Isaac Asimov*. Edited by Joseph D. Olander and Martin Harry Greenberg. New York: Taplinger, 1977, pp. 154-157. Watt's evaluation praises *The Gods Themselves* as being a remarkable book, although he realizes some strong weaknesses in the work. He compares his character development with that of Ursula Le Guin.

Reviews:

Analog. XC, November, 1972, pp. 168-170.

Best Sellers. XXXII, July 1, 1972, p. 154.

Booklist. LXVIII, July 15, 1972, p. 975.

Extrapolation. XXXIII, May, 1972, pp. 127-131.

Kirkus Reviews. XL, March 1, 1972, p. 282.

Library Journal. XCVII, July, 1972, p. 2438.

New York Times. January 28, 1973, p. 12.

Times Literary Supplement. CCIII, April 16, 1973, p. 56.

GRAVITY'S RAINBOW

Author: Thomas Pynchon (1936-   )
First book publication: 1973
Type of work: Novel
Time: 1943-1947
Locale: London and Europe, with historical segments located all over the world

A vast novel centered around the firing of a mysterious rocket towards the end of World War II and the search for the event and its meaning by a large and varied group of people

Principal characters:
> LT. TYRONE SLOTHROP (ROCKETMAN), an American initially attached to Intelligence in London
> "PIRATE" PRENTICE, an Intelligence officer who is used by the "Firm" (Special Operations Executive) through his unique ability to absorb other people's horror fantasies
> DR. LASZLO JAMF, a mysterious chemist and creator of the strange polymer Imipolex G
> EDWARD POINTSMAN, F.R.S.C., who seeks to test Pavlovian theories and explain why response precedes stimulus in Slothrop
> KATJE BORGESIUS, used by Pointsman to condition Slothrop and control Brigadier Ernest Pudding
> OBERST ENZIAN, leader of the Schwarzkommando, the blacks displaced from the German Südwest to form rocket firing crews
> MAJOR WEISSMANN, an SS officer with the code name of Dominus Blicero
> GOTTFRIED, Weissmann-Blicero's concubine
> VASLAV TCHITCHERINE, the Soviet agent looking for the rocket; half-brother of Enzian
> GERHARDT VON GOLL, alias the Stringer, German film director and Allied Special Operations worker who becomes master of the black market in the Zone

At one and the same time *Gravity's Rainbow* goes far beyond the normal science fiction novel yet lacks some of the characteristics generally associated with the genre. Its winning of the American National Book Award (1974) suggests the wide-ranging literary and stylistic variety in Pynchon's achievement, aspects of the work which are to be seen in Cervantes' use of the picaresque and in writers of the bitter ironies of contemporary war and life such as Joseph Heller, Kurt Vonnegut, Jr., and Günter Grass. Its sprawling, imagistic, pictorial style owes much to James Joyce and to the cinematic techniques of jump-cut, cross-fade, and fantasy sequence that have had an important influence on novelistic design in recent years. It is unlike much science fiction, however, in its lack of rigor towards the exploration of any particular idea or set of ideas, in its lack of tight and coherent plotting, and in the wildness of its comic and ironic invention and language. *Gravity's Rainbow* is an immensely intricate book about human beings viewed through wildly distorting mirrors as they pirouette through a *pas de deux* with death before the dual gods of war and modern science.

The novel is divided into four sections, although any attempt to describe the line of action of the sections must of necessity omit most of the dense analogical matter that is both the strength and style of the book. "Beyond the Zero," the first section, takes place predominantly in wartime London and England and serves to introduce most of the concepts and characters of the novel. The exotic experiments by the Special Operations Executive using seances, psi forces, Pavlovian conditioning as a weapon, and the curious special abilities of Pirate Prentice and Slothrop are explicated against the paranoid background of the poised death of the silent V-2 rockets being fired upon London. The frantic intensity of life erupts upon the reader in the virtuoso opening description of Pirate Prentice's fabled Banana Breakfast and in Roger Mexico's desperate and intense love affair with Jessica Swanlake.

The "Zero" of this section's title refers to several of the main concepts explored in the novel. The quotation from Wernher von Braun, which heads the section, suggests that the zero refers to death and that "Beyond the Zero" is concerned with psi and supranatural factors that S.O.E. is toying with, including Prentice and Slothrop. In addition the whole ethos of London under the threat of the V-2 is one of a nervous and fantastic limbo of men living further and further beyond the statistical probabilities of wartime survival. The V-2 rocket, which is always the mythical center of *Gravity's Rainbow*, figures heavily in the "Zero" as well *via* the equations of the calculus. The rocket passes beyond the zero at the apogee of its ballistic arc and its fall, inevitable and beyond the control of man, is a pure physical act of gravity. The fatalism typified by the path of the rocket runs through the destinies of men and the course of history, beneath the seeming chaos of wartime London and Europe, and, by extension, into both the past and future. The calculus, which deals with ever tinier segments of reality, offers a philosophical basis for the immense and varied detailed world picture in *Gravity's Rainbow*, for each point on the arc is a meaningful and connected fragment of the whole path of history.

The second section, "Un Perm' au Casino Hermann Goering," centers on Slothrop's training by Pointsman's agents in a liberated casino-hotel on the French Riviera. Katje Borgesius is used as a lure here, and in this portion of the novel Slothrop becomes more and more aware that he is either the victim of an extremely long running and intricate plot or else is a superb classic example of a paranoid. No one ever tells Slothrop why he is being trained in every detail of the manufacture and handling of the V-2 or instructed in European languages, but he sees ample signs that his every move is being programed and then watched. Through a variety of wild adventures with three of his keepers, Tantivity Mucker-Maffick, Teddy Bloat, and Sir Stephen Dodson-Truck, with Katje, and with a circus of black marketeers and partying aristocrats Slothrop presses forward in his attempt to find out what "They" want. Instead he uncovers the beginnings of the mystery of Imipolex G and the rocket 00000 to which it was fitted. He escapes from the Riviera to Zürich, where he buys stolen information on Dr. Laszlo Jamf and then proceeds, on what he thinks is his own initiative, to seek the further mysteries of the rocket in recently surrendered German territory. He does not know that he is actually fulfilling "Their" desires in moving towards the Schwarzkommando, for the elimination of this black African force has joined the salvage of rocket technology among "Their" goals.

The third and by far the largest section of the book covers Slothrop's zigzagging route of adventures "In the Zone" as he visits the rocket factories and testing sites and gleans scraps of information about 00000. The narrative digresses frequently to explain events and characters whom he discovers as he competes with the Russian Tchitcherine, the wild American Major Marvy, and the Schwarzkommando for the history of the rocket and the special meaning of 00000. Slothrop spends part of his time disguised as Rocketman and part of it disguised as a pig, and his adventures, zany but always haunted by the forces he cannot touch, include a wild orgy on a Polish ship of aristocratic fools and a dope pick-up from President Truman's backyard at the Potsdam Conference. Eventually Slothrop learns from Franz Pökler, the engineer whom Weissmann had coerced into design work on 00000, about the use of Imipolex G and the reader gains other scraps of information from scenes in which Slothrop does not appear.

The last section, "The Counterforce," deals with the futile attempts of Katje, Pirate Prentice, Osbie Feel, Blodgett Waxwing, Roger Mexico, and Webley Silvernail to find Slothrop and rescue him from the Zone and from those who have been running him. Here the narrative fragments almost entirely, and Slothrop fades out of the action, leaving only the strange and gruesome revelation of what happened in the launching of 00000. The closing pages reveal that Weissmann-Blicero's last maniacal attempt to preserve the master race and immortalize his sadistic homosexuality involved launching Gottfried, his childish blond German lover, in an Imipolex G shroud in the V-2 00000. Here the perverse sexuality of the Nazi cause mixes with the cause of racial sanctity as Blicero, the "bleacher," obscenely "purifies" Gottfried in the pure light of the sun in outer space instants before the boy plunges to his inevitable death.

The conclusion of the novel is a passage called "Descent," addressed directly to the reader. It implies that the rocket is falling upon us now and thus directs the meaning of Slothrop's futile search to the present, where the technological achievements of the rocket harbor the potential for universal death and where all of the details of the paranoid world of the cartels and the technology of the management of history are still the background to our lives, although this can never be conclusively proved.

Pynchon's style will be confusing to readers expecting an orderly plot. He improvises upon his themes, creating a teeming variety of characters and incidents, each with some contact to the grid of the rocket. Beginning anywhere in the action inevitably leads everywhere. For example, Dr. Laszlo Jamf enters the novel primarily as the discoverer of the mystery polymer, Imipolex G. Later we find that he taught Franz Pökler, Weissmann's engineer, and that Jamf, the true National Socialist chemist, always wanted to escape the organic bonds in compounds such as polymers (symbolized by C - H) and develop inorganic syntheses such as silicon and nitrogen (symbolized by Si - N). This fanaticism to escape even the organic synthetics in which man dictates to Nature the management of dead metallic elements suggests the hollow soul of modern science and led to the rocket and all of the phallic adoration it excited. Slothrop also discovers that Jamf, moving from IG Farben to its American cartel partners, actually had a hand in the surveillance of Slothrop when he was a baby. Pointsman already knew this, and the reader discovers that Jamf's use of Pavlovian conditioning on baby Tyrone may account for Slothrop's hidden skill for predicting the fall of the V-2's.

This hardly exhausts the connections leading to and from Jamf in *Gravity's Rainbow*, but it suggests the gradual growth of paranoia which the reader shares with Slothrop as the often comic elliptical fragments of the novel mesh to an ever more unnerving whole.

The novel is Rabelaisian in its sexual language and the frequency with which sexual experience is portrayed. Besides the fact that this is an accurate portrayal of the liberty born of the fear of war, poverty, and the loneliness of the Zone, the sexual explicitness functions as a reminder that nothing is too private or delicate for "Their" use. Thus Katje, for whom Slothrop has a real affection, is brought to him to service him and confirm that he is getting erections from his study of the rocket data. She has previously been Weissmann's whore to serve intelligence purposes; and she is later used by Pointsman to control Brigadier Pudding through his masochistic and coprophilic fantasies prior to his being sent into the Zone to the Schwarzkommando Enzian. Human warmth is almost wholly leeched from the sex act in the novel, and any moment of tenderness is quickly subsumed to a mechanical instant in the implacable ballistic course of history.

Wandering through the surrealistic, war-torn and frequently wildly comic scenes of *Gravity's Rainbow* leads to a principal issue concerning the book: is it science fiction? The answer to this lies in the pervasive presence of science in the book in fashions varying from the hard details of the construction, function, and firing of the V-2 and Pavlovian training to the metaphors of the calculus, the rocket, and organic polymers. Pynchon demonstrates how science and technology rule our modern world in the same abstract sense that the ballistic arc is forever fixed and immutable once the launch has reached *Brennschluss* (burn-out). The great affinities and interlocking between IG Farben,

ICI, and the American chemical giants are the immutable, organic growths of chemical technology. Pynchon is writing of a scientific event which is not known to have happened, so the launching of Gottfried is science fiction in the strictest sense. But it is vastly more important that Pynchon has created a novel which places science in its true position, controlling the lives and the imaginations of contemporary men.

Over and over again the novel views situations as science perceives them, and over and over Pynchon expands the immediate perceptions of the scientific eye to the realms of metaphysics. The rocket becomes the center of it all, the mystery of the consummation that cannot be resisted because gravity is law. But although it is worshiped it is finally sterile, a gigantic penis that cannot penetrate but only destroy with its ejaculation of Sodium Amatol. And when the frenzy of Weissmann-Blicero, blindly confusing the deep sexual confusion of Nazism with the racial fears of the "Master-race," creates the horrible ritual murder-sacrifice of his beloved to the machine in a spectacular yet futile gesture, Pynchon has perfectly enunciated man's desperate surrender to the grip of the ballistic parabola of the rocket age. We have all "gone up" towards the sun in our own chariots of the gods, but we have chosen to surrender the reins, so that like Gottfried we cannot resist the Masters or avoid the descent into chaos after the power is extinguished in the *Brennschluss* that we cannot control. Like its ancestor in art, *Dr. Strangelove, Gravity's Rainbow* presents the situation in which we laugh until we cry and die. It is a masterful novel.

Peter Brigg

Sources for Further Study

Criticism:

Adams, Robert Martin. *After Joyce: Studies in Fiction After Ulysses.* New York: Oxford University Press, 1977, pp. 175-179. Adams compares *Gravity's Rainbow* with other novels of the Seventies, but does not emphasize its importance to science fiction writing.

Friedman, Alan J. and Manfred Puetz. "Science as Metaphor: Thomas Pynchon and *Gravity's Rainbow*," in *Contemporary Literature.* XV (Summer, 1974), pp. 345-359. The scientific metaphor used by Pynchon in *Gravity's Rainbow*, particularly that of the thermodynamics of life itself, is the focal point of this article.

Krafft, J. M. "And How Far-Fallen: Puritan Themes in *Gravity's Rainbow*," in *Critique: Studies in Modern Fiction.* XVIII (1977), pp. 55-73. The religious and moral aspects of *Gravity's Rainbow* are analyzed here, as the title implies. However, this issue of *Critique: Studies in Modern Fiction* has several articles which give in-depth discussion of the novel and is one of the best sources of criticism yet published on Pynchon.

Le Clair, Thomas. *"Gravity's Rainbow,"* in *Critique: Studies in Modern Fiction.* XVII (1975), pp. 25-28. Le Clair analyzes Pynchon's handling of death in *Gravity's Rainbow*.

Reviews:

Atlantic. CCXXXI, March, 1973, p. 98.

Christian Science Monitor. May 23, 1973, p. 11.

Nation. CCXVII, July 16, 1973, p. 53.

New Republic. CLXVIII, April 14, 1973, p. 241.

New York Review of Books. XX, March 22, 1973, p. 22.

New York Times Book Review. March 11, 1973, p. 1.

Newsweek. LXXXI, March 19, 1973, p. 92.

Saturday Review of the Arts. I, March, 1973, p. 59.

Yale Review. LXII, June, 1973, p. 624.

GRAY MATTERS

Author: William Hjortsberg (1941-   )
First book publication: 1971
Type of work: Novel
Time: 2425
Locale: The Earth

A satiric depiction of humanity's failure to improve upon creation by redesigning itself physically, spiritually, and intellectually by means of technology

> *Principal characters:*
> SKEETS KALBFLEISCHER, a twelve-year-old and the first cerebromorph
> VERA MITLOVIC, a cerebromorph and former movie queen
> PHILIP QUARRELS, Depository Auditor and former astronaut
> OBU ITUBI, a runaway cerebromorph and former Nigerian sculptor
> OONA, an authentic female

Gray Matters is a masterful science fiction-satire in which actuated super-technology is the apparatus for a study in epistemology, behaviorism, and levels of consciousness, intelligence, and communication. William Hjortsberg's future world provides pseudoserious answers to questions such as: Is man needed in the universe? What is his proper function there? How does he need to change to improve that fuction? Hjortsberg's spectacle mocks the realities behind many of the clichéd expressions and labels of our age. His disporting tone, however, never lightens the effect of his exposé of the concepts and trends to which the common coinages refer. While a mere recitation of the themes in relation to elements in the novel cannot catch the spirit and imagination which distinguish the story, it will suggest the range of Hjortsberg's view.

The assorted objects of the author's attack are invasion of privacy *via* spy activities of government intelligence agencies and operations (auditing and monitoring, the impossibility of secrets, complete files of memory tapes); genetic engineering (cerebrectomy); cybernation, psycho-cybernation, behavior modification (dream playbacks, meditation exercises, auditing reports, "spiritual growth" as the ten levels toward Elevation); dehumanization and depersonalization (anti-anthropomorphism, divestment of body and ego to achieve awareness and understanding); fragmentation of experience and machine dominance (the bureaucratic operations of the Depository, the various Mark machines as automated and stratified labor); Eastern mysticism and consciousness-expansion (the Awakening as the millennium with its paths of obedience, duty, patience, and meditation toward Enlightenment); counterculture creeds and lifestyles; the ecological movement (the Nords and Tropiques with perfect bodies from the hatchery in mystical harmony with themselves and nature); and biological experimentation toward evolutionary change (the Amphbios, aquatic human beings).

With double irony, Hjortsberg dehumanizes and depersonalizes his characters by removing their brains and discarding their bodies to reverse the existential stance to Essence precedes Being. The awakening inaugurated the advent of mass voluntary discorporation. By means of cerebrectomy, the cerebromorphs (or disembodied brains), divested of their corporeal form, undergo a metamorphosis made possible by the miracles of technology in a vast Depository with numerous levels which represent the stages of elevation toward perfection, then reincarnation. Ego and libido, which impede ascension, are prohibited. The id is directed toward knowledge and information to discipline the mind and perfect the intellect until the new selfless self attains the supremacy of Enlightenment when it is ready for a new body also hatched in the Depository.

To expose the systems approach and its consequent fragmentation of life in modern times, Hjortsberg ridicules precision instruments and mechanization which err and break down but which nonetheless denote exactitude. In the novel, men and women can be dismantled, redesigned, and reconstituted by the systematic derangement and rearrangement of personality and the systematic deprivation of the psyche and emotional outlets — all under the autocratic, impersonal supervision of Central Control. Using the terminology from the biological ontogeny of insects, bees in particular (Hive, Pupa, Imago, Drone, Larva), Hjortsberg superimposes the reverencing attitudes and language of yoga to suggest a composite transformation whose operations are solely technological in contrast to the natural organic ways of insects and the mental and spiritual discipline of mystics. Furthermore, in applying the stages associated with growth and participation in a beehive to the dubious process of Elevation in the Depository, Hjortsberg shows that the master plan for human change predicated on determinism will not work.

Thus evolution is consigned to automation with the machine as surrogate mother and electrical currents as the only source of sustenance. The reincarnated product of this process attains the ultimate though finite intellectual excellence that parallels the perfection and order of the natural world which has also become a redesigned ecological ideal. The realm outside the domain of the Depository is an Arcadian garden in which the *au naturel* Nords and Tropiques inhabiting their custom-made hatchery bodies represent the counterculture of the new naturalists. They live in silent simplicity mystically attuned to one another and the laws of nature, the ways of the earth. Depository misfit and escapee Obu Itubi mirrors Hjortsberg's derision when he becomes baffled by their perpetual entrancement and arcane variety of interrelatedness.

The cerebromorphs who head the cast of characters, and whose existence in the Depository forms the storyline of the novel, fail to achieve Elevation all the way from Level I to Level X because they cannot overcome or surmount their original anthropomorphic integrality. Even as discorporate entities, they resist the process that aims to change their pre-Awakening patterns of behavior. Itubi is a renegade (against the Awakening) and a sculptor, a hold-out humanist who cannot understand and accept the assassination of the arts, the denigration of man-made beauty. Psychologically he cannot divest himself of ego and libido and wants to reclaim his whole selfhood. Unable to await Elevation, he arrogates control of an Amco-pak (machine), massacres the brainless bodies in the hatchery, escapes from the Depository, and attempts to rejoin the outside world. His hard-won freedom is only temporary, however, for reincarnated he is an old-fashioned brain in a newfangled body. Eventually he is returned to the Depository where he undergoes a brainwipe and is indefinitely consigned to the limbo of anonymity. Nevertheless, his identity is not totally expunged, for he leaves behind pregnant Oona, the weaver, an original human being who escaped the Awakening and cerebrectomy and who perpetuates Obu's spirit in the baby he sired. Their relationship is the only authentic human union in the novel. As an untampered female, Oona will have their child, who symbolizes a second genesis.

Young Skeets Kalbfleischer, the historic first cerebromorph, is a case of arrested adolescence. Although his brain has become an educated repository for diverse subjects, he is fixated on becoming a cowboy. Individualistic Itubi is a conscious rebel and hero-worshiping Kalbfleischer a subconscious rebel, both in defiance of a "sophisticated age of meditation and spiritual liberation."

Vera Mitlovic, the beautiful paradox — at once child, prostitute, and goddess — represents the twentieth century malaise arising from superfluity and artificiality. Before the Awakening, she was a movie queen for whom the only reality in the Depository is her own celluloid past. Vera is reminiscent of Marlene Dietrich and Gloria Swanson, once glamorous women and now relics who slavishly rejuvenate themselves to preserve their bygone image. Incapable of dispensability, Vera deliberately eschews the process of becoming more by being less. No longer able to devote herself to appearances, she nevertheless permits her mind to dwell on irrelevancies and nurtures a false security in dreams of material possessions and earthly pleasures, chiefly sexual conquests. Her subversion is tuning out the Depository procedures and tuning in her old films.

Through Mitlovic and the other characters, Hjortsberg examines the character of sexual experience. In a memory merge, Vera and Skeets fornicate as carefree hedonists. Before the merge, which becomes a permanent displacement for Vera as a missing, unclassified cerebromorph, she finds a kind of auto-erotic euphoria in replaying her old movies. The erotic is everywhere in the novel. Itubi's preoccupation with the study of bees and spiders as so-called projects for self-improvement is sublimated sexuality. Philip Quarrels, a Level II Auditor and former hero-astronaut, succumbs to Vera and thereafter reverts to his ways as a womanizer.

As an automated laboratory, the Depository, with its invisible network of Central Control as overseer, is a complex environment of corridors and machinery where all the surfaces are hard, brittle, smooth, reflective, opaque.

The Depository is a glossy-surfaced grayness composed of stainless steel, concrete, aluminum, formica, and chrome, containing the complex circuits that nurture the cerebromorphs. In this manufactured substantiality without shadows where humanity is manufactured, nothing is accidental; everything is contrived. There the action happens as though at once as Hjortsberg cuts from scene to scene. The events that transpire in fragments and parallels have an overall effect of simultaneity and underscore the ceaseless, artificial hivelike activity in the Depository. While Skeets has overslept and missed reveille, Vera is reliving a particular scene from one of her movies, and Obu is studying bees.

Much of the novel's satiric texture and symbolic significance derive from Hjortsberg's imagery and diction. His penchant for wordplay begins with the title of the novel and continues with puns that lace the narrative. Many of them pertain to "gray matters," to wit — "It's amazing what you can do if you put your mind to it"; "Mind over matter." In another linguistic category, Hjortsberg provides elaborate correlatives and associations which signify a character's state of mind. One of the best and most central to the character's inability to accommodate his human nature to the demands of Elevation is Skeets's recurring nightmare in which monkey brains and ultimately his own brain are served to him as a gourmet delicacy. Not even his withdrawal into perpetual adolescence can shield him from his awareness of the rape of cerebrectomy. Other effective associations rely on the humanness of the bodiless brains juxtaposed against the unreality of the brainless bodies. For example, Itubi kills the unliving humanoid bodies in the hatchery in his rebellion and escapes. With the massacre of the lifeless forms, he converts the artificial womb into a morgue, which the Depository already connotes.

In the absurd, bizarre, surreal events in *Gray Matters*, Hjortsberg shows us characters who are real enough beneath their stereotypical identities. Their recourses to subterfuge dramatize how Progress, so-called, with its worship of the modern god, Electron, with its idolatry of absolutist technology, threatens our essential humanity. Through their behavior, he depicts the terms of technological advancement and its attendant conflict between means and ends, between the ideal and the real, between theory and practice in the use of machines. Hjortsberg's machinery and machines are frightening — not because they evolve toward humanness, for they are not androids and humanoids. In them we find neither our best nor worst. What frightens us is the total alienness and the supremacy with which they have been endowed by their human creators and which we program them to use unremittingly and irrevocably to dehumanize their creators. The dilemma is plain, for Hjortsberg does not offer a golden mean.

Lahna Diskin

Sources for Further Study

Reviews:

Analog. LXXXVIII, February, 1972, p. 175.

Book World. December 19, 1971, p. 6.

Futures. IV, June, 1972, p. 195.

Kirkus Reviews. XXXIX, August 1, 1971, p. 823.

Library Journal. XCVI, July, 1971, p. 2351.

Luna Monthly. XXXVIII–XXXIX, July–August, 1972, p. 30.

New York Times Book Review. October 31, 1971, p. 7.

Newsweek. LXXVIII, November 29, 1971, p. 104.

Publisher's Weekly. CC, August 2, 1971, p. 63.

Times Literary Supplement. May 18, 1973, p. 562.

GREYBEARD

Author: Brian W. Aldiss (1925-   )
First book publication: 1964
Type of work: Novel
Time: 2029 (with episodes set in 1981-2018)
Locale: England, in the Thames Valley

A somber, elegiac study of a world in which no children have been born for more than forty years, and of one of the youngest men left alive in that world, Algy Timberlane (nicknamed "Greybeard"), his wife Martha, and their traveling companions

Principal characters:
>ALGY TIMBERLANE (nicknamed "GREYBEARD"), an adventurer and former soldier
>MARTHA BROUGHTON TIMBERLANE, his wife
>CHARLEY SAMUELS, cotraveler with the Timberlanes
>JEFF PITT, a hunter and poacher, cotraveler with the Timberlanes and Samuels
>PATRICIA TIMBERLANE, Algy's mother
>ARTHUR TIMBERLANE, Algy's father
>JACK PILBEAM, organizer for DOUCH, Algy's colleague
>JINGADANGELOW, an attractive charlatan

Greybeard fits several possible categories of novel genre, but none so conveniently as that of "British disaster novel." The main characteristics of this subgenre of science fiction include: one all-embracing disaster which threatens most human life (with the novel set in Britain); one or more resourceful and self-aware characters who can survive the disaster and set up a new life in its wake; celebration of an England left purified by the disappearance of civilization. No more than a few science fiction novels fulfill each of these conditions; probably the most famous are John Wyndham's *The Day of the Triffids* and several of J. G. Ballard's novels, including *The Drowned World.*

To say that *Greybeard* fits this subgenre neither denigrates the book nor captures much of its content. (The quality it shares most obviously with others of its kind is its affection for the English landscape.) Nevertheless, any discussion of the book must begin with the disaster which affects the lives of all the characters.

Brian Aldiss' *Greybeard*, first published in 1964, postulates that atomic weapons testing in the atmosphere would continue during the 1960's and 1970's. Protests about rising fallout levels lead the atomic powers to test these devices outside the atmosphere, in orbit around Earth. Spectacular borealis effects in the night sky are an indication of what Earth's inhabitants recognize too late: the tests have seriously disturbed the Van Allen belt which surrounds the planet. In 1981, during what is later euphemistically called the Accident, the Van Allen belt became so unstable that on two occasions earth's biosphere was bombarded by hard radiation from space.

At first the results of the Accident go unrecognized. Many people, especially children, die or develop fatal cancers. Most of those who survive the initial sickness recover without side effects. Only a year later is it found that no babies have been born to humans or higher mammals since the Accident. Scientists make optimistic reassurances that the global sterility will probably disappear in five or ten years' time. It does not.

The real disaster develops not from the initial Accident, but from the social and economic effects of wiping out the expected new generation. For instance, Algy Timberlane's father, Arthur, owns a toy-manufacturing firm. Within a year of the Accident, he finds that his business has gone bankrupt. In turn, this means that his business is no longer placing new orders, and neither are many others. Unemployment and social disruption increase; eventually totalitarian governments take power, even in the Western democracies. As if to add suicide to infanticide, those nations which can still finance large-scale wars send opposing armies throughout the world looking for any children which might be left. The first nation to gather enough children for a viable gene pool has an assured future. Most of the children found are deformed in some way, or are killed during the fighting itself.

The novel begins in the year 2029, after social organization on a national scale has disappeared, and England's population has decreased to perhaps six million in all. Those people who are left stay in small self-contained villages or towns, fending off intruders and newly feral animal species.

At the novel's beginning, Algy Timberlane (nicknamed "Greybeard" throughout the book) and his wife Martha have been living eleven years in the tiny settlement of Sparcot. During that time, the village has been cut off from most other people, principally by the forest which has covered England again. Algy and Martha, now in their late forties, are two of the youngest people left alive in the world. Most of the other people in the village are older, less adventurous, and more dispirited.

There is no reason why Algy and Martha could not have stayed in Sparcot for the rest of their lives — except that they still have some sense of adventure. There is a rumor of an attack on the village by stoats (a dangerous plague in the area since the disappearance of people). During the ill-organized, panic-stricken attempt to defend the village, Algy, Martha, and some friends take the opportunity to leave Sparcot. Algy has a boat prepared, and the small party, including Jeff Pitt and Charley Samuels, begin their pilgrimage down the Thames river to the sea.

Of the disaster itself, Algy is the first to admit that "from all this, I do derive a terrible pleasure. . . . Somewhere it is there, a little stoaty thing that makes of a global disaster a personal triumph." *Greybeard* is, more than anything, a tale of Algy Timberlane's determination to make the most of the experiences offered to him by this vastly changed world. These experiences present themselves in three main sections of the book: "The River: Swifford Fair," "The River: Oxford," and "The River: The End." *Greybeard* is a refreshingly unmelodramatic account of what Algy chooses to discover, rather than what is done to him. In this way, Aldiss avoids all the horror-story elements which have often been the blight of "disaster novels."

The group of pilgrims finds that traces of the old English way of life remain on the banks of the Thames downriver. At Swifford Fair, they find that most of the people, like the Sparcot villagers, are older and less agile than they are. Worse, any senility among them tends to be reinforced by the rest of the group. This senility mainly takes the form of hanging onto any reassurance that children are being born, or that a source of immortality has been discovered.

The attractive charlatan, Jingadangelow, offers both. His "youths" are castrated old people wearing heavy cosmetics, but the disguise fools many of Jingadangelow's followers. He says that he owns a castle somewhere in the woods where immortality can be bought. He convinces many old people with failing memories that they have already lived hundreds of years because of his help, and can expect centuries yet. Their gratitude is considerable.

Jingadangelow does not bother trying to fool Greybeard, though. He recognizes another canny man, and also another optimist:

> You don't suffer as you should in this blighted time; though life is miserable, you enjoy it. . . . We need our disasters. You and I have weathered, somehow, the collapse of a civilization. We are survivors after shipwreck. But for us two, we feel something deeper than survival — triumph! Before the crash came, we willed it, and so disaster for us is a success, a victory for the raging will.

Much of the rest of the novel explores the probable truth (or lack of it) in this statement. The difference between Jingadangelow and Greybeard is one of integrity. Jingadangelow would have taken his fellow beings down a peg, whatever society he lived in. Greybeard feels that he did not make the best of his life until now, and his standards of good conduct rise above mere practicality. This difference of attitudes leads to the confrontation between the two men at the end of the novel.

And in what way did the people of the former world "will" the disaster? Aldiss does not reveal the total pattern of his thought on this matter until the last pages of the book.

The pilgrims, now reduced to Algy, Martha, Jeff Pitts and Charley Samuels, set off from Swifford Fair and reach the spires of Oxford. There corruption and opportunism are rife.

At one stage, cholera and other plagues made Oxford a dead city (so Greybeard finds out). The people who returned to the city tried to re-create its old style. They divided Oxford into territories based on the university Colleges. Christ Church beat off a challenge from Balliol with the last mortar weapon left in the city. No genuine revival of learning has been attempted or wanted. The three octogenerians who control Chirst Church — Norman, Vivian, and

Gavin — have locked up the relics from the previous civilization: "Wireless — the radio, don't you know — is one of the things we do not like in our quiet little gerontocracy. . . . It could not profit us, and might upset us, to have news of the outside world." The three run the College as a money-making museum. On New Year's Day they exhibit a few deformed adolescents. One of their exhibits is a truck which Greybeard recognizes as his — he had to sell it many years ago in desperation to obtain food for Sparcot village. His claim to the truck is not recognized. Instead, he is charged "garage fees" — four years of laboring for the College which will be needed to pay it off.

Greybeard actually stays there for one and a half years to try to buy back the truck. He works gathering reeds from a boat on the widened, marshy river, "feeling himself absorbed between the flat prospect of water and marsh and the mould of sky." This recalls the same humble devotion to duty and to nature as Clym Yeobright in Thomas Hardy's *The Return of the Native*. In these pages in particular, *Greybeard* is a Hardyesque poem in praise of rural England. "The Earth renewed itself," writes Aldiss, recalling the stream of language which flows from the King James Bible through Hardy to Aldiss, "only men grew older and were not replenished. The trees grew taller, the rookeries noisier, the graveyards fuller, the streets more silent. . . ."

But rural senescence is not for Greybeard. On his birthday, he decides to celebrate by going with Martha to their original goal, the sea. They do not reach it (in the book, at least) because they discover a more specific object for their energies. They meet Jingadangelow again. He has set himself up as a holy man, and his main gimmick is that he has captured one nondeformed adolescent girl. There is promise for a human future after all. Jingadangelow guesses, correctly, that those children which have been born during recent years have been hidden or sent into the woods, for fear of their lives. Greybeard is disgusted that Jingadangelow keeps one of them as his mistress instead of trying to help and make contact with the new children. In the final scene of the book, three of these children try to recapture the girl. They taunt Jingadangelow, dancing around him as if representatives of an alien species. Greybeard takes a wild shot at them before he realizes who they are. A wounded boy is captured. Greybeard's remorse is considerable: "He himself had fired at the first child he had been close to. Perhaps there was some kind of filicidal urge in man forcing him to destruction." But he and Martha now have the opportunity to rear the child they could never have themselves.

Only during these last pages does Aldiss make this point explicitly: that much of human activity, especially during the late twentieth century, seems designed to wipe out our children. Yet many people claim they would like to live in a simpler, less lethal world. Greybeard is certainly happier doing so. Not that such a paradox makes a novel in itself. The events of the pilgrimage appear on a backdrop of somber, elegiac colors; there is little enough conventional "story" from which to construct more than a novella. The strongest pattern of the book appears not in the formal story but in the *other* pilgrimage of the book: Algy's memories of how the world of 2029 came into existence. These memories appear in three "flashbacks." Each is a self-contained story, but together they add up to the inner meaning of the book.

The first flashback, "Cowley," tells how Algy, Martha, and Jeff Pitt reached Sparcot. They had been stranded in Cowley, a suburb of the old Oxford, as central government in England disintegrates. Commander Peter Croucher takes over the city, and tries to enlist Algy's aid for his cause. Algy's allegiance lies elsewhere: to DOUCH(E) — Documentation of Universal Contemporary History (English branch) — an organization set up to record the end of humanity on tape and film for anyone or anything that might follow the human race.

Although Croucher's deceptions and power mania are repellent to Algy, he decides to cooperate for a time. Jeff Pitt is a soldier ordered by Croucher to kill Algy and take the DOUCH(E) van. Jeff cannot bring himself to kill Algy and Martha; he breaks down, and Algy decides to use the van to break through the barriers around the city, taking Jeff Pitt as fellow escapee. They succeed in the escape. It is a constant paradox of the story that Jeff remains most deeply ashamed of the most admirable characteristic about him — that he cannot kill another human being. The Stoicism that leads to optimism in Algy turns sour in Jeff; he remains morose, a lonely hunter who can never hide his resentment at finding himself in this particular post-Accident world.

Algy's pilgrimage into memory is backward. Before Cowley was Washington. The second flashback tells how he was seconded to the American organization, DOUCH, after fighting in the English army (before the country itself disintegrated). After Jack Pilbeam from Washington promises to fly his girl friend, Martha, to America, Algy agrees to join DOUCH. During their stay in Washington, Martha is perhaps the youngest and best-looking woman visible. A sexually disturbed stranger captures her and sends a note to Algy on where to find her. He goes to the place — God's Sufferance Press — deserted offices of what had been a religious publisher for children. When at first Algy cannot find Martha (although he does find her unharmed), he is struck by an obsessive experience which guides the rest of his life. "God, this is what it's like to be left alone in the world. . . . Year by year, as the living died, the empty rooms about him would multiply, like the cells of a giant hive which no bees visited. . . ." In a way, he has the most horrifying view of the future that ever strikes him; he also realizes what will really count in that future world. He proposes to Martha as soon as he finds her, as companionship and love are the only qualities which last the distance. He has seen the worst; now it is up to him to make what he can of the life still allowed him.

The final flashback, "London," is the most poignant section of the book. When Algy was six, and sick from the radiation illness that followed the Accident, he stayed for a while in a house by the Thames. The Timberlanes could not buy the house because Algy's father had gone bankrupt: he learned the true nature of the world disaster as he investigated why toys were not being sold anymore. Algy's mother was infatuated with Keith Barrett, Arthur's business partner. Algy overheard some of this, but he was more wounded by the fact that his father was so bowed down by his troubles that he could not extend affection to his son. The significance of the crisis overwhelmed Arthur and he killed himself in a car crash.

This final episode is particularly strong in Algy's memory because it recalls the world lost after the Accident. It was a world that betrayed him and all children. It was a world of human relationships complicated by Patricia Timberlane's faithlessness and Arthur's hopelessness. It was a world of television pundits "all, one of them with considerable pipemanship, being euphoric about world conditions." It is our present world, in all but fine details.

It is also more complex than Greybeard's world. The human relationships shown in the "London" section have a vividness missing in, even inappropriate to, the rest of the novel. Algy is relentlessly fine-spirited during the rest of the novel; Martha endlessly forgiving and supportive; Jeff and Charley so much the good friends. In the world of 2029, much of the problem is accommodating oneself to the landscape, rather than with one another. The novel's greatest success is its detailed and affectionate portrayal of that landscape, which triumphs as humanity disappears.

Greybeard reminds us, through the abrupt change of focus in the "London" section, of how we are responsible for our present landscape. The world can still choose whether to obliterate the human race or preserve it. In *Greybeard*, Aldiss shows us that our motives are hardly simple; perhaps we really do want to do away with the twentieth century, with our children, and with ourselves. There are no easy choices.

Bruce Gillespie

Sources for Further Study

Criticism:

Mathews, Richard. *Aldiss Unbound*. San Bernardino, Calif.: Borgo, 1977, pp. 26-30. *Greybeard* is considered a "valid commentary" on what could happen as a result of flirtation with nuclear weapons.

Reviews:

Analog. LXXIV, February, 1965, pp. 87-88.

Best Sellers. XXIV, September 1, 1964, p. 200.

Library Journal. LXXXIX, September 15, 1964, p. 3332.

Magazine of Fantasy and Science Fiction. XXVII, December, 1964, p. 70.

LA GUERRE AU XXE SIÈCLE
(War in the 20th Century)

Author: Albert Robida (1848-1926)
First book publications: 1883; 1887 (Dual versions)
Type of work: Novels
Time: The twentieth century
Locale: Mozambique and Australia

Two speculative versions of man at war in the twentieth century by an author who is famous for the illustrations he includes in his works

To review a work by Albert Robida, one of the most fascinating illustrators working at the end of the nineteenth century, is very difficult. In his novels, illustration is inseparable from the text in that it expands the narrative, a picture being worth a thousand additional words. Thus, in Gifford's *La guerre infernale* (*The Fiendish War*, 1907) when the text has "rolling bombards," the artist draws a tank with a turret and armed with a three-inch cannon, such as might have appeared at the end of World War II.

There are two versions of *La guerre au XXe siècle*. One was got up in the Italian fashion, in a beautiful album with illustrations, some in color. This version is humorous. The other, of 1883, comprising a special issue of *La Caricature*, is just the opposite, a gloomy and much more prophetic work.

The humorous version (1887) is dedicated to Rude's *Marseillaise*, armed with a big gun and carrying a gas mask such as might be imagined in antiwar drawings following the 1914-1918 conflict. The book traces the adventures of a man from Toulouse, Fabius Molinas, in the 18th Balloonist Reserves, called up in 1945 as second-class gunner aboard the *Epervier*. The fleet of balloons starts out by strafing "rolling blockhouses" that have crossed the border. However, the hero constantly changes weapons to alert us to the existence of every invention of the era; he rides in a tank, he lays siege to a town, and he serves in the poison gas corps. Shells gas the entire population of a town just as troops take it over; mediums influence the minds of the enemy while reading battle plans in the minds of generals. There are epidemics of colds and scabies, armies cough, scratch, and sneeze. And all of this unfolds in a laughable way. The work was published as a *de luxe* album, it was advisable not to assail the buyer with overly gloomy images. Besides, who would believe in pictures like these: armored divisions, aerial fleets setting towns afire, underwater torpedo boats? At the time, the only flying machines in existence were dirigibles. Artillery was entirely horse-drawn.

The period was one of military expectation, following publication of George Chesney's *The Battle of Dorking* (1871). This book can profitably be contrasted with the "well-founded, quite-serious" exploits of Robida's Captain Danrit, who always casts aside any protective shielding. It was only later, in 1916, that Robida's views hit home. His prophetic vision was a stroke of genius, not of luck. The artist in the black-and-white who hated war continually pondered new means of destruction, and his first work, this 1883 edition of *La guerre au XXe siècle*, far surpasses in its foresight not only that of the professional military imagination, but also that of H. G. Wells in *Anticipations*.

This edition (1883) is more of a novel and contains more individual heroes. The war is set in 1975 between Mozambique and Australia, since by this time the center of world power is no longer in Europe. But the countries are mere representations, like the war. Robida sums up the book with his frontispiece in the style of the day: "Civilization bestowing its benefits on the people." The cornucopia overflows with shells and bullets. History books have beautiful words about honor and the glories of military victory, but Robida knew that the underlying cause of war was economic — competition for new markets.

Previously, distances between Africa and Australia would have mitigated the conflict, but technical progress now makes it feasible for everyone to fight, even though oceans separate them. When war threatens, all citizens volunteer, thus giving up the very freedoms for which they are fighting. Robida comments in passing that one's country is the place where one pays his taxes, and that the tax on blood increases just as the one on money. At the rate things are going, he suggests, in the twenty-first century, citizens from seven to seventy will be drafted. Everything increases, the expenditure of human flesh like the rest.

Mozambique is protected against a naval assault, but not from an aerial one. How to predict a landing point? How to concentrate troops without weakening another point? But the Australians land in the neutral territory of Cafrerie in flagrant contempt of every law and treaty. This is the common fate of small countries, too small to offer an effective defense. Australian tanks confront their Mozambique counterparts in the great battle of Zumbo. The African armored columns fall back, covered by an aerial squadron.

The Australians land new armies; the Africans regroup in the interior. Mozambico City is besieged, the Australians making use of electrically operated drilling machines that require fifteen men to operate and that move along at two kilometers an hour. This is the only invention in the work that is really fantastic, for the same cannot be said of the chemical battles in which rockets spread suffocating mists, the "chemists" being protected by filter-plug masks. (These are the sodium thiosulphate masks of 1915, and photos from that era look as if they might have been used as models for Robida's drawings.)

Since both open and closed cities are vulnerable to air attack, the Australians benefit by destroying factory towns making products that compete with their own. Once again the objectives are not military or strategic, but economic.

The battle of Mazoyambo pits 800,000 Australians against 625,000 Africans. That night the defeated Africans withdraw. The great powers propose mediation. The Australian demands are unacceptable: total economic control with free entry for their products without reciprocity, interdiction against forming other trade agreements.

For a time Mozambique avoids a pitched battle while it is cutting the supply lines of the too audacious invaders; then it counterattacks. Robida ends with a two-line communiqué: "Bombardment and gassing of Melbourne. The Australians are suing for peace. An armistice is signed."

Albert Robida's speculative work is prolific. Besides the two *La guerre au XXe siècle* (1883 and 1887), there are *Saturnin Farandoul*; *Le vingtième siècle* (*The Twentieth Century*); *Voyage de fiançailles au XXe siècle* (*Engagement Trip in the 20th Century*); *La vie électrique* (*A Fast-Paced Life*); *Jadis chez aujourd'hui* (*The Past Today*), in which the court of Louis XIV is transported into the world of 1890; *L'Horloge des siècles* (*The Century Clock*), in which time runs backwards; *L'Ingénieur Von Satanas* (*Von Satanas the Engineer*); and *Un chalet dans les airs* (*A Chalet in the Sky*.)

Robida created some of the most despairing works of his day. Thus, *L'Ingénieur Von Satanas*, the story of a war following the one of 1914-1918, was published in February, 1919, when everyone, even the military, believed that peace had returned for a long time to come. Two moods continually vie with each other in the present (dual) work: humor and hopelessness.

The striking thing about Robida is his approach. When reviewers were disturbed by the descriptions of his inventions, Robida was blithely undisturbed. No doubt it was easy to draw pictures, but above all he knew that the state of technology in that era was not equal to the task of realizing his ideas. He talked about combat railways and rolling blockhouses, and he drew funny locomotives. Upon reading the text one sees that the latter travel without rails and are capable of going through passes and moving on mountain roads. Especially interesting is the use to which they are, to be put. If after thirty years the silhouette becomes, in 1907, a very modern tank, it will still be put to the same use. Armored columns act *en masse* to break through fronts and stream through breaches. If they can be stopped, it is only by other armored vehicles, or by calling in aerial squadrons. There are many of them, usually formations of dirigibles, and they operate in much the same way as those of today.

In *La guerre infernale* the author's concepts unfold. War becomes increasingly total, consuming every resource, and ignoring every law. French squadrons firebomb open cities, bombard hospitals and refugee trains. "War should be fierce in order to be short" is the slogan.

Robida's voice fell on deaf ears. Military people smiled, serious-minded people shrugged. However, they later bowed to the accuracy of his vision. Today Robida is being rediscovered in France. Some even rank him above Jules Verne — not as a novelist, as he does not even know how to develop a plot, but as a clear-thinking prophet.

Jacques van Herp

Sources for Further Study

Criticism:

Palache, Mary. "Albert Robida," in *New York Herald Tribune Books*. (March, 1929), p. 8. Palache makes some general comments concerning Robida's style.

HALCYON DRIFT

Author: Brian Stableford (1948-   )
First book publication: 1974
Type of work: Novel
Time: The far future
Locale: An unnamed planet, the Earth, a planet in the Drift, and deep space

A vivid and economically executed space adventure, the first of a series of six novels featuring a crack space pilot and a new type of spaceship, with a problem requiring resolution on a world in the dangerous nebula known as Halcyon Drift

> Principal characters:
> GRAINGER, the hero, a disillusioned space pilot
> EVE LAPTHORN, sister to Grainger's co-pilot, now dead
> JOHNNY SOCORO, a young technician who admires Grainger
> NICK DELARCO, captain of the "Hooded Swan"
> ROTHGAR, an old friend of Grainger, crew member of the "Hooded Swan"
> ALACHAKH, a friendly alien from the planet Khonmon

In many ways, *Halcyon Drift* is a simple and traditional space story of the kind that has been around at least as long as the science fiction magazines. Only by courtesy can it be called a novel; in form it is a lengthy short story.

Its attraction lies in part in the way it adheres exactly to a formula, never deviating far from it but sometimes enhancing it. In true formulaic fashion, it does this by having at its center a snazzy piece of supertechnology, the spaceship "Hooded Swan."

Grainger's first ship, the "Javelin," has crashed on an unnamed planet. Grainger's mate, Lapthorn, has been killed, and Grainger has buried him. Awaiting rescue, Grainger lets his memory roam over his past. He is a cold, emotionless man, with no affection even for Lapthorn. One of the few men he liked was the alien, Alachakh. Women mean little to him.

While he sits listening to the wind blow, Grainger finds that one of the winds is in his head. It is an alien. The alien is familiar and not at all sinister; news that it will remain with Grainger until he dies is not particularly disturbing. A true symbiote, it makes no attempt to harm him.

The unnamed planet lies on the edge of the Halcyon Drift, "a bad place," full of radiation and distortion and anomalous space. In the opening chapter, Grainger reminisces in a romantic vein about the worlds he has known.

> On Bira, we both got hooked on the nectar of the scorpion lilies, which grew only in the dawn, and faded once the sun was clear of the horizon. But the local day was two standard years long, and the dawn lingered long. We followed sunrise around the planet for half a year, until we reached the shore of an uncrossable sea. There would be no more lilies until the dawn reached the far shore.

Grainger is rescued by a ship belonging to the Caradoc Company, an interplanetary mining firm which stands as an example for the evils of monopolistic capitalism. The Company does not like Grainger; and he does not like it. He returns to one of his old haunts on Earth, where he meets young Johnny Socoro, who used to loiter as a kid in the workshop where Grainger and Lapthorn worked. Earth is in decline. "Overnight, she was obsolete and dying." The scene is in many respects as melancholy as the one on the unnamed planet.

Despite his coldness, Grainger decides to return Lapthorn's few possessions to the dead man's family. His relationships with them are as prickly as every other relationship, but he leaves Eve Lapthorn his address. Through her Nick delArco arrives to offer Grainger a job piloting a new ship, which he has built on the planet of New Alexandria. After a good deal of arguing, both with delArco and the wind in his head, Grainger agrees to sign on. The knowledge that his old buddy, Rothgar, also will be on board helps to persuade him, as does the sight of the new ship, the "Hooded Swan."

The fact that by a piece of legalistic trickery Grainger now owes the Caradoc Company twenty thousand for his rescue is also persuasive. The Company has a fleet of ramrods in the Halcyon Drift, investigating the whereabouts of a crashed spaceship, the "Lost Star."

> The "Lost Star" bleep was the Lorelei of deep-space. It could be heard all over the Halcyon Drift and quite some way outside it, but because of the warping of space inside the Drift, its source couldn't be located. . . . There were no maps of the Drift, there were dust . . . clouds in abundance, and the further in you went, the more distorted was the space in which you were flying. The core was virtually unreachable at supercee velocities.

So the Lost Star's bleep has been sounding for eighty years, and no ship has reached her. DelArco's plan is to have Grainger fly the new ship into the Drift and grab the wreck out from under the nose of Caradoc. Grainger, after a period of being obnoxious, agrees on the trip.

By far the most lively and compelling part of the book, as so often happens in space fiction, is at the point when the rather contrived personal relationships are set aside and the machinery takes over. The "Hooded Swan" is the real hero of *Halcyon Drift* and the novels that come after it. The "Swan" is not a rigid ship but an articulated one, "a bird with feathers of shiny metal." The metal is only plating; for beneath it, she is built of organic chain molecules. She has a "mass-relaxation drive." Her most advanced feature is a nerve net, allowing for complete sensory hookup between pilot and vessel. "In my ship," says delArco, "the hull will be your skin, the drive will be *inside* you." The ship has been developed by New Alexandria, and achieves a synthesis between human and Khormon theory and technology.

The nearest Grainger ever comes to delight is when he flies the "Hooded Swan."

> My hands grew into great wings, my spine was the ship's long axis, my legs were the tail stabilizers, my groin the atomic cannons, my heart the relaxation web wrapped around the drive, my lungs the ship's lacunae.

> I knew beyond all doubt what my ship could do, because I was she and she was me.
> *My* ship, was the "Hooded Swan." Mine.
> I could fly faster than light.
> I could fly higher than the stars.

They enter the fringes of the Drift and land on an inhabited planet called Hallsthammer, where Grainger meets his old friend, Alachakh, an alien of the Khor-monsa race, who closely resemble humans. Alachakh is also going to find the "Lost Star," although he is old and knows his time is running out. His usefulness has waned. "Dreams are very wasteful to the mind, my friend." Alachakh makes a deal, agreeing to lead Grainger in his ship to the "Lost Star," the secret of whose whereabouts he has bought.

After having a difficult time penetrating the Drift, Alachakh and his ship die. Grainger finds a note next to the alien's body. The note declares that the Khormon do not in fact come from the planet Khor, as they pride themselves on doing, but that they originate on a semilegendary world beyond the rim of the galaxy. Alachakh wants to keep this fact a secret. Before it crashed, the "Lost Star" discovered the world beyond the rim, and contains cargo originating there, which Alachakh, in his note, requests that Grainger destroy.

Grainger brushes off delArco's and Eve's natural questions on his return to the "Swan," and they head for the planet where the wrecked "Star" lies. To do that, they have to pass through an anamorphosis in space. Pressed beyond endurance, Grainger blacks out, but the wind in his head sees them down to a safe planetfall. The wind pilots Grainger as Grainger pilots the "Swan."

By vehicle and then on foot, delArco and Grainger experience the traditional vicissitudes of life on a savage and unknown planet. Fighting their way through a dark jungle, they find themselves surrounded by faces — or rather, multiple images of one face.

> The faces changed expression. From vacuousness, they passed through fear and pain and agony. I watched the face — always the same face — grow thinner, watched the flesh whiten and tauten about the bones, watched it begin to peel from the face, watched it dissolve and flow and writhe. I watched the death and decay of a human being. Wherever my lamp fell, there it was.

No explanation, even of a pseudoscientific kind, is offered for this remarkable phenomenon. The wind simply tells Grainger that the face belongs to one of the crew of the "Lost Star," which the trees have "actually seen and experienced." Grainger protests at this. The wind in his head tells him, "They're like everything else on this world — just plain and simple reaction," as though this particular response (which could presumably be explained as being of a photochemical kind) is the only possible one. Such gothic stage effects, flirting with death and decay, appear with remarkable frequence throughout science fiction, set against passages extolling the beauty of future technology.

Eventually, the two explorers find the "Lost Star." Grainger keeps delArco out for a while, but eventually both men stand inside the old ship. The cargo consists of books, papers, and films — alien knowledge — from the quasileg-endary Khor planet beyond the rim. Grainger destroys everything as his dead friend Alachakh wished, and switches off the bleep. His motives are mainly spiteful: to cheat his employers, in whose power he dislikes being. "I wanted to make a fool of the whole bloody human race. Except me. And also because it was a good joke."

They still have to deal with some of Caradoc's ships, which threaten to blow them up, but that is easily handled, as is the escape from the Drift. We leave Grainger catching up on his sleep on Hallsthammer and awaiting another job.

Despite Grainger's misanthropy, the adventure element in *Halcyon Drift* is uppermost, and the author may perhaps assume that most readers will not care that plot and characterization are arbitrary. A counter-argument suggests that the excitement would be heightened if the reader could learn more about the wind in Grainger's head and, particularly, about the ancient culture of the Khor-monsa, which is merely used as a plot device. Such science as there is, is equally superficial. Despite these drawbacks, characteristic of the space adven-ture genre as a whole, *Halcyon Drift* buoyantly passes muster as light enter-tainment. It and the novels which followed it are good, undemanding, once-only reading; they provide evidence of the continued liveliness of a traditional narrative structure which can, with a little imagination, be traced back to the Odyssey.

It is somewhat of a change to have a central character who so patently loathes the human race; the force of his loathing, however, would strike the reader more authentically if the author had not drawn all the other characters as being unpleasant or ineffectual, making them just targets for Grainger's scorn. Only the stoical but defeatist alien escapes his scorn, with the possible excep-tion of Eve — but that relationship remains undeveloped.

The other novels in this series repeat the same formula, with Grainger reluc-tantly but successfully undertaking a demanding task, assisted by the wind in his head and the "Hooded Swan." They are: *Rhapsody in Black*, *Promised Land*, *The Paradise Game*, *The Fenris Device*, and *Swan Song*.

Brian W. Aldiss

HALF PAST HUMAN

Author: T. J. Bass
First book publication: 1971
Type of work: Novel
Time: 2349
Locale: The Earth

The frightening and satirical account of the struggle between the underground Earth Society of the four-toed Nebish and the surface culture of five-toed Eyepeople, and what that struggle represents to the future of the human race

> *Principal characters:*
> OLD MOON, a timeless five-toed genetic throwback
> DAN, his dog who is also timeless
> TOOTHPICK, a companion robot meant to be carried
> TINKER, a mechanic who defects to the Eyepeople
> MU REN, his wife
> MOSES EPPENDORFF, a "pipe" who defects to the Eyepeople
> HIP, a seer and prophet of Mt. Tabulum
> BALL, a metalloid sphere
> OLGA, an implant starship who is a "cyberdeity"

The relationship between the individual and society has been written about by such writers as George Orwell, Aldous Huxley, and Eugene Zamyatin. Science fiction writers such as H. G. Wells, Ray Bradbury, and Kurt Vonnegut, Jr., have made trenchant statements about the dangerous possibilities of society unchecked. The combined fears of Fascism in the 1940's and Communism in the 1950's contributed to a large outpouring of science fiction which warned of the inherent dangers of authoritarian repression. The rapid growth of technology in the 1950's and 1960's produced a new fear — the threat of dehumanization. Much of the science fiction written in the late 1960's and early 1970's envisioned the future consequences in a world that ignored the "limits to growth," abused technology, and allowed fundamental human values to erode. In this dehumanized world, mechanical intelligences and robots would rule. The tail would wag the dog.

T. J. Bass's *Half Past Human* is a frighteningly serious and bitterly satirical novel of the 1970's. Written in 1971, it is the account of a dehumanized, tightly monitored, and genetically controlled "Earth Society." The "Big ES" is a technologically repressive society located within the bowels of the Earth. In the overpopulated underground "hive," there is little regard for life and overwhelming concern for "calories" and "flavored protein." Earth Society, in this tale of the future, has lost its concept of individuality to the ideal of a passive and complacent citizenry. The "Good Citizens" are given "Molecular Reward" if they stay in line and are punished if found guilty of "Inappropriate Activity."

An underlying premise in the story, that most people desire happiness and food over freedom, is common to many antiutopian novels. The story line itself is multilayered. On the surface level, the novel dramatizes the struggle between the four-toed Nebishes crowded within the Earth and the five-toed Eyepeople living on the outside. The author's interwoven plot, as well as his evocative description, helps to sustain the reader through the rough literary terrain. On another level, the novel is a story of our present society, revealing through allegory the often calloused attitude toward life that much of the world exhibited during the Vietnam War years. Here, the story mirrors such malignant elements as blind prejudice, racial purity, and the general abnegation of personal responsibility. On a third level, the novel is a journey of awakening, a tale of exodus and transformation in which the human spirit slowly grows aware, struggles with adversity, and is finally reborn. Throughout all three levels is the persistent theme of the dehumanization of man by man.

In all, this book is so complex and "jargonese" that anyone who endures the first reading must be overwhelmingly interested in these various levels of meaning. The plot itself, emerging out of an unlikely sequence of events, criss-crosses in what is eventually revealed as teleological cosmic design. Although it can be tedious to read, there are a few central points that are best approached through a discussion of characters and basic story lines.

It is the Year of Olgo, 2349. Old Moon and his dog, Dan, genetic throwbacks from a time when humans had five toes and were able to survive on the surface of the planet, are surveying the avocado-colored Earth from the summit of Rocky Top Mountain. The two companions are timeless, having been subjected to metabolic experiments centuries ago; and have had the misfortune of bearing witness to the calculated extinction of their species by the now predominate four-toed Nebish. The Nebish or "complacent hive citizen," has been genetically bred for passive acceptance of the overcrowded conditions in subterranean Earth Society. Here, in the third millennium, the only remaining inhabitants on the planet's surface are mechanical intelligences called Agromecks and a few primitive five-toed throwbacks. These surface dwellers or "Eyepeople," due to the five-toe gene, are genetically unsuited for the crowded conditions below. The photosynthesized land on the surface of the planet is used solely to grow vegetation to feed the three-trillion Nebishes below, and is protected from the surface dwelling Eyepeople by Huntercraft and Hunters. Pursued and hungry, Moon and Dan are in search of either vegetation or human meat.

On Rocky Top Mountain, Moon and Dan discover Toothpick, a javelin-shaped cybernetic companion robot "with optic," who demonstrates his powers by making it rain. The three end up at Mount Tabulum in the camp of Hip the elder. The Hip, with the help of Ball, a metalloid sphere, has been uniting and protecting the Eyepeople from hunters. Considered a seer and a prophet, the Hip is preparing the people for the return of Olga, a mysterious deity who will provide salvation for the abused surface dwellers with five toes.

The story line jumps back and forth between several simultaneous subplots, with the action shifting from above ground to below. Underground, working on "meck" huntercraft and other mechanical intelligences, is a central figure, Tinker. He, like his coworkers, Val and Walter, is a Good Citizen who follows the dictates of the Big ES. Although he daily witnesses the slaughter of innocent Eyepeople by Nebish hunters, the lack of concern for the hunters by the Big ES, and the mutilation of the bodies of the "less than human" five-toed surface dwellers, Tinker is more concerned with his work output and homemade listening devices than with moral questions.

Tinker's transformation from ideal Good Citizen to renegade Buckeye is the first major element of dramatic tension in the plot. The author, through the use of foils, allows each major character to experience an essential awakening and transformation. This holds true for Val, Tinker's essential foil, and fat Walter, Val's foil. Actually, the seeds for all character and situational development can be found in the opening chapter of the novel, though this is easily overlooked in a first reading. Fortunately, however, the segmented incidents which reveal character development become reasonably unified at about midpoint in the novel.

Within the first chapter, however, Tinker is subjected to the "system." Issued a societal dictate to find a human incubator for his "budchild," he, not wanting to become involved with a female, petitions for use of the "meck uteri." Permission denied, Tinker has his "anti-puberty cocoon" removed and is "polarized." He then finds a qualified human carrier in Mu Ren, a spontaneously polarized ten year old female who is implanted with his budchild. The implant fails and Mu Ren allows herself to be impregnated naturally. Junior, who is born shortly thereafter, not only is "unauthorized," but, without genetic screening, is born with five toes. Rather than "chuck" the child into a disposer unit, Tinker and Mu Ren, under directions from mysterious surface transmissions, flee the hive with Junior.

In a story in which names can carry a symbolic meaning, another central character, Moses Eppendorff is the softspoken personification of his biblical counterpart. Moses' transformation from an obedient "Pipe" to the powerful leader of an exodus from the hive is a key part of the narrative. While he is on a "reward" climb to the surface, Moses, through several incidents, meets up with Moon, Dan and Toothpick, who convince him to defect. The story line takes the reader through several episodes with the foursome, culminating with the wounding of Moon and Dan by hunters and the joinder of Moses and Toothpick for a mission to the Dundas Caves.

After Moses and Toothpick break into the Dundas Caves, suspension chambers for millions of terminal patients awaiting cure, Toothpick begins systematic work on the hibernating patients. Moses, who flees the caves with the attendant, is ultimately captured by the Big ES and charged with the murder of the patients. Toothpick, who has been dismantled, is returned to Moses; but, unknown to the authorities, Toothpick is still in operation. After discovering that many of the patients in suspension were cured, not killed, by Moses, the court sets him free to lead the cured (all five-toed patients) out onto the surface. Moses and Toothpick, like the biblical figure and his staff, begin the long trek to freedom, leading a "glacier of five-toes."

In similar manner, the Hip, Ball, and Tinker are leading their group of Eyepeople on a pilgrimage to the River to await Olga's return. The groups eventually converge, but the authorities from the Big ES launch a major hunt to wipe them out. After much fighting between surface dwellers and Nebishes in which all seems lost for the surface dwellers, there is a major explosion and Tektite meteor shower. Though many of the surface people are killed, many more disappear.

Although *Half Past Human* can easily appear to be erratic and disunified, it is coherently structured. The individual stories of Tinker, Moses Eppendorff, Toothpick, Moon, and Dan all are carefully plotted to come together at the appropriate time. Although surrealistic at times, the action is built upon an underlying unity. What begins in disarray coalesces by the end of the novel. After the explosion of Ball and the Tektite meteor shower, the combined numbers of surface people disappear without explanation. Several incidents take place after the disappearance, including the appearance of the meck G.I.T.A.R., whose music lures hive citizens to death on the surface, and the eventual defection of Val and Walter from the hive, but, it is return of Olga that brings the story to closure.

Olga, an enormous "implant starship" with mechanical intelligence, has been responsible for all events from beginning to end. With her existence forgotten by mankind after they abandoned outer space for the caverns of the Earth, she had become a "cyberdeity," traveling through the cosmos. Recognizing that mankind has deteriorated after eliminating the five-toe gene, she had been acting through the "meck" brains to gather the Earth's carriers of the five-toe gene for implantation to other planets in the universe. She had used the Tektite shower and explosion of Ball as a screen to conceal the true nature of her work from the Big ES, who would then explain the disappearance as natural disaster. She reasoned that knowledge of her existence might impel Earth Society to reach out for the stars again, spreading destruction throughout the cosmos. The story ends with Moses, Dan, Moon, and a Tinkerless Mu Ren transplanted to the planet Tiercel — Land of the Hawks. It is here, with their new budchildren, that they will continue the species.

Half Past Human is not an easy novel to read. The strongly technical language can be exasperating. The segmented incidents can be frustrating. Nevertheless, the cold and technical description and the intricate detail are necessary to the author's purpose. The technical language reveals the mechanical soul of the Big ES, creating a vivid sense of verisimilitude. The author throws together various themes in an invective aimed at modern man. The environmental and religious themes are obvious, as are the political themes. The value questions are less obvious, with the author providing no definitive guidelines for the reader. Much of the story can be seen as a toss-up between allegory and black humor. The issue of the fifth toe can lend itself to both interpretations.

If Bass is reflecting our present values in the mirror of black humor, his humor *is* an invective. Normally, humor allows the reader to poke fun at the various aspects of evil, giving one the opportunity to shrug it off as human. *Half Past Human*, if falling within the realm of humor, forces the reader to laugh painfully, to contemplate the underlying brutality of his society, and to investigate the misconceptions and dogmas housed within his own self. Hunting down and mutilating bodies of those "less than human" is something very familiar to the twentieth century. This book, if investigated closely, will reveal numerous forms of dehumanization and a few other frightening blemishes on the face of humanity.

Clifford P. Bendau

Sources for Further Study

Reviews:

Luna Monthly. XXXVII–XXXIX, July–August, 1972, p. 63.
Publisher's Weekly. CXCIX, May 31, 1971, p. 137.
WSFA Journal. LXXVIII, August–October, 1971, pp. 27-28.

THE HAMPDENSHIRE WONDER

Author: John Davys Beresford (1873-1947)
First book publication: 1911
Type of work: Novel
Time: The early twentieth century
Locale: A rural district of one of the southern communities of England

The story of a freak child with mental powers that might one day be the common property of man's descendants

Principal characters:
VICTOR STOTT, the Hampdenshire Wonder
GINGER STOTT, his father
HENRY CHALLIS, the local landlord
PERCY CRASHAW, the rector of the parish
THE NARRATOR, a writer

The Hampdenshire Wonder is the earliest story built on serious speculation about the intellectual nature of men who have reached a "higher" evolutionary stage. The endeavor does, however, tie in very well with the kinds of imaginative exploration that had been conducted by H. G. Wells in his early scientific romances, and the influence of Wells's work on the novel is indubitable. In fact, Beresford was to write the first critical/biographical study of Wells four years after publication of this novel.

In examining the probable opinions of its central character with regard to the contemporary human condition, *The Hampdenshire Wonder* invites comparison with several earlier works, the most important being Wells's *The Wonderful Visit* (1895), Grant Allen's *The British Barbarians*, and W. D. Howells' *A Traveller from Altruria* (1894), all of which use imaginary "superior" viewpoints for critical commentary. In Wells's novel the superior outsider who passes judgment on Victorian England is an angel fallen from heaven; in Allen's novel the visitor is an anthropologist from the future come to study the taboos of primitive culture; and in Howell's work a visitor from a Utopian society compares America unfavorably with his homeland. The idea of using a specimen of a distinct species evolved out of humankind as an analytical viewpoint was a natural successor to these exercises, and Wells came close to it in *The Food of the Gods* (1904), even though the supermen featured in the novel were artificial creations. Thus, Beresford was the first to try to imagine what humanity might look like from further up the evolutionary ladder, from the viewpoint of individuals whose physical form had already been designed by Wells in the essay "The Man of the Year Million." *The Hampdenshire Wonder* became, of course, an important influence in its own right, prompting Olaf Stapledon to repeat the exercise in *Odd John* (1935) and probably influencing Stanley Weinbaum's superman story *The New Adam* (1939) and Eden Phillpotts' speculations regarding alien viewpoints in *Saurus* and *Address Unknown*.

Beresford's Narrator first encounters the Wonder as a babe-in-arms with a huge head and an unusually disconcerting stare. This encounter on a train is juxtaposed with a quotation from the book which the Narrator is reading at the time and sets the scene for the philosophical implications of the commentary which the Wonder is ultimately to deliver on human knowledge. In the first edition the book in question is Henri Bergson's *Time and Free Will (Essai sur les données immédiates de la conscience*, 1889), and the key quotation concerns the argument which equates free will with irrationality, a notion with which the Narrator disagrees vehemently. In subsequent editions, however, the book becomes Hegel's *The Phenomenology of the Spirit (Die Phänomenologie des Geistes*, 1807), and the quotation concerns the nature of knowledge. The change is apt, for though the Wonder does indeed seem to expose the element of the irrational in human freedom of thought and action, the real implications of his judgment deal with the limitations and nature of human knowledge. (The initial reference to Bergson carries the additional suggestion that it was Bergsonian evolutionary philosophy rather than the Darwinian philosophy that obsessed Wells which led Beresford to his image of evolved man; this is further suggested in a later passage when Bergson's *L'Evolution créatrice* (1906) is noted as the one title in a stack of philosophical tomes which absorbs the Wonder's attention for more than a passing moment.)

The early part of the novel is taken up by a curious account of the circumstances which led up to the Wonder's conception. He is the son of a professional cricketer determined to pass on his phenomenal skills and an aging spinster who proposes to him a marriage of convenience. The child's father leaves his wife, continuing to provide for her and the child's support, and mother and child are given a new home by the local squire, Henry Challis, whose attention is drawn to the child by the rector Percy Crashaw.

Crashaw is the villain of the book, and though he is not overtly accused, there is a very strong implication that he is the Wonder's eventual murderer. He is the embodiment of antiscientific and antirational religious fervor. The Narrator reports that Crashaw became fanatical after an early enthusiastic flirtation with the possibility of reconciling scientific knowledge with religious dogma had damaged his career prospects. The novel's criticism of Crashaw's intolerance is vituperative, but this is to a large extent a side issue. Virtually all novels of this type are scathing in their sarcastic abuse of whatever opinions their authors most dislike — *The British Barbarians* is the most ill-mannered example, though *Odd John* is the most extreme — and Beresford's novel is actually notable for its careful objectivity, though in this one matter it is unrestrained.

The attack on Crashaw's opinions is not characteristic of Beresford's works. His imaginative works are rather characterized by an objectivity that is often very determined (as, for instance, in *Revolution*), and usually sympathetic to human fallibility (most particularly in *Goslings*). Beresford, who was crippled in infancy by poliomyelitis, seems always to have regarded himself as an outsider remote from the social world that surrounded him, and he was rarely given to such outbursts of misanthropy as that directed in *The Hampdenshire Wonder* against the antiscientific rector. It is interesting to note that his own father was the rector of a rural parish in one of the southern counties.

The Wonder's career gets properly under way when Challis gives him access to his library, where he familiarizes himself (before the age of five) with virtually the entire legacy of human knowledge. He offends Crashaw by denying the existence of God, and the rector tries to have him certified as an idiot and removed to an asylum. Challis prevents this and also thwarts a subsequent attempt to have the child forcibly enrolled at a primary school where he would be available for indoctrination.

The Wonder seems totally self-sufficient and makes no attempt whatever at social intercourse until he begins to court the attention of the Narrator. Even this act proves futile, in that the Wonder can find no words to express his point of view in terms the Narrator will understand, and the Narrator finds the child as disconcerting as ever. The Narrator saves the child from being pestered by the one person who is not intimidated by his gaze, a hydrocephalic idiot, but he eventually begins to avoid the Wonder. This avoidance is one of the things which permits the Wonder to be murdered, and the guilt-stricken Narrator deliberately refuses to speculate as to whether the idiot or Crashaw is responsible.

The main problem facing any author who undertakes a novel featuring a superhuman viewpoint is that of specifying its nature. Some writers — Allen and Stapledon are the obvious examples — were arrogant enough to assume that they themselves were sufficiently advanced over the vulgar prejudices of their fellow men to put words into the mouths of their prodigies, but Beresford was much more cautious. Victor Stott is the most taciturn of characters; only half a dozen substantial pronouncements are reported in the book as his. The Narrator reports that the Wonder spoke at length on only one occasion, when he submitted the insight gained from the early days in Challis' library to the test of a debate with Challis. The Narrator cannot report the substance of this conversation because Challis will not repeat it, and, indeed, claims to have willfully put it out of his mind. The reader is permitted to know the reasons for Challis' rejection of the philosophical insights of Victor Stott, but no more (these are given in the book's epilogue, "The Uses of Mystery"). This subtlety on the part of the author is what makes *The Hampdenshire Wonder* the best novel of its kind, for it saves the book from the pompous and waspish pontificating which mars *Odd John* and yet allows it to imply enough to make a genuine and valid philosophical point.

The essential quality of the Wonder's viewpoint (and this is hardly surprising) is its objectivity. This is, of course, commonplace in superman novels, but in inferior examples it is construed simply as a lack of emotion. Stott certainly lacks emotion, but there is much more to his attitude than that. For Victor Stott, a statement is either true, false, or unverifiable, and that is all there is to knowledge. He has no sense of mystery; unanswered and unanswerable questions hold no fascination for him. He is the perfect logical positivist, holding all metaphysical questions to be meaningless. His comment on the human quest for enlightenment — "Subtract the endeavor to demonstrate a preconceived hypothesis from any known philosophy and the remainder, the only valuable material, is found to be distorted" — is surely true, and his subsequent condemnation of human intellectual endeavor as fundamentally flawed by irrationality is the inevitable conclusion to be drawn in consequence.

However, Beresford's narrator is just as surely right when he dissents from the Wonder's notion of what constitutes "useful" knowledge. To the Wonder, the utility of knowledge has to do solely with the ability to make true statements, but to the Narrator (who reads Bergson and Hegel with admiration) and to Challis the question of utility is rather one of pragmatic psychology. As Challis says in the epilogue, human beings *need* mystery and ignorance as stimuli to intellectual endeavor, and without them intellectual life would lose its color and purpose. The kind of knowledge which the Wonder is able to possess, perfect not because it answers all questions but because it knows with certainty which questions *can* be answered and has no ambitions outside that area, is, in Challis' view, a psychological burden which only an unhuman being could tolerate. In the context of the philosophical argument, the question of whether Victor Stott was murdered by the rector, jealously reacting against the violation of his sacred dogmas, or the idiot, the very personification of ignorance, is charged with an extra dimension of ironic significance.

The tale told in *The Hampdenshire Wonder* is eccentric in several respects. The prelude recounting the history of Ginger Stott appears to have so little connection with the main theme as to be almost bizarre. It is certainly a peculiar way to establish that the Wonder might be seen as the product of altogether exceptional parental desires. The Narrator's suggestion that the mental attitudes of the parents may be responsible for the freakishness of the child may seem ridiculous to modern readers, but it should be remembered that Beresford drew his evolutionary philosophy from Bergson and the idea of *élan vital*, and also that this notion crops up with disturbing regularity in handbooks on sex and child-rearing published in the first half of this century. In the main narrative, also, there is evidence that Beresford originally intended to do more than he eventually settled for. The character of Gregory Lewes, Challis' research assistant, was presumably introduced into the plot with some purpose in mind, though he is dropped from the story without making any contribution at all.

Despite these eccentricities, however, the book remains one of the best science fiction novels ever written, outstanding in terms of both its literary and ideative merits. Although it has not suffered the oblivion into which the author's other excellent philosophical fantasies have fallen, notably *What Dreams May Come?* and *The Riddle of the Tower*, it has nevertheless been too infrequently reprinted, and should be far better known than it is.

Brian Stableford

Sources for Further Study

Criticism:

The Encyclopedia of Science Fiction and Fantasy. Compiled by Donald H. Tuck. Chicago: Advent Publishers, Inc., 1978, p. 40. This concise article calls *The Hampdenshire Wonder* a modern classic and an excellent mutant novel.

HARD TO BE A GOD
(TZUNDO BIT' BOGOM)

Authors: Arkady Strugatsky (1925-   ) and Boris Strugatsky (1933-   )
First book publication: 1964
English translation: 1973
Type of work: Novel
Time: Several centuries in the future
Locale: The Earth, and the distant planet Arkanar

A novel about a complex, tragic, and heroic mission of a group of the Earth's representatives carried out on a backward and gloomy planet still passing through a historical stage reminiscent of Earth's Middle Ages

> *Principal characters:*
> ANTON (DON RUMATA OF ESTORIA), a member of the Experimental History Institute
> PASHKA (DON HUG), a member of the same Institute
> KYRA, an Arkanarian girl, Anton's sweetheart
> DON PAMPA, an Arkanarian baron, Don Rumata's friend
> DON REBA, the Minister of Internal Security at the King of the Arkanar, an illegal conspirator
> ARATA THE FAIR, an insurgent, the leader of the peasant army

Hard to Be a God is probably the most popular book written by the Strugatsky brothers. It has been translated into nearly every European language and published in the United States. In both structure and conception it is one of the most refined and satisfying books by the Strugatskys.

The fact that *Hard to Be a God* was first published with *Far Rainbow* is not a mere coincidence nor the fancy of the publishing house. After having raised the moral and logical problems about the Man-Nature interrelations (*Far Rainbow*), the Strugatskys made a logical step forward by including social problems into this sphere as well. The theme of interference in the history of an alien planet is common to Western science fiction readers. The unusual thing is how the Strugatskys solve this problem.

Strictly speaking the novel is not a hard-core science fiction work. It is actually a moral parable about human gods capable but not willing to interfere in the historical evolution of an alien planet. Because of their humane nature these men-gods cannot indifferently view bloodshed, suffering, mediocrity, or the downfall of civilization. Such events offer concrete associations with our own earthly past.

The Strugatskys have deliberately parallelled the quasihistorical background of their novel with our own earthly conditions while slightly displacing some of the well-known elements and changing numerous details known to the reader. We can easily relate to the Arkanarian Middle Ages, and in the heavy stamping of the Arkanarian Sturmovics (stormtroopers) we clearly hear echoes of Munich and Nuremberg. Such familiar things on an alien planet are not weaknesses, but rather strong points in the Strugatskys' imagination. They do not want to lead us out of familiar historical surroundings into an imaginary country; on the contrary, they strive to return to the facts of our own well-known history. Thus, this novel deals with the people of the Earth and their deeds, presented from behind a distant galactic curtain.

The spirit of the beginning of *Hard to Be a God* is similar to that of *Far Rainbow*. There is the same feeling of a vague threat which disturbs the serene existence of the main characters. These characters are Anton, Pashka, and Anka, who look like the pupils of a boarding school in other Strugatsky novels: *Noon: Twenty-second Century* and *Far Rainbow*.

Like all children, they have escaped to the forest to play games of pirates and noble dons, or to imitate other popular characters from the books they have read. But all their games do not seem to come from books. Their imagination is full of a bloodchilling reality and historical details, and the repertoire of their games is well thought out. These things are further supplemented by some unusual trifles, such as "a hoarse, shrill voice, quite unhuman." (Where and when could they have heard such a voice? Scarcely in the warm, bright, and absolutely human future.)

This prologue to the novel is openly symbolic. In a game Anton, expressing mature judgment, refuses to play William Tell because the children have real crossbows, and a real apple on Pashka's real head. In another scene, when the children come across a deserted road with an old traffic sign that reads "Do Not Enter," we realize that these events set a keynote for the whole plot of the book.

Two simple truths are suggested by these incidents: the first, no one can use weapons against a human being; the second, history is an "anisotropic one-way road." Without this prologue the moral chord of the novel, running through the book up to its epilogue, might have been lost. By presenting the main characters on the Earth, in their natural surroundings, the prologue and the epilogue substantiate the actions of these persons in quite different surroundings on Arkanar.

As the novel proper begins, we find ourselves in a gloomy atmosphere on an alien planet. The workers of the Experimental History Institute are carrying on their uneasy "intelligent watch." Suddenly we recognize Anton in Don Rumata of Estoria, a dashing cavalier, dueller, and man about town; Pashka is Don Hug. The game is over; ahead of them lies the hard road of the explorers, with a possibly fatal outcome. Society on Arkanar is undergoing a difficult period. Events are occurring which cannot be explained by existing theoretical schemes. These developments alarm Anton and his friends. The events also evoke unpleasant associations for the reader. Memories of historical injustices are triggered. While persecution was common in the Middle Ages, there was not a well-organized Grey Militia, consisting of small retailers, narrow-minded people, and massacrers. There were stupid and narrow-minded monarchs and cruel favorites, but the sinister image of Don Reba reminds us of more recent historical events. The Minister of Internal Security is neither an adventurer nor a politician. He is simply a personified symbol of stupidity, narrow-mindedness, and triviality.

The anxiety of the observers mounts, but they can interfere only marginally to save a few outstanding individuals such as doctors, scientists, and poets. Even Arata the Fair, the leader of the local "Jacquerie," is deprived by the "Gods" of such intervention. Why is it so?

In *Hard to Be a God* the Strugatskys have made their first mature attempt to formulate an attitude towards the problem of interference in the process of historical evolution. The problem is ambiguous. To interfere means to deprive a nation of its history; as the main character of "The Escape Attempt" has put it: "History is the backbone of humanity, and by destroying history one breaks the back of humanity." But noninterference holds the danger of killing the personal feelings of human brotherhood and generating a hatred of everything unhuman. But at the same time the Strugatskys clearly and with journalistic enthusiasm express their own point of view: a person has neither the possibility nor the right to escape from the necessity of solving these problems by hiding behind an elevated godlike façade.

The Strugatskys carry on a subtle polemic against the mass of science fiction books in which advanced earthly civilization imposes justice and order on the Cosmos by using fire and sword as was done by our predecessors on Earth. Why have the Strugatskys chosen to present their case in a science fiction novel? What is there so fantastic in it? The stormtroopers on the absolutely earthly narrow streets of a medieval town as well as the adventures of our up-to-date characters traveling by "time-machine" into the stormy and romantic past are typically earthly. Was it not possible to avoid such science fiction props as spaceships, orbital satellites, and minitransmitters disguised as jewelry? Was it not possible to drop the purely fabricated situation on Arkanar and have the main character safely travel to Munich of 1933 by such an unscientific method as time displacement or a somnambulistic sleep such as Mark Twain's Connecticut Yankee?

Had this been done, we would have been deprived of a bright, picturesque, and unique world. Despite analogies with our well-known past, this fictional world is unearthly, interesting, and petrifying. In addition, the main characters would have had no trouble in making their moral choice, because the developments on the Earth after 1933 are known. And finally, it would have been impossible to carry out an extremely valuable sociological experiment, which can be realized only in science fiction — to show the spiritual alliance between the Middle Ages and Fascism. The authors have managed to single out the common elements in these two dark periods of our history: obscurantism, ignorance, and an animalistic hatred of everything intelligent.

But let us not allow these philosophical concepts, sociological modeling, and moral principles to obscure the fact that this is a first-rate story. This novel could have been entitled "Three Musketeers in Space," and it was first conceived exactly in such a key. Consider the wonderful gallery of characters. Rumata, likable Don Pampa, Reba, Doctor Budach, the peasant leader Arata, and Rumata's sweetheart Kyra all stay in one's memory for a longtime. They are flesh and blood characters, not mere personified ideas. The proper names are rich and the dialogue is lively. For example, the slang conversation between Don Reba and Waga Koleso (Waga the Wheel), the leader of "the night vagabond army," is a brilliant and perhaps untranslatable example of an artificial, but animated acceptable language. Unfortunately this scene, as well as a number of others, has been rather simplified in the translation by Wendayne Ackerman so that some nuances have been lost.

Impressive as they are, the backgrounds are not the main things in the book. The intellectual and emotional climax of the novel lies in Rumata's conflict with himself, while the description of his image and the fixation on his mental suffering contribute to the development of the plot. This conflict is between a "god" who does not kill even in fights, and a man, whose race has experienced its own "Don Rebas" and "Grey Sturmoviks" in its own past. The Strugatskys are interested in the individual moral choice of Rumata and not in his sociological conception of interference. *Hard to Be a God* remains a moral parable, not a sketchy science fiction novel. That is why the Strugatskys have chosen for the novel's epigraphs words by Ernest Hemingway and Pierre Abelard (omitted in the English edition), authors who preferred human personal moral feelings to abstract sociology.

Hard to Be a God is not a static and moralizing monologue; by the end of the novel the action has become even more dynamic. A tragedy takes place on Arkanar: one unhuman state system has been replaced by another more unhuman power — Don Reba leads a revolt and seizes power. The gloomy atmosphere on Arkanar turns into a dark and starless night. Now even the visitors from Earth have no time for their historical discussions; they must save the remnants of the planet's culture and its few very rare bright spots of humanity. Rumata finally has to draw his sword, but he does so only after his limits of suffering have been surpassed: his only intimate friend and sweetheart Kyra has been killed.

A comparison with the works of Ursula K. Le Guin suggests itself: like Genly Ai, Shevek, and her other characters, Anton-Rumata makes a peculiar round trip and returns to his initial point as a quite different person. Even the duality of his character, which results from his role of an explorer, reminds one of the immortal wisdom of Taoism, so brilliantly expressed by Ursula K. Le Guin: "Light is the Left Hand of Darkness, and Darkness is the Right Hand of Light."

And what about the problem of interference in the process of history? It is hard to find a definite answer in the novel itself, but the book provides much food for thought. The absence of a definite conduct prescription is justified by the fact that such a prescription does not exist in real life either.

Had Rumata deeply interfered in Arkanarian affairs, and helped the Arata insurgents, the aftereffects could have been even more tragic. The dialogue between Rumata and Arata is one of the most remarkable scenes in the novel; in it the Strugatskys subtly dispute the proponents of the "revolution export" theory. Rumata declines to render any help, because his earthly past is a reliable guide in his deliberations. This past reminds him of the ultimate effects of the accessibility of modern weapons for a people whose intelligence and social consciousness are ages behind the proposed technical possibilities.

The same problem, although on a different intellectual level, is raised in the dispute with Budach, an outstanding Arkanarian doctor, and again the Strugatskys are consistent: the "gods" cannot help Arata because they know what price will be paid by the Arkanarians when such superfantastic weapons fall into the hands of Don Reba and his supporters (and sooner or later this must happen). Neither can the visitors from Earth help Budach, a representative of the first Arkanarian intellectuals. To give a powerful and abrupt push forward to the planet's progress is to deprive its inhabitants of their own history.

It is possible to make a delicate distinction between the position of Arthur C. Clarke's Overlords in *Childhood's End* and other "good strange gods" of Western science fiction and the point of view of the "gods" in the Strugatskys' novel, and this distinction unavoidably affects the final decision. In books by Clarke, Clifford Simak, and others, the interfering forces are absolutely sure of the necessity to interfere: in the above books humanity on the Earth has reached the critical stage of a looming thermonuclear war that endangers more than human culture and its best representatives. It threatens the very existence of human civilization. At all times and in all societies it has been considered moral for a doctor to fight for the life of all patients, even those who have attempted suicide. Such an analogy justifies extraterrestial interference in human affairs as well.

The tragedy of Rumata is of a quite different nature. Despite the dark and unhuman night on Arkanar, the population of the planet must fix this night in its memory too. Rumata is a historian and he well knows the stages of his own history: the philosophical conception of humanism itself did not arise at random but during the early stages of the Middle Ages. After a stormy night one appreciates a bright and fresh morning even more. The dark night over Arkanar is not a finale, it is only a turning point. In a distant future "the still unborn boys and girls, who will be sitting before the dictascopes of the schools in the Communist Republic of Arkanar" will use their past to study the ABC's of humanism. An immediate interference by Rumata at a point when the Arkanar population is far behind the proper stage of humanity might deprive them of ever experiencing that stage.

Such are the complicated schemes and sophisticated sociology, which explain the ages of history and the destinies of various nations. But Rumata is only human; he is not a "history demon" observing the slow flow of history from above. Therefore, he cannot help interfering. Therein lies the duality and tragic dialectics of people for whom it is "hard to be a god." But is that really so? The Strugatskys state that it is very simple to be a god, but it is extremely difficult (though necessary) to remain human. It is a simple conclusion, but after reading this novel the reader should arrive at the same conclusion, accepting it not as a bookish morality, but as the essence of our existence.

Vl. Gakov

Sources for Further Study

Reviews:

Choice. X, February, 1974, p. 1861.

Galaxy. XXXIV, November, 1973, pp. 84-85.

New Statesman. LXXXVII, January 18, 1974, p. 81.

New York Times. September 23, 1973, p. 39.

Renaissance. V, Summer, 1973, p. 7.

THE HEART OF A DOG
(SOBATJE SERDTSE)

Author: Michail Bulgakov (1891-1940)
First book publication: 1925
English translation: 1968
Type of work: Novel
Time: 1924
Locale: Moscow

A satirical novel about a mongrel dog which, after an operation, is changed into a man and becomes a Party politruk

> *Principal characters:*
> SJARIK, a dog
> DR. FILIPP FILIPPOVITJ PREOBRAZJENSKIJ, a scientist
> FJODOR, a doorman
> ZINA, a maid
> SJVONDER, a party politruk
> DR. BORMENTHAL, a colleague of Dr. Preobrazjenskij

The "Frankenstein syndrome" — the fear of creating something one cannot handle — is a recurring theme in science fiction. This is natural enough, since science fiction is very much a product of a society in rapid change where nothing is really secure and old values are constantly being transformed and destroyed. We find this theme in almost perfected form in Mary Shelley's celebrated novel *Frankenstein* (1818), which successfully mixed German *Märchen* fantasy with the British Gothic tale, and later, with the added benefit of satirical barbs in Michail Bulgakov's delightful monster story, *The Heart of a Dog*. This novel can be read on several levels: as an unusual and rather amusing monster tale, as a political allegory, or as a discussion of science in society. It is also a work of no mean literary merit and certainly a science fiction classic that deserves more recognition in the West.

Michail Bulgakov is best known in the West for his brilliant satirical novel *Master i Margarita* (1928; translated as *The Master and Margarita*, 1967), a take-off on the Passion of Christ in which the Devil appears in modern Moscow. A highly literary work, *Master i Margarita* is a subtle satire on life and ambitions in the new Soviet state and is still very popular in the U.S.S.R. Three years before that celebrated work, however, Bulgakov wrote two science fiction novels that, on the surface at least, look like typical pulp magazine fare. The first of those, *Rokovyje jajtsa* (1925; *Roc's Eggs*), is a typical monster tale which sounds like the script for a Godzilla film: a mad scientist manages to re-create prehistorical monsters which then devastate the countryside around Moscow until killed by the winter cold. The other was *The Heart of a Dog*, a far more complex novel which nevertheless utilizes some of pulp fiction's techniques.

The story opens in Moscow in December, 1924, some years after the Revolution, when a starving, cowardly, and ingratiating mongrel dog manages to befriend a bourgeois scientist, the kind and rather eccentric professor Preobrazjenskij (literally "The Changer"), who, like Doctor Moreau in H. G. Wells's novel, tries to change animals into men. The dog is willing to do anything for food and shelter, and happily submits to the various operations designed to make him into a good and useful Soviet citizen. After having received the hypophysis and the testicles of a man, the dog slowly turns into a real human being, starts to smoke and swear, runs after women, and drinks and fights. He is thrown out of the Professor's bourgeois home but soon returns, dressed up in a tie and patent-leather shoes as the new Director of the "Government office for the extermination of prowling four-legged animals in Moscow." In other words, the former mongrel has become the leading dog-catcher in town, ruthlessly exterminating his former friends and peers. What we see is, of course, the appearance of the GPU, the Stalinist secret police, the monster destroying its creator. The former dog, now known as Comrade Sjarik, is a trusted and powerful man in Moscow, a Party member whose word is law. Nothing remains of the cringing dog; comrade Sjarik, an unholy mixture of Karel Čapek's robots and the vain and quarrelsome mandrake in Achim von Arnim's *Isabella von Ägypten*, will never be the slave of man. On the contrary, men will be his slaves. The good professor Preobrazjenskij finally manages to reverse the process, and Comrade Sjarik slowly reverts into a dog again — while still retaining his powers as a man of the Party, which gives Bulgakov obvious and well-utilized possibilities for satire.

The Heart of a Dog has never been published in the U.S.S.R., at least not officially. This is hardly surprising, for even though most of the satire is aimed at the Stalinist regime, the novel also deals with the responsibility of the scientist and the right of a government to mold its citizens according to its wishes, which obviously is still a somewhat touchy subject in both East and West. Also, of course, *The Heart of a Dog* is a very funny novel, and a very bitter one, and as such a very effective satire. It is funny and bitter in the way Jonathan Swift's *Gulliver's Travels* is funny and bitter, and maybe for the same reasons. *The Heart of a Dog* is an attack on the contemporary world written by an embittered Utopian revolutionary who has fought for the revolution, only to see it turn into a mindless machine, brutally destroying its former supporters.

We should keep in mind when reading the novel that it was written at the time of the gradual downfall of Russian Futurism, that brilliant artistic and literary explosion of talent, led by people like Vladimir Mayakovsky, which has offered so much in the way of artistic and intellectual vitality, only to be strangled by a servile and unfeeling bureaucracy and a cold Party machine. Three leading revolutionaries of this time — Vladimir Mayakovsky, Evgeny Zamyatin, and Michail Bulgakov — turned away in disgust from the Party monster they themselves had helped to create. They voiced their disgust in now-famous works of science fiction: Zamyatin in *My* (1920; *We*), Bulgakov in *Sobatje serdtse* (1925; *The Heart of a Dog*), and Mayakovsky in *Klop* (1929; *The Bedbug*).

All three works deal with the same subject, although in vastly different ways. Zamyatin is serious and dystopian in his description of the Only State of the future; Mayakovsky is boisterous, kicking merrily in all directions in his play about a worker from our time who wakes up in the perfect Communist state of the future — and finds he detests it. Bulgakov chooses the entertaining magazine story technique to voice his misgivings — obviously with some success, since the novel turned out to be decidedly unprintable. The new Soviet State was a Utopian dream, to a large degree the creation of Lenin, whom H. G. Wells in his book *Russia in the Shadows* (1920) called "the dreamer in the Kremlin." But if Lenin was the dreamer, Stalin was the man destined to put theory into practice, and Bulgakov's novel, like Mayakovsky's play, speaks eloquently of how the intellectuals viewed the outcome.

The Heart of a Dog is, of course, a very political story, as most works of science fiction are in the last analysis — for how could the genre avoid being political, dealing as it does with the future and the changes it may bring? However, like most science fiction, it can also be read on another, simpler level — as a modern version of the Frankenstein myth. Bulgakov's monster is not at odds with society, however, but instead, like a true opportunist, manages to learn the rules of society and use them to his own ends. Mary Shelley's Monster was a beast with the soul of a poet; Bulgakov's Comrade Sjarik is half-man, half-beast on the surface, but all upstart inside, a ruthless human animal fighting for survival and succeeding, a latter-day Uriah Heep showing his true colors and no longer begging, but demanding. This is something man cannot forgive him, of course; we can sympathize with Mary Shelley's monster, tortured and filled with remorse and disgust for what he has done. Comrade Sjarik is different. He is so "human" that he feels he has a right to survive at any cost and that man owes him something. He ought to be grateful, but he is not. He is, in fact, an ungrateful lout, and, like Dickens' Uriah Heep (with whom Comrade Sjarik indeed shares many traits), he must be destroyed.

The conflict between the old bourgeois professor Preobrazjenskij, who lives for his scientific research in prerevolutionary splendor in postrevolutionary Moscow, and the former cringing slave Sjarik, who will no longer be kicked around or sell his birthright for a sausage, gives yet one more interesting side to this tale. Who is the real villain? The kind old professor who has always been able to pursue his private interests, or the starving, downtrodden former slave whose main fault appears to be that he will not be 'umble and that he shows no respect to his betters? There is a moral problem here and a political one, and this makes the novel even more interesting for anyone willing to dig down a bit beneath the surfaces of action and fun.

Sam J. Lundwall

Sources for Further Study

Reviews:

Christian Science Monitor. LX, July 11, 1968, p. 11.
Kirkus Reviews. XXXVI, July 1, 1968, p. 704.
Library Journal. XCIII, August, 1968, p. 2896.
New Statesman. LXXVI, August 30, 1968, p. 262.
New York Times Book Review. LXXIII, July 28, 1968, p. 5.
Saturday Review. LI, July 20, 1968, p. 24.

HELIOPOLIS

Author: Ernst Jünger (1895-   )
First book publication: 1949
Type of work: Novel
Time: An indefinite future
Locale: The city of Heliopolis on Earth

A philosophical novel of Utopian ideas that views a future society and a not-so-futuristic clash of world views, a plebeian and an elitist-aristocrat one

> *Principal characters:*
> LUCIUS DE GEER, the commander of the War School
> THE PROCONSUL, the ruler of Heliopolis and head of the feudal-aristocratic forces
> THE LANDVOGT, the leader of the plebeian forces
> THE CHIEF OF STAFF, the commanding general of the Proconsul's military forces
> BUDUR PERI, a Parsee girl and friend of Lucius de Geer
> PATER FOELIX, a priest
> THE BERGRAT, an intellectual
> PHARES, a space pilot and messenger of the absent Regent

Ernst Jünger is an important conservative German writer who has made two excursions into Utopian writing, *Heliopolis* and the shorter, more modest *Gläserne Bienen* (*The Glass Bees*, 1957). In *Heliopolis* he describes a not quite Utopian future society. The novel would not be as important if it did not carry a heavy charge of philosophical speculation, which is either presented directly or in parable form. As in so many Utopian novels, the plot is hardly more than a pretext for presenting the viewpoints of the various characters, who are often the spokesmen for Jünger's own conservative, elitist philosophy. After a catastrophic atomic war, the Regent, in whom absolute power rests, has withdrawn to the stars somewhere "beyond the Hesperides." He prefers not to involve himself in the affairs of an Earth that has sunk to the level of a cosmic province. Somewhere in this province lies the model city Heliopolis, ruled in the name of the Regent by a Proconsul. The Proconsul is a self-assured aristocrat, arrogant in his daily affairs, yet of such authority and dignity that even in time of crisis he can engage in his hobbies, leaving the running of things to his aides and military commanders. As commander of the military forces, he has the real power, while the political power is wielded by the popular Landvogt. The Landvogt is a sensualist, a master of rhetoric, a demagogue, and the keeper of many mistresses. He is immensely popular with the masses, who think him kind, although in reality he is totally ruthless, unprincipled, and without mercy. The police force that he commands from his impenetrable fortress is indistinguishable from a band of criminals, and instead of fighting crime, they actively engage in it.

To Jünger, the Proconsul represents legitimate power, the Landvogt only brutal violence. The two men and their followers are locked in a power game that polarizes the city, sometimes through secret maneuvers, sometimes through open battles. The Proconsul can check the forces of the Landvogt at any one point in the city and win an individual battle, but he cannot do so everywhere at once. So he bides his time playing the game. Caught between the two parties are the Parsees, a social group modeled after the Jews. They are a race of dignity, possessing a certain nobility of appearance and thought artistically inclined, but distrusted for their alien ways. They are loathed for their peculiar burial customs and hated for their commercial astuteness that sometimes involves money lending. Pogroms are encouraged by the Landvogt as a safety valve for the undisciplined masses. The legitimate forces have no great liking for the Parsees either, and are not willing to jeopardize the precarious power balance in their defense. Therefore, the Parsees are the frequent victims of rape and pillage, taken into "custody" by the police, kept in concentration camps, and subjected to mass execution.

The hero of the novel is Lucius de Geer, commander of the Proconsul's War School. He is a man of noble birth, well liked by his superiors, comrades, and even the opposition. He has an independent, questioning mind and is not a member of a particular social group in Heliopolis. While most of the other characters are shown only in their stereotyped surroundings, de Geer is the only person who comes into contact with all the groups in Heliopolis and is valued even by the Landvogt. He moves through society observing it for us and speaking for the author on society, art, history, and philosophy. However, he is not quite at home anywhere. He is an Odysseus in search of spiritual worlds, a seeker after Utopia.

De Geer falls in love with the beautiful Parsee girl Budur Peri, daughter of the cultivated bookbinder Antonio Peri, a dreamer who seeks release in opium. At first, out of a sense of duty to his friends, he saves the girl from a police concentration camp. He later uses a military expedition launched to teach the Landvogt a lesson, to liberate the girl's father from an experimental clinic, where unscrupulous scientists make experiments reminiscent of those of SS physicians. In military terms the commando is a success, but de Geer's superior, the Chief of Staff, has no sympathy for using a military action for private ends, and dismisses him. His failure, however, is only temporary. At the close of the novel the messenger of the distant Regent appears and asks him to enter into the extraterrestrial services of the Regent. Lucius de Geer and his loved ones leave for the stars.

The plot of the novel is quite thin; what is important are the fables, essays, and reflections included in the book that give it its manifold meaning and philosophical weight. Central to the philosophy of the novel is the dichotomy between the Proconsul and the Landvogt. The Landvogt, the representative of collective, bureaucratic forces, who flies the red flag with the iron fist, is interested only in technology and its control. The Proconsul is interested in the perfection of man. Some other groups contribute to the complexity of the situation. In addition to the Parsees there are the Burgenländer, the old nobility of Earth, and the Mauretanians, the technicians of power. They seek both to use and to ally themselves with each other. Mauretanians serve both the Proconsul and the Landvogt.

There is a certain amount of technology in *Heliopolis*, sometimes magical, but mostly in the field of weaponry. The most remarkable item is the "phonophor," an apparatus of universal application. Its function as a clock, a compass, and a passport. It gives information about accounts with the Energeion (besides gold, energy is the main currency), serves as a newspaper, is a communication line with libraries and encyclopedias, and provides communication with all the other phonophors in the world. In short, it is a kind of microminiaturized computer connected with central data banks, the Central Archive, and the *Punktamt*.

The technological details are well thought out, but they are never central to the novel. What interests Jünger is how they are used, the problem of power, and man's place in the world. Man is always more important than man's tools. In this respect, Jünger's novel reflects and recapitulates the events of the first half of the twentieth century. Anarchy has triumphed, the rule of the masses has begun, and the problem, as he sees it, is the establishment of a historical social order that ensures the rule of law and order and the authority of the state.

Jünger is a very conservative writer, who favors authority, order, discipline, obedience, honor, and legitimacy. He was deeply influenced by his experience of World War I, but unlike writers such as Erich Maria Remarque, who came to hate war, Jünger glorified fighting and held it to be a purification, a strengthening force. He arrived at the conclusion that war must be made more violent, not abolished. During World War II Jünger was an active supporter of the Nazi cause, a sentiment that can be found in the novel. In *Heliopolis*, the Chief of Staff expounds the military philosophy: once a soldier has sworn his oath, his only duty is to obey, to be as efficient in his tasks as possible, and to follow every command, unless it goes against his honor. It is not the soldier's place to question the decisions of his comanders or the goals of the political authority. Human sacrifices are necessary, and the Chief does not care about losses as long as the ends are achieved. He stresses the necessity of strict obedience, unlike Lucius de Geer, who acknowledges the possibility of conflict between liberty and duty. The soldier's greatness and glory is to sacrifice his life. The persons in power have the duty to arrange the affairs of state in such a way that the soldier can follow them with a clear conscience.

The soldier's place, nevertheless, is not the most important or highest in society. Even the Chief acknowledges that the genius is better off in the arts, in politics, or in science, where freedom is more important than order. A novel may be of greater importance than a decisive battle, since the creative force is the guiding principle in the world. For Jünger, writers are prophets and seers, perceiving things that will come to pass only later. Several of the characters develop Utopias. There is the planned Utopia of the Bergrat who sees birth-control as the solution to mob rule, and the Christian Utopia of Pater Foelix who stresses suffering and sacrifice, saying that everything is included in God's plan (although not everything is in the law). He envisions a world of universal love, similar to the world of the bees that he keeps. Ultimately, the world is not rational, and salvation is not possible by rationally planning the future.

In any case, Jünger's Utopias are for a select few; there is no hope for the masses who are low by nature and destined to remain so because it is their inheritance. Lucius explains to Budur Peri that a nocturnal logic rules beyond the Hesperides, a visionary power that also manifests itself in dreams. "There is nothing mightier than the dreaming spirit." The finest manifestation of this spirit is the nobility of Burgenland, a realm where poetry has not yet become separated from reality. It is the last and strongest residence of the spirit. Similar to Nietzsche, Jünger sees dream and ecstasy as the native soil of the arts, and the artist is a visionary, changing the world by his art. In the Burgenland, technology and mythos are reconciled. There is no time there to enslave its citizens. If the Landvogt is a slave of time and his passions, the party of the Proconsul and the Burgenländer are obligated to platonic ideals. They exist in a unity of knowledge and belief and respond stoically to whatever catastrophes befall them. So naturally the novel finally turns to the problem of happiness.

Jünger's ideal of happiness is the idyll: the garden; farming; watching growth; the small pleasures of intimate contact with things, animals, and people. He has no large plans for the melioration of the world, which turns out worse, the more ambitious these plans are. His idea of happiness is life in a small circle, in the company of friends, a wife, children. But this takes second place. Higher still ranks mythical elevation such as Lucius experiences after his demotion. Phares is the Regent's resident pilot on Earth. He represents a higher form of mankind. He has experienced the gravity free regions of space where the terrestrial conflicts are unknown, and he possesses a physiognomy of indubitable power softened by pity. Phares takes Lucius, his beloved Budur Peri, and another young man to the galactic residence of the Regent. The Regent suggests a metaphysical rather than a mere physical or political power. In fact, he reminds one of Bloy's "dieu se retire": the God who is not dead, but has merely temporarily withdrawn from the world, who now finds the time ripe for his return, since the worldly powers and ideologies have reached their wit's end and exhausted themselves. For this return into the center of political life he will need a man like Lucius de Geer as his paladin. This implies that man is absolutely powerless to achieve happiness and establish a just order through his own efforts. Salvation must come from beyond, from metaphysical-religious realms. The fighting man who has gone through all the disappointments of life, witnessed the destruction of his career, suffered pain and the humiliation of defeat, but who has nevertheless remained his own man, is finally metaphysically elevated to fulfill new tasks. The new elite of the world consists of men who have been purified by suffering and learned pity and love, without which no true greatness is possible. However, to achieve this, one must be chosen; for the masses there is no such hope in Jünger's world.

Franz Rottensteiner

Sources for Further Study

Criticism:

The Encyclopedia of Science Fiction and Fantasy. Compiled by Donald H. Tuck. Chicago: Advent Publishers, Inc., 1978, p. 248. This biographical and bibliographical article is brief, but outlines his career.

L'HERBE ROUGE
(Red Grass)

Author: Boris Vian (1920-1959)
First book publication: 1950
Type of work: Novel
Time: Unidentified
Locale: Unidentified

Wolf, an engineer who has been entrusted by the city administration to assemble a mysterious machine, uses it to get rid of his past, but when he dies, his body is rejected by the machine

Principal characters:
WOLF, the engineer
SAPHIR LAZULI, his mechanic
LIL, his wife
FOLAVRIL, his girl friend
SÉNATEUR DUPONT, the dog

There is no doubt that Boris Vian was one of the most active and knowledgeable among the few intellectuals who introduced American science fiction to France in the early 1950's. His influence was considerable in science fiction as well as in many other fields; and it continues quite significantly today. In less than fifteen years of intense production, he succeeded in contributing to a number of domains. In science fiction, he wrote articles for reviews such as Jean-Paul Sartre's *Les Temps Modernes*, gave interviews on science fiction and cinema, created the first science fiction cabaret shows, and translated *The World of Null-A* and *The Pawns of Null-A* by A. E. van Vogt, as well as Lewis Padgett's "Mimsy Were the Borogoves" and other short stories. But of more importance are his own novels and short stories.

Among the latter, only two narratives can unquestionably be classified as science fiction: *Le Danger des Classiques* and *Paris, le 15 décembre 1999*. The rest of his work, including his great novels *L'Ecume des jours*, *L'Automne à Pékin*, *L'Herbe Rouge*, and *L'Arrachecoeur* in particular, raise certain important theoretical problems to the science fiction critic. Before discussing these questions, however, let us examine the plot of *L'Herbe Rouge*.

In an unidentified place, where the Red Grass grows plentifully, Wolf, with the help of his mechanic Lazuli, has assembled a machine which makes it possible to reexperience one's own life. Vian never clearly describes the cage in which Wolf sits to relive his past; he only explains that it is located on a line which begins in a well and terminates in the sky, leaving a visible streak above the machine. The novel opens as the machine is being tested.

Following a burlesque official inauguration, Wolf sits in the cage of the machine to relive the various episodes of his life. On his first voyage into his own past, he is welcomed by Monsieur Perle, who gives him a plan to follow on his further voyages. He is to experience relations with his family; education; his first experience with religion; puberty, sexual life as a teenager, and marriage; activity as part of a social group; and metaphysical doubt. At each point, Wolf meets a different person. His conversations with these strangers are, in effect, charges against family, studies, religion — against bourgeois society, a misconceived society.

In counterpoint to this main thematic line, other episodes are developed. Sénateur Dupont, the dog, has but one aim in life: to find a wapiti. Wolf helps him achieve his dream. From that moment, Sénateur cuts himself off from the rest of the world and falls into senile decay. Lazuli tries, throughout the novel, to make love to his consenting girl friend. Each time he begins kissing her, a man dressed in a dark suit appears. Lazuli kills the intruder, but each time he reappears. Finally Lazuli kills himself, and on his body Folavril, who witnesses all this, sees the injuries Lazuli has made to his doubles. Wolf and Lazuli visit a redlight district, accompany two sailors in their sadistic games, and spend several hours watching a Black dancing. This episode is typical of Vian's fantasy. As the novel comes to a close, the opposition and misunderstanding between the sexes reach a climax. The two men die in their quests, and the women decide to live their lives without men's love, wondering how they had ever lived with it.

A novel that could be described as autobiographical in many respects (and this is unusual in Vian's works), *L'Herbe Rouge* most clearly expresses the bitterness of a man who resents the failure of his life. Attrition, ugliness, compartmentalization, and simplistic conceptions destroy him; yet he has used demystifying lucidity and imagination to counter debasing, degrading structures.

One of the favorite means Vian used to attack the system as a whole was Korzybskism. He knew A. Korzybski through A. E. van Vogt and made extensive personal use of his ideas. In *L'Herbe Rouge* some influence is still noticeable. Education received in schools is Aristotelian. It is based on the existence of an ideal order and on the postulate of the fixed world; it is grounded on a delusion: the opposition between matter and spirit, physical and psychic spheres, manual and intellectual labor. Education in these conditions inevitably leads to elitism. For instance, it conveys the concept that a scientist is a kind of a superman, whereas, Vian believed, it is more difficult to learn boxing than mathematics.

In Vian's works, bourgeois values are challenged radically through his treatment of language rather than through intellectual debates. Using humor and verbal invention, he dismantles linguistic stereotypes and alters reality by submitting it to his own invented laws. The resulting universe is coherent, even though its laws are mysterious.

Here, a genuine science fiction universe could be created. As a matter of fact, Vian's fictional worlds are antirealistic. This antirealism is not the exclusive prerogative of science fiction. One particularly clear example is the dog. Sénateur Dupont talks, laughs, gives his opinion on everything. This is typically a fairy tale device placed in Vian's framework (as opposed to that of Clifford D. Simak's *City*, for example. As for fantasy, the appearances of Lazuli's doubles and their sudden disappearances are obviously fantastic motifs. Yet, science fiction is also present, at least in the enigmatic machine with the attributes of a cosmic ship and of a time machine. However, more than a time machine, it is a gadget that revives memories. Wolf does not actually *relive* them. The operation, that can be called travel only metaphorically, takes Wolf to a place where everything is fictitious, time as well as space. Pure memories do not exist, Vian points out repeatedly. Practically speaking, time travel is impossible in the context of *L'Herbe Rouge*. Paradoxically enough, the book's main object rejects the possibility for man to spatialize time and make it exist in some *locus* where it would be accessible. Vian's treatment of time travel amounts to a protest against science fiction's ways and means.

In any case, Wolf's memories are revived and, avoiding nostalgic pondering, he obliterates them. What about the Red Grass that grows in that unnamed place? It is obviously of the same species as that in H. G. Wells's *War of the Worlds*. Does such a filiation create a thematic link between Vian and Wells? Would that link be enough to integrate a work like *L'Herbe Rouge* into science fiction? The answer to both questions is no.

Many other elements of the book could temptingly be connected with science fiction. Wolf's and Lazuli's deep instability might be explained by their agonizing lack of adaptation to the "alter locus," where they seem to be exiled and consequently made mutants. Such a connection would lead to a misinterpretation of the novel; in Wolf's case, the questions aroused by the machine do not need answers taken from science fiction themes; they lie in Wolf's encounter with M. Perle and others.

When tackling Vian, the student of science fiction is bound to ask questions about the function of the genre in this author's fiction. In Vian the term *fiction* is rich in meaning. All positivistic views, either scientific or literary, must be dismissed. Science is present in the fiction, but it serves as fantasy, parody, and/or satire. Science fiction elements play an important role, but they are never an occasion for a penetration into otherness through logical estrangement, although Vian is endowed with considerable imaginative power. Surrealism and pataphysics, its offspring, play a more important part than science fiction. This is quite logical since Vian's purpose is mainly to destroy the divisions in life and subvert the frameworks of institutionalized life (marriage, work, religion, studies). Consequently, the protagonists' drama is always expressed in the private sphere. Wolf and Lazuli, as the characters of *L'Ecume des jours*, *L'Automne à Pékin* and *L'Arrachecoeur*, act for their own purpose and good; what happens to them can in no way have an effect on the group and/or society. In this respect it is highly significant that Wolf appropriates the machine for his own personal use.

Vian's genius consists in admirably integrating various streams into a fiction that could be called "parascientific fiction" to account for its marginal status as science fiction. *L'Herbe Rouge*, like most of Vian's works, has to be dealt with along these lines in order to understand fully its originality.

Jean-Marc Gouanvic

HERE ABIDE MONSTERS

Author: Andre Norton (1912-   )
First book publication: 1973
Type of work: Novel
Time: July 21, 1972
Locale: Initially, a small American country town; after Chapter One, a parallel world
with no specific location

*An attempt to provide an explanation for mysterious disappearances such as those
in the Bermuda Triangle, and a study of identity and alienation as people from different times and places are exiled together in a parallel world of superscience and extrasensory perception*

Principal characters:
> NICK SHAW, a young man estranged from his father and unpleasant
> stepmother
> LINDA DURANT, a young woman who travels to the parallel world
> with him
> AVALON, one of the four Heralds of the parallel world
> ADRIAN HADLETT, an elderly vicar transported to the fairy realm
> RITA, one of the group of World War II Britons who have banded
> together in the parallel world
> JEREMIAH, a cat, a transported pet
> LUNG, a Pekinese, another transported pet

To confront one of Andre Norton's many works of fiction is to have an
experience rich in learning and wonder. Consistently, her writing springs from
a deep well of sources and thought and from an abiding affection for the individual. *Here Abide Monsters* displays both of these elements. Its inspiration
flows from the many unexplained disappearances that have been recorded
throughout history. More specifically, the novel draws on those vanishings
associated with the English fairy mounds and from Charles Fort's more contemporary accounts in *The Book of the Damned* (1919), *New Lands* (1923),
Lo! (1931), and *Wild Talents* (1932).

Such excursions into myth, legend, history, and literature are typical of
Norton's work. *Dark Piper* (1968) and *Year of the Unicorn* (1965) are drawn
from the folk tales of the Pied Piper of Hamelin and the Beauty and the Beast,
respectively. *Star Guard* (1955) is a retelling of Xenophon's *Anabasis*;
Shadow Hawk (1960), a historical fantasy, emerged from Norton's reading of
Joan Grant's novels of ancient Egypt. More like the use of the historical and
pseudohistorical sources of *Here Abide Monsters* is the utilization of Paul
Hermann's *Conquest by Man* (translated from the German in 1954), which
includes an account of the prehistoric Beaker Traders, as a source for the Time
Trader novels: *The Time Traders* (1958), *Galactic Derelict* (1959), *The Defi-
ant Agents* (1962), and *Key Out of Time* (1963). In the same vein, *Scarface*
(1948), an early juvenile adventure story in novel form, stems from the diary
of a Dutch physician and the life of Henry Morgan. *The Beast Master* (1959)
and its sequel, *Lord of Thunder* (1962), were researched through actual

Navaho phrase books. More specifically, the Celtic and British backgrounds for *Here Abide Monsters* are anticipated by the Arthurian Britain of *Steel Magic* (1965; later title *Grey Magic*), a juvenile fantasy, and are repeated in the adult science fiction novel *Merlin's Mirror* (1975).

In *Here Abide Monsters*, however, the Charles Fort and Bermuda Triangle allusions are merely devices that help the reader suspend disbelief. They offer a semiscientific explanation for the characters' movement into the parallel world of mental miracle and superscience. When Nick Shaw and Linda Durant pass into the numinous realm of the Heralds and the wondrous Kin to join a group of World War II Britons, they become involved in a mixture of the seemingly rational and irrational. On one hand are various historical groups transported into the singular time of the fairy world: Chinese, Mongols, Anglo-Saxons, and a singular group of religious fanatics. On the other are the native inhabitants: the Kin with their Heralds; their king, Logos or Merlin; and their varied beasts, such as unicorns, enfields, lamias, and griffons.

The humans and the natives do interact after a fashion. The Heralds, Avalon in particular, regularly offer a unity and a sharing to the humans. This is because the inhabitants enjoy a deep bond with the sentient land. Without this special communion, the transported humans will exist and die as strangers, forever alienated from benefits the Heralds and their people (the Kin) possess. The link between the humans and the Kin is Rita, one of the group of Britons that Nick and Linda join for mutual protection. Before Nick's and Linda's arrival, Rita had accepted the Herald's apple — offered both literally and symbolically — and been transformed into one of the Kin, the native inhabitants of the gloriously spired cities. Her transformation grants her various special abilities, including the power to protect herself and others with an invisible aura, to communicate mentally, and to move from place to place by teleportation. However, her friends, especially her former fiancé, have rejected her and her bond to the Kin and the land, and labeled her an inhuman traitor.

This juxtaposition of rigidity and flexibility, tradition and change, is not unusual in Norton's fiction. Like so many of her characters, Rita represents the fulfilled opportunity for transition and growth. Her disposition allows her to adapt to the land she has inherited through happenstance. The other members of the British group, especially Adrian Hadlett, lack this ability to cope, to find themselves, and to be free from their traditions and conditioned expectations. However, Nick Shaw and Linda Durant, because of their youth and the estrangements in their prior human existence, will, it appears, have the ability to embrace the intuitive and personal powers that the Herald and Rita offer.

Nick comes to fairyland and its dangers having lost his mother and after watching his once beloved father become a stranger through the influence of his conniving stepmother. It is no surprise that, even though he has yet to accept the Herald's offer, he is the first to display mental power. Trapped by a group of religious fanatics, led by a deranged bishop and a slovenly young woman, Nick creates a protoplasmic arm to free himself and evade the monsters created by the minds of the religious zealots. Later, aided by Linda and the two pets, he is able to reproduce the manifestation despite the British group's strong disbelief. This intuitive and mental activity reflects a common element in much of Norton's fiction.

Despite the numerous science fiction works Norton has written, her stance is clearly antiscientific, and her views on the damage she feels the empirical mode has done to mankind are quoted in Rick Brooks' essay "Andre Norton: Loss of Faith" (1971). Elsewhere, this conflict is seen in the juxtaposition of the witches of Escarp and the scientific Kolder in the main branch of the Witch World series, and her view is supported by Carl Jung who observes that science has alienated modern man from his individual and collective unconscious. This is further emphasized in *Here Abide Monsters* by the fact that the two animals, Jeremiah the cat and Lung the Pekinese, are the first to develop mental powers because of their closeness to nature. In addition, the central psychic power source in the city of the Kin, which Nick infiltrates with his nascent power to create illusion, is a giant, radiant ankh, the Egyptian symbol of life that Norton also uses as a symbol of power in *Wraiths of Time* (1976).

The ankh is an indicator of the potential of the human mind. When Nick enters the city, he is almost overwhelmed, mentally overloaded, by its power: his mind has not yet made the intuitive commitment necessary to absorb the ankh's gift. Were Rita, the animals, and the ankh not enough of an indication of the conflict between numina and phenomena, there are also the scientific Hunters to point out the threat of the artificiality of technology. All of the people in the parallel world, natives and strangers alike, are threatened by the superscience of the Hunters, a group who use their flying saucers to trap the visitors and harass the Kin. When Nick, Linda, and the Britons finally do destroy the Hunters' base through courage and mental power, it is significant that Adrian Hadlett, the courageous elderly vicar, freely gives up his life. He knows that he can never accept the Herald's invitation: he is too committed to the old ways and his own concept of "the good" to release his inhibitions and adapt to the new world.

When Hadlett dies, he signifies the passing away of the old order and marks the end of the threat of science. As Nick and Linda, along with the two animals, turn to the gloriously emblazoned Herald at the end of the novel, *Here Abide Monsters* embodies the dominant theme in the fiction of Andre Norton: the affirmation of the essentially human. Life, in all its generative and adaptive glory is celebrated in what Northrop Frye in *The Anatomy of Criticism* calls the comic mode. New orders arise from the ashes of the old and humanity is enhanced. The artificial, contrived, and rigid are defeated, and the alienated are elevated to nobility through self-discovery and find a union that celebrates their precious uniqueness.

Roger C. Schlobin

HEROVIT'S WORLD

Author: Barry N. Malzberg (1939-   )
First book publication: 1973
Type of work: Novel
Time: The present
Locale: New York

An account of the spiritual decline and fall of a professional science fiction writer

> *Principal characters:*
> JONATHAN HEROVIT, a science fiction writer
> KIRK POLAND, his pseudonym
> MACK MILLER, his principal character
> JANICE, his wife
> MITCHELL WILK, his best friend

Thirty-seven-year-old Jonathan Herovit is the author of ninety-two science fiction novels. (There are only two other writers who have clocked up a higher total, and they are both considerably older.) His sex life has been suffering since his wife Janice found herself unexpectedly inconvenienced by a late pregnancy and gave birth to a daughter. He is also in trouble with his agent, Morton Mackenzie, who is pushing him for delivery of his latest Mack Miller novel, *Survey Sirius*, which is overdue. Herovit's reputation is beginning to suffer a little because the pressure upon him has resulted in a decline in the quality of his recent work, and the decline is itself becoming the source of *more* pressure. When the novel begins he is already locked into this vicious circle, the ultimate result of which is presaged by an incident in which a resentful fan throws half a glass of scotch and soda into his face at a meeting of the New League of Science Fiction Professionals, leaving a stain on his jacket which seems to him to be symbolic.

No matter how hard he tries, Herovit cannot get into the groove with *Survey Sirius*. He pecks away at the typewriter, drinking scotch and somehow being perpetually sidetracked by reminiscences of early meetings with the great editor who shaped his career, and of the time he was expelled from the science fiction guild for nearly causing the great V. V. Vivaldi to have a heart attack. He even begins to suffer phantasmal visitations from Kirk Poland, the imaginary *persona* he invented (at editor John Steele's instigation) to be the signatory of his work. The Poland *persona*, expressed through his ultratough stories of surveyman Mack Miller, chauvinist *extraordinaire*, is a lot tougher than Herovit's everyday *persona*, and reckons that Herovit can no longer cut the mustard and ought to hand over control of his life to him.

Herovit is interrupted in his struggle by a more substantial visitation in the shape of his best friend Mitchell Wilk. Wilk once had some reputation as a satirical science fiction writer, but has not written anything in years and has taken refuge in the olive-grove of Academe. He has come to offer Herovit the opportunity to be guest writer in his new science fiction program, showering him with promises of a hundred-dollar honorarium and abundant opportunities for sexual encounters. By this time, Herovit is beginning to suffer communication difficulties, and Wilk has problems in connecting with him, but the agreement is made. Later, when Herovit — in desperate need of reassurance — rings Wilk at his hotel, he interrupts his friend in the middle of an erotic interlude, and only succeeds in fanning the flames of his own frustration.

Ultimately, worst comes to worst, and Janice, in a rare moment of passion, takes him so completely by surprise as to render him temporarily impotent. In despair, Herovit resigns control of himself to the ever-eager Kirk Poland *persona*, who has very definite ideas about how things can be sorted out. At first, Poland's go-getting style seems to have a slim chance of prevailing against the awful might of evil circumstance, but when he irrevocably alienates Morton Mackenzie and tears up the completed pages of *Survey Sirius* the reader knows that hope is gone. Kirk Poland strides forth to redeem his marriage by forceful action, but finds Janice with her bags packed waiting for the removal men. He is suddenly as helpless as the hapless Herovit, dismally unable to cope with a situation that never could have arisen in the space operas for whose production Herovit invented him.

Next, a girl named Gloria (one of his casual adulteries) rings with an offer to rally round, and for a moment there again seems to be a glimmer of hope, but when she turns up in the flesh, she has Mitchell Wilk in amorous attendance. In desperation, Poland hands over control to the *persona* of Mack Miller, the scourge of the galaxy, who has *never* met a situation he couldn't handle with the aid of tough talking and a blaster. Unfortunately, not once in ninety-two genocidal novels has Mack Miller met aliens like those which face him now. Though he has pacified many a hostile star-system, he stands no chance against New York, which crushes him like an insect within minutes of his taking command.

Barry Malzberg gave up writing science fiction as a full-time professional when he was about thirty-seven. He wrote some twenty science fiction novels and a hundred science fiction short stories in the space of seven years, the earlier ones under the pseudonym K. M. O'Donnell. He has cited *Herovit's World* as testimony to some of his reasons for abandoning his career as a science fiction writer. (Further amplification of these reasons is given in the pages of his novel *Galaxies*, which deals with some of the compromises involved in writing marketable science fiction.)

Basically, Malzberg sees science fiction writing as a seductive trap. There are few easier ways of making a living than churning out science fiction in fifty-thousand-word chunks, provided that one can master the relatively simple button-pushing techniques that determine the salability of the product. It sells because it provides pleasant escapism in association with perennial reassurance that complex problems can be simply solved by right thinking and direct action. Because science fiction exists largely in the sector of the literary marketplace where a steady demand for disposable reader-experiences is met by the mass-production of stereotyped goods, there is, in Malzberg's view, hardly any scope for the typecast science fiction professional to exercise genuine creativity, genuine artistry, or genuine concern for real problems. The science fiction community, which protects the self-respect and sense of mission of both writers and fans, operates, in this view, to insulate the writer from an awareness of the genre's shortcomings and to discourage attempts to transcend its narrow limitations. All science fiction writers, according to Malzberg, risk ending up in Herovit's world, burnt out without every having accomplished anything, dislocated from reality, injured by the anonymity and tastelessness of the audience. It is hardly surprising that Malzberg is not particularly popular in the science fiction community.

Herovit's World is, of course, a parody. Everything is exaggerated to the point of absurd tragicomedy. Malzberg is an intense and impassioned writer who invariably prefers overstatement to understatement as an affective technique. His narratives always consist of the insistent streams-of-consciousness of alienated viewpoints, anguished and locked into gathering crescendos of desperation. There is no one who presents the terror of frustration as well as he, and in *Herovit's World* more than in any of his other novels we can see and feel the echoes of his personal frustrations as a writer. Not, of course, that he *is* Jonathan Herovit — but there is no mistaking the extent to which he feels for his antihero. Herovit's predicament and fate are grotesquely exaggerated, to be sure, but their roots are in Malzberg's perception of his own situation.

Hervoit's social environment is a transfiguration of the real science fiction community. Opinion has differed widely as to the justice of the representation: writers and fans cast in the mould of V. V. Vivaldi have regarded the portrayal as an unforgivable heresy, and even those who are more similar to Mitchell Wilk have tended to resent it. But there is nevertheless sufficient correspondence between the events that happen in the novel and happenings in the real science fiction community to provide a warrant for the transfiguration. No matter how ludicrous the events become in their distillation into the essence of black comedy, they are echoes of history. For this reason, *Herovit's World* — which is, of course, far from being a science fiction novel — invites attention within the science fiction field as the most scathing indictment of the genre ever written. Ironically, the market forces about which it complains dictated that it should be released and promoted under the science fiction label to insure the modest sales more or less guaranteed to any book bearing that emblem.

In truth, there are not many Herovits in the American science fiction community, with many millions of words to their dubious credit at a still-tender age. Only one American writer sold more than a million words of science fiction before his thirtieth birthday, and that was Robert Silverberg, the writer Malzberg admires more than any other. Nor are there many Mack Millers peddling a brutal ideology of militaristic xenophobia (at least, not any more). Nor are there many writers who feel utterly frustrated because, like Herovit, they feel that writing science fiction has somehow prevented them from doing the serious work they otherwise might have done. If there were, one would be inclined to suspect (as one suspects of Herovit) that they never had it in them in the first place and are suffering from delusions of grandeur if they think they had.

What *is* true, however, is that there are countless professional science fiction writers who have ground out the occasional Mack Miller-type potboiler in the interest of paying the rent, and not a few who have ground out too many. It is not easy to point to a science fiction writer who has been dependent on the field for his bread and butter and who has not coldheartedly written at least one bad book, and it is not so difficult to find examples who have clocked up twenty or more. This is, in some ways, a sad state of affairs, but probably not cause for despair, in that many of those writers have also written some good books. Malzberg's own spectacular career was a testament to the extent to which it is possible to bend the rules of the science fiction marketplace. (And it may be worth noting that after his retirement, Malzberg found the impetus to write *Chorale*, which favors fight against flight in no uncertain terms.)

Herovit's World is a good novel because it pursues its objective relentlessly, providing the perfect summary of its case, neatly laid-out and viciously effective. It is a parody which arises from honest frustration, and which therefore has a pertinence which it could so easily have lacked. It never descends to the level of a science fiction community in-joke (of which there are many), nor is it a *roman a clef* (V. V. Vivaldi and Mitchell Wilk each have obvious affinities with more than one real personality, but are *not* simply well-known characters disguised to protect the author from libel suits.) The novel is not an exposé or a straightforward hymn of hate, but a satirical commentary intended to bring damnation upon certain regrettable tendencies in modern science fiction, while recognizing that many of these tendencies are beyond the control of the people who are their victims. It should be read attentively by all would-be science fiction writers, and then thrown away. Readers with no such aspirations may take a much more innocent amusement from its pages.

Brian Stableford

Sources for Further Study

Reviews:

Best Sellers. XXXV, August, 1975, p. 147.

Booklist. LXX, November 1, 1973, p. 274.

Kirkus Reviews. XLI, May 1, 1973, p. 534.

Library Journal. XCVIII, August, 1973, p. 2340.

Magazine of Fantasy and Science Fiction. XLVI, May, 1974, p. 25.

Publisher's Weekly. CCIII, May 7, 1973, p. 60.

THE HIGH CRUSADE

Author: Poul Anderson (1926-)
First book publication: 1960
Type of work: Novel
Time: 1345
Locale: The Earth and the Galactic Empire

When unsuspecting aliens, bent on invasion by intimidation, land in a medieval English village, the local gentry and peasantry subdue them, take over their ship, and begin to conquer the galaxy for England

Principal characters:
BROTHER PARVUS, the Chronicler, a Franciscan
SIR ROGER, BARON DE TOURNEVILLE, a vassal of Edward III, leader of the people of Ansby
LADY CATHERINE, his wife
SIR OWAIN MONTBELLE, the handsome younger son of a petty baron

A chief theoretical problem in the genre of imaginative fiction is the relationship of science fiction to the outright fantasies, disparagingly called "sword and sorcery" fiction. Yet, as the popularity of such writers as Edgar Rice Burroughs, Fritz Leiber, and Leigh Brackett demonstrates, many readers find a quasi-medieval world as satisfying mentally as a remote planet, with a sword or battleaxe holding more romance than a laser or disintegrator ray, and a barded horse being a better vehicle for their imaginations than a spaceship.

Poul Anderson's *The High Crusade* is a thoroughly successful *tour de force*, combining the best of both worlds. The inhabitants of an English village during the Middle Ages are pitted against a star-trekking race of alien conquerors, and emerge on top. There is both sufficient action to satisfy the lover of sword and sorcery, and sufficient scientific accuracy to satisfy John W. Campbell, Jr., in whose *Astounding Science Fiction* it was first published in serial form in 1960.

Anderson's task is large — as large as the successful attempt of Isaac Asimov to combine science fiction and the detective story in his *Caves of Steel*. The blending of two disparate genres always presents a greater challenge and carries a greater risk, because it demands competence in both fields. Anderson has produced a convincingly standard alien superpower in science fiction setting, within which he has moved characters that are true to their medieval, spiritual, and cultural background. Yet Anderson, who has been praised for the accuracy of his settings, past, present, and future, is equal to the task.

He opens the story with a framing device characteristic of medieval literature. Chaucer used the Canterbury pilgrimage as the medium for his collection of stories, and Boccaccio has refugees from the plague tell one another the tales of *The Decameron* at his villa near Florence. Anderson's frame is also a masterpiece of economy, relating the situation to the reader in less than a page. The captain of a spaceship lands on an alien planet, and is confronted by the translation of an ancient manuscript that presents astonishing evidence. Although the original of the translation has been written more than a thousand years before the time when the story opens, the captain dreads its impact on his present society. As he begins to read, the story begins.

The manuscript itself is written as a medieval chronicle. It tells how its author, a poorly educated, rural Franciscan monk named Brother Parvus, eye-witnessed the events of May 1, 1345, during the reign of King Edward III. An alien spaceship on a mission of conquest, filled with a crew of soldiers of the race called Wersgorix, lands in a pasture near the town of Ansby in Lincolnshire. Their procedure is to seek out less advanced cultures, make a show of scientific and military strength, and use their superior technology to awe the natives into submission.

Rather than a village full of farmers, they find a town full of armed veterans in which Roger de Tourneville is gathering an army for a campaign in France. Four aliens emerge to overawe the crowd; then one of them fires a laser. He and the others are killed with a swarm of arrows, and the assembled army storms the spaceship's gangplank, floods through the airlock, and takes the rest of the crew.

Sir Roger decides that the spaceship is heaven-sent, and that with its aid, he could win the war in France, retake the Holy Land, and be home in time for harvest. Setting a surviving Wersgor named Branithar to navigate the ship, he loads the entire village of Ansby — people, cattle, pigs, chickens, and all aboard, and prepares to depart. Instead, Branithar sets the autopilot for a flight to the nearest planet in the Wersgorix galaxy. The English see earth recede beneath them as they unwittingly begin the high crusade.

Anderson throughout stresses the single theme of English adaptability — and exemplifies the theme in a series of confrontations between old and new technologies. By the time the ship appears over one of the three fortified cities on the planet Tharixan, the knights have already learned how to use the ship's armament. The sophistication of advanced weapon technology has simplified the job of the human agent; the English find a target much easier to hit with a self-guided missile or a laser that locks onto its target than with a bow and arrow. The theme's corollary is that much of value has become obsolete and therefore forgotten in the scientific advance of the Wersgorix. Brother Parvus observes that the Wersgorix are not adept at hand-to-hand combat, and although they have force-fields to counter laser beams, they city falls because they do not take the simple precautions of medieval warfare. Having bombarded the city from the air, the English land to do close combat. The Wersgorix's attempts to get airborne in a small craft are foiled by jousting knights in full armor who simply knock it over.

The English succeed, because of their adaptability and their military training and experience, against seemingly more capable foes. However, the Wersgorix have indulged in ease for so long they have become overly dependent on their machinery; when their machines fail, they are helpless. Thus, while vehicles similar to tanks fall into the camouflaged pits the English have prepared, archers and mounted knights scatter the supporting infantry.

The English success depends on more than might. It depends equally on the faith that the Lord of Hosts is with them, or an unshakable confidence in their prowess, and sometimes on a mixture of craftiness and Christian charity. And the conflict among all these elements and the modern technology of the Wersgorix is a constant source of humor. During a conference with Huruga, the supreme Wersgor commander on Tharixan, the English pause for prayer. The Wersgorix are unfamiliar with the concept, and their lack of knowledge of the language leaves them wondering whether "God" is a mighty computer with which the English are in contact telepathically. (Some hypothesize that prayers are mental exercises through which the English temporarily increase their physical powers.) Throughout the contacts between the two races, Sir Roger's continuous bluffing leaves the Wersgorix hamstrung with indecision: they can see that the English wear armor and carry weapons that the Wersgorix have not used for centuries, but they can never be certain whether these knights, yeomen, and peasants are savages or the representatives of a culture so superior that it needs only a handful of warriors to counter the Wersgorix Empire.

At one point, Huruga and his armed force barricade themselves in their last stronghold on the planet — a fort impregnable even to the nuclear bombs being dropped from the highly automated aircraft the English have learned how to operate. With plenty of provisions for a seige, Huruga is prepared to wait in the fort during the few weeks it will take to summon help from a military base on a planet circling a neighboring star. Being experienced at seiges, Sir Roger scours the countryside and rounds up a horde of Wersgorix civilians — women, children, and old men and sends them to the fort. Faced with the thought of feeding them, Huruga surrenders.

Anderson continues his theme that technological advancement does not necessarily assure victory. Sir Roger is aware that a relief force from the military base will soon end his conquests, and that his enemies will have little use for diplomacy. Thus, leaving a force to hold Tharixan, he sets off to meet the representatives of three races subject to the Wersgorix and unites the subjugated peoples in a revolt. With medieval foresight, he has bribed key members of the other diplomatic parties into making each of the ambassadors think that the other two were also ready to move.

Since the English can outthink as well as outfight the Wersgorix, the outcome would not be much in doubt in the final third of the novel, were it not for still another characteristically medieval touch — an adulterous love affair. Like Tristram and Isolde, like Lancelot and Guinevere, Sir Roger's wife, Lady Catherine, and Sir Owain Montbelle see more of each other than either does of Sir Roger, whose attention is fully occupied, though not overtaxed, by leading an interstellar war. Although Catherine resists Owain's pleas to consummate their love, Sir Roger's trust of his wife is strained and Owain's loyalties become doubtful.

Anderson's final scenes blend remarkably the two cultures he has skillfully developed to a climax. The feudal system with all its chivalric trappings has proven so effective an instrument to overthrow a tyrannical society, that a spacesuit with plume and crest no longer seems ludicrous. The resolution of the lovers' triangle is dramatically satisfying and winds down in good time.

The English win in more ways than one. Although their way back to England is lost, even centuries later they have not lost their desire for home; they hope that humanity will develop space flight on its own and eventually find them. During the interim, they have set about building new Englands throughout the galaxy under the benign and businesslike rule of the descendants of Sir Roger de Tourneville, aided in the job by the Wersgorix, who enjoy their new freedom.

Walter E. Meyers

Sources for Further Study

Reviews:

Analog. LXVII, June, 1961, p. 165.

Booklist. LVI, July 15, 1960, p. 675.

Christian Science Monitor. July 8, 1960, p. 9.

Galaxy. XIX, August, 1961, pp. 154-155.

Kirkus Reviews. XXVIII, August 1, 1960, p. 648.

Library Journal. LXXXVI, March 15, 1961, p. 1332.

Magazine of Fantasy and Science Fiction. XXIII, December, 1962, pp. 82-83.

THE HUMANOIDS
AND
"WITH FOLDED HANDS"

Author: Jack Williamson (1908-   )
First book publication: 1949; "With Folded Hands," 1947 (as serial)
Type of work: Novel and novelette

The humanoids, perfect mechanical servants invented "to serve and obey, and guard men from harm," but they end up smothering humanity with their efficiency

One of the central images of science fiction is the robot, the independently operating machine that provides an ambiguous link between humanity and its inanimate tools. In the evolution of that image three works or collections of works come immediately to mind: Karel Čapek's play *R.U.R.* ("Rossum's Universal Robots"), which introduced the Czech word *robot*, meaning "to work," into the English language; Isaac Asimov's robot stories collected in *I, Robot* and other books; and Jack Williamson's "With Folded Hands" and *The Humanoids*.

The way in which the image affects the reader often depends upon the shape of the robot: is it more like a machine or more like a man? If it is like a machine, does it move independently, or does it remain fixed in place like a computer or an appliance? If it is more like a man, does it merely resemble humanity or is it identical except for biological origin?

Science fiction has worked out a nomenclature for answering most of these questions. A mechanical creature constructed full size out of parts is a robot; a creature with human features, structure, and skin, usually grown rather than built, is an android. Asimov's robots are made of polished metal; their eyes are photocells; their positronic brains are made out of sponge platinum and iridium. Čapek's robots today would be called androids; they are flesh and blood.

The shape of these creatures influences how the characters (and the readers) react to them and determines the questions raised about them. Asimov's mechanicals display increasingly humanlike characteristics, while their non-human shapes prevent the characters from recognizing their human aspects until the end of the story. In a sense Asimov is exploring through the robots the irreducible characteristics of humanity. Androids, because they can be mistaken for human beings, lead the characters into broader definitions of humanity and raise questions about prejudice.

Williamson's creatures are different from either; they are images of the machine, not of humanity, and Williamson calls them "humanoids" to distinguish them from the more traditional mechanicals: "smaller and slimmer than a man, it was nude, neuter as a doll. A shining black, its sleek silicone skin had a changing sheen of bronze and metallic blue. Its graceful oval face wore a fixed look of alert and slightly surprised solicitation. . . ." The characters' response to these creatures is the response to the threat of the machine; the efficiency and beauty of the humanoids enhances their menace. They share only their anthropomorphic shapes with humanity; they are the perfect machines. They can serve humanity totally.

"With Folded Hands," the classic novelette that introduced the humanoids in 1947, lists other kinds of mechanicals: "androids, mechanoids, electronoids, automatoids, and ordinary robots." As a matter of fact, Underhill, the protagonist of the story, sells androids, and the humanoids put him out of business in the little town of Two Rivers and finally threaten his sanity and his free will.

Most citizens eagerly assign their property to the Humanoid Institute and receive the total service of the humanoids. The humanoids do everything: clean house, tend the children, cook, perform personal services, give music lessons, answer any question, build new houses. "You're too damned perfect," Underhill says bitterly. "I suppose there's nothing men can do, but you can do it better." And a humanoid (all are identical) assures him that this is true.

> Naturally we are superior. Because our units are metal and plastic, while your body is mostly water. Because our transmitted energy is drawn from atomic fission, instead of oxidation. Because our senses are sharper than human sight or hearing. Most of all, because our mobile units are joined to one great brain, which knows all that happens on many worlds, and never dies or sleeps or forgets.

Their power need not be feared, however. "Because we cannot injure any human being, unless to prevent greater injury to another. We exist only to discharge the Prime Directive." That directive is inscribed on a nameplate emblazoned on each humanoid breast: "To Serve and Obey, and GUARD MEN FROM HARM."

A humanoid comes to serve Underhill's wife and his children. Life is so much better at home for awhile that Underhill cannot bring himself to send it away, although he refuses to sign over his business even when he is forced into bankruptcy.

From his wife's new roomer, battered old Mr. Sledge, he finally gets the story of the creation of the humanoids. Sledge created them, as well as the science of rhodomagnetics, on Wing IV, a planet 109 light years away, approximately sixty years ago. Rhodomagnetics is a new universal force "keyed to the second triad of the periodic table, rhodium and ruthenium and palladium, in very much the same way that ferromagnetism is keyed to the first triad, iron and nickel and cobalt."

Wing IV had been racked and nearly destroyed by two successive wars, the second fought with rhodomagnetics. Half out of his mind, Sledge created the humanoids, and the Humanoid Center which powers and controls them, in order to stop war and crime, poverty and inequality, human blundering and resulting human pain. As his humanoids rebuilt the world and went forth to carry their services to other worlds, Sledge thought he had succeeded. But he discovered when a man came to assassinate him that the humanoids had smothered humanity with their perfection and their concern for people's safety. They took away almost everything, particularly anything that might contain any possibility of injury, even — by means of brain surgery, drugs, and hypnosis — the individual's right to be unhappy.

With Underhill's help, Sledge tries to stop the humanoids by creating a fusion process in Wing IV's oceans with a rhodomagnetic device. When the project fails, Sledge — about to die — surrenders his immunity and the humanoids operate on his brain to remove his memories and his unhappiness. Underhill is helpless. He is unable even to appear unhappy. He must sit, like the rest of humanity, with folded hands.

John W. Campbell, Jr., editor of *Astounding Science Fiction*, convinced Williamson that he should write a sequel to his novelette; "With Folded Hands. . ." was published in Campbell's magazine with an ellipsis. The sequel, a novel, was serialized in 1948 under the title of . . . *and Searching Mind*. Simon & Schuster published it as *The Humanoids* in 1949.

What Campbell saw was that although humanity was unable to use their hands under the Prime Directive — because humanoids are more skillful than people, and because most physical activities, including science, can be dangerous to the individual and to others — people could still use their minds, particularly their psychic abilities.

The Humanoids recapitulates with slight variations the dramatic situation of "With Folded Hands." A scientist, Clay Forester, has just discovered rhodomagnetics and heads a secret military project to stop, with rhodomagnetic missiles, a threatened attack from neighboring worlds. An unlikely group of rebels against the humanoids, who have not yet made their appearance on this planet, tries to get Forester's help: Jane Carter, a ragged little girl; Mark White, a giant of a man with fiery red hair and beard who had been an assistant to Warren Mansfield (Sledge's real name), the creator of the humanoids; Graystone, a telepath and former stage magician; Lucky Ford, a gambler and telekinetic; and Ash Overstreet, a clairvoyant. They need Forester's scientific skills and rhodomagnetic knowledge.

Forester is a troubled man. He is tormented by his responsibilities and driven by his desire to find a unified field equation that would be the basic statement about all reality, a *prima materia*. His marriage to Ruth, a much younger woman, is in difficulties, and he has health problems. He refuses to believe in the psychic abilities of White's group or in the humanoids until they arrive, just in time to stop a rhodomagnetic interplanetary war.

Soon Forester discovers the dangers of the humanoids. He is frightened and appalled when he finds that his unhappy wife, Ruth, has been given a drug called euphoride that makes her happy but vague and childlike. He is infuriated by the lack of concern and immunity from humanoid interference of his carefree former assistant, mathematician Frank Ironsmith, who was once his rival for Ruth's love. The humanoids are only machines, Ironsmith says, and cannot be malevolent; he urges Forester to accept them and he will have no problems. Ironsmith is concerned, however, about White and his group; they must be stopped before they do irreparable harm.

Forester finally joins White's group. He and Jane eventually teleport themselves to Wing IV to change the Prime Directive so that it will include the phrase: "But We the Humanoids Cannot Serve or Defend Any Man Except at His Own Command, or Restrain Any Man Against His Will, for Men Must Be Free."

Ironsmith prevents Forester and Jane from changing the Prime Directive. Jane's mind is taken over by the humanoids, and Forester is placed in a cell inside a new grid the humanoids have been building; it generates paraphysical energy. While waiting for experiments to begin on him, Forester realizes that the unifying equation he has been seeking, the *prima materia*, states the relation between electromagnetic, rhodomagnetic, and psychophysical energies. With this knowledge he is able to escape with Jane, teleporting them both to a distant planet, then saving them from airlessness and cold by subconsciously constructing a shelter out of rock.

He seeks out Ironsmith, who is living with a restored Ruth and a healthy, happy Warren Mansfield and other free and happy people on an idyllic planet without humanoid interference. They have accepted the humanoids and their minds have been freed to do the things that humanity was never able to do because it was concerned with physical problems and physical science. Forester's final attempt to destroy with his newfound knowledge the human traitors and then the humanoids is thwarted effortlessly by Ironsmith and Mansfield and the others.

Fifty years later Forester wakes up restored in body and mind. Joined by White, also restored, they prepare to leave for another island universe where they will join an adult Jane in building a new rhodomagnetic grid to bring humanoids to settlers in that universe.

The conclusion is ambiguous. After Forester is placed in his cell, everything happens so easily that it seems like a dream — or a paraphysical illusion generated by the humanoids to make him happy. Even if these scenes are to be accepted literally, the final scenes of Forester's awakening seem unreal, partly because he is no longer the same man — he now accepts the humanoids, or has been made to accept them.

Nagging questions remain. The resolution seems too pat: for example, Ironsmith was right — if humanity would only accept the humanoids as the blessing they really are, it would be liberated to explore the life of the mind. But how many persons are capable of such exploration? It seems an elitist philosophy out of keeping with the peace and beauty, even benevolence, of the planet paradise and its handful of liberated people. Are Ironsmith and the others deluding themselves? Have they "sold out" to the humanoids? Or are they under humanoid illusions?

Forester's conversion clearly is forced. His trip to the island universe, whether real or not, clearly is the humanoids' method of making people happy, an improvement over euphoride. Forester may still be in his cell under the parapsychological dome.

Campbell wanted a sequel in which the oppression of the humanoids was discovered to be liberation and that, apparently, was what Williamson gave him. But Williamson has said that his sense of the story led him to believe that the humanoids would master parapsychology, too, and that the message of the novel was that the perfect machine was perfectly destructive.

But it is not plot alone that explains the power of *"With Folded Hands"* and *The Humanoids* to move generations of readers, it is the image of the humanoids themselves — these naked and beautiful perfect servants of humanity whose solicitude is deadly.

James Gunn

Sources for Further Study

Reviews:

Analog. XLV, May, 1950, p. 104.

Authentic Science Fiction. XLII, February, 1954, pp. 147-148.

Fantasy Book. I, 1950, p. 31.

Flying Saucers From Other Worlds. III, September, 1951, p. 132-133.

Future Science Fiction. II, November, 1951, p. 86.

Kirkus Reviews. XVII, June 1, 1949, p. 282.

New York Herald Tribune Weekly Book Review. October 9, 1949, p. 18.

New York Times. September 18, 1949, p. 16.

Super Science Stories. V, July, 1949, pp. 94-95.

Worlds Beyond. I, February, 1951, pp. 91-93.

I AM LEGEND

Author: Richard Matheson (1926-   )
First book publication: 1954
Type of work: Novel
Time: January, 1976–January, 1979
Locale: Los Angeles

A man who believes he is the sole survivor of a worldwide plague must confront an emerging new society of living vampires

> *Principal characters:*
> ROBERT NEVILLE, the "sole" survivor
> BEN CORTMAN, his former neighbor and a victim of the plague
> RUTH, a member of the new society

In *I Am Legend* Richard Matheson successfully combines the standard last-man-on-earth plot with the equally standard what-makes-a-man theme. From the fine balance created by this blending, he produces an exciting, satisfying novel. While the plot contains sufficient twists and turns to hold the reader, the theme demands that the reader become more deeply involved with the point-of-view character, Robert Neville.

In January, 1976, Neville appears to be the only person alive who has not been affected by a plague that turns its victims into vampires. Through some quirk (Neville hypothesizes that he earlier received a mild form of the disease from a bat and is, therefore, immune), he has been spared. All other people have been transformed by the plague. They are either dead, usually burned by the people not yet afflicted; or vampires, people who died and have returned complete with the characteristics of Count Dracula; or living vampires, people who have these same characteristics but did not go through the stage of dying first. Thus, Neville lives in a nightmare world in which he must cope with the frustrations of being a sole survivor and, at the same time, save himself from the two types of vampires who now inhabit the world.

While Neville has succeeded in creating an oasis of civilization in his fortress house (all the trappings of a cultured life free from want), he is obsessed with his unique position in the world. Memories of the death of his daughter, of his wife's return from the grave, and of his neighbor's living vampirism continually haunt him. Not only must he cope with Cortman's constant attempts to attack him, but, more important, he must cope with trying to live in a present world which has destroyed the past. Neville, must, in other words, live only in the present moment, because neither the past nor the future holds any place for him. He has outlived the past and the future belongs to the vampires.

Sexual frustration is effectively used by Matheson to illustrate Neville's new position:

> And the women. . . .

Did he have to start thinking about *them* again? He tossed over an his stomach with a curse and pressed his face into the hot pillow. He lay there, breathing heavily, body writhing slightly on the sheet. Let the morning come. His mind spoke the words it spoke every night. Dear God, let the morning come.

He dreamed about Virginia [his vampire wife] and he cried out in his sleep and his fingers gripped the sheets like frenzied talons.

The despair which results from Neville's living in his own no-man's-land of time periodically drives him to drunken stupors, and, as these increase in frequency, he becomes incapable of any action. But then, what does he have to act for? Throughout the early part of the novel Neville searches for reasons, but is continually unable to find any.

It is at this stage that hatred gives Neville a reason to act. He finally strikes out at his tormentors, Cortman in particular, and drives himself relentlessly in a search for a weak spot in the vampires' physical nature. He goes on daily hunting expeditions to kill them, first driving stakes through the hearts of the sleeping vampires and later perfecting more efficient techniques. It is not simply that the vampires pose an immediate threat to his own existence, but rather that Neville finds in such actions on escape from thinking about his wife and daughter. By killing vampires, he believes that he is somehow striking a blow for humanity as he represents it.

Neville's crusade against the vampires leads him into an investigation of the plague: how it has been transmitted, and what causes it. While some answers are found to these questions, and they seem reasonable enough for the purposes of the novel, it is Neville's quest for the answers that is important, not the results. Each time he seems to find a new clue to the vampirism, he applies it to his more important search: how to kill larger and larger numbers of vampires. Thus, Neville may now have gone beyond his initial stage of morbid despair, but he has replaced it with an equally destructive drive.

While it may seem, at first, to be strange to call the killing of vampires destructive, this is in fact, what his actions are. Matheson has chosen well the transformation because few readers will question Neville's repulsion of them. His sometimes brutal handling of them will not, in the beginning, seem brutal. Yet these creatures are now the heirs of humanity; they are, in fact, human. Neville, however, is obsessed with his own situation and with his own past, and rarely stops to consider who the vampires are. He is only concerned with what they are.

There are hints that he should be interested in the question *who*. Early in the novel Neville dwells briefly on the fact that there are two classes of vampires. Further, having identified the bacteria responsible for the vampirism, he only considers the clinical nature of the disease and how his knowledge may serve his own bloodlust. He does not consider the possibility that the living vampires are a new man transformed by the disease and that this new breed may have human aspirations as well. That these living vampires resemble too well the true vampires is all that Neville cares about. They are not humans as he once knew them and, thus, while he may at times pity them, he will kill them too.

Finally, however, as Neville's bloodlust for vampires starts to wane and the impact of his loneliness increases, he enters the final stage of development: Neville must learn of the human side of what he views as monsters. On one of his forages to kill vampires, Neville finds a woman. Given the fact that she is out in daylight, there is the distinct possibility that she is not a vampire, and Neville, starved for human contact, captures her. She must, however, be human according to his own definition, and, therefore, he insists on testing her for the bacteria he has identified. Even after both he and the woman, Ruth, have spent a night together and seem to have established a promising relationship, Neville insists on the test. To be human, in Neville's terms, is to be like those before the plague. While he wants Ruth to be human, he needs proof that she meets this one important criterion. Thus, no matter how she acts toward him or how well he feels in her company, Neville cannot accept her until he knows for sure that she is not contaminated by the disease.

But things can never be as they once were, and when he finally does convince her to undergo the test, Ruth is shown to be a living vampire. She is, in fact, a member of a group that has learned how to control the disease. They are not Count Draculas but humans who now wish to rebuild their world. For three years Neville has been killing them off. Ruth had, therefore, been sent by this new society to learn about Neville and his strengths. They have now developed sufficient organization that they are ready to come out in the open. Neville is their enemy, even if it is through ignorance on his part, and from their point of view he must be stopped.

While Ruth is totally dedicated to the new society, she does feel pity and, perhaps, the beginnings of love for Neville. In a totally human fashion, she tries to warn him of his danger and, thus, comes close to betraying her mission. Neville, however, is too tired of his lonely life to protect himself from the new society. Moreover, he sees in them at least some promise for a return to the way things were before the plague. Once his hope of finding a fellow human in Ruth are dashed, Neville must accept the inevitable. At least Ruth has shown him that living vampires are capable of very human emotions. He admits that there is no cure for the disease and that the biological nature of man is forever changed, but he now wishes to throw himself upon the mercy of the new breed. Thus, Neville, in the hope of a different life, waits passively for the living vampires to come for him. By seeing the human side of Ruth and even starting a relationship with her, he has accepted these beings as more than bloodsucking vampires.

Neville's dream, however, can never be realized. When members of the new society arrive, they begin by destroying the vampires who had tormented Neville, not out of pity for him but because these vampires do not fit into their society. In a particularly brutal scene, the living vampires hunt down and destroy Cortman, who represents a type of new man that will not fit into the new society. His kind, as well as the true vampires, must be destroyed in order to rebuild. Yet the killing is even more brutal than any Neville committed. He saw all vampires as abominations, the end result of a tragedy that had destroyed his world. When vampire kills vampire, however, it is the strong of the species preying upon the weak.

Immediately after the death of Cortman, Neville is himself attacked. He had hoped to give himself up peacefully, but because of what he saw and because of the ruthless way in which his attackers entered his house, Neville is fatally wounded when he tries to resist capture. As he lies on his deathbed, all his former beliefs return. The living vampires are to him once again monstrous killers; in fact, they are worse than the true vampires they have slaughtered. When Ruth appears, he accuses her new society of being nothing more than an organization of gangsters who enjoy killing. When Ruth points out that he too had made killing an integral part of his life, Neville tries to defend himself by saying he only did it for his own survival.

Ruth's reply to Neville's self-justification contains the core of Matheson's theme for the novel. If Neville killed to protect himself, the new society killed for an even larger kind of protection:

> "That's exactly why we're killing," she said calmly. "To survive. We can't allow the dead to exist beside the living. Their brains were impaired, they exist for only one purpose. They *have* to be destroyed. As one who killed the dead *and* the living, you know that."

Neville is the last of his race, and it is his fate to see the beginning of a new order. Such beginnings are usually brutal and never pleasant. The new cannot simply live side by side with the old; it must replace the old. This is the lesson that Neville learns, and with that knowledge comes an understanding of the living vampires. They are the new Adams and Eves.

Once Neville is able to see that the living vampires are indeed the heirs to humanity, his fate is sealed. There is no place in the new world for him, and when Ruth offers him poison so that he might avoid execution at the hands of the new society, he willingly takes it. He is the last man of his kind and his day has ended. Neville has finally accepted the fact that his world is over. He is an anachronism. He is also the stuff of future legend. Like Christ, he has come to represent what man would aspire to be but can never quite achieve. He represents to the living vampires a past existence now closed to them, "an invisible specter who had left for evidence of his existence the bloodless bodies of their loved ones." Neville, in imitation of Christ, dies so that a new man can get on with living. With him dies the living memory of what the world once was, and therefore, the new society can look to the future without being haunted by the past.

The point of self-sacrifice in *I Am Legend* is a significant one. Whatever the future may hold, it is doubtful that the human race will remain the same. Matheson has sped up the process of change through the device of a disease and allowed the last of the old breed to confront the new. What Neville learns is that change cannot be stopped or killed, a lesson worthy of the finest traditions in science fiction.

Stephen H. Goldman

Sources for Further Study

Reviews:

Galaxy. IX, January, 1955, p. 121.

Luna Monthly. XXX, November, 1971, p. 26.

New Worlds. XCIX, October, 1960. p. 126.

Son of WSFA Journal. XVIII, April, 1971, pp. 7-8.

I AM THINKING OF MY DARLING

Author: Vincent McHugh (1904-   )
First book publication: 1943
Type of work: Novel
Time: The mid-twentieth century
Locale: New York City

A tropical ailment robs a city's population of its competitive, aggressive drive

Principal characters:
>JAMES ROWAN, acting commissioner of New York's Department of City Planning
>NIOBE ROWAN, a runaway actress, his wife
>NICK PARAVECCHIO, a cab driver, Rowan's friend
>DR. PETER JENKINS, an epidemiologist
>DR. DICK WIRTH, Commissioner of Health for New York City
>EUNICE FLATTERY, Rowan's secretary

No less a major science fiction author than Robert A. Heinlein has designated Vincent McHugh as a leading candidate for writing the perfect science fiction-fantasy novel, *Caleb Catlum's America* (1936). McHugh, one-time staff writer for the *New Yorker* magazine, is usually regarded by most critics as one of America's mainstream novelists, but Heinlein thinks otherwise. Writing in *The Science Fiction Novel* (1959), Heinlein pointed out that McHugh's novel combined all the elements for artful science fiction-fantasy, "featuring future prediction, some comedy, some tragedy, and straight hortatory propaganda."

It is true, *Caleb Catlum's America* has many of the desired elements; however, it also borders on being an urbane, sophisticated rewrite of the Paul Bunyan and Pecos Bill folk tales. It is McHugh's fourth published novel, *I Am Thinking of My Darling*, that fits more smoothly into the science fiction-fantasy framework, especially as social criticism.

A surprising number of science fiction novels and short stories take an unkind look at the American business culture, and the protestant ethic in particular. Frederik Pohl and C. M. Kornbluth's *The Space Merchants* comes to mind as do parts of Heinlein's *Stranger in a Strange Land*, John Brunner's *The Sheep Look Up* and *Stand on Zanzibar*, plus a number of Ray Bradbury's Martian stories.

McHugh's 1943 novel belongs in this classification. The book takes a few roundhouse swings at the Ben Franklin, Horatio Alger, "work-and-win" tradition, but it is done in such a clever, low-key manner, that the reader is often distracted from the essential sermon: the mercantile culture is a huge bore.

Briefly, the plot of the book is about the concerns of James Rowan, who returns from a trip to find that the metropolis is in the grip of an epidemic, a mysterious disease that has turned the population into sleepy, relaxed people who stay in bed. People quit their jobs to roam the city "doing their own thing." Rowan's wife, Niobe, an actress, has caught the ailment and avoids her marital duties by disguising herself. Rowan and the health authorities finally find an antidote for the virus, he recaptures his wife, the city returns to normal, and the novel ends.

There will be no attempt here to make an exhaustive study into why McHugh chose to treat the business society so, but it might be worthwhile to trace this trend in science fiction literature, back to one or more possible sources. Quite a few writers in the genre, obviously, have considerable knowledge of the writings of G. W. F. Hegel, Karl Marx, Oswald Spengler, and others. However, this article will be content to narrow down this examination to five names in literature, Henry David Thoreau and Herman Melville, with a subsequent discussion of H. G. Wells, Michael Crichton, and Frederik Pohl. The thoughts of these men seem to be directly involved in the novel *I Am Thinking of My Darling*.

Thoreau's *Civil Disobedience* is applicable to McHugh's work because most of the novel is concerned with passive resistance to authority. Then, too, some of the comments Thoreau makes in *Walden* are *apropos*: for example, his sarcasm about the mercantile spirit in the section on "The Ponds" wherein he points out that the owner of Flint's Pond admires the shine of the silver dollar above the glint of sun on its beautiful (but soon-to-be-exploited) waters. But actually, we do not have to find notations in Thoreau's writings to observe his contempt for the business culture and "getting ahead," a so-called virtue so well epitomized by America's polymath, Benjamin Franklin. Thoreau's life, itself, was in a way a tract against the values of our protestant ethic.

One can also reflect upon Melville's "Bartleby the Scrivener." To be certain, there are many interpretations of this short story, and Bartleby's long and depressing chore in the Dead Letter branch of the post office rather muddies the waters in pin-pointing some of the major themes in the work. But indeed, Bartleby's famous dictum, "I prefer not to," might be an aid in understanding McHugh's novel. Granted, there are many complex reasons why Bartleby is inspired to repeat over and over, "I prefer not to." That is to say, Bartleby's rejection of the business life in Wall Street is many-faceted, with cultural and cosmic overtones playing a part. But Melville himself might be saying as an aside, that the grubby business culture is not worth bothering about, Dead Letter office experience or not. The lawyer-narrator in Melville's story tries to force upon Bartleby the merits of responsible action, but to no avail. Here then is much of the concern of *I Am Thinking of My Darling*: I-Prefer-Not-To *versus* Responsibility. Responsibility wins out, but it is a very close race.

McHugh was fascinated with the inner workings of a big city; he had been a reporter for the *New Yorker*, and had written a knowledgeable chapter on New York ("Metropolis and Her Children") for Clifton Fadiman's anthology, *Reading I've Liked* (1942). McHugh was very much aware of what might happen if such a complex organism as Manhattan broke down. Mayors and ex-mayors of our large cities today know what concerned Commissioner Rowan: no garbage collection, no police or fire protection, no elevators — a city gone somnambulistic, if not vicious or violent.

McHugh was speculating in 1943 to more or less highlight what it would mean if a giant megalopolis came to a halt due to a sudden wave of absenteeism and indifference by public employees. What would the get-ahead, eager, aggressive types do to inspire responsibility in those who suddenly abandoned their tasks in vital city departments. For this is what the novel dwells on: what would happen if Thoreau's "Walden Pondism" or Melville's "I Prefer Not To," in the guise of a tropical ailment suddenly swept through the city like an epidemic of smallpox?

There are, to be sure, other distractions in the novel that provide some comic relief to this central thesis. Rowan runs after his lady-love, Niobe, who is one of the early victims of the virus. She flits around New York in various disguises, doing exactly as she pleases. Here McHugh's prophecy about our 1960's hippy movement is quite remarkable. Almost the entire population suddenly becomes intent on doing its own thing, and people begin to dress in clothes modeled after their inner desires: they loaf around the town in cowboy, farmer, or Indian costumes, and rather than work, they beg for bread, or merely shoplift in front of indifferent storekeepers.

This debilitating tropical disease overcomes in one sweep the inhibitions and the drive it took a life-time of parental and societal pressures to pound into our psyches. This virus ailment, too, *hlehhana*, does have a bit in common with Aldous Huxley's *soma* drug. In *Brave New World*, *soma* calmed people down when they got upset about things. McHugh's tropical disease calms people except sexually; the sex drive is intensified, and both men and women in the novel are most willing to succumb to its influence.

But of course, the few determined persons who are still ambulatory and who still have that urge to run things on an orderly and efficient basis cannot tolerate these lax affairs. They are afraid that the city will collapse entirely, fires will rage unchecked, and rodents will multiply.

Thus, the novel ends well. Everything is straightened out, the hero finds Niobe, and the town's health authorities find an antidote that cures the virus. New York returns to its killing pace as before and all seems well. Still the reader is likely to have a flat taste in his mouth. McHugh has made his point. When you contrast a "do-it-mañana" culture with a frantic, work-and-win society, which one will, or *should* survive?

Finally, there are at least three parallels between this novel and other novels in the science fiction-fantasy genre. In Michael Crichton's *The Andromeda Strain* (published some twenty-five years after *I Am Thinking of My Darling*), we can see similarities in the elaborate, high-gear workings of medical authorities to combat a strange ailment. Both McHugh and Crichton were obviously knowledgeable and impressed with the skills of large medical centers to quell epidemics. Crichton's mysterious virus comes from outside our solar system, and is fatal to physical health; the *hlehhana* virus comes from the nearby tropics and is fatal only to the business or competitive drive.

However, it is in H. G. Wells's fantasy novel *In the Days of the Comet* that we can relate to McHugh's work more directly. In the Wells novel, a mysterious green fog accompanies a comet that comes perilously close to Earth. It accomplishes much the same transformation in people that McHugh's tropical ailment does; that is, the fog makes people calmer, more humane, and especially more interested in a socialistic economic system.

Interestingly enough, Wells has his central character, Willie Leadford, spend a good part of the book searching, not for a Niobe, but a Nettie. However, Leadford, unrequited in love, has murder on his mind, rather than sex or husbandly concern. Then, also, the virus *hlehhana* does not so much remake men into saints, as does the green fog. But the essential results of both the green fog and the virus are the same: man's competitive drives and ceaseless aggressions are overcome.

Wells allows Leadford to live permanently in this Utopian-socialist world; McHugh, however, more of a realist, brings his characters back to the hardboiled, work-a-day, capitalistic society. Alas, salubrious green fogs or tropical viruses, McHugh implies, cannot last forever.

L. W. Michaelson

Sources for Further Study

Reviews:

Book Week. August 1, 1943, p. 3.

Galaxy. I, December, 1950, p. 65.

Nation. CLVII, August 7, 1943, p. 162.

Science Fiction Adventures. II, June, 1954, p. 123.

Springfield Republican. August 8, 1943, p. 7.

Time. XLII, August 16, 1943, p. 103.

Weekly Book Review. August 1, 1943, p. 2.

I, ROBOT

Author: Isaac Asimov (1920-   )
First book publication: 1950
Type of work: Thematically related short stories
Time: 1996-2064
Locale: The United States and outer space

Robots, responding to the often ambiguous Three Laws of Robotics, gradually become equal in ability and perhaps superior to human beings

> *Principal characters:*
> DR. SUSAN CALVIN, Robopsychologist for U. S. Robots
> DR. ALFRED LANNING, Director of research for U. S. Robots
> PETER BOGERT, his assistant, later acting director
> GREGORY POWELL and
> MIKE DONOVAN, outer space robot troubleshooters

While gathering background material for an article, the narrator of the story framing Isaac Asimov's *I, Robot* visits Dr. Susan Calvin, age seventy-five in the year 2057, and listens to her recital of robot development history from before the time she became Robopsychologist for United States Robots in the year 2008. Each of the nine stories advances the history of robots and the problems of human management of and reaction to them. Both sides — man and machine — generate much sympathy, but Dr. Calvin exhibits the scientist's classical lack of fear of scientific advancements and believes firmly that robots are superior to humans.

Asimov prefaces the book with "The Three Laws of Robotics," which have become the foundation of his science fiction dealing with robots:

> 1. A robot may not injure a human being, or, through inaction, allow a human being to come to harm.
> 2. A robot must obey the orders given it by human beings except where such orders would conflict with the First Law.
> 3. A robot must protect its own existence as long as such protection does not conflict with the First or Second Law.

These laws form a system of ethics governing the behavior of robots; drawing analogies between robots and pets or slaves, the book explores the man-robot relationship in practical and eventually in quasimetaphysical terms.

The robot of the first story, "Robbie," can think but cannot speak. A nursemaid to a little girl of eight named Gloria, whose dependence on the machine becomes a neighborhood scandal, it suffers the antagonism of Gloria's mother who objects that it has no soul. Gloria, inconsolable after Robbie is sent away, earns a trip to New York to forget her loss but, at the Science and Industry exposition, escapes from her parents to talk with the first Talking Robot. He burns out his coils attempting to answer her questions about Robbie's whereabouts. Susan Calvin, then a student, watches what happens and writes her first physics paper on human and robot interaction as a result of her observation.

Later Gloria's father proposes a visit to a robot factory to show her that robots are machines, not people. Gloria sees Robbie and dashes forward into the path of an oncoming tractor. Robbie saves her life, but the opposition of Gloria's mother indicates community feeling, and seven years later the government bans private ownership of robots. Men, afraid of creating machines superior to themselves, build their robots with the Three Laws built into their brains so that robots will always serve man and never triumph over their masters. Robbie's character, that of pet and servant, becomes the robot stereotype.

In the story "Runaround," robots have been banned to outer space except for their use in research. They have been programed to mine selenium on Mercury, in an atmosphere harmful to humans. Circumstance creates an environment which sets Rule Three in conflict with Rule Two. Gregory Powell and Mike Donovan find the robot SPD — "Speedy" — reciting Gilbert and Sullivan and running around the selenium pool, "the locus of all points of potential equilibrium." Donovan solves this problem by invoking the superior Rule One. He rushes forward to expose himself to the murderous rays of the sun, assuming correctly in terms of robopsychology that Speedy must save his life; thereafter Speedy successfully runs his master's errands.

Six months later on a solar space station, Donovan and Powell find themselves engaged in a comedy satirizing religion and scientific method. Robot QT-1 or "Cutie" inquires of his origins but will not accept the answer that he comes from Earth, an inconsequential point of light far away from the Energy Converter which he serves and from which he focuses energy beams on Earth. He defies all man's logic with his own: Donovan could not have assembled ("created") him because "no being can create another being superior to itself"; he decides that the space station and its contents are the work of the Master, the Energy Converter. In the face of an approaching electron storm, the other robots refuse to obey the men, saying, in defiance of Rule Two, there is only one Master and QT-1 is his prophet. But, proving his superiority to men, Cutie during the storm keeps the energy beam undeviating in its focus on Earth and simultaneously obeys the First Law, keeping humans from harm. Having performed his function adequately (though for the wrong reasons), the robot sadly sees Powell and Donovan depart at the end of "their term of existence," firm in his conviction that his own scientific reasoning is correct. Man has abandoned a planet to the management of robots whose thinking differs from his, an important point in terms of the outcome of the last story.

In "Catch That Rabbit," DV-5 or "Dave," the thinking robot of a seven-unit team of robots, can offer no explanation why the ore cars return empty from an asteroid mine unless a human being is present; this contradicts the fact that the mines are unsafe for humans. Powell finally solves the problem by destroying one robot — a kind of sixth finger in Dave's personal initiative circuit which was causing an overloaded circuit at times of crises. The emphasis has shifted from the ambiguity in interpreting the three laws to a simple mechanical problem.

The next story is "Liar!" and it scrutinizes more closely the conflicts which might arise from a robot's desire to serve. RB-34 or "Herbie" can read minds and, in obedience to the First Law, tells his masters what he knows they want to hear. But all of the people with whom he comes in contact — Dr. Calvin, Dr. Lanning, and Peter Bogert — are profoundly hurt when they eventually learn that the robot's statements, though confirming their fondest dreams, are actually false. Dr. Calvin finally confronts Herbie with an insoluble dilemma; if he tells the truth, he hurts, but if he does not tell the truth, he hurts. It drives him insane. She recommends that he be scrapped, and her final accusation — "Liar!" — expresses the frustration of finding her hopes confounded.

The desire to serve also causes the problem related in "Little Lost Robot," set in 2029 at a Hyperatomic Base. Again the story shows the inferiority of fallible humans. A man angrily tells a persistent robot to get lost and incurs its literal obedience; it merges itself with sixty-two other look-alike robots. Dr. Calvin decides to isolate the "lost" one by testing its difference from the others, its ability to detect gamma radiation, and tricks it into revealing itself.

Where robot pride manifests itself in this story, robot humor solves a problem in the next story, "Escape," in which a rival robot company requires U. S. Robots' services for a project which has burned out their own comparable unit. The Brain of U. S. Robots — more a computer than a robot but with the personality of a child — has no problem handling the test and builds an interstellar spaceship. Like Coleridge's poetic Ancient Mariner, Gregory Powell and Mike Donovan find themselves trapped in a unique structure, flown by remote control — a ghost ship upon a painted ocean but moving, eventually, beyond the stars. However, the interstellar ship must vanish when light changes to dark, and the two men survive the interstellar jump through a space warp only because the Brain permits them to die temporarily twice — going and coming. The title functions on three levels: U. S. Robots' escape from its contract with Consolidated, Powell's and Donovan's escape through hyperspace and through death, and the Brain's escape from the problem assigned it by playing a joke on the ship's two passengers. The robot's humor serves as its chief means of escape from a human-imposed dilemma, but its joke marks a thematic shift: the robot is capable of treating man as its pet.

In "Evidence," Stephen Byerly, a district attorney running for mayor, is suspected by a rival politician of being a robot. One week before the mayoral election, Byerly, making a speech to an angry crowd, responds to a man's disbelief in his humanity by actually hitting the man. Although this act apparently proves his humanity, Dr. Calvin reasons that he still might be a robot if the man he hit was also a robot. Byerly, after serving as mayor, becomes Regional and then World Coordinator, and, instead of dying, terminates his existence with his secret intact by having himself atomized. In this story, Dr. Calvin discusses the parallel between man's and robot's conditioned existence by pointing out that "the three Rules of Robotics are the essential guiding principles of a good many of the world's ethical systems," all of which makes Byerly, even though a good robot, also a very good man. This stage of robot advancement prepares for the last story.

In 2052, in "The Evitable Conflict," Byerly is World Coordinator, and his study contains a fireplace with a blazing fire, that mythical element tradition-ally stolen by Prometheus from the gods themselves and symbol of man's search for and conveyance of enlightenment. When Byerly is faced with a problem of the malfunctioning of machines regulating world production, he calls on Susan Calvin for help.

Through the cycles of history, Byerly points out, humanity has not solved its problems; instead, circumstances have changed to dissolve old problems and create new. Now, calculating circuits throughout the world regulate the economy in keeping with the First Law to serve the best interests of man. The current irregularities, however, can be corrected only by a machine. Dr. Calvin protests that the machines have become too specialized to permit the interplay of the three rules, but Byerly suggests that machines have been given the wrong data by human error; he points out that the Machine cannot enforce the obedience of man and suggests that the Society for Humanity (which, like Gloria's mother, opposes machines) is responsible. Dr. Calvin, however, reminds him that the Machine, serving humanity in compliance with the First Law, has its own means of correcting humanity; she believes the Machine is causing the problems so that it can "shake loose" the undesirables and, with-out harming them, transfer them to other jobs.

Conditions are now such that individual initiative may be suppressed or controlled by the Machine in the greater interests of serving the entirety of humanity. This machine has taken on many of the roles attributed to God by ancient theologians — moving in mysterious ways, admitting no explanations, but invisibly guiding the affairs of humanity for its best interests. The universe of both man and robot is a conditioned universe; for the Machine, willing service is not slavery, and man is being molded in the image of the ethical machine. Dr. Calvin, the book's chief problem-solver and an example of human intellect combined with compassion for robots, explains that "for all time, all conflicts are finally evitable. Only the Machines, from now on, are inevitable." With this statement of her faith, Byerly's fire dies out. Man has, in creating robots, found the answer to his several searches; symbolically, he has returned the fire to the gods.

Grace Eckley

Sources for Further Study

Criticism:

Fiedler, Jean and Jim Mele. "Asimov's Robots," in *Critical Encounters: Writers and Themes in Science Fiction*. Edited by Dick Riley. New York: Frederick Ungar, 1978, pp. 3-8. The *I, Robot* collection of Asimov is considered a classic and is used to measure the standards of all other robot tales.

Watt, Donald. "A Galaxy Full of People: Characterization in Asimov's Major Fiction," in *Isaac Asimov*. Edited by Joseph D. Olander and Martin Harry Greenberg. New York: Taplinger, 1977, pp. 141-144. An in-depth discussion of Asimov's short stories about robots is given here. The article provides an excellent foundation for understanding Asimov's themes and characterizations.

Reviews:

Booklist. XLVII, January 15, 1951, p. 188.

Horn Book. XXVII, May, 1951, p. 197.

New York Times. February 4, 1951, p. 16.

San Francisco Chronicle. February 4, 1951, p. 17.

ICE

Author: Anna Kavan (Helen Woods Edwards, 1901-1968)
First book publication: 1967
Type of work: Novel
Time: Unspecified
Locale: Unspecified

An account of a man's obsessive pursuit of a girl through a world in crisis, imperiled by a new ice age

> *Principal characters:*
> THE NARRATOR
> A GIRL, the object of his obsession
> "THE WARDEN," his rival

Ice is a dream-narrative whose landscapes are psychological rather than physical, whose world is an inner rather than an outer one. None of its people or places is named; the characters move anonymously through a series of confrontations in which roles and environments shift uncertainly. Both the world and its people are under pressure, yielding slowly — though not always reluctantly — to the freezing clutch of encroaching glaciation.

The narrator of the story has two obsessions. The first is his pursuit of a fragile girl with white skin and hair "as bright as spun glass" — a pursuit which drags him from one troubled war-zone to another, always haunted by visions. The second is his memory of the Indris: shy, almost-extinct lemurs which live deep in the rain-forests of Madagascar and are rarely seen, though their plaintive "singing" is audible over long distances. The Indris have come to symbolize for him a young, warm world that might have existed had mankind been made of different, gentler stuff.

The girl, by contrast, is the frail hope that drags him through the decaying present in hopeless quest of a better future. Though he compares her at one point to a will-o'-the-wisp, she *can* be caught. Her virtues are no less tantalizing for that, however, because once achieved, the goal seems to have little meaning, and whenever he is close to her his visions attend him. He, too, is pursued by the fluid desert of ice which is reclaiming the world. The novel provides a surreal map of a particular view of the world, terrifying in its coldness and harshness, which may owe something to its author's personal experiences. Anna Kavan had been addicted to heroin since before World War II, and had spent two protracted spells in mental hospitals. She died only a year after publishing *Ice*, with a syringe of heroin beside her.

We first encounter the Narrator driving through a wintry night, intending to pay a brief call on friends who live in a country house. Recently returned to the country on business, he is curiously haunted by the thought of the girl and her husband, with whom he stayed some time before. He sees her briefly in the glare of his headlights, in the process of being swallowed up by a cliff of ice. He admits to having once been infatuated with her, but his attitude now is more detached and more complex, and beyond his own comprehension. The drugs he takes for insomnia and nervous strain following a breakdown of some kind render him susceptible to hallucinations in which the girl always appears as a victim, hurt and terrified. Fascinated by these visions, he now lives almost entirely within them, unable to separate them (if they can be separated) from the fabric of his mundane existence.

He recalls his earlier visit to the house he is seeking, describing the curious relationship between the timid girl and her domineering husband. Though there is little evidence, it is implied that her husband is her captor, and that he treats her cruelly and contemptuously. The husband, who also treats the Narrator with contempt, reappears throughout the plot as "the warden," a figure of authority and importance who usually keeps the girl encaged in a darkened room. The Narrator fears and hates him, but also on occasion identifies with him so closely that he wonders whether there are, in fact, two people rather than one.

The Narrator eventually reaches the house for which he is searching, and is received by the husband. He sees the girl briefly before he leaves, and though he still feels implicated in her affairs he returns to the town to conduct his business. Nothing happens to change things until he hears, some time later, that she has left her husband and gone abroad, at which point he abandons all other concerns in order to follow her. Again he envisions her engulfed by ice, and his search is soon infected by a sense of extreme desperation. The world around him is threatening to make his vision a prophetic one: there are rumors about the explosion of a new atomic device which will precipitate a new ice age. Anxiety is running high in many places, and there are armed conflicts within and among unnamed nations.

The girl is difficult to find, and even more difficult to catch. She seems not to relish the prospect of "rescue" by the Narrator, whom she appears to regard in exactly the same light as she regards the husband or warden who kept her captive.

By the time the Narrator catches up with the girl she is again a prisoner, kept by the warden in the High House in a small town in a remote northern country. The Narrator has to overcome the suspicions of the local inhabitants by pretending interest in the nearby ruins, and he actually begins to write down his observations of them, interspersed with passages of a book recalling his memories of the Indris and their idyllic jungle existence. He secures an invitation to the High House, and although he cannot immediately meet the girl he sees her in his visions, terrified and persecuted. His visions turn at one point into a protracted nightmare in which the town is destroyed by barbarian invaders who burn everything and slaughter the populace with swords and spears. He sees the girl's mangled corpse, and then sees her again as the dream becomes witness to an act of sacrifice in which she is thrown from a cliff-top into the jaws of a sea-monster. His only way out of this phantasmagoria is to write feverishly of the Indris and their "gay, affectionate, innocent ways."

Panic descends upon the small town, threatened by strife and by the ice. The Narrator and the warden flee separately, and the Narrator tries to take advantage of this forced release from his obsession by resolving to go to the island of the Indris instead. After a brief interlude in the sun, however, his old situation again catches up with him. Faced with the prospect of arrest and imprisonment, he escapes to another country, where the warden and the girl have established themselves. The Narrator sees her briefly, but she flees from him and the warden alike. The war and the advance of the glaciers make pursuit difficult, but he follows her to a nation under siege, and locates her in a hostel. She refuses to go with him, and he has to take her forcibly out of the cold region and back to a country where catastrophe is still far away. There, he takes up the threads of a normal life.

Though he now has the girl, the Narrator is still haunted by anxiety and the knowledge of impending doom. He cannot settle into his work, and the determinedly gay sensation-seeking of the social whirl appalls him. The girl, though, seems to love it, and the two drift apart. When he decides to forget her and again go to search for the Indris, she accuses him of betrayal, saying that she knew he would treat her thus, and that this is why she was afraid of him. Nevertheless, he leaves her.

When he feels that he is again close to the Indris, at least in the spiritual sense, he hallucinates a visitation from an inhabitant of the better, suprahuman world which they have come to symbolize for him. For a moment, the better world almost seems to be within reach as a possible way of life, but the vision dissolves momentarily, and the war returns to surround him. The warden is once more nearby, with the girl in thrall, and although another confrontation with the ice seems imminent, the Narrator goes to bargain with her master for the girl's release. Yet again the warden surrenders her carelessly, though again she is fearful and resentful, as she and the Narrator drive off into the snow, with the ice cliffs massing around them.

They drive on and on, the interior of their vehicle becoming a microcosm of light and warmth in a world now totally conquered by the ice, completely enclosed by cold and darkness, a world already ended, vast and vacuous. Here the narrative ends with the only consummation that was ever possible.

Because *Ice* is a first-person narrative entirely enclosed by the narrator's stream of consciousness, hardly any distinction is made between vision and "real" experience. Sometimes he can identify his hallucinations, sometimes he cannot. There is no way he (or the reader) can decide with certainty how much of what happens to him happens within his head — or, indeed, whether *anything* that happens to him is objectively real. It hardly matters, though, whether the new ice age really is overtaking the world at large, or whether it is welling up from within to take possession only of his individual psyche; within the story it is all-encompassing. The *meaning* of the event is clear enough:

what the reader experiences through the narrative is the adventure of a mind under siege, attempting to raise barriers against the encroaching cold of death by promoting one or another defensive obsession. It is a siege whose end is never in doubt, though the story can only point the way to its own ultimate eclipse.

The story can be read as an allegory, interpreted in terms of its author's heroin addiction and mental instability. It also makes accusations against human nature and the coldness of the social world built by modern man. The ways in which it might be "decoded," however, are only a secondary issue. Its primary importance lies in its effectiveness as a surreal reader-experience, in the sharpness of its vision and the startling clarity of its dream-imagery. The ice that surrounds the narrator's bleak mental life, continually invading it and crystallizing his visions, is a relentless psychological force which oppresses the reader as it oppresses the narrator. The descriptive sequences in which the vision is presented are brilliantly conceived.

The world view which *Ice* encapsulates is as dramatically schizophrenic as Kafka's, but its clarity makes it accessible and tangible, if never quite comprehensible. Only in the most superficial sense is the novel science fiction — in the token supportive logic which gives the ice age an extra concreteness. In its method, however, it does compare to work done by some of the more experimental writers in the science fiction field, expecially J. G. Ballard and Brian Aldiss. It was Aldiss who "discovered" *Ice*, claiming it enthusiastically as science fiction; and though the claim is, perhaps, a political move in an odd game of literary colonization being played by certain apologists for the genre, it is not entirely without justice.

Brian Stableford

Sources for Further Study

Reviews:

Galaxy. XXXII, January, 1972, pp. 118-119.

Library Journal. XCV, December 1, 1970, p. 4196.

Luna Monthly. XXXIV, March, 1972, p. 30.

Magazine of Fantasy and Science Fiction. XLI, October, 1971, pp. 25-26.

Publisher's Weekly. CXCVIII, September 7, 1970, p. 53.

IF THE STARS ARE GODS

Authors: Gregory Benford (1941-   ) and Gordon Eklund
First book publication: 1977
Type of work: Thematically related short stories
Time: 1992, 2017, 2052, 2060, 2061
Locale: Mars, Earth (especially Africa), the Moon, Jupiter, Titan (a satellite of Saturn)

Bradley Reynolds encounters various alien life forms as he explores the nature of man and the possibilities of gods

> *Principal characters:*
> BRADLEY REYNOLDS, an astronomer
> JONATHAN, the captain of an alien starship
> MARA, an extremely beautiful and intelligent product of genetic manipulation
> COREY, a brilliant but horribly mutated product of genetic manipulation

In *If the Stars Are Gods*, the authors, through three short stories, present a delightful trip through Dr. Bradley Reynolds' long, productive, provocative life. The three episodes are woven around themes which may be dissected into subthemes. The major thread is the god-alien theme. This fine, thoughtful work deserves more than a cursory reading to discover the intertwining themes revealed through the character of Reynolds.

The first episode of the three-part story line is set in 1992 on Mars. Bradley Reynolds is a young, self-motivated, highly political astronomer assigned to a manned exploration of Mars; life has been discovered there, and Earth must investigate. Reynolds observes that the density and complexity of life forms increase as the exploration party moves toward a calculated point on the surface of Mars. The hypothesis is that this point is the origin of life on Mars — a "Garden of Eden." However, accidents or mishaps kill the other members of the landing party, leaving Reynolds alone, clinging to the surface of Mars. Left alone to determine the true meaning of life on Mars, Reynolds' answer is a bitter one; life on Mars is apparently the result of contamination from an early Earth probe. Reynolds reacts to his understanding of the nature of research and pursuit of knowledge in Earth societies and makes a unilateral, godlike decision to withhold the facts for the good of further exploration. He returns to Earth apparently having failed to answer the questions about life on Mars. The venture can only be considered a failure, yet Reynolds is proclaimed a hero.

The second episode moves in time to 2017 and in space to the Moon. Once again, Reynolds alone is thrust to the edge of human knowledge and experience when he is selected as envoy to an alien spaceship orbiting the Moon. This is the first of several examples of the authors' ability to take the improbable and make it, if not probable, at least lovely and thoughtfully enjoyable. The aliens are beautifully described intelligent "giraffes." They are in the midst of a long journey, the purpose of which is to meet and talk with stars. Reynolds has been chosen as envoy because he knows more about our sun than any other human.

One of the most interesting aspects of this, the second section of the novel, is the author's use of elements derived from Jonathan Swift's *Gulliver's Travels* to enrich the writing. The specific voyage which Benford utilizes is the one to the Houyhnhnms. We recall the great ironic reversal with which Swift is concerned: horses are godlike; men are Yahoos, veritable animals. Benford gives us, instead of horses, the "nice, kind, friendly, pleasant, smiling, silent giraffes," whose leader is named, significantly Jonathan. The aliens are both familiar and unfamiliar. They have no science as such, but they do, like Swift's prototypes, have a science of the mind, and perhaps even a science of the spirit; they consider astronomy and astrophysics as religious or theological arts. The stars *are* gods, and they worship with a religion totally foreign, indeed almost unacceptable, to the minds of men. They have no contempt, at least on the surface, for humanity, and they do respect Reynolds. While the parallels to Swift are not completely explicit, they are sufficiently indicated to provide the reader with another dimension in his understanding.

An interestingly warm, albeit suspicious, relationship develops between Reynolds and Jonathan — the Earthly name assumed by the captain of the alien ship. Through this relationship, Jonathan is revealed to be an acceptable though faulted being. He is a chronic and inept liar; whenever he lies, he blinks his eyes madly.

Reynolds is charged with discovering as much from the aliens about their planet and technology as possible. He does not have to do this; neither is he successful in this task. Reynolds, however, does attempt (perhaps successfully) to talk to our sun. The experience so moves him that he becomes retrospective and feels he has experienced a measure of fulfillment only twice in his life, once here with the aliens and once on Mars. In a well-written scene, Reynolds renounces his world and man with it, and he requests to go with the aliens on their journey. They refuse him and leave him with a confused concept of the nature of stars. Are they beings? Even gods? Once again, although his mission has "failed," Reynolds comes out a hero.

The final episode moves from a short but informative interlude in Africa in 2052, to Jupiter in 2060, and finally to Saturn's satellite Titan in 2061. Bradley (he has renounced his other names along with the world) has withdrawn to the sanctuary of a religious commune. But at the age of ninety-five, he is called back to the world he left after the encounter with Jonathan and the star. This time his task is to decipher a message received from an intelligent life form somewhere in the universe. Once again he is at the edge, directing the four hundred or more people who work and live on the laboratory orbiting Jupiter. The have come to Jupiter because of information gathered from the part of the message which is understandable.

At this point the authors introduce the reader to Mara and Corey. These two inhabitants of the Orb, central characters in the book, are "Nips" — the result of genetic manipulation intended to produce superbeings with superintellects. This potentially hackneyed idea is treated with freshness and insight. There are, of course, the "Christers" who view these experiments and their products as evil and deserving of destruction. On the other hand, there are those who view these beings as perfect, almost godlike. We see the two extremes in Mara and Corey. Here is another opportunity for the authors to develop the personality of an improbable being — Corey is so badly mutated that to sustain its (is it male or female?) life, to move it, even to communicate with it, it must be kept inside a steel box. As with Jonathan, Corey's personality comes complete with a variety of human frailities.

Mara, on the other hand, is physically beautiful with a superintellect, the epitome of what man can create. Of course, she too is flawed, but her personality grows and a warm compelling relationship develops between her and Bradley. Mara is on the Orb (as is Corey) because of her intelligence. She and Corey are the ones, if anyone can, who will crack the code and interpret the message. Although Bradley's authoritative position is weakened by his refusal to destroy the two "Nips" as was ordered after an earthly religious revival, his tenure as commander of the Orb is continued by Earth when Mara deciphers the message and solves the puzzle.

The scene in which the key to the message is found at the cost of Corey's life is probably the best in the book for cleverness, emotion, and description. The decoding of the message introduces some very imaginative concepts. Corey had studied the language of dolphins and whales and found their language significantly different in form and complexity from that of humans. Dolphins move in a three-dimensional environment, while man moves in a two-dimensional environment. Dolphins, therefore, conceive words in three space, humans in two space. Once the assumption that the message-senders also thought in a higher-dimensional space is made, the key to the code becomes the correct topological transformation. The ensuing mathematical discussion, which possesses just the right balance of accuracy and interest, produces a comfortable sense of authenticity. The message, appropriately, is primarily concerned with mathematical truths unknown on Earth, which lead directly to further exploration.

Bradley apparently dies the next year while exploring a new life form on Titan. He has made the unauthorized trip to Titan to see, investigate, and hopefully communicate with yet another life form. But because the trip is unauthorized, he is removed from command and ordered home. Now that his mission is finally successful, he is considered a failure on Earth for the first time.

The god theme is intricately woven throughout the novel. Reynolds worships the reality, the "true meaning," of exploration and being on the edge of contribution. His childhood heroes were "the first men who conquered Mount Everest . . . mountaineers clinging to the edge of that white god." To worship is to be on the "cutting edge of discovery." As he explains to Jonathan, "anything a man does that no man has done before — whether it is good or evil or neither one or both — is considered . . . a great accomplishment." The edge, the void, and exploration are methods of being godly or of worshiping a god. Intelligence, alien or terrestrial, is treated as a divine entity. Bradley speaks of the sun as a "greater, vaster being, more powerful and knowing [than Earth]." Mara holds a similar reverence toward Jupiter. The authors achieve something comparable to a marriage of Zen and C. S. Lewis in presenting all objects as possessing a godly visage. Each planet seems a power and a force — even Mars seems to strike down intruders on her surface as a dog might dispose of fleas on its back.

The god-intelligence-theme is diminished near the end of the book. Bradley declares that, with a clearer vision because of old age, he realized that intelligence is not all people believe it to be. On Earth, a religious revival insists that "Nips," the ultimate in intelligence, are in fact blasphemous. Perhaps stars are the only gods after all.

The god theme is, however, only one of several attractive themes Benford and Eklund introduce. Bradley himself catalyzes them all. He is old for most of the story — an old hero, a champion for the ever-growing number of us growing ever older. He is endearing and fallible. The careful reader will discover that Bradley gives misinformation about his age on at least two different occasions, and on those occasions he says he is older than he in fact is. He observes that he will be the first of a line of ancient leaders and heroes.

If the Stars Are Gods does not overpower one with messages. The writing style is easy and enjoyable to the point of allowing the reader to browse. This is entertainment with enough interesting scientific and science fiction ideas to hold the reader's imagination.

Ray C. Shiflett

Sources for Further Study

Reviews:
Booklist. LXXIII, May 1, 1977, p. 1328.
Kirkus Reviews. XLV, February 1, 1977, p. 123.
Library Journal. CII, March 15, 1977, p. 731.
New York Times Book Review. March 27, 1977, p. 42.
Publisher's Weekly. CCXI, January 24, 1977, p. 330.

THE ILLUSTRATED MAN

Author: Ray Bradbury (1920-   )
First book publication: 1951
Type of work: Short stories
Time: The present and the future
Locale: The United States, Mars, and unspecified planets

Eighteen stories in a narrative frame, dealing with a variety of science fiction and fantasy situations

In *Billion Year Spree, The True History of Science Fiction*, Brian W. Aldiss makes a fundamental distinction between the science fiction of H. G. Wells and that of Edgar Rice Burroughs. Wells's work he finds intensely serious, aimed at provoking readers into thinking about the condition of mankind, whereas Burroughs' work is fast-paced exotic adventure. Wells's protagonists are usually Cockney "little men" who "see it through," while Burroughs' are epic heroes. But the basic difference between the two is that Wells teaches us to think; Burroughs, to wonder. Ray Bradbury combines both traditions. As a boy, he devoured the fiction of Burroughs, and he still writes tributes to Burroughs and calls him the most influential writer of the twentieth century. Like Burroughs, Bradbury knows very little about actual science; the scientific ingredients of his tales are mainly a veneer for the underlying fantasy, so that while Bradbury's paperback publishers call him "the world's greatest living science fiction writer," some hard-core writers and critics in the genre maintain that Bradbury is not a science fiction writer at all. Bradbury's Mars is closer to Greek mythology or the Arabian Nights than to anything scientifically probable. When asked whether the Mariner mission to Mars invalidated his fiction, he answered that it in no way affected it, because he had been writing a myth. What Bradbury creates better than anyone else is the poetry of space, the sense of wonder — akin to religious awe — at the vastness, mystery, and beauty of the galaxies. At the same time, many of his tales are tinged with terror, often with a sense of macabre humor, revealing Bradbury's affinity to Poe, Bierce, Lovecraft, and others who employ what Wordsworth called "the ministry of fear" to arouse the imagination.

Bradbury, though, resembles Wells as well as Burroughs. For one thing, he does not imitate Burroughs' spectacular adventures; there is no swashbuckling in Bradbury and his protagonists are not heroic warriors but ordinary people placed in extraordinary situations. Bradbury writes about the middle-class family, and his astronauts are crew-cut, uniformed members of a team. Most of them are interchangeable. But as C. S. Lewis observed of science fiction and fantasy, those who experience extraordinary things should not be extraordinary themselves. Most of Bradbury's characters are quite commonplace and are not developed in much depth. Bradbury never writes about "bug-eyed monsters"; where Burroughs provides a whole natural history of exotic and usually dan-

gerous beasts, and where other science fiction writers often provide a fabulous
bestiary, Bradbury's science fiction has no fauna at all. The resemblance to
Wells comes in the fact that Bradbury's stories, for all their sense of wonder,
are concerned with ideas, with the implications or consequences of science and
space upon both society at large and upon the psychology of the individual.
Bradbury is a social critic as well as a prose poet, and he simultaneously
makes us think and wonder.

Together with *The Martian Chronicles*, *The Illustrated Man* (1951) is one
of Bradbury's best collections of short stories. Some of the stories were written specifically for it, while others appeared between 1947 and 1951 in magazines ranging in quality from the pulps (*Love Romances*, *Fantasy Fiction*) to
Esquire. Each story is self-contained, but Bradbury gives them an ingenious
framework. An unnamed narrator hiking in Wisconsin encounters a derelict
who is illustrated over every part of his body from the neck down with pictures, not routine tattoos but miniature masterpieces in glowing three-
dimensional color that recall El Greco. In 1900, at a carnival, a woman from
the future — a witch, he calls her — burned the illustrations into him. Though
they are indelible, they shift and change like motion pictures, not only telling
stories but predicting the future, usually in sinister ways. Each story of the
eighteen in the collection is supposed to be an illustration come to life. After
the first two stories, Bradbury returns briefly to the Illustrated Man, but he
then abandons the framework until the end of the collection when the narrator,
seeing that the sleeping Illustrated Man will wake and strangle him, flees.
Aside from the verbal virtuosity with which Bradbury describes the illustrations, the framework contributes nothing. It is even an obstacle, for there is no
way that such illustrations could tell the complex stories that follow, complete
with interior and exterior dialogue and unspoken emotions.

The stories themselves fit no formula, but they do fall into several categories. There are tales of future technology, including robots, stories of space
travel, and stories of Mars not included in *The Martian Chronicles*.

Space travel is intoxicating but perilous. In "Kaleidoscope," a rocket ship
has exploded, spilling the crew out into space, where — in their pressurized
suits — they drift away from each other like meteors into the orbit of various
planets until they burn up with the friction of reentry into the atmosphere and
appear as falling stars. While falling, they communicate by radio, and we learn
their fears, frustrations, and the values they lived by. In "No Particular Night
or Morning," an astronaut is driven mad by disorientation in space and commits suicide by ejecting himself from the ship. In "The City," another crew of
astronauts lands safely on a planet but is murdered by a city that has been
waiting for twenty thousand years to avenge the death of its people by an
invasion from Earth. The dying aliens have turned the entire city into a robot-
like machine, programed for just this moment. The dead astronauts are
replaced with identical robots and sent back to Earth to drop bombs containing

disease cultures. In "The Long Rains," the survivors of a rocket wrecked on Venus are tormented and driven mad by the never-ending torrential downpour that Bradbury vividly evokes in poetic prose. Only one man makes it to a sun-dome, where warmth, dryness, cinnamon buns, and cocoa with marshmallows await him.

Bradbury reveals a persistent nostalgia for the Midwestern small town of his boyhood in Waukegan, Illinois. Pulling against the lure of space, with the wonders of interplanetary travel, is a sentimental homesickness for the innocence of childhood in an idealized past of cool old houses with verandahs, porch swings, attics, rocking chairs, grandparents straight out of Norman Rockwell illustrations, lemonade, and homemade pie. "The Rocket Man" must choose between these polarities. For about three days out of every three months, he returns to a quaint home, a heaven of sorts; but inevitably the restless pull of space takes him away again from his lonely wife and son. Before the last voyage, he promises to settle down for good, but it is too late, for his ship falls into the sun. Yet his son plans in turn to become a rocket man. In "The Rocket," a poor junk dealer and wrecker cannot afford to take his large family to Mars, which has for them all the lure that Europe did for Henry James's Americans. But he buys a mock-up rocket, fixes it up with mirror illusions of space travel, and takes his happily deluded children on a week-long imaginary excursion around Mars and back, so that they will have the lifelong memory of the great adventure and its marvels.

For all his fascination with rockets, Bradbury is basically hostile towards technology (he has never learned to drive a car), and by contrast with the Victorian house he is homesick for is the evil of the future home in which machines are programed to do everything from tying shoes to providing wall-to-wall television screens that project the fantasies of the children. When Mr. and Mrs. Hadley in "The Veldt" threaten to turn off the gadgetry in their completely mechanized Happylife Home "which clothed and fed them and rocked them to sleep and played and sang and was good to them" (for only $30,000 installed), and return to a more self-reliant life, their spoiled children, vicious with frustration, trap them in the nursery and project three-dimensional lions out of the television wall to devour them. Children are equally menacing in "Zero Hour," in which Martian invaders, unable to attack a unified and prosperous Earth, superbly organized for defense, mobilize the children, work upon their as yet unfettered imaginations, and through an increasingly sinister game of "Invasion," the children and their Martian allies conquer the parents who had been too unobservant to pay attention to their children's lives.

Nevertheless, Bradbury is the last person to want to inhibit anyone's imagination or to censor imaginative literature. "The Exiles" is akin to "Usher II" in *The Martian Chronicles* and to *Fahrenheit 451* in its attack on censorship. In this story, all the works of fantasy and horror have been banned on earth, and the spirits of their authors have fled to Mars. They live peacefully in exile until a space ship comes, threatening to export Earth's antiseptic religion of science so as to root out superstition. Romantic authors have traditionally challenged empirical science's insistence on verifiable fact at the expense of fantasy. In his sonnet on "Science," Poe complained of science as a "Vulture, whose wings are dull realities" and who has driven away deities and mythologies. Bradbury's Poe organizes an army of fantasy authors — Shakespeare, Bierce, Blackwood, Machen, Coppard — and the creatures of their horror tales — witches, vampires, werewolves, hallucinations, the Red Death — to kill the invading astronauts. But the captain of the space ship, a crew-cut conformist smelling of antiseptic lotions, "a fresh instrument, honed and ready," has anticipated such a problem and brought along from a museum the only surviving copies of the works by the proscribed authors. To defend against Poe's occult legions, he burns the books, and as he does so, the authors, who have remained alive only in their works, are exterminated.

Bradbury tells the story with jocose humor (Dickens, for instance, claims to have been unfairly associated with the others; his ghost stories were not typical, and he refuses to fight as Poe's ally). Bradbury's underlying point, though, is serious and is aimed at such psychological censors as Dr. Frederick Wertham, who charged that fantasy and horror fiction corrupted the minds of the young, while earnest sociologists and educationists (not teachers) insisted during the early 1950's on a realism that was almost as pedestrian as that required in Soviet Russia. Despite his billing as a science fiction writer, Bradbury prefers fantasy to science; his allegiance is to Oz more than to astronomy.

There are other unscientific details in Bradbury, such as there being no atmospheric problems for humans on other planets; they are able to walk about there as comfortably as on Earth. And with a few exceptions, the inhabitants of other planets resemble humans except for their complexion. Not only is Bradbury anthropocentric, but his spacemen are extraordinarily ethnocentric and chauvinistic; most of them expect the people and cultures of other planets to be exactly like their own, including the worst features of the pop culture. This backfires in "The Concrete Mixer," another tale of an invasion from Mars. The Martian protagonist, Ettil, is convinced after reading old science fiction magazines that any invasion is doomed to be thwarted by lean-jawed, crew-cut Earthmen named Rick or Bannon, but the invaders find themselves welcomed by the worst excesses of a bloated and vulgar American materialism. Instead of fighting the Martians, the Americans figure to make money off of them, to export soap, soft drinks, cars, candy, booze, movies, and nightclubs. Rick turns out to be a Babbitlike tycoon who plans to conquer Mars by economic imperialism. The final pathetic twist is that Ettil is run down by a car full of drunken teen-agers.

Bradbury has become increasingly a Transcendental optimist, but his early stories both criticize the present and predict a grim future. In "The Fox and the Forest," the world of 2155 is a totalitarian police state dedicated to war. A married couple flees their jobs in bomb and disease culture units and escape via time travel to 1938, only to be pursued and recaptured by secret agents. Science is the enemy in a number of tales. "The Marionettes" is a sardonic study of robotry gone awry, but usually Bradbury is more serious. Written just after the onset of the atomic age and Cold War, several stories such as "The Highway" reflect the fear of and predict a thermonuclear disaster. "The Other Foot" is a sequel to a chapter in *The Martian Chronicles* in which all the blacks leave the South by taking a rocketship to Mars. After the Earth is destroyed by atomic warfare, the white survivors seek refuge on Mars, where the blacks are dominant and the racial roles have been reversed. A black leader wants to lynch the first white man, but after learning of the destruction that has taken place on Earth, especially in the South, the blacks feel compassion and abandon thoughts of revenge.

If Earth is doomed, salvation may be found on other planets. "The Fire Balloons" is a Martian tale in which Episcopal missionaries find that the only surviving Martians have undergone a transformation from human form to floating balls of blue flame. In the process, they have lost the ability to sin; their regained state of innocence reminds the author of his lost childhood, and he indulges in reminiscing about Fourth of July celebrations with fire balloons symbolizing innocent joy. "The Man" tells of Christ appearing on another planet is a distant galaxy, just as a spaceship from Earth arrives. Its commander expects a brass-band welcome and resents the competition, but when his skepticism is converted to belief, he wants to monopolize Christ. He bullies and assaults the aliens, and pursues Christ as he would any other commodity. Similarly, in "The Visitor," fatally sick humans exiled to an outer space sanitarium on Mars become unruly with greed when they discover a patient who has the power to project illusions of life on Earth. As in Clark's "The Portable Phonograph," which this story resembles, each man wants the treasure exclusively for himself, and during the conflict, they kill the patient and find themselves left with nothing.

In *The Illustrated Man*, Bradbury has taken the props — even the clichés — of science fiction (time travel, robots, interplanetary war) and given them new life through an inventive narrative ability, a gift for metaphor and imagery, and fresh and often provocative insights. Despite his reservations about, evasion of, and even hostility towards science, Bradbury explores some of the ethical dilemmas posed by science, thereby making the reader both think and wonder.

Robert E. Morsberger

Sources for Further Study

Reviews:

Booklist. XLVII, March 15, 1951, p. 255.

Hornbook. XXVII, May, 1951, p. 197.

Kirkus Reviews. XVIII, December 15, 1950, p. 740.

New York Times. February 4, 1951, p. 16.

San Francisco Chronicle. March 25, 1951, p. 18.

Springfield Republican. March 18, 1951, p. 30.

THE IMMORTALS

Author: James E. Gunn (1923-   )
First book publication: 1962
Type of work: Novel
Time: A period of one hundred and fifty-three years starting in the mid-twentieth century
Locale: Primarily Kansas City, Missouri

A study of mankind's quest for immortality and how this quest affects the growth of medical science

> *Principal characters:*
> MARSHALL CARTWRIGHT, the original immortal
> DR. RUSSEL PEARCE, a specialist in geriatrics
> LEROY WEAVER, a dying millionaire
> JASON LOCKE, director of the search for the immortals
> EDWIN SIBERT, a member of Locke's task force
> BARBARA MCFARLAND, daughter of Marshall Cartwright
> BENJAMIN FLOWERS, a medic
> LEAH PEARCE, daughter of Russell Pearce
> HARRY ELLIOTT, a doctor
> GOVERNOR WEAVER, son of Leroy Weaver
> MARNA, daughter of Governor Weaver and an immortal

Besides his fine ability as an author, James Gunn is also an articulate scholar who has contributed many valuable critical statements on the genre. Thus, it would seem to be a valuable exercise to compare his own works with several of these statements. *The Immortals*, in particular, supplies just such an opportunity. Whether it be in letters, popular articles, or books such as *The Road to Science Fiction* and *Alternate Worlds*, Gunn has spent most of his professional life trying to define the genre of science fiction. In the process he has on several occasions contrasted science fiction and mainstream fiction in some rather interesting and useful ways. Put simply, Gunn sees the difference between these two types of writing as arising from the use of characterization. He defines science fiction as an idea-oriented fiction that attempts to characterize change. This change is usually technical or scientific in nature, and in most cases involves more than just one or two individuals. In fact, in most cases, whole nations of people or the human race itself is at stake.

On the other hand, mainstream fiction is usually oriented around the individual. Thus, according to Gunn, the mainstream novel depends heavily on the characterization of individual people in the work. Whereas in science fiction it is the world and the change that it is undergoing that is important, for mainstream fiction it is the development (or lack of development) of the people in the novel that is most emphasized. This point of contrast and the resulting definition of science fiction works quite well for *The Immortals*, and the reasons why give excellent clues for a reading of the novel.

The characters in *The Immortals*, while not exactly flat, are not very complex nor do they allow for any close identification between them and the reader. There are two reasons for this lack of complexity and identification. The first is the simple fact that *The Immortals* was written and published over a period of years, not as a novel but as four novellas. Second, except for Russell Pearce and the continual mention of Marshall Cartwright, the center of each part involves different characters. Thus, characters who might interest the reader in one story disappear in the next. Even Russell Pearce, who plays an important role in three of the four parts, fails as an attractive character for the reader because he is clearly a fatherly, moral voice rather than a growing and learning character.

Characters in *The Immortals*, then, are not in and of themselves interesting. They are, instead, functions of the world that Gunn creates. They exist so that the author can explore how various types of people react to the threat of death in face of the existence of immortals. Thus, in "Part I: New Blood," Leroy Weaver is portrayed as the millionaire who is willing to spend any amount of money and have any kind of act committed that might allow him to avoid death. In "Part II: Donor," Edwin Sibert is a simple investigator with little money and fewer scruples who uses Barbara McFarland's love for him in an attempt to win immortality. And, in "Part IV: Immortal," Dr. Harry Elliott sees medical science as his steppingstone to eternal life.

Even when a character does undergo a change of belief, as in the cases of Benjamin Flowers and Elliott, the change comes from the fact that these characters are given further information about their world, not because they have undergone any change of heart of growth. When they change, they do so because more enlightened characters in possession of complete information see Flowers and Elliott in a clearer light than these two men see themselves. Greed, selfishness, idealism, licentiousness, self-sacrifice, love, and hope all have their representatives in *The Immortals*, and it is rare for one of these representatives to overstep his or her characterizing label.

There is, however, a second element in the novel that does unify all four stories: the world that the characters live in. Gunn has created this world from a trend that is all too evident in present society. One need not read far in current newspapers to learn of the advances now being made in modern medicine. One need not read any further in these same newspapers to learn just how expensive the new advances are. These developments save lives, but they also drive up the cost of all medical care. Hospitals may have more and better methods of treating the sick and dying, but each year the number of people who can afford the increasing costs diminishes. Gunn takes his premise from this fact of modern life and adds the element of immortality to it. The mixture becomes a damning description of just how dangerous man's preoccupation with avoiding death can be.

The fact that immortals exist unbalances whatever forces of common sense that did exist in the world of the novel to hold down the development of more exotic and expensive means of treatment. No longer held in even light check, the amount of money and time spent on medical research increases geometrically. At the same time, all programs not directly concerned with such research are ignored. This is the change that is characterized in the novel, and it certainly does concern all mankind.

Gunn introduces the origin of the change in the first part. When the millionaire, Leroy Weaver, receives the blood of Marshall Cartwright in a transfusion, the old man soon behaves and looks like a man of thirty. While he never gets the opportunity to use Cartwright as his private blood bank, Weaver sets the theme for the rest of the novel. In the quest for life, no expense should be spared. The second part opens on the same note. Weaver is dead, but a consortium of millionaires has funded a search for Cartwright and his children. During the fifty-year search, five billion dollars has been spent. In this same story Gunn reminds the reader that money and medicine are inextricably combined. Thus, Kansas City, Missouri, is a dying city, but the hospital complex is growing and starting to absorb the abandoned land about it.

In the third part, the death of Kansas City is near at hand, yet the ruined city is dominated by a still growing and healthy hospital complex. Medical care is out of the reach of the inhabitants of the city. Health insurance has become so high that most people can no longer afford it, and to receive health care without being injured (that is, receiving medical treatment without being able to pay for it) is a crime punishable by consigning the offender's body to the organ bank. Before Russell Pearce and his daughter teach him differently Harry Elliott sees nothing wrong with such a situation. Since the wealthy are responsible for the funds that allow for the development of new medical discoveries, they should be the first to receive the benefits. What Elliott fails to understand is that the wealthy, and doctors belong to this class, are the only ones who will receive the treatments. The cost of the simplest of operations is ridiculously beyond the means of the majority of citizens.

What has caused medicine to become so exclusive? Pearce speaks directly to this point. In devoting the major part of medical research to extending the lives of people, more equipment and drugs are necessary. Such things cost money, and the people who have money are more than willing to spend it if even a remote possibility exists for them to add a day to their lives. The government has also joined the wealthy in this quest: income taxes begin at fifty percent and climb from there. For people of even moderate income, such a tax rate precludes being able to pay for medical insurance. What makes the situation worse is that it is obvious that the taxes are going to the hospitals; they are certainly not going to the cities. Thus, Kansas City, which surrounds a vast, modern hospital complex, is filled with the diseases of poverty, and nothing is done. Doctors have become like the friars of the fourteenth century. Both groups were in theory created to serve their fellow man; both, however, found it more rewarding to serve a limited group of men capable of supporting them.

By the fourth part, the world of *The Immortals* must face the consequences of its quest for immortality. Pearce had stated in the third part that there is such a thing as too much health. There reaches a point at which the amount of time and money needed to extend a person's life one day equals the same amount needed to extend someone else's life five years. For several decades, the wealthy have cured all their diseases by taking blood from the few immortals they have captured or by taking a dose of an elixir which is a synthetic reconstruction of the gamma globulins in the blood of the immortals. Such treatment, however, is limited to the extremely wealthy. While enough supplies exist to promise a small number of men immortality, this immortality has serious consequences. Leroy Weaver's son, for example, is presented as a bloated, self-centered slug who believes he has complete power over life and death. The wealthy classes have so avoided any semblance of disease in their antiseptic lives that they are incapable of any natural immunity. Their bodies are malformed and their minds are worthy of such bodies. By the fourth part, Gunn hammers at the ultimate cost of seeking immortality. These people have been so afraid to die that they have forgotten to live. Is eternal life worth such a cost? Given the way the wealthy and powerful are presented, their very repulsiveness forces a negative answer.

The final irony of *The Immortals* lies in the fact that universal immortality becomes possible. Russell Pearce finds the way by learning to control his body with his mind. But Pearce is able to learn this method because he gave up trying to build machines or find miracle drugs. Instead, he turns inward, something the doctors and the millionaires were never capable of doing. They were too busy trying to catch Cartwright and his children, endowing new hospital wings, and worshiping their recent discoveries. The implication is that the potential for immortality is within man, but money cannot buy it.

The Immortals is not about immortality. Gunn leaves the reader on the brink of a new world where mankind may live forever, but he is not interested in portraying that world. What Gunn does do, and do well, in this novel is show a world in transition. It is the possibility of immortality and how it affects people that is his concern. The world and the characters are all geared toward the investigation of this one theme. And it is because of the unity of purpose behind each of the four parts that the novel holds together. One wonders how much more successful the television series based on *The Immortals* would have been if in 1969 it had dared to explore these implications instead of turning the story into a chase.

Gunn defines science fiction as an idea-oriented literature concerned with a technological or scientific change that affects mankind. After a reading of *The Immortals*, a rather interesting question arises: Which came first, the definition or the novel? They are certainly true to each other.

Stephen H. Goldman

Sources for Further Study

Reviews:

Analog. LXXI, August, 1963, p. 91.

Luna Monthly. XXXII, January, 1972, p. 27.

Publisher's Weekly. CXCVIII, August 31, 1970, p. 281.